BRINGING MANY SONS INTO GLORY

GOD'S PLAN, PURPOSE AND INSTRUCTIONS
HOLY BIBLE STUDY RESOURCES

Volume 1
God Preserves His Chosen People

KING JAMES VERSION BIBLE COMPILED

BY THE DISCIPLE OF CHRIST AND THE GOD OF ISRAEL
Herminia Sendon Ramos

HERMINIA RAMOS, SELF PUBLISHING
Panorama City 91402

1 Chronicles 29:11

Thine, O LORD, is the greatness, and the power, and the glory, and the victory, and the majesty: for all that is in the heaven and in the earth is thine; thine is the kingdom, O LORD, and thou art exalted as head above all.

Printed in United States of America.

ISBN Soft Cover
978-0-692-34266-4

ISBN eBook
978-0-9964734-0-8

HERMINIA RAMOS, SELF PUBLISHING
Panorama City 91402

For information to buy a copy of this book and a quantity discounts with bulk purchase for a bible study group, educational or sale promotional use, go to email:
minniesendon52@yahoo.com or contact HERMINIA RAMOS
Tel: 818-392-9637 or call 202-664-4718

DEDICATION
1Timothy 1:12

And I thank Christ Jesus our Lord, who hath enabled me, for that he counted me faithful, putting me into the ministry;13 Who was before a blasphemer, and a persecutor, and injurious: but I obtained mercy, because I did it ignorantly in unbelief.

Firstly, *I highly dedicate these books volume 1,2&3 to my LORD, the God of Israel who gave me life and hope to be with Him in the last days.*

I praise you LORD, my God, for answering my long time prayer, Ephesians 1:17-20 and supplications for two years to help me know You, and to reveal Yourself to me, who didn't know You at all for nineteen years.

The best honor is to You my LORD and truly I glorify Your greatest name by sending your Holy Spirit to guide me in compiling Your word from the Bible, to give me full understanding on how well and perfect Your works are and Your plan of salvation of soul. It is truly wonderful and amazing, LORD that You continuously implementing Your greatest plan from the beginning of time to bring many sons into glory in the LORD's day. Your calling is so powerful and overwhelming, by entrusting me, Your lowly servant to put into writings the mysteries, biblical events and knowing all the persons involved in Your plan both the earthly and spiritual beings, written in the Bible. Even though, You didn't predestinate me first, to attend any theological school for critical and comprehensive study of the scriptures, neither leading me to have a deeper religious or church involvement but rather uplifted and helped me to grow spiritually through the power of Your grace. Unknowingly, The Holy Spirit filled my understanding and thoughts the details of the flow of Your messages and instructions to the chosen, both the Jews and Gentiles alike from the day of creation up to the second coming of my dear LORD Jesus. Bless you my God of Israel, through your grace my LORD, You became my only perfect mentor and my loving rabbi.

1Timothy 1:17 *Now unto the King eternal, immortal, invisible, the only wise God, be honour and glory for ever and ever. Amen.*

Secondly, *to all the readers of these books*

May the Holy Spirit give you peace, joy, wisdom and understanding. May the LORD reveal himself to you fully through His Word and I pray that He may help you in your journey to eternal life. Praise the LORD God for His will to allow His Word to be written by prophets of different generations so that everyone could understand His great plan of salvation of souls of the chosen people: first to the Jews and to the gentiles.

I pray that everyone who is predestined to be the children of God will continue to read the Holy Bible, to keep God's Word, to be obedient, and to remain faithful to our LORD Jesus for the rest of our short lives.

Thirdly, *to my dearest family: my loving husband, Francisco Ramos Jr., my beloved children, Liwanag, Diwa, Sinag, Laya, Bayan and Pilipinas, son -inlaw, Vermon Ferre; my most loved grandchildren, Bea, Shawn and Liam Francis and all the descendants to come; and my fourteen siblings; Agnes, Samuel, Susana, Nomelita, Zoe, Maria Salome,, Salvemin,, Marife, Archimedes, Lelibeth, Eudelia, Floreden, Lourdes, and Lenlen, including the whole Sendon clan, the whole Ramos family and to to the loving memory of my parents: Amando I. Sendon, and Rufina E. Villanueva who became first in the family to become the true followers of Christ.*

By the grace of the LORD, these books volume 1,2 &3 will serve as a rich Bible study guide resources along with our Bible. These books were compiled according to God's purpose is my best gift to all of you and to all our descendants to come that they might also, be fully equipped with the word of God, May the LORD bless us to have the mind of Christ that will make our family powerful and victorious against the attack and workings of the devil while we are waiting for the second coming of our LORD Jesus Christ.

PRAISING GOD FOR HIS WONDERFUL PLAN FOR HIS CHILDREN

I thank you God, for Your wonderful plan that when You created us, You breathed your spirit of life and made us the living soul. Thank you Father for sending your beloved Son who died on the cross to save myr soul. I accept Him in my heart. I ask you God for the forgiveness of all my sins, cleanse me with the power of your WORD and sanctify me fully, my body, soul and spirit through the power of the Holy Ghost Thank you my Lord for giving me comfort Through Your grace, I shall experience the joy and peace because you are with me in my short journey from this physical life to life everlasting.I praise you for giving me the real hope of the beauty of the resurrection from the dead and in the blink of an eye, You will cloth me with a new glorious body. Through Your grace I will be joined together with the heavenly hosts according to Your promise. Praise God, all of us who believe and keep your WORD could inherit Your kingdom and Your son our LORD Jesus will be the King of all kings and the LORD of all hosts.

In the mighty name of the LORD Jesus Christ, I pray and praise and love Thee with all my heart, with all my mind with all my soul, and with all my strength. Amen and Amen.

05/31/20014

Acts 13:16

Then Paul stood up, and beckoning with his hand said, **Men of Israel, and ye that fear God,** *give audience.*
17The God of this people of Israel chose our fathers, and exalted the people when they dwelt as strangers in the land of Egypt, and with an high arm brought he them out of it.
18And about the time of forty years suffered he their manners in the wilderness.
19And when he had destroyed seven nations in the land of Chanaan, he divided their land to them by lot.
20And after that he gave unto them judges about the space of four hundred and fifty years, until Samuel the prophet.
21And afterward they desired a king: and God gave unto them Saul the son of Cis, a man of the tribe of Benjamin, by the space of forty years.
22And when he had removed him, he raised up unto them David to be their king; to whom also **he gave testimony,** *and said,* **I have found David** *the son of Jesse, a man after mine own heart,* **which shall fulfil all my will.**
23 Of this man's seed hath God according to his promise raised unto Israel a Saviour, Jesus:

VOLUME 1 TABLE OF CONTENTS
GOD PRESERVES HIS CHOSEN PEOPLE

PART 1
GOD'S WORD TO ALL GENERATIONS

CHAPTER I THE HOLY BIBLE WAS WRITTEN

===

PART 1
GOD'S WORD TO ALL GENERATIONS

CHAPTER II IMPORTANCE OF THE HOLY SCRIPTURES

===

PART 2
THE SCRIPTURES SPEAK ABOUT GOD'S PLAN

CHAPTER I GOD'S PLAN FOR HIS CHOSEN

===

PART 2
THE SCRIPTURES SPEAK ABOUT GOD'S PLAN

CHAPTER II **IMPLEMENTATION OF GOD'S PLAN**

===

PART 2
THE SCRIPTURES SPEAK ABOUT GOD'S PLAN

CHAPTER III **MYSTERY OF GOD'S CREATION**

===

PART 2
THE SCRIPTURES SPEAK ABOUT GOD'S PLAN

CHAPTER IV SEPARATION OF ANCIENT MEN FROM HIS CREATOR

===

PART 3
GOD CALLED HIS PEOPLE

CHAPTER I GOD CHOSE HIS PEOPLE FROM THE BEGINNING

==

PART 3
GOD CALLED HIS PEOPLE

CHAPTER II **SEED**

==

PART 3
GOD CALLED HIS PEOPLE

CHAPTER III **GOD REVEALED HIMSELF TO GENTILES**

PART 4
FIRST AGREEMENT TO THE NATION OF ISRAEL

CHAPTER I **THE ORDINANCES OF GOD**

===

PART 4
FIRST AGREEMENT TO THE NATION OF ISRAEL

CHAPTER II **FEASTS AND TRADITIONS**

===

PART 4
FIRST AGREEMENT TO THE NATION OF ISRAEL

CHAPTER III **GOD CHOSE LEVITES TO BE THE PRIEST**

===

PART 4
FIRST AGREEMENT TO THE NATION OF ISRAEL

CHAPTER IV **THE BLOOD COVENANT**

===

PART 4
FIRST AGREEMENT TO THE NATION OF ISRAEL

CHAPTER V **THE LAW OF SABBATH**

PART 4
THE FIRST AGREEMENT TO THE NATION OF ISRAEL

CHAPTER VI **OTHER LAWS FOR SANCTIFICATION**

PART 4
THE FIRST AGREEMENT TO THE NATION OF ISRAEL

CHAPTER VII **GOD'S ECONOMY**

===

PART 5
TEST OF FAITH

CHAPTER I JOB'S SUFFERINGS

===

PART 5
TEST OF FAITH

CHAPTER II A BLESSING OR A CURSE

==

PART 6
GOD ANOINTED DELIVERERS

CHAPTER 1 **TO PRESERVE GOD'S CHOSEN**

==

PART 6
GOD ANOINTED DELIVERERS

CHAPTER II **THE JUDGES**

===

PART 6
GOD ANOINTED DELIVERERS

CHAPTER III **THE KINGS OF ISRAEL**

===

PART 6
GOD ANOINTED DELIVERERS

CHAPTER IV **GOD REVEALED HIS PLAN TO HIS PROPHETS**

===

PART 6
GOD ANOINTED DELIVERERS

CHAPTER V **GOD GAVE POWERS TO THE PROPHETS OF ISRAEL**

A. Filled with the Spirit
    1.Of Might and Power To do Miracles
    Moses   337-338
    Elijah   338
      The Widow from Zeraphath   338
      Elijah sent Obadiah to King Ahab   338-339
        Ahab met Elijah   339-340
        Elijah Challenged the False Prophets and their False
          Gods   340-341
        Elijah Prayed to the Lord to Reveal His Power   341
        The Abundance of Rain Came   342
        Elijah was taken to Heaven Alive   342-343
        Elias and Elijah the Same Person   343-344
      Elisha
        Water of Jordan was parted   344
        Water was healed in Jericho   344-345
        The Dead Child was risen from Dead   345
    2. To Anoint Kings

==

PART 7
THE CHILDREN OF DISOBEDIENCE

CHAPTER I IDOLATERS

==

===

PART 8
GOD RENDERS PUNISHMENT
.
CHAPTE IV **GOD'S PUNISHMENT TO MOSES' PEOPLE**

==

PART 8
GOD RENDERS PUNISHMENT

CHAPTER V **ISRAEL'S DISOBEDIENCE**

==

PART 8
GOD RENDERS PUNISHMENT

CHAPTER VI **KINGS' DISOBEDIENCE AND ABOMINATION**

===

PART 8
GOD RENDERS PUNISHMENT

CHAPTER VII **THE DIVIDED KINGDOMS LED TO CAPTIVITY**

PART 8
GOD RENDERS PUNISHMENT
.
CHAPTER VI1I **FALSE PROPHET**

PART 8
GOD RENDERS PUNISHMENT

CHAPTER IX **GOD LEFT HIS CHOSEN**

PART 8
GOD RENDERS PUNISHMENT

CHAPTER X **JUDGMENT OF SOUL UPON DEATH**

===

PART 9
MYSTERY OF THE BODY, SOUL AND SPIRIT

CHAPTER 1 **THE LIVING SOUL**

PART 9
MYSTERY OF BODY, SOUL AND SPIRIT

CHAPTER II **SPIRIT OF GOD IN MAN**

===

VOLUME 2
GOD'S WORD BECAME FLESH

PART 10
THE SAVIOR OF SOUL

CHAPTER I **GOD SENT THE REDEEMER**

3. To Bring Many Sons into Glory
   By Lord's Obedience Many Will Become Righteous
4. To Redeem Israel under the Law and Gives Light to
      Gentiles
   The Lord's body will be the Sacrifice for Sin
   The Lord Came for the Sinners to Repentance
5. Lord Jesus the Shepherd
   The Lost Sheep
      a. House of Israel
      b. Gentiles
6. Fulfilling God's Plan (Volume1 Part 2 Chapter1)
      a. To Save the Lost
      b. All Things will be in Subjection under the Lord
      c. The Elect and Host of Heaven Together in Christ
      d. To Destroy the Power of Death
      e. No More Curse on Earth

==

PART 10
THE SAVIOR OF SOUL

CHAPTER II **THE COMING OF THE MESSIAH WRITTEN IN THE SCRIPTURES**

Revelation of Christ's Mystery
The Spirit of Christ was in the Prophets
Biblical Prophecies Written in the Old Testament
The Word of God Will Become Flesh
A. Redeemer, Everlasting Father and God
B. The Messiah
   1. The Seed of Eve
   2. The Descendant of Shem
   3. The King Will Come from Juda's Family
   4. Descendant of David
   5. Born by the Virgin in Bethlehem
C. Fasting in the Wilderness
   Praising God during Fasting
D. The Spirit of the Lord will be Upon Him
   1. To Preach the Good News
   2. The Light to the Gentiles and Restorer of Israel

3 The Lord Could Hear the Thoughts of Men
E. Will Teach about the Everlasting Kingdom
F. Lord Will Be the Shepherd
G. The King Will Be Riding on a Donkey
  Lord's Prayer
  To Strengthen His Soul
H. One of the Apostle will turn against Him
  The Amount shall be paid to betray the Lord
  The Amount shall be Casted out in the House of the Lord

===

PART 10
THE SAVIOR OF SOUL

CHAPTER III **PROPHECIES OF THE DEATH AND RESURRECTION OF CHRIST**

A. Rejected by Men
B. Sufferings of the Messiah
  1. Shall be accused by False Witness
    Lord's Prayer
  2. The Lord shall be Mocked and Insulted
    Lord's Prayer
  3. The Lord shall be Wounded and Bruise
  4. The Lord will never answer the Inquisitors
    Lord's Prayer: in the Councils of Accusers
    The Lord's Prayer when the non-believers shall be Insulting
      Him
C. The Crucifixion on the Cross
  Lord's Prayer while hanging on the Cross
  1. The Soldiers shall cast Lots to His Garments
  2. The Messiah's Last Words on the Cross
  3. The Lord will die on the Cross
    The Lord's Death will bear the Sins of Many
  4. The Lord will visit the Captive
D. Christ will be Risen from the Dead
  Dead Men will be Risen along with Christ's Resurrection
  The Lord will be the High Priest
E. A Messenger of God to Come
F. The Second Coming of Christ

1. Sceptre shall Rise out of Israel, will Destroy Nations against Israel
2. The Lord's Kingdom will be Upon the Holy Hill of Zion
3. Resurrection of the Dead
4. The Lord will be the Judge
   a. Will Render Punishment to the Hosts/Angels
   b. He will bring Forth Judgment
   To His People (Jews)
   To The Heathen (Evildoers)
5. Christ will Rule as King of kings forever
6. The Lord will give Blessings to the Children of God
7. The Lord will be worshiped

===

PART 10
THE SAVIOR OF SOUL

CHAPTER IV **FULFILLMENT OF BIBLICAL PROPHECIES RECORDED IN THE NEW TESTAMENT**

The Word of God Became Flesh
A. The Messiah was Born
   1. The Good News to the Virgin Mary
   2. Lord Jesus was Born in Bethlehem
   3. The Generations of Joseph the Husband of Mary
      a. Noe /Noah Came From Enoch the Son of Seth
      b. Abraham Came from Shem, Son of Noah
      c. Phares, Son of Judah and Tamar the Ancestor of Boaz
      d. The Generations of the Sons of Judah
      e. David the Son of Abraham
   4. Jesus the Son of David
B. Prophet Will Prepare the Way of the Lord
   John the Baptist
   Testimony of John the Baptist
C. Lord Jesus Fasted in Wilderness
D. Jesus Entered Jerusalem Riding on a Donkey
E. Judas Iscariot, Turned against Lord Jesus
   The Amount were Casted out in the House of the Lord
   Judas Hanged Himself

PART 10
THE SAVIOR OF SOUL

CHAPTER V **THE SUFFERINGS AND DEATH ON THE CROSS OF CHRIST JESUS**

A. Wounded and Bruised
   The Soldiers Braided a Crown of Thorns to Christ's Forehead
B. The Lord Never Answered Back
   Condemned The Lord To Death
C. The Crucifixion on the Cross
   1. The Chief Priests and Scribes Mocked And Insulted the Lord
   2 Soldiers Threw Lots for the Lord's Clothing
      The Lord Prayed for the Forgiveness of Sin
   3 The Lord's Last Words, before His Death
   4. Lord Jesus' Bones were Not Broken
   5. The Lord was pierced
      The Body of the Lord Jesus was Put Down from the Tree

==

PART 10
THE SAVIOR OF SOUL

CHAPTER VI **RESURRECTION OF THE LORD**

The Saints Were Risen Up After the Lord's Resurrection
The Lord was Risen from the Dead
Lord Jesus, the First One who was Risen Up from the Dead
Lord Jesus Upon Resurrection has a Glorious Body
 Disciples Received the Holy Ghost
 The Risen Lord Commanded the Disciples To Teach all Nations
      and Baptize them
Jesus Christ was Taken Up to Heaven
Jesus Prophecy His Coming in the clouds of Heaven(Rapture)
The Chief Priest Paid the Soldiers to Spread False Claim about
      the Stolen Cadaver of Christ

==

CHAPTER VII **LORD JESUS WAS FILLED WITH THE HOLY GHOST**

The Grace of God was Upon Him
The Lord Started His Ministry
A. The Lord Preached the Gospel
   Lord Said No Prophet is Accepted in His Own Country
B. Lord Jesus has the Power to forgive Sins
   1. The Man Sick with Palsy
   2. The Woman with Perfumed Ointment.
C. Lord Jesus Performed the Mighty Power of God
   1. Turned the Water into Wine
   2. Casted Out Devils
   3. The Power to Hear the Thoughts of Men
   4. Catching the Multitude of Fish
   5. Bringing People Back to Life
      Lazarus
      The Son of the Widow
      The Ruler of the Synagogue's daughter
   6. The Lord Walked on the Sea
   7 The Lord Fed The Multitude
      a. Four Thousand People
      b Five Thousand People
   8. The Lord Healed the Sick
   9. The Lord Stopped the Storm
   10. Jesus Cursed the Fig Tree
   11.Lord Jesus Gave Power to the Apostles
      The Lord's Apostles
      No Fasting for the Disciples of the Lord
   12. Lord Jesus was with /Moses and Elias
D. The Lord Prophecy His Death and Resurrection
E. The Lord Prophecy of His Authority to Executejudgment
F. The Spirit Christ went to the Captives (the spirits in prison)

PART 10
THE SAVIOR OF SOUL

CHAPTER VIII **LORD JESUS IS THE ONLY WAY TO THE FATHER**

A. Lord Jesus the Mediator Between Chosen and Father God
B. Only Lord Jesus will Bring us to Paradise
C. Lord Jesus is the High Priest In Heaven
D.The Lord is the Mediator of the New Testament and the New
     Covenant
   Lord Jesus Brings our Prayers to the Most Holy Place
   The Lord Make Reconciliation for the Sins of the People

PART 10
THE SAVIOR OF SOUL

CHAPTER IX **THE LORD IS WORTHY OF PRAISE AND WORSHIP**

Lord Jesus, the Foundation of Our Faith is Alive
Lord Jesus is the Lord of the Living and the Dead
Worshipers of Christ
A. Angels
B. The Believers
     1. The Wise Men Worshiped the New born Christ
     2. The Blind Man
     3. The Leper
     4. Canaan Woman
     5. The Disciples
          a. During the Lord's Ministry
          b. The Disciples Worshiped The Risen Lord
          c. The Lord was Lifted Up to Heaven
     6. The Ruler
C. The Unclean Spirit
Must Pray to Save the Soul of All Men
Prayer to the Lord Who Redeemed Our Souls

PART 11
THE GOSPEL OF CHRIST

CHAPTER1 THE GOOD NEWS OF SALVATION TO JEWS AND GENTILES

The Gospel of the Lord from Heaven
Jesus Christ Brought Life through the Gospel
The Gospel of God is the Gospel of Christ
Full Gospel of Christ
1. Gospel of the Kingdom of Heaven (The preaching of Christ Jesus)
    The Lord was Speaking in Parables to the None-believers
    Parable:The Kingdom of God is Within You
    The nonbelievers Has Spiritual Blindness
    Kingdom Of Heaven Explained In Parables
    a. The Parable of the Sower
    b. The Parable of the Man that Sowed Good Seed
    c. Parable of the Grain of Mustard Seed
    d. The Kingdom of Heaven is Like the Treasure Hidden in a Field
    e. The Parable of the Merchant Man, Seeking Goodly Pearls
    f. The Kingdom of Heaven is like unto a Net
    g. The Kingdom Of Heaven is Like unto a Man that is a Householder
    h. Like Leaven
    The Gospel of Christ unto Salvation
2. Gospel of the Death and Resurrection of Christ
    a. Made Peace to God through the Cross
    b. The Lord Nailed our Sins in the Cross
        Sickness was Not Nailed on the Cross
        1. Apostle Paul Suffered Infirmities in His Flesh
        2. Tabitha the Follower of Christ Got Sick and Died
        Sickness is for the Glory of God
    c. The Blood on the Cross Reconcile both Things in Heaven and on Earth
    d. The Blood of Lord Jesus Purged the Sin
    Forgiveness of Sin Through the Lord's Blood

3. Gospel of Grace (since the day of Pentecost)
   Saving Grace through Faith
   Build the Foundation of Faith through Grace
   Grace reign through Righteousness by Jesus Christ Our
       Lord.
   Spiritual Blessings through Grace (Part16, Chapter I-VII)
       a. Grace Brings Salvation both to Jews and Gentiles
       b. Sealed with the Holy Spirit of Promise
       c. Apostleship Comes from the Power of Grace
       d. The Saved by Grace has No Dominion of Sin
       e. Will Deliver the Elect from the Wrath to Come
4. Gospel of the Kingdom of God (Last Days)
       a. The Kingdom of God in New Earth (In God's Time)
       b. Everlasting Dominion of the Lord
       c. Not Everyone Who Called to God will enter the
           kingdom
       d. The Children of God will enter the Kingdom
       e. Celebration in the Kingdom Of God
           The Feast of Unleavened Bread
       f. One Pure Language for the Children of God in His
           Kingdom
       g. The Kingdom of God to come will be in Israel
======================================

PART 11
THE GOSPEL OF CHRIST

CHAPTER II THE MYSTERY OF THE KINGDOM OF HEAVEN

Lord's Kingdom is not of this World
God is the Builder of the Kingdom of Heaven
A. The Kingdom of Heaven is Still in Heaven
B. Kingdom of Heaven is a Place
   1 Lord Jesus is the Prince in the Heavenly Kingdom
   2. God's Kingdom
   3 The Kingdom is a Paradise
   4 The Temple of God
       The Glimpse of the Sanctuary of God in Heaven
   The Ark of the Covenant
       a. Pattern of the Tabernacle

b. Two Cherubs are in the Ends of the Mercy Seat of God
c. Vessels and Everything in Heavenly Sanctuary are Made of Gold
d. Spiritual Garments in the Kingdom
    The Cloths of Service of Aaron
    Joshua was given a New Spiritual Garments
C Heavenly Kingdom is a City
    1. There are Mansions in the Heavenly City
    2. The City of New Jerusalem
        Size of the City of God
        Gates of New Jerusalem
        Foundations of the Wall of New Jerusalem
D. The Souls Live in the Kingdom of Heaven
E. There is Food in the Kingdom Of Heaven
Lord Jesus' Prayer for the Kingdom to come

===

PART 11
THE GOSPEL OF CHRIST

CHAPTER III **PREACH THE GOSPEL AND BAPTIZE THE BELIEVERS**

The Risen Lord Commanded The Disciples To Teach All Nations
    And Baptize Them
Feed the Flock of God
These Signs Shall Follow To Them That Believe
The Lord Commanded The Witnesses To Preach
Today God is Calling His Chosen
The Gospel is preached to enter God's Rest
    1. Preach the Gospel of Peace
    2. Bring Good Tidings to the Chosen
      Preach the Gospel to the Gentiles
        Paul Preach The Gospel Of The Death And Resurrection Of Christ
        The Mystery of Salvation that Comes to Gentiles
        Boast Not Christian Gentiles)Against The Natural Branch (Unbelieving Jews)That Was Broken Off
        Salvation to the Gentiles
    3.Preach the Word

Speak the Wisdom of God in a Mystery
4. Publish the Gospel among All Nations
    Preaching of the Cross is the Power of God

==

PART 12
THE DOCTRINES OF CHRIST

CHAPTER I DOCTRINE OF WATER BAPTISM

The Principles of the Doctrine Of Christ
1. Confess the Sins and Repent
    Parable of the Prodigal Son
    The Loving And Forgiving Father
2.Baptism of Repentance
3. To Fulfill All Righteousness
    a. Lord Jesus Was Baptized Before His Ministry
    b. The Apostles Baptized The Followers Of Christ
        The Prison Keeper was baptized
Prayer For God's Mercy

==

PART 12
THE DOCTRINES OF CHRIST

CHAPTER II THE LAWS ARE YOKE TO THE CHOSEN

The First Agreement with Moses and the Israelites
1. The Law Purged with Blood
2 The High Priest (Levites) Chosen by God
3. Tabernacle: Patterns Of Things In The Heaven
4. Keeping the Sabbath Holy
    Gatherings of Manna for Six Days
    Death Punishment for Not Keeping the Sabbath
5. Sect of Pharisee would Like to Implement the Law to
        Gentiles
6. The Laws are Yoke or Burden to the Chosen
7. The Law of Sin to the Flesh
    Chosen Who are Debtor to the Law

8.There is Still a Veil Covering the Face of the Chosen (Children of Israel)

==

CHAPTER III **THE NEW AGREEMENT**
(To Israel)

Doctrine Of Christ Is From God The Father
Doctrine Taught in Parables
Parables of the Old and the New Agreement
A. New Agreement (to Israel)
   1. Christ will redeem His Seed who are Under the Law (Israel)
   2. Blotting Out Ordinances by Nailing it to the Cross
   3. Building the Tabernacle of David with New Agreement
   4. Dead To The Law By The Body Of Christ
*God's Instructions to both Jews and Gentiles
B. The New Testament (Jews and gentiles)
C. New Covenant (to the Jews and Gentiles)
   The New Covenant that will Take Away the Sins
   Knowing The Truth, No More Sacrifice For Sin
   The Most Glorious Covenant
      1. The Spirit of the Lord is upon the Seed and the Coming Generation
      2. Righteousness through the Blood of the Lord
      3. Heirs According to the Promise.
      The Death of Testator Makes the Children Heirs
      4. Save from God's Wrath (rapture)

==

CHAPTER IV **LAW OF THE SPIRIT OF LIFE IN CHRIST**

(SEE: Vol 1 Part 5 Test Of Faith; Chapter III)
Free from the Law of Sin and Death.

Law of the Spirit of Life in Christ
A. Lord Jesus is the Lord of the Sabbath
   Lord Jesus Healed The Man On Sabbath
      1.The Blind Man
      2.The Man With Withered Hand
B. Food is Sanctify by the Word of God
C. Tithing is not enough to please the Lord
   The Offering that will please the Lord
   Give according to Your Heart's Desire
===

PART 12
THE DOCTRINES OF CHRIST

CHAPTER V **CHRIST ABOLISHED THE LAW OF COMMANDMENTS CONTAINED IN ORDINANCES**

The Lord Reconciled Both Unto God In One Body By The Cross
. The Great Three Commandments of the Lord
      1. First Great Commandment: Thou shalt Love the Lord Thy God with All Thy Heart, and with All Thy Soul, and with   All Thy Mind.
      2. Second Great Commandment: Thou shalt Love Thy Neighbour as Thyself
      The Law is fulfilled
      3. New Commandment: Love One Another
===

PART 12
THE DOCTRINES OF CHRIST

CHAPTER VI **OBEDIENCE TO THE COMMANDMENTS OF CHRIST**

Keep The Commandments Of The Lord
A. First Great Commandment: Thou Shalt Love the Lord Thy God with All Thy Heart, and with All Thy Soul, and   With All Thy Mind.
   Serve One Master

==

PART 12
THE DOCTRINES OF CHRIST

CHAPTER VII **BE A DOER OF THE WORD**

4. Be a Doer of the Word Not a Hearer Only
5. Sowing the Seed (Word of God)
   The Parables of Sowing Seed
6. Relationship with Christ
Save Soul by the Word of Truth
Clean by the Word
Be Fruitful in the Knowledge of the Lord
Be Perfect, and Peace shall be with you.

==

PART 12
THE DOCTRINES OF CHRIST

CHAPTER VIII **LIVE BY GRACE**

A. Give Your Worries to the Lord
   1. The Life is More than Meat
   2. God will Supply According to His Will
   3. Be Established by Grace Not with Meats
B. The Apostles Lived by Grace Not by Treasures
   1. Supply the Necessity of the Saints
   2. The Apostles Are Partakers of the Blessings of Provisions
      Blessings to the Ministers of Seed to the Sower
C. God's provisions both to Master and Slave
D. Warning Not to Store Worldly Treasures
E. Serve God Not Money (False God of Riches)
   1. Trust in Riches is Hard to enter the Kingdom of God
   2. Love the Word Not the Worldly Riches
F. Take the Cross and Follow the Lord
Man Does Not Live by Bread Alone
Lord Jesus is the Bread of Life

==

PART 12
THE DOCTRINES OF CHRIST

CHAPTER IX **PRAYING AND FASTING**

A. Praying to the LORD God
   Kneel Down and Pray

Pray with Joy
Pray with Thanksgiving
Pray by Lifting Hands and No Doubting
Pray in Secret
Pray Not in Repetitions
Forgive then Pray
Pray in the Spirit
Always Pray to the Faithful God

B. God Answers the Prayers
   1. At the Appointed Time
   2. Prayers of Two or More Praying Together
   3. Praying and Fasting
     a. Lord Jesus Fasted Before His Ministry
     b. Ordained Elders in Every Church (Gentiles)
     c. Brethren were called to do Apostolic Works
     d. For Safe Trip
     e. Asking for God's Mercy to preserve Lives
     f. Daniel Fasted During Captivity
       Angel Gabriel was sent to Daniel
       Daniel Had Vision in the Last Days

C. . Kind Of Prayers
   1. Prayer for the Forgiveness of Sin
   2. Praising God for Forgiving Our Iniquities
   3. Prayer for Mercy
   4. Prayer for Peace
   5. Pray not to enter into Temptation
   6. Prayer for Peace to Jerusalem
   7. Prayer for Spiritual Blessings of Might and Power

D. God Hears And Open To Prayers
Take Away the Yoke of Vanity and Selfishness

E.. The Holy Spirit will come to the Followers
   1. God Sent an Angel
   2. God Showed Visions
   3. Prayers Healed the Sick
   Hezekiah was Healed
   4. Through Prayers God Raised the Dead
   5 God Will Forgive and Bless His People
     Confess With Our Mouth That Jesus Is Our Lord

F.. God Answered
   1. Jonah's Prayer
   2. Elija/ Elias' Prayer

==

PART 12
THE DOCTRINES OF CHRIST

CHAPTER X NEVER GO WITH THE FALSE DOCTRINE

==

PART 13
THE CHILDREN OF GOD

CHAPTER I ELECT

Elect is the Branch of the True Vine (Lord Jesus)
Ambassadors for Christ
The Lord Covenant to the Elect
God's Election through Grace
Calling and Election of God
The Holy Calling to abide in Christ
Bringing Every Thought to the Obedience to Christ
C. God's Elect
  1. The Save
  2. The Anointed
     God will Listen and Hear the Prayers of His Anointed
     The Elect has the Power of the Word
     Elect Lives by the Word of God
       a. Word Gives Life Eternal
       b. The Elect will be holding the Lord's Glory
       c. Protected from Evil
       d. The Anointed Could Cast Out Devils
  3. Sanctified and Holy through Christ Jesus
     Sanctified of the Spirit
     Speak in Christ
The Lord Prayed for Sanctification of the Elect

==

PART 13
THE CHILDREN OF GOD

CHAPTER II **MINISTERS OF NEW TESTAMENT**

Minister and Good Steward of Grace
Apostles' Doctrine and Fellowship
Ministers of New Testament
Ministry Of Saints
  1. The Lord's Apostles
  2. Ministers
     Paul Was Called
     Apostle Paul Preached the Gospel of Grace and the Kingdom
       of God
  3. The Preacher
       The Preacher Should Live of the Gospel
  4. Disciples of Christ
     Disciples Abide in Christ

No Fasting For The Diciples While The Lord Was With Them
The Sermon Of The Lord On The Mount
Prayer to the Elect Who Answered the Calling

==

PART 13
THE CHILDREN OF GOD

CHAPTER III **TEMPLE OF GOD**

Elects are the First fruits of the Spirit
Firstfruits Will Be The First One To Rise From The Dead
The Elect's Body
     1. Temple of God
     2. No Agreements of the Body with the Idols
     3 The Body is for the Lord
     4 Body must be Holy
     5. Body as Living Sacrifice to God
     6. The Body Must Flee Fornications
       Epistle of Paul Not to go with Fornicators
       The Thought of Foolishness is Sin
     7. Shine as Light of the World
     8. Salt of the Earth
       Elect is Waiting for the Lord's Second Coming
Sufferings of the Elect
The Elects Comfort Themselves
Elect Loves His Brother
Showing Kindness and Mercy to Others

==

PART 13
THE CHILDREN OF GOD

CHAPTER IV **ELECTS THE BODY OF CHRIST**

The Body of Christ
The Unity of the Body of the Elects
Being many, are in One Body of Christ
Christ is the Head of the Body
Lord Jesus is the Head of the Body of Christ

Joining Together of Jews and Gentiles in One Body
Disciples were called Christians
Baby Christians to Matured Christians
Fellowship of Christians

===

PART 13
THE CHILDREN OF GOD

CHAPTER V **ELECTS THE CHURCH OF CHRIST**

Grace Be Unto The Church Of Christ
A. Christ is the Rock and Head of the Church
    Elects were called Church
B.God is the Rock of Israel
    The Rock of Salvation
    Rock Gave Strength to His Elect (Church)
    1. Joseph Son of Jacob
    2. Christ was with Moses
    3. Christ was with the Prophets
Persecutions of the Elect (Church of Christ)
A. The Church of God and the Church of Christ of the Jews
    1. The Church in the Wilderness (Time of Moses)
    2. Churches of Judea
    3. Church in Jerusalem
B. Apostle Paul Established Churches of Christ for the Gentiles
(Churches of Asia)
    1. Church in Cenchrea (Rome)
    2. Church in Corinth
    3. Churches of Galatia
    4. Church in Philippi
    5. Church in Colosse
    6. Church of the Thessalonians
    7. Church of the Cretians
    8. Church in Antioch
C. . Lord Jesus Is The Advocate Of The Church/ Elect To The
Father
    1. Church of Ephesus: Repent
    2. Church of Smyrna Remain Faithful to Christ
    3. Church of Pergamos: Repent

4. Church of Thyatira: Repent and Keep Up the Works for Christ

5 Church of Sardis Repent, be Watchful and Strengthen

6. Church of Philadelphia: Keep the Word of the Lord

7. Church of Laodiceans: Repent

Apostle Peter Repented for Denying Christ Three Times

Prayer for Repentance

==

PART 14
THE POWER OF DARKNESS

CHAPTER 1 **KNOWING SATAN**

Satan was a Perfect Cherub

Satan Sinned against God

God Casted Out Satan from the Holy Mountain

Satan is the Profane Wicked Prince of Israel

War in Heaven

Satan and His Angels Were Cast Out into the Earth

Jesus Witnessed the fall of Satan and His Fallen Angels from Heaven

Satan Stature was like a Cedar Tree in the Garden of God

The Coming Judgement and Punishment to Satan

==

PART 14

THE POWER OF DARKNESS

CHAPTER II THE ENEMY OF THE CHOSEN AND ELECT

A. The Prince of the Devils and of This World (Satan)
   Responsible to Make the World into Wilderness

B, Satan the Deceiver and Liar
   Planted Seed of Doubt and Disobedience against God
   1. The Cleverness and the Workings of the Devil against the Children of God
   2. Satan against the Elect
   Job,
   David

Apostle Peter
Satan Hindered The Ministry Of Apostle Paul
3. The Accuser of Holy People
4. To Take Away All the Blessings of the Elect
   a. Blessings of Provisions
   b. Behind Evil Thoughts of Men to Harm the Chosen and Elect
   c. Bring Natural Disaster to the Elect's Household and Property
   d. Bring Sickness
   e. Satan Inputs Suicidal Thoughts
      Tried to deceive Lord Jesus in the Wilderness
      Judas Iscariot Killed Himself
C. Satan against Lord Jesus
   1. Tempted the Lord in the Wilderness
   2. Behind the Arrest and Murder of Lord Jesus
D. Behind the Man of Evil and His False Prophet (End Times)
E. Satan will make War with the Almighty in the End Times

==

PART 14
THE POWER OF DARKNESS

CHAPTER III VAIN DECIET

Behind False Prophets
Enticing and Misleading the Chosen
Prophets Lied Perverted the Words of God
False Prophesy
False Prophets Deceive the Chosen
False Prophet with Lying Divination

==

PART 14
THE POWER OF DARKNESS

CHAPTER IV DECEITFUL WORKERS OF SATAN

Behind False Apostles , Deceitful Workers
   1. Behind False Teachings

2.False Teachers with False Religions (Cult, Pagans, Christian
Pagans and Anti- Christ)
3. Behind False Ministers that Love Money more than the
Creator
4. Behind False Ministers that Serve Idols
==

PART 14
THE POWER OF DARKNESS

CHAPTER V **SATAN BLINDED THE SOUL OF THE CHOSEN**

A. Satan wants our Soul to sin against God
1. Satan Entered into Judas Iscariot to betray the Lord
The Lord Exposed the Coming of Betrayal during the Last
Supper
Judas Betrayed the Lord with a Kiss
2. Ananias and Wife Sappira
B. Satan Influences Rebellion against God
C. Behind Spiritual Blindness of the Lost Soul
1 Nonbelievers
2. Hate His Brother or a Sister in Christ
3. Does Not Follow God's Commands
4. The One that Continues Sinning
D. Behind the Murderers of God's Saints (Jews and Christians)
E. Hindered the Preaching of the Gospel of Christ to the Gentiles
==

PART 14
THE POWER OF DARKNESS

CHAPTER VI **BONDAGE OF SINS AND CURSES**

THURSDAY, Dec. 26, 2013 12:06 PM CA TIME (Posted In FB
Casting out the Generation of Curses)
Sin of Disobedience
1. Adam Disobeyed God
2. Worshiping Idols
3. Tampering the Commandments of the Lord

4. Disobedience Because of Ignorance
5. To Preach another Gospel
    a. Teaching the Commandments of Men
    b. Followers of the Word of Men Not of God
6. Nonbelievers to Christ the Saviour
7. Sin of Denial
8. Work of the Flesh
No Peace for the None-Believers and Wicked

===

PART 14
THE POWER OF DARKNESS

CHAPTER VII **THE DEVILS**

The Devils Need a Body to Dwell On
    1. Possessed People
       Unclean Spirits (The Spirits of Devils)
       Legions of Unclean Spirits
    2. Devils Possessed None-believers of Christ
    3. Dwell inside People of Wicked Generation
    4. Caused Sickness
       Spirit of Infirmity
       Dumb and Deaf Spirit (Foul Spirit)
    5. Oppressed People
       Spirit of Jealousy
          Saul was jealous of David
       Spirit of Envy
          a. Against own Brother
             1. Cain
             2. Sons of Jacob: Ten Brothers of Joseph
          b. The Presidents and Princes of Medes and Persia
             against Daniel
          c. The Pharisees Accused the Lord Jesus
          d. The Jews Speaks against Apostle Paul and the
          Followers of Christ
       Spirit of Bondage
       Spirit of Fear
       Spirit of Error
       Seducing Spirits
       Spirit of Lust

===

PART 15
VICTORY OVER THE POWER OF DARKNESS

CHAPTER I GOD WILL GIVE FAITH TO THE ELECT

3. Victory over the Power of Darkness
4. Through Faith God will answer Our Prayers
        Physical Healing
    a. The Samaritan
    b. The Woman with the Issue of Blood for Twelve
        Years
    c. The Blind Men
5. Inherit the Promise of God
Live by Faith
Be Not Faithless but Believing
Fight the Good Fight of Faith
May Christ Dwell in your Heart by Faith

==

PART 15
VICTORY OVER THE POWER OF DARKNESS

CHAPTER II **DELIVERANCE FROM BONDAGE OF SINS**

Victory over the Devil
The Holy People is at War with the Rulers of This World
Be Vigilant
Withstanding the Attack of the Devil
A. The Comforter will help the Elect
    Take the Full Armor of God
B. Deliverance
    1. Fear the Lord
        Fear Not
    2. Trust in the Name of the Lord
    3. Commit Yourself to the Lord
        The Lord Gives Strength
    4. Always Depend on the Lord
C. Resisting the Devil Using the Word of God
Victory over the Devils
    Spirit of Bondage
    Foul Spirit (Spirit of Epilepsy Dumb and Deaf Spirit)-
    Deceiving Spirits
    Spirit of Fear
    Spirit of Lust

Teachings and Instructions
5. Seek the Lord
D. Never Give Place to the Devil
　　The Sins Are Conceive from Temptations
　　　a. Slow to Anger
　　　b. Be Strong against Temptations
　　Temptations Not from God
　　　a. Body Language Shows Temptations
　　　b. Lustful Eyes Lead to Temptations
　　　c. Tongue is a Fire Leads to Sin
　　　　The Proud Tongue
　　　　Sharp Tongue
　　　　Lying Tongue
　　　　Unruly Tongue
　　　　Perverse Tongue
God Delivers the Tongue
Prayer for the Deliverance of Tongues

==

PART 15
VICTORY OVER THE POWER OF DARKNESS

CHAPTER III **WALK IN THE SPIRIT NOT OF THE FLESH**

A. Repent And Seek The Lord
　　1. Cleanse Our Selves
　　　Confess the Iniquity, and the Iniquity of the Fathers
　　2. Purge the Old Self of Malice and Wickedness
　　3. Flee from Youthful Lusts
B. Be Sanctified, a Vessel into Honor
　　1. Fulfill the Law of Christ
　　2. Watch and Pray
　　3. Listen to Apostles' Warning
　　4. Stop Ignoring God's
Prayer for Forgiveness of Sins and Deliverance from the Evil
One(Shared by Lelibeth S. Alveza)

==

PART 15
VICTORY OVER THE POWER OF DARKNESS

CHAPTER IV **RECONCILE TO THE GOD OF PEACE AND PRINCE OF PEACE**

Peace Comes from God
The God of Peace (Posted In FB Dec. 22, 2013; 2:19 pm Sunday CA Time)
God will break the Curse and Turned It into Blessing
Free From Sin through Lord Jesus
Perfecting Holiness
Become the Servant of Righteousness
  1. Serve the Law of God through Christ
  2. The Elect Must Live with Christ
  3. Obey from the Heart the Doctrine of Christ
May the Lord Take Charge

===

VOLUME 3
SANCTIFICATION, BLESSINGS AND RESURRECTION

PART 16
SPIRITUAL BLESSINGS ACCORDING TO GOD'S GRACE

CHAPTER I SALVATION OF SOUL

Rejoice In His Salvation
Saving Grace
A. Through Faith
    Abel (Second Son of Adam and Eve),
    Enoch
    Noah
    Abraham
    Isaac and Jacob
    Joseph, Son of Jacob
    Parents of Moses
    Moses
    Joshua
    Rahab
    Sufferings Of The Prophets
    Judges, Barak, David and the Prophets
    David

B. Through Christ
 The World through the Lord shall be saved
 The Lord Redeems the Soul
 Spiritual Drink of Israel through Lord Jesus Christ
 Spiritual Blindness of Israel
 Salvation Comes to the Gentiles
 Gentiles Were Grafted into Salvation by Faith
 Gentiles Must Have Lowly Spirit
Man is justified by Faith Not by Works
The Joy of Salvation

===

PART 16
SPIRITUAL BLESSINGS ACCORDING TO GOD'S GRACE

CHAPTER II **HOPE OF THE CHILDREN OF GOD**

The Blessed Hope
The Hope through Grace
A. Shall be saved from the Wrath of God
 All the Meek of the Earth shall be saved
 All of Israel shall be saved in the Fullness of the Gentiles
 The Mercy of the Deliverer to Israel
 The Gatherings of the Elect (Rapture)
B. Redemption of the Body
 No Flesh and Blood Could Inherit God's Kingdom
  1. The Elect shall become the Children of God
  2. The Children of God shall Rise Up from the Dead
   The Resurrected Children of God
    a. Shall be the Bride of Christ
     Christ is the Bridegroom
    b. Live Like Angels
C. God Shall Reward His Children
 The Heirs of the Kingdom of God
 Have the Right to eat the Fruit of the Tree of Life
 Shall Drink the Water of Life in God's Kingdom
Prayer of Thanksgiving

===

PART 16
SPIRITUAL BLESSINGS ACCORDING TO GOD'S GRACE

CHAPTER III **BAPTISM OF THE HOLY GHOST**

The Comforter
A. To Receive the Holy Ghost
    1. Repent and be baptized with Water
    2. Apostles Prayed And Laid Their Hands On Them
        a. Holy Spirit Came Upon the Elect
        b. The Believers of Christ were baptized by the Holy
           Ghost
B. Filled by the Holy Spirit
    1 Fruits of the Holy Spirit
    2 Gifts of the Holy Spirit
    3 The Manifestations of the Spirit Filled
      Gift Of Utterance Is Diversities Of Tongues
        a. To Make Known The Mystery Of The Gospel And Of
           Christ
           Keep Silence if there be no Interpreter
        b. Praying In Spirit That The Word May Have Free
           Course, And Be Glorified
           Gifts of Tongues without Water Baptism
           Short Prayer to ask for the Utterance of Tongue
    4. Baptized in One Body into One Spirit
    5. Edification through Praying
    6. Elect Becomes a Spiritual person
        a. The Opening of Spiritual Eyes
        b. Renewed the Mind of the Elect
        c. Born of the Spirit
        d. The Holy Spirit will renew the Spirit
        e. Become a Born Again
        f. New Man, a New Creature in Christ

==

PART 16
SPIRITUAL BLESSINGS ACCORDING TO GOD'S GRACE

CHAPTER IV **GOD'S BLESSINGS AND FAVOR TO THE ELECT**

A. Lord Jesus is the Blessing
B. Inherit a Blessing
    God's Blessings through Faith
    Noah

Abraham
Abraham Believed and Trusted God
God's Covenant to Abraham
Abraham Chose to obey God and was Blessed
Abraham Obeyed God
God Stablished His Covenant to Sarah's Son Isaac
Sarah, Wife of Abraham was also blessed
 God's Blessings Passed to the Offspring
1. Ishmael, Son of Abraham
The Sons of Ishmael
Other Sons of Abraham
2. The Lord Blessed Isaac
3. God Blessed Jacob
a. Generations of Kings will come from Jacob's Ancestry
b. God Gave Jacob the Land of Israel
C. Elect Blessed His Sons
1. Isaac Blessed Jacob
2. Israel Blessed Ephraim and Manasseh
3. God Blessed Jacob
a. Generations Of Kings Will Come From Jacob's Ancestry
b. God Gave Jacob The Land Of Israel
D. Elect Blessed His Sons
1. Isaac Blessed Jacob
2. Israel Blessed Ephraim And Manasseh
E. In Time of Trouble the Elect Received God's Favor
Joseph Was Blessed Inside the Prison
F. God Provided the Needs both the Chosen and Elect
In the Wilderness
Manna from Heaven
G. Wealth Comes from God

===

PART 16
SPIRITUAL BLESSINGS ACCORDING TO GOD'S GRACE

CHAPTER V PROVISIONS ACCORDING TO GOD'S PORPUSE

Sufficiency in All Things
1. Provisions to Abraham and Lot
*God's Instruction to Abraham
Hundreds of Abraham's Trained Servants Rescued Lot

2. Joseph was the Governor over the Land of Egypt
3. God Bless Those Who Blessed the Elects
   a. Joseph brought Blessings to Potiphar, the Egyptian
   b. Naomi brought Blessings to Ruth, the Moabite
     Naomi and the Two Daughters -in Law
     Ruth the Moabite was a Chosen
     Naomi and Ruth went to Bethlehem
     Boaz, the Kinsman of Elimelech
     Ruth Found Favor in the Eyes of Boaz
     Naomi Gave Instruction to Ruth
     Ruth Obedience to Naomi
     Boaz Settled with Naomi's Nearer Kin
     The Law of Redeeming
     Purpose of Redeeming
   c. Boaz and Ruth were the Ancestors of David's Family
4. Solomon Prospered through His Obedience to the Lord God
5. Daniel Became the Chief of the Governors of Babylon (See Vol. 1 Part 6 Chapter IV)
6. Joseph of Arimathea

==

PART 16
SPIRITUAL BLESSINGS ACCORDING TO GOD'S GRACE

CHAPTER VI **GOD PROTECTS HIS ELECT**

A God Saved His Elect from God's Wrath
    1. Noah and the Great Flood
      God's Covenant to Noah
    2. The Destruction of Sodom and Gomorrah
    Abraham Made a Bargain with the Lord
 The Angels Saved Lot and Family
B. God Rescued the Lives of His Elect
    1. Isaac's Life was spared
    2. Jacob and His Sons Saved from Famine
    3 Daniel and His Friends
      a. From the Blazing Furnace
        Three Friends of Daniel Did not Worship the Image of the King
        Three Friends were casted in the Fiery Furnace

b. Daniel was saved from the Lions
C. God Sent Angel to restrain Balaam of Cursing the People of Israel
D. God Preserves Life from Fear of the Enemy
E. No Harm Came to Paul when the Snake Fastened on His Hand

==

PART 16
SPIRITUAL BLESSINGS ACCORDING TO GOD'S GRACE

CHAPTER VII **GOD ASSIGNED ANGELS TO THE ELECT**

A. In Charge of the Elect
   An Angel Was With Moses And His People
   The Angel Led the Apostle to the Chosen
   There is an Angel in the Church of Christ
B. The Word of God is confirmed by Angels
   1. To Answer the Prayer of the Elect
   2. To Announce the Birth of the Elect
      a. Samson
      b. John the Baptist
      c. Lord Jesus
    The Angel of the Lord Appeared to Joseph in His Dream
   3. To Bring Good Tidings
   4. To Announce the Good News
      The Resurrection of the Lord
      Christ will be coming back
   5. To Save the Life of his Elect
      Abraham Showed His Obedience to the Lord
      God Sent Angel to Save Peter from Herod
   6. God's Blessing to His Elect
   7. To Fight against the Princess Of Darkness
   8. To Bring Healing to His Chosen
   9. Takes Care of Prophet Elijah
   10. Every Nations has a Prince Angel
   11. Will blow the Trumpet in the End Times
       To Warn the People
       a. Gatherings of the Elect
       b. Blowing of Six Trumpets in Gods Wrath to come

c. The Coming of the Lord Jesus Christ
d. Rising of the Dead in the End Days.

===

PART 17
THE HOLY GHOST

CHAPTER 1 POWERFUL WORKINGS OF THE HOLY SPIRIT

3/23/2013

The Holy Spirit is Alive and has Feelings
A. The Holy Spirit gave instructions to the Elect
    1. The Holy Spirit spoke to the Prophet
    2. Holy Spirit was speaking to the Apostles
    3. The Holy Spirit speaks about the Latter Times
    4. The Holy Spirit as a Person: Speaking about Truth
B. The Holy Spirit Helps the Elect how to pray
C. Knowing the Holy Spirit
    1. The Creator of Earth and Man
       The Holy Spirit is the Spirit of Life
    2. The Wonderful Works of the Holy Spirit to His Chosen
       a. The Holy Spirit did Wonders and Signs in Egypt
       b. Divided the Red Sea
       c. The Holy Spirit gives a Place to rest
       d. The Coming of the Savior
          1. The Holy Ghost came upon Mary
          2. Lord Jesus was filled with the Holy Spirit
            a. Child Jesus
      b Lord Jesus was Thirty Years Old
    3. The Holy Spirit Raised Up Jesus Christ from the Dead
D. The Holy Spirit Witness to the New Covenant
    1. The Holy Spirit gives the Church an Overseers
    2. Demonstration of Spirit and Power
    3. Made the Elects Ministers of the New Testament
E. The Elect Receives a New Strength in Tribulation
F. God gave us His Love through the Holy Spirit
G. The Holy Spirit will gather His People
H. The Holy Spirit will give Life to the Resurrected Body
I. The Holy Ghost will give a New Heart to the Children of God

J. The Holy Spirit Witness that we are Children of God
K Spirit of Judgment
L. The King of kings is Filled with the Holy Spirit of God
==

PART 17
THE HOLY GHOST

CHAPTER II RECEIVING THE HOLY SPIRIT OF GOD

Pouring Out The Holy Spirit
A. The Holy Spirit of God Freely Given
   Meek and Quite Spirit
     Moses was Very Meek
   Spirit of Meekness
   Faithful Spirit
   Spirit of Adoption
   Humble Spirit
   Contrite Spirit
   Spirit of Prophecy
   Excellent Spirit
   Spirit of Obedience
   Sorrowful Spirit
   Spirit of Righteousness
B. The Holy Spirit Manifests According to His. Blessings
   1. Spirit of Wisdom, Understanding and Workmanship
     a. Spirit of Wisdom
     b. Spirit of Workmanship
      Bezaleel and Aholiab
      King David was given the Pattern of the House of God
   2. The Spirit of Might
   Judges
   Othniel
   Gideon
   Samson
   3. Spirit of Knowledge and Fear of the Lord
   4. Spirit of Grace and Truth
   5. Spirit of Prophecy
     Azariah's Prophecy: Nation That Forsake God Will Be In
     Trouble

Seventy Elders of Israel
Made Saul a Prophet
   6. The Holy Spirit showed visions to the Prophet and Seers
      Hanani
      Michaiah
      Ezekiel
   7. Understanding about Visions
      Balaam blessed Israel
      Prophecy to Nations that will Raise Up against Israel
C. Spiritual Blessings to the Offspring
D. The Holy Spirit will give Peace and Joy

==

PART 18
BIBLICAL PROPHECIES OF THE FINAL PLAN OF GOD

CHAPTER I THE BEGINNING OF END TIMES

Lord Jesus Is Coming To Establish His Kingdom
A. The Time to open and To Lose the Seal of the Book
   1. God will order to lose the Seal of the Book
   2. The Lamb Will Open the Seven Seals of the Book
   3. The Four Spirits of Heaven will come down to Earth
      First Seal: To Conquer
      Second Seal: God will take peace from the Earth
      Third Seal: Troubles to People without the Seal of God
      Fourth Seal: Hunger and Death to People
B. The Signs before End Times
   1. Spoken by the Prophets
      Ten Tribes of Israel shall come back home
      Pestilence will come
   2. Spoken by the Lord
     a. Wars and Disasters to many Nations
     b. Gospel of the Kingdom shall be preached in all the World
     c. Many False Prophets shall rise
     d. The Son of Perdition shall be revealed first
C. Anti-Christ shall lead upon Nations
   1. The Rise to Power of the King from the North and the Rising Sun (Northeast)

2. The King shall consolidate His Power to Rule
3. He will declare to Bring Good Tidings to Jerusalem
4. The Man of Perdition will establish His Kingdom in the Glorious Land
5. The King will come from Jewish Origin
   The Seed Of The Beast In The House Of Judah

==

PART 18
BIBLICAL PROPHECIES OF THE FINAL PLAN OF GOD

CHAPTER II **GREAT TRIBULATION PERIOD OF THE SAINTS (31/2 YEARS)**

Fulfillment of Prophecies of the Reigning 666
A. The King will exalt Himself as God
   The King Is Against The Holy Covenant
   The King will be the Beast
B. False Prophet shall be Helping the Beast
   1. The Great Image of Abomination in Jerusalem
   2. Jerusalem shall be compassed of 666 Armies
   3. Will Deceive the Earth to Worship the Beast and His Image
   4. Will Force All to Receive the Mark of the Beast (666)
C. The Two Witnesses in Jerusalem
     Prophecies of the Second Coming of the Lord
D. The Great Tribulation of the Holy People (31/2 Years)
   The Beginning of Sorrow
   The Sufferings for Righteousness
   Patience to Receive the Promise
   Fear God Not the Anti-Christ
   The Suffering Christians Shall Rejoice to the Lord
   Trusting the Lord Jehovah
   In Tribulations the Saints shall have Hope
The Fifth Seal in Heaven
The Souls of the Saints In Heaven
 Prayer for Comfort

==

PART 18
BIBLICAL PROPHECIES OF THE FINAL PLAN OF GOD

CHAPTER III **GOD'S FINAL WARNING**

God's Warning
    1. People of Israel
    2. People of Edom and Teman
    3. People of All Nations
    4. Nations which has Perpetual Hatred against Israel
Nations shall join together to Destroy Israel
The Lord will persecute them

===

PART 18
BIBLICAL PROPHECIES OF THE FINAL PLAN OF GOD

CHAPTER IV **ELECT WILL BE DELIVERED FROM GOD'S WRATH**

The Elect Is Crying Out To God During Tribulation
God's People shall be delivered from the Time of Great Trouble
    1. The Book of Remembrance shall be opened
    2. Seal the Elect
A. Troubles to People without the Seal of God
    Third Seal
        First Trouble: Smoke Locust
        Second Trouble: Great Earthquake in Jerusalem
B. The Death of Two Witnesses
C. The Land of Magog shall plan to attack Israel
    The Evil Plan of Gog
    Great Earthquake in Israel
    The Mountains shall be Thrown Down
    Elect shall be saved from God's Wrath
        a. The Lord will come down from the Clouds of Heaven
        b. First Rising of the Dead
            The Resurrected Saints shall reign with Christ for a
                thousand   Years
        c. Gatherings both the Living and Resurrected Saints
            Gathering Of Elects In Different Time Zone
The Great Crowd in Heaven shall be coming out from Great
        Tribulation
The Saints Praising God in Heaven
Praising God for Preserving His Saints

PART 18
BIBLICAL PROPHECIES OF THE FINAL PLAN OF GOD

CHAPTER V **GREAT TROBLE FROM GOD**

The Coming of the Wrath of God
A. The Sixth Seal
   The Sun shall become Black and the Moon as Blood
B. Seventh Seal
   One Half Hour of Silence in Heaven
   God's pouring of His Wrath
        To the Earth
      1. Vials of Wrath
         a. Against People with the Mark of the Beast
         b. Water Becomes Blood
         c. Thunders, Lightings and Earthquake
      2. Seven Trumpets shall be sounded in Heaven
         a. Third Parts of Trees and All Grass shall be burned up
         b. Third Part of the Sea shall become blood
         c. Third Part of the Fresh Water shall become bitter
         d. Third Part of the Sun, the Moon and the Stars shall be
         darkened

===

PART 18
BIBLICAL PROPHECIES OF THE FINAL PLAN OF GOD

CHAPTER VI **THE SECOND COMING OF CHRIST**

Blow the Trumpet in Zion
A. The Lord Will Come Down from Heaven
   David's Vision of the Coming of Christ
   Second Coming of Christ
   The Troops of the LORD
      a. Angels
      b. Saints
   The Great Day of the Lord
   The Coming of the Day of Terror to the Wicked
   Watchman Must Warn The People of Israel
B. Spirits of Devils shall gather the kings of the Whole World

The 666 shall gather Nations against Christ
C. Battle of Armageddon
   The Angels shall fight against the Multitude
   The Lord will teach the Saints the Ways of War
   God's Fury against the Armies of Nations
   Those That Shall Escape Shall Be Declaring The Glory Of
      The Lord Among The Gentiles

==

PART 18
BIBLICAL PROPHECIES OF THE FINAL PLAN OF GOD

CHAPTER VII THE DAY OF MOURNING IN JERUSALEM

Abominations in Jerusalem
A. The Lord will Recompense His Enemies
   The People Who Did Abominations will be ashamed
   In that Day They Shall Recognize the Lord
B. The Lord will come with Fire
   The Lord will smite Israel from Head to Tail in One Day
   1. God will destroy People and Their Idols
   2. The Lord will destroy the Residue of the Heathen
   3. The Lord will cut off Their Remembrance of Idols
   4. In that Day the Prophets shall be ashamed
   5. The Lord will slay Two Parts of the People in Jerusalem
      The Whole City shall Hide Themselves with Great Fear

==

PART 18
BIBLICAL PROPHECIES OF THE FINAL PLAN OF GOD

CHAPTER VIII THE LORD WILL BRING PUNISHMENT TO ALL NATIONS

A. Shall Be Destroying Nations that Worship Idols
   1. Wrath against Moab
   2. Wrath against Samaria
B. Destroying Nations which are against Israel
   1. The Lord against Tyre
   2. The Lord Will Destroy The Philistines
   3. The Lord God against Zidon

4. The Land Of Edom (The Land Of Esau)

5. Wrath against Ammon

6. Damascus

7. Destroy With Fire the City Of Babylon the Great

The Second Seal:

God Will Take Peace from the Earth

God's Voice will Roar against the Inhabitants of Nations

1. Heavenly Armies shall come to slay 1/3 Part of Men
   Sound of Trumpet

2. Slain the Proud and Lofty
   Frightened Idol Worshipers shall throw away their Idols
   Wrath Of God Against People Who Rely On
   Enchantments

Fourth Seal

God will give power to Death and Hell

. 3. Smite the Wicked of the Earth
   Hell shall meet the Wicked Souls

===

PART 18
BIBLICAL PROPHECIES OF THE FINAL PLAN OF GOD

CHAPTER IX **THE FALL OF THE 666, FALSE PROPHET, SATAN AND THE PRINCES OF DARKNESS**

The Beast and the False Prophet shall be thrown into the Lake of
   Fire

The Army of Satan and the Beast shall be slain by the Lord

Defeat of Satan and His Angels/ Devils

After the Wrath of God

The Great Trumpet shall be blown

The Righteous shall be glad

Heavenly Beings shall be rejoicing

===

PART 18
BIBLICAL PROPHECIES OF THE FINAL PLAN OF GOD

CHAPTER X **NEW EARTH AND NEW HEAVEN**

Prior to the Coming Down of the Kingdom of Heaven

A. The Heavens shall be rolled together

B. Earth shall be destroy
C. Creation of New Earth and Heaven
D. The New Earth shall become Paradise
E. The Lord will build Cities in the Land of Israel
   The Mercy of the Lord on Jacob
   The Cities shall be inhabited
   Nation of Israel shall become One Nation again
   Shall be Gathering the Lost Sheep (Nation of Israel)
   The Lord will divide by Lots the Land of Israel for Inheritance
   God's Plan for Samaria

===

PART 18
BIBLICAL PROPHECIES OF THE FINAL PLAN OF GOD

CHAPTER XI THE MILLENNIAL KINGDOM OF CHRIST

Elect shall be Waiting for God's Kingdom to Come
*Promise of Lord Jesus to His Elect
God's Heavenly Kingdom shall be Adorned Like a Bride
New Jerusalem the Kingdom from Heaven
The Lord God shall be coming from the Way to the East
Lord God will give Light to the City
Inside the Kingdom of God
A. The Lord of Hosts will dwell in the Midst of Jerusalem
   Praising Father God
B. The Lord will be the King of All kings
   he Lord King will Judge the People Fairly
   The King will be worshiped
   The Heathen shall Serve and Obey the Lord
C. Lord Jesus is the Lord of Hosts
   *The Lord's Instructions to His People
D. The Life of People during One Thousand Years
    1. Shall live a Joyful Life
    2. Shall have a Longer Life
    3. People shall live in Peace
    4. The Lord will blessed the People that Fears Him
    5. Prosperity to the Land
    6. David will be the Prince of the Nation of Israel
    7. Safety Living

Nations shall come to Worship in the Temple of New
Jerusalem
Punishment to Nations that shall not Come up to Worship
Praising God in New Jerusalem
8. A Cheerful Feast in New Jerusalem
Sing Praise to the Lord
Blessed be the Lord's Glorious Name For Ever
=======================================

PART 18
BIBLICAL PROPHECIES OF THE FINAL PLAN OF GOD

CHAPTER XII **THE RESURRECTION OF THE DEAD**

After the Thousand Years
A. Satan shall deceive and shall Gather Nations against the Lord
The Lord will defend Jerusalem
The Bands of Gog shall fall upon the Mountain of Israel
The Lord God Will Send Fire In The Land Of Magog
The Angel Shall Announce The Day of Judgment
B. Jesus will raise up the Dead
Second Rising of the Dead
1. The Children of God shall rise first
Gentiles (Children of God)
The Children of God shall have Glorious Bodies
Resurrected Children of God are looking upon Zion
Death shall be swallowed up in Victory
Prayer of Thanksgiving
2. Death and Hell shall deliver up the Dead
===

PART 18
BIBLICAL PROPHECIES OF THE FINAL PLAN OF GOD

CHAPTER XIII **THE DAY OF JUDGMENT**

The Throne shall be ready for the Judgment
A. The Lord will Execute Judgment
The Lord will Judge in Righteousness
B. The Saints shall Judge the Twelve Tribes of Israel
The Saints shall be Joyful in the Glory of the Lord

Judgment Day
Valley of Decision
C. The Lord will Open Up the Books
   The Books of Works and Book of Life shall Be Opened
   1. Names of the Children of God Written in the Book of Life
   2. Names not Written in the Book of Life
      No More Excuses and Escape to the Unsaved
   3. Names were Blotted Out from the Book of Life
      a. Idol Worshippers
      b. Workers of Iniquity (Sinners)
      c. The People who Persecuted the Lord
   4. Names not found in the Book of Life
      Separating the Righteous from the Wicked
      Blessing of Life Forever to the Resurrected Children of
         God
      Let The Saints Be Joyful In Glory

===

PART 18
BIBLICAL PROPHECIES OF THE FINAL PLAN OF GOD

CHAPTER XIV THE LORD WILL ENTER INTO JUDGMENT AND WILL EXECUTE PUNISHMENT

.

A. The Devil and the Fallen Angels
   1. Satan
   2. The Angels that Sinned against God
B The Dead shall be Judged according to the Book of Works
C. Judgment According to the Law and Gospel of Christ
   1. Judgment to the Chosen People
      The House of Israel shall be Judged First, followed by the
         Gentiles
      The Place of Punishment
   2. Punishment to Wicked
      a. They shall Perish
         1.The Righteous turned away from His Righteousness
         2. Worshipers of the Hosts of Heaven
         3. The Proud and the Wicked
      b. Eternal Punishment (Lake of Fire)
         1. Nonbeliever

2. People that do not obey the Gospel of Christ
3. Pharisees and Scribes who persecuted the Prophets
4. Children of Disobedience
  Rebellion is against God
5. They that walked according to the Flesh
6. Idolaters, Ungodly and Evildoers
7. With Evil Tongue
8 Man who received the Mark of the Beast
c. Shall be transported to the Darkest Part of the Lake of
    Fire
  False Teachers with False Religions
  Angels shall be gathering the Wicked into the Lake of
    Fire

The Weight of Eternal Punishment
Lake of Fire the Second Death

==

PART 18
BIBLICAL PROPHECIES OF THE FINAL PLAN OF GOD

CHAPTER XV GOD AND THE HEIRS OF HIS KINGDOM

Lord Jesus Christ will be the King of Saints
The Glory of the Lord
The Redeemed shall come Rejoicing into Zion
Welcoming the Children of God
The Household of God
A. The Children of God shall inherit the Earth Forever
  1. The Saints of the Most High
  2. Shall be Rulers and Kings
    3. David shall be the Prince of the Nation Of Israel
B. Heavenly Way of Living for the Children of the Resurrection
    1. No More Sorrow and Death
    2 Shall be Living Together with the Heavenly Hosts
  Hosts of Heaven: Ministering Spirits
      1. Angels
      a. Seraphim
      b. Cherubim
      Some Names of the Angels
      Michael
        1. Prince Angel of Israel

85

INTRODUCTION

Luke 10:*21 In that hour Jesus rejoiced in spirit, and said, I thank thee, O Father, Lord of heaven and earth, **that thou hast hid these things from the wise and prudent, and hast revealed them unto babes**: even so, Father; for so it seemed good in thy sight.*
22 All things are delivered to me of my Father: and no man knoweth who the Son is, but the Father; and who the Father is, but the Son, and he to whom the Son will reveal him.
23 And he turned him unto his disciples, and said privately, Blessed are the eyes which see the things that ye see:
24 For I tell you, that many prophets and kings have desired to see those things which ye see, and have not seen them; and to hear those things which ye hear, and have not heard them.

These books **Volume 1, 2 &3** the **compilation of verses from the KJV Bible will serve as a rich study bible guide using only the Holy Bible as the main source of knowledge and wisdom with the guidance of the Holy Spirit.**
According to the Bible, the word of God will not go in vain. The Scriptures were written by many prophets of different generations with the guidance of the Holy Ghost, Through His word, God reveals Himself, to all generations His single plan was written in the scriptures both in the Old and New Testament. He gave instructions according to his purpose to bring many sons into His glory in order to glorify Him and to abide to His calling to preach the Gospel of Christ and baptize the believers both the Jews and Gentiles *(03/02/14)*
God implements His single plan from the ancient times to the last of days about the great hope of salvation of souls to everyone called chosen people whom God's love dearly.
This is how God implements his single plan , in Volume 1, God reveals Himself to people of all generations, by creation of heavens, hosts of heaven , His Kingdom, earth and man. He anointed His prophets to write down His plan and instructions and anointed deliverers to preserve His chosen. He gave the first agreement to His chosen to test their faith and obedience.The chosen chose to disobey so God rendered punishment to the

children of disobedience. In Volume 2, God redeemed the souls of His chosen who were lost(Israelites and Gentles) through the death and resurrection of Christ.This book also expose the workings of the devils against God's chosen and elect. Volume 3 speaks about God's grace of giving spiritual blessings to the elect by the workings of the Hoy Ghost. The last part, are compilation of verses about the prophecies of the second coming of Christ in the last days. After the resurrection of the dead, He will render judgment with punishment to the nonbelievers, idolaters and wicked according to the gospel of Christ. He will otherwise give rewards to the heirs of His kingdom that will last forever.

Through prayers and Bible studies, people of all generations are encourage to read and teach our children and children's children the Scriptures and to remain faithful to the living God until the second coming of our LORD Jesus Christ. **Through God's grace, the readers will be enlightened how to spiritually discern the false prophets and to avoid following the doctrines of ma**n to avoid the destruction of souls and eternal punishment.

These is the course on how God' plan is being implemented after creation up to the second coming of Christ as written in the Bible:

BRINGING MANY SONS INTO GLORY
(God's Plan, Purpose and Instructions)
VOLUME 1
GOD PRESERVES HIS CHOSEN PEOPLE

THE IMPORTANCE OF HOLY SCRIPTURES
PART 1   GOD'S WORD TO ALL GENERATIONS
PART 2   THE SCRIPTURES SPEAK ABOUT GOD'S PLAN

PREDESTINATION OF THE CHOSEN PEOPLE
PART 3   GOD CALLED HIS PEOPLE

GOD PRESERVED HIS CHOSENPEOPLE
PART 4   FIRST AGREEMENT TO THE NATION OF ISRAEL
PART 5   TEST OF FAITH
PART 6   GOD ANOINTED DELIVERERS

GOD'S PUNISHMENT
PART 7   THE CHILDREN OF DISOBEDIENCE
PART 8   GOD RENDERS PUNISHMENT
DESTINATION OF SOUL AND SPIRIT
PART 9   MYSTERY OF THE BODY, SOUL AND SPIRIT

==

VOLUME 2
GOD'S WORD BECAME FLESH

GOD'S PURPOSE OF SENDING THE MESSIAH
PART 10 THE SAVIOR OF SOUL

THE GOSPEL OF GOD IS THE GOSPEL OF CHRIST
PART 11   THE GOSPEL OF CHRIST
PART 12   THE DOCTRINES OF CHRIST

THE CHURCH/ELECT ARE THE FOLLOWERS OF CHRIST
PART 13   THE CHILDREN OF GOD

SATAN AND THE FALLEN ANGELS IN THIS WORLD
PART 14   THE POWER OF DARKNESS

GOD IS IN CONTROL
PART 15 VICTORY OVER THE POWER OF DARKNESS

==

VOLUME 3
SANCTIFICATION, BLESSINGS AND RESURRECTION

THE POWERFUL WORKINGS OF THE HOLY SPIRIT
PART 16   SPIRITUAL BLESSINGS   ACCORDING TO GOD'S GRACE
PART 17   THE HOLY GHOST

PROPHECIES OF THE SECOND COMING OF CHRIST

PART 18 BIBLICAL PROPHECIES OF THE FINAL PLAN OF GOD

The prophecies of the end times

1. Signs before the tribulation period of the saints
2. 31/2 Years Tribulations of the Saints
3. Signs before the second coming of the LORD
   Gatherings of the Elect
4. The wrath of GOD
a. Armageddon
b. Wrath against nations
5. Creation of new heaven and earth
6. Millennial Kingdom of Christ
7 Resurrection of the Dead
8. Day of Judgment
9. Lake of Fire Final Punishment
10. Final plan of God

Glory to God!

First, God is giving His wisdom to His follower who prayed deeply and unceasingly with a fervent desire to learn and to reveal the mysteries in the Scriptures.

1. Godliness
2. God's creation
3. Predestination
4. Body, soul and spirit
5. Kingdom of heaven and the kingdom of God
6. Power of darkness
7. Gatherings of the elect
8. Resurrection of the dead
9. Angels and the heavenly hosts

Second: these books are the answer of God's calling that He must be worshiped, His people must keep His word and must spread the Gospel of Christ.

Third: These books are also powerful testimonies that spiritual understanding of the depths of God's word is not only a sole privilege to the expert of biblical studies. Amazingly, the Holy Ghost gave the gifts of wisdom, understanding and revelation of Christ through His Word to the compiler. for free through God's will and grace. The Holy Spirit worked miraculously without the intervention of human understanding, interpretation and indoctrination of man in absorbing the doctrines of religion. The compilation of the verses show that a servant of God has no need to expound, to interpolate, to interpret and to use her own word and understanding to expose the message from the Bible. Hence, avoiding the unintentional tampering of the word of God which spiritually violates the very essence of what the LORD's instructions that the Scriptures is not subject for any private interpretation and it is prohibited to add or to take away any of His Word from the Scriptures. The verses from the Scriptures are perfectly enough to explain God's instructions to His chosen and elect, for His Word is pure and all his works are perfect. God is not the author of confusion but the God of truth as what the Bible says.

Jesus said, these things hidden to the wise and prudent but gave revelations to the babes, Even though the compiler has no formal training or intensive education in Theology, and not affiliated to any religious group, the power of the Holy Spirit worked hand in hand with His servant to finish the book with three volumes.

The power of God through the workings of the Holy Spirit manifested to the compiler by spiritually guiding her, giving her insights on how to organize and how to compile the verses from the Holy Bible KJV. His Word is wisdom. By learning the truth of God's instructions on how He is continuously, implementing His plan of salvation from the beginning up to the last day was amazingly unbelievable, priceless and eternal.

According to His Word, the chosen are predestined to be an heir and will become His children. Through God's grace, children of God have a great hope, that LORD Jesus will resurrect them from the dead and God will give them a new life, with a new glorious body. The Bible says, No flesh and blood could inherit His kingdom. He will join the resurrected children of God together with the hosts of heaven to His heavenly household wherein Christ will be the head forever.

Through this magnificent revelation of what the Holy Bible teaches, the compiler excitedly started the manuscript. She began to compile PART 18 BIBLICAL PROPHECIES OF THE FINAL PLAN OF GOD of fifteen chapters. At first, she had no idea of what the text was all about. After reading all the chapters, she was sorely afraid, felt goosebumps and dreaded the pouring out of God's wrath to idol worshipers, nonbelievers and sinners in the last days. Uncontrollably, she cried out and sob three times, because of fear to what will happen when God 's time comes. She prayed that may the LORD reveals himself to people without faith and praying that many people will be save and have eternal life.

This incredible knowledge and revelations from the Holy Bible. was a real supernatural experience. The compiler is now giving glory to God by abiding to His holy calling that the Gospel of God must be preach at Hs appointed time. Deeper spiritual understanding of His Word leads to loving Him more, worshipping and thanking and praising Him above all names.

Isaiah 6:3 *Holy holy, holy is the Lord of Hosts, the whole earth is full of your glory.*

May the LORD bless this book and the other two volumes to last until the Gospel of the kingdom of God be preached to all nations and then the end will come as it was written in the Bible.

Lastly, before embarking to study this compilation of the Holy Bible verses, the compiler is encouraging everyone to pray and ask God for the guidance of the Holy Ghost to give His power of wisdom, understanding and revelation.

PRAYER FOR STRENGTH

2Timothy 4:17 *Notwithstanding the Lord stood with me, and strengthened me; that by me the preaching might be fully known, and that all the Gentiles might hear: and I was delivered out of the mouth of the lion.*
18 And the Lord shall deliver me from every evil work, and will preserve me unto his heavenly kingdom: to whom be glory for ever and ever. Amen and Amen.

VOLUME 1
GOD PRESERVES HIS CHOSEN PEOPLE

PART 1
GOD'S WORD TO ALL GENERATIONS

CHAPTER I **THE HOLY BIBLE WAS WRITTEN**

1Corinthians 10:11
*Now all this things happened unto them for ensamples: and **they are written for our admonition,** upon whom the ends of the world are come.*

THE HOLY SCRIPTURES: GOD IS THE AUTHOR

Isaiah 41:4 *Who hath wrought and done it, calling the generations from the beginning? I the LORD, the first, and with the last; I am he.*

1Corinthians 14:33 **For God is not the** *author of confusion,* **but of peace**, as in all churches of the saints.
Deuteronomy 32:4 He is the Rock, **his work is perfect**: for all his ways are judgment: a *God of truth* **and without iniquity, just and right is he.**

A. THE HOLY GHOST MOVED THE PROPHETS

Hebrews 1:1 *God, who at sundry times **and in divers manners spake in time past unto the fathers by the prophets,***

2Samuel 23:2 **The Spirit of the LORD spake by me, and his word was in my tongue.**

Ezekiel 2:1 And he said unto me, Son of man, stand upon thy feet, and I will speak unto thee.

2 **And the spirit entered into me when he spake unto me**, and set me upon my feet, **that I heard him that spake unto me.**

Ezekiel 3:10 Moreover **he said unto me, Son of man, all my words that I shall speak unto thee receive in thine heart, and hear with thine ears.**

Ezekiel 3:24 **Then the spirit entered into me, and set me upon my feet, and spake with me,** and said unto me, Go, shut thyself within thine house.

25 But thou, O son of man, behold, they shall put bands upon thee, and shall bind thee with them, and thou shalt not go out among them:

26 **And I will make thy tongue cleave to the roof of thy mouth, that thou shalt be dumb**, and shalt not be to them a reprover: for they *are* a rebellious house.

27 **But when I speak with thee, I will open thy mouth, and thou shalt say unto them, Thus saith the Lord GOD; He that heareth, let him hear; and he that forbeareth, let him forbear: for they** *are* **a rebellious house.**

2Peter 1:21 **For the** *prophecy* **came not in old time by the will of man: but holy men of God spake as they were moved by the Holy Ghost.**

Luke 1:70 **As he spake by the mouth of his holy prophets, which have been since the world began:**

71 That we should be saved from our enemies, and from the hand of all that hate us;

72 To perform the mercy *promised* to our fathers, and to remember his holy covenant;

73 The oath which he sware to our father Abraham,

74 That he would grant unto us, that we being delivered out of the hand of our enemies might serve him without fear,

75 In holiness and righteousness before him, all the days of our **life.**

* B. GOD'S INSTRUCTIONS TO THE PROPHETS

1. WRITE DOWN THE WORDS

Psalms 102:18 *This shall be written for the generation to come: and the people which shall be created shall praise the LORD.*

Jeremiah 36:2 **Take thee a roll of a book, and write therein all the words that I have spoken unto thee** against Israel, and against Judah, and against all the nations, from the day I spake unto thee, from the days of Josiah, even unto this day.

4 Then Jeremiah called Baruch the son of Neriah: and **Baruch wrote from the mouth of Jeremiah all the words of the LORD, which he had spoken unto him, upon a roll of a book.**

Habakkuk 2:2 And **the LORD answered me, and said**, *Write the vision, and make it plain upon tables, that he may run that readeth it.*

3 *For the vision is yet for an appointed time, but at the end it shall speak, and not lie: though it tarry, wait for it; because it will surely come, it will not tarry.*

Isaiah 8:1 Moreover **the LORD said unto me. Take thee a great roll, and write in it with a man's pen** concerning Ma-her-shalal-hash-baz.

Isaiah 30:8 **Now go, write it before them in a table, and note it in a book, maybe for the time to come forever and ever:**

2 HEAR GOD'S INSTRUCTIONS

Deuteronomy 32:1 Give ear, O ye heavens, and I will speak; and **hear, O earth the words of my mouth.**

2 **My doctrine shall drop as the rain, my speech shall distil as the dew, as the small rain upon the tender herb, and as the showers upon the grass:**

3 Because **I will publish the name of the LORD:** ascribe ye greatness unto our God.

Proverb 8:32 **Now therefore hearken unto me, O ye children**: for blessed *are they that* keep my ways.

33 **Hear instruction, and be wise, and refuse it not**.

34 **Blessed** *is* **the man that heareth me, watching daily at my gates, waiting at the posts of my doors.**

35 **For whoso findeth me findeth life**, and **shall obtain favour of the LORD**.

36 But *he that sinneth against me wrongeth his own soul:* **all they that hate me love death**.

C. LORD JESUS WARNS NOT TO ALTER THE WORD OF GOD

Proverbs 30:6 **Add thou not unto his words,** he lest he reprove thee, and thou be found a liar.

1. BLASPHEMY AGAINST THE HOLY GHOST

Matthew 12:31 Wherefore I say unto you, **All manner of sin and blasphemy shall be forgiven** unto men: but the blasphemy against the Holy Ghost shall not be forgiven unto men.

32 And whosoever speaketh a word against the Son of man, it shall be forgiven him: **but whosoever speaketh against the Holy Ghost, it shall not be forgiven him, neither in this world, neither in the world to come.**

Mark 3:29 But he that shall blaspheme against the Holy Ghost hath never forgiveness, but **is in danger of eternal damnation.**

30 Because they said, **He hath an unclean spirit.**

2. THE LORD SHALL BLOT OUT NAME FROM UNDER THE HEAVEN.

2Peter 1:20 Knowing this first, **that no prophecy of the scripture is of any private interpretation.**

21 For the prophecy came not in old time by the will of man: but holy men of God spake *as they were* moved by the Holy Ghost.

Exodus 32:33 And the LORD said unto Moses**, Whoever hath sinned against me, him will I blot out of my book.**

Revelation 22:18 For I testify unto every man that heareth the words of the prophecy of this book, **If any man shall add unto these things, God shall add unto him the plagues that are written in this book:**

19 **And if any man shall take away from the words of the book of this prophecy, God shall take away his part out of the book of life, and out of the holy city, and** *from* **the things which are written in this book.**

Deuteronomy 29:20 **The LORD will not spare him, but then the anger of the LORD and his jealousy shall smoke against that man, and all the curses that are written in this book shall lie upon him, and the LORD shall** *blot out* **his name from under heaven.**

PART 1
GOD'S WORD TO ALL GENERATIONS

CHAPTER II **IMPORTANCE OF THE HOLY SCRIPTURES**

Isaiah 55:11
*So shall **my word** be **that goeth forth out of my mouth**: it shall **not return unto me void**, but it shall accomplish **that which I please**, and **it shall prosper in the thing whereto I sent it.***

A. GOD'S WORD IS WISDOM
Proverbs 2:10 When wisdom entereth into thine heart, and knowledge is **pleasant unto thy soul**;
11 Discretion shall preserve thee, understanding shall keep thee:
Proverbs 8:6 Hear; for *I will speak* of excellent things; and the opening of my lips shall be right things.
7 **For my mouth *shall speak* truth**; and wickedness is an abomination to my lips.
8 **All the words of my mouth are in righteousness**; there is nothing froward or perverse in them.
9 **They are all plain to him that understandeth, and right to them that find knowledge.**
10 **Receive my instruction**, and not silver; **and knowledge** rather than choice gold.
11 **For wisdom is better than rubies; and all the things that may be desired are not to be compared to it.**

THE LORD GIVES WISDOM TO UNDERSTAND GOD'S WORD

Proverbs 2:6 *For the LORD giveth wisdom: out of his mouth cometh knowledge and understanding.*

Colossians 2:2 That their hearts might be comforted, being knit together in love, and unto all riches of the full assurance of understanding, **to the acknowledgement of the mystery of God, and of the Father, and of Christ;**

3 **In whom are hid all the treasures of wisdom and** knowledge.

WISDOM FROM ABOVE IS PURE AND PEACEFUL

Daniel 2:20 Daniel answered and said, **Blessed be the name of God forever and ever: for wisdom and might are his:**

James 3:17 **But the wisdom that is from above is first pure, then peaceable, gentle, and easy to be intreated, full of mercy and good fruits, without partiality, and without hypocrisy.**

GOD GIVES WISDOM THAT REVEALS THE DEEP AND SECRET THINGS

Daniel 2:21 And **he changeth the times and the seasons:** he removeth kings, and setteth up kings: **he giveth wisdom unto the wise, and knowledge to them that know understanding**:

22 **He revealeth the deep and secret things**: he knoweth what *is* in the darkness, and the light dwelleth with him.

IF ANY ONE LACK WISDOM, LET HIM ASK GOD IN FAITH

Mark 9:23 *Jesus said unto him, If thou canst believe, all things are possible to him that believeth.*

Jeremiah 33:3 **Call unto me, and I will answer thee, and shew thee great and mighty things, which thou knowest not.**

James 1:5 **If any one lack wisdom, let him ask of God, that giveth to all men liberally, and upraideth not; and it shall be given him.**

6 **But let him ask in faith, nothing wavering.** For he that wavereth is like a wave of the sea driven with the wind and tossed.

PRAYER FOR WISDOM AND UNDERSTANDING

Ephesians 1:17 *That the God of our Lord Jesus Christ, the Father of glory, may give unto you the spirit of wisdom and revelation in the knowledge of him:*

18 The eyes of your understanding being enlightened; that ye may know what is the hope of his calling, and what the riches of the glory of his inheritance in the saints,

19 And what is the exceeding greatness of his power to us-ward who believe, according to the working of his mighty power,

20 Which he wrought in Christ, when he raised him from the dead, and set him at his own right hand in the heavenly places,, Amen and Amen.

DANIEL PRAISING GOD
Daniel 2:23 *I thank thee, and praise thee, O thou God of my fathers, who hast given me wisdom and might, and hast made known unto me now what we desired of thee: for thou hast now made known unto us the king's matter.*

B. THE WORD OF GOD WILL LAST FOREVER

1. BREAD FROM HEAVEN
Matthew 4:4 But he answered and said, It is written, **Man shall not live by bread alone, but by every word that proceedeth out of the mouth of God.**
John 6:32 Then Jesus said unto them, Verily, verily, I say unto you, Moses gave you not that bread from heaven; but my Father giveth you the true bread from heaven.
33 **For the bread of God is** *he* **which cometh down from heaven, and giveth life unto the world.**

2. THE WORD OF GOD IS PURE
Proverbs 30:5 Every **word of God is pure: he** is **a shield unto them that put their trust in him.**
2Samuel 22:31 **As for God, his way is perfect; the word of the LORD is tried:** he is a buckler to all them that trust him.
Psalms 18:30 **As for God, his way is perfect; the word of the LORD is tried:** he is a buckler to all those that trust in him.
Psalms 12:6 **The words of the LORD are pure words**: as silver tried in a furnace of earth, purified seven times.

3. THE WORD OF GOD IS TRUE FROM THE BEGINNING
John 17:17 *Sanctify them through thy truth: thy word is truth.*
Psalm 119:160 **Thy word is true from the beginning**; and every one of thy righteous judgments endureth forever.
1Thessalonians 2:13 **For this cause also thank we God without ceasing, because, when ye received the word of God which ye heard of us, ye received** *it* **not** *as* **the word of men, but as it is in truth, the word of God, which effectually worketh also in you that believe.**

4. THE WORD OF GOD SHALL NOT PASS AWAY

Luke 21:33, Matthew 24:35 and Mark 13:31 Heaven and earth shall pass away: but **my words shall not pass away.**

Isaiah 40:8 The grass withereth, the flower fadeth: but **the word of our God shall stand for ever.**

Isaiah 55: 11 So shall my word be that goeth forth out of my mouth: it shall not return unto me void, but it shall accomplish that which I please, and it shall prosper *in the thing* whereto I sent it.

C. THE SCRIPTURES IS ALL ABOUT GOD

Revelation 1:8. *I am Alpha and Omega, the beginning and the ending, saith the Lord, which is, and which was, and which is to come, the Almighty.*

Revelation 22:13 *I am Alpha and Omega, the beginning and the end, the first and the last.*

1. GOD GIVES HOPE AND MERCY

Romans 5:5 **And hope maketh not ashamed; because the love of God is shed abroad in our hearts by the Holy Ghost which is given unto us.**

Romans 11:32 **For God hath concluded** *them all in unbelief,* **that he might have mercy upon all.**

Romans 15:4 **For whatsoever things were written aforetime were written for our learning, that we through patience and comfort of the scriptures might have hope.**

2. GOD GIVES EVERLASTING LIFE

John 4:14 But whosoever drinketh of the water that I shall give him shall never thirst; but the water that **I shall give him shall be in him a well of water springing up into everlasting life.**

Psalms 36:9 **For with thee is the fountain of life: in thy light shall we see light.**

*D. FOR INSTRUCTION IN RIGHTEOUSNESS

2Timothy 3:16 **All scripture** *is* **given by inspiration of God,** and *is* profitable for doctrine, for reproof, for correction, for instruction in righteousness:

17 That the man of God may be perfect, throughly furnished unto all good works.

E. GOD SHOWS ALL HIS WONDERFUL WORKS

Psalms 111:6 *He hath shewed his people the power of his works, that he may give them the heritage of the heathen.*

Psalms 111:**4 He hath made his wonderful works to be remembered**: the LORD is gracious and full of compassion.

Psalms 111:3 His work *is* honourable and glorious: and his righteousness endureth for ever.

1Samuel 2:2 *There is* none holy as the LORD: for *there is* none beside thee: **neither *is there* any rock like our God.**

Deuteronomy 32:4 *He is* the Rock, **his work *is* perfect:** for all his ways *are* judgment: a God of truth and without iniquity, just and right *is* he.

F. THE PLAN OF GOD

Romans 16:26 **But now is made manifest, and by the scriptures of the prophets, according to the commandment of the everlasting God, made known to all nations for the obedience of faith:**

Proverbs 2:8 **He keepeth the paths of judgment, and preserveth the way of his saints.**

9 Then shalt thou understand righteousness, and judgment, and equity; *yea*, every good path.

Psalms 102:26 **They shall perish, but thou shalt endure: ye all of them shall wax old like a garment; as a vesture shalt thou change them, and they shalt be changed:**

Psalms 33:11 **The counsel of the LORD standeth for ever, the thoughts of his heart to all generations.**

Proverbs 19:21 *There are* many devices in a man's heart; **nevertheless the counsel of the LORD, that shall stand.**

REVELATION OF LORD JESUS CHRIST

Hebrews 10:7 *Then said I, Lo,* **I come (in the volume of the book it is written of me,) to do thy will, O God.**

Luke 24:27 **And beginning at Moses and all the prophets, he expounded unto them in all the scriptures the things concerning himself.**

Galatians 3:22 **But the Scripture hath concluded all under sin, that the promise by faith of Jesus Christ must be given to them that believe.**

Romans 10:11 For the scripture saith, **Whosoever believeth on him shall not be ashamed.**

John 5:39 **Search the scriptures**; for in them ye think ye have eternal life: and **they are they which testify of me.**

Acts 18:28 For he mightily convinced the Jews, and that publickly, **shewing by the scriptures that Jesus was Christ.**

LEADS TO GOSPEL OF CHRIST

1Peter 1: 25 But the word of the LORD endureth for ever. And this is the word which by the gospel is preached unto you.

2Timothy 3:15 **And that from a child thou hast known the holy scriptures, which are able to make thee wise unto salvation through faith which is in Christ Jesus.**

1Thessalonians 1:5 **For our gospel came not unto you in word only, but also in power, and in the Holy Ghost,** and as much assurance; as ye know what manner of men we were among you for your sake.

6 And ye became followers of us, and of the Lord, having received the word in much affliction, with joy of the Holy Ghost:

G. THE LORD'S REMINDER TO ALL GENERATIONS

Deuteronomy 32:5 **They have corrupted themselves, their spot** *is* **not** *the spot* **of his children:** *they are* **a perverse and crooked generation.**

6 Do ye thus requite the LORD, O foolish people and unwise? *is* **not he thy father** *that* **hath bought thee? hath he not made thee, and established thee?**

7 **Remember the days of old,** consider the years of many generations: **ask thy father, and he will shew thee; thy elders, and they will tell thee.**

1. GOD WILL ALWAYS HELP AND STRENGTHEN HIS CHILDREN

Psalms 127:1 (A Song of degrees for Solomon.) **Except the LORD build the house, they labour in vain that build it: except the LORD keep the city, the watchman waketh** *but* **in vain.**

2 *It is* vain for you to rise up early, to sit up late, to eat the bread of sorrows: *for* so he giveth his beloved sleep.

3 Lo, children *are* an heritage of the LORD: *and* the fruit of the womb *is his* reward.

4 As arrows *are* in the hand of a mighty man; so *are* children of the youth.

5 Happy *is* the man that hath his quiver full of them: they shall not be ashamed, but they shall speak with the enemies in the gate.

Isaiah 41:10 Fear thou not; for I *am* with thee: be not dismayed; for I *am* thy God: I will strengthen thee; yea, I will help thee; yea, I will uphold thee with the right hand of my righteousness.

11 Behold, all they that were incensed against thee shall be ashamed and confounded: they shall be as nothing; and they that strive with thee shall perish.

2. COMING OF THE WRATH OF GOD

2Chronicles 34:21 Go, inquire of the LORD for me, and for them that are left in Israel and in Judah, **concerning the words of the book that is found: for great is the wrath of the LORD** that is poured out upon us, because our fathers have not kept the word of the LORD, to do after **all that is written in this book.**

2Kings 22:13 Go ye, inquire of the LORD for me, and for the people, and for all Judah, concerning the words of this book that is found: for great is the wrath of the LORD that is kindled against us, because **our fathers have not hearkened unto the words of this book, to do according unto all that which is written concerning us.**

ALL GENERATIONS MUST PRAISE GOD

Psalms 145:4 One generation shall praise thy works to another, and shall declare thy mighty acts.

5 I will speak of the glorious honour of thy majesty, and of thy wondrous works.

6 And *men* shall speak of the might of thy terrible acts: and **I will declare thy greatness**.

7 They shall abundantly utter the memory of thy great goodness, and shall sing of thy righteousness.

8 **The LORD *is* gracious, and full of compassion**; slow to anger, and of great mercy.

9 The LORD *is* good to all: and his tender mercies *are* over all his works.

10 All thy works shall praise thee, O LORD; and thy saints shall bless thee.

11 **They shall speak of the glory of thy kingdom, and talk of thy power;**

12 To make known to the sons of men his mighty acts, and the glorious majesty of his kingdom.

13 Thy kingdom *is* an everlasting kingdom, and thy dominion *endureth* throughout all generations.

PRAYER TO PRAISE GOD (posted in FB Oct.11,2014 9:12am CA time)

Psalms 145:1 **I will extol thee, my God, O king; and I will bless thy name for ever and ever.**

2 **Everyday will I bless thee; and I will praise thy name for ever and ever.**

3 **Great is the LORD, and greatly to be praised; and his greatness is unsearchable.** *Amen.*

=====================================

===

PART 2
THE SCRIPTURES SPEAK ABOUT GOD'S PLAN

CHAPTER I GOD'S PLAN FOR HIS CHOSEN

Ephesians 1:9
Having made known unto us the mystery of his will, according to his good pleasure which he hath purposed in himself: 10 *That in the dispensation of the fullness of times* **he might gather together** *in one all things* **in Christ, both which are in heaven, and which are on earth; even in him:**

SINGLE PLAN OF GOD FOR ALL HIS CHOSEN

Isaiah 64:4 **For since the beginning of the world** *men* **have not heard, nor perceived by the ear, neither hath the eye seen, O God, beside thee**, *what* **he hath prepared for him that waiteth for him.**

5 Thou meetest him that rejoiceth and worketh righteousness, *those that* remember thee in thy ways: behold, thou art wroth; for we have sinned: in those is continuance, and **we shall be saved.**

Romans 16:25 Now to him that is of power to stablish you according to my gospel, and **the preaching of Jesus Christ, according to the revelation of the mystery**, which was kept secret since the world began,

26 But now is made manifest, and by the scriptures of the prophets, according to the commandment of the everlasting God, made known to all nations for the obedience of faith:

2Peter 3:7 **But the heavens and the earth which are now**, *by the same word* **are kept in store, reserved unto fire against the day of judgment and perdition of ungodly men.**

Acts 17:31 **Because he hath appointed a day, in the which he will judge the world in righteousness** by *that* man whom he hath ordained; *whereof* he hath given assurance unto all *men*, in that he hath raised him from the dead.

Hebrews 9:26 For then **must he often have suffered since the foundation of the world: but now once in the end of the world hath he appeared to put away sin by the sacrifice of himself**.
28 So **Christ was once offered to bear the sins of many**; and unto them that look for him **shall he appear the second time without sin unto salvation.**

THE LORD GOD WILL LIVE AMONG HIS PEOPLE

1Kings 8:27 But will God indeed dwell on the earth? behold, the heaven and heaven of heavens cannot contain thee; how much less this house that I have builded?
2Chronicles 6:18 But will God in very deed dwell with men on the earth? behold, heaven and the heaven of heavens cannot contain thee; how much less this house which I have built!

1. TABERNACLE OF THE CONGREGATION IN WILDERNESS

Leviticus 26:11 And **I will set my tabernacle among you: and my soul shall not abhor you**.
12 And I will walk among you, and will be your God, and ye shall be my people.

2. THE LORD'S TABERNACLE WILL BE IN MOUNT ZION

Psalms 15:1 (A Psalm of David.) LORD, who shall abide in thy tabernacle? **who shall dwell in thy holy hill?**
2 He that walketh uprightly, and worketh righteousness, and speaketh the truth in his heart.
3 *He that* backbiteth not with his tongue, nor doeth evil to his neighbour, nor taketh up a reproach against his neighbour.
4 In whose eyes a vile person is contemned; but he honoureth them that fear the LORD. *He that* sweareth to *his own* hurt, and changeth not.
5 *He that* putteth not out his money to usury, nor taketh reward against the innocent. He that doeth these *things* shall never be moved.
Isaiah 16:5 And in mercy shall the throne be established: and he shall sit upon it in truth in the tabernacle of David, judging, and seeking judgment, and hasting righteousness.

ZION WILL BE THE HABITATION OF GOD

Psalms 132:11 The LORD hath sworn *in* truth unto David; he will not turn from it; **Of the fruit of thy body will I set upon thy throne.**

12 If thy children will keep my covenant and my testimony that I shall teach them, their children shall also sit upon thy throne for evermore.

13 For **the LORD hath chosen Zion**; **he hath desired** *it* **for his habitation**.

14 This *is* my rest for ever: here will I dwell; for I have desired it.

15 I will abundantly bless her provision: I will satisfy her poor with bread.

16 I will also clothe her priests with salvation: and her saints shall shout aloud for joy.

17 T**here will I make the horn of David to bud**: I have ordained a lamp for mine anointed.

18 His enemies will I clothe with shame: but upon himself shall his crown flourish.

Psalms 122:5 For **there are set thrones of judgment**, the thrones of the house of David.

INHERITANCE OF THE SAINTS

James 2:5 Hearken, my beloved brethren**, Hath not God chosen the poor of this world rich in faith, and heirs of the kingdom** which he hath promised to them that love him?

1Peter 1:4 To an inheritance incorruptible, and undefiled, and that fadeth not away, reserved in heaven for you,

5 Who are kept by the power of God through faith unto salvation ready to be revealed in the last time.

 PRAYER PRAISING THE LORD'S FAITHFULNESS

Psalms 89:5 *And the heavens shall praise thy wonders, O LORD: thy faithfulness also in the congregation of the saints.*

6 For who in the heaven can be compared unto the LORD? who among the sons of the mighty can be likened unto the LORD?

Revelation 1:6 *And* ***hath made us kings and priests unto God and his Father; to him be glory and dominion for ever and ever***. Amen.

CHAPTER II **IMPLEMENTATION OF GOD'S PLAN**

A. GOD REVEALED HIMSELF

1John 5:7 For there are three that bear record in heaven, *the Father, The Word* **and** *the Holy Ghost***: and** *these three are one.*
8 And **there are three that bear witness in earth,** *the Spirit***, and** *the water***, and** *the blood: and these three agree in one.*
6 This is He that came by water and blood, even **Jesus Christ; not by water only, but by water and blood.** And it is **the Spirit that beareth witness, because the Spirit is truth.**

THE MYSTERY OF GODLINESS

1Timothy 3:16 *And without controversy great is the mystery of godliness:* **God was manifest in the flesh, justified in the Spirit,** *seen of angels, preached unto the Gentiles, believed on in the world, received up into glory.*

John 4:24 **God** *is* **a Spirit:** and they that worship him must worship *him* in spirit and in truth.
2Corinthians 3:17 **Now the Lord is that Spirit:** and where the Spirit of the Lord *is*, there *is* liberty.
Ephesians 3:5 Which in other ages was not made known unto the sons of men, as it is now revealed unto his holy apostles and prophets by the Spirit;

1. GOD IN HEAVENLY KINGDOM

Psalms 8:1 (To the chief Musician upon Gittith, A Psalm of David.) *O LORD our Lord,* **how excellent is thy name in all the earth! who has set thy glory above the heavens.**
Isaiah 45:5 I *am* **the LORD, and** *there is* **none else,** *there is* **no God beside me**: I girded thee, though thou hast not known me:

6 That they may know from the rising of the sun, and from the west, **that *there is* none beside me. I *am* the LORD, and *there is* none else.**

7 **I form the light, and create darkness: I make peace, and create evil: I the LORD do all these things.**

Exodus 3:14 And God said unto Moses**, I AM THAT I AM**: and he said, Thus shalt thou say unto the children of Israel**, I AM *hath sent me unto you*.**

15 And God said moreover unto Moses, Thus shalt thou say unto the children of Israel, **The LORD God of your fathers, the God of Abraham, the God of Isaac, and the God of Jacob, *hath sent me unto you*:** this *is* my name for ever, and this *is* my memorial unto all generations.

Exodus 6:3 And I appeared unto Abraham, unto Isaac, and unto Jacob, by **the name of God Almighty, but by my name JEHOVAH was I NOT known to them.**

Psalms 83:18 That men may know that thou, **whose name alone is JEHOVAH, art the most high over all the earth.**

Isaiah 26:4 Trust ye in the Lord forever: for in **the LORD JEHOVAH** is everlasting strength:

Isaiah 12:2 Behold, God *is* my salvation; I will trust, and not be afraid: for the **LORD JEHOVAH** *is* my strength and *my* song; he also is become my salvation.

Genesis 22:14 And **Abraham called the name of that place JEHOVAHJIREH**: as it is said *to* this day, **In the mount of the LORD it shall be seen**.

Exodus 17:15 And **Moses built an altar**, and called the name of it **JEHOVAH-NIS-S**I:

16 For he said, Because the LORD hath sworn *that* the LORD *will have* war with Amalek from generation to generation.

Judges 6:24 Then **Gideon built an altar** there unto the LORD, and called it **JEHOVAH-SHA-LOM**: unto this day it *is* yet in Oph-rah of the A-bi-ez-rites.

Psalms 68:4 Sing unto God, sing praises to his name: extol him that rideth upon the heavens by his name **JAH**, and rejoice before him**.**

Psalms 113:4 The LORD *is* high above all nations, *and* his glory above the heavens.

CREATOR OF HEAVENS

Genesis 1:1 In the beginning God created the heaven and the earth.

Genesis 1:8 And God called the firmament Heaven. And the evening and the morning were the second day.

Isaiah 50:3 I clothe the heavens with blackness, and I make sackcloth their covering.

Isaiah 48:13 Mine hand also hath laid the foundation of the earth, and my right hand hath spanned the heavens: *when* I call unto them, they stand up together.

Psalms 103:19 The LORD hath prepared his throne in the heavens; and his kingdom ruleth over all.

Job 26:9 He holdeth back the face of his throne, *and* spreadeth his cloud upon it.

Deuteronomy 10:14 Behold, the h*eaven and the heaven of heavens* is the LORD'S thy God, the earth also, with all that therein is.

Matthew 5:34 But I say unto you, Swear not at all; neither by heaven; for it is *God's throne:*

2. GOD'S WORD

John 1:1 ***In the beginning was the Word, and the Word was with God, and the Word was God. 2 The same was in the beginning with God.***

1Peter 1:20 **Who verily was** *foreordained* **before the foundation of the world, but was manifest in these last times for you,**

21 Who by him do believe in God, that raised him up from the dead, and gave him glory; that your faith and hope might be in God.

Proverbs 8:22 **The LORD possessed me in the beginning of his way, before his works of old.**

23 I was set up from everlasting, from the beginning, or ever the earth was.

24 When *there were* no depths, I was brought forth; when *there were* no fountains abounding with water.

25 Before the mountains were settled, before the hills was I brought forth:

26 While as yet he had not made the earth, nor the fields, nor the highest part of the dust of the world.

27 **When he prepared the heavens, I** *was* **there: when he set a compass upon the face of the depth:**

28 When he established the clouds above: when he strengthened the fountains of the deep:

29 When he gave to the sea his decree, that the waters should not pass his commandment: when he appointed the foundations of the earth:

30 **Then I was by him**, *as* one brought up *with him*: and I was daily *his* delight, rejoicing always before him;

31 Rejoicing in the habitable part of his earth; and my delights *were* with the sons of men.

LORD JESUS THE WORD OF GOD

Hebrews 11:3 ***Through faith*** *we understand that the worlds* ***were framed by the word of God,*** *so that the things which are seen were not made of things which do appear.*

Colossians 1:15 Who is the image of the invisible God, the firstborn of every creature:

16 For by him were all things created, that are in heaven, and that are in earth, visible and invisible, whether *they be* thrones, or dominions, or principalities, or powers: all things were created by him, and for him:

17 And he is before all things, and by him all things consist.

John 1:3 **All things were made by him; and without him was not anything made that was made**.

John 1:10 He was in the world, and the world was made by him, and the world knew him not.

11 He came unto his own, and his own received him not.

12 **But as many as received him, to them gave he power to become the sons of God,** *even* **to them that believe on his name:**

13 Which were born, not of blood, nor of the will of the flesh, nor of the will of man, but of God.

14 And **the Word was made flesh, and dwelt among us,** (and we beheld his glory, the glory as only **begotten son of the Father,) full of grace and truth.**

3. HOLY SPIRIT IS GOD'S BREATH

Psalms 33:6 By **the WORD of the LORD were the heavens made; and** *all the host* **of them by** *the breath of his mouth.*

CREATOR OF THE HOSTS OF HEAVEN

Job 26:13 *By His Spirit he hath garnished the heavens: his hands hath formed the crooked serpent.*

Psalms104:4 Who maketh **the angels spirits; his ministers a flaming fire**:
Nehemiah 9:6 **Thou, even** *thou, art LORD alone***; thou hast made** *heaven, the heaven of heavens***, with all their host,** the earth, and all the things that are therein, the seas, and all that is therein, and thou preservest them all; **and the** *host of heaven* **worshippeth thee.**
Isaiah 40:26 Lift up your eyes on high, and behold **who hath created these things, that bringeth out their** *host by number***;** *he calleth them all by names* **by the greatness of his might,** for that **he is strong in power; not one faileth**.
Jeremiah 33:22 **As the** *host of heaven* **cannot be numbered**, neither the sand of the sea measured: **so will I multiply the seed of David my servant, and the Levites that minister unto me.**
1Kings 22:19 And he said, Hear thou therefore the word of the LORD: I saw the LORD sitting on his throne, **and all the host of heaven standing by him on his right hand and on his left.**

THE HOSTS OF HEAVEN WAS SEEN BY JACOB
Genesis 32:1 And Jacob went on his way, **and the angels of God met him.**
 2 And **when Jacob saw them, he said, This is** *God's host*; and he called the place *Mahanaim.*

PRAYER PRAISING GOD FOR HIS WORKS IN ALL
PLACES OF HIS DOMINION

Psalms 148:1 *Praise ye the LORD. Praise ye the LORD from the heavens: praise him in the heights.*
2 *Praise ye him, all his angels, praise ye him, all his host*
Psalms 103:19 T*he LORD hath prepared his throne in the heavens; and his kingdom ruleth over all.*

20 *Bless the LORD, ye his angels, that excel in strength, that do his commandments, hearkening unto the voice of his word.*

21 *Bless ye the LORD**, all ye his hosts; ye ministers of his,** that do his pleasure.*

22 *Bless the LORD, all his works in all places of his dominion: bless the LORD, O my soul. Amen.*

B. GOD THE CREATOR OF EARTH AND MAN

Psalms 115:15 **Ye are blessed by the Lord which made heaven and earth.**

Proverbs 3:19 The LORD **by** *wisdom* **hath founded the earth; by** *understanding* **hath he established the heavens.**

20 By his *knowledge* the depths are broken up, and the clouds drop down the dew.

Psalms 90:2 ***Before the mountains were brought forth, or ever thou hadst formed the earth and the world, even from everlasting to everlasting, thou art God.***

Isaiah 46:9 **Remember the former things of old;** *for I am God***, and** *there is none else***; I am God, and there is none like me,**

10 Declaring the end from the beginning, and from ancient times *the things* that are not *yet* done, saying, My counsel shall stand, and I will do all my pleasure:

Zechariah 12:1 The burden of the word of the LORD for Israel, saith **the LORD, which stretcheth forth the** *heavens,* **and layeth the** *foundation of the earth,* **and formeth the** *spirit of man* **within him.**

C. THE MIGHTY GOD

Deuteronomy 10:**17** For the LORD your God *is* God of gods, and Lord of lords, a great God, a mighty, and a terrible, which regardeth not persons, nor taketh reward:

PART 2
THE SCRIPTURES SPEAK ABOUT GOD'S PLAN

CHAPTER III MYSTERY OF GOD'S CREATION

Job 37: 12
*And **it is turned round about by his COUNSELS**: that **THEY may do whatsoever he commandeth THEM** upon the face of the world in the earth.*

Psalms 19:1 (To the chief Musician, A Psalm of David.) The heavens declare the glory of God; and the firmament sheweth his handywork.

2 **Day unto day uttereth speech, and night unto night sheweth knowledge**.

3 *There is* no speech nor language, *where* **THEIR VOICE** is not heard.

4 **THEIR LINE** is gone out through all the earth, and **THEIR WORDS** to the end of the world. **IN THEM** hath he set a tabernacle for the sun,

5 Which *is* as a bridegroom coming out of his chamber, *and* rejoiceth as a strong man to run a race.

6 His going forth *is* from the end of the heaven, and his circuit unto the ends of it: and there is nothing hid from the heat thereof.

IN THE BEGINNING

1. CREATION OF EARTH

2Peter 3:5 *For this they willingly are ignorant of, **that by the WORD OF GOD the heavens were of old, and the earth standing out of the water and in the water**:*

Genesis 1:2 And the earth was without form, and void; and darkness *was* upon the face of the deep. And **the Spirit of God** moved upon the face of the waters.

Jeremiah 51:15 He hath made the earth by *his power*, he hath established the world by *his wisdom*, and hath stretched out the heaven by *his understanding* .

Jeremiah 10:12 He hath made the earth by his power, he hath established the world by his wisdom, and hath stretched out the heavens by his discretion.

Psalms 115:15 Ye are blessed by **the LORD which made heaven and earth**.

Psalms 104:5 **Who laid the foundations of the earth, that it should not be removed for ever.**

6 Thou coveredst it with the deep as *with* a garment: the waters stood above the mountains.

Job 38: 4 Where was thou when I laid the foundations of the earth? declare, if thou hast   understanding.

5 Who hath laid the measures thereof, if thou knowest? or who hath stretched the line upon it?

6 Whereupon are the foundations thereof fastened? or who laid the corner stone thereof?

7 **When the *morning stars sang together*, and all the sons of God shouted for joy?**

Job 26:7 He stretcheth out the north over the empty place, and hangeth the earth upon nothing.

8 **He bindeth up the waters in his thick clouds**:and the clouds is not rent under them.

9 He holdeth back the face of his throne, and spreadeth his cloud upon it.

10 **He hath compassed the waters with bounds, until the day and night come to an end**.

11 The pillars of heaven tremble and are astonished at his reproof.

12 **He divideth the sea with *his power*,** and by *his understanding* he smiteth through the proud.

a. THROUGH GOD'S WORD EVERYTHING WAS CREATED

Psalms 33:9 For **he spake**, and **it was done; he commanded and it stood fast.**

Job 37:2 Hear attentively **the noise of his voice, and the sound that goeth out of his mouth.**

3 He directeth it under the whole heaven, and his lightning unto the ends of the earth.

4 After it *a voice* roareth: he thundereth with the voice of the excellency; and he will not stay them when his voice is heard.

5 God thundereth marvelously with his voice; great things doeth he, which we cannot comprehend.

*First Day: THERE WAS LIGHT

Genesis 1:3 And God said, *Let there be light: and there was light.*

4 and God saw the light, that it was good: and God divided the light from darkness

5 And God called the light Day, and the darkness he called Night. And *the evening and the morning were the first day.*

Job 38:1 Then the LORD answered Job out of the whirlwind, and said,

Job 38:12 Hast thou commanded the morning since thy days; and caused the dayspring to know his place;

13 That it might take hold of the ends of the earth, that the wicked might be shaken out of it?

Job 38:24 By what way is the light parted, which scattereth the east wind upon the earth?

*Second Day: A FIRMAMENT IN THE MIDST OF THE WATERS

Genesis 1:6 And God said, *Let there be a firmament in the midst of the waters, and let it divide the waters from the waters.*

7 And God made the firmament, and divided the waters which were under the firmament from the waters which were above the firmament: and it was so.

8 And God called the firmament HEAVEN *And the evening and the morning were the second day.*

Jeremiah 51:16 When he uttereth *his voice*, there is a multitude of waters in the heavens; and he causeth the vapours to ascend from the ends of the earth: he maketh lightnings with rain, and bringeth forth the wind out of his treasures.

Jeremiah 10:13 When he uttereth his voice, *there is* a multitude of waters in the heavens, and he causeth the vapours to ascend from the ends of the earth; he maketh lightnings with rain, and bringeth forth the wind out of his treasures.

Psalms 147:8 Who covereth the heaven with clouds, who prepareth rain for the earth, who maketh grass to grow upon the mountains.

Job 37:6 **For he saith to the snow, Be thou *on* the earth**; likewise to the small rain, and to the great rain of his strength.

Job 37:16 Dost thou know the balancing of the clouds, the wondrous works of him which is perfect in knowledge?

17 How thy garments *are* warm, when **he quieteth the earth by the south *wind*?**

Job 38:9 **When I made the cloud the garment thereof, and thick darkness, a swaddling band for it.**

10 And break up for it my decreed place, and **set bars and doors,**

Job 37:10 **By the *breath of God* (Holy Spirit) frost is given; and the breath of the waters is straitened.**

11 **Also by watering he wearieth the thick cloud: he scattereth his bright cloud:**

Psalms 147:16 He giveth snow like a wool: he scattereth the hoarfrost like ashes.

17 He casteth fort his ice like morsels: who can stand before his cold?

18 **He sendeth out *his word*, and melteth them**: he causeth his wind to blow, and the waters flow.

*Third Day: THE WATERS UNDER THE HEAVEN BE GATHERED TOGETHER

Genesis 1:9 And **God said**, *Let the waters under the heaven be gathered together unto one place, and* **let the dry land appear**: *and it was so.*

Job 38:11 **And said, Hitherto shalt thou come, but no further: and here shall thy proud waves be stayed?**

Job 38:8 Or who shut up the sea with doors, when it brake forth, as if it had issued out of the womb?

2Samuel 22:16 And the channels of the sea appeared, **the foundations of the world were discovered, at the rebuking of the LORD, at the blast of the breath of his nostrils.**

Psalms 18:15Then the channels of waters were seen, and the foundations of the world were discovered at **thy rebuke, O LORD, at the blast of the breath of thy nostrils.**

Genesis 1:10 And **God called all the dry land EARTH**; and **the gathering together of waters, called he SEAS:** and God saw that it was good.

Job 38:25 Who hath divided a watercourse for the overflowing of waters, or a way of lightning of thunder;
26 To cause it to rain on the earth, *where* no man.is; on the wilderness, wherein there is no man;
27 To satisfy the desolate and waste ground; and to cause the bud of the tender herb to spring forth?

Genesis 1:11 And **God said**, *Let the earth bring forth grass, the herb yielding seed, and the fruit tree yielding fruit after his kind, whose seed is in itself, upon the earth: and it was so.*
12 And the earth brought forth grass, and herb yielding seed after his kind, and the tree yielding fruit, whose seed was in itself, after his kind: and God saw that *it was* good.
13 **And the evening and the morning were the third day.**

Fourth Day: **LIGHTS IN HEAVEN TO DIVIDE THE DAY FROM THE NIGHT**
Genesis 1:14 And **God said**, *Let there be lights in the firmament of the heaven to divide the day from the night; and let them be for signs, and for seasons, and for days, and years*:
15 *And let them be for lights in the firmament of the heaven to give light upon the earth:* and it was so.
16 And God made two great lights; the greater light to rule the day, and the lesser light to rule the night: *he made* the stars also.
17 And God set them in the firmament of the heaven to give light upon the earth,
18 And to rule over the day and over the night, and to divide the light from the darkness: and God saw that *it was* good.
19 **And the evening and the morning were the fourth day.**

THE STARS IN HEAVEN
Job 38:31 Canst thou bind the sweet influences of **Pleiades,** or loose the bands of **Orion?**
32 Canst thou bring forth **Mazzaroth** in his season? or canst thou guide **Arcturus** with his sons?
33 **Knowest thou the ordinances of heaven**? canst thou set the dominion thereof in the earth?

Fifth Day: **WATERS BRING FORTH ABUNDANTLY THE MOVING CREATURE AND FOWLS THAT FLY ABOVE THE EARTH**

Genesis 1:20 And **God said**, *Let the waters bring forth abundantly the moving creature that hath life, and fowl that may fly above the earth in the open firmament of heaven.*

21 And God created great whales, and every living creature that moveth, which the waters brought forth abundantly, after their kind, and every winged fowl after his kind: and God saw that *it was* good.

22 And **God blessed them, saying**, *Be fruitful, and multiply, and fill the waters in the seas, and let fowl multiply in the earth.*

23 And **the evening and the morning were the fifth day.**

Sixth Day**: GOD CREATED MAN IN HIS OWN IMAGE AND FORMED EVERY BEAST OF THE FIELD**

Genesis 1:27 **So God created man in his *own* image, in the image of God created he him; male and female created he them**.

Genesis 2:18 And the LORD God said**,** *It is not good that the man should be alone; I will make him an help meet for him.*

19 And out of the ground the LORD God formed every beast of the field, and every fowl of the air; and brought *them* unto Adam to see what he would call them: and whatsoever Adam called every living creature, that *was* the name thereof.

Genesis 1:24 **And God said,** *Let the earth bring forth the living creature after his kind, cattle and creeping thing, and beast of the earth after his kind, and it was so.*

25 **And God made the beast of the earth after his kind, and cattle after their kind, and every thing that creepeth upon the earth after his kind: and God saw that *it was* good.**

Genesis 1:31 And God saw every thing that he had made, and, behold, *it was* very good. *And the evening and the morning were the sixth day.*

Seventh Day: **GOD BLESSED THE SEVENTH DAY AND RESTED**

Genesis 2:1 **Thus the heavens and the earth were finished, and all the host of them.**

2 And on the seventh day God ended his work which he had made; and he rested on the seventh day from all his work which he had made.

3 And God blessed the seventh day, and sanctified it: because that in it he had rested from all his work which God created and made.

b. GOD CREATED EARTH FOR THE CHILDREN OF MEN

Isaiah 45:18 For thus saith the LORD that created the heavens; **God himself that formed the earth and made it; he hath established it**, he created it not in vain, **he formed it to be inhabited**: *I am the LORD; and there is none else.*

Isaiah 48:13 *Mine hand also hath laid the foundation of the earth, and my right hand hath spanned the heavens:* **when I call unto them, they stand up together.**

Psalms 115:16 The heaven, *even* the heavens, *are* the LORD'S: but **the earth hath he given to the children of men.**

c. NO EARTHLY BEING COMES FROM HEAVEN EXCEPT THE SON OF MAN

Isaiah 45:12 I have made the earth, and created man upon it: I, *even* my hands, have stretched out the heavens, and all their host have I commanded.

John 3:13 **And no man hath ascended up to heaven, but he that came down from heaven,** *even* **the Son of man which is in heaven.**

John 3: 31 He that cometh from above is above all: he that is of the earth is earthly, and speaketh of the earth: **he that cometh from heaven is above all.**

Proverbs 30:4 Who hath ascended up into heaven, or descended? who hath gathered the wind in his fists? who hath bound the waters in a garment? who hath established all the ends of the earth? what *is* his name, and what *is* his son's name, if thou canst tell?

Psalms 33:13 **The LORD looketh from heaven**; he beholdeth all the sons of men.

14 From the place of his habitation **he looketh upon all the inhabitants of the earth.**

2. THE CREATION OF MAN

Genesis 1:26 And God said, **Let us make man in our image, after our likeness**: and let them have dominion over the fish of the sea, and over the fowl of the air, and over the cattle, and over all the earth, and over every creeping thing that creepeth upon the earth.

a. GOD GAVE US LIFE WHICH IS HIS SPIRIT OF LIFE

Genesis 2:7 **And the LORD God formed man** *of* **the dust of the ground, and breathed into his nostrils the breath of life; and man became a living soul.**

Job 33:4 the **Spirit of God hath made me, and the breath of the almighty hath given me life.**

Psalms 119:25 DALETH. **My soul cleaveth unto the dust: quicken thou me according to thy word.**

Isaiah 42:5 Thus saith God the LORD, he that created the heavens, and stretched them out; he that spread forth the earth, and that which cometh out of it**; he that giveth breath unto the people upon it, and spirit to them that walk therein:**

b. MAN WAS FORMED FROM DUST

Genesis 1:27 So God created man in his own image, in the image of God created he him; male and female created he them.

Psalm 33:15 **He fashioneth their hearts alike; he considereth all their works**.

Job 42:2 **I** know that thou canst do everything, and that **no thought can be withholden from thee.**

Psalms 103:14 For **he knoweth our frame; he remembereth that we are** *dust.*

3. THE WORKS OF GOD FOR HIS PEOPLE
(According to God's plan and purpose)

James 1:18_Of his own will begat he us with the word of truth, that we should be a kind of firstfruits of his creatures.

Job 35:11 Who teacheth us more than the beasts of the earth, and maketh us wiser than the fowls of heaven?

a. MAN WAS CREATED IN GOD'S OWN IMAGE AND LIKENESS

1.GOD IS BEAUTIFUL

Psalms 27:4 One *thing* have I desired of the LORD, that will I seek after; that I may dwell in the house of the LORD all the days of my life, **to behold the beauty of the LORD**, and to enquire in his temple.

Psalms 29:2 Give unto the LORD the glory due unto his name; worship the LORD in the beauty of holiness.

Psalms 50:2 Out of Zion, **the perfection of beauty, God hath shined.**

Psalms 90:17 **And let the beauty of the LORD our God be upon us: and establish thou the work of our hands upon us;** yea, the work of our hands establish thou it.

Psalms 96:9 O worship the LORD in the beauty of holiness: fear before him, all the earth.

Isaiah 33:17 Thine eyes shall see the king in his beauty: they shall behold the land that is very far off.

Psalms 104:1 Bless the LORD, O my soul. O LORD my God, thou art very great; **thou art clothed with honour and majesty.**

GOD'S BEAUTY MANIFESTS IN HIS CREATION

Romans 1:19 Because that which may be known of God is manifest in them; for God hath shewed *it* unto them.

20 **For the invisible things of him from the creation of the world are clearly seen, being understood by the things that are made,** *even* his eternal power and Godhead; so that they are without excuse:

2.THE FIRST MAN WITH EVERLASTING LIFE

Genesis 2:16 And the LORD God commanded the man, saying, Of every tree of the garden thou mayest freely eat:

17 But of the tree of the knowledge of good and evil, thou shalt not eat of it: for in the day that thou eatest thereof **thou shalt surely die.**

Genesis 3:22 And the LORD God said, **Behold, the man is become as one of us**, to know good and evil: and **now, lest he put forth his hand, and take also of the tree of life, and eat, and live for ever:**

3. ADAM'S DOMINION OVER GOD'S CREATIONS

Genesis 1:26 And God said, Let us make man in our image, after our likeness**: And let them have dominion** over the fish of the sea, and over the fowl of the air, and over the cattle, and over all the earth, and over every creeping thing that creepeth the earth.

Genesis 2:20 And Adam gave names to all the cattle, and to the fowl of the air, and to every beast of the field; **but Adam there was not found an help meet for him.**

THE FIRST MAN UNDERSTAND AND COULD TALK TO ANIMALS

Genesis 3:1 Now the serpent was more subtil than any beast of the field which the LORD God had made. And he said unto the woman, *Yea, hath God said, Ye shall not eat of every tree of the garden?*

2 And the woman said unto the serpent, *We may eat of the fruit of the trees of the garden:*

3 *But of the fruit of the tree which is in the midst of the garden, God hath said, Ye shall not eat of it, neither shall ye touch it, lest ye die.*

4 And the serpent said unto the woman, *Ye shall not surely die:*

5 *For God doth know that in the day ye eat thereof, then your eyes shall be opened, and ye shall be as gods, knowing good and evil.*

b. GOD CREATED A WOMAN AS THE HELPER OF MAN

Genesis 2:21 And **the LORD God caused a deep sleep to fall upon Adam,** and he slept: and **he took one of his ribs, and closed up the flesh instead thereof;**

22 **And the rib, which the LORD God had taken from man, made he a woman**, and brought her unto the man.

23 **And Adam said, This *is* now bone of my bones, and flesh of my flesh**: she shall be called Woman, because she was taken out of Man.

24 **Therefore shall a man leave his father and his mother, and shall cleave unto his wife: and they shall be one flesh.**

GOD BLESSED THE FIRST MAN TO BE FRUITFUL

Genesis 1:28 And **God blessed them, and God said unto them,** *Be fruitful, and multiply, and replenish the earth*, and subdue it: and have dominion over the fish of the sea, and over the fowl of the air, and over every living thing that moveth upon the earth.

c. GOD WAS VISIBLE AND COMMUNED WITH ADAM AND EVE

Genesis 3:8 And they heard the voice of the LORD God walking in the garden in the cool of the day: and Adam and his wife hid themselves from the presence of the LORD God amongst the trees of the garden.

9 And the LORD God called unto Adam, and said unto him, *Where art thou?*

d. LORD GOD THE PROVIDER

Psalms 103:13 *Like as a father pitieth his children,* ***so the LORD pitieth them that fear him.***

Genesis 2:8 And the LORD God planted a garden eastward in Eden; and there he put the man whom he had formed.

Genesis 2:9 And out of the ground made the LORD God to grow every tree that is pleasant to the sight, and good for food; **the tree of life also in the midst of the garden**, and the tree of knowledge of good and evil.

Genesis 1:29 And God said, *Behold, I* ***have given you every herb bearing seed,*** *which is upon the face of all the earth, and* ***every tree, in the which is the fruit of a tree yielding seed;*** *to you it shall be* ***for meat.***

30 *And to every beast of the earth, and to every fowl of the air, and to everything that creepeth upon the earth, wherein there is life, I have given* ***every green herb for meat***: and it was so.

GOD THAT MADE THE WORLD AND ALL THINGS THEREIN

 Acts 17:24 God that made the world and all things therein, seeing that he is Lord of heaven and earth, dwelleth not in temples made with hands;

25 Neither is worshipped with men's hands, as though he needed any thing, seeing he giveth to all life, and breath, and all things;

26 And hath made of one blood all nations of men for to dwell on all the face of the earth, and **hath determined the times before appointed,** and the bounds of their habitation;

27 That they should seek the Lord, if haply they might feel after him, and find him, though he be not far from every one of us:

GOD'S LANGUAGE WAS THE ONLY LANGUAGE OF MEN

Genesis 11:1 **And the whole earth was of one language, and of one speech.**

PRAISING GOD FOR ALL HIS WONDERFUL CREATIONS

Psalms 148:1 *Praise ye the LORD. Praise ye the LORD from the heavens: praise him in the heights.*

*2 **Praise ye him, all his angels: praise ye him, all his hosts**.*

3 Praise ye him, sun and moon: praise him, all ye stars of light.

4 Praise him, ye heavens of heavens, and ye waters that be above the heavens.

*5 **Let them praise the name of the LORD:** for he commanded, and they were created.*

6 He hath also stablished them for ever and ever: he hath made a decree which shall not pass.

*Psalms 69:34 **Let the heaven and earth praise him, the seas, and everything that moveth therein.***

Psalms 104:24 O LORD, how manifold are thy works! in wisdom hast thou made them all: the earth is full of thy riches.

25 So is this great and wide sea, wherein are things creeping innumerable, both small and great beasts.

26 There go the ships: there is that leviathan, whom thou hast made to play therein.

27 These wait all upon thee; that thou mayest give them their meat in due season.

28 That thou givest them they gather: thou openest thine hand, they are filled with good.

29 Thou hidest thy face, they are troubled: thou takest away their breath, they die, and return to their dust.

30 Thou sendest forth thy spirit, they are created: and thou renewest the face of the earth.

31 The glory of the LORD shall endure for ever: the LORD shall rejoice in his works.

***Psalms 148:**7 Praise the LORD from the earth, ye dragons, and all deeps:*

8 Fire, and hail; snow, and vapour; stormy wind fulfilling his word

9 Mountains, and all hills; fruitful trees, and all cedars:

10 Beasts, and all cattle; creeping things, and flying fowl:

11 Kings of the earth, and all people; princes, and all judges of the earth:

12 Both young men, and maidens; old men, and children:

13 Let them praise the name of the LORD: for his name alone is excellent; his glory is above the earth and heaven.

14 He also exalteth the horn of his people, the praise of all his saints; even of the children of Israel, a people near unto him. Praise ye the LORD.

===

PART 2
THE SCRIPTURES SPEAK ABOUT GOD'S PLAN

CHAPTER IV **SEPARATION OF ANCIENT MEN FROM HIS CREATOR**

Isaiah 40: 2*2*
It is he that sitteth upon the circle of the earth, and the inhabitants thereof are as grasshoppers; that stretcheth out the heavens as a curtain, and spreadeth them out as a tent to dwell in:

*FIRST INSTRUCTION OF GOD
Genesis 2:16And **the LORD God commanded the man, saying,**
Of every tree of the garden thou mayest freely eat:
17 ***But of the tree of the knowledge of good and evil, thou shalt not eat of it: for in the day that thou eatest thereof thou shalt surely die.***

A. DISOBEDIENCE OF THE FIRST MAN
Genesis 3:6 And **when the woman saw that the tree *was* good for food, and that it *was* pleasant to the eyes, and a tree to be desired to make *one* wise, she took of the fruit thereof, and did eat, and gave also unto her husband with her; and he did eat.**
7 And the eyes of them both were opened, and they knew that they *were* naked; and they sewed fig leaves together, and made themselves aprons.
8 And they heard the voice of the LORD God walking in the garden in the cool of the day: and Adam and his wife hid themselves from the presence of the LORD God amongst the trees of the garden.
9 And the LORD God called unto Adam, and said unto him, *Where art thou?*
10 And he said, *I heard thy voice in the garden, and I was afraid, because I was naked; and I hid myself.*

11 And he said, *Who told thee that thou wast naked? Hast thou eaten of the tree, whereof I commanded thee that thou shouldest not eat?*

12 And the man said, *The woman whom thou gavest to be with me, she gave me of the tree, and I did eat.*

13 And **the LORD God said unto the woman, *What is this that thou hast done?* And the woman said, *The serpent beguiled me, and I did eat.***

ADAM AND EVE WERE SENT OUT FROM THE GARDEN OF EDEN

Genesis 3:22 And **the LORD God said**, *Behold, the man **is become as one of us**, to know good and evil: and now, lest he put forth his hand, and take also of the tree of life, and eat, and live for ever:*

23 Therefore the LORD God sent him forth from the garden of Eden, to till the ground from whence he was taken.

24 So he drove out the man; and **he placed at the east of the garden of Eden Cherubims, and a flaming sword which turned every way, to keep the way of the tree of life.**

*GOD'S INSTRUCTION TO NOAH

Genesis 9:4 But **flesh with the life thereof, *which is* the blood thereof, shall ye not eat.**

5 And surely **your blood of your lives will I require**; at the hand of every beast will I require it, and at the hand of man; at the hand of every man's brother will I require the life of man.

6 Whoso sheddeth man's blood, by man shall his blood be shed: for in the image of God made he man.

B. AFTER NOAH'S FLOOD

Genesis 11:2 And it came to pass, as they journeyed from the east, that they found a plain in the land of Shinar; and they dwelt there.

3 And they said one to another, *Go to, let us make brick, and burn them throughly.* And they had brick for stone, and slime had they for morter.

4 And **they said, *Go to, let us build us a city and a tower, whose top may reach unto heaven; and let us make us a name, lest we be scattered abroad upon the face of the whole earth.***

C. THE LORD GOD IMPLEMENTED HIS POWER TO ALL MEN

1. GOD CONFOUNDED THE LANGUAGE OF MAN

Genesis 11:1 **And the whole earth was of one language, and of one speech.**

5 And the LORD came down to see the city and the tower, which the children of men builded.

6 And **the LORD said**, *Behold, the people is one, and they have all one language; and this they begin to do: and now nothing will be restrained from them, which they have imagined to do.*

7 *Go to,* **let us go down***, and there confound their language, that they may not understand one another's speech.*

2. GOD SCATTERED PEOPLE ABROAD UPON THE FACE OF THE EARTH

Genesis 11:8 So the LORD scattered them abroad from thence upon the face of all the earth: and they left off to build the city.

9 Therefore is the name of it called Babel; because the LORD did there confound the language of all the earth: and from thence did the LORD scatter them abroad upon the face of all the earth.

Genesis 10:5 **By these were the isles of the Gentiles divided in their lands; every one after his tongue, after their families, in their nations.**

GOD DIVIDED THE NATIONS IN THE DAYS OF PELEG

Genesis 10:1 Now **these** *are* **the generations of the sons of Noah**, **Shem,** Ham, and Japheth: and unto them were sons born after the flood.

Genesis 10:21 Unto **Shem** also, the father of all the children of Eber, the brother of Japheth the elder, even to him were *children* born.

22 The children of Shem; Elam, and Asshur, and **Arphaxad,** and Lud, and Aram.

23 And the children of Aram; Uz, and Hul, and Gether, and Mash.

24 And Arphaxad begat **Salah**; and Salah begat Eber.

25 And unto **Eber were born two sons**: the name of one *was* **Peleg; for in his days was the earth divided;** and his brother's name *was* Joktan.

1 Chronicles 1:19 And unto Eber were born two sons: the name of the one *was* Peleg; because in his days the earth was divided: and his brother's name *was* Joktan.

THE GENERATIONS OF SHEM

Genesis 11:10 These *are* the generations of Shem: **Shem *was* an hundred years old, and begat Arphaxad two years after the flood:**

11 And **Shem lived after he begat Arphaxad five hundred years, and begat sons and daughters**.

12 And **Arphaxad lived five and thirty years, and begat Salah:**

13 And **Arphaxad lived after he begat Salah four hundred and three years**, and begat sons and daughters.

14 And **Salah lived thirty years, and begat Eber:**

15 And **Salah lived after he begat Eber four hundred and three years**, and begat sons and daughters.

16 And **Eber lived four and thirty years, and begat Peleg**:

17 And **Eber lived after he begat Peleg four hundred and thirty years**, and begat sons and daughters.

18 And **Peleg lived thirty years, and begat Reu:**

19 **And Peleg lived after he begat Reu two hundred and nine years,** and begat sons and daughters.

3. GOD DIVIDED TO THE NATIONS THEIR INHERITANCE

Deuteronomy 32:8 **When the Most High divided to the nations their inheritance, when he separated the sons of Adam, he set the bounds of the people *according to the number of the children of Israel.***

9 **For the LORD'S portion *is* his people; Jacob *is* the lot of his inheritance.**

Acts 17:26 And hath made of one blood all nations of men for to dwell on all the face of the earth, and hath determined the times before appointed, and the bounds of their habitation;

27 That they should seek the Lord, if haply they might feel after him, and find him, though he be not far from every one of us:

Genesis 10: 32 These *are* the families of the sons of Noah, after their generations, in their nations: and **by these were the nations divided in the earth after the flood.**

a. THE SONS OF SHEM

KINGDOM OF ASSYRIA

Genesis 10:21 Unto **Shem** also, the father of all the children of Eber, the brother of Japheth the elder, even to him were *children* born.

22 The **children of Shem**; Elam, and **Asshur**, and Arphaxad, and Lud, and Aram.

Genesis 10:11 **Out of that land went forth Asshur, and builded Nineveh, and the city Rehoboth, and Calah,**

12 And **Resen between Nineveh and Calah: the same** *is* **a great city**.

KINGS IN THE LAND OF EDOM FROM THE SONS OF ESAU

1Chronicles 1:34 And   **Abraham begat Isaac**. **The sons of Isaac**; **Esau** and Israel.

35 The sons of Esau; Eliphaz, Reuel, and Jeush, and Jaalam, and Korah.

36 The sons of Eliphaz; Teman, and Omar, Zephi, and Gatam, Kenaz, and Timna, and Amalek.

37 The sons of Reuel; Nahath, Zerah, Shammah, and Mizzah.

38 And **the sons of Seir**; Lotan, and Shobal, and Zibeon, and Anah, and Dishon, and **Eze**r, and Dishan.

39 And the sons of Lotan; Hori, and Homam: and Timna *was* Lotan's sister.

40 The sons of Shobal; Alian, and Manahath, and Ebal, Shephi, and Onam. And the sons of Zibeon; Aiah, and Anah.

41 The sons of Anah; Dishon. And the sons of Dishon; Amram, and Eshban, and Ithran, and Cheran.

42 The **sons of Ezer**; Bilhan, and Zavan, *and* Jakan. The sons of Dishan; Uz, and Aran.

43 **Now these** *are* **the kings that reigned in the land of Edom before** *any* **king reigned over the children of Israel**; **Bela the son of Beor**: and **the name of his city** *was* **Dinhabah.**

44 And when Bela was dead, **Jobab the son of Zerah** of Bozrah reigned in his stead.

45 And when Jobab was dead, **Husham of the land of the Temanites** reigned in his stead.

46 And when Husham was dead, **Hadad the son of Bedad**, which smote Midian in the field of Moab, reigned in his stead: and **the name of his city** *was* **Avith**.

47 And when Hadad was dead, **Samlah of Masrekah** reigned in his stead.

48 And when Samlah was dead, **Shaul of Rehoboth by the river** reigned in his stead.

49 And when Shaul was dead, **Baalhanan the son of Achbor** reigned in his stead.

50 And when Baalhanan was dead, **Hadad** reigned in his stead: and **the name of his city** *was* **Pai** and his wife's name *was* Mehetabel, the daughter of Matred, the daughter of Mezahab.

DUKES OF EDOM
1Chronicles 1:51 Hadad died also. And the dukes of Edom were; **duke Timnah, duke Aliah, duke Jetheth,**
52 **Duke Aholibamah, duke Elah, duke Pinon,**
53 **Duke Kenaz, duke Teman, duke Mibzar,**
54 **Duke Magdiel, duke Iram**. These *are* the dukes of Edom.

b. THE SONS OF HAM

KINGDOM OF BABEL (Babylon)
Genesis 10:6 And **the sons of Ham**; **Cush,** and Mizraim, and Phut, and Canaan.

7 And the sons of Cush; Seba, and Havilah, and Sabtah, and Raamah, and Sabtecha: and the sons of Raamah; Sheba, and Dedan.

8 And **Cush begat Nimrod**: he began to be a mighty one in the earth.

9 He was a mighty hunter before the LORD: wherefore it is said, Even as Nimrod the mighty hunter before the LORD.

10 And **the beginning of his kingdom was Babel**, and Erech, and Accad, and Calneh, in the land of Shinar,

SODOM, GOMORRAH AND NATIONS OF CANAAN
Genesis 10:6 And **the sons of Ham**; Cush, and Mizraim, and Phut, and **Canaan**
13 And **Mizraim begat Ludim**, and Anamim, and Lehabim, and Naphtuhim,

14 And Pathrusim, and Casluhim, (out of whom came Philistim,) and Caphtorim.

15 And **Canaan begat** Sidon his firstborn, and Heth,

16 And the **Jebusite, and the Amorite, and the Girgasite,**

17 And the Hivite, and the Arkite, and the Sinite,

18 And the Arvadite, and the Zemarite, and the Hamathite: and **afterward were the families of the Canaanites spread abroad.**

19 And **the border of the Canaanites** was from Sidon, as thou comest to Gerar, unto Gaza; **as thou goest, unto Sodom, and Gomorrah,**

PHILISTINES

1Chronicles 1:9 And **the sons of Cush**; Seba, and Havilah, and Sabta, and Raamah, and Sabtecha. And the sons of Raamah; Sheba, and Dedan.

10 And **Cush begat Nimrod**: **he began to be mighty upon the earth**.

11 And **Mizraim** begat Ludim, and Anamim, and Lehabim, and Naphtuhim,

12 And Pathrusim, and **Casluhim, (of whom came the Philistines**,) and Caphthorim.

c. THE SONS OF JOPETH

Genesis 10:2 and The sons of Japheth; **Gomer, and Magog, and Madai, and Javan, and Tubal, and Meshech, and Tiras.**

3 And the sons of Gomer; Ashkenaz, and Riphath, and Togarmah.

4 And the sons of Javan; Elishah, and Tarshish, Kittim, and Dodanim.

4. THE MOST HIGH GOD RULES OVER THE KINGDOMS OF MEN

Daniel 4:17 This matter is by the decree of the watchers, and the demand by the word of the holy ones: **to the intent that the living may know that the most High ruleth in the kingdom of men, and giveth it to whomsoever he will,** and setteth up over it the basest of men.

KING SOLOMON

1Chronicles 28:5 And of all my sons, (for the LORD hath given me many sons,) he hath chosen Solomon my son to sit upon the throne of the kingdom of the LORD over Israel.

6 And he said unto me, **Solomon thy son**, he shall build my house and my courts: **for I have chosen him to be my son, and I will be his father.**

KING NEBUCHADNEZAR OF BABYLON

Daniel 4:25 That they shall drive thee from men, and thy dwelling shall be with the beasts of the field, and they shall make thee to eat grass as oxen, and they shall wet thee with the dew of heaven, and seven times shall pass over thee, till thou know **that the most High ruleth in the kingdom of men, and giveth it to whomsoever he will.**

Daniel 5:21 And he was driven from the sons of men; and his heart was made like the beasts, and his dwelling *was* with the wild asses: they fed him with grass like oxen, and his body was wet with the dew of heaven; till he knew **that the most high God ruled in the kingdom of men, and *that* he appointeth over it whomsoever he will.**

===

PART 3
GOD CALLED HIS PEOPLE

CHAPTER I GOD CHOSE HIS PEOPLE FROM THE BEGINNING

Ephesians 1: 4
*According as **he hath chosen us in him before the foundation of the world,** that **we should be holy and without blame** before him in love: 5 **Having predestinated** us unto the adoption of children by Jesus Christ to himself, according to the good pleasure of his will, 6 **To the praise of the glory of his grace,** wherein he hath made us accepted in the beloved.*

THE MYSTERY OF ADOPTION

A. NAMES WRITTEN IN HEAVEN
Hebrews 12:23 **To the general assembly and church of the firstborn, which are written in heaven,** and to God the Judge of all, and to the spirits of just men made perfect,
24 And to Jesus the mediator of the new covenant, and to the blood of sprinkling, that speaketh better things than *that of* Abel.
25See that ye refuse not him that speaketh. For if they escaped not who refused him that spake on earth, much more *shall not* we *escape*, if we turn away from him that *speaketh* from heaven:
Isaiah 8:18 Behold, **I and the children whom the LORD hath given me are for signs and for wonders in Israel from the LORD of hosts, which dwelleth in Mount Zion.**

B. PREDESTINATED ACCORDING TO THE PURPOSE OF HIM

Romans 9:11 (***For the children being not yet born, neither having done any good or evil, that the purpose of God according to election might stand, not of works, but*** *of him that calleth;)*

Matthew 20:16 So the last shall be first, and the first last: for many be called, but few chosen.

Ephesians 1:11 In whom also we have obtained an inheritance, **being predestinated according to the purpose of him who worketh all things after the counsel of his own will**:

Romans 8:28 And we know that all things work together for good **to them that love God, to them who are the called according to *his* purpose.**

29 **For whom he did foreknow**, he also did predestinate *to be* **conformed to the image of his Son,** that he might be the firstborn among many brethren.

30 **Moreover whom he did predestinate, them he also called: and whom he called, them he also justified: and whom he justified, them he also glorified.**

2Timothy 1:9 Who hath saved us, and called *us* with an holy calling, not according to our works, but **according to his own purpose and grace, which was given us in Christ Jesus before the world began,**

10 But is now made manifest by the appearing of our Saviour Jesus Christ, who hath abolished death, and hath brought life and immortality to light through the gospel:

2Thessalonians 2:13 But we are bound to give thanks alway to God for you, brethren beloved of the Lord**, because God hath from the beginning chosen you to salvation through sanctification of the Spirit and belief of the truth:**

14 Whereunto he called you by our gospel, to the obtaining of the glory of our Lord Jesus Christ.

Ephesians 2:10 **For we are his workmanship, created in Christ Jesus unto good works, which God hath before ordained that we should walk in them.**

*GOD'S INSTRUCTION TO THE CHOSEN (NATION OF ISRAEL)

Exodus 19:5 Now therefore, **if ye will obey my voice indeed, and keep my covenant, then ye shall be a peculiar treasure unto me above all people**: for all the earth *is* mine:

6 **And ye shall be unto me a kingdom of priests, and an holy nation**. These *are* the words which thou shalt speak unto the children of Israel.

GOD CHOSE THE PRINCES OF THE TRIBES OF ISRAEL

Numbers 1:16 These *were* the renowned of the congregation, princes of the tribes of their fathers, **heads of thousands in Israel.**

Genesis 32:28 And he said, Thy name shall be called no more **Jacob**, **but Israel:** for as a prince hast thou power with God and with men, and hast prevailed.

Ezekiel 34:24 And I the LORD will be their God, and **my servant David a prince among them;** I the LORD have spoken *it*.

1Kings 11:34 Howbeit I will not take the whole kingdom out of his hand: but I will make him prince all the days of his life **for David my servant's sake, whom I chose**, because he kept my commandments and my statutes:

GOD CHOOSE THE POOR AND FOOLISH THINGS OF THIS WORLD

1Corinthians 1:26 **For ye see your calling, brethren**, how that not many wise men after the flesh, not many mighty, not many noble, are called:

27 **But God hath chosen the foolish things of the world to confound the wise; and God hath chosen the weak things of the world to confound the things which are mighty;**

28 And base things of the world, and things which are despised, hath God chosen, yea, and things which are not, to bring to nought things that are:

29 That no flesh should glory in his presence.

30 But of him are ye in Christ Jesus, who of God is made unto us wisdom, and righteousness, and sanctification, and redemption:

James 2:5 Hearken, my beloved brethren, **Hath not God chosen the poor of this world rich in faith, and heirs of the kingdom which he hath promised to them that love him?**

1Thessalonians 4:7 For God hath not called us unto uncleanness, but unto holiness.

THE MYSTERY OF GOD'S MIND

Isaiah 55:8 **For my thoughts *are* not your thoughts, neither *are* your ways my ways**, saith the LORD.

9 For *as* the heavens are higher than the earth, so are my ways higher than your ways, and my thoughts than your thoughts.

Job 42:2 I know that thou canst do every *thing*, and *that* no thought can be withholden **thee.**

1. GOD IS THE POTTER, PEOPLE ARE CLAY

Isaiah 64:8 But now, O LORD, thou art our father, **we are the clay, and thou our potter**; we are all the work of thy hand.

Jeremiah 18:4 And **the vessel that he made of clay was marred** in the hand of the potter: **so he made it again another vessel,** as seemed good to the potter to make it.

2Timothy 2:20 But in a great house there are not only vessels of gold and of silver, but also of wood and of earth; and some to honour, and some to dishonour.

21 If a man therefore purge himself from these, he shall be a vessel unto honour, sanctified, and meet for the master's use, *and* prepared unto every good work.

Isaiah 45:9 Woe unto him that striveth with his Maker! *Let* the potsherd *strive* with the potsherds of the earth. Shall the clay say to him that fashioneth it, What makest thou? or thy work, He hath no hands?

10 Woe unto him that saith unto *his* father, What begettest thou? or to the woman, What hast thou brought forth?

11 Thus saith the LORD, the Holy One of Israel, and his Maker, Ask me of things to come concerning my sons, and concerning the work of my hands command ye me.

Romans 9:18 **Therefore hath he mercy on whom he will have mercy, and whom he will be hardeneth.**

19 Thou wilt say then unto me, Why doth he yet find fault? For who hath resisted his will?

20 Nay but, **O man, who art thou that repliest against God? Shall the thing formed say to him that formed *it*, Why hast thou made me thus?**

21 **Hath not the potter power over the clay**, of the same lump to make one vessel unto honour, and another unto dishonour?

22 *What* if God, willing to shew *his* wrath, and to make his power known, endured with much longsuffering the vessels of wrath fitted to destruction:

23 And **that he might make known the riches of his glory on the vessels of mercy, which he had afore prepared unto glory,**

24 **Even us, whom he hath called, not of the Jews only, but also of the Gentiles?**

GOD FASHIONED MAN FROM DUST

Job 10:8 Thine hands have made me and fashioned me together round about; yet thou dost destroy me.

9 Remember, I beseech thee, that thou hast made me as the clay; and wilt thou bring me into dust again?

11 Thou hast clothed me with skin and flesh, and hast fenced me with bones and sinews.

12 Thou hast granted me life and favour, and thy visitation hath preserved my spirit.

Job 33: 6 **Behold, I am according to thy wish in God stead: I also am formed out of the clay.**

Job 12:10 In whose hand is *the soul* of every living thing, and the breath of all mankind.

Jeremiah 18:6 O house of Israel, cannot I do with you as this potter? saith the LORD. **Behold, as the clay *is* in the potter's hand, so *are* ye in mine hand, O house of Israel.**

Isaiah 29:16 Surely your turning of things upside down shall be esteemed as the potter's clay: for shall the work say of him that made it, He made me not? or shall the thing framed say of him that framed it, He had no understanding?

2. GOD KNOWS THE HEART OF PEOPLE

Proverbs 15:3 The eyes of the LORD *are* in every place, beholding the evil and the good.

1Samuel 16:7 But the LORD said unto Samuel, **Look not on his countenance, or on the height of his stature;** because I have refused him: for *the LORD seeth* not as man seeth; for man looketh on the outward appearance, **but the LORD looketh on the heart.**

Jeremiah 17:10 **I the LORD search the heart, *I* try the reins, even to give every man according to his ways, *and* according to the fruit of his doings.**

1John 3:19 And hereby we know that we are of the truth, and shall assure our hearts before him.

20 For if our heart condemn us, **God is greater than our heart, and knoweth all things.**

21 Beloved, if our heart condemn us not, *then* have we confidence toward God.

1Kings 8:38 What prayer and supplication soever be *made* by any man, *or* by all thy people Israel, which shall know every man the plague of his own heart, and spread forth his hands toward this house:

39 Then hear thou in heaven thy dwelling place, and forgive, and do, and give to every man according to his ways, **whose heart thou knowest**; (for thou, *even* **thou only, knowest the hearts of all the children of men**;)

3. GOD KNOWS HIS CHOSEN

Psalms 100:3 Know ye that **the LORD he is God: It is he that hath made us,** and **not we ourselves; we are his people,** and **the sheep of his pasture.**

Ezekiel 11:5 **And the Spirit of the LORD fell upon me, and said unto me, Speak; Thus saith the LORD; Thus have ye said, O house of Israel: for I know the things that come into your mind,** *every one of* **them.**

John 6: 64 **But there are some of you that believe not. For Jesus** *knew from the beginning* **who they were that believed not, and who should betray him.**

Psalms 1:6 For the LORD knoweth the way of the righteous: but the way of the ungodly shall perish.

Psalms 37:18 The LORD knoweth the days of the upright: and their inheritance shall be for ever.

Psalms 44:21 Shall not God search this out? for he knoweth the secrets of the heart.

Psalms 94:11 The LORD knoweth the thoughts of man, that they *are* vanity.

Hebrews 4:13 Neither is there any creature that is not manifest in his sight: but all things *are* naked and opened unto the eyes of him with whom we have to do.

a. INSIDE THE MOTHER'S WOMB

Psalms 139:13 For thou hast possessed my reins: thou hast covered me in my mother's womb.

14 **I will praise thee; for I am fearfully and wonderfully made: marvelous are thy works; and that my soul knoweth right well.**

15 **My substance was not hid from thee, when I was made in secret,** and curiously wrought in the lowest parts of the earth.

16 **Thine eyes did see my substance, yet being unperfect; and in thy book all my members were written, which in**

continuance were fashioned, when as yet there was none of them.

1.GOD CHOSE ISAAC BEFORE HE WAS BORN

Genesis 17:19 And **God said, Sarah thy wife shall bear thee a son indeed; and thou shalt call his name Isaac:** and I will establish my covenant with him for an everlasting covenant, *and* with his seed after him.

Genesis 17:21 **But my covenant will I establish with Isaac**, which **Sarah shall bear unto thee at this set time in the next year.**

JACOB AND ESAU

Genesis 25:21 And Isaac intreated the LORD for his wife, because she *was* barren: and the LORD was intreated of him, and Rebekah his wife conceived.

22 **And the children struggled together within her; and she said, If** *it be* **so, why** *am* **I thus? And she went to enquire of the LORD**.

23 **And the LORD said unto her, Two nations** *are* **in thy womb, and two manner of people shall be separated from thy bowels; and** *the one* **people shall be stronger than** *the other* **people; and the elder shall serve the younger.**

2.GOD CHOSE JACOB

Romans 9:13 **As it is written, Jacob have I loved, but Esau have I hated.**

14 What shall we say then? *Is there* **unrighteousness with God?** God forbid.

15 **For he saith to Moses, I will have mercy on whom I will have mercy, and I will have compassion on whom I will have compassion.**

16 So then *it is* not of him that willeth, nor of him that runneth, but of God that sheweth mercy.

17 **For the scripture saith unto Pharaoh, Even for this same purpose have I raised thee up, that I might shew my power in thee, and that my name might be declared throughout all the earth.**

Isaiah 44:2 **Thus saith the LORD that made thee, and formed thee from the womb,** *which* **will help thee; Fear not, O Jacob, my servant; and thou, Jesurun, whom I have chosen.**

Psalms 135:4 For the LORD hath chosen Jacob unto himself, *and* Israel for his peculiar treasure.

Isaiah 41:8 But thou, Israel, *art* my servant, **Jacob whom I have chosen, the seed of Abraham my friend.**

9 *Thou* whom I have taken from the ends of the earth, and called thee from the chief men thereof, and said unto thee, Thou *art* my servant; I have chosen thee, and not cast thee away.

3.SAMSON

Judges 13:1 And **the children of Israel did evil again in the sight of the LORD; and the LORD delivered them into the hand of the Philistines forty years.**

2 And there was a certain man of Zorah, of the family of the Danites, whose name *was* Manoah; and his wife *was* barren, and bare not.

3 And **the angel of the LORD appeared unto the woman, and said unto her, Behold now, thou *art* barren, and bearest not: but thou shalt conceive, and bear a son.**

4 Now therefore beware, I pray thee, and drink not wine nor strong drink, and eat not any unclean *thing*:

5 **For, lo, thou shalt conceive, and bear a son; and no razor shall come on his head: for the child shall be a Nazarite unto God from the womb: and he shall begin to deliver Israel out of the hand of the Philistines.**

4. GOD CHOSE SOLOMON BEFORE HE WAS BORN

1Kings 8:16 Since the day that I brought forth my people Israel out of Egypt, I chose no city out of all the tribes of Israel to build an house, that my name might be therein; **but I chose David to be over my people Israel.**

17 And it was in the heart of David my father to build an house for the name of the LORD God of Israel.

18 And the LORD said unto David my father, Whereas it was in thine heart to build an house unto my name, thou didst well that it was in thine heart.

19 Nevertheless thou shalt not build the house; **but thy son that shall come forth out of thy loins**, he shall build the house unto my name.

20 And the LORD hath performed his word that he spake, and I am risen up in the room of David my father, and sit on the throne

of Israel, as the LORD promised, and have built an house for the name of the LORD God of Israel.

b. NO ONE COULD ESCAPE FROM THE POWER OF GOD

Jeremiah 23:23 Am I a God at hand, saith the LORD, and not a God afar off?

24 Can any hide himself in secret places that I shall not see him? saith the LORD. Do not I fill heaven and earth? saith the LORD.

Job 23:13 But he *is* in one *mind*, and who can turn him? and *what* his soul desireth, even *that* he doeth.

14 **For he performeth *the thing that is* appointed for me**: and many such *things are* with him.

Psalms 139:9 *If* I take the wings of the morning, *and* dwell in the uttermost parts of the sea;

10 **Even there shall thy hand lead me, and thy right hand shall hold me**.

11 If I say, Surely the darkness shall cover me; even the night shall be light about me.

12 Yea, the darkness hideth not from thee; but the night shineth as the day: the darkness and the light *are* both alike *to thee*.

Job 34:16 **If now *thou hast* understanding, hear this**: hearken to the voice of my words.

17 Shall even he that hateth right govern? and wilt thou condemn him that is most just?

18 *Is it fit* to say to a king, *Thou art* wicked? *and* to princes, *Ye are* ungodly?

19 *How much less to him* that accepteth not the persons of princes, nor regardeth the rich more than the poor? **for they all *are* the work of his hands**.

20 **In a moment shall they die, and the people shall be troubled at midnight, and pass away: and the mighty shall be taken away without hand.**

21 **For his eyes *are* upon the ways of man, and he seeth all his goings.**

22 ***There is* no darkness, nor shadow of death, where the workers of iniquity may hide themselves.**

23 For he will not lay upon man more *than right*; **that he should enter into judgment with God.**

24 **He shall break in pieces mighty men without number**, and set others in their stead.

25 **Therefore he knoweth their works**, and he overturneth *them* in the night, so that they are destroyed.

26 **He striketh them as wicked men in the open sight of others;**
27 **Because they turned back from him, and would no**t **consider any of his ways:**

28 So that they cause the cry of the poor to come unto him, and he heareth the cry of the afflicted.

29 **When he giveth quietness, who then can make trouble? and when he hideth** *his* **face, who then can behold him? whether** *it* *be done* **against a nation, or against a man only:**

c. GOD KNOWS THE THOUGHTS AND IMAGINATIONS OF MAN

1Chronicles 28:9 And thou, Solomon my son, know thou the God of thy father, and serve him with a perfect heart and with a willing mind: for **the LORD searcheth all hearts, and understandeth all the imaginations of the thoughts:** if thou seek him, he will be found of thee; but if thou forsake him, he will cast thee off for ever.

Psalms 69:**5** O God, thou knowest my foolishness; and my sins are not hid from thee.

d. GOD KNOWS WHERE THE SOUL GOES AFTER DEATH

Psalms 139:7 Whither shall I go from thy spirit? or whither shall I flee from thy presence?

8 If I ascend up into heaven, thou *art* there: if I make my bed in hell, behold, thou *art there*.

THE WHOLE DUTY OF MAN

Ecclesiastes 12:13 Let us hear the conclusion of the whole matter: **Fear God, and keep his commandments:** for this *is* the whole *duty* of man.

14 For God shall bring every work into judgment, with every secret thing, whether *it be* good, or whether *it be* evil.

THE CHOSEN MUST ALWAYS READY TO MEET THE LORD

PARABLES OF THE WISE AND FOOLISH VIRGINS

Matthew25:1 Then shall the kingdom of heaven be likened unto ten virgins, which took their lamps, and went forth to meet the bridegroom.

2 And **five of them were wise**, and **five** *were* **foolish**.

3 They that *were* **foolish took their lamps, and took no oil with them**:

4 But **the wise took oil in their vessels with their lamps**.

5 While the bridegroom tarried, they all slumbered and slept.

6 And **at midnight there was a cry made**, Behold, the bridegroom cometh; go ye out to meet him.

7 Then all those virgins arose, and trimmed their lamps.

FOOLISH VIRGINS NOT ALLOWED TO BE WITH THE BRIDEGROOM

Matthew 25:8 And the foolish said unto the wise, Give us of your oil; for our lamps are gone out.

9 But the wise answered, saying, *Not so*; lest there be not enough for us and you: but go ye rather to them that sell, and buy for yourselves.

10 And while they went to buy, the bridegroom came; and they that were ready went in with him to the marriage: and the door was shut.

11 Afterward came also the other virgins, saying, **Lord, Lord, open to us**.

12 **But** *he* **answered and said,** *Verily I say unto you, I know you not.*

13 **Watch therefore, for ye know neither the day nor the hour wherein the Son of man cometh.**

PEOPLE WILL PASSED AWAY LIKE GRASS

2Peter 3:8 But, beloved, be not ignorant of this one thing, that one day *is* **with the Lord as a thousand years, and a thousand years as one day.**

Psalm 90:4 For a thousand years in thy sight *are but* as yesterday when it is past, and *as* a watch in the night.

5 Thou carriest them away as with a flood; they are *as* a sleep: in the morning *they are* like grass *which* groweth up.

6 In the morning it flourisheth, and groweth up; in the evening it is cut down, and withereth.

7 For we are consumed by thine anger, and by thy wrath are we troubled.

8 Thou hast set our iniquities before thee, our secret *sins* in the light of thy countenance.

9 For all our days are passed away in thy wrath: we spend our years as a tale *that is told*.

10 The days of our years *are* threescore years and ten; and if by reason of strength *they be* fourscore years, yet *is* their strength labour and sorrow; for it is soon cut off, and we fly away.

Psalms 103: 15 *As for* **man, his days** *are* **as grass: as a flower of the field, so he flourisheth.**

16 **For the wind passeth over it, and it is gone**; and the place thereof shall know it no more.

REMEMBER THE CREATOR WHILE WE ARE YOUNG

Ecclesiastes 12:1 Remember now thy Creator in the days of thy youth, while the evil days come not, nor the years draw nigh, when thou shalt say, I have no pleasure in them;

2 While the sun, or the light, or the moon, or the stars, be not darkened, nor the clouds return after the rain:

3 **In the day when the keepers of the house shall tremble**, and the strong men shall bow themselves, and the grinders cease because they are few, and **those that look out of the windows be darkened,**

4 And the doors shall be shut in the streets, when the sound of the grinding is low, and he shall rise up at the voice of the bird, and all the daughters of musick shall be brought low;

5 Also *when* they shall be afraid of *that which is* high, and fears *shall be* in the way, and the almond tree shall flourish, and the grasshopper shall be a burden, and desire shall fail: because man goeth to his long home, and the mourners go about the streets:

6 Or ever the silver cord be loosed, or the golden bowl be broken, or the pitcher be broken at the fountain, or the wheel broken at the cistern.

PRAYER TO THE ALL KNOWING GOD

Psalms 139:1 *(To the chief Musician, A Psalm of David.) O LORD, thou hast searched me, and known me.*

2 Thou knowest my downsitting and mine uprising, thou understandest my thought afar off.

3 Thou compassest my path and my lying down, and art acquainted with all my ways.

4 For there is not a word in my tongue, but, lo, O LORD, thou knowest it altogether.

5 Thou hast beset me behind and before, and laid thine hand upon me.

6 Such knowledge is too wonderful for me; it is high, I cannot attain unto it.

7 Whither shall I go from thy spirit? or whither shall I flee from thy presence?

---

*Help me O God in all my ways. In the mighty name of the LORD Jesus Christ I Pray thee. Amen.

PART 3
GOD CALLED HIS PEOPLE

CHAPTER II **SEED**

Acts 3:25
Ye are the children of the prophets, and of the covenant which
*God made with our fathers, **saying unto Abraham**, And **in thy***
seed shall all the kindreds of the earth be blessed.

GOD CALLED HIS CHOSEN PEOPLE, SEED
Matthew 13:38 **The field is the world; the good seed are the**
children of the kingdom; but the *tares* **are the children of the**
wicked one;
39 The enemy that sowed them is the devil; the harvest is the end
of the world; and the reapers are the angels.
Psalms 105:6 O ye seed of Abraham his servant, **ye children of**
Jacob his chosen.
Numbers 23:21 He hath not beheld iniquity in Jacob, neither hath
he seen perverseness in Israel: **the LORD his God *is* with him**,
and the shout of a king *is* among them.
23 Surely *there is* no enchantment against Jacob, neither *is*
there any divination against Israel: according to this time it shall
be said of Jacob and of Israel, What hath God wrought!

GOD'S COVENANT TO ABRAHAM AND HIS SEED
Genesis 17:1 And when Abram was ninety years old and nine,
the LORD appeared to Abram, and said unto him, I *am* the
Almighty God; walk before me, and be thou perfect.
2 **And I will make my covenant between me and thee, and will**
multiply thee exceedingly.
3 And Abram fell on his face: and God talked with him, saying,
4 **As for me, behold, my covenant *is* with thee, and thou shalt**
be a father of many nations.
5 **Neither shall thy name any more be called Abram, but thy**
name shall be Abraham; for a father of many nations have I
made thee.

6 And I will make thee exceeding fruitful, and I will make nations of thee, and kings shall come out of thee.

7 **And I will establish my covenant between me and thee and thy seed after thee in their generations for an everlasting covenant, to be a God unto thee, and to thy seed after thee.**

9 And God said unto Abraham, **Thou shalt keep my covenant therefore, thou, and thy seed after thee in their generations.**

A. GOD GAVE THE PROMISE LAND TO ABRAHAM AND HIS SEED

Genesis 15:18 In the same day the LORD made a covenant with Abram, saying, **Unto thy seed have I given this land, from the river of Egypt unto the great river, the river Euphrates:**

19 The Kenites, and the Kenizzites, and the Kadmonites,

20 And the Hittites, and the Perizzites, and the Rephaims,

21 And the Amorites, and the Canaanites, and the Girgashites, and the Jebusites.

GOD GAVE THE LAND OF CANAAN (ISRAEL) TO ISAAC SEED

Genesis 17:8 And **I will give unto thee, and to thy seed after thee, the land wherein thou art a stranger, all the land of Canaan, for an everlasting possession; and I will be their God.**

Deuteronomy 34:4 And the LORD said unto him, **This** *is* **the land which I sware unto Abraham, unto Isaac, and unto Jacob,** saying, I will give it unto thy seed: I have caused thee to see *it* with thine eyes, but thou shalt not go over thither.

Deuteronomy 1:8 Behold, I have set the land before you: go in and possess the land which the LORD sware unto your fathers, Abraham, Isaac, and Jacob, to give unto them and to their seed after them.

Genesis 28:13 And, behold, the LORD stood above it, and said**, I** *am* **the LORD God of Abraham thy father, and the God of Isaac**: **the land whereon thou liest, to thee will I give it, and to thy seed;**

Genesis 13:15 For **all the land which thou seest, to thee will I give it, and to thy seed for ever.**

Exodus 33:1 And the LORD said unto Moses, Depart, *and* go up hence, thou and the people which thou hast brought up out of the land of Egypt, unto the land which I sware unto Abraham, to Isaac, and to Jacob, saying, Unto thy seed will I give it:

Genesis 35:12 And the land which I gave Abraham and Isaac, to thee I will give it, and to thy seed after thee will I give the land.

B. THE CHOSEN PEOPLE

ISAAC THE PROMISE OF GOD WAS MADE
Genesis 26:24 And the LORD appeared unto him the same night, and said, I *am* the God of Abraham thy father: fear not, for I *am* with thee, and will bless thee, and multiply thy seed for my servant Abraham's sake.
Genesis 28:4 And give thee the blessing of Abraham, to thee, and to thy seed with thee; that thou mayest inherit the land wherein thou art a stranger, which God gave unto Abraham.
Genesis 21:12 And **God said unto Abraham**, Let it not be grievous in thy sight because of the lad, and because of thy bondwoman; in all that Sarah hath said unto thee, hearken unto her voice; **for in Isaac shall thy seed be called.**

1. THE SEED OF PROMISE FROM ISAAC
Isaiah 61:9 **And their seed shall be known among the Gentiles, and their offspring among the people:** all that see them shall acknowledge them, that **they** *are* **the seed** *which* **the LORD hath blessed.**
Joshua 24:3 And I took your father Abraham from the other side of the flood, and led him throughout all the land of Canaan, and multiplied his seed, and gave him Isaac.
Romans 9:7 Neither, because they are the seed of Abraham, *are they* all children: **but, In Isaac shall thy seed be called.**
8 That is, **They which are the children of the flesh, these** *are* **not the children of God: but the children of the promise are counted for the seed.**
9 For this *is* the word of promise, At this time will I come, and Sara shall have a son.
10 And not only *this*; but when Rebecca also had conceived by one, *even* by our father Isaac;
12 It was said unto her, The elder shall serve the younger.

Isaiah 46:3 *Hearken unto me, O house of Jacob, and all the remnant of the house of Israel,* which are borne by me from the belly, which are carried from the womb:

4 And even to your old age I am he; and even to hoar hairs will I carry you: I have made, and I will bear; even I will carry, and will deliver you.

Isaiah 44:1 Yet now hear, **O Jacob my servant; and Israel, whom I have chosen**:

Isaiah 41:8 But thou, Israel, *art* my servant, **Jacob whom I have chosen, the seed of Abraham my friend.**

Hosea 1:10 **Yet the number of the children of Israel shall be as the sand of the sea, which cannot be measured nor numbered**; and it shall come to pass, *that* in the place where it was said unto them, **Ye** *are* **not my people,** *there* **it shall be said unto them,** *Ye are* **the sons of the living God.**

Deuteronomy 7:6 For thou *art* an holy people unto the LORD thy God: the LORD **thy God hath chosen thee to be a special people unto himself, above all people that** *are* **upon the face of the earth.**

7 **The LORD did not set his love upon you, nor choose you**, because ye were more in number than any people; for ye *were* the fewest of all people:

8 **But because the LORD loved you, and because he would keep the oath which he had sworn unto your fathers,** hath the LORD brought you out with a mighty hand,

10 **And repayeth them that hate him to their face, to destroy them: he will not be slack to him that hateth him, he will repay him to his face.**

2Samuel 7:23 **And what one nation in the earth** *is* **like thy people,** *even* **like Israel, whom God went to redeem for a people to himself, and to make him a name,** and to do for you great things and terrible, for thy land, before thy people, which thou redeemedst to thee from Egypt, *from* the nations and their gods?

24 **For thou hast confirmed to thyself thy people Israel** *to be* **a people unto thee for ever: and thou, LORD, art become their God.**

Deuteronomy 4:37 And **because he loved thy fathers, therefore** *he chose* **their seed after them**, and brought thee out in his sight with his mighty power out of Egypt;

38 To drive out nations from before thee greater and mightier than thou *art*, to bring thee in, to give thee their land *for* an inheritance, as *it is*this day.

Deuteronomy 10:15 Only the LORD had a delight in thy fathers to love them, and he chose their seed after them, *even* you above all people, as *it is* this day.

1Peter 2:9 But *ye are a chosen generation,* **a royal priesthood, an holy nation,** a peculiar people; that ye should shew forth the praises of him *who hath called you* out of darkness into his marvelous light:

THE LORD CAME FROM THE TRIBE OF JUDAH

Psalms 78:68 But *chose* the tribe of Judah ,the Mount Zion which he loved.

Hebrews 7:14 **For** *it is* **evident that our Lord sprang out of Juda**; of which tribe Moses spake nothing concerning priesthood.

Isaiah 65:9 And **I will bring forth a seed out of Jacob, and out of Judah; an inheritor of my mountains: and mine elect** shall inherit it, and my servants shall dwell there.

GOD CHOSE DAVID TO BE THE KING OF ISRAEL FOREVER (End times)

1Chronicles 28:4 Howbeit **the LORD God of Israel chose me before all the house of my father to be king over Israel for ever: for he hath chosen Judah** *to be* **the ruler; and of the house of Judah, the house of my father**; and among the sons of my father he liked me to make *me* king over all Israel:

THE FAMILY OF ISRAEL (GOD'S CHOSEN)

Romans 3:1 *What advantage then hath* **the Jew?** *or what profit is there of circumcision? 2 Much everyway: chiefly* **because that unto them were committed the oracles of God.**

Genesis 28:1 And Isaac called Jacob, and blessed him, and charged him, and said unto him, Thou shalt not take a wife of the daughters of Canaan.

2 Arise, go to Padanaram, to the house of Bethuel thy mother's father; and **take thee a wife from thence of the daughters of Laban thy mother's brother.**

3 And God Almighty bless thee, and make thee fruitful, and multiply thee, that thou mayest be a multitude of people;

4 And give thee the blessing of Abraham, to thee, and to thy seed with thee; that thou mayest inherit the land wherein thou art a stranger, which God gave unto Abraham.

Isaiah 45:4 **For Jacob my servant's sake, and Israel mine elect, I have even called thee by thy name: I have surnamed thee, though thou hast not known me.**

a. JACOB'S TWO WIVES AND TWO HANDMAIDS

Genesis 29:16 And **Laban had two daughters**: the name o**f the elder** *was* **Leah,** and the name o**f the younger** *was* **Rachel.**

17 Leah *was* tender eyed; but Rachel was beautiful and well favoured.

18 And **Jacob loved Rachel; and said, I will serve thee seven years for Rachel thy younger daughter.**

19 And Laban said, *It is* better that I give her to thee, than that I should give her to another man: abide with me.

20 And **Jacob served seven years for Rachel**; and they seemed unto him *but* a few days, for the love he had to her.

21 And Jacob said unto Laban, Give *me* my wife, for my days are fulfilled, that I may go in unto her.

22 And Laban gathered together all the men of the place, and made a feast.

23 And it came to pass **in the evening, that he took Leah his daughter, and brought her to him; and he went in unto her.**

24 And **Laban gave unto his daughter Leah Zilpah** his maid *for* **an handmaid**.

25 And it came to pass, **that in the morning, behold, it** *was* **Leah**: and **he said to Laban, What** *is* **this thou hast done unto me? did not I serve with thee for Rachel? wherefore then hast thou beguiled me?**

26 And **Laban said, It must not be so done in our country, to give the younger before the firstborn.**

27 **Fulfil her week, and we will give thee this also for the service which thou shalt serve with me yet seven other years**.

28 And Jacob did so, and fulfilled her week: and he gave him Rachel his daughter to wife also.

29 And **Laban gave to Rachel his daughter Bilhah his handmaid to be her ma**id.

30 And he went in also unto Rachel, and **he loved also Rachel more than Leah, and served with him yet seven other years.**

31 **And when the LORD saw that Leah** *was* **hated, he opened her womb: but Rachel** *was* **barren.**

b. TWELVE SONS OF JACOB (TWELVE TRIBES OF ISRAEL)

LEAH'S FOUR SONS: REUBEN, SIMEON, LEVI AND JUDAH

Genesis 29:32 And **Leah conceived**, and bare a son, and she called **his name Reuben**: for she said, **Surely the LORD hath looked upon my affliction; now therefore my husband will love me.**

33 And **she conceived again**, and bare a son; and said, **Because the LORD hath heard that I** *was* **hated,** he hath therefore given me this *son* also: and she called **his name Simeon**.

34 And **she conceived again**, and bare a son; and said, **Now this time will my husband be joined unto me,** because I have born him three sons: therefore was **his name called Levi**.

35 And **she conceived again**, and bare a son: and she said, **Now will I praise the LORD**: therefore **she called his name Judah**; and left bearing.

BILHAH'S (Rachel's handmaid) TWO SONS: DAN, AND NAPHTALI

Genesis 30:1 And when Rachel saw that she bare Jacob no children, **Rachel envied her sister**; and said unto Jacob, Give me children, or else I die.

2 And Jacob's anger was kindled against Rachel: and he said, *Am* I in God's stead, who hath withheld from thee the fruit of the womb?

3 And **she said, Behold my maid Bilhah, go in unto her**; and **she shall bear upon my knees, that I may also have children by her.**

4 And **she gave him Bilhah her handmaid to wife**: and Jacob went in unto her.

5 And **Bilhah conceived, and bare Jacob a son.**

6 And **Rachel said, God hath judged me, and hath also heard my voice,** and hath given me a son: therefore called **she his name Dan.**

7 And **Bilhah Rachel's maid conceived again, and bare Jacob a second son.**

8 And **Rachel said, With great wrestlings have I wrestled with my sister, and I have prevailed:** and **she called his name Naphtali.**

ZILPAH'S (Leah's handmaid) TWO SONS: GAD AND ASHER
Genesis 30:9 **When Leah saw that she had left bearing, she took Zilpah her maid, and gave her Jacob to wife.**

10 And **Zilpah Leah's maid bare Jacob a son**.

11 And Leah said, **A troop cometh**: and she called **his name Gad.**

12 And Zilpah Leah's maid bare Jacob a second son.

13 And **Leah said, Happy am I, for the daughters will call me blessed**: and she called his name **Asher**.

LEAH'S OTHER TWO SONS AND A DAUGHTER (ISSACHAR AND ZEBULUN)
Genesis 30:14 And Reuben went in the days of wheat harvest, and found mandrakes in the field, and brought them unto his mother Leah. Then Rachel said to Leah, Give me, I pray thee, of thy son's mandrakes.

15 And she said unto her, *Is it* a small matter that thou hast taken my husband? and wouldest thou take away my son's mandrakes also? And Rachel said, Therefore he shall lie with thee to night for thy son's mandrakes.

16 And Jacob came out of the field in the evening, and Leah went out to meet him, and said, Thou must come in unto me; for surely I have hired thee with my son's mandrakes. And he lay with her that night.

17 And God hearkened unto **Leah, and she conceived**, and **bare Jacob the fifth son**.

18 And **Leah said, God hath given me my hire, because I have given my maiden to my husband**: and **she called his name Issachar.**

19 And **Leah conceived again, and bare Jacob the sixth son**.

20 And **Leah said, God hath endued me *with* a good dowry; now will my husband dwell with me**, because I have born him six sons: and she called his name **Zebulun**.

21 And **afterwards she bare a daughter, and called her name Dinah**.

TWO SONS OF RACHEL (JOSEPH AND BENJAMIN)

Genesis 30:22 And God remembered Rachel, and God hearkened to her, and opened her womb.

23 And **she conceived, and bare a son; and said, God hath taken away my reproach**:

24 And **she called his name Joseph**; and said, The LORD shall add to me another son.

Genesis 35:16 And they journeyed from Bethel; and there was but a little way to come to Ephrath: and Rachel travailed, and she had hard labour.

17 And it came to pass, when she was in hard labour, that the midwife said unto her, Fear not; thou shalt have this son also.

18 **And it came to pass, as her soul was in departing, (for she died) that she called his name Benoni: but his father called him Benjamin**.

2. GENTILES THE OTHER CHOSEN

Acts 10:34 Then Peter opened his mouth, and said, Of a truth I perceived that **God is no respecter of persons**:

35 **But in every nation he that feareth him, and worketh righteousness, is accepted with him**.

GENTILES THE WORSHIPERS OF IDOLS

1Corinthians 10:20 But I *say*, **that the things which the Gentiles sacrifice, they sacrifice to devils, and not to God**: and I would not that ye should have fellowship with devils.

1Corinthians 12:2 Ye know that **ye were Gentiles, carried away unto these dumb idols, even as ye were led**.

Ephesians 2:11 Wherefore remember, that ye *being* in time past Gentiles in the flesh, who are called Uncircumcision by that which is called the Circumcision in the flesh made by hands;

12That at that time ye were without Christ, being aliens from the commonwealth of Israel, and strangers from the covenants of promise, having no hope, and without God in the world:

THE GENTILES WERE CALLED TO BECOME THE CHILDREN OF GOD

Romans 9:24 Even us, whom he hath called, not of the Jews only, but also of the Gentiles?

25 **As he saith also in Osee, I will call them my people, which were not my people; and her beloved, which was not beloved**.

26 And it shall come to pass, *that* in the place where it was said unto them, **Ye *are* not my people; there shall they be called the children of the living God.**

Genesis 22:18 **And in thy seed shall all the nations of the earth be blessed; because thou hast obeyed my voice.**

Galatians 3:8 And the scripture, foreseeing that God would justify the heathen through faith, preached before the gospel unto Abraham, *saying*, In thee shall all nations be blessed.

PART 3
GOD CALLED HIS PEOPLE

CHAPTER III **GOD REVEALED HIMSELF TO GENTILES**

Psalm 33:12
Blessed is the nation whose God is the LORD; and the people whom he hath chosen for his own inheritance.

GOD FREED HIS CHOSEN FROM BONDAGE

A. GOD SENT JOSEPH TO EGYPT (The Land of Ham)
Psalms 105:16 Moreover he called for a famine upon the land: he brake the whole staff of bread.

17 He sent a man before them, *even* **Joseph,** *who* **was sold for a servan**t:

18 **Whose feet they hurt with fetters: he was laid in iron**:

19 **Until the time that his word came: the word of the LORD tried him**.

20 The king sent and loosed him; *even* the ruler of the people, and let him go free.

21 **He made him lord of his house, and ruler of all his substance**:

22 To bind his princes at his pleasure; and teach his senators wisdom.

B. GOD OF ISRAEL SENT MOSES TO PHARAOH
Psalms 105:23 Israel also came into Egypt; and Jacob sojourned in the land of Ham.

24 And he increased his people greatly; and made them stronger than their enemies.

25 **He turned their heart to hate his people, to deal subtly with his servants.**

26 **He sent Moses his servant; and Aaron whom he had chosen.**

Exodus 7:1 And the LORD said unto Moses, **See, I have made thee a god to Pharaoh: and Aaron thy brother shall be thy prophet.**

2 **Thou shalt speak all that I command thee: and Aaron thy brother shall speak unto Pharaoh,** that he send the children of Israel out of his land.

3 And I will harden Pharaoh's heart, and multiply my signs and my wonders in the land of Egypt.

4 But Pharaoh shall not hearken unto you, that I may lay my hand upon Egypt, and bring forth mine armies, *and* my people the children of Israel, out of the land of Egypt by great judgments.

5 **And the Egyptians shall know that I** *am* **the LORD, when I stretch forth mine hand upon Egypt, and bring out the children of Israel from among them.**

6 And Moses and Aaron did as the LORD commanded them, so did they.

7 And Moses *was* fourscore years old, and Aaron fourscore and three years old, when they spake unto Pharaoh.

Exodus 6:1 Then the LORD said unto Moses, **Now shalt thou see what I will do to Pharaoh: for with a strong hand shall he let them go, and with a strong hand shall he drive them out of his land**.

Exodus 6:10 And the LORD spake to Moses, saying,

11 **Go in, speak unto Pharaoh king of Egypt, that he let the children of Israel go out of his land**.

Exodus 5:1 And afterward Moses and Aaron went in, and told Pharaoh, Thus saith the LORD God of Israel, *Let my people go*, that they may hold a feast unto me in the wilderness.

2 And Pharaoh said, *Who is the LORD, that I should obey his voice to let Israel go? I know not the LORD, neither will I let Israel go.*

3 And they said, The God of the Hebrews hath met with us: let us go, we pray thee, three days' journey into the desert, and sacrifice unto the LORD our God; lest he fall upon us with pestilence, or with the sword.

C. GOD SHOWED HIS POWER TO GENTILES

Acts 7:36 **He brought them out, after that he had shewed wonders and signs in the land of Egypt, and in the Red sea, and in the wilderness forty years**.

Jeremiah 32:20 Which hast set signs and wonders in the land of Egypt, *even* unto this day, and in Israel, and among *other* men; and hast made thee a name, as at this day;

21 And hast brought forth thy people Israel out of the land of Egypt with signs, and with wonders, and with a strong hand, and with a stretched out arm, and with great terror;

Deuteronomy 4:34 Or hath God assayed to go *and* take him a nation from the midst of *another* nation, by temptations, by signs, and by wonders, and by war, and by a mighty hand, and by a stretched out arm, and by great terrors, according to all that the LORD your God did for you in Egypt before your eyes?

Deuteronomy 7:19 The great temptations which thine eyes saw, and the signs, and the wonders, and the mighty hand, and the stretched out arm, whereby the LORD thy God brought thee out: so shall the LORD thy God do unto all the people of whom thou art afraid.

Deuteronomy 26:8 And the LORD brought us forth out of Egypt with a mighty hand, and with an outstretched arm, and with great terribleness, and with signs, and with wonders:

Deuteronomy 34:11 In all the signs and the wonders, which the LORD sent him to do in the land of Egypt to Pharaoh, and to all his servants, and to all his land,

12 And in all that mighty hand, and in all the great terror which Moses shewed in the sight of all Israel.

Deuteronomy 6:22 And the LORD shewed signs and wonders, great and sore, upon Egypt, upon Pharaoh, and upon all his household, before our eyes:

LORD DID SIGNS AND WONDERS IN EGYPT

Psalms 105:27 They shewed his signs among them, and wonders in the land of Ham.

1. TURNED THEIR WATER INTO BLOOD

Psalms 105:29 **He turned their waters into blood, and slew their fish**.

Exodus 7:17 Thus saith the LORD, *In this thou shalt know that I am the LORD: behold, I will smite with the rod that is in mine hand upon the waters which are in the river, and they shall be turned to blood.*

18 And the fish that *is* in the river shall die, and the river shall stink; and the Egyptians shall lothe to drink of the water of the river.

19 And the LORD spake unto Moses, *Say unto Aaron, Take thy rod, and stretch out thine hand upon the waters of Egypt, upon their streams, upon their rivers, and upon their ponds, and upon all their pools of water, that they may become blood; and that there may be blood throughout all the land of Egypt, both in vessels of wood, and in vessels of stone.*

20 And Moses and Aaron did so, as the LORD commanded; and he lifted up the rod, and smote the waters that *were* in the river, in the sight of Pharaoh, and in the sight of his servants; and **all the waters that *were* in the river were turned to blood.**

21 And the fish that *was* in the river died; and the river stank, and the Egyptians could not drink of the water of the river; and there was blood throughout all the land of Egypt.

22 And the magicians of Egypt did so with their enchantments: and Pharaoh's heart was hardened, neither did he hearken unto them; as the LORD had said.

23 And Pharaoh turned and went into his house, neither did he set his heart to this also.

24 And all the Egyptians digged round about the river for water to drink; for they could not drink of the water of the river.

25 **And seven days were fulfilled**, after that the LORD had smitten the river.

2. BROUGHT FORTH FROGS IN ABUNDANCE

Psalms 105:30 **Their land brought forth frogs in abundance**, in the chambers of their kings.

Exodus 8:1 And **the LORD spake unto Moses**, *Go unto Pharaoh, and say unto him, Thus saith the LORD,* **Let my people go, that they may serve me**.

2 *And if thou refuse to let them go, behold, I will smite all thy borders with frogs:*

3 *And the river shall bring forth frogs abundantly, which shall go up and come into thine house, and into thy bedchamber, and upon thy bed, and into the house of thy servants, and upon thy people, and into thine ovens, and into thy kneading troughs*:

4 *And the frogs shall come up both on thee, and upon thy people, and upon all thy servants.*

5 And **the LORD spake unto Moses,** *Say unto Aaron, Stretch forth thine hand with thy rod over the streams, over the rivers, and over the ponds, and cause frogs to come up upon the land of Egypt.*

6 And **Aaron stretched out his hand over the waters of Egypt; and the frogs came up, and covered the land of Egypt.**

7 And the magicians did so with their enchantments, and brought up frogs upon the land of Egypt.

8 Then Pharaoh called for Moses and Aaron, and said, *Intreat the LORD, that he may take away the frogs from me, and from my people; and I will let the people go, that they may do sacrifice unto the LORD.*

9 And Moses said unto Pharaoh, *Glory over me: when shall I intreat for thee, and for thy servants, and for thy people, to destroy the frogs from thee and thy houses, that they may remain in the river only?*

10 And he said, **To morrow.** *And he said, Be it according to thy word: that thou mayest know that there is none like unto the LORD our God.*

11 *And the frogs shall depart from thee, and from thy houses, and from thy servants, and from thy people; they shall remain in the river only.*

12 And Moses and Aaron went out from Pharaoh: and Moses cried unto the LORD because of the frogs which he had brought against Pharaoh.

13 And the LORD did according to the word of Moses; and the frogs died out of the houses, out of the villages, and out of the fields.

14 And they gathered them together upon heaps: and the land stank.

3. THERE CAME DIVERS SORTS OF FLIES AND LICE FROM DUST

Psalms 105:31 **He spake**, and **there came divers sorts of flies, *and* lice in all their coasts**.

Exodus 8:16 **And the LORD said unto Moses,** *Say unto Aaron, Stretch out thy rod, and smite the dust of the land, that it may become lice* throughout all the land of Egypt.

17 And they did so; for Aaron stretched out his hand with his rod, and smote the dust of the earth, and it became lice in man, and in

beast; all the dust of the land became lice throughout all the land of Egypt.

18 And **the magicians did so with their enchantments to bring forth lice, but they could not: so there were lice upon man, and upon beast.**

19 Then the magicians said unto Pharaoh, *This is the finger of God:* and Pharaoh's heart was hardened, and he hearkened not unto them; as the LORD had said.

20 And **the LORD said unto Moses**, *Rise up early in the morning, and stand before Pharaoh; lo, he cometh forth to the water; and say unto him*, *Thus saith the LORD*, *Let my people go, that they may serve me.*

Exodus 8:21 *Else, if thou wilt not let my people go, behold, I will send swarms of flies upon thee, and upon thy servants, and upon thy people, and into thy houses: and the houses of the Egyptians shall be full of swarms of flies, and also the ground whereon they are.*

22 *And I will sever in that day the land of Goshen, in which my people dwell, that no swarms of flies shall be there; to the end thou mayest know that I am the LORD in the midst of the earth.*

23 *And I will put a division between my people and thy people:* ***to morrow*** *shall this sign be.*

24 And the LORD did so; and there came a grievous swarm *of flies* into the house of Pharaoh, and *into* his servants' houses, and into all the land of Egypt: the land was corrupted by reason of the swarm *of flies.*

25 And Pharaoh called for Moses and for Aaron, and said, *Go ye, sacrifice to your God in the land*

4. PLAGUE TO THE ANIMALS OF THE EGYPTIANS

Exodus 9:1 Then the LORD said unto Moses, *Go in unto Pharaoh, and tell him, Thus saith the LORD God of the Hebrews, Let my people go, that they may serve me.*

2 *For if thou refuse to let them go, and wilt hold them still,*

3 *Behold,* **the hand of the LORD is upon thy cattle which is in the field, upon the horses, upon the asses, upon the camels, upon the oxen, and upon the sheep: there shall be a very grievous murrain.**

4 *And the LORD shall sever between the cattle of Israel and the cattle of Egypt: and there shall nothing die of all that is the children's of Israel.*

5 And the LORD appointed a set time, saying, *To morrow the LORD shall do this thing in the land.*

6 And the LORD did that thing on the morrow, and all the cattle of Egypt died: but of the cattle of the children of Israel died not one.

7 And Pharaoh sent, and, behold, there was not one of the cattle of the Israelites dead. And the heart of Pharaoh was hardened, and he did not let the people go.

8 And **the LORD said unto Moses and unto Aaron,** *Take to you handfuls of ashes of the furnace, and let Moses sprinkle it toward the heaven in the sight of Pharaoh.*

5. BOIL BREAKING FORTH WITH BLAINS UPON EGYPTIANS

Exodus 9:9 *And it shall become small dust in all the land of Egypt, and shall be a boil breaking forth with blains upon man, and upon beast, throughout all the land of Egypt.*

10 And **they took ashes of the furnace, and stood before Pharaoh; and Moses sprinkled it up toward heaven; and it became a boil breaking forth *with* blains upon man, and upon beast.**

11 And the magicians could not stand before Moses because of the boils; for **the boil was upon the magicians, and upon all the Egyptians.**

12 And the LORD hardened the heart of Pharaoh, and he hearkened not unto them; as the LORD had spoken unto Moses.

13 And the LORD said unto Moses, *Rise up early in the morning, and stand before Pharaoh, and say unto him, Thus saith the LORD God of the Hebrews,* **Let my people go, that they may serve me.**

14 *For I will at this time send all my plagues upon thine heart, and upon thy servants, and upon thy people; that thou mayest know that there is none like me in all the earth.*

15 *For now I will stretch out my hand, that I may smite thee and thy people with pestilence; and thou shalt be cut off from the earth.*

16 *And in very deed for this cause have I raised thee up, for to shew in thee my power; and that my name may be declared throughout all the earth.*

17 *As yet exaltest thou thyself against my people, that thou wilt not let them go?*

6. HAIL FOR RAIN, AND FLAMING FIRE IN THEIR LAND

Psalms 105:32 **He gave them hail for rain,** *and* **flaming fire in their land.**

Exodus 9:22 And the LORD said unto Moses, *Stretch forth thine hand toward heaven, that there may be hail in all the land of Egypt, upon man, and upon beast, and upon every herb of the field, throughout the land of Egypt.*

23 And Moses stretched forth his rod toward heaven: and the LORD sent thunder and hail, and the fire ran along upon the ground; and the LORD rained hail upon the land of Egypt.

24 So there was hail, and fire mingled with the hail, very grievous, such as there was none like it in all the land of Egypt since it became a nation.

25 And the hail smote throughout all the land of Egypt all that *was* in the field, both man and beast; and the hail smote every herb of the field, and brake every tree of the field.

26 **Only in the land of Goshen, where the children of Israel** *were***, was there no hail.**

27 And Pharaoh sent, and called for Moses and Aaron, and said unto them, *I have sinned this time: the LORD is righteous, and I and my people are wicked.*

28 *Intreat the LORD (for it is enough) that there be no more mighty thunderings and hail; and I will let you go, and ye shall stay no longer.*

29 And Moses said unto him, *As soon as I am gone out of the city, I will spread abroad my hands unto the LORD; and the thunder shall cease, neither shall there be any more hail; that thou mayest know how that the earth is the LORD'S.*

30 *But as for thee and thy servants, I know that ye will not yet fear the LORD God.*

 31 And the flax and the barley was smitten: for the barley *was* in the ear, and the flax *was* bolled.

32 But the wheat and the rie were not smitten: for they *were* not grown up

33 And Moses went out of the city from Pharaoh, and spread abroad his hands unto the LORD: and the thunders and hail ceased, and the rain was not poured upon the earth.

34 And when Pharaoh saw that the rain and the hail and the thunders were ceased, he sinned yet more, and hardened his heart, he and his servants.

7. THE LOCUSTS AND CATERPILLARS DEVOURED THE KINGDOM'S FARM

Psalms 105:34 **He spake, and the locusts came, and caterpillers, and that without number,**

35 And did eat up all the herbs in their land, and devoured the fruit of their ground.

Exodus 10:12 And the LORD said unto Moses, *Stretch out thine hand over the land of Egypt for the locusts, that they may come up upon the land of Egypt, and eat every herb of the land, even all that the hail hath left.*

13 And Moses stretched forth his rod over the land of Egypt, and the LORD brought an east wind upon the land all that day, and all *that* night; *and* when it was morning, the east wind brought the locusts.

14 And the locusts went up over all the land of Egypt, and rested in all the coasts of Egypt: very grievous *were they*; before them there were no such locusts as they, neither after them shall be such.

15 For they covered the face of the whole earth, so that the land was darkened; and they did eat every herb of the land, and all the fruit of the trees which the hail had left: and there remained not any green thing in the trees, or in the herbs of the field, through all the land of Egypt.

16 Then Pharaoh called for Moses and Aaron in haste; and he said, *I have sinned against the LORD your God, and against you.*

17 *Now therefore forgive, I pray thee, my sin only this once, and intreat the LORD your God, that he may take away from me this death only.*

18 And he went out from Pharaoh, and intreated the LORD.

19 And the LORD turned a mighty strong west wind, which took away the locusts, and cast them into the Red sea; there remained not one locust in all the coasts of Egypt

8. THREE DAYS OF THICK DARKNESS IN ALL THE LAND OF EGYPT

Exodus 10:20 But the LORD hardened Pharaoh's heart, so that he would not let the children of Israel go.

21 And the LORD said unto Moses, *Stretch out thine hand toward heaven, that there may be darkness over the land of Egypt, even darkness which may be felt.*

22 And Moses stretched forth his hand toward heaven; and there was a thick darkness in all the land of Egypt three days:

23 They saw not one another, neither rose any from his place for three days: but all the children of Israel had light in their dwellings.

24 And Pharaoh called unto Moses, and said, *Go ye, serve the LORD; only let your flocks and your herds be stayed: let your little ones also go with you.*

25 And Moses said, *Thou must give us also sacrifices and burnt offerings, that we may sacrifice unto the LORD our God.*

26 *Our cattle also shall go with us; there shall not an hoof be left behind; for thereof must we take to serve the LORD our God; and we know not with what we must serve the LORD, until we come thither.*

27 But the LORD hardened Pharaoh's heart, and he would not let them go.

28 And Pharaoh said unto him, *Get thee from me, take heed to thyself, see my face no more; for in that day thou seest my face thou shalt die.*

29 And Moses said, *Thou hast spoken well, I will see thy face again no more.*

9. THE LORD'S PASSOVER TO ALL THE FIRSTBORN OF EGYPT

Psalms 105:36 **He smote also all the firstborn in their land, the chief of all their strength.**

Exodus 11:1 And the LORD said unto Moses, *Yet will **I bring one plague more upon Pharaoh, and upon Egypt**; afterwards he will let you go hence: when he shall let you go, he shall surely thrust you out hence altogether.*

2 ***Speak now in the ears of the people, and let every man borrow of his neighbour, and every woman of her neighbour, jewels of silver, and jewels of gold.***

3 And the LORD gave the people favour in the sight of the Egyptians. Moreover the man Moses *was* very great in the land of Egypt, in the sight of Pharaoh's servants, and in the sight of the people.

4 And Moses said, Thus saith the LORD, ***About midnight will I go out into the midst of Egypt:***

5 ***And all the firstborn in the land of Egypt shall die, from the firstborn of Pharaoh that sitteth upon his throne, even unto the***

firstborn of the maidservant that is behind the mill; and all the firstborn of beasts.

6 *And there shall be a great cry throughout all the land of Egypt, such as there was none like it, nor shall be like it any more.*

7 *But against any of the children of Israel shall not a dog move his tongue, against man or beast: that ye may know how that the LORD doth put a difference between the Egyptians and Israel.*

8 *And all these thy servants shall come down unto me, and bow down themselves unto me,* saying, Get thee out, and all the people that follow thee: and after that I will go out. And he went out from Pharaoh in a great anger.

Exodus 12:1 And the LORD spake unto Moses and Aaron in the land of Egypt, saying,

2 *This month shall be unto you the beginning of months: it shall be the first month of the year to you.*

3 *Speak ye unto all the congregation of Israel, saying,* **In the tenth day of this month they shall take to them every man a lamb, according to the house of their fathers, a lamb for an house**:

4 *And if the household be too little for the lamb, let him and his neighbour next unto his house take it according to the number of the souls; every man according to his eating shall make your count for the lamb.*

5 *Your lamb shall be without blemish, a male of the first year: ye shall take it out from the sheep, or from the goats:*

6 *And ye shall keep it up until the fourteenth day of the same month: and the whole assembly of the congregation of Israel shall kill it in the evening.*

7 *And* **they shall take of the blood, and strike it on the two side posts and on the upper door post of the houses, wherein they shall eat it.**

8 *And they shall eat the flesh in that night, roast with fire, and unleavened bread; and with bitter herbs they shall eat it.*

9 *Eat not of it raw, nor sodden at all with water, but roast with fire; his head with his legs, and with the purtenance thereof.*

10 *And ye shall let nothing of it remain until the morning; and that which remaineth of it until the morning ye shall burn with fire.*

11 *And **thus shall ye eat it; with your loins girded, your shoes on your feet, and your staff in your hand; and ye shall eat it in haste: it is the LORD'S passover**.*

12 *For I will pass through the land of Egypt this night, and will smite all the firstborn in the land of Egypt, both man and beast; and against all the gods of Egypt I will execute judgment: I am the LORD.*

13 *And **the blood shall be to you for a token upon the houses where ye are: and when I see the blood, I will pass over you, and the plague shall not be upon you to destroy you**, when I smite the land of Egypt.*

Exodus 12: 21 Then Moses called for all the elders of Israel, and said unto them, *Draw out and **take you a lamb according to your families, and kill the passover.***

22 ***And ye shall take a bunch of hyssop, and dip it in the blood that is in the bason, and strike the lintel and the two side posts with the blood that is in the bason; and none of you shall go out at the door of his house until the morning.***

23 ***For the LORD will pass through to smite the Egyptians;** and when he seeth the blood upon the lintel, and on the two side posts, the LORD will pass over the door, and will not suffer the destroyer to come in unto your houses to smite you.*

24 ***And ye shall observe this thing for an ordinance to thee and to thy sons for ever.***

25 *And it shall come to pass, when ye be come to the land which the LORD will give you, according as he hath promised, that ye shall keep this service.*

26 *And it shall come to pass, when your children shall say unto you, What mean ye by this service?*

27 *That ye shall say, **It is the sacrifice of the LORD'S passover, who passed over the houses of the children of Israel in Egypt,** when he smote the Egyptians, and delivered our houses. And the people bowed the head and worshipped*

28 And the children of Israel went away, and did as the LORD had commanded Moses and Aaron, so did they.

29 And it came to pass, **that at midnight the LORD smote all the firstborn in the land of Egypt**, from the firstborn of Pharaoh that sat on his throne unto the firstborn of the captive that *was* in the dungeon; and all the firstborn of cattle.

30 And Pharaoh rose up in the night, he, and all his servants, and all the Egyptians; and there was a great cry in Egypt; for *there was* not a house where *there was* not one dead.

THE FEAST OF GOD'S PASSOVER THROUGH OUT ALL GENERATIONS

Exodus 12:14 And **this day shall be unto you for a memorial; and ye shall keep it a feast to the LORD throughout your generations; ye shall keep it a feast by an ordinance for ever**.

15 Seven days shall ye eat unleavened bread; even the first day ye shall put away leaven out of your houses: for whosoever eateth leavened bread from the first day until the seventh day, that soul shall be cut off from Israel.

16 And **in the first day** *there shall be* **an holy convocation, and in the seventh day there shall be an holy convocation to you;** no manner of work shall be done in them, save *that* which every man must eat, that only may be done of you.

OBSERVANCE OF THE FIRST FEAST OF UNLEAVENED BREAD

Exodus 12:17 And **ye shall observe** *the feast of* **unleavened bread;** for in this selfsame day have I brought your armies out of the land of Egypt: **therefore shall ye observe this day in your generations by an ordinance for ever.**

18 **In the first** *month*, **on the fourteenth day of the month at even, ye shall eat unleavened bread, until the one and twentieth day of the month at even.**

19 **Seven days shall there be no leaven found in your houses: for whosoever eateth that which is leavened, even that soul shall be cut off from the congregation of Israel, whether he be a stranger, or born in the land.**

20 Ye shall eat nothing leavened; in all your habitations shall ye eat unleavened bread.

10. THE RED SEA PARTED

Exodus 14:18 *And* **the Egyptians shall know that I am the LORD, when I have gotten me honour upon Pharaoh, upon his chariots, and upon his horsemen.**

Exodus 14:4 And I will harden Pharaoh's heart, that he shall follow after them; and I will be honoured upon Pharaoh, and upon all his host; that the Egyptians may know that I *am* the LORD. And they did so.

5 And it was told the king of Egypt that the people fled: and the heart of Pharaoh and of his servants was turned against the people, and they said, Why have we done this, that we have let Israel go from serving us?

6 And he made ready his chariot, and took his people with him:

7 And he took six hundred chosen chariots, and all the chariots of Egypt, and captains over every one of them.

8 And **the LORD hardened the heart of Pharaoh king of Egypt, and he pursued after the children of Israel: and the children of Israel went out with an high hand.**

9 But the Egyptians pursued after them, all the horses *and* chariots of Pharaoh, and his horsemen, and his army, and overtook them encamping by the sea, beside Pihahiroth, before Baalzephon.

10 And when Pharaoh drew nigh, the children of Israel lifted up their eyes, and, behold, the Egyptians marched after them; and they were sore afraid: and the children of Israel cried out unto the LORD.

11 And they said unto Moses, Because *there were* no graves in Egypt, hast thou taken us away to die in the wilderness? wherefore hast thou dealt thus with us, to carry us forth out of Egypt?

12 *Is* not this the word that we did tell thee in Egypt, saying, Let us alone, that we may serve the Egyptians? For *it had been* better for us to serve the Egyptians, than that we should die in the wilderness.

13 And Moses said unto the people, **Fear ye not, stand still, and see the salvation of the LORD, which he will shew to you to day:** for the Egyptians whom ye have seen to day, ye shall see them again no more for ever.

14 **The LORD shall fight for you, and ye shall hold your peace**.

15 And **the LORD said** unto Moses, Wherefore criest thou unto me? **speak unto the children of Israel, that they go forward**:

16 **But lift thou up thy rod, and stretch out thine hand over the sea, and divide it:** and the children of Israel shall go on dry *ground* through the midst of the sea.

17 And I, behold, I will harden the hearts of the Egyptians, and they shall follow them: and I will get me honour upon Pharaoh, and upon all his host, upon his chariots, and upon his horsemen.

19 And **the angel of God, which went before the camp of Israel,** removed and went behind them; and the pillar of the cloud went from before their face, and stood behind them:

20 And it came between the camp of the Egyptians and the camp of Israel; and it was a cloud and darkness *to them*, but it gave light by night *to these*: so that the one came not near the other all the night.

21 **And Moses stretched out his hand over the sea; and the LORD caused the sea to go *back* by a strong east wind all that night, and made the sea dry *land*, and the waters were divided.**

22 And the children of Israel went into the midst of the sea upon the dry *ground*: and the waters *were* a wall unto them on their right hand, and on their left.

23 **And the Egyptians pursued, and went in after them to the midst of the sea, *even* all Pharaoh's horses, his chariots, and his horsemen.**

24 And it came to pass, that in the morning watch the LORD looked unto the host of the Egyptians through the pillar of fire and of the cloud, and troubled the host of the Egyptians,

25 And took off their chariot wheels, that they drave them heavily: so that the Egyptians said, Let us flee from the face of Israel; for the LORD fighteth for them against the Egyptians.

26 And the LORD said unto Moses, Stretch out thine hand over the sea, that the waters may come again upon the Egyptians, upon their chariots, and upon their horsemen.

27 **And Moses stretched forth his hand over the sea, and the sea returned to his strength when the morning appeared; and the Egyptians fled against it; and the LORD overthrew the Egyptians in the midst of the sea.**

28 And the waters returned, and covered the chariots, and the horsemen, *and* all the host of Pharaoh that came into the sea after them; there remained not so much as one of them.

29 But the children of Israel walked upon dry *land* in the midst of the sea; and the waters *were* a wall unto them on their right hand, and on their left.

30 Thus the LORD saved Israel that day out of the hand of the Egyptians; and Israel saw the Egyptians dead upon the sea shore.

31 And Israel saw that great work which the LORD did upon the Egyptians: and the people feared the LORD, and believed the LORD, and his servant Moses.

D. DANIEL UNDER BABYLONIAN CAPTIVITY

KING NEBUDCHANEZZAR'S DREAMS TROUBLED HIM

Daniel 2:1 And in the second year of the reign of Nebuchadnezzar Nebuchadnezzar dreamed dreams, wherewith his spirit was troubled, and his sleep brake from him.

2 Then the king commanded to call the magicians, and the astrologers, and the sorcerers, and the Chaldeans, for to shew the king his dreams. So they came and stood before the king.

3 And the king said unto them, I have dreamed a dream, and my spirit was troubled to know the dream.

4 Then spake the Chaldeans to the king in Syriack, O king, live for ever: tell thy servants the dream, and we will shew the interpretation.

5 The king answered and said to the Chaldeans, The thing is gone from me: if ye will not make known unto me the dream, with the interpretation thereof, ye shall be cut in pieces, and your houses shall be made a dunghill.

6 But if ye shew the dream, and the interpretation thereof, ye shall receive of me gifts and rewards and great honour: therefore shew me the dream, and the interpretation thereof.

10 The Chaldeans answered before the king, and said, There is not a man upon the earth that can shew the king's matter: therefore *there is* no king, lord, nor ruler, *that* asked such things at any magician, or astrologer, or Chaldean.

11 And *it is* a rare thing that the king requireth, and there is none other that can shew it before the king, except the gods, whose dwelling is not with flesh.

12 For this cause the king was angry and very furious, and commanded to destroy all the wise *men* of Babylon.

13 And the decree went forth that the wise *men* should be slain; and they sought Daniel and his fellows to be slain.

DANIEL PRAYED AND GAVE THANKS TO THE LORD

Daniel 2:17 Then Daniel went to his house, and made the thing known to Hananiah, Mishael, and Azariah, his companions:

18 That they would desire mercies of the God of heaven concerning this secret; that Daniel and his fellows should not perish with the rest of the wise *men* of Babylon.

19 Then was the secret revealed unto Daniel in a night vision. Then Daniel blessed the God of heaven.

20 Daniel answered and said, *Blessed be the name of God for ever and ever: for wisdom and might are his:*

21 And he changeth the times and the seasons: he removeth kings, and setteth up kings: he giveth wisdom unto the wise, and knowledge to them that know understanding:

22 He revealeth the deep and secret things: he knoweth what is in the darkness, and the light dwelleth with him.

23 I thank thee, and praise thee, O thou God of my fathers, who hast given me wisdom and might, and hast made known unto me now what we desired of thee: for thou hast now made known unto us the king's matter.

GOD REVEALED SECRETS IN THE LATTER DAYS

Daniel 2:27 Daniel answered in the presence of the king, and said, The secret which the king hath demanded cannot the wise *men*, the astrologers, the magicians, the soothsayers, shew unto the king;

28 **But there is a God in heaven that revealeth secrets, and maketh known to the king Nebuchadnezzar what shall be in the latter days**. Thy dream, and the visions of thy head upon thy bed, are these;

29 As for thee, O king, thy thoughts came *into thy mind* upon thy bed, what should come to pass hereafter: and he that revealeth secrets maketh known to thee what shall come to pass.

30 **But as for me, this secret is not revealed to me for** *any* **wisdom that I have more than any living, but for** *their* **sakes that shall make known the interpretation to the king, and that thou mightest know the thoughts of thy heart**.

THE KING NEBUCHADNEZZAR'S DREAMS

1. THE GREAT IMAGE

Daniel 2:31 Thou O king, sawest, and behold **a great image.** This great image, whose brightness was excellent, stood before thee: and the form thereof was terrible.

32 This image *head* was of fine **gold,** his *breast* and his *arms* **of silver,** his *belly* and his *thighs* of **brass,**
33 His *legs* of **iron,** his *feet* **part of iron and part of clay**.

2. THE STONE CUT OUT WITHOUT HANDS
Daniel 2:34 **Thou sawest till that a stone was cut out without a hands, which smote the image upon his feet, that were of iron and clay, and brake them into pieces.**
35 Then was the iron, the clay, the brass, the silver, and the gold, broken to pieces together, and became like the chaff of the summer threshing floors; and the wind carried them away, that no place was found for them: and the stone that smote the image became a great mountain, and filled the whole earth.

DANIEL INTERPRETED THE DREAMS
Daniel 2:36 This *is* the dream; and we will tell the interpretation thereof before the king.
37 Thou, **O king,** *art* **a king of kings: for the God of heaven hath given thee a kingdom, power, and strength, and glory.**
38 And wheresoever the children of men dwell, the beasts of the field and the fowls of the heaven hath he given into thine hand, and hath made thee ruler over them all. **Thou** *art* **this head of gold.**
39 And **after thee shall arise another kingdom inferior to thee, and another third kingdom of brass, which shall bear rule over all the earth.**
40 And **the fourth kingdom shall be strong as iron**: forasmuch as iron breaketh in pieces and subdueth all *things*: and as iron that breaketh all these, shall it break in pieces and bruise.
41 And **whereas thou sawest the feet and toes, part of potters' clay, and part of iron, the kingdom shall be divided**; but there shall be in it of the strength of the iron, forasmuch as thou sawest the iron mixed with miry clay.
42 And *as* the toes of the feet *were* part of iron, and part of clay, *so* the kingdom shall be partly strong, and partly broken.
43 And whereas thou sawest iron mixed with miry clay, they shall mingle themselves with the seed of men: but they shall not cleave one to another, even as iron is not mixed with clay.

THE COMING OF THE KINGDOM OF GOD IN THE NEW
EARTH
Daniel 2:44 And **in the days of these kings shall the God of
heaven set up a kingdom, which shall never be destroyed:** and
the kingdom shall not be left to other people, *but* it shall break in
pieces and consume all these kingdoms, and it shall stand for
ever.
45 Forasmuch as thou sawest that the stone was cut out of the
mountain without hands, and that it brake in pieces the iron, the
brass, the clay, the silver, and the gold; the great God hath made
known to the king what shall come to pass hereafter: and the
dream *is* certain, and the interpretation thereof sure.

E. SAUL/PAUL WAS CALLED TO MINISTER THE GENTILES (After the Resurrection of the Lord Jesus)

Acts 22:21 And he said unto me, **Depar**t: **for I will send thee far
hence unto the Gentiles.**
Acts 22:14 And he said, **The God of our fathers hath chosen
thee**, that thou shouldest know his will, and see that Just One, and
shouldest hear the voice of his mouth.
15 **For thou shalt be his witness unto all men of what thou
hast seen and heard**.
16 And now why tarriest thou? **arise, and be baptized, and wash
away thy sins, calling on the name of the Lord.**

THE TESTIMONY OF PAUL

1. PAUL WAS NAMED SAUL OF TARSUS

Acts 22:1 Men, brethren, and fathers, hear ye my defence *which I
make* now unto you.
2 (And when they heard that he spake in the Hebrew tongue to
them, they kept the more silence: and he saith,)
3 I am verily a man *which am* a Jew, born in Tarsus, *a city* in
Cilicia, yet brought up in this city at the feet of Gamaliel, *and*
taught according to the perfect manner of the law of the fathers,
and was zealous toward God, as ye all are this day.
4 **And I persecuted this way unto the death, binding and
delivering into prisons both men and women.**
5 As also the high priest doth bear me witness, and all the estate
of the elders: from whom **also I received letters unto the**

176

brethren, and went to Damascus, to bring them which were there bound unto Jerusalem, for to be punished.

2. LORD JESUS BLINDED SAUL

Acts 22:6 And it came to pass, that, as I made my journey, and was come nigh unto Damascus about noon, suddenly there shone from heaven a great light round about me.

7 And I fell unto the ground, and heard a voice saying unto me, *Saul, Saul, why persecutest thou me?*

8 And I answered, Who art thou, Lord? And **he said unto me, *I am Jesus of Nazareth, whom thou persecutest.***

9 And **they that were with me saw indeed the light**, and were afraid; **but they heard not the voice of him that spake to me.**

10 And I said, *What shall I do, Lord?* And the Lord said unto me, *Arise, and go into Damascus; and there it shall be told thee of all things which are appointed for thee to do.*

11 And when I could not see for the glory of that light, being led by the hand of them that were with me, I came into Damascus.

12 And one Ananias, a devout man according to the law, having a good report of all the Jews which dwelt *there*,

13 Came unto me, and stood, and said unto me, Brother Saul, receive thy sight. And the same hour I looked up upon him.

SAUL BECAME THE APOSTLE OF CHRIST

1Timothy1:12 And I thank Christ Jesus our Lord, who hath enabled me, for that he counted me faithful, putting me into the ministry;

13 Who was before a blasphemer, and a persecutor, and injurious: but I obtained mercy, because I did *it* ignorantly in unbelief.

15 This *is* a faithful saying, and worthy of all acceptation, that Christ Jesus came into the world to save sinners; of whom I am chief.

16 Howbeit for this cause I obtained mercy, that in me first Jesus Christ might shew forth all longsuffering, for a pattern to them which should hereafter believe on him to life everlasting.

1Timothy2:7 Whereunto I am ordained a preacher, and an apostle, (I speak the truth in Christ, *and* lie not;) a teacher of the Gentiles in faith and verity.

8 I will therefore **that men pray every where, lifting up holy hands, without wrath and doubting**.

PAUL'S TEACHING AGAINST IDOLATRY

Acts 17:22 Then Paul stood in the midst of Mars' hill, and said, *Ye* men of Athens, I perceive that in all things ye are too superstitious.

23 For as I passed by, and beheld your devotions, I found an altar with this inscription, TO THE UNKNOWN GOD. Whom therefore ye ignorantly worship, him declare I unto you.

24 **God that made the world and all things therein, seeing that he is Lord of heaven and earth, dwelleth not in temples made with hands;**

25 **Neither is worshipped with men's hands, as though he needed any thing, seeing he giveth to all life, and breath, and all things;**

26 And hath made of one blood all nations of men for to dwell on all the face of the earth, and hath determined the times before appointed, and the bounds of their habitation;

27 That they should seek the Lord, if haply they might feel after him, and find him, though he be not far from every one of us:

28 For in him we live, and move, and have our being; as certain also of your own poets have said, For we are also his offspring.

29 Forasmuch then **as we are the offspring of God, we ought not to think that the Godhead is like unto gold, or silver, or stone, graven by art and man's device.**

30 And the times of this ignorance God winked at; but now commandeth all men every where to repent:

31 **Because he hath appointed a day, in the which he will judge the world in righteousness by** *that* **man whom he hath ordained;** *whereof* **he hath given assurance unto all** *men*, **in that he hath raised him from the dead.**

PRAYER OF APOSTLE PAUL FOR THE GENTILES BELIEVERS (Posted in FB Oct 13, 2014 9:23am CA time)

Ephesians 3:14 *For this cause I bow my knees unto the Father of our Lord Jesus Christ,*

15 Of whom the whole family in heaven and earth is named,

16 That he would grant you, according to the riches of his glory, to be strengthened with might by his Spirit in the inner man;

17 That Christ may dwell in your hearts by faith; that ye, being rooted and grounded in love,

18 May be able to comprehend with all saints what is the breadth, and length, and depth, and height;

19 And to know the love of Christ, which passeth knowledge, that ye might be filled with all the fulness of God.

20 Now unto him that is able to do exceeding abundantly above all that we ask or think, according to the power that worketh in us,

21 Unto him be glory in the church by Christ Jesus throughout all ages, world without end. Amen.

===

==

PART 4
FIRST AGREEMENT TO THE NATION OF ISRAEL

CHAPTER I **THE ORDINANCES OF GOD**

Nehemiah 9:13
*Thou camest down also upon mount Sinai, and **spakest with them from heaven,** and gavest them right judgments, and true laws, good statutes and commandments:*

GOD SHOWED HIS GLORY TO MOSES AND OTHERS
Exodus 24:9 Then went up **Moses, and Aaron, Nadab, and Abihu, and seventy of the elders of Israel**:
10 And they saw the God of Israel: and *there was* under his feet as it were a paved work of a sapphire stone, and as it were the body of heaven in *his* clearness.
11 And upon the nobles of the children of Israel he laid not his hand: also they saw God, and did eat and drink.
12 And the LORD said unto Moses, Come up to me into the mount, and be there: and I will give thee tables of stone, and a law, and commandments which I have written; that thou mayest teach them.
13 And Moses rose up, and his minister Joshua: and Moses went up into the mount of God.
14 And he said unto the elders, Tarry ye here for us, until we come again unto you: and, behold, Aaron and Hur *are* with you: if any man have any matters to do, let him come unto them.
15 And Moses went up into the mount, and a cloud covered the mount.
16 And the glory of the LORD abode upon mount Sinai, and the cloud covered it six days: and the seventh day he called unto Moses out of the midst of the cloud.
17 And **the sight of the glory of the LORD *was* like devouring fire on the top of the mount in the eyes of the children of Israel**.

18 And Moses went into the midst of the cloud, and gat him up into the mount: and Moses was in the mount forty days and forty nights.

GOD COMMANDED MOSES TO CUT TWO TABLES OF STONE

Psalms 94:12 *Blessed is the man whom thou chastenest, O LORD, and teachest him out of thy law;*

Exodus 34:1 And the LORD said unto Moses, Hew thee two tables of stone like unto the first: and I will write upon *these* tables the words that were in the first tables, which thou brakest.

2 And be ready in the morning, and come up in the morning unto mount Sinai, and present thyself there to me in the top of the mount.

3 And no man shall come up with thee, neither let any man be seen throughout all the mount; neither let the flocks nor herds feed before that mount.

4 **And he hewed two tables of stone like unto the first**; and Moses rose up early in the morning, and went up unto mount Sinai, as the LORD had commanded him, and took in his hand the two tables of stone.

5 And the LORD descended in the cloud, and stood with him there, and proclaimed the name of the LORD.

6 And the LORD passed by before him, and proclaimed, The LORD, **The LORD God, merciful and gracious, longsuffering, and abundant in goodness and truth,**

7 **Keeping mercy for thousands, forgiving iniquity and transgression and sin, and that will by no means clear** *the guilty*; **visiting the iniquity of the fathers upon the children, and upon the children's children, unto the third and to the fourth** *generation*.

8 And **Moses made haste, and bowed his head toward the earth, and worshipped**.

9 And he said, *If now I have found grace in thy sight,* **O LORD, let my LORD, I pray thee, go among us;** *for it is a stiff necked people;* **and pardon our iniquity and our sin, and take us for thine inheritance.**

10 **And he said,** *Behold, I make a covenant: before all thy people I will do marvels, such as have not been done in all the earth, nor in any nation:* and all the people among which thou art shall see the work of the LORD: *for it is a terrible thing that I will do with thee.*

THE FIRST BLOWING OF TRUMP

GOD WILL SHOW HIMSELF TO THE PEOPLE OF ISRAEL
Exodus 19:9 And the LORD said to Moses, Lo I come unto thee in a thick cloud that the people may hear when I speak with thee, and believe thee forever. And Moses told the words of the people unto the LORD.

PEOPLE MUST SANCTIFY AND WEAR CLEAN CLOTHES BEFORE SEEING THE LORD
Exodus 19:10 And the LORD said unto Moses, Go unto the people, and sanctify them to day and to morrow, and let them wash their clothes,

11 And be ready against the third day: for the third day the LORD will come down in the sight of all the people upon mount Sinai.

12 And thou shalt set bounds unto the people round about, saying, Take heed to yourselves, *that ye* go *not* up into the mount, or touch the border of it: whosoever toucheth the mount shall be surely put to death:

13 There shall not an hand touch it, but he shall surely be stoned, or shot through; whether *it be* beast or man, it shall not live: when the trumpet soundeth long, they shall come up to the mount.

14 And Moses went down from the mount unto the people, and sanctified the people; and they washed their clothes.

15 And he said unto the people, Be ready against the third day: come not at *your* wives.

16 And it came to pass **on the third day in the morning**, that **there were thunders and lightnings, and a thick cloud upon the mount, and the voice of the trumpet exceeding loud**; so that all the people that *was* in the camp trembled.

17 And Moses brought forth the people out of the camp to meet with God; and they stood at the nether part of the mount.

THE LORD CAME DOWN TO GIVE HIS LAWS

Deuteronomy 33:2 And he(Moses) said**, The LORD came from Sinai, and rose up from Seir unto them; he shined forth from mount Paran**, and **he came with ten thousands of saints: from his right hand came a fiery law for them.**

3 Yea, he loved the people; all his saints *are* in thy hand: and they sat down at thy feet**;** *every one* **shall receive of thy words.**

4 **Moses commanded us a law,** *even* **the inheritance of the congregation of Jacob.**

Exodus 19:18 And mount Sinai was altogether on a smoke, because the LORD descended upon it in fire: and the smoke thereof ascended as the smoke of a furnace, and the whole mount quaked greatly.

19 And when the voice of the trumpet sounded long, and waxed louder and louder, Moses spake, and God answered him by a voice.

20 And the LORD came down upon mount Sinai, on the top of the mount: and the LORD called Moses *up* to the top of the mount; and Moses went up.

21 And the LORD said unto Moses, Go down, charge the people, lest they break through unto the LORD to gaze, and many of them perish.

22 And let the priests also, which come near to the LORD, sanctify themselves, lest the LORD break forth upon them.

23 And Moses said unto the LORD, The people cannot come up to mount Sinai: for thou chargedst us, saying, Set bounds about the mount, and sanctify it.

24 And the LORD said unto him, Away, get thee down, and thou shalt come up, thou, and Aaron with thee: but let not the priests and the people break through to come up unto the LORD, lest he break forth upon them.

25 So Moses went down unto the people, and spake unto them.

Exodus 20:18 And all the people saw the thunderings, and the lightnings, and the noise of the trumpet, and the mountain smoking: and when the people saw *it*, they removed, and stood afar off.

19 And they said unto Moses, Speak thou with us, and we will hear: but let not God speak with us, lest we die.

20 And Moses said unto the people, Fear not: for God is come to prove you, and that his fear may be before your faces, that ye sin not.

21 And the people stood afar off, and Moses drew near unto the thick darkness where God *was*.

THE ORDINANCES OF GOD

Deuteronomy 4:2 *Ye shall not add unto the word which I command you, neither shall ye diminish ought from it, that ye may keep the commandments of the LORD your God which I command you.*

Deuteronomy 4:7 For what nation *is* *there* *so* great, who *hath* God *so* nigh unto them, as the LORD our God *is* in all *things that* we call upon him *for*?
8 **And what nation *is* *there* *so* great, that hath statutes and judgments *so* righteous as all this law, which I set before you this day?**
Deuteronomy 9:10 And **the LORD delivered unto me two tables of stone written with the finger of God; and on them *was written* according to all the words, which the LORD spake with you in the mount out of the midst of the fire in the day of the assembly.**
Deuteronomy 6:1 Now these *are* the commandments, the statutes, and the judgments, which the LORD your God commanded to teach you, that ye might do *them* in the land whither ye go to possess it:

THE TEN COMMANDMENTS
First Commandment: **THOU SHALT HAVE NONE OTHER gods BEFORE ME**
Exodus 20:1 And **God spake all these words , saying,**
2 I *am* the LORD thy God, which brought thee out of the land of Egypt, out of the house of bondage.
3 Thou shalt have no other gods before me.
Deuteronomy 5:6 I *am* the LORD thy God, which brought thee out of the land of Egypt, from the house of bondage.
7 Thou shalt have none other gods before me.

Second Commandment: **THOU SHALT NOT BOW DOWN AND SERVE THE IDOLS**

Exodus 20:4 Thou shalt not make unto thee any graven image, or any likeness *of any thing* that *is* in heaven above, or that *is* in the earth beneath, or that *is* in the water under the earth:

5 Thou shalt not bow down thyself to them, nor serve them: for I the LORD thy God *am* **a jealous God, visiting the iniquity of the fathers upon the children unto the third and fourth** *generation* **of them that hate me;**

6 And shewing mercy unto thousands of them that love me, and keep my commandments.

Deuteronomy 5:8Thou shalt not make thee *any* graven image, *or* any likeness *of any thing* that *is* in heaven above, or that *is* in the earth beneath, or that *is* in the waters beneath the earth:

9 Thou shalt not bow down thyself unto them, nor serve them: for I the LORD thy God *am* a jealous God, visiting the iniquity of the fathers upon the children unto the third and fourth *generation* of them that hate me,

10 And shewing mercy unto thousands of them that love me and keep my commandments.

Third Commandment: **THOU SHALT NOT TAKE THE NAME OF THE LORD THY GOD IN VAIN**

Exodus 20:7 **Thou shalt not take the name of the LORD thy God in vain;** for the Lord will not hold him guiltless that taketh his name in vain.

Deuteronomy 5:11 Thou shalt not take the name of the LORD thy God in vain: for the LORD will not hold *him* guiltless that taketh his name in vain.

Fourth Commandment: **KEEP THE SABBATH DAY**

Deuteronomy 5:12 **Keep the sabbath day to sanctify it, as the LORD thy God hath commanded thee.**

13 Six days thou shalt labour, and do all thy work:

14 But the seventh day *is* the sabbath of the LORD thy God: *in it* thou shalt not do any work, thou, nor thy son, nor thy daughter, nor thy manservant, nor thy maidservant, nor thine ox, nor thine ass, nor any of thy cattle, nor thy stranger that *is* within thy gates; that thy manservant and thy maidservant may rest as well as thou.

Exodus 20: 8 Remember the sabbath day, to keep it holy.

9 Six days shalt thou labour, and do all thy work:

10 But the seventh day *is* the sabbath of the LORD thy God: *in it* thou shalt not do any work, thou, nor thy son, nor thy daughter,

thy manservant, nor thy maidservant, nor thy cattle, nor thy stranger that *is* within thy gates:

11 For *in* six days the LORD made heaven and earth, the sea, and all that in them *is*, and rested the seventh day: wherefore the LORD blessed the sabbath day, and hallowed it.

Fifth Commandment: HONOUR THY FATHER AND THY MOTHER

Deuteronomy 5:16 **Honour thy father and thy mother, as the LORD thy God hath commanded thee; that thy days may be prolonged,** and that it may go well with thee, in the land, which the LORD thy God giveth thee.

Exodus 20:12 Honour thy father and thy mother: that thy days may be long upon the land which the LORD thy God giveth thee.

Sixth Commandment: THOU SHALT NOT KILL

Deuteronomy 5:17 Thou shalt Not Kill

Exodus 20:13 Thou shalt not kill.

Seventh Commandment: THOU SHALT NOT COMMIT ADULTERY

Deuteronomy 5:18 Neither shalt thou commit adultery.

Exodus 20:14 Thou shalt not commit adultery.

Eighth Commandment: THOU SHALT NOT STEAL.

Deuteronomy 5:19 Neither shalt thou steal,

Exodus 20:15 Thou shalt not steal.

Ninth Commandment: THOU SHALT NOT BEAR FALSE WITNESS AGAINST THY NEIGHBOUR.

Deuteronomy 5:20 Neither shalt thou bear false witness against thy neighbor..

Exodus 20:16 Thou shalt not bear false witness against thy neighbour.

Tenth Commandment: NEITHER SHALT THOU DESIRE THY NEIGHBOR'S WIFE

Deuteronomy 5:21 Neither shalt thou desire thy neighbour's wife, neither shalt thou covet thy neighbour's house, his field, or his manservant, or his maidservant, his ox, or his ass, or any *thing* that *is* thy neighbour's.

Exodus 20:17 Thou shalt not covet thy neighbour's house, thou shalt not covet thy neighbour's wife, nor his manservant, nor his maidservant, nor his ox, nor his ass, nor any thing that *is* thy neighbour's.

*GOD'S INSTRUCTIONS TO THE NATION OF ISRAEL

Deuteronomy 10:12 *And now, Israel, what doth the LORD thy God require of thee, but **to fear the LORD thy God, to walk in all his ways, and to love him, and to serve the LORD thy God with all thy heart and with all thy soul,** 13To keep the commandments of the LORD, and his statutes, which I command thee this day for thy good?*

1. KEEP THE COMMANDMENTS AND LAWS
Psalms 19:7 The law of the LORD is perfect, converting the soul: the testimony of the LORD is sure, making wise the simple.
Proverbs 7:1 My son, keep my words, and lay up my commandments with thee.
2 **Keep my commandments, and live; and my law as the apple of thine eye.**
3 Bind them upon thy fingers, write them upon the table of thine heart.
Deuteronomy 7:10 And repayeth them that hate him to their face, to destroy them: he will not be slack to him that hateth him, he will repay him to his face.
11 Thou shalt therefore keep the commandments, and the statutes, and the judgments, which I command thee this day, to do them.
Deuteronomy 4:5 Behold, I have taught you statutes and judgments, even as the LORD my God commanded me, that **ye should do so in the land whither ye go to possess it.**
6 **Keep therefore and do *them*; for this *is* your wisdom and your understanding in the sight of the nations, which shall hear all these statutes**, and say, Surely this great nation *is* a wise and understanding people.

2. OBEY THE COMMANDMENTS
Psalms 19:8 *The statutes of the LORD are right, rejoicing the heart: the commandment of the LORD is pure, enlightening the eyes.*

Deuteronomy 5:32 Ye shall observe to do therefore as the LORD your God hath commanded you: ye shall not turn aside to the right hand or to the left.

33 Ye shall walk in all the ways which the LORD your God hath commanded you, that ye may live, and *that it may be* well with you, and *that* ye may prolong *your* days in the land which ye shall possess.

Deuteronomy 6:2 That thou mightest fear the LORD thy God, to keep all his statutes and his commandments, which I command thee, thou, and thy son, and thy son's son, all the days of thy life; and that thy days may be prolonged.

3 Hear therefore, O Israel, and observe to do *it*; that it may be well with thee, and that ye may increase mightily, as the LORD God of thy fathers hath promised thee, in the land that floweth with milk and honey.

4 Hear, O Israel: **The LORD our God *is* one LORD**:

5 **And thou shalt love the LORD thy God with all thine heart, and with all thy soul, and with all thy might.**

6 And these words, which I command thee this day, shall be in thine heart:

3 THE PEOPLE MUST NOT MAKE IDOLS of gods

Exodus 20:22 And the LORD said unto Moses, Thus thou shalt say unto the children of Israel, Ye have seen that I have talked with you from heaven.

23 **Ye shall not make with me gods of silver, neither shall ye make unto you gods of gold.**

Isaiah 42:5 Thus saith God the LORD, he that created the heavens, and stretched them out; he that spread forth the earth, and that which cometh out of it; he that giveth breath unto the people upon it, and spirit to them that walk therein:

6 I the LORD have called thee in righteousness, and will hold thine hand, and will keep thee, and give thee for a covenant of the people, for a light of the Gentiles;

7 To open the blind eyes, to bring out the prisoners from the prison, *and* them that sit in darkness out of the prison house.

8 **I *am* the LORD: that *is* my name: and my glory will I not give to another, neither my praise to graven images.**

Leviticus 26:1 Ye shall make you no idols nor graven image, neither rear you up a standing image, neither shall ye set

up *any* image of stone in your land, to bow down unto it: for I *am* the LORD your God.

4. DO NOT WORSHIP THE HOSTS OF HEAVEN AND ANY GRAVEN IMAGES

Deuteronomy 4:15 Take ye therefore good heed unto yourselves; for ye saw no manner of similitude on the day *that* the LORD spake unto you in Horeb out of the midst of the fire:

16 **Lest ye corrupt *yourselves*, and make you a graven image, the similitude of any figure, the likeness of male or female,**

17 The likeness of any beast that *is* on the earth, the likeness of any winged fowl that flieth in the air,

18 The likeness of any thing that creepeth on the ground, the likeness of any fish that *is* in the waters beneath the earth:

19 **And lest thou lift up thine eyes unto heaven, and when thou seest the sun, and the moon, and the stars, *even* all the host of heaven, shouldest be driven to worship them, and serve them**, *which the LORD thy God hath divided unto all nations under the whole heaven.*

Deuteronomy 17:3 And hath gone and served other gods, and worshipped them, either the sun, or moon, or any of the host of heaven, which I have not commanded;

4 And it be told thee, and thou hast heard *of it*, and enquired diligently, and, behold, *it be* true, *and* the thing certain, *that* such abomination is wrought in Israel:

Colossians 2:18 **Let no man beguile you** of your reward in a voluntary humility and **worshipping of angels**, intruding into those things which he hath not seen, vainly puffed up by his fleshly mind,

5. TEACH THE CHILDREN THE COMMANDMENTS AND FEAR OF THE LORD

Deuteronomy 31:12 Gather the people together, men, and women, and children, and thy stranger that *is* within thy gates, that they may hear, and that they may learn, and fear the LORD your God, and observe to do all the words of this law:

13 And *that* **their children, which have not known *any thing*, may hear, and learn to fear the LORD your God, as long as ye live in the land whither ye go over Jordan to possess it.**

Deuteronomy 4:9 Only take heed to thyself, and keep thy soul diligently, lest thou forget the things which thine eyes have seen, and lest they depart from thy heart all the days of thy life: but teach them thy sons, and thy sons' sons;

10 *Specially* the day that thou stoodest before the LORD thy God in Horeb, when the LORD said unto me, *Gather me the people together, and I will make them hear my words, that they may learn to fear me all the days that they shall live upon the earth, and that they may teach their* children.

11 And ye came near and stood under the mountain; and the mountain burned with fire unto the midst of heaven, with darkness, clouds, and thick darkness.

Psalms 78:1 (Maschil of Asaph.) **Give ear, O my people, *to* my law: incline your ears to the words of my mouth.**

2 **I will open my mouth in a parable: I will utter dark sayings of old:**

3 Which we have heard and known, and our fathers have told us.

4 We will not hide *them* from their children, shewing to the generation to come the praises of the LORD, and his strength, and his wonderful works that he hath done.

5 For he established a testimony in Jacob, and appointed a law in Israel, which he commanded our fathers, that they should make them known to their children:

6 **That the generation to come might know *them, even* the children *which* should be born; *who* should arise and declare *them* to their children**:

7 **That they might set their hope in God, and not forget the works of God, but keep his commandments:**

8 And might not be as their fathers, a stubborn and rebellious generation; a generation *that* set not their heart aright, and whose spirit was not stedfast with God.

Deuteronomy 6:7 **And thou shalt teach them diligently unto thy children**, and shalt talk of them when thou sittest in thine house, and when thou walkest by the way, and when thou liest down, and when thou risest up.

8 And thou shalt bind them for a sign upon thine hand, and they shall be as frontlets between thine eyes.

9 And thou shalt write them upon the posts of thy house, and on thy gates.

PART 4
FIRST AGREEMENT TO THE NATION OF ISRAEL

CHAPTER II FEASTS AND TRADITIONS COMMANDED BY GOD

THE ARK OF THE COVENANT

Exodus 25:16 And thou shalt put into the ark the testimony which I shall give thee.

17 And thou shalt make a mercy seat *of* pure gold: two cubits and a half *shall be* the length thereof, and a cubit and a half the breadth thereof.

18 And thou shalt make two cherubims *of* gold, *of* beaten work shalt thou make them, in the two ends of the mercy seat.

19 And make one cherub on the one end, and the other cherub on the other end: *even* of the mercy seat shall ye make the cherubims on the two ends thereof.

20 And the cherubims shall stretch forth *their* wings on high, covering the mercy seat with their wings, and their faces *shall look* one to another; toward the mercy seat shall the faces of the cherubims be.

21 And thou shalt put the mercy seat above upon the ark; and in the ark thou shalt put the testimony that I shall give thee.

22 And there I will meet with thee, and I will commune with thee from above the mercy seat, from between the two cherubims which *are* upon the ark of the testimony, of all *things* which I will give thee in commandment unto the children of Israel.

MOVING OUT OF THE ARK OF THE COVENANT OF THE LORD

Numbers 10:33 And they departed from the mount of the LORD three days' journey: and the ark of the covenant of the LORD went before them in the three days' journey, to search out a resting place for them.

34 And the cloud of the LORD *was* upon them by day, when they went out of the camp.

35 And it came to pass, when the ark set forward, that Moses said, *Rise up, LORD, and let thine enemies be scattered; and let them that hate thee flee before thee.*
36 And when it rested, he said, *Return, O LORD, unto the many thousands of Israel.*

FEASTS OF THE LORD

Deuteronomy 16:12 And thou shalt remember that thou wast a bondman in Egypt: and **thou shalt observe and do these statutes.**

Leviticus 23:1 And the LORD spake unto Moses, saying,

2 Speak unto the children of Israel, and say unto them, *Concerning* the feasts of the LORD, which ye shall proclaim *to be* holy convocations, *even* these *are* my feasts.

3 Six days shall work be done: but the seventh day *is* the sabbath of rest, an holy convocation; ye shall do no work *therein*: it *is* the sabbath of the LORD in all your dwellings.

4 These *are* the feasts of the LORD, *even* holy convocations, which ye shall proclaim in their seasons.

1. LORD'S PASSOVER: Leviticus 23:5 In the fourteenth *day* of the first month at even *is* the LORD'S passover.

Exodus 13:3 And Moses said unto the people, Remember this day, in which ye came out from Egypt, out of the house of bondage; for by strength of hand the LORD brought you out from this *place*: there shall no leavened bread be eaten.

4 This day came ye out in the month Abib.

Deuteronomy 16:1 **Observe the month of Abib,** and keep the passover unto the LORD thy God: for in the month of Abib the LORD thy God brought thee forth out of Egypt by night.

2 Thou shalt therefore sacrifice the passover unto the LORD thy God, of the flock and the herd, in the place which the LORD shall choose to place his name there.

3 Thou shalt eat no leavened bread with it; seven days shalt thou eat unleavened bread therewith, *even* the bread of affliction; for thou camest forth out of the land of Egypt in haste: that thou mayest remember the day when thou camest forth out of the land of Egypt all the days of thy life.

4 And there shall be no leavened bread seen with thee in all thy coast seven days; neither shall there *any thing* of the flesh, which

thou sacrificedst the first day at even, remain all night until the morning.

5 Thou mayest not sacrifice the passover within any of thy gates, which the LORD thy God giveth thee:

6 But at the place which the LORD thy God shall choose to place his name in, there thou shalt sacrifice the passover at even, at the going down of the sun, at the season that thou camest forth out of Egypt.

7 And thou shalt roast and eat *it* in the place which the LORD thy God shall choose: and thou shalt turn in the morning, and go unto thy tents.

8 Six days thou shalt eat unleavened bread: and on the seventh day *shall be* a solemn assembly to the LORD thy God: thou shalt do no work *therein*.

9 Seven weeks shalt thou number unto thee: begin to number the seven weeks from *such time as* thou beginnest *to put* the sickle to the corn.

10 And thou shalt keep the feast of weeks unto the LORD thy God with a tribute of a freewill offering of thine hand, which thou shalt give *unto the LORD thy God*, according as the LORD thy God hath blessed thee:

11 And thou shalt rejoice before the LORD thy God, thou, and thy son, and thy daughter, and thy manservant, and thy maidservant, and the Levite that *is* within thy gates, and the stranger, and the fatherless, and the widow, that *are* among you, in the place which the LORD thy God hath chosen to place his name there.

2. FEAST OF TRUMPET: **Leviticus 23**:23 And the LORD spake unto Moses, saying,

24 Speak unto the children of Israel, saying, **In the seventh month, in the first *day* of the month, shall ye have a sabbath, a memorial of blowing of trumpets**, an holy convocation.

25 Ye shall do no servile work *therein*: but ye shall offer an offering made by fire unto the LORD.

3. DAY OF ATONEMENT (Forgiveness of Sin)**Leviticus 23:27** Also **on the tenth *day* of this seventh month *there shall be* a day of atonement**: it shall be an holy convocation unto you; and ye shall afflict your souls, and offer an offering made by fire unto the LORD.

28 And ye shall do no work in that same day: for it *is* a day of atonement, to make an atonement for you before the LORD your God.

29 For whatsoever soul *it be* that shall not be afflicted in that same day, he shall be cut off from among his people.

30 And whatsoever soul *it be* that doeth any work in that same day, the same soul will I destroy from among his people.

31 **Ye shall do no manner of work:** *it shall be* a statute for ever throughout your generations in all your dwellings.

32 It *shall be* unto you a sabbath of rest, and ye shall afflict your souls: in the ninth *day* of the month at even, from even unto even, shall ye celebrate your sabbath.

4. FEAST OF DEDICATION: John 10:22 And it was in Jerusalem the feast of dedication, and it was winter.

5. FEASTS OF SHELTERS: FEAST OF BOOTHS' OR FEAST OF TENTS'**Leviticus 23**:42 Ye shall dwell in booths seven days; all that are Israelites born shall dwell in booths:

43 That your generations may know that I made the children of Israel to dwell in booths, when I brought them out of the land of Egypt: I *am* the LORD your God.

44 And Moses declared unto the children of Israel the feasts of the LORD.

6. FEAST OF PURIM: **Esther 9**:17 On the thirteenth day of the month Adar; and on the fourteenth day of the same rested they, and made it a day of feasting and gladness.

18 But the Jews that *were* at Shushan assembled together on the thirteenth *day* thereof, and on the fourteenth thereof; and on the fifteenth *day* of the same they rested, and made it a day of feasting and gladness.

19 Therefore the Jews of the villages, that dwelt in the unwalled towns, made the fourteenth day of the month Adar *a day of* gladness and feasting, and a good day, and of sending portions one to another.

20 And Mordecai wrote these things, and sent letters unto all the Jews that *were* in all the provinces of the king Ahasuerus, *both* nigh and far,

21 To stablish *this* among them, that they should keep the fourteenth day of the month Adar, and the fifteenth day of the same, yearly,

THE LORD COMMANDED HIS PEOPLE TO APPEAR BEFORE HIM

Deuteronomy16:16 Three times in a year shall all thy males appear before the LORD thy God in the place which he shall choose; **in the feast of unleavened bread, and in the feast of weeks, and in the feast of tabernacles**: and **they shall not appear before the LORD empty:**

17 **Every man *shall give* as he is able, according to the blessing** of the LORD thy God which he hath given thee.

7. FEAST OF UNLEAVENED BREAD: **Leviticus 23**:6 And on the fifteenth day of the same month *is* the feast of unleavened bread unto the LORD: seven days ye must eat unleavened bread.

7 In the first day ye shall have an holy convocation: ye shall do no servile work therein.

8 But ye shall offer an offering made by fire unto the LORD seven days: in the seventh day *is* an holy convocation: ye shall do no servile work *therein.*

8. THE FEAST OF WEEKS OF THE FIRSTFRUITS OF WHEAT HARVEST

Numbers 28:26 **Also in the day of the first fruits**, when ye bring a new meat offering unto the LORD, after your weeks be out, ye shall have a holy convocation; ye shall do no servile work:.

Exodus 23:16 And **the feast of harvest**, the firstfruits of thy labours, which thou hast sown in the field: and the feast ingathering, which is in the end of the year, when thou hast gathered in thy labours out of the field.

Exodus 23:19 The first of the firstfruits of thy land thou shalt bring into the house of the LORD thy God. Thou shalt not seethe a kid in his mother's milk.

Exodus 34:22 And thou shalt observe **the feast of weeks, of the firstfruits of wheat harvest, and the feast of ingathering at the year's end.**

Exodus 34:26 The first of the firstfruits of thy land thou shalt bring unto the house of the LORD thy God. Thou shalt not seethe a kid in his mother's milk.

9. THE FEAST OF TABERNACLES: **Leviticus 23**:34 Speak unto the children of Israel, saying, **The fifteenth day of this seventh month** *shall be* **the feast of tabernacles** *for* **seven days unto the LORD**.

35 On the first day *shall be* an holy convocation: ye shall do no servile work *therein*.

36 Seven days ye shall offer an offering made by fire unto the LORD: on the eighth day shall be an holy convocation unto you; and ye shall offer an offering made by fire unto the LORD: it *is* a solemn assembly; *and* ye shall do no servile work *therein*.

37 **These** *are* **the feasts of the LORD, which ye shall proclaim** *to be* **holy convocations, to offer an offering made by fire unto the LORD, a burnt offering, and a meat offering, a sacrifice, and drink offerings, every thing upon his day:**

38 Beside the sabbaths of the LORD, and beside your gifts, and beside all your vows, and beside all your freewill offerings, which ye give unto the LORD.

Deuteronomy16:13 Thou shalt observe **the feast of tabernacles** seven days, after that thou hast gathered in thy corn and thy wine:

14 And thou shalt rejoice in thy feast, thou, and thy son, and thy daughter, and thy manservant, and thy maidservant, and the Levite, the stranger, and the fatherless, and the widow, that *are* within thy gates.

15 Seven days shalt thou keep a solemn feast unto the LORD thy God in the place which the LORD shall choose: because the LORD thy God shall bless thee in all thine increase, and in all the works of thine hands, therefore thou shalt surely rejoice.

Leviticus 23:39 Also in the fifteenth day of the seventh month, when ye have gathered in the fruit of the land, ye shall keep a feast unto the LORD seven days: on the first day *shall be* a sabbath, and on the eighth day *shall be* a sabbath.

40 And ye shall take you on the first day the boughs of goodly trees, branches of palm trees, and the boughs of thick trees, and willows of the brook; and ye shall rejoice before the LORD your God seven days.

41 And ye shall keep it a feast unto the LORD seven days in the year. *It shall be* a statute for ever in your generations: **ye shall celebrate it in the seventh month.**

PART 4
FIRST AGREEMENT TO THE NATION OF ISRAEL

CHAPTER III **GOD CHOSE LEVITES TO BE THE PRIEST**

Leviticus 16:16 And he shall make an atonement for the holy place, because of the uncleanness of the children of Israel, and because of their transgressions in all their sins: and so shall he do for the tabernacle of the congregation, that remaineth among them in the midst of their uncleanness.

AARON WAS THE HEAD OF THE HOUSE OF LEVI
Numbers 17:1 And **the LORD spake unto Moses**, saying,
2 Speak unto the children of Israel, and take of every one of them a rod according to the house of *their* fathers, of all their princes according to the house of their fathers twelve rods: write thou every man's name upon his rod.
3 And **thou shalt write Aaron's name upon the rod of Levi: for one rod *shall be* for the head of the house of their fathers.**
4 And **thou shalt lay them up in the tabernacle of the congregation before the testimony, where I will meet with you.**
5 And it shall come to pass, *that* **the man's rod, whom I shall choose, shall blossom**: and I will make to cease from me the murmurings of the children of Israel, whereby they murmur against you.
6 And Moses spake unto the children of Israel, and **every one of their princes gave him a rod a piece, for each prince one, according to their fathers' houses, *even* twelve rods: and the rod of Aaron *was* among their rods.**
7 And Moses laid up the rods before the LORD in the tabernacle of witness.
8 And it came to pass, that on the morrow Moses went into the tabernacle of witness; and, **behold, the rod of Aaron for the house of Levi was budded, and brought forth buds, and bloomed blossoms, and yielded almonds.**

9 And Moses brought out all the rods from before the LORD unto all the children of Israel: and they looked, and took every man his rod.

10 And **the LORD said unto Moses, Bring Aaron's rod again before the testimony, to be kept for a token against the rebels**; and thou shalt quite take away their murmurings from me, that they die not.

11 And Moses did *so*: as the LORD commanded him, so did he.

AARON AND HIS SONS THE ANOINTED PRIESTS OF ISRAEL

Numbers 18:1 And **the LORD said unto Aaron, Thou and thy sons and thy father's house with thee shall bear the iniquity of the sanctuary: and thou and thy sons with thee shall bear the iniquity of your priesthood.**

2 And **thy brethren also of the tribe of Levi, the tribe of thy father, bring thou with thee, that they may be joined unto thee, and minister unto thee: but thou and thy sons with thee *shall minister* before the tabernacle of witness.**

3 And **they shall keep thy charge**, and the charge of all the tabernacle: only they shall not come nigh the vessels of the sanctuary and the altar, that neither they, nor ye also, die.

4 And they shall be joined unto thee, and keep the charge of the tabernacle of the congregation, for all the service of the tabernacle: and a stranger shall not come nigh unto you.

5 And **ye shall keep the charge of the sanctuary, and the charge of the altar**: **that there be no wrath any more upon the children of Israel.**

6 And I, behold, I have taken your brethren the Levites from among the children of Israel: to you *they are* given *as* a gift for the LORD, to do the service of the tabernacle of the congregation.

7 Therefore thou and thy sons with thee shall keep your priest's office for every thing of the altar, and within the vail; and ye shall serve: **I have given your priest's office *unto you* as a service of gift: and the stranger that cometh nigh shall be put to death**.

8 And the LORD spake unto Aaron, **Behold, I also have given thee the charge of mine heave offerings of all the hallowed things of the children of Israel**; unto thee have I given them by reason of the anointing, and to thy sons, **by an ordinance for ever.**

Deuteronomy 21:5 And **the priests the sons of Levi shall come near; for them the LORD thy God hath chosen to minister unto him, and to bless in the name of the LORD**; and **by their word shall every controversy and every stroke be** *tried*:

A. THE HIGH PRIEST AND PRIEST

Exodus 40:12 And **thou shalt bring Aaron and his sons unto the door of the tabernacle of the congregation, and wash them with water.**

13 And **thou shalt put upon Aaron the holy garments, and anoint him, and sanctify him;** that he may minister unto me in the priest's office.

14 And thou shalt bring his sons, and clothe them with coats:

15 And thou shalt anoint them, as thou didst anoint their father, that they may minister unto me in the priest's office: **for their anointing shall surely be an everlasting priesthood throughout their generations**.

Exodus 40:27 And he burnt sweet incense thereon; as the LORD commanded Moses.

28 And he set up the hanging *at* the door of the tabernacle.

29 And he put the altar of burnt offering *by* the door of the tabernacle of the tent of the congregation, and offered upon it the burnt offering and the meat offering; as the LORD commanded Moses.

30 And he set the laver between the tent of the congregation and the altar, and put water there, to wash *withal*.

31 And Moses and Aaron and his sons washed their hands and their feet thereat:

32 When they went into the tent of the congregation, and when they came near unto the altar, they washed; as the LORD commanded Moses.

GOD TOOK LEVITES TO DO THE SERVICE IN THE TABERNACLE

Numbers 8:13 And **thou shalt set the Levites before Aaron, and before his sons, and offer them** *for* **an offering unto the LORD.**

14 Thus shalt thou separate the Levites from among the children of Israel: and **the Levites shall be mine.**

15 And after that **shall the Levites go in to do the service of the tabernacle of the congregation**: and thou shalt cleanse them, and offer them *for* an offering.

16 For they *are* wholly given unto me from among the children of Israel; instead of such as open every womb, *even instead of* the firstborn of all the children of Israel, have I taken them unto me.

17 **For all the firstborn of the children of Israel *are* mine, *both* man and beast:** on the day that I smote every firstborn in the land of *Egypt* **I sanctified them for myself.**

18 **And I have taken the Levites for all the firstborn of the children of Israel.**

19 And I have given the Levites *as* a gift to Aaron and to his sons from among the children of Israel, to do the service of the children of Israel in the tabernacle of the congregation, and **to make an atonement for the children of Israel:** *that there be no plague* **among the children of Israel, when the children of Israel come nigh unto the sanctuary.**

THE MINISTER OF CONGREGATION

Numbers 8:23 **And** the LORD spake unto Moses, saying,

24 This *is it* that *belongeth* unto the Levites: **from twenty and five years old and upward they shall go in to wait upon the service of the tabernacle of the congregation**:

25 And **from the age of fifty years they shall cease waiting upon the service *thereof*,** and shall serve no more:

26 But **shall minister with their brethren in the tabernacle of the congregation, to keep the charge, and shall do no service.** Thus shalt thou do unto the Levites touching their charge.

THE HOLY GARMENT OF THE PRIEST

Leviticus 8:6 And Moses brought Aaron and his sons, and washed them with water.

7 And he put upon him the coat, and girded him with the girdle, and clothed him with the robe, and put the ephod upon him, and he girded him with the curious girdle of the ephod, and bound *it* unto him therewith.

8 And he put the breastplate upon him: also he put in the breastplate the Urim and the Thummim.

9 And he put the mitre upon his head; also upon the mitre, *even* upon his forefront, did he put the golden plate, the holy crown; as the LORD commanded Moses.

12 And he poured of the anointing oil upon Aaron's head, and anointed him, to sanctify him.

13 And Moses brought Aaron's sons, and put coats upon them, and girded them with girdles, and put bonnets upon them; as the LORD commanded Moses.

THE SHARE OF THE PRIEST

Leviticus 7:33 He among the sons of Aaron, that offereth the blood of the peace offerings, and the fat, shall have the right shoulder for *his* part.

B. RULES ABOUT TITHES

Leviticus 27:30 And **all the tithe of the land,** *whether* **of the seed of the land,** *or* **of the fruit of the tree,** *is* **the LORD'S:** *it is* **holy unto the LORD.**

31 **And if a man will at all redeem** *ought* **of his** tithes, he shall add thereto the fifth *part* thereof.

32 And concerning the tithe of the herd, or of the flock, *even* of whatsoever passeth under the rod, the tenth shall be holy unto the LORD.

Deuteronomy 12:5 But unto the place which the LORD your God shall choose out of all your tribes to put his name there, *even* unto his habitation shall ye seek, and thither thou shalt come:

6 And thither ye shall bring your burnt offerings, and your sacrifices, and your tithes, and heave offerings of your hand, and your vows, and your freewill offerings, and the firstlings of your herds and of your flocks:

7 And there ye shall eat before the LORD your God, and ye shall rejoice in all that ye put your hand unto, ye and your households, wherein the LORD thy God hath blessed thee.

Deuteronomy 14:22 Thou shalt truly tithe all the increase of thy seed, that the field bringeth forth year by year.

23 **And thou shalt eat before the LORD thy God, in the place which he shall choose to place his name there, the tithe of thy corn, of thy wine, and of thine oil, and the firstlings of thy herds and of thy flocks**; that thou mayest learn to fear the LORD thy God always.

24 And if the way be too long for thee, so that thou art not able to carry it; *or* if the place be too far from thee, which the LORD thy God shall choose to set his name there, when the LORD thy God hath blessed thee:

25 Then shalt thou turn *it* into money, and bind up the money in thine hand, and shalt go unto the place which the LORD thy God shall choose:

26 And thou shalt bestow that money for whatsoever thy soul lusteth after, for oxen, or for sheep, or for wine, or for strong
drink, or for whatsoever thy soul desireth: and thou shalt eat there before the LORD thy God, and thou shalt rejoice, thou, and thine household,

27 And the Levite that *is* within thy gates; thou shalt not forsake him; for he hath no part nor inheritance with thee.

28 At the end of three years thou shalt bring forth all the tithe of thine increase the same year, and shalt lay *it* up within thy gates:

29 And the Levite, (because he hath no part nor inheritance with thee,) and the stranger, and the fatherless, and the widow, which *are* within thy gates, shall come, and shall eat and be satisfied; that the LORD thy God may bless thee in all the work of thine hand which thou doest.

TITHES BE GIVEN TO THE SONS OF LEVI

Hebrews 7:5 *And verily they that are of **the sons of Levi, who receive the office of the priesthood, have a commandment to take tithes of the people according to the law,** that is, of their brethren, though they come out of the loins of Abraham:*

Deuteronomy 26:12 When thou hast made an end of tithing **all the tithes of thine increase the third year, *which is* the year of tithing, and hast given *it* unto the Levite**, the stranger, the fatherless, and the widow, that they may eat within thy gates, and be filled;

13 Then thou shalt say before the LORD thy God, I have brought away the hallowed things out of *mine* house, and also have given them unto the Levite, and unto the stranger, to the fatherless, and to the widow, according to all thy commandments which thou hast commanded me: I have not transgressed thy commandments, neither have I forgotten *them*:

FIRST TITHE:ABRAHAM TO THE HIGH PRIEST OF GOD

Hebrews 7:1 For this Melchisedec, king of Salem, priest of the most high God, who met Abraham returning from the slaughter of the kings, and blessed him;

2 To whom also Abraham gave a tenth part of all; first being by interpretation King of righteousness, and after that also King of Salem, which is, King of peace;

3 Without father, without mother, without descent, having neither beginning of days, nor end of life; but made like unto the Son of God; abideth a priest continually.

4 Now consider how great this man *was*, unto whom even the patriarch Abraham gave the tenth of the spoils.

MELCHIZEDEK BLESSED ABRAM

Genesis 14:18 And Melchizedek king of Salem brought forth bread and wine: and he *was* the priest of the most high God.

19 And he blessed him, and said, Blessed *be* Abram of the most high God, possessor of heaven and earth:

20 And blessed be the most high God, which hath delivered thine enemies into thy hand. And he gave him tithes of all.

C. THE FIRSTFRUITS OFFERINGS OF ISRAEL TO THE LORD

Leviticus 23:10 *Speak unto the children of Israel, and say unto them,* **When ye be come into the land which I give unto you, and shall reap the harvest thereof, then ye shall bring a sheaf of the firstfruits of your harvest unto the priest:**

 Deuteronomy 26:1 And it shall be, when thou *art* come in unto the land which the LORD thy God giveth thee *for* an inheritance, and possessest it, and dwellest therein;

2 **That thou shalt take of the first of all the fruit of the earth, which thou shalt bring of thy** land that the LORD thy God giveth thee, and shalt put *it* in a basket, and shalt go unto the place which the LORD thy God shall choose to place his name there.

3 And **thou shalt go unto the priest that shall be in those days, and say unto him**, *I profess this day unto the LORD thy God, that I am come unto the country which the LORD sware unto our fathers for to give us.*

4 **And the priest shall take the basket out of thine hand, and set it down before the altar of the LORD thy God**.

5 And thou shalt speak and say before the LORD thy God, A Syrian ready to perish *was* my father, and he went down into Egypt, and sojourned there with a few, and became there a nation, great, mighty, and populous:

6 And the Egyptians evil entreated us, and afflicted us, and laid upon us hard bondage:

7 And when we cried unto the LORD God of our fathers, the LORD heard our voice, and looked on our affliction, and our labour, and our oppression:

8 And **the LORD brought us forth out of Egypt with a mighty hand, and** with an outstretched arm, and with great terribleness, and with signs, and with wonders:

9 And **he hath brought us into this place, and hath given us this land,** *even* **a land that floweth with milk and honey.**

Leviticus 2:12 As for the oblation of the firstfruits, ye shall offer them unto the LORD: but they shall not be burnt on the altar for a sweet savour.

13 And every oblation of thy meat offering shalt thou season with salt; neither shalt thou suffer the salt of the covenant of thy God to be lacking from thy meat offering: with all thine offerings thou shalt offer salt.

14 And if thou offer a meat offering of thy firstfruits unto the LORD, thou shalt offer for the meat offering of thy firstfruits green ears of corn dried by the fire, *even* corn beaten out of full ears.

15 And thou shalt put oil upon it, and lay frankincense thereon: it *is* a meat offering.

16 And the priest shall burn the memorial of it, *part* of the beaten corn thereof, and *part* of the oil thereof, with all the frankincense thereof:*it is* an offering made by fire unto the LORD.

Numbers 18:12 All the best of the oil, and all the best of the wine, and of the wheat, the firstfruits of them which they shall offer unto the LORD, them have I given thee.

13 *And* whatsoever is first ripe in the land, which they shall bring unto the LORD, shall be thine; every one that is clean in thine house shall eat *of* it.

14 Every thing devoted in Israel shall be thine.

Deuteronomy 26:10 And now, behold, I have brought the firstfruits of the land, which thou, O LORD, hast given me. And thou shalt set it before the LORD thy God, **and worship before the LORD thy God**:

GOD CLAIMED THE FIRSTBORN BOTH OF MAN AND OF BEAST

Exodus 13:2 Sanctify unto me all the firstborn, whatsoever openeth the womb among the children of Israel, *both* of man and of beast: it *is* mine.

Exodus 13:15 And it came to pass, when Pharaoh would hardly let us go, that the LORD slew all the firstborn in the land of Egypt, both the firstborn of man, and the firstborn of beast: therefore I sacrifice to the LORD all that openeth the matrix, being males; but all the firstborn of my children I redeem.

Numbers 18:15 Every thing that openeth the matrix in all flesh, which they bring unto the LORD, *whether it be* of men or beasts, shall be thine**: nevertheless the firstborn of man shalt thou surely redeem, and the firstling of unclean beasts shalt thou redeem**.

16 And those that are to be redeemed from a month old shalt thou redeem, according to thine estimation, for the money of five shekels, after the shekel of the sanctuary, which *is* twenty gerahs.

17 But **the firstling of a cow, or the firstling of a sheep, or the firstling of a goat, thou shalt not redeem; they** *are* **holy: thou shalt sprinkle their blood upon the altar, and shalt burn their fat** *for* **an offering made by fire, for a sweet savour unto the LORD.**

18 And the flesh of them shall be thine, as the wave breast and as the right shoulder are thine.

19 All the heave offerings of the holy things, which the children of Israel offer unto the LORD, have I given thee, and thy sons and thy daughters with thee, by a statute for ever: **it** *is* **a covenant of salt for ever before the LORD unto thee and to thy seed with thee.**

PRAYER OFFERING THE FIRST FRUITS OF THE LAND

Deuteronomy 26:10 *And now, behold, I have brought the firstfruits of the land, which thou, O LORD, hast given me.* And thou shalt set it before the LORD thy God, and worship before the LORD thy God:

D. THE LORD COMMANDED ISRAEL TO MAKE THEIR OWN TRUMPETS

Numbers 10:1 And the LORD spake unto Moses, saying,

2 Make thee two trumpets of silver; of a whole piece shalt thou make them: that thou mayest use them for the calling of the assembly, and for the journeying of the camps.

3 And when **they shall blow with them, all the assembly shall assemble themselves to thee at the door of the tabernacle of the congregation.**

*GOD'S INSTRUCTIONS IN BLOWING THE TRUMPET

Numbers 10:8 And the sons of Aaron, the priests, shall blow with the trumpets; and they shall be to you for an ordinance for ever throughout your generations.

THE PURPOSE OF BLOWING THE TRUMPET

Nehemiah 4:20 In what place thereof ye hear **the sound of the trumpet**, resort ye thither unto us: **our God shall fight for us.**

1. JOURNEY FROM MOUNT SINAI

Numbers 10:4 And if they blow *but* with one *trumpet*, then the princes, *which are* heads of the thousands of Israel, shall gather themselves unto thee.

5 When ye blow an alarm, then the camps that lie on the east parts shall go forward.

6 When ye blow an alarm the second time, then the camps that lie on the south side shall take their journey: they shall blow an alarm for their journeys.

7 But when the congregation is to be gathered together, ye shall blow, but ye shall not sound an alarm.

2. IN THE DAY OF FEAST AND CELEBRATION

Numbers 10:10 Also in the day of your gladness, and in your solemn days, and in the beginnings of your months, ye shall blow with the trumpets over your burnt offerings, and over the sacrifices of your peace offerings; **that they may be to you for a memorial before your God: I *am* the LORD your God.**

Psalm 81:3 Blow a trumpet in the new moon, in the time appointed, on our solemn feast day.

3. TO GO WAR WITHIN THE LAND OF ISRAEL

Numbers 10:9 And if ye go to war in your land against the enemy that oppresseth you**, then ye shall blow an alarm with the trumpets; and ye shall be remembered before the LORD your God, and ye shall be saved from your enemies**.

*GOD'S INSTRUCTIONS ABOUT THE FALL OF JERICO

Joshua 6:2 And the LORD said unto Joshua, See, I have given into thine hand Jericho, and the king thereof, *and* the mighty men of valour.

3 And ye shall compass the city, all *ye* men of war, *and* go round about the city once. Thus shalt thou do six days.

4 And seven priests shall bear before the ark seven trumpets of rams' horns: and the seventh day ye shall compass the city seven times, and the priests shall blow with the trumpets.

5 And it shall come to pass, that when they make a long *blast* with the ram's horn, *and* when ye hear the sound of the trumpet, all the people shall shout with a great shout; and the wall of the city shall fall down flat, and the people shall ascend up every man straight before him.

6 And Joshua the son of Nun called the priests, and said unto them, Take up the Ark of the Covenant, and let seven priests bear seven trumpets of rams' horns before the ark of the LORD.

7 And he said unto the people, Pass on, and compass the city, and let him that is armed pass on before the ark of the LORD.

8 And it came to pass, when Joshua had spoken unto the people, that the seven priests bearing the seven trumpets of rams' horns passed on before the LORD, and blew with the trumpets: and the ark of the covenant of the LORD followed them.

9 And the armed men went before the priests that blew with the trumpets, and the rereward came after the ark, *the priests* going on, and blowing with the trumpets.

10 And Joshua had commanded the people, saying, Ye shall not shout, nor make any noise with your voice, neither shall *any* word proceed out of your mouth, until the day I bid you shout; then shall ye shout.

THE BLOWING OF TRUMPETS

1. THE FALL OF JERICO **Joshua 6**:11 So the ark of the LORD compassed the city, going about *it* once: and they came into the camp, and lodged in the camp.

12 And Joshua rose early in the morning, and the priests took up the ark of the LORD.

13 And **seven priests bearing seven trumpets of rams' horns before the ark of the LORD went on continually, and blew with the trumpets:** and the armed men went before them; but the rereward came after the ark of the LORD, *the priests* going on, and blowing with the trumpets.

14 And the second day they compassed the city once, and returned into the camp: so they did six days.

15 And it came to pass on the seventh day, that they rose early about the dawning of the day, and compassed the city after the same manner seven times: only on that day they compassed the city seven times.

16 And it came to pass at the seventh time, when the priests blew with the trumpets, Joshua said unto the people, Shout; for the LORD hath given you the city.

17 And the city shall be accursed, *even* it, and all that *are* therein, to the LORD: only Rahab the harlot shall live, she and all that *are* with her in the house, because she hid the messengers that we sent.

18 And ye, in any wise keep *yourselves* from the accursed thing, lest ye make *yourselves* accursed, when ye take of the accursed thing, and make the camp of Israel a curse, and trouble it.

19 But all the silver, and gold, and vessels of brass and iron, *are* consecrated unto the LORD: they shall come into the treasury of the LORD.

20 So the people shouted when *the priests* blew with the trumpets: and it came to pass, when the people heard the sound of the trumpet, and the people shouted with a great shout, that the wall fell down flat, so that the people went up into the city, every man straight before him, and they took the city.

21 And they utterly destroyed all that *was* in the city, both man and woman, young and old, and ox, and sheep, and ass, with the edge of the sword.

2. THE TRUMPET SOUNDED FOR VICTORY AGAINST MOAB **Judges 3**:27 And it came to pass, when he was come, that he blew a trumpet in the mountain of Ephraim, and the children of Israel went down with him from the mount, and he before them.

28 And he said unto them, Follow after me: for the LORD hath delivered your enemies the Moabites into your hand. And they went down after him, and took the fords of Jordan toward Moab, and suffered not a man to pass over.

29 And they slew of Moab at that time about ten thousand men, all lusty, and all men of valour; and there escaped not a man.

30 So Moab was subdued that day under the hand of Israel. And the land had rest fourscore years.

3. THE SPIRIT OF THE LORD CAME UPON GIDEON AGAINST MIDIANITES **Judges 6**:33 Then all the Midianites and the Amalekites and the children of the east were gathered together, and went over, and pitched in the valley of Jezreel.

34 But the Spirit of the LORD came upon Gideon, and he blew a trumpet; and Abiezer was gathered after him.

35 And he sent messengers throughout all Manasseh; who also was gathered after him: and he sent messengers unto Asher, and unto Zebulun, and unto Naphtali; and they came up to meet them.

Judges 7:16 And **he divided the three hundred men *into* three companies, and he put a trumpet in every man's hand,** with empty pitchers, and lamps within the pitchers.

17 And he said unto them, Look on me, and do likewise: and, behold, when I come to the outside of the camp, it shall be *that*, as I do, so shall ye do.

18 **When I blow with a trumpet, I and all that *are* with me, then blow ye the trumpets also on every side of all the camp, and say, *The sword* of the LORD, and of Gideon**.

19 So Gideon, and the hundred men that *were* with him, came unto the outside of the camp in the beginning of the middle watch; and they had but newly set the watch: and they blew the trumpets, and brake the pitchers that *were* in their hands.

20 And the three companies blew the trumpets, and brake the pitchers, and held the lamps in their left hands, and the trumpets in their right hands to blow *withal*: and they cried, The sword of the LORD, and of Gideon.

21 And they stood every man in his place round about the camp: and all the host ran, and cried, and fled.

22 **And the three hundred blew the trumpets, and the LORD set every man's sword against his fellow, even throughout all the host: and the host fled to Bethshittah in Zererath, *and* to the border of Abelmeholah, unto Tabbath**.

23 And the men of Israel gathered themselves together out of Naphtali, and out of Asher, and out of all Manasseh, and pursued after the Midianites.

24 And Gideon sent messengers throughout all mount Ephraim, saying, Come down against the Midianites, and take before them the waters unto Bethbarah and Jordan. Then all the men of Ephraim gathered themselves together, and took the waters unto Bethbarah and Jordan.

25 And they took two princes of the Midianites, Oreb and Zeeb; and they slew Oreb upon the rock Oreb, and Zeeb they slew at the winepress of Zeeb, and pursued Midian, and brought the heads of Oreb and Zeeb to Gideon on the other side Jordan.

4 VICTORY OF KING SAUL AND JONATHAN AGAINST PHILISTINES1Samuel 13:3 And Jonathan smote the garrison of the Philistines that *was* in Geba, **and the Philistines heard** *of it.* **And Saul blew the trumpet throughout all the land**, saying, **Let the Hebrews hear.**

4 And all Israel heard say *that* Saul had smitten a garrison of the Philistines, and *that* Israel also was had in abomination with the Philistines. And the people were called together after Saul to Gilgal

5 BLOWING THE TRUMPET STOPPED THE FIGHTS BETWEEN PEOPLE OF ISRAEL AND JUDAH (After the Death of King Saul) **2samuel 2:10 Ishbosheth Saul's son** *was* **forty years old when he began to reign over Israel, and reigned two years**. But the house of Judah followed David.

12 And Abner the son of Ner, and the servants of Ishbosheth the son of Saul, went out from Mahanaim to Gibeon.

13 And Joab the son of Zeruiah, and the servants of David, went out, and met together by the pool of Gibeon: and they sat down, the one on the one side of the pool, and the other on the other side of the pool.

14 And Abner said to Joab, Let the young men now arise, and play before us. And Joab said, Let them arise.

15 Then there arose and went over by number twelve of Benjamin, which *pertained* to Ishbosheth the son of Saul, and twelve of the servants of David.

16 And they caught every one his fellow by the head, and *thrust* his sword in his fellow's side; so they fell down together:

wherefore that place was called Helkathhazzurim, which *is* in Gibeon.

17 And there was a very sore battle that day; and Abner was beaten, and the men of Israel, before the servants of David.

18 And there were three sons of Zeruiah there, Joab, and Abishai, and Asahel: and Asahel *was as* light of foot as a wild roe.

19 And Asahel pursued after Abner; and in going he turned not to the right hand nor to the left from following Abner.

20 Then Abner looked behind him, and said, *Art* thou Asahel? And he answered, I *am*.

21 And Abner said to him, Turn thee aside to thy right hand or to thy left, and lay thee hold on one of the young men, and take thee his armour. But Asahel would not turn aside from following of him.

22 And Abner said again to Asahel, Turn thee aside from following me: wherefore should I smite thee to the ground? how then should I hold up my face to Joab thy brother?

23 Howbeit he refused to turn aside: wherefore Abner with the hinder end of the spear smote him under the fifth *rib*, that the spear came out behind him; and he fell down there, and died in the same place: and it came to pass, *that* as many as came to the place where Asahel fell down and died stood still.

24 Joab also and Abishai pursued after Abner: and the sun went down when they were come to the hill of Ammah, that *lieth*before Giah by the way of the wilderness of Gibeon.

25 And the children of Benjamin gathered themselves together after Abner, and became one troop, and stood on the top of an hill.

26 Then Abner called to Joab, and said, Shall the sword devour for ever? knowest thou not that it will be bitterness in the latter end? how long shall it be then, ere thou bid the people return from following their brethren?

27 And Joab said, *As* God liveth, unless thou hadst spoken, surely then in the morning the people had gone up every one from following his brother.

28 So Joab blew a trumpet, and all the people stood still, and pursued after Israel no more, neither fought they any more.

6. THE PRIESTS AS WATCHMAN SHALL BLOW THE TRUMPHET IN THE SECOND COMING OF CHRIST
(Volume 3 Part 18 Chapter VI)

═══

CHAPTER IV **THE BLOOD COVENANT**

Leviticus 4:20"
And he shall do with the bullock as he did with the bullock for a
sin offering, so shall he do with this: and the priest shall make an
atonement for them, and it shall be forgiven them."

ATONEMENT OF SIN

Leviticus 4:5 And **the priest that is anointed shall take of the bullock's blood,** and bring it to the tabernacle of the congregation:

1 Chronicles 6:49 But Aaron and his sons offered upon the altar of the burnt offering, and on the altar of incense, *and were appointed* for all the work of the *place* most holy, and to make an atonement for Israel, according to all that Moses the servant of God had commanded.

2 Chronicles 29:24 And the priests killed them, and they made reconciliation with their blood upon the altar, to make an atonement for all Israel: for the king commanded *that* the burnt offering and the sin offering *should be made* for all Israel. Leviticus 4:31 And he shall take away all the fat thereof, as the fat is taken away from off the sacrifice of peace offerings; and the priest shall burn *it* upon the altar for a sweet savour unto the LORD; and the priest shall make an atonement for him, and it shall be forgiven him.

THE PLACE TO OFFER THE BURNT OFFERINGS

Deuteronomy 12:13 Take heed to thyself that **thou offer not thy burnt offerings in every place that thou seest:**

14 But in the place which **the LORD shall choose** in one of thy tribes, there thou shalt offer thy burnt offerings, **and there thou shalt do all that I command thee**.

Deuteronomy 12:26 Only thy holy things which thou hast, and thy vows, thou shalt take, and go unto the place which the LORD shall choose:

THE ALTAR

Exodus 20:24 An altar of earth thou shalt make unto me, and shalt sacrifice thereon thy burnt offerings, and thy peace offerings, thy sheep, and thine oxen: in all places where I record my name I will come unto thee, and I will bless thee.

25 And **if thou wilt make me an altar of stone, thou shalt not build it of hewn stone: for if thou lift up thy tool upon it, thou hast polluted it**.

26 Neither shalt thou go up by steps unto mine altar, that thy nakedness be not discovered thereon.

Exodus 40:6 And thou shalt set the altar of the burnt offering before the door of the tabernacle of the tent of the congregation.

7 And thou shalt set the laver between the tent of the congregation and the altar, and shalt put water therein.

8 And thou shalt set up the court round about, and hang up the hanging at the court gate.

9 And thou shalt take the anointing oil, and anoint the tabernacle, and all that *is* therein, and shalt hallow it, and all the vessels thereof: and it shall be holy.

10 And thou shalt anoint the altar of the burnt offering, and all his vessels, and sanctify the altar: and it shall be an altar most holy.

11 And thou shalt anoint the laver and his foot, and sanctify it.

Leviticus 8:10 And Moses took the anointing oil, and anointed the tabernacle and all that *was* therein, and sanctified them.

11 And he sprinkled thereof upon the altar seven times, and anointed the altar and all his vessels, both the laver and his foot, to sanctify them.

SPRINKLE THE BLOOD AROUND THE ALTAR

Leviticus 1:5 And he shall kill the bullock before the LORD: and the priests, Aaron's sons, shall bring the blood, and sprinkle the blood round about upon the altar that *is by* the door of the tabernacle of the congregation.

Leviticus 8:15 And he slew *it*; and Moses took the blood, and put *it* upon the horns of the altar round about with his finger, and purified the altar, and poured the blood at the bottom of the altar, and sanctified it, to make reconciliation upon it.

Leviticus 8:19 And he killed *it*; and Moses sprinkled the blood upon the altar round about.

Exodus 24:8 And **Moses took the blood, and sprinkled *it* on the people, and said, Behold the blood of the covenant, which the LORD hath made with you** concerning all these words.

*Exodus 23:18 **Thou shalt not offer the blood of my sacrifice with leavened bread; neither shall the fat of my sacrifice remain until the morning**.

Exodus 34:25 Thou shalt not offer the blood of my sacrifice with leaven; neither shall the sacrifice of the feast of the passover be left unto the morning.

Leviticus 4:16 And the priest that is anointed shall bring of the bullock's blood to the tabernacle of the congregation:

18 And **he shall put *some* of the blood upon the horns of the altar** which *is* before the LORD, that *is* in the tabernacle of the congregation, and shall pour out all the blood at the bottom of the altar of the burnt offering, which *is at* the door of the tabernacle of the congregation.

Leviticus 4:6 And **the priest shall dip his finger in the blood, and sprinkle of the blood seven times before the LORD**, before the vail of the sanctuary.

Leviticus 4:17 And the priest shall dip his finger *in some* of the blood, and sprinkle *it* seven times before the LORD, *even* before the vail.

Leviticus 4:30 And **the priest shall take of the blood thereof with his finger, and put *it* upon the horns of the altar of burnt offering**, and **shall pour out all the blood thereof at the bottom of the altar.**

Leviticus 4:7 And the priest shall put *some* of the blood upon the horns of the altar of sweet incense before the LORD, which *is* in the tabernacle of the congregation; and shall pour all the blood of the bullock at the bottom of the altar of the burnt offering, which *is at* the door of the tabernacle of the congregation.

Exodus 24:6 And Moses took half of the blood, and put *it* in basons; and half of the blood he sprinkled on the altar.

Leviticus 1:11 And he shall kill it on the side of the altar northward before the LORD: and the priests, Aaron's sons, shall sprinkle his blood round about upon the altar.

Leviticus 1:15 And the priest shall bring it unto the altar, and wring off his head, and burn *it* on the altar; and the blood thereof shall be wrung out at the side of the altar:

Leviticus 3:2 And he shall lay his hand upon the head of his offering, and kill it *at* the door of the tabernacle of the congregation: and Aaron's sons the priests shall sprinkle the blood upon the altar round about.

Leviticus 3:8 And he shall lay his hand upon the head of his offering, and kill it before the tabernacle of the congregation: and Aaron's sons shall sprinkle the blood thereof round about upon the altar.

Leviticus 3:13 **And he shall lay his hand upon the head of it, and kill it before the tabernacle of the congregation: and the sons of Aaron shall sprinkle the blood thereof upon the altar round about.**

Leviticus 7:14 And of it he shall offer one out of the whole oblation *for* an heave offering unto the LORD, *and* it shall be the priest's that sprinkleth the blood of the peace offerings.

PREPARATION OF THE BURNT OFFERING

Leviticus 8:14 And he brought the bullock for the sin offering: and Aaron and his sons laid their hands upon the head of the bullock for the sin offering.

15 And he slew *it*; and Moses took the blood, and put *it* upon the horns of the altar round about with his finger, and purified the altar, and poured the blood at the bottom of the altar, and sanctified it, to make reconciliation upon it.

16 And **he took all the fat that *was* upon the inwards, and the caul *above* the liver, and the two kidneys, and their fat, and Moses burned *it* upon the altar.**

17 But the bullock, and his hide, his flesh, and his dung, he burnt with fire without the camp; as the LORD commanded Moses.

18 And he brought the ram for the burnt offering: and Aaron and his sons laid their hands upon the head of the ram.

19 And he killed *it*; and Moses sprinkled the blood upon the altar round about.

20 And he cut the ram into pieces; and Moses burnt the head, and the pieces, and the fat.

21 And he washed the inwards and the legs in water; and Moses burnt the whole ram upon the altar: it *was* a burnt sacrifice for a sweet savour, *and* an offering made by fire unto the LORD; as the LORD commanded Moses.

22 And he brought the other ram, the ram of consecration: and Aaron and his sons laid their hands upon the head of the ram.

23 And he slew *it*; and Moses took of the blood of it, and put *it* upon the tip of Aaron's right ear, and upon the thumb of his right hand, and upon the great toe of his right foot.

24 And he brought Aaron's sons, and Moses put of the blood upon the tip of their right ear, and upon the thumbs of their right hands, and upon the great toes of their right feet: and Moses sprinkled the blood upon the altar round about.

25 And he took the fat, and the rump, and all the fat that *was* upon the inwards, and the caul *above* the liver, and the two kidneys, and their fat, and the right shoulder:

26 And out of the basket of unleavened bread, that *was* before the LORD, he took one unleavened cake, and a cake of oiled bread, and one wafer, and put *them* on the fat, and upon the right shoulder:

27 And he put all upon Aaron's hands, and upon his sons' hands, and waved them *for* a wave offering before the LORD.

28 And Moses took them from off their hands, and burnt *them* on the altar upon the burnt offering: they *were* consecrations for a sweet savour: it *is* an offering made by fire unto the LORD.

29 And Moses took the breast, and waved it *for* a wave offering before the LORD: *for* of the ram of consecration it was Moses' part; as the LORD commanded Moses.

30 And Moses took of the anointing oil, and of the blood which *was* upon the altar, and sprinkled *it* upon Aaron, *and* upon his garments, and upon his sons, and upon his sons' garments with him; and sanctified Aaron, *and* his garments, and his sons, and his sons' garments with him.

31 And Moses said unto Aaron and to his sons, Boil the flesh *at* the door of the tabernacle of the congregation: and there eat it with the bread that *is* in the basket of consecrations, as I commanded, saying, Aaron and his sons shall eat it.

32 And that which remaineth of the flesh and of the bread shall ye burn with fire.

33 And ye shall not go out of the door of the tabernacle of the congregation *in* seven days, until the days of your consecration be at an end: for seven days shall he consecrate you.

34 As he hath done this day, *so* the LORD hath commanded to do, to make an atonement for you.

35 Therefore shall ye abide *at* the door of the tabernacle of the congregation day and night seven days, and keep the charge of the LORD, that ye die not: for so I am commanded.

36 So Aaron and his sons did all things which the LORD commanded by the hand of Moses.

THE BURNT OFFERINGS

Leviticus 7:2 In the place where they kill the burnt offering shall they kill the trespass offering: and **the blood thereof shall he sprinkle round about upon the altar**.

 Deuteronomy15:21 And if there be *any* blemish therein, *as if it be* lame, or blind, *or have* any ill blemish, thou shalt not sacrifice it unto the LORD thy God.

22 **Thou shalt eat it within thy gates**: the unclean and the clean *person shall eat it* alike, as the roebuck, and as the hart.

23 **Only thou shalt not eat the blood thereof; thou shalt pour it upon the ground as water.**

Deuteronomy 12: 27 **And thou shalt offer thy burnt offerings, the flesh and the blood, upon the altar of the LORD thy God**: **and the blood of thy sacrifices shall be poured out upon the altar of the LORD thy God, and thou shalt eat the flesh**.

Leviticus 6:27 Whatsoever shall touch the flesh thereof shall be holy: and when there is sprinkled of the blood thereof upon any garment, thou shalt wash that whereon it was sprinkled in the holy place.

Deuteronomy 12:15 Notwithstanding thou mayest kill and eat flesh in all thy gates, whatsoever thy soul lusteth after, according to the blessing of the LORD thy God which he hath given thee: the unclean and the clean may eat thereof, as of the roebuck, and as of the hart.

16 **Only ye shall not eat the blood; ye shall pour it upon the earth as water.**

18 But thou must eat them before the LORD thy God in the place which the LORD thy God shall choose, thou, and thy son, and thy daughter, and thy manservant, and thy maidservant, and the Levite that *is* within thy gates: and thou shalt rejoice before the LORD thy God in all that thou puttest thine hands unto.

19 **Take heed to thyself that thou forsake not the Levite as long as thou livest upon the earth.**

MEAT OFFERINGS

Leviticus 2:1 And when any will offer a meat offering unto the LORD, his offering shall be *of* fine flour; and he shall pour oil upon it, and put frankincense thereon:

2 And he shall bring it to Aaron's sons the priests: and he shall take thereout his handful of the flour thereof, and of the oil thereof, with all the frankincense thereof; and the priest shall burn the memorial of it upon the altar, *to be*an offering made by fire, of a sweet savour unto the LORD:

3 And the remnant of the meat offering *shall be* Aaron's and his sons': *it is* a thing most holy of the offerings of the LORD made by fire.

4 And if thou bring an oblation of a meat offering baken in the oven, *it shall be* unleavened cakes of fine flour mingled with oil, or unleavened wafers anointed with oil.

1. BREAD OFFERINGS

Numbers 28:1 And the LORD spake unto Moses, saying,

2 Command the children of Israel, and say unto them, **My offering, *and* my bread for my sacrifices made by fire,*for* a sweet savour unto me,** shall ye observe to offer unto me in their due season.

Leviticus 23:17 Ye shall bring out of your habitations two wave loaves of two tenth deals: they shall be of fine flour; they shall be baken with leaven; *they are* the firstfruits unto the LORD.

Leviticus 23:20 And the priest shall wave them with the bread of the firstfruits *for* a wave offering before the LORD, with the two lambs: they shall be holy to the LORD for the priest.

2. TWO LAMBS FOR CONTINUAL OFFERING

Numbers 28:3 And thou shalt say unto them, This *is* the offering made by fire which ye shall offer unto the LORD; **two lambs of the first year without spot day by day, *for* a continual burnt offering.**

4 **The one lamb shalt thou offer in the morning, and the other lamb shalt thou offer at even**;

5 And a tenth *part* of an ephah of flour for a meat offering, mingled with the fourth *part* of an hin of beaten oil.

6 *It is* **a continual burnt offering, which was ordained in mount Sinai** for a sweet savour, a sacrifice made by fire unto the LORD.

7 **And the drink offering thereof *shall be* the fourth *part* of an hin for the one lamb**: in the holy *place* shalt thou cause the strong wine to be poured unto the LORD *for* a drink offering.

8 And the other lamb shalt thou offer at even: as the meat offering of the morning, and as the drink offering thereof, thou shalt offer *it*, a sacrifice made by fire, of a sweet savour unto the LORD.

3. SABBATH OFFERING
Numbers 28:9 And **on the sabbath day two lambs of the first year without spot, and two tenth deals of flour *for* a meat offering, mingled with oil**, and the drink offering thereof:
10 *This is* the burnt offering of every sabbath, beside the continual burnt offering, and his drink offering.

4. BEGINNING OF MONTH'S OFFERING
Numbers 28:11 And **in the beginnings of your months ye shall offer a burnt offering unto the LORD; two young bullocks, and one ram, seven lambs of the first year without spot;**
12 And **three tenth deals of flour *for* a meat offering, mingled with oil, for one bullock; and two tenth deals of flour *for* a meat offering, mingled with oil, for one ram;**
13 **And a several tenth deal of flour mingled with oil *for* a meat offering unto one lamb**; *for* a burnt offering of a sweet savour, a sacrifice made by fire unto the LORD.
14 **And their drink offerings shall be half an hin of wine unto a bullock, and the third *part* of an hin unto a ram, and a fourth *part* of an hin unto a lamb:** this *is* the burnt offering of every month throughout the months of the year.

5. SIN OFFERING (ATONEMENT)

Leviticus 5:9 *And he shall sprinkle of the blood of the sin offering upon the side of the altar; and the rest of the blood shall be wrung out at the bottom of the altar: it is a sin offering.*

Numbers 28:15 And **one kid of the goats for a sin offering unto the LORD shall be offered, beside the continual burnt offering, and his drink offering.**
22 And one goat *for* a sin offering, to make an atonement for you.
23 Ye shall offer these beside the burnt offering in the morning, which *is* for a continual burnt offering.
Leviticus 6:30 And no sin offering, whereof *any* of the blood is brought into the tabernacle of the congregation to reconcile *withal* in the holy *place*, shall be eaten: **it shall be burnt in the fire.**

Leviticus 4:25 And **the priest shall take of the blood of the sin offering with his finger, and put** *it* **upon the horns of the altar of burnt offering**, and shall pour out his blood at the bottom of the altar of burnt offering.

Leviticus 4:34 And the priest shall take of the blood of the sin offering with his finger, and put *it* upon the horns of the altar of burnt offering, and shall pour out all the blood thereof at the bottom of the altar:

6. PASSOVER OFFERING

Numbers 28:16 And **in the fourteenth day of the first month** *is* **the passover of the LORD**.

17 And **in the fifteenth day of this month** *is* **the feast: seven days shall unleavened bread be eaten.**

18 In **the first day** *shall be* **an holy convocation; ye shall do no manner of servile work** *therein*:

19 But ye shall **offer a sacrifice made by fire** *for* **a burnt offering unto the LORD; two young bullocks, and one ram, and seven lambs of the first year: they shall be unto you without blemish:**

20 And **their meat offering** *shall be of* **flour mingled with oil: three tenth deals shall ye offer for a bullock, and two tenth deals for a ram;**

21 A several tenth deal shalt thou offer for every lamb, throughout the seven lambs:

7. SEVENTH MONTH ON THE FIRST DAY OFFERING

Numbers 29:1 And in the seventh month, on the first *day* of the month, ye shall have an holy convocation; ye shall do no servile work**: it is a day of blowing the trumpets unto you**.

2 And **ye shall offer a burnt offering for a sweet savour unto the LORD; one young bullock, one ram,** *and* **seven lambs of the first year without blemish:**

3 **And their meat offering** *shall be of* **flour mingled with oil, three tenth deals for a bullock,** *and* **two tenth deals for a ram,**

4 **And one tenth deal for one lamb, throughout the seven lambs:**

5 **And one kid of the goats** *for* **a sin offering, to make an atonement for you:**

6 Beside the burnt offering of the month, and his meat offering, and the daily burnt offering, and his meat offering, and their drink

offerings, according unto their manner, for a sweet savour, a sacrifice made by fire unto the LORD.

8. TENTH DAY OF THIS SEVENTH MONTH HOLY CONVOCATION

Numbers 29:7 And ye shall have on **the tenth** *day* **of this seventh month an holy convocation**; and ye shall afflict your souls: ye shall not do any work *therein*:

8 But ye shall offer a burnt offering unto the LORD *for* a sweet savour; one young bullock, one ram, *and* seven lambs of the first year; they shall be unto you without blemish:

9 And their meat offering *shall be of* flour mingled with oil, three tenth deals to a bullock, *and* two tenth deals to one ram,

10 A several tenth deal for one lamb, throughout the seven lambs:

11 **One kid of the goats** *for* **a sin offering; beside the sin offering of atonem**ent, and **the continual burnt offering, and the meat offering of it, and their drink offerings.**

9. FIFTEENTH DAY OF THE SEVENTH MONTH
First Day

Numbers 29:12 And on the fifteenth day of the seventh month ye shall have an holy convocation; ye shall do no servile work, and ye shall keep a feast unto the LORD seven days:

13 And ye shall offer a burnt offering, a sacrifice made by fire, of a sweet savour unto the LORD; thirteen young bullocks, two rams, *and* fourteen lambs of the first year; they shall be without blemish:

14 And their meat offering *shall be of* flour mingled with oil, three tenth deals unto every bullock of the thirteen bullocks, two tenth deals to each ram of the two rams,

15 And a several tenth deal to each lamb of the fourteen lambs:

16 And one kid of the goats *for* a sin offering; beside the continual burnt offering, his meat offering, and his drink offering.

Second Day

Numbers 29:17 And on the second day *ye shall offer* twelve young bullocks, two rams, fourteen lambs of the first year without spot:

18 And their meat offering and their drink offerings for the bullocks, for the rams, and for the lambs, *shall be* according to their number, after the manner:

19 And one kid of the goats *for* a sin offering; beside the continual burnt offering, and the meat offering thereof, and their drink offerings.

Third Day
Numbers 29:20 And on the third day **eleven bullocks, two rams, fourteen lambs of the first year without blemish;**
21 And their meat offering and their drink offerings for the bullocks, for the rams, and for the lambs, *shall be* according to their number, after the manner:
22 **And one goat** *for* **a sin offering; beside the continual burnt offering, and his meat offering, and his drink offering.**

Fourth Day
Numbers 29:23 And on the fourth day **ten bullocks, two rams, *and* fourteen lambs of the first year without blemish:**
24 Their meat offering and their drink offerings for the bullocks, for the rams, and for the lambs, *shall be* according to their number, after the manner:
25 **And one kid of the goats** *for* **a sin offering; beside the continual burnt offering, his meat offering, and his drink offering**

Fifth Day
Numbers 29:26 And on the fifth day nine bullocks**, two rams, *and* fourteen lambs of the first year without spot:**
27 And their meat offering and their drink offerings for the bullocks, for the rams, and for the lambs, *shall be* according to their number, after the manner:
28 **And one goat** *for* **a sin offering; beside the continual burnt offering, and his meat offering, and his drink offering.**

Sixth Day
Numbers 29:29 And on the sixth day **eight bullocks, two rams, *and* fourteen lambs of the first year without blemish:**
30 And their meat offering and their drink offerings for the bullocks, for the rams, and for the lambs, *shall be* according to their number, after the manner:
31 And **one goat** *for* **a sin offering; beside the continual burnt offering, his meat offering, and his drink offering.**

Seventh Day

Numbers 29:32 And on the seventh day **seven bullocks, two rams,** *and* **fourteen lambs of the first year without blemish:**

33 And their meat offering and their drink offerings for the bullocks, for the rams, and for the lambs, *shall be* according to their number, after the manner:

34 **And one goat** *for* **a sin offering; beside the continual burnt offering, his meat offering, and his drink offering.**

Eight Day

Number 29:35 On the eighth day ye shall have a solemn assembly: ye shall do no servile work *therein*:

36 But ye shall offer a burnt offering, a sacrifice made by fire, of a sweet savour unto the LORD: **one bullock, one ram, seven lambs of the first year without blemish**:

37 Their meat offering and their drink offerings for the bullock, for the ram, and for the lambs, *shall be* according to their number, after the manner:

38 **And one goat** *for* **a sin offering; beside the continual burnt offering, and his meat offering, and his drink offering**.

39 These *things* ye shall do unto the LORD in your set feasts, beside your vows, and your freewill offerings, for your burnt offerings, and for your meat offerings, and for your drink offerings, and for your peace offerings.

OFFERINGS FOR DEFILING THE LAW

1. SINNED BY THE DEAD

Numbers 6:9 And if any man die very suddenly by him, and he hath defiled the head of his consecration; then he shall shave his head in the day of his cleansing, on the seventh day shall he shave it.

10 And on the eighth day he shall bring two turtles, or two young pigeons, to the priest, to the door of the tabernacle of the congregation:

11 And the priest shall offer the one for a sin offering, and the other for a burnt offering, and make an atonement for him, for that he sinned by the dead, and shall hallow his head that same day.

2. LAW OF SEPARATION DEFILED

Numbers 6:12 And he shall consecrate unto the LORD the days of his separation, and shall bring a lamb of the first year for a trespass offering: but the days that were before shall be lost, because his separation was defiled.

13 And this *is* the law of the Nazarite, when the days of his separation are fulfilled: he shall be brought unto the door of the tabernacle of the congregation:

3. PEACE OFFERINGS

Numbers 6:14 And he shall offer his offering unto the LORD, one he lamb of the first year without blemish for a burnt offering, and one ewe lamb of the first year without blemish for a sin offering, and one ram without blemish for peace offerings,

15 And a basket of unleavened bread, cakes of fine flour mingled with oil, and wafers of unleavened bread anointed with oil, and their meat offering, and their drink offerings.

16 And **the priest** shall bring *them* before the LORD, and **shall offer his sin offering, and his burnt offering:**

17 And he shall **offer the ram *for* a sacrifice of peace offerings unto the LORD, with the basket of unleavened bread: the priest shall offer also his meat offering, and his drink offering.**

18 And **the Nazarite shall shave the head of his separation** *at* the door of the tabernacle of the congregation, and **shall take the hair of the head** of his separation, and **put** *it* **in the fire which** *is* **under the sacrifice of the peace offerings.**

19 And the priest shall take the sodden shoulder of the ram, and one unleavened cake out of the basket, and one unleavened wafer, and shall put *them* upon the hands of the Nazarite, after *the hair of* his separation is shaven:

20 And the priest shall wave them *for* a wave offering before the LORD: this *is* holy for the priest, with the wave breast and heave shoulder: and after that the Nazarite may drink wine.

21 **This** *is* **the law of the Nazarite who hath vowed,** *and of* **his offering unto the LORD for his separation**, beside *that* that his hand shall get: according to the vow which he vowed, so he must do after the law of his separation.

PART 4
FIRST AGREEMENT TO THE NATION OF ISRAEL

CHAPTER V **THE LAW OF SABBATH**

Psalms 19:7
The law of the LORD is perfect, converting the soul: the
testimony of the LORD is sure, making wise the simple.

Psalm 119:1 ALEPH. Blessed *are* the undefiled in the way, who
walk in the law of the LORD.
2 Blessed *are* they that keep his testimonies, *and that* seek him
with the whole heart.

*GOD'S INSTRUCTIONS
Deuteronomy 11:16 Take heed to yourselves, that **your heart be
not deceived, and ye turn aside, and serve other gods, and
worship them;**
Leviticus 26:2 Ye shall keep my sabbaths, and reverence my
sanctuary: I *am* the LORD.

THE LAW OF SABBATH GIVEN TO NATION OF ISRAEL
Exodus 31:13 Speak thou also unto the children of Israel, saying,
Verily my sabbaths ye shall keep: for it *is* a sign between me and
you throughout your generations; that *ye* may know that I *am* the
LORD that doth sanctify you.
Exodus 31:16 Wherefore the children of Israel shall keep the
sabbath, to observe the sabbath throughout their generations, *for* a
perpetual covenant.
Deuteronomy 5:15 And remember that thou wast a servant in the
land of Egypt, and *that* the LORD thy God brought thee out
thence through a mighty hand and by a stretched out arm:
therefore the LORD thy God commanded thee to keep the sabbath
day.
Leviticus 24:8 Every sabbath he shall set it in order before the
LORD continually, *being taken* from the children of Israel by an
everlasting covenant.

DAYS OF SABBATH HOLY CONVOCATION

Leviticus 23:24 Speak unto the children of Israel, saying, In **the seventh month, in the first** *day* **of the month**, shall ye have a sabbath, **a memorial of blowing of trumpets, an holy convocation.**

Leviticus 23:32 It *shall be* unto you a sabbath of rest, and ye shall afflict your souls: **in the ninth** *day* **of the month at even, from even unto even**, shall ye celebrate your sabbath.

Leviticus 23:39 **Also in the fifteenth day of the seventh month,** when ye have gathered in the fruit of the land, ye shall keep a feast unto the LORD seven days: on the first day *shall be* a sabbath, and on the eighth day *shall be* a sabbath.

Leviticus 25:4 But **in the seventh year shall be a sabbath of rest unto the land**, a sabbath for the LORD: thou shalt neither sow thy field, nor prune thy vineyard.

Leviticus 25:8 And **thou shalt number seven sabbaths of years unto thee, seven times seven years; and the space of the seven sabbaths of years shall be unto thee forty and nine years**.

9 Then **shalt thou cause the trumpet of the jubile to sound on the tenth** *day* **of the seventh month, in the day of atonement shall ye make the trumpet sound throughout all your land.**

IMPLEMENTING THE LAW OF SABBATH

Exodus 20:11 For *in* six days the LORD made heaven and earth, the sea, and all that in them *is*, and rested the seventh day: wherefore the LORD blessed the sabbath day, and hallowed it.

1. KEEP IT HOLY

Exodus 20:8 Remember the sabbath day, to keep it holy.

Leviticus 19:30 Ye shall keep my sabbaths, and reverence my sanctuary: I *am* the LORD.

Leviticus 26:2 Ye shall keep my sabbaths, and reverence my sanctuary: I *am* the LORD.

2. NO WORK FOR EVERYBODY

Exodus 20:10 But the seventh day *is* the sabbath of the LORD thy God: *in it* thou shalt not do any work, thou, nor thy son, nor thy daughter, thy manservant, nor thy maidservant, nor thy cattle, nor thy stranger that *is* within thy gates:

Leviticus 23:3 Six days shall work be done: but the seventh day *is* the sabbath of rest, an holy convocation; ye shall do no work *therein*: it *is* the sabbath of the LORD in all your dwellings.

Deuteronomy 5:14 But the seventh day *is* the sabbath of the LORD thy God: *in it* thou shalt not do any work, thou, nor thy son, nor thy daughter, nor thy manservant, nor thy maidservant, nor thine ox, nor thine ass, nor any of thy cattle, nor thy stranger that *is* within thy gates; that thy manservant and thy maidservant may rest as well as thou.

3. BAKE FOOD BEFORE THE DAY OF SABBATH
Exodus 16:23 And he said unto them, This *is that* which the LORD hath said, To morrow *is* the rest of the holy sabbath unto the LORD: bake *that* which ye will bake *to day*, and seethe that ye will seethe; and that which remaineth over lay up for you to be kept until the morning.

4. NO MAN GO OUT OF HIS PLACE ON SABBATH
Exodus 16:29 See, for that the LORD hath given you the sabbath, therefore he giveth you on the sixth day the bread of two days; abide ye every man in his place, let no man go out of his place on the seventh day.

5. NO KINDLING OF FIRE IN THE DAY OF SABBATH
Exodus 35:3 Ye shall kindle no fire throughout your habitations upon the sabbath day.

6. OBSERVE SABBATH IN THE PROMISE LAND
Leviticus 25:2 **Speak unto the children of Israel, and say unto them, When ye come into the land which I give you, then shall the land keep a sabbath unto the LORD.**
Leviticus 25:6 And the sabbath of the land shall be meat for you; for thee, and for thy servant, and for thy maid, and for thy hired servant, and for thy stranger that sojourneth with thee,

7. THE EAST GATE OF THE INNER COURT WILL BE OPENED ON SABBATH
Ezekiel 46:1 Thus saith the Lord GOD; The gate of the inner court that looketh toward the east shall be shut the six working days; but on the sabbath it shall be opened, and in the day of the new moon it shall be opened.

3 Likewise the people of the land shall worship at the door of this gate before the LORD in the sabbaths and in the new moons.

8.THE PRINCE PART TO GIVE THE BURNT OFFERINGS DURING SABBATH

Ezekiel 45:17 And it shall be the prince's part *to give* burnt offerings, and meat offerings, and drink offerings, in the feasts, and in the new moons, and in the sabbaths, in all solemnities of the house of Israel: **he shall prepare the sin offering, and the meat offering, and the burnt offering, and the peace offerings, to make reconciliation for the house of Israel.**

Ezekiel 46:4 And the burnt offering that **the prince shall offer unto the LORD in the sabbath day** *shall be* **six lambs without blemish, and a ram without blemish.**

Ezekiel 46:12 Now when **the prince shall prepare a voluntary burnt offering or peace offerings** voluntarily unto the LORD, *one* shall then open him the gate that looketh toward the east, and he shall prepare his burnt offering and his peace offerings, as he did on the sabbath day: then he shall go forth; and after his going forth *one* shall shut the gate.

GOD WILL BLESS THOSE WHO KEEP THE SABBATH

Isaiah 56:1 Thus saith the LORD, Keep ye judgment, and do justice: for my salvation *is* near to come, and my righteousness to be revealed.

2 Blessed *is* the   man *that* doeth   this,   and   the   son   of man *that* layeth hold on it; that keepeth the sabbath from polluting it, and keepeth his hand from doing any evil.

3 Neither let the son of the stranger, that hath joined himself to the LORD, speak, saying, The LORD hath utterly separated me from his people: neither let the eunuch say, Behold, I *am* a dry tree.

4 For thus saith the LORD unto the eunuchs that keep my sabbaths, and choose *the things* that please me, and take hold of my covenant;

5 **Even unto them will I give in mine house and within my walls a place and a name better than of sons and of daughters: I will give them an everlasting name, that shall not be cut off.**

6 Also the sons of the stranger, that join themselves to the LORD, to serve him, and to love the name of the LORD, to be

his servants, every one that keepeth the sabbath from polluting it, and taketh hold of my covenant;

7 **Even them will I bring to my holy mountain, and make them joyful in my house of prayer: their burnt offerings and their sacrifices *shall be* accepted upon mine altar; for mine house shall be called an house of prayer for all people**.

PUNISHMENT TO ISRAELITES WHO VIOLATES THE SABBATH

1. PUT TO DEATH

Exodus 31:14 Ye shall keep the sabbath therefore; for it *is* holy unto you: every one that defileth it shall surely be put to death: for whosoever doeth *any* work therein, that soul shall be cut off from among his people.

15 Six days may work be done; but in the seventh *is* the sabbath of rest, holy to the LORD: whosoever doeth *any* work in the sabbath day, he shall surely be put to death.

Exodus 35:**2 Six days shall work be done, but on the seventh day there shall be to you an holy day, a sabbath of rest to the LORD: whosoever doeth work therein shall be put to death.**

2. AFFLICT THE SOUL

Leviticus 16:31 It *shall be* a sabbath of rest unto you, and ye shall afflict your souls, by a statute for ever.

PART 4
THE FIRST AGREEMENT TO THE NATION OF ISRAEL

CHAPTER VI **OTHER LAWS FOR SANCTIFICATION**

*GOD'S INSTRUCTIONS:** ORDINANCES OF THE COMMANDMENTS
Read the book of Leviticus 20

A. DO NOT EAT BLOOD
Deuteronomy12:23 **Only be sure that thou eat not the blood: for the blood *is* the life**; and thou mayest not eat the life with the flesh.

24 Thou shalt not eat it; thou shalt pour it upon the earth as water.

25 Thou shalt not eat it; that it may go well with thee, and with thy children after thee, when thou shalt do *that which is* right in the sight of the LORD.

Leviticus 7:26 **Moreover ye shall eat no manner of blood, *whether it be* of fowl or of beast,** in any of your dwellings.

Leviticus 3:17 *It shall be* **a perpetual statute for your generations throughout all your dwellings, that ye eat neither fat nor blood.**

Leviticus 7:27 Whatsoever soul *it be* that eateth any manner of blood, even that soul shall be cut off from his people.

B. MEAT THAT CAN BE EATEN
Deuteronomy 14:4 These *are* the beasts which ye shall eat: the ox, the sheep, and the goat,

5 The hart, and the roebuck, and the fallow deer, and the wild goat, and the pygarg, and the wild ox, and the chamois.

6 And every beast that parteth the hoof, and cleaveth the cleft into two claws, *and* cheweth the cud among the beasts, that ye shall eat.

ANIMALS WHICH THE ISRAELITES NOT ALLOW TO EAT

Deuteronomy14:3 **Thou shalt not eat any abominable thing.**

7 Nevertheless these ye shall not eat of them that chew the cud, or of them that divide the cloven hoof; *as* the camel, and the hare, and the coney: for they chew the cud, but divide not the hoof; *therefore* they *are* unclean unto you.

8 And the swine, because it divideth the hoof, yet cheweth not the cud, it *is* unclean unto you: ye shall not eat of their flesh, nor touch their dead carcase.

9 These ye shall eat of all that *are* in the waters: all that have fins and scales shall ye eat:

10 And **whatsoever hath not fins and scales ye may not eat; it** *is* **unclean unto you**.

11 *Of* all clean birds ye shall eat.

12 But these *are they* of which ye shall not eat: the eagle, and the ossifrage, and the ospray,

13 And the glede, and the kite, and the vulture after his kind,

14 And every raven after his kind,

15 And the owl, and the night hawk, and the cuckow, and the hawk after his kind,

16 The little owl, and the great owl, and the swan,

17 And the pelican, and the gier eagle, and the cormorant,

18 And the stork, and the heron after her kind, and the lapwing, and the bat.

19 And every creeping thing that flieth *is* unclean unto you: they shall not be eaten.

20 *But of* all clean fowls ye may eat.

21 **Ye shall not eat** *of* **any thing that dieth of itself**: thou shalt give it unto the stranger that *is* in thy gates, that he may eat it; or thou mayest sell it unto an alien: for thou *art* an holy people unto the LORD thy God. Thou shalt not seethe a kid in his mother's milk.

C. LAW OF NAZARITE

Numbers 6:1 And the LORD spake unto Moses, saying,

2 Speak unto the children of Israel, and say unto them, When either man or woman shall separate *themselves* to vow a vow of a Nazarite, to separate *themselves* unto the LORD:

3 **He shall separate** *himself* **from wine and strong drink, and shall drink no vinegar of wine, or vinegar of strong drink,**

neither shall he drink any liquor of grapes, nor eat moist grapes, or dried.

4 All the days of his separation shall he eat nothing that is made of the vine tree, from the kernels even to the husk.

5 All the days of the vow of his separation **there shall no razor come upon his head**: until the days be fulfilled, in the which he separateth *himself* unto the LORD, he shall be holy, *and* shall let the locks of the hair of his head grow.

6 All the days that he separateth *himself* unto the LORD he shall come at no dead body.

7 He shall not make himself unclean for his father, or for his mother, for his brother, or for his sister, when they die: because the consecration of his God *is* upon his head.

8 All the days of his separation he *is* holy unto the LORD.

D. LAWS ABOUT THE GENTILES

Deuteronomy 23:3 **An Ammonite or Moabite shall not enter into the congregation of the LORD; even to their tenth generation** shall they not enter into the congregation of the LORD for ever:

4 **Because they met you not with bread and with water in the way, when ye came forth out of Egypt; and because they hired against thee Balaam the son of Beor of Pethor of Mesopotamia, to curse thee.**

7 **Thou shalt not abhor an Edomite; for he *is* thy brother: thou shalt not abhor an Egyptian; because thou wast a stranger in his land.**

8 The children that are begotten of them shall enter into the congregation of the LORD in their third generation.

E. MAKE THE CAMP OF THE CHOSEN HOLY

Deuteronomy 23:14 For the LORD thy God walketh in the midst of thy camp, to deliver thee, and to give up thine enemies before thee; therefore shall thy camp be holy: that he see no unclean thing in thee, and turn away from thee

15 Thou shalt not deliver unto his master the servant which is escaped from his master unto thee:

16 He shall dwell with thee, *even* among you, in that place which he shall choose in one of thy gates, where it liketh him best: thou shalt not oppress him.

17 There shall be no whore of the daughters of Israel, nor a sodomite of the sons of Israel.

18 Thou shalt not bring the hire of a whore, or the price of a dog, into the house of the LORD thy God for any vow: for even both these *are* abomination unto the LORD thy God.

Deuteronomy 23:1 He that is wounded in the stones, or hath his privy member cut off, shall not enter into the congregation of the LORD.

2 A bastard shall not enter into the congregation of the LORD; even to his tenth generation shall he not enter into the congregation of the LORD.

F. THE LAW OF MARRYING THE WIDOW

Deuteronomy 25:4 Thou shalt not muzzle the ox when he treadeth out *the corn*.

5 **If brethren dwell together, and one of them die, and have no child, the wife of the dead shall not marry without unto a stranger: her husband's brother shall go in unto her, and take her to him to wife, and perform the duty of an husband's brother unto her.**

6 **And it shall be, *that* the firstborn which she beareth shall succeed in the name of his brother *which is* dead, that his name be not put out of Israel**.

7 And if the man like not to take his brother's wife, then let his brother's wife go up to the gate unto the elders, and say, My husband's brother refuseth to raise up unto his brother a name in Israel, he will not perform the duty of my husband's brother.

8 Then the elders of his city shall call him, and speak unto him: and *if* he stand *to it*, and say, I like not to take her;

9 Then shall his brother's wife come unto him in the presence of the elders, and loose his shoe from off his foot, and spit in his face, and shall answer and say, So shall it be done unto that man that will not build up his brother's house.

10 And his name shall be called in Israel, The house of him that hath his shoe loosed.

11 When men strive together one with another, and the wife of the one draweth near for to deliver her husband out of the hand of him that smiteth him, and putteth forth her hand, and taketh him by the secrets:

12 Then thou shalt cut off her hand, thine eye shall not pity *her*.

G. NOT ALLOWED TO CUT HAIR FOR THE DEAD

Deuteronomy 14:1 Ye are the children of God; ye shall not cut yourselves, nor make any baldness between your eyes for the dead.

H. LAW OF PUNISHMENT FOR THE WICKED

Deuteronomy 25:1 If there be a controversy between men, and they come unto judgment, that *the judges* may judge them; then they shall justify the righteous, and condemn the wicked.

2 And it shall be, if the wicked man *be* worthy to be beaten, that the judge shall cause him to lie down, and to be beaten before his face, according to his fault, by a certain number.

3 Forty stripes he may give him, *and* not exceed: lest, *if* he should exceed, and beat him above these with many stripes, then thy brother should seem vile unto thee.

I. DIVORCE

Leviticus 22:13 But if the priest's daughter be a widow, or divorced, and have no child, and is returned unto her father's house, as in her youth, she shall eat of her father's meat: but there shall no stranger eat thereof.

Deuteronomy 24:1When a man hath taken a wife, and married her, and it come to pass that she find no favour in his eyes, because he hath found some uncleanness in her: then let him write her a bill of divorcement, and give *it* in her hand, and send her out of his house.

2 And when she is departed out of his house, she may go and be another man's *wife*.

3 And *if* the latter husband hate her, and write her a bill of divorcement, and giveth *it* in her hand, and sendeth her out of his house; or if the latter husband die, which took her *to be* his wife;

4 Her former husband, which sent her away, may not take her again to be his wife, after that she is defiled; for that *is* abomination before the LORD: and thou shalt not cause the land to sin, which the LORD thy God giveth thee *for* an inheritance.

5 When a man hath taken a new wife, he shall not go out to war, neither shall he be charged with any business: *but* he shall be free at home one year, and shall cheer up his wife which he hath taken.

PART 4
THE FIRST AGREEMENT TO THE NATION OF ISRAEL

CHAPTER VII **GOD'S ECONOMY**

*GOD'S INSTRUCTIONS:

A. TAKING CARE OF ANIMALS
Leviticus 19:19 Ye shall keep my statutes. Thou shalt not let thy cattle gender with a diverse kind: thou shalt not sow thy field with mingled seed: neither shall a garment mingled of linen and woollen come upon thee.

B THE LEND UPON USURY
Deuteronomy 23:19 **Thou shalt not lend upon usury to thy brother; usury of money**, usury of victuals, usury of any thing that is lent upon usury:

20 **Unto a stranger thou mayest lend upon usury**; but unto thy brother thou shalt not lend upon usury: that the LORD thy God may bless thee in all that thou settest thine hand to in the land whither thou goest to possess it.

21 **When thou shalt vow a vow unto the LORD thy God, thou shalt not slack to pay it:** for the LORD thy God will surely require it of thee; and it would be sin in thee.

22 But if thou shalt forbear to vow, it shall be no sin in thee.

23 **That which is gone out of thy lips thou shalt keep and perform**; *even* a freewill offering, according as thou hast vowed unto the LORD thy God, which thou hast promised with thy mouth.

Leviticus 25:36 Take thou no usury of him, or increase: but fear thy God; that thy brother may live with thee.

37 Thou shalt not give him thy money upon usury, nor lend him thy victuals for increase.

C. RULES ABOUT GATHERING THE NEIGHBORS CROPS

Deuteronomy 23:24 When thou comest into thy neighbour's vineyard, then thou mayest eat grapes thy fill at thine own pleasure**; but thou shalt not put *any* in thy vessel.**

25 When thou comest into the standing corn of thy neighbour, then thou mayest pluck the ears with thine hand; **but thou shalt not move a sickle unto thy neighbour's standing corn.**

D. THE SEVENTH YEAR THE YEAR OF RELEASE

Deuteronomy 15:10 *Thou shalt surely give him, and thine heart shall not be grieved when thou givest unto him: because that for this thing the LORD thy God shall bless thee in all thy works, and in all that thou puttest thine hand unto.*

Deuteronomy 15:15 And thou shalt remember that thou wast a bondman in the land of Egypt, and the LORD thy God redeemed thee: therefore I command thee this thing to day.

Deuteronomy 15:4 **Save when there shall be no poor among you**; for the LORD shall greatly bless thee in the land which the LORD thy God giveth thee *for* an inheritance to possess it:

Deuteronomy 15:1 **At the end of *every* seven years thou shalt make a release.**

2 And this *is* the manner of the release: **Every creditor that lendeth *ought* unto his neighbour shall release *it*; he shall not exact *it* of his neighbour, or of his brother; because it is called the LORD'S release.**

3 Of a foreigner thou mayest exact *it again*: but *that* which is thine with thy brother thine hand shall release;

Deuteronomy 15:9 **Beware that there be not a wicked thought in thy heart, saying, The seventh year, the year of release, is at hand, and thine eye be evil against thy poor brother**, and thou givest him nought; and he cry unto the LORD against thee, and it be sin against thee.

10 Thou shalt surely give him, and thine heart shall not be grieved when thou givest unto him: because that for this thing the LORD thy God shall bless thee in all thy works, and in all that thou puttest thine hand unto.

11 For the poor shall never cease out of the land: therefore I command thee, saying, Thou shalt open thine hand wide unto thy brother, to thy poor, and to thy needy, in thy land.

12 *And* if thy brother, an Hebrew man, or an Hebrew woman, be sold unto thee, and serve thee six years; then in the seventh year thou shalt let him go free from thee.

13 And when thou sendest him out free from thee, thou shalt not let him go away empty:

14 Thou shalt furnish him liberally out of thy flock, and out of thy floor, and out of thy winepress: *of that* wherewith the LORD thy God hath blessed thee thou shalt give unto him.

E. THE SEVENTH YEAR, THE SABBATH OF REST

Leviticus 25:1 **And the LORD spake unto Moses in mount Sinai, saying,**

2 Speak unto the children of Israel, and say unto them, When ye come into the land which I give you, then shall the land keep a sabbath unto the LORD.

3 Six years thou shalt sow thy field, and six years thou shalt prune thy vineyard, and gather in the fruit thereof;

4 **But in the seventh year shall be a sabbath of rest unto the land, a sabbath for the LORD: thou shalt neither sow thy field, nor prune thy vineyard**.

5 That which groweth of its own accord of thy harvest thou shalt not reap, neither gather the grapes of thy vine undressed: *for* it is a year of rest unto the land.

6 And the sabbath of the land shall be meat for you; for thee, and for thy servant, and for thy maid, and for thy hired servant, and for thy stranger that sojourneth with thee,

7 And for thy cattle, and for the beast that *are* in thy land, shall all the increase thereof be meat.

BLESSINGS COMES IN THE SIXTH YEAR

Leviticus 25:20 And if ye shall say, What shall we eat the seventh year? behold, we shall not sow, nor gather in our increase:

21 **Then I will command my blessing upon you in the sixth year, and it shall bring forth fruit for three years.**

22 And ye shall sow the eighth year, and eat *yet* of old fruit until the ninth year; until her fruits come in ye shall eat *of* the old *store*.

F. YEAR OF JUBILE

Leviticus 25:17 **Ye shall not therefore oppress one another; but thou shalt fear thy God: for I *am* the LORD your God.**

Leviticus 25:23 **The land shall not be sold for ever**: for the land *is* mine; for ye *are* strangers and sojourners with me.

Leviticus 25: **8 And thou shalt number seven sabbaths of years unto thee, seven times seven years; and the space of the seven sabbaths of years shall be unto thee forty and nine years.**

9 Then shalt thou cause the trumpet of the jubile to sound on the tenth *day* of the seventh month, in the day of atonement shall ye make the trumpet sound throughout all your land.

10 And **ye shall hallow the fiftieth year, and proclaim liberty throughout *all* the land unto all the inhabitants thereof: it shall be a jubile unto you; and ye shall return every man unto his possession, and ye shall return every man unto his family.**

11 A jubile shall that fiftieth year be unto you: ye shall not sow, neither reap that which groweth of itself in it, nor gather *the grapes* in it of thy vine undressed.

12 For it *is* the jubile; it shall be holy unto you: ye shall eat the increase thereof out of the field.

13 In the year of this jubile ye shall return every man unto his possession.

14 And if thou sell ought unto thy neighbour, or buyest *ought* of thy neighbour's hand, ye shall not oppress one another:

15 According to the number of years after the jubile thou shalt buy of thy neighbour, *and* according unto the number of years of the fruits he shall sell unto thee:

16 According to the multitude of years thou shalt increase the price thereof, and according to the fewness of years thou shalt diminish the price of it: for *according* to the number *of the years* of the fruits doth he sell unto thee.

REDEMPTION OF THE POSSESSION

Leviticus 25:24 And in all the land of your possession ye shall grant a redemption for the land.

25 **If thy brother be waxen poor, and hath sold away *some* of his possession, and if any of his kin come to redeem it, then shall he redeem that which his brother sold.**

26 And **if the man have none to redeem it, and himself be able to redeem it;**

27 Then let him count the years of the sale thereof, and restore the overplus unto the man to whom he sold it; that he may return unto his possession.

28 But if he be not able to restore *it* to him, then that which is sold shall remain in the hand of him that hath bought it until the year of jubile: and in the jubile it shall go out, and he shall return unto his possession.

29 And **if a man sell a dwelling house in a walled city, then he may redeem it within a whole year after it is sold; *within* a full year may he redeem it.**

30 And **if it be not redeemed within the space of a full year, then the house that *is* in the walled city shall be established for ever to him that bought it throughout his generations: it shall not go out in the jubile**.

31 But the houses of the villages which have no wall round about them shall be counted as the fields of the country: they may be redeemed, and they shall go out in the jubile.

32 Notwithstanding the cities of the Levites, *and* the houses of the cities of their possession, may the Levites redeem at any time.

33 And if a man purchase of the Levites, then the house that was sold, and the city of his possession, shall go out in *the year of* jubile: for the houses of the cities of the Levites *are* their possession among the children of Israel.

34 But the field of the suburbs of their cities may not be sold; for it *is* their perpetual possession.

35 And if thy brother be waxen poor, and fallen in decay with thee; then thou shalt relieve him: *yea, though he be* a stranger, or a sojourner; that he may live with thee.

38 I *am* the LORD your God, which brought you forth out of the land of Egypt, to give you the land of Canaan, *and* to be your God.

NEVER FORCE THE POOR BROTHER TO BECOME YOUR SLAVE

Leviticus 25:55 **For unto me the children of Israel *are* servants; they *are* my servants whom I brought forth out of the land of Egypt: I *am* the LORD your God**.

Leviticus 25:39 And if thy brother *that dwelleth* by thee be waxen poor, and be sold unto thee; thou shalt not compel him to serve as a bondservant:

40 *But* as an hired servant, *and* as a sojourner, he shall be with thee, *and* shall serve thee unto the year of jubile:

41 And *then* shall he depart from thee, *both* he and his children with him, and shall return unto his own family, and unto the possession of his fathers shall he return.

42 For they *are* my servants, which I brought forth out of the land of Egypt: they shall not be sold as bondmen.

43 Thou shalt not rule over him with rigour; but shalt fear thy God.

44 Both thy bondmen, and thy bondmaids, which thou shalt have, *shall be* of the heathen that are round about you; of them shall ye buy bondmen and bondmaids.

REDEEMING CHILDREN OF THE STRANGERS

Leviticus 25:45 Moreover of the children of the strangers that do sojourn among you, of them shall ye buy, and of their families that *are* with you, which they begat in your land: and they shall be your possession.

46 And ye shall take them as an inheritance for your children after you, to inherit *them for* a possession; they shall be your bondmen for ever: but over your brethren the children of Israel, ye shall not rule one over another with rigour.

47 And if a sojourner or stranger wax rich by thee, and thy brother *that dwelleth* by him wax poor, and sell himself unto the stranger *or* sojourner by thee, or to the stock of the stranger's family:

48 After that he is sold he may be redeemed again; one of his brethren may redeem him:

49 Either his uncle, or his uncle's son, may redeem him, or *any* that is nigh of kin unto him of his family may redeem him; or if he be able, he may redeem himself.

50 And he shall reckon with him that bought him from the year that he was sold to him unto the year of jubile: and the price of his sale shall be according unto the number of years, according to the time of an hired servant shall it be with him.

51 If *there be* yet many years *behind*, according unto them he shall give again the price of his redemption out of the money that he was bought for.

52 And if there remain but few years unto the year of jubile, then he shall count with him, *and* according unto his years shall he give him again the price of his redemption.

53 *And* as a yearly hired servant shall he be with him: *and the other* shall not rule with rigour over him in thy sight.

54 **And if he be not redeemed in these *years*, then he shall go out in the year of jubile, *both* he, and his children with him.**

MOSES WROTE THE WORDS AND LAW OF THE COVENANT

Exodus 34:27 And the LORD said unto Moses, Write thou these words: for after the tenor of these words I have made a covenant with thee and with Israel.

28 And he was there with the LORD forty days and forty nights; he did neither eat bread, nor drink water. And he wrote upon the tables the words of the covenant, the ten commandments.

29 And it came to pass, when Moses came down from mount Sinai with the two tables of testimony in Moses' hand, when he came down from the mount, that Moses wist not that the skin of his face shone while he talked with him.

31 And Moses called unto them; and Aaron and all the rulers of the congregation returned unto him: and Moses talked with them.

32 And afterward all the children of Israel came nigh: and he gave them in commandment all that the LORD had spoken with him in mount Sinai.

33 And *till* Moses had done speaking with them, he put a vail on his face.

34 But when Moses went in before the LORD to speak with him, he took the vail off, until he came out. And he came out, and spake unto the children of Israel *that* which he was commanded.

35 And the children of Israel saw the face of Moses, that the skin of Moses' face shone: and Moses put the vail upon his face again, until he went in to speak with him.

Deuteronomy 31:9 And Moses wrote this law and delivered it unto the priests the sons of Levi, which bare the ark of the covenant of the LORD, and unto all the elders of Israel.

10 And Moses commanded them, saying **at the end of every seven years, in the solemnity of the day of release, in the feast of tabernacles,**

11 When all the Israel is come to appear before the LORD thy God in the place which he shall choose, **thou shalt read this law before all Israel in their hearing.**

PART 5
TEST OF FAITH

CHAPTER I JOB'S SUFFERINGS

JOB'S LIFE BEFORE GOD CALLED HIM

Job 29:5 When the Almighty *was* yet with me, *when* my children *were* about me;

6 When I washed my steps with butter, and the rock poured me out rivers of oil;

7 When I went out to the gate through the city, *when* I prepared my seat in the street!

8 The young men saw me, and hid themselves: and the aged arose, *and* stood up.

9 The princes refrained talking, and laid *their* hand on their mouth.

10 The nobles held their peace, and their tongue cleaved to the roof of their mouth.

11 When the ear heard *me*, then it blessed me; and when the eye saw *me*, it gave witness to me:

12 Because I delivered the poor that cried, and the fatherless, and *him that had* none to help him.

GOD GAVE JOB WISDOM AND UNDERSTANDING

Proverbs 3:13 *Happy is **the man that findeth wisdom**, and **the man that getteth understanding.***

Job 29:4 As **I was in the days of my youth, when the secret of God was upon my tabernacle;**

Job 27:3 All the while my breath *is* in me, and the spirit of God *is* in my nostrils;

4 My lips shall not speak wickedness, nor my tongue utter deceit.

6 My righteousness I hold fast, and will not let it go: my heart shall not reproach *me* so long as I live.

Job 29:13The blessing of him that was ready to perish came upon me: and I caused the widow's heart to sing for joy.

14 I put on righteousness, and it clothed me: my judgment *was* as a robe and a diadem.

15 I was eyes to the blind, and feet *was* I to the lame.

16 I *was* a father to the poor: and the cause *which* I knew not I searched out.

Job 28:12 But where shall wisdom be found? and where *is* the place of understanding?

13 Man knoweth not the price thereof; neither is it found in the land of the living.

28 And unto man he said, Behold, **the fear of the Lord, that *is* wisdom; and to depart from evil *is* understanding.**

JOB WAS BLESSED WITH PROVISIONS AND CHILDREN

Job 1:1 There was a man in the land of Uz, whose name *was* Job; and that man was perfect and upright, and one that feared God, and eschewed evil.

2 And there were born unto him seven sons and three daughters.

3 His substance also was seven thousand sheep, and three thousand camels, and five hundred yoke of oxen, and five hundred she asses, and a very great household; so that this man was the greatest of all the men of the east.

SATAN BROUGHT TRAGEDIES TO JOB

(See the workings of Satan to Job Volume 2 Part 14 Chapter 1)

Job 1:13 And there was a day when his sons and his daughters *were* eating and drinking wine in their eldest brother's house:

14 And there came a messenger unto Job, and said, The oxen were plowing, and the asses feeding beside them:

15 And the Sabeans fell *upon them*, and took them away; yea, they have slain the servants with the edge of the sword; and I only am escaped alone to tell thee.

16 While he *was* yet speaking, there came also another, and said, The fire of God is fallen from heaven, and hath burned up the sheep, and the servants, and consumed them; and I only am escaped alone to tell thee.

17 While he *was* yet speaking, there came also another, and said, The Chaldeans made out three bands, and fell upon the camels, and have carried them away, yea, and slain the servants with the edge of the sword; and I only am escaped alone to tell thee.

18 While he *was* yet speaking, there came also another, and said, Thy sons and thy daughters *were* eating and drinking wine in their eldest brother's house:

19 And, behold, there came a great wind from the wilderness, and smote the four corners of the house, and it fell upon the young men, and they are dead; and I only am escaped alone to tell thee.

20 Then Job arose, and rent his mantle, and shaved his head, and fell down upon the ground, and worshipped,

21 And said, Naked came I out of my mother's womb, and naked shall I return thither: **the LORD gave, and the LORD hath taken away; blessed be the name of the LORD.**

22 **In all this Job sinned not**, nor charged God foolishly.

JOB GOT SICKNESS

Job 2:9 Then said his wife unto him, Dost thou still retain thine integrity? curse God, and die.

10 But he said unto her, Thou speakest as one of the foolish women speaketh. **What? shall we receive good at the hand of God, and shall we not receive evil? In all this did not Job sin with his lips.**

Job 30:17 My bones are pierced in me in the night season: and my sinews take no rest.

18 By the great force *of my disease* is my garment changed: it bindeth me about as the collar of my coat.

19 He hath cast me into the mire, and I am become like dust and ashes.

30 My skin is black upon me, and my bones are burned with heat.

THREE FRIENDS OF JOB CONDEMNED HIM

Job 2:11 Now when Job's three friends heard of all this evil that was come upon him, they came every one from his own place; **Eliphaz the Temanite**, and **Bildad the Shuhite, and Zophar the Naamathite:** for they had made an appointment together to come to mourn with him and to comfort him.

12 And when they lifted up their eyes afar off, and knew him not, they lifted up their voice, and wept; and they rent every one his mantle, and sprinkled dust upon their heads toward heaven.

13 So they sat down with him upon the ground seven days and seven nights, and none spake a word unto him: for they saw that *his* grief was very great.

Job 3:1 After this opened Job his mouth, and cursed his day.

25 **For the thing which I greatly feared is come upon me, and that which I was afraid of is come unto me.**

26 I was not in safety, neither had I rest, neither was I quiet, yet trouble came.

1. ELIPHAZ THE TEMANITE

Job 4:1 Then **Eliphaz, the Temanite** answered and said,

8 Even as I have seen, **they that plow iniquity, and sow wickedness, reap the same**.

9 By the blast of God they perish, and by the breath of his nostrils are they consumed.

2. BILDAD THE SHUHITE

Job 8:1 Then answered **Bildad the Shuhite,**

3 Doth God pervert judgment? or doth the Almighty pervert justice?

4 If thy children have sinned against him, and he have cast them away for their transgression;

13 **So *are* the paths of all that forget God; and the hypocrite's hope shall perish**:

20 Behold, God will not cast away a perfect *man*, neither will he help the evil doers:

22 They that hate thee shall be clothed with shame; and the dwelling place of the wicked shall come to nought.

3. ZOPHAR THE NAAMATHITE

Job 11:1 Then answered Zophar the Naamathite, and said,

2 Should not the multitude of words be answered? and should a man full of talk be justified?

3 Should thy lies make men hold their peace? and when thou mockest, shall no man make thee ashamed?

4 **For thou hast said, My doctrine *is* pure, and I am clean in thine eyes**.

5 But oh that God would speak, and open his lips against thee;

Job 11:11 For he knoweth vain men: he seeth wickedness also; will he not then consider *it*?

13 If thou prepare thine heart, and stretch out thine hands toward him;

14 If iniquity *be* in thine hand, put it far away, and let not wickedness dwell in thy tabernacles.

20 But the eyes of the wicked shall fail, and they shall not escape, and their hope *shall be as* the giving up of the ghost.

JOB'S OWN RIGHTEOUSNESS

Job 34:4 Let us choose to us judgment: let us know among ourselves what *is* good.

5 **For Job hath said, I am righteous**: and God hath taken away my judgment.

6 Should I lie against my right? my wound *is* incurable without transgression.

GOD'S WRATH AGAINST PERSON WITH A PROUD HEART

Job 40:10 Deck thyself now *with* majesty and excellency; and array thyself with glory and beauty.

11 **Cast abroad the rage of thy wrath: and behold every one** *that is* **proud, and abase him.**

12 **Look on every one** *that is* **proud,** *and* **bring him low; and tread down the wicked in their place**.

13 Hide them in the dust together; *and* bind their faces in secret.

14 **Then will I also confess unto thee that thine own right hand can save thee**

ELIHU WITNESSED THE EXCHANGED BETWEEN JOB AND HIS FRIENDS

Job 32:2 Then was kindled the wrath of Elihu the son of Barachel the Buzite, of the kindred of Ram: against Job was his wrath kindled, **because he justified himself rather than God.**

3 **Also against his three friends was his wrath kindled, because they had found no answer, and** *yet* **had condemned Job.**

JOB REPENTED

Job 42:1 Then Job answered the LORD, and said,

2 I know that thou canst do every *thing*, and *that* no thought can be withholden from thee.

3 Who *is* he that hideth counsel without knowledge? therefore have I uttered that I understood not; things too wonderful for me, which I knew not.

4 **Hear, I beseech thee, and I will speak: I will demand of thee, and declare thou unto me**.

5 I have heard of thee by the hearing of the ear: but **now mine eye seeth thee.**

6 **Wherefore I abhor *myself*, and repent in dust and ashes.**

THE LORD BLESSED JOB TWICE AS MUCH AS HE HAD BEFORE.

Job 42:7 And it was *so*, that after the LORD had spoken these words unto Job, the LORD said to Eliphaz the Temanite, My wrath is kindled against thee, and against thy two friends: for ye have not spoken of me *the thing that is* right, as my servant Job *hath*.

8 Therefore take unto you now seven bullocks and seven rams, and go to my servant Job, and offer up for yourselves a burnt offering; and my servant Job shall pray for you: for him will I accept: lest I deal with you *after your* folly, in that ye have not spoken of me *the thing which is* right, like my servant Job.

9 So Eliphaz the Temanite and Bildad the Shuhite *and* Zophar the Naamathite went, and did according as the LORD commanded them: the LORD also accepted Job.

10 And the LORD turned the captivity of Job, when he prayed for his friends: also the LORD gave Job twice as much as he had before.

11 Then came there unto him all his brethren, and all his sisters, and all they that had been of his acquaintance before, and did eat bread with him in his house: and they bemoaned him, and comforted him over all the evil that the LORD had brought upon him: every man also gave him a piece of money, and every one an earring of gold.

12 So the LORD blessed the latter end of Job more than his beginning: for he had fourteen thousand sheep, and six thousand camels, and a thousand yoke of oxen, and a thousand she asses.

13 He had also seven sons and three daughters.

14 And he called the name of the first, Jemima; and the name of the second, Kezia; and the name of the third, Kerenhappuch.

15 And in all the land were no women found *so* fair as the daughters of Job: and their father gave them inheritance among their brethren.

16 After this lived Job an hundred and forty years, and saw his sons, and his sons' sons, *even* four generations.

17 So Job died, *being* old and full of days.

ELIHU WROTE DOWN THE BOOK OF JOB

Job 32:15 They were amazed, they answered no more: they left off speaking.

16 **When** *I* **(Elihu) had waited**, (for they spake not, but stood still, and answered no more;)

17 I said, I **will answer also my part,** *I* **also shew mine opinion**.

Job 19:23 **Oh that my words were now written! oh that they were printed in a book.**

Job 31:35 Oh that one would hear me! behold, my desire *is, that* the Almighty would answer me, and *that* **mine adversary had written a book.**

36 Surely I would take it upon my shoulder, *and* bind it *as* a crown to me.

37 I would declare unto him the number of my steps; as a prince would I go near unto him.

PART 5
TEST OF FAITH

CHAPTER II **A BLESSING OR A CURSE**

Deuteronomy 30:19
*I call heaven and earth to record this day against you, **that I have set before you life and death, blessing and cursing: therefore choose life, that both thou and thy seed may live:***

OBEDIENCE TO ESTABLISH GOD'S COVENANT TO ISRAEL

Leviticus 25:18 *Wherefore ye shall do my statutes, and keep my judgments, and do them; and ye shall dwell in the land in safety.*

Leviticus 26:9 **For I will have respect unto you, and make you fruitful, and multiply you, and establish my covenant with you.**
11 And I will set my tabernacle among you: and my soul shall not abhor you.
12 And I will walk among you, and will be your God, and ye shall be my people.
13 I *am* the LORD your God, which brought you forth out of the land of Egypt, that ye should not be their bondmen; and I have broken the bands of your yoke, and made you go upright.
Deuteronomy 30:20 That thou mayest love the LORD thy God, *and* that thou mayest obey his voice, and that thou mayest cleave unto him: for he *is* thy life, and the length of thy days: that thou mayest dwell in the land which the LORD sware unto thy fathers, to Abraham, to Isaac, and to Jacob, to give them.
Isaiah 1:19 If ye be willing and obedient, ye shall eat the good of the land**:**
Deuteronomy   7:11   Thou   shalt   therefore   keep   the commandments, and the statutes, and the judgments, which I command thee this day, to do them.

12 Wherefore it shall come to pass, if ye hearken to these judgments, and keep, and do them, that the LORD thy God shall keep unto thee the covenant and the mercy which he sware unto thy fathers:

Deuteronomy 12:28 Observe and hear all these words which I command thee, that it may go well with thee, and with thy children after thee for ever, when thou doest *that which is* good and right in the sight of the LORD thy God.

1Kings 2:3 And **keep the charge of the LORD thy God, to walk in his ways, to keep his statutes, and his commandments, and his judgments, and his testimonies,** as it is written in the law of Moses, **that thou mayest prosper in all that thou doest, and whithersoever thou turnest thyself:**

*GOD'S INSTRUCTIONS UPON REACHING CANAAN

Deuteronomy 12:32 *What thing soever I command you, observe to do it: thou shalt not add thereto, nor diminish from it.*

Deuteronomy 14:2 **For thou *art* an holy people unto the LORD thy God, and the LORD hath chosen thee to be a peculiar people unto himself, above all the nations that *are* upon the earth.**

Deuteronomy 12:29 When the LORD thy God shall cut off the nations from before thee, whither thou goest to possess them, and thou succeedest them, and dwellest in their land;

30 **Take heed to thyself that thou be not snared by following them**, after that they be destroyed from before thee; **and that thou enquire not after their gods**, saying, How did these nations serve their gods? even so will I do likewise.

31 Thou shalt not do so unto the LORD thy God: for every abomination to the LORD, which he hateth, have they done unto their gods; for even their sons and their daughters they have burnt in the fire to their gods.

1. DESTROY THOSE SEVEN NATIONS

Deuteronomy 9:5 *Not for thy righteousness, or for the uprightness of thine heart, dost thou go to possess their land: **but for the wickedness of these nations the LORD thy God doth drive them out from before thee, and that he may perform the*** *word which the LORD sware unto thy fathers, Abraham, Isaac, and Jacob.*

Deuteronomy 7:1 When the LORD thy God shall bring thee into the land whither thou goest to possess it, and hath cast out many nations before thee, **the Hittites**, and the **Girgashite**s, and the **Amorites**, and the **Canaanites,** and the **Perizzites**, and the **Hivite**s, and the **Jebusites**, seven nations greater and mightier than thou;

2 And when the LORD thy God shall deliver them before thee; **thou shalt smite them, *and* utterly destroy them; thou shalt make no covenant with them, nor shew mercy unto them:**

Psalms 78:54 And he brought them to the border of his sanctuary, *even to* this mountain, *which* his right hand had purchased.

55 He cast out the heathen also before them, and divided them an inheritance by line, and made the tribes of Israel to dwell in their tents.

2. NEVER MARRY SONS AND DAUGHTERS OF OTHER NATIONS

Deuteronomy 7:3 Neither shalt thou make marriages with them: thy daughter thou shalt not give unto his son, nor his daughter shalt thou take unto thy son.

4 **For they will turn away thy son from following me, that they may serve other gods: so will the anger of the Lord be kindled against you, and destroy you suddenly**.

3. DON'T MAKE MOLTEN gods

Exodus 34:15 **Lest thou make a covenant with the inhabitants of the land, and they go a whoring after their gods, and do sacrifice unto their gods, and *one* call thee, and thou eat of his sacrifice;**

16 And thou take of their daughters unto thy sons, and their daughters go a whoring after their gods, and make thy sons go a whoring after their gods.

17 Thou shalt make thee no molten gods.

4. DON'T OFFER THE SON OR DAUGHTER AS SACRIFICE TO FALSE god

Deuteronomy 12:31 Thou shalt not do so unto the LORD thy God: for every abomination to the LORD, which he hateth, have they done unto their gods; for even **their sons and their daughters they have burnt in the fire to their gods.**

Deuteronomy 18:10 There shall not be found among **you** *any* *one* **that maketh his son or his daughter to pass through the fire,** *or* **that useth divination,** *or* **an observer of times, or an enchanter, or a witch,**

5. DON'T TALK TO THE SPIRIT OF THE DEAD AND TO CONSULT WIZARD

Deuteronomy 18:11 Or a charmer, or a consulter with familiar spirits, or a wizard, or a necromancer.

6. DESTROY THE IDOLS IN THE LAND

Exodus 34:11 Observe thou that which I command thee this day: behold, I drive out before thee the Amorite, and the Canaanite, and the Hittite, and the Perizzite, and the Hivite, and the Jebusite.

12 Take heed to thyself, lest thou make a covenant with the inhabitants of the land whither thou goest, lest it be for a snare in the midst of thee:

13 But ye shall destroy their altars, break their images, and cut down their groves:

Deuteronomy 12:1 These *are* the statutes and judgments, which ye shall observe to do in the land, which the LORD God of thy fathers giveth thee to possess it, all the days that ye live upon the earth.

2 Ye shall utterly destroy all the places, wherein the nations which ye shall possess served their gods, upon the high mountains, and upon the hills, and under every green tree:

3 And ye shall overthrow their altars, and break their pillars, and burn their groves with fire; and ye shall hew down the graven images of their gods, and destroy the names of them out of that place.

Deuteronomy 7:**5 But thus shall ye deal with them; ye shall destroy their altars, and break down their images, and cut down their groves, and burn their graven images with fire.**

2Kings 23:4 And the king commanded Hilkiah the high priest, and the priests of the second order, and the keepers of the door, to bring forth out of the temple of the LORD all the vessels that were made for Baal, and for the grove, and for all the host of heaven: and he burned them without Jerusalem in the fields of Kidron, and carried the ashes of them unto Bethel.

7. ISRAEL NOT ALLOWED TO ATTEND BURIAL OF THE OTHER NATIONS

Isaiah 14:20 Thou shalt not be joined with them in burial, because thou hast destroyed thy land, *and* slain thy people: the seed of evildoers shall never be renowned.

TWO CHOICES FOR THE CHOSEN

Deuteronomy11:26 Behold, I set before you this day a blessing and a curse;

27 A blessing, if ye obey the commandments of the LORD your God, which I command you this day:

28 And a curse, if ye will not obey the commandments of the LORD your God, but turn aside out of the way which I command you this day, to go after other gods, which ye have not known.

A. BLESSINGS TO ISRAEL UPON OBEDIENCE TO THE LAWS

Deuteronomy 28:2 *And **all these blessings shall come on thee, and overtake thee, if thou shalt hearken unto the voice of the LORD thy God**.*

1. PROSPERITY TO THE FAMILY OF ISRAEL

Deuteronomy 29:9 Keep therefore the words of these covenant, and do them, that ye may prosper in all that ye do.

Deuteronomy 7:13 **And he will love thee, and bless thee, and multiply thee: he will also bless the fruit of thy womb, and the fruit of thy land, thy corn, and thy wine, and thine oil, the increase of thy kine, and the flocks of thy sheep, in the land which he sware unto thy fathers to give thee.**

Deuteronomy 28:8 The LORD shall command the blessing upon thee in thy storehouses, and in all that thou settest thine hand unto; and he shall bless thee in the land which the LORD thy God giveth thee.

12 The LORD shall open unto thee his good treasure, the heaven to give the rain unto thy land in his season, and to bless all the

work of thine hand: and thou shalt lend unto many nations, and thou shalt not borrow.

Deuteronomy 28:5 Blessed shall be thy basket and thy store.

Leviticus 26:3 If ye walk in my statutes, and keep my commandments, and do them;

4 Then I will give you rain in due season, and the land shall yield her increase, and the trees of the field shall yield their fruit.

5 And your threshing shall reach unto the vintage, and the vintage shall reach unto the sowing time: and ye shall eat your bread to the full, and dwell in your land safely.

2. GOD WILL BLESS ISRAEL WITH GOOD HEALTH

Deuteronomy 7:14 Thou shalt be blessed above all people: there shall not be male or female barren among you, or among your cattle.

Deuteronomy 28:3 Blessed *shalt* thou *be* in the city, and blessed *shalt* thou *be* in the field.

4 Blessed *shall be* the fruit of thy body, and the fruit of thy ground, and the fruit of thy cattle, the increase of thy kine, and the flocks of thy sheep.

6 Blessed *shalt* thou *be* when thou comest in, and blessed *shalt* thou *be* when thou goest out.

3. NO ENEMY COULD HARM THEM

Deuteronomy 7:15 **And the LORD will take away from thee all sickness, and will put none of the evil diseases of Egypt, which thou knowest, upon thee; but will lay them upon all *them* that hate thee.**

Deuteronomy 28:7 The LORD shall cause thine enemies that rise up against thee to be smitten before thy face: they shall come out against thee one way, and flee before thee seven ways.

Exodus 23:22 But if thou shalt indeed obey his voice, and do all that I speak; then I will be an enemy unto thine enemies, and an adversary unto thine adversaries.

23 For mine Angel shall go before thee, and bring thee in unto the Amorites, and the Hittites, and the Perizzites, and the Canaanites, the Hivites, and the Jebusites: and I will cut them off.

Leviticus 26:6 And I will give peace in the land, and ye shall lie down, and none shall make *you* afraid: and I will rid evil beasts out of the land, neither shall the sword go through your land.

7 And ye shall chase your enemies, and they shall fall before you by the sword.

8 And five of you shall chase an hundred, and an hundred of you shall put ten thousand to flight: and your enemies shall fall before you by the sword.

FEAR NOT THE REPROACH OF MEN
Isaiah 51:7 Hearken unto me, ye that know righteousness, the people in whose heart *is* my law; fear ye not the reproach of men, neither be ye afraid of their revilings.

SALVATION WILL CONTINUE FOREVER
Isaiah 51:8 For the moth shall eat them up like a garment, and the worm shall eat them like wool: but my righteousness shall be for ever, and my salvation from generation to generation.

GOD IS IN CONTROL
Isaiah 51:13 **And forgettest the LORD thy maker**, that hath stretched forth the heavens, and laid the foundations of the earth; and hast feared continually every day because of the fury of the oppressor, as if he were ready to destroy? and where *is* the fury of the oppressor?

GOD WILL GIVE COMFORT
Isaiah 51:12 I, *even* I, *am* he that comforteth you: who *art* thou, that thou shouldest be afraid of a man *that* shall die, and of the son of man *which* shall be made *as* grass;

GOD WILL COVER THE CHOSEN
Psalms 105:7 He *is* the LORD our God: his judgments *are* in all the earth.

8 He hath remembered his covenant for ever, the word *which* he commanded to a thousand generations.

9 Which *covenant* he made with Abraham, and his oath unto Isaac;

10 And confirmed the same unto Jacob for a law, *and* to Israel *for* an everlasting covenant:

11 Saying, Unto thee will I give the land of Canaan, the lot of your inheritance:

12 When they were *but* a few men in number; yea, very few, and strangers in it.

13 When they went from one nation to another, from *one* kingdom to another people;

14 **He suffered no man to do them wrong: yea, he reproved kings for their sakes**;

15 *Saying*, **Touch not mine anointed, and do my prophets no harm.**

1Chronicles 16:16 *Even of the covenant* which he made with Abraham, and of his oath unto Isaac;

17 And hath confirmed the same to Jacob for a law, *and* to Israel *for* an everlasting covenant,

18 **Saying, Unto *thee will I give the land of Canaan, the lot of your inheritance;***

19 When ye were but few, even a few, and strangers in it.

20 And *when* they went from nation to nation, and from *one* kingdom to another people;

21 He suffered no man to do them wrong: yea, he reproved kings for their sakes,

22 *Saying*, **Touch not mine anointed, and do my prophets no harm.**

4. THE BLESSING OF LONG LIFE AND PEACE

Proverbs 3:1 My son, forget not my law; but let thine heart keep my commandments:

2 For length of days, and long life, and peace, shall they add to thee.

3 Let not mercy and truth forsake thee: bind them about thy neck; write them upon the table of thine heart:

4 So shalt thou find favour and good understanding in the sight of God and man.

5 Trust in the LORD with all thine heart; and lean not unto thine own understanding.

6 In all thy ways acknowledge him, and he shall direct thy paths.

7 Be not wise in thine own eyes: fear the LORD, and depart from evil.

LENGTHEN THE DAYS OF LIFE OF THE ELECT AND OFFSPRINGS

1Kings 3:14 And if thou wilt walk in my ways, to keep my statutes and my commandments, as thy father David did walk, then **I will lengthen thy days**.

Deuteronomy 4:40 Thou shalt keep therefore his statutes, and his commandments, which I command thee this day, that it may go well with thee, and with thy children after thee, and that thou mayest prolong *thy* days upon the earth, which the LORD thy God giveth thee, for ever.

Deuteronomy 6:2 That thou mightest fear the LORD thy God, to keep all his statutes and his commandments, which I command thee, thou, and thy son, and thy son's son, all the days of thy life; and that thy days may be prolonged.

3 Hear therefore, O Israel, and observe to do *it*; that it may be well with thee, and that ye may increase mightily, as the LORD God of thy fathers hath promised thee, in the land that floweth with milk and honey.

5. THE LORD WILL ESTABLISH ISRAEL AS A HOLY NATION

Deuteronomy 28:13 And **the LORD shall make thee the head, and not the tail**; and thou shalt be above only, and thou shalt not be beneath; if that thou hearken unto the commandments of the LORD thy God, which I command thee this day, to observe and to do *them*:

14 **And thou shalt not go aside from any of the words which I command thee this day, *to* the right hand, or *to* the left, to go after other gods to serve them.**

Deuteronomy 26:16 This day the LORD thy God hath commanded thee to do these statutes and judgments: thou shalt therefore keep and do them with all thine heart, and with all thy soul.

17 Thou hast avouched the LORD this day to be thy God, and to walk in his ways, and to keep his statutes, and his commandments, and his judgments, and to hearken unto his voice:

18 And the LORD hath avouched thee this day to be his peculiar people, as he hath promised thee, and that *thou* shouldest keep all his commandments;

19 And to make thee high above all nations which he hath made, in praise, and in name, and in honour; and that thou mayest be an holy people unto the LORD thy God, as he hath spoken.

Deuteronomy 28:1 And it shall come to pass, if thou shalt hearken diligently unto the voice of the LORD thy God, to observe *and* to do all his commandments which I command thee this day, that the LORD thy God will set thee on high above all nations of the earth:

Deuteronomy 28:9 **The LORD shall establish thee an holy people unto himself**, as he hath sworn unto thee, if thou shalt keep the commandments of the LORD thy God, and walk in his ways.

10 **And all people of the earth shall see that thou art called by the name of the LORD; and they shall be afraid of thee**.

GOD BLESSED ISRAEL

Number 6:22 And the LORD spake unto Moses, saying,

23 Speak unto Aaron and unto his sons, saying, On this wise ye shall bless the children of Israel, saying unto them,

24 The LORD bless thee, and keep thee:

25 The LORD make his face shine upon thee, and be gracious unto thee:

26 The LORD lift up his countenance upon thee, and give thee peace.

27 And they shall put my name upon the children of Israel; and I will bless them.

MOSES BLESSED ISRAEL BEFORE HIS DEATH

Deuteronomy 33:1 And **this** *is* **the blessing, wherewith Moses the man of God blessed the children of Israel before his death.**

2 And he said, **The LORD came from Sinai, and rose up from Seir unto them; he shined forth from mount Paran, and he came with ten thousands of saints: from his right hand** *went* **a fiery law for them.**

3 Yea, he loved the people; all his saints *are* in thy hand: and they sat down at thy feet; *every one* **shall receive of thy words.**

4 Moses commanded us a law, *even* the inheritance of the congregation of Jacob.

5 And he was king in Jeshurun, when the heads of the people *and* the tribes of Israel were gathered together.

6 Let **Reuben live, and not die; and let** *not* **his men be few.**

7 **And this** *is the blessing* **of Judah: and he said, Hear, LORD, the voice of Judah, and bring him unto his people: let his hands be sufficient for him; and be thou an help** *to him* **from his enemies.**

8 And **of Levi he said,** *Let* **thy Thummim and thy Urim** *be* **with thy holy one, whom thou didst prove at Massah,** *and with* **whom thou didst strive at the waters of Meribah**;

9 Who said unto his father and to his mother, I have not seen him; neither did he acknowledge his brethren, nor knew his own children: for they have observed thy word, and kept thy covenant.

10 They shall teach Jacob thy judgments, and Israel thy law: they shall put incense before thee, and whole burnt sacrifice upon thine altar.

11 Bless, LORD, his substance, and accept the work of his hands: smite through the loins of them that rise against him, and of them that hate him, that they rise not again.

12 *And* **of Benjamin he said, The beloved of the LORD shall dwell in safety by him;** *and the LORD* **shall cover him all the day long, and he shall dwell between his shoulders**.

13 And **of Joseph he said, Blessed of the LORD** *be* **his land, for the precious things of heaven, for the dew, and for the deep that coucheth beneath**,

14 **And for the precious fruits** *brought forth* **by the sun, and for the precious things put forth by the moon,**

15 **And for the chief things of the ancient mountains, and for the precious things of the lasting hills,**

16 And for the precious things of the earth and fulness thereof, and *for* the good will of him that dwelt in the bush: **let** *the blessing* **come upon the head of Joseph, and upon the top of the head of him** *that was* **separated from his brethren.**

17 **His glory** *is* *like* **the firstling of his bullock, and his horns** *are like* **the horns of unicorns: with them he shall push the people together to the ends of the earth: and they** *are* **the ten thousands of Ephraim, and they** *are* **the thousands of Manasseh**.

18 And of Zebulun he said, **Rejoice, Zebulun, in thy going out; and, Issachar, in thy tent**s.

19 **They shall call the people unto the mountain; there they shall offer sacrifices of righteousness: for they shall suck** *of* **the abundance of the seas, and** *of* **treasures hid in the sand.**

20 And of **Gad he said, Blessed** *be* **he that enlargeth Gad: he dwelleth as a lion, and teareth the arm with the crown of the head**.

21 And he provided the first part for himself, because there, *in* a portion of the lawgiver, *was he* seated; and he came with the heads of the people, he executed the justice of the LORD, and his judgments with Israel.

22 And of Dan he said, **Dan *is* a lion's whelp: he shall leap from Bashan**.

23 And of Naphtali he said, **O Naphtali, satisfied with favour, and full with the blessing of the LORD: possess thou the west and the south.**

24 And of Asher he said, ***Let* Asher *be* blessed with children; let him be acceptable to his brethren, and let him dip his foot in oil.**

25 Thy shoes *shall be* iron and brass; and as thy days, *so shall* thy strength *be*.

26 *There is* none like unto the God of Jeshurun, *who* rideth upon the heaven in thy help, and in his excellency on the sky.

27 **The eternal God *is thy* refuge, and underneath *are* the everlasting arms: and he shall thrust out the enemy from before thee; and shall say, Destroy *them*.**

28 Israel then shall dwell in safety alone: the fountain of Jacob *shall be* upon a land of corn and wine; also his heavens shall drop down dew.

29 **Happy *art* thou, O Israel: who *is* like unto thee, O people saved by the LORD, the shield of thy help, and who *is* the sword of thy excellency! and thine enemies shall be found liars unto thee; and thou shalt tread upon their high places**.

B. CURSES DUE TO DISOBEDIENCE

Exodus 34:7 Keeping mercy for thousands, forgiving iniquity and transgression and sin, and that will by no means clear *the guilty*; **visiting the iniquity of the fathers upon the children, and upon the children's children, unto the third and to the fourth *generation*.**

1. POVERTY AND PESTILENCE TO HERDS AND PLANTS

Deuteronomy 28:15 But it shall come to pass, **if thou wilt not hearken unto the voice of the LORD thy God, to observe to do all his commandments and his statutes which I command thee this day; that all these curses shall come upon thee, and overtake thee:**

16 Cursed *shalt* thou *be* in the city, and cursed *shalt* thou *be* in the field.

17 Cursed *shall be* thy basket and thy store.

18 Cursed *shall be* the fruit of thy body, and the fruit of thy land, the increase of thy kine, and the flocks of thy sheep.

19 Cursed *shalt* thou *be* when thou comest in, and cursed *shalt* thou *be* when thou goest out.

20 The LORD shall send upon thee cursing, vexation, and rebuke, in all that thou settest thine hand unto for to do, until thou be destroyed, and until thou perish quickly; because of the wickedness of thy doings, whereby thou hast forsaken me.

21 The LORD shall make the pestilence cleave unto thee, until he have consumed thee from off the land, whither thou goest to possess it.

2. ISRAEL WILL SUFFER FROM SICKNESS.

Deuteronomy 28:22 The LORD shall smite thee with a consumption, and with a fever, and with an inflammation, and with an extreme burning, and with the sword, and with blasting, and with mildew; and they shall pursue thee until thou perish.

23 And thy heaven that *is* over thy head shall be brass, and the earth that is under thee *shall be* iron.

24 The LORD shall make the rain of thy land powder and dust: from heaven shall it come down upon thee, until thou be destroyed.

25 The LORD shall cause thee to be smitten before thine enemies: thou shalt go out one way against them, and flee seven ways before them: and shalt be removed into all the kingdoms of the earth.

26 And thy carcase shall be meat unto all fowls of the air, and unto the beasts of the earth, and no man shall fray *them* away.

27 The LORD will smite thee with the botch of Egypt, and with the emerods, and with the scab, and with the itch, whereof thou canst not be healed.

28 The LORD shall smite thee with madness, and blindness, and astonishment of heart:

29 And thou shalt grope at noonday, as the blind gropeth in darkness, and thou shalt not prosper in thy ways: and thou shalt be only oppressed and spoiled evermore, and no man shall save *thee*.

30 Thou shalt betroth a wife, and another man shall lie with her: thou shalt build an house, and thou shalt not dwell therein: thou shalt plant a vineyard, and shalt not gather the grapes thereof.

3. THE ENEMIES WILL COME TO DESTROY ISRAEL

Deuteronomy 28:31 Thine ox *shall be* slain before thine eyes, and thou shalt not eat thereof: thine ass *shall be* violently taken away from before thy face, and shall not be restored to thee: thy sheep *shall be* given unto thine enemies, and thou shalt have none to rescue *them*.

32 Thy sons and thy daughters *shall be* given unto another people, and thine eyes shall look, and fail *with longing* for them all the day long: and *there shall be* no might in thine hand.

33 The fruit of thy land, and all thy labours, shall a nation which thou knowest not eat up; and thou shalt be only oppressed and crushed alway:

34 So that thou shalt be mad for the sight of thine eyes which thou shalt see.

35 The LORD shall smite thee in the knees, and in the legs, with a sore botch that cannot be healed, from the sole of thy foot unto the top of thy head.

36 The LORD shall bring thee, and thy king which thou shalt set over thee, unto a nation which neither thou nor thy fathers have known; and there shalt thou serve other gods, wood and stone.

37 And thou shalt become an astonishment, a proverb, and a byword, among all nations whither the LORD shall lead thee.

4. POVERTY WILL NEVER LEFT THEM

Deuteronomy 28:38 Thou shalt carry much seed out into the field, and shalt gather *but* little in; for the locust shall consume it.

39 Thou shalt plant vineyards, and dress *them*, but shalt neither drink *of* the wine, nor gather *the grapes*; for the worms shall eat them.

40 Thou shalt have olive trees throughout all thy coasts, but thou shalt not anoint *thyself* with the oil; for thine olive shall cast *his fruit*.

41 Thou shalt beget sons and daughters, but thou shalt not enjoy them; for they shall go into captivity.

42 All thy trees and fruit of thy land shall the locust consume.

43 The stranger that *is* within thee shall get up above thee very high; and thou shalt come down very low.

44 He shall lend to thee, and thou shalt not lend to him: he shall be the head, and thou shalt be the tail.

45 **Moreover all these curses shall come upon thee, and shall pursue thee, and overtake thee, till thou be destroyed; because thou hearkenedst not unto the voice of the LORD thy God, to keep his commandments and his statutes which he commanded thee:**

46 **And they shall be upon thee for a sign and for a wonder, and upon thy seed for ever.**

47 Because thou servedst not the LORD thy God with joyfulness, and with gladness of heart, for the abundance of all *things*;

48 Therefore shalt thou serve thine enemies which the LORD shall send against thee, in hunger, and in thirst, and in nakedness, and in want of all *things*: and he shall put a yoke of iron upon thy neck, until he have destroyed thee.

5. OTHER NATIONS WILL BRING THEM INTO CAPTIVITY

Deuteronomy 28:49**The LORD shall bring a nation against thee** from far, from the end of the earth, *as swift* as the eagle flieth; a nation whose tongue thou shalt not understand;

50 A nation of fierce countenance, which shall not regard the person of the old, nor shew favour to the young:

51 And he shall eat the fruit of thy cattle, and the fruit of thy land, until thou be destroyed: which *also* shall not leave thee *either* corn, wine, or oil, *or* the increase of thy kine, or flocks of thy sheep, until he have destroyed thee.

52 And he shall besiege thee in all thy gates, until thy high and fenced walls come down, wherein thou trustedst, throughout all thy land: and he shall besiege thee in all thy gates throughout all thy land, which the LORD thy God hath given thee.

53 And thou shalt eat the fruit of thine own body, the flesh of thy sons and of thy daughters, which the LORD thy God hath given thee, in the siege, and in the straitness, wherewith thine enemies shall distress thee:

54 *So that* the man *that is* tender among you, and very delicate, his eye shall be evil toward his brother, and toward the wife of his bosom, and toward the remnant of his children which he shall leave:

55 So that he will not give to any of them of the flesh of his children whom he shall eat: because he hath nothing left him in

the siege, and in the straitness, wherewith thine enemies shall distress thee in all thy gates.

56 The tender and delicate woman among you, which would not adventure to set the sole of her foot upon the ground for delicateness and tenderness, her eye shall be evil toward the husband of her bosom, and toward her son, and toward her daughter,

57 And toward her young one that cometh out from between her feet, and toward her children which she shall bear: for she shall eat them for want of all *things* secretly in the siege and straitness, wherewith thine enemy shall distress thee in thy gates.

6. ISRAEL WILL SUFFER PLAGUES FROM THE LORD

Deuteronomy 28:58 If thou wilt not observe to do all the words of this law that are written in this book, that thou mayest fear this glorious and fearful name, THE LORD THY GOD;

59 Then the LORD will make thy plagues wonderful, **and the plagues of thy seed,** *even* **great plagues, and of long continuance, and sore sicknesses, and of long continuance**.

60 Moreover he will bring upon thee all the diseases of Egypt, which thou wast afraid of; and they shall cleave unto thee.

61 Also every sickness, and every plague, which *is* not written in the book of this law, them will the LORD bring upon thee, until thou be destroyed.

62 And ye shall be left few in number, whereas ye were as the stars of heaven for multitude; because thou wouldest not obey the voice of the LORD thy God.

63 And it shall come to pass, *that* as the LORD rejoiced over you to do you good, and to multiply you; so the LORD will rejoice over you to destroy you, and to bring you to nought; and ye shall be plucked from off the land whither thou goest to possess it.

7. ISRAEL WILL LIVE WITH WORRIES AND A TREMBLING HEART

Deuteronomy 28:64 And the LORD shall scatter thee among all people, from the one end of the earth even unto the other; and there thou shalt serve other gods, which neither thou nor thy fathers have known, *even* wood and stone.

65 And among **these nations shalt thou find no ease, neither shall the sole of thy foot have rest: but the LORD shall give**

thee there a trembling heart, and failing of eyes, and sorrow of mind:

66 And thy life shall hang in doubt before thee; and thou shalt fear day and night, and shalt have none assurance of thy life:

67 In the morning thou shalt say, Would God it were even! and at even thou shalt say, Would God it were morning! for the fear of thine heart wherewith thou shalt fear, and for the sight of thine eyes which thou shalt see.

68 And the LORD shall bring thee into Egypt again with ships, by the way whereof I spake unto thee, Thou shalt see it no more again: and there ye shall be sold unto your enemies for bondmen and bondwomen, and no man shall buy *you*.

8. WRATH OF GOD WILL COME TO PEOPLE OF DISOBEDIENCE

2Chronicles 34:21 **Go, enquire of the LORD for me**, and for them that are left in Israel and in Judah, concerning the words of the book that is found: **for great *is* the wrath of the LORD that is poured out upon us, because our fathers have not kept the word of the LORD, to do after all that is written in this book.**

2Kings 22:13 Go ye, enquire of the LORD for me, and for the people, and for all Judah, concerning the words of this book that is found: **for great *is* the wrath of the LORD that is kindled against us, because our fathers have not hearkened unto the words of this book, to do according unto all that which is written concerning us.**

JUDGMENT TO ISRAEL UPON BREAKING THE COVENANT

Leviticus 26:15 And if ye shall despise my statutes, or if your soul abhor my judgments, so that ye will not do all my commandments, ***but* that ye break my covenant**:

1. WILL BREAK THE PRIDE OF THEIR POWER

Leviticus 26:16 I also will do this unto you; I will even appoint over you terror, consumption, and the burning ague, that shall consume the eyes, and cause sorrow of heart: and ye shall sow your seed in vain, for your enemies shall eat it.

17 And I will set my face against you, and ye shall be slain before your enemies: they that hate you shall reign over you; and ye shall flee when none pursueth you.

18 And if ye will not yet for all this hearken unto me, then I will punish you seven times more for your sins.

19 And **I will break the pride of your power**; and I will make your heaven as iron, and your earth as brass:

20 And your strength shall be spent in vain: for your land shall not yield her increase, neither shall the trees of the land yield their fruits.

21 And if ye walk contrary unto me, and will not hearken unto me; I will bring seven times more plagues upon you according to your sins.

22 I will also send wild beasts among you, which shall rob you of your children, and destroy your cattle, and make you few in number; and your *high* ways shall be desolate.

23 And if ye will not be reformed by me by these things, but will walk contrary unto me;

24 Then will I also walk contrary unto you, and will punish you yet seven times for your sins.

2. PESTILENCE WILL COME AND BE DELIVERED IN THE HAND OF THEIR ENEMIES

Leviticus 26:25 And I will bring a sword upon you, that shall avenge the quarrel of *my* covenant: and when ye are gathered together within your cities, I will send the pestilence among you; and ye shall be delivered into the hand of the enemy.

26 *And* when I have broken the staff of your bread, ten women shall bake your bread in one oven, and they shall deliver *you* your bread again by weight: and ye shall eat, and not be satisfied.

27 And if ye will not for all this hearken unto me, but walk contrary unto me;

28 Then I will walk contrary unto you also in fury; and I, even I, will chastise you seven times for your sins.

29 And ye shall eat the flesh of your sons, and the flesh of your daughters shall ye eat.

30 And I will destroy your high places, and cut down your images, and cast your carcases upon the carcases of your idols, and my soul shall abhor you.

31 And I will make your cities waste, and bring your sanctuaries unto desolation, and I will not smell the savour of your sweet odours.

32 And I will bring the land into desolation: and your enemies which dwell therein shall be astonished at it.

33 And I will scatter you among the heathen, and will draw out a sword after you: and your land shall be desolate, and your cities waste.

34 Then shall the land enjoy her sabbaths, as long as it lieth desolate, and ye *be* in your enemies' land; *even* then shall the land rest, and enjoy her sabbaths.

35 As long as it lieth desolate it shall rest; because it did not rest in your sabbaths, when ye dwelt upon it.

36 And upon them that are left *alive* of you I will send a faintness into their hearts in the lands of their enemies; and the sound of a shaken leaf shall chase them; and they shall flee, as fleeing from a sword; and they shall fall when none pursueth.

37 And they shall fall one upon another, as it were before a sword, when none pursueth: and ye shall have no power to stand before your enemies.

38 And ye shall perish among the heathen, and the land of your enemies shall eat you up.

39 And they that are left of you shall pine away in their iniquity in your enemies' lands; and also in the iniquities of their fathers shall they pine away with them.

40 If they shall confess their iniquity, and the iniquity of their fathers, with their trespass which they trespassed against me, and that also they have walked contrary unto me;

3. ISRAEL WILL BE BROUGHT TO THE LAND OF THEIR ENEMIES

Leviticus 26:41 And *that* I also have walked contrary unto them, and have brought them into the land of their enemies; if then their uncircumcised hearts be humbled, and they then accept of the punishment of their iniquity:

42 Then will I remember my covenant with Jacob, and also my covenant with Isaac, and also my covenant with Abraham will I remember; and I will remember the land.

43 The land also shall be left of them, and shall enjoy her sabbaths, while she lieth desolate without them: and they shall accept of the punishment of their iniquity: because, even **because they despised my judgments, and because their soul abhorred my statutes.**

44 And yet for all that, when they be in the land of their enemies, I will not cast them away, neither will I abhor them, to destroy them utterly, and **to break my covenant with them: for I *am* the LORD their God**.

45 But I will for their sakes remember the covenant of their ancestors, whom I brought forth out of the land of Egypt in the sight of the heathen, that I might be their God: I *am* the LORD.

46 **These *are* the statutes and judgments and laws, which the LORD made between him and the children of Israel in mount Sinai by the hand of Moses.**

THE ELECT BLESSED THE LORD

1Chronicles 29:10 *Wherefore David blessed the LORD before all the congregation: and David said, Blessed be thou, LORD God of Israel our father, for ever and ever.*

11 Thine, O LORD, is the greatness, and the power, and the glory, and the victory, and the majesty: for all that is in the heaven and in the earth is thine; thine is the kingdom, O LORD, and thou art exalted as head above all.

12 Both riches and honour come of thee, and thou reignest over all; and in thine hand is power and might; and in thine hand it is to make great, and to give strength unto all.

*13 **Now therefore, our God, we thank thee, and praise thy glorious name.***

Amen

==

PART 6
GOD ANOINTED DELIVERERS

CHAPTER I **TO PRESERVE GOD'S CHOSEN**

A. GOD WOULD NOT LIKE HIS PEOPLE TO PERISH

JONAH WAS SENT TO NINEVEH (GENTILES)

Jonah 3:1 And the word of the LORD came unto Jonah the second time, saying,

2 **Arise, go unto Nineveh, that great city, and preach unto it the preaching that I bid thee.**

3 So Jonah arose, and went unto Nineveh, according to the word of the LORD. Now Nineveh was an exceeding great city of three days' journey.

4 **And Jonah began to enter into the city a day's journey, and he cried, and said, Yet forty days, and Nineveh shall be overthrown**.

5 **So the people of Nineveh believed God, and proclaimed a fast, and put on sackcloth, from the greatest of them even to the least of them.**

6 For word came unto the king of Nineveh, and he arose from his throne, and he laid his robe from him, and covered *him* with sackcloth, and sat in ashes.

7 And he caused *it* to be proclaimed and published through Nineveh by the decree of the king and his nobles, saying, Let neither man nor beast, herd nor flock, taste any thing: let them not feed, nor drink water:

8 But let man and beast be covered with sackcloth, and cry mightily unto God: yea, let them turn every one from his evil way, and from the violence that *is* in their hands.

9 Who can tell *if* God will turn and repent, and turn away from his fierce anger, that we perish not?

GOD SHOWED HIS REASON TO JONAH

Jonah 3:10 And **God saw their works, that they turned from their evil way; and God repented of the evil, that he had said that he would do unto them; and he did** *it* **not.**

Jonah 4:1 But **it displeased Jonah exceedingly, and he was very angry**.

2 And he prayed unto the LORD, and said, I pray thee, O LORD, *was* not this my saying, when I was yet in my country? Therefore I fled before unto Tarshish: for I knew that thou *art* a gracious God, and merciful, slow to anger, and of great kindness, and repentest thee of the evil.

3 Therefore now, O LORD, take, I beseech thee, my life from me; for *it is* better for me to die than to live.

4 Then said **the LORD, Doest thou well to be angry**?

5 So Jonah went out of the city, and sat on the east side of the city, and there made him a booth, and sat under it in the shadow, till he might see what would become of the city.

6 And **the LORD God prepared a gourd, and made** *it* **to come up over Jonah, that it might be a shadow over his head, to deliver him from his grief. So Jonah was exceeding glad of the gourd**.

7 **But God prepared a worm when the morning rose the next day, and it smote the gourd that it withered**.

8 **And it came to pass, when the sun did arise, that God prepared a vehement east wind; and the sun beat upon the head of Jonah, that he fainted, and wished in himself to die, and said,** *It is* **better for me to die than to live.**

9 And **God said to Jonah, Doest thou well to be angry for the gourd? And he said, I do well to be angry,** *even* **unto death**.

10 **Then said the LORD, Thou hast had pity on the gourd, for the which thou hast not laboured, neither madest it grow; which came up in a night, and perished in a night:**

11 **And should not I spare Nineveh, that great city, wherein are more than sixscore thousand persons that cannot discern between their right hand and their left hand**; and *also* much cattle?

B. GOD'S ELECT WILL INHERIT THE LAND OF ISRAEL

Isaiah 65:9 **And I will bring forth a seed out of Jacob, and out of Judah** an inheritor of my mountains: **and mine elect shall inherit it,** and my servants shall dwell there.

C. GOD ANOINTED DELIVERERS OF ISRAEL

1. MOSES AGAINST AMALEK

Exodus 17:8 Then came Amalek, and fought with Israel in Rephidim.

9 And Moses said unto Joshua, Choose us out men, and go out, fight with Amalek: to morrow I will stand on the top of the hill with the rod of God in mine hand.

10 So Joshua did as Moses had said to him, and fought with Amalek: and Moses, Aaron, and Hur went up to the top of the hill.

11 And it came to pass, **when Moses held up his hand, that Israel prevailed: and when he let down his hand, Amalek prevailed**.

12 But Moses' hands *were* **heavy; and they took a stone, and put** *it* **under him, and he sat thereon; and Aaron and Hur stayed up his hands, the one on the one side, and the other on the other side; and his hands were steady until the going down of the sun.**

13 And Joshua discomfited Amalek and his people with the edge of the sword.

14 And **the LORD said unto Moses**, *Write this for a memorial in a book, and rehearse it in the ears of Joshua: for I will utterly put out the remembrance of Amalek from under heaven.*

15 And Moses built an altar, and called the name of it *Jehovahnissi:*

16 For he said, Because the LORD hath sworn *that* the LORD *will have* war with Amalek from generation to generation.

MOSES' VICTORIES AGAINST KINGS OF HESHBON AND OF BASHAN

Deuteronomy 29:2 And Moses called unto all Israel, and said unto them, Ye have seen all that the LORD did before your eyes in the land of Egypt unto Pharaoh, and unto all his servants, and unto all his land;

3 The great temptations which thine eyes have seen, the signs, and those great miracles:

4 Yet the LORD hath not given you an heart to perceive, and eyes to see, and ears to hear, unto this day.

5 And I have led you forty years in the wilderness: your clothes are not waxen old upon you, and thy shoe is not waxen old upon thy foot.

6 Ye have not eaten bread, neither have ye drunk wine or strong drink: that ye might know that I *am* the LORD your God.

7 And when ye came unto this place, Sihon the king of Heshbon, and Og the king of Bashan, came out against us unto battle, and we smote them:

8 And we took their land, and gave it for an inheritance unto the Reubenites, and to the Gadites, and to the half tribe of Manasseh.

MOSES LAID HAND ON JOSHUA TO TAKE CHARGE

Numbers 27:18 And **the LORD said unto Moses, Take thee Joshua the son of Nun, a man in whom** *is* **the spirit, and lay thine hand upon him;**

19 And set him before Eleazar the priest, and before all the congregation; and give him a charge in their sight

20 And thou shalt put *some* of thine honour upon him, that all the congregation of the children of Israel may be obedient.

21 And he shall stand before Eleazar the priest, who shall ask *counsel* for him after the judgment of Urim before the LORD: at his word shall they go out, and at his word they shall come in, *both* he, and all the children of Israel with him, even all the congregation.

22 And Moses did as the LORD commanded him: and he took Joshua, and set him before Eleazar the priest, and before all the congregation:

23 And **he laid his hands upon him, and gave him a charge, as the LORD commanded by the hand of Moses.**

Deuteronomy 3:28 **But charge Joshua, and encourage him, and strengthen him: for he shall go over before this people, and he shall cause them to inherit the land which thou shalt see.**

Deuteronomy 34:9 And **Joshua the son of Nun was full of the spirit of wisdom; for Moses had laid his hands upon him: and the children of Israel hearkened unto him, and did as the LORD commanded Moses**

2. JOSHUA, THE SON OF NUN

Joshua 1:5 *There shall not any man be able to stand before thee all the days of thy life: as I was with Moses, so I will be with thee: I will not fail thee, nor forsake thee.*

LED THE ISRAELITES INTO THE PROMISE LAND (CANAAN)

Joshua 1:1 Now after the death of Moses the servant of the Lord it came to pass, **that the LORD spake unto Joshua the son of Nun, Moses' minister, saying,**

2 **Moses my servant is dead; now therefore arise, go over this Jordan, thou, and all this people, unto the land which I do give to them,** *even* **to the children of Israel.**

3 Every place that the sole of your foot shall tread upon, that have I given unto you, as I said unto Moses.

4 From the wilderness and this Lebanon even unto the great river, the river Euphrates, all the land of the Hittites, and unto the great sea toward the going down of the sun, shall be your coast.

5 There shall not any man be able to stand before thee all the days of thy life: as I was with Moses, *so* I will be with thee: I will not fail thee, nor forsake thee.

6 Be strong and of a good courage: for unto this people shalt thou divide for an inheritance the land, which I sware unto their fathers to give them.

7 Only be thou strong and very courageous, that thou mayest observe to do according to all the law, which Moses my servant commanded thee: turn not from it *to* the right hand or *to* the left, that thou mayest prosper whithersoever thou goest.

8 This book of the law shall not depart out of thy mouth; but thou shalt meditate therein day and night, that thou mayest observe to do according to all that is written therein: for then thou shalt make thy way prosperous, and then thou shalt have good success.

9 Have not I commanded thee? Be strong and of a good courage; be not afraid, neither be thou dismayed: for the LORD thy God *is* with thee whithersoever thou goest.

GOD WAS WITH JOSHUA THE ELECT

a. JORDAN RIVER DRIED UP

Joshua 3:7 And the LORD said unto Joshua, This day will I begin to magnify thee in the sight of all Israel, that they may know that, as I was with Moses, *so* I will be with thee.

8 And thou shalt command the priests that bear the ark of the covenant, saying, When ye are come to the brink of the water of Jordan, ye shall stand still in Jordan.

9 And Joshua said unto the children of Israel, Come hither, and hear the words of the LORD your God.

10 And Joshua said, **Hereby ye shall know that the living God** *is* **among you, and** *that* **he will without fail drive out from before you the Canaanites, and the Hittites, and the Hivites, and the Perizzites, and the Girgashites, and the Amorites, and the Jebusites.**

11 **Behold, the ark of the covenant of the Lord of all the earth passeth over before you into Jordan.**

12 Now therefore take you twelve men out of the tribes of Israel, out of every tribe a man.

13 **And it shall come to pass, as soon as the soles of the feet of the priests that bear the ark of the LORD, the Lord of all the earth, shall rest in the waters of Jordan,** *that* **the waters of Jordan shall be cut off** *from* **the waters that come down from above; and they shall stand upon an heap.**

14 And it came to pass, when the people removed from their tents, to pass over Jordan, and the priests bearing the ark of the covenant before the people;

15 And as they that bare the ark were come unto Jordan, and the feet of the priests that bare the ark were dipped in the brim of the water, (for Jordan overfloweth all his banks all the time of harvest,)

16 **That the waters which came down from above stood** *and* **rose up upon an heap very far from the city Adam, that** *is* **beside Zaretan: and those that came down toward the sea of the plain,** *even* **the salt sea, failed,** *and* **were cut off: and the people passed over right against Jericho.**

17 **And the priests that bare the ark of the covenant of the LORD stood firm on dry ground in the midst of Jordan, and all the Israelites passed over on dry ground, until all the people were passed clean over Jordan.**

TWELVE STONES FOR THE MEMORIAL IN JORDAN

Joshua 4:1 And it came to pass, when all the people were clean passed over Jordan, that the LORD spake unto Joshua, saying,

2 Take you twelve men out of the people, out of every tribe a man,

3 And command ye them, saying, Take you hence out of the midst of Jordan, out of the place where the priests' feet stood firm,

twelve stones, and ye shall carry them over with you, and leave them in the lodging place, where ye shall lodge this night.

4 Then Joshua called the twelve men, whom he had prepared of the children of Israel, out of every tribe a man:

5 And Joshua said unto them, Pass over before the ark of the LORD your God into the midst of Jordan, and take ye up every man of you a stone upon his shoulder, according unto the number of the tribes of the children of Israel:

6 That this may be a sign among you, *that* when your children ask *their fathers* in time to come, saying, What *mean* ye by these stones?

7Then ye shall answer them, That the waters of Jordan were cut off before the ark of the covenant of the LORD; when it passed over Jordan, the waters of Jordan were cut off: and these stones shall be for a memorial unto the children of Israel for ever.

8 And the children of Israel did so as Joshua commanded, and took up twelve stones out of the midst of Jordan, as the LORD spake unto Joshua, according to the number of the tribes of the children of Israel, and carried them over with them unto the place where they lodged, and laid them down there.

9 And Joshua set up twelve stones in the midst of Jordan, in the place where the feet of the priests which bare the ark of the covenant stood: and they are there unto this day.

Joshua 4:20 And those twelve stones, which they took out of Jordan, did Joshua pitch in Gilgal.

b. GOD WAS WITH JOSHUA IN JERICHO

RAHAB HID THE MESSENGERS OF ISRAEL

Joshua 2:1 And Joshua the son of Nun sent out of Shittim two men to spy secretly, saying, Go view the land, even Jericho. And they went, and came into an harlot's house, named Rahab, and lodged there.

2 And it was told the king of Jericho, saying, Behold, there came men in hither to night of the children of Israel to search out the country.

3 And the king of Jericho sent unto Rahab, saying, Bring forth the men that are come to thee, which are entered into thine house: for they be come to search out all the country.

4 And the woman took the two men, and hid them, and said thus, There came men unto me, but I wist not whence they *were*:

5 And it came to pass *about the time* of shutting of the gate, when it was dark, that the men went out: whither the men went I wot not: pursue after them quickly; for ye shall overtake them.

6 But she had brought them up to the roof of the house, and hid them with the stalks of flax, which she had laid in order upon the roof.

7 And the men pursued after them the way to Jordan unto the fords: and as soon as they which pursued after them were gone out, they shut the gate.

8 And before they were laid down, she came up unto them upon the roof;

9 And **she said unto the men**, I know that the LORD hath given you the land, and that your terror is fallen upon us, and that all the inhabitants of the land faint because of you.

10 For we have heard how the LORD dried up the water of the Red sea for you, when ye came out of Egypt; and what ye did unto the two kings of the Amorites, that *were* on the other side Jordan, Sihon and Og, whom ye utterly destroyed.

11 And as soon as we had heard *these things*, our hearts did melt, neither did there remain any more courage in any man, because of you: for the LORD your God, he *is* God in heaven above, and in earth beneath.

12 *Now therefore, I pray you, swear unto me by the LORD, since I have shewed you kindness, that ye will also shew kindness unto my father's house, and give me a true token:*

13 ***And that ye will save alive my father, and my mother, and my brethren, and my sisters, and all that they have, and deliver our lives from death.***

14 And the men answered her, Our life for yours, if ye utter not this our business. And it shall be, when the LORD hath given us the land, that we will deal kindly and truly with thee.

15 Then she let them down by a cord through the window: for her house *was* upon the town wall, and she dwelt upon the wall.

16 And she said unto them, Get you to the mountain, lest the pursuers meet you; and hide yourselves there three days, until the pursuers be returned: and afterward may ye go your way.

17 And the men said unto her, We *will be* blameless of this thine oath which thou hast made us swear.

18 Behold, *when* we come into the land, thou shalt bind this line of scarlet thread in the window which thou didst let us down by:

and thou shalt bring thy father, and thy mother, and thy brethren, and all thy father's household, home unto thee.

19 And it shall be, *that* whosoever shall go out of the doors of thy house into the street, his blood *shall be* upon his head, and we *will be* guiltless: and whosoever shall be with thee in the house, his blood *shall be* on our head, if *any* hand be upon him.

20 And if thou utter this our business, then we will be quit of thine oath which thou hast made us to swear.

21 And she said, According unto your words, so *be* it. And she sent them away, and they departed: and she bound the scarlet line in the window.

22 And they went, and came unto the mountain, and abode there three days, until the pursuers were returned: and the pursuers sought *them* throughout all the way, but found *them* not.

23 So the two men returned, and descended from the mountain, and passed over, and came to Joshua the son of Nun, and told him all *things* that befell them:

24 And they said unto Joshua, Truly the LORD hath delivered into our hands all the land; for even all the inhabitants of the country do faint because of us.

RAHAB AND HER FAMILY WERE SPARED IN THE FALL OF JERICHO

Joshua 6:6 And Joshua the son of Nun called the priests, and said unto them, Take up the ark of the covenant, and let seven priests bear seven trumpets of rams' horns before the ark of the LORD.

7 And he said unto the people, Pass on, and compass the city, and let him that is armed pass on before the ark of the LORD.

8 And it came to pass, when Joshua had spoken unto the people, that the seven priests bearing the seven trumpets of rams' horns passed on before the LORD, and blew with the trumpets: and the ark of the covenant of the LORD followed them.

9 And the armed men went before the priests that blew with the trumpets, and the rereward came after the ark, *the priests* going on, and blowing with the trumpets.

10 And Joshua had commanded the people, saying, Ye shall not shout, nor make any noise with your voice, neither shall *any* word proceed out of your mouth, until the day I bid you shout; then shall ye shout.

Joshua 6:22 But Joshua had said unto the two men that had spied out the country, Go into the harlot's house, and bring out thence the woman, and all that she hath, as ye sware unto her.

23 And the young men that were spies went in, and brought out Rahab, and her father, and her mother, and her brethren, and all that she had; and they brought out all her kindred, and left them without the camp of Israel.

24 And they burnt the city with fire, and all that *was* therein: only the silver, and the gold, and the vessels of brass and of iron, they put into the treasury of the house of the LORD.

25 **And Joshua saved Rahab the harlot alive, and her father's household, and all that she had; and she dwelleth in Israel *even* unto this day; because she hid the messengers, which Joshua sent to spy out Jericho.**

26 And Joshua adjured *them* at that time, saying, Cursed *be* the man before the LORD, that riseth up and buildeth this city Jericho: he shall lay the foundation thereof in his firstborn, and in his youngest *son* shall he set up the gates of it.

27 So the LORD was with Joshua; and his fame was *noised* throughout all the country.

c. GOD FOUGHT FOR ISRAEL AGAINST FIVE KINGS

Joshua 10:5 Therefore the five kings of the Amorites, the king of Jerusalem, the king of Hebron, the king of Jarmuth, the king of Lachish, the king of Eglon, gathered themselves together, and went up, they and all their hosts, and encamped before Gibeon, and made war against it.

6 And the men of Gibeon sent unto Joshua to the camp to Gilgal, saying, Slack not thy hand from thy servants; come up to us quickly, and save us, and help us: for all the kings of the Amorites that dwell in the mountains are gathered together against us.

7 So Joshua ascended from Gilgal, he, and all the people of war with him, and all the mighty men of valour.

8 And the LORD said unto Joshua, Fear them not: for I have delivered them into thine hand; there shall not a man of them stand before thee.

9 Joshua therefore came unto them suddenly, *and* went up from Gilgal all night.

10 And the LORD discomfited them before Israel, and slew them with a great slaughter at Gibeon, and chased them along the way that goeth up to Bethhoron, and smote them to Azekah, and unto Makkedah.

11 And it came to pass, as they fled from before Israel, *and* were in the going down to Bethhoron, **that the LORD cast down great stones from heaven upon them unto Azekah, and they died**: *they were* more which died with hailstones than *they* whom the children of Israel slew with the sword.

12 Then spake Joshua to the LORD in the day when the LORD delivered up the Amorites before the children of Israel, and he said in the sight of Israel, *Sun, stand thou still upon Gibeon; and thou, Moon, in the valley of Ajalon.*

13 And the sun stood still, and the moon stayed, until the people had avenged themselves upon their enemies. *Is* not this written in the book of Jasher? **So the sun stood still in the midst of heaven, and hasted not to go down about a whole day.**

14 And there was no day like that before it or after it, that the LORD hearkened unto the voice of a man: for the LORD fought for Israel.

16 But these five kings fled, and hid themselves in a cave at Makkedah.

17 And it was told Joshua, saying, The five kings are found hid in a cave at Makkedah.

18 And Joshua said, Roll great stones upon the mouth of the cave, and set men by it for to keep them:

19 And stay ye not, *but* pursue after your enemies, and smite the hindmost of them; suffer them not to enter into their cities: for the LORD your God hath delivered them into your hand.

20 And it came to pass, when Joshua and the children of Israel had made an end of slaying them with a very great slaughter, till they were consumed, that the rest *which* remained of them entered into fenced cities.

22 Then said Joshua, Open the mouth of the cave, and bring out those five kings unto me out of the cave.

23 And they did so, and brought forth those five kings unto him out of the cave, the king of Jerusalem, the king of Hebron, the king of Jarmuth, the king of Lachish, *and* the king of Eglon.

24 And it came to pass, when they brought out those kings unto Joshua, that Joshua called for all the men of Israel, and said unto the captains of the men of war which went with him, Come near, put your feet upon the necks of these kings. And they came near, and put their feet upon the necks of them.

25 And Joshua said unto them, Fear not, nor be dismayed, be strong and of good courage: for thus shall the LORD do to all your enemies against whom ye fight.

26 And afterward Joshua smote them, and slew them, and hanged them on five trees: and they were hanging upon the trees until the evening.

27 And it came to pass at the time of the going down of the sun,*that* Joshua commanded, and they took them down off the trees, and cast them into the cave wherein they had been hid, and laid great stones in the cave's mouth, *which remain* until this very day.

28 And that day Joshua took Makkedah, and smote it with the edge of the sword, and the king thereof he utterly destroyed, them, and all the souls that *were* therein; he let none remain: and he did to the king of Makkedah as he did unto the king of Jericho.

29 Then Joshua passed from Makkedah, and all Israel with him, unto Libnah, and fought against Libnah:

39 And he took it, and the king thereof, and all the cities thereof; and they smote them with the edge of the sword, and utterly destroyed all the souls that *were* therein; he left none remaining: as he had done to Hebron, so he did to Debir, and to the king thereof; as he had done also to Libnah, and to her king.

40 So Joshua smote all the country of the hills, and of the south, and of the vale, and of the springs, and all their kings: he left none remaining, but utterly destroyed all that breathed, as the LORD God of Israel commanded.

41 And Joshua smote them from Kadeshbarnea even unto Gaza, and all the country of Goshen, even unto Gibeon.

42 And all these kings and their land did Joshua take at one time, because the LORD God of Israel fought for Israel.

D. ESTHER WAS DESTINED TO SAVE THE LIVES OF JEWS

Esther 2:5 *Now* in Shushan the palace **there was a certain Jew, whose name *was* Mordecai, the son of Jair, the son of Shimei, the son of Kish, a Benjamite;**

6 Who had been carried away from Jerusalem with the captivity which had been carried away with Jeconiah king of Judah, whom Nebuchadnezzar the king of Babylon had carried away.

7 And **he brought up Hadassah, that** *is*, **Esther, his uncle's daughter**: for she had neither father nor mother, and the maid *was* fair and beautiful; whom Mordecai, when her father and mother were dead, took for his own daughter.

Esther 2:15 Now when the turn of Esther, the daughter of Abihail the uncle of Mordecai, who had taken her for his daughter, was come to go in unto the king, she required nothing but what Hegai the king's chamberlain, the keeper of the women, appointed. And Esther obtained favour in the sight of all them that looked upon her.

16 So Esther was taken unto king Ahasuerus into his house royal in the tenth month, which *is* the month Tebeth, in the seventh year of his reign.

17 And **the king loved Esther above all the women, and she obtained grace and favour in his sight more than all the virgins; so that he set the royal crown upon her head, and made her queen** instead of Vashti.

THE KING ORDERED TO KILL ALL THE JEWS IN ONE DAY

Esther 3:13 And the letters were sent by posts into all the king's provinces, to destroy, to kill, and to cause to perish, all Jews, both young and old, little children and women, in one day, *even* upon the thirteenth *day* of the twelfth month, which is the month Adar, and *to take* the spoil of them for a prey.

14 The copy of the writing for a commandment to be given in every province was published unto all people, that they should be ready against that day.

Esther 4:1 When Mordecai perceived all that was done, Mordecai rent his clothes, and put on sackcloth with ashes, and went out into the midst of the city, and cried with a loud and a bitter cry;

2 And came even before the king's gate: for none *might* enter into the king's gate clothed with sackcloth.

3 **And in every province, whithersoever the king's commandment and his decree came,** *there was* **great mourning among the Jews, and fasting, and weeping, and wailing; and many lay in sackcloth and ashes.**

4 So Esther's maids and her chamberlains came and told *it* her. Then was the queen exceedingly grieved; and she sent raiment to clothe Mordecai, and to take away his sackcloth from him: but he received *it* not.

5 Then called Esther for Hatach, *one* of the king's chamberlains, whom he had appointed to attend upon her, and gave him a commandment to Mordecai, to know what it *was*, and why it*was*.

6 So Hatach went forth to Mordecai unto the street of the city, which *was* before the king's gate.

7 And Mordecai told him of all that had happened unto him, and of the sum of the money that Haman had promised to pay to the king's treasuries for the Jews, to destroy them.

8 Also he gave him the copy of the writing of the decree that was given at Shushan to destroy them, to shew *it* unto Esther, and to declare *it* unto her, and to charge her that she should go in unto the king, to make supplication unto him, and to make request before him for her people.

9 And Hatach came and told Esther the words of Mordecai.

10 Again Esther spake unto Hatach, and gave him commandment unto Mordecai;

11 All the king's servants, and the people of the king's provinces, do know, that whosoever, whether man or woman, shall come unto the king into the inner court, who is not called, *there is* one law of his to put *him* to death, except such to whom the king shall hold out the golden sceptre, that he may live: but I have not been called to come in unto the king these thirty days.

12 And they told to Mordecai Esther's words
.

MORDECAI ASKED ESTHER FOR DELIVERANCE OF ALL THE JEWS

Esther 4:13 Then Mordecai commanded to answer Esther, Think not with thyself that thou shalt escape in the king's house, more than all the Jews.

14 **For if thou altogether holdest thy peace at this time,** *then* **shall there enlargement and deliverance arise to the Jews from another place; but thou and thy father's house shall be destroyed:** and who knoweth whether thou art come to the kingdom for *such* a time as this?

15 Then Esther bade *them* return Mordecai *this answer,*

16 **Go, gather together all the Jews that are present in Shushan, and fast ye for me, and neither eat nor drink three days, night or day: I also and my maidens will fast likewise; and so will I go in unto the king, which *is* not according to the law: and if I perish, I per**ish.

17 So Mordecai went his way, and did according to all that Esther had commanded him.

ESTHER EXPOSED THE EVIL PLAN OF HAMAN

Esther 7:2 And the king said again unto Esther on the second day at the banquet of wine, What *is* thy petition, queen Esther? and it shall be granted thee: and what *is* thy request? and it shall be performed, *even* to the half of the kingdom.

3 Then Esther the queen answered and said, If I have found favour in thy sight, **O king, and if it please the king, let my life be given me at my petition, and my people at my request:**

4 **For we are sold, I and my people, to be destroyed, to be slain, and to perish. But if we had been sold for bondmen and bondwomen, I had held my tongue, although the enemy could not countervail the king's damage.**

5 Then **the king Ahasuerus** answered and said unto Esther the queen, Who is he, and where is he, that durst presume in his heart to do so?

6 And Esther said, The adversary and enemy *is* this wicked Haman. Then Haman was afraid before the king and the queen.

7 And the king arising from the banquet of wine in his wrath *went* into the palace garden: and Haman stood up to make request for his life to Esther the queen; for he saw that there was evil determined against him by the king.

8 Then the king returned out of the palace garden into the place of the banquet of wine; and Haman was fallen upon the bed whereon Esther *was*. Then said the king, Will he force the queen also before me in the house? As the word went out of the king's mouth, they covered Haman's face.

9 And Harbonah, one of the chamberlains, said before the king, Behold also, the gallows fifty cubits high, which Haman had made for Mordecai, who had spoken good for the king, standeth in the house of Haman. Then the king said, Hang him thereon.

10 **So they hanged Haman on the gallows that he had prepared for Mordecai**. Then was the king's wrath pacified.

PART 6
GOD ANOINTED DELIVERERS

CHAPTER II **THE JUDGES**

Judges 2:18
*And **when the LORD raised them up judges, then the LORD was with the judge, and delivered them out of the hand of their enemies** all the days of the judge; for it repented the LORD because of their groanings by reason of them that oppressed them and vexed them.*

NATIONS WITHIN THE PROMISE LAND
Judges 2:22 That through them I may prove Israel, whether they will keep the way of the LORD to walk therein, as their fathers did keep it, or not.
Judges 2:21 I also will not henceforth drive out any from before them of the nations which Joshua left when he died:
 23Therefore **the LORD left those nations, without driving them out hastily; neither delivered he them into the hand of Joshua.**
Judges 3:1 Now these *are* the nations which the LORD left, to prove Israel by them, *even* **as many** *of Israel* **as had not known all the wars of Canaan;**
2 Only that the generations of the children of Israel might know, to teach them war, at the least such as before knew nothing thereof;
3 *Namely*, five lords of the Philistines, and all the Canaanites, and the Sidonians, and the Hivites that dwelt in mount Lebanon, from mount Baalhermon unto the entering in of Hamath.
4 And they were to prove Israel by them, to know whether they would hearken unto the commandments of the LORD, which he commanded their fathers by the hand of Moses.
5 And the children of Israel dwelt among the Canaanites, Hittites, and Amorites, and Perizzites, and Hivites, and Jebusites:
Acts 13:19 **And when he had destroyed seven nations in the land of Canaan, he divided their land to them by lot.**

ISRAEL CRIED FOR GOD'S HELP

Judges 3:9 And when the children of Israel cried unto the LORD, the LORD raised up a deliverer to the children of Israel, who delivered them, *even* Othniel the son of Kenaz, Caleb's younger brother..

Acts 13:20 And after that **he gave *unto them* judges about the space of four hundred and fifty years,** until Samuel the prophet.

Judges 2:16 Nevertheless the LORD raised up judges, which delivered them out of the hand of those that spoiled them.

17 And yet they would not hearken unto their judges, but they went a whoring after other gods, and bowed themselves unto them: they turned quickly out of the way which their fathers walked in, obeying the commandments of the LORD; *but* they did not so.

19 And it came to pass, when the judge was dead, *that* they returned, and corrupted *themselves* more than their fathers, in following other gods to serve them, and to bow down unto them; they ceased not from their own doings, nor from their stubborn way.

THE JUDGES OF ISRAEL

2Samuel 7:10 Moreover I will appoint a place for my people Israel, and will plant them, that they may dwell in a place of their own, and move no more; neither shall the children of wickedness afflict them any more, as beforetime,

11 **And as since the time that I commanded judges *to be* over my people Israel, and have caused thee to rest from all thine enemies**. Also the LORD telleth thee that he will make thee an house.

1. OTHNIEL AGAINST THE KING OF MESOPOTAMIA

Judges 3:10 And **the Spirit of the LORD came upon him, and he judged Israel**, **and went out to war: and the LORD delivered Chu-shan-rish-a-tha-im king of Mesopotamia into his hand; and his hand prevailed** against **Chu-shan-rish-a-tha-im**

11 And the land had rest forty years. And Othaniel the son of Kenaz died.

2. EHUD AGAINST THE KING OF MOAB

Judges 3:12 And **the children of Israel did evil again in the sight of the LORD: and the LORD strengthened Eglon the king of Moab against Israel, because they had done evil in the sight of the LORD.**

13 And he gathered unto him the children of Ammon and Amalek, and went and smote Israel, and possessed the city of palm trees.

14 **So the children of Israel served Eglon the king of Moab for eighteen years**.

16 But Ehud made him a dagger which had two edges, of a cubit length; and he did gird it under his raiment upon his right thigh.

17 And he brought the present unto Eglon king of Moab: and Eglon *was* a very fat man.

18 And when he had made an end to offer the present, he sent away the people that bare the present.

19 But he himself turned again from the quarries that *were* by Gilgal, and said, I have a secret errand unto thee, O king: who said, Keep silence. And all that stood by him went out from him.

20 And Ehud came unto him; and he was sitting in a summer parlour, which he had for himself alone. And Ehud said, I have a message from God unto thee. And he arose out of *his* seat.

21 And Ehud put forth his left hand, and took the dagger from his right thigh, and thrust it into his belly:

22 And the haft also went in after the blade; and the fat closed upon the blade, so that he could not draw the dagger out of his belly; and the dirt came out.

23 Then Ehud went forth through the porch, and shut the doors of the parlour upon him, and locked them.

24 When he was gone out, his servants came; and when they saw that, behold, the doors of the parlour *were* locked, they said, Surely he covereth his feet in his summer chamber.

25 And they tarried till they were ashamed: and, behold, he opened not the doors of the parlour; therefore they took a key, and opened *them*: and, behold, their lord *was* fallen down dead on the earth.

26 And Ehud escaped while they tarried, and passed beyond the quarries, and escaped unto Seirath.

27 And it came to pass, when he was come, that he blew a trumpet in the mountain of Ephraim, and the children of Israel went down with him from the mount, and he before them.

28 And he said unto them, Follow after me: for the LORD hath delivered your enemies the Moabites into your hand. And they went down after him, and took the fords of Jordan toward Moab, and suffered not a man to pass over.

29 And they slew of Moab at that time about ten thousand men, all lusty, and all men of valour; and there escaped not a man.

30 **So Moab was subdued that day under the hand of Israel. And the land had rest fourscore years.**

3. SHAMGAR AGAINST PHILISTINES

Judges 3:31 And after him was Shamgar the son of Anath, **which slew of the Philistines six hundred men with an ox goad: and he also delivered Israel.**

4. DEBORAH AGAINST CAPTAIN SISERA OF THE CANAANITES

Judges 4:1 And the children of Israel **again did evil in the sight of the LORD,** when Ehu was dead.

2 And **the LORD sold them into the hand of Jabin king of Canaan**, that reigned in Hazor; **the captain of whose host was Sisera,** which dwelt in Harosheth of the Gentiles.

3 **And the children of Israel cried unto the LORD: for he had nine hundred chariots of iron; and twenty years he mightily oppressed the children of Israel**.

4 And Deborah, a prophetess, the wife of Lap-i-doth, she judged Israel at that time.

5 And she dwelt under the palm tree of Deborah between Ramah and Bethel in mount Ephraim: and **the children of Israel came up for her for judgment**.

6 And **she sent and called Barak the son of Abinoam out of Kedeshnaphtali, and said unto him, Hath not the LORD God of Israel commanded,** *saying***, Go and draw toward mount Tabor, and take with thee ten thousand men of the children of Naphtali and of the children of Zebulun**?

7 And **I will draw unto thee to the river Kishon Sisera, the captain of Jabin's army, with his chariots and his multitude; and I will deliver him into thine hand**.

8 And **Barak said unto her**, If thou wilt go with me, then I will go: **but if thou wilt not go with me,** *then* **I will not go.**

9 And **she said,** I **will surely go with thee: notwithstanding the journey that thou takest shall not be for thine honour; for the**

LORD shall sell Sisera into the hand of a woman. And Deborah arose, and went with Barak to Kedesh.

10 And **Barak called Zebulun and Naphtali to Kedesh; and he went up with ten thousand men at his feet: and Deborah went up with him**.

11 Now Heber the Kenite, *which was* of the children of Hobab the father in law of Moses, had severed himself from the Kenites, and pitched his tent unto the plain of Zaanaim, which *is* by Kedesh.

12 And they shewed Sisera that Barak the son of Abinoam was gone up to mount Tabor.

13 And Sisera gathered together all his chariots, *even* nine hundred chariots of iron, and all the people that *were* with him, from Harosheth of the Gentiles unto the river of Kishon.

14 And Deborah said unto Barak, Up; for this *is* the day in which the LORD hath delivered Sisera into thine hand: is not the LORD gone out before thee? So Barak went down from mount Tabor, and ten thousand men after him.

15 And **the LORD discomfited Sisera, and all *his* chariots, and all *his* host, with the edge of the sword before Barak; so that Sisera lighted down off *his* chariot, and fled away on his feet.**

16 But Barak pursued after the chariots, and after the host, unto Harosheth of the Gentiles: and all the host of Sisera fell upon the edge of the sword; *and* there was not a man left.

17 **Howbeit Sisera fled away on his feet to the tent of Jael the wife of Heber the Kenite**: for *there was* peace between Jabin the king of Hazor and the house of Heber the Kenite.

18 And Jael went out to meet Sisera, and said unto him, Turn in, my lord, turn in to me; fear not. And when he had turned in unto her into the tent, she covered him with a mantle.

19 And he said unto her, Give me, I pray thee, a little water to drink; for I am thirsty. And she opened a bottle of milk, and gave him drink, and covered him.

20 Again he said unto her, Stand in the door of the tent, and it shall be, when any man doth come and enquire of thee, and say, Is there any man here? that thou shalt say, No

21 **Then Jael Heber's wife took a nail of the tent, and took an hammer in her hand, and went softly unto him, and smote the nail into his temples, and fastened it into the ground: for he was fast asleep and weary. So he died.**

22 And, behold, as Barak pursued Sisera, Jael came out to meet him, and said unto him, Come, and I will shew thee the man

whom thou seekest. And when he came into her *tent*, behold, Sisera lay dead, and the nail *was* in his temples.

23 So God subdued on that day Jabin the king of Canaan before the children of Israel.

24 And the hand of the children of Israel prospered, and prevailed against Jabin the king of Canaan, until they had destroyed Jabin king of Canaan.

5. GIDEON AGAINST MIDIAN

Judges 6:1 And the children of Israel did evil in the sight of the LORD: and **the LORD delivered them into the hand of Midian seven years.**

2 And **the hand of Midian prevailed against Israel:** *and* **because of the Midianites the children of Israel made them the dens which** *are* **in the mountains, and caves, and strong holds**.

3 And *so* it was, when Israel had sown, that the Midianites came up, and the Amalekites, and the children of the east, even they came up against them;

4 And they encamped against them, and destroyed the increase of the earth, till thou come unto Gaza, and left no sustenance for Israel, neither sheep, nor ox, nor ass.

5 **For they came up with their cattle and their tents, and they came as grasshoppers for multitude;** *for* **both they and their camels were without number: and they entered into the land to destroy it.**

6 **And Israel was greatly impoverished because of the Midianites; and the children of Israel cried unto the LORD**.

7 And it came to pass, when the children of Israel cried unto the LORD because of the Midianites

THE ANGEL OF THE LORD APPEARED TO GIDEON

Judges 6:11 And there came an angel of the LORD, and sat under an oak which *was* in Ophrah, that *pertained* unto Joash the Abiezrite: and his son Gideon threshed wheat by the winepress, to hide *it* from the Midianites.

12 And the angel of the LORD appeared unto him, and said unto him, The LORD *is* with thee, thou mighty man of valour.

13 And Gideon said unto him, Oh my Lord, if the LORD be with us, why then is all this befallen us? and where *be* all his miracles which our fathers told us of, saying, Did not the LORD bring us

up from Egypt? but now the LORD hath forsaken us, and delivered us into the hands of the Midianites.

14 And the LORD looked upon him, and said, Go in this thy might, and thou shalt save Israel from the hand of the Midianites: have not I sent thee?

15 And he said unto him, Oh my Lord, wherewith shall I save Israel? behold, my family *is* poor in Manasseh, and I *am* the least in my father's house.

16 And the LORD said unto him, Surely I will be with thee, and thou shalt smite the Midianites as one man.

17 And he said unto him, If now I have found grace in thy sight, then shew me a sign that thou talkest with me.

18 Depart not hence, I pray thee, until I come unto thee, and bring forth my present, and set *it* before thee. And he said, I will tarry until thou come again.

19 And Gideon went in, and made ready a kid, and unleavened cakes of an ephah of flour: the flesh he put in a basket, and he put the broth in a pot, and brought *it* out unto him under the oak, and presented *it*.

20 And the angel of God said unto him, Take the flesh and the unleavened cakes, and lay *them* upon this rock, and pour out the broth. And he did so.

21 Then the angel of the LORD put forth the end of the staff that *was* in his hand, and touched the flesh and the unleavened cakes; and there rose up fire out of the rock, and consumed the flesh and the unleavened cakes. Then the angel of the LORD departed out of his sight.

22 And when Gideon perceived that he *was* an angel of the LORD, Gideon said, Alas, O Lord GOD! for because I have seen an angel of the LORD face to face.

THE LORD'S MESSAGE TO GIDEON

Judges 6:23 And the LORD said unto him, Peace *be* unto thee; fear not: thou shalt not die.

24 Then Gideon built an altar there unto the LORD, and called it Jehovahshalom: unto this day it *is* yet in Ophrah of the Abiezrites.

25 And it came to pass the same night, that the LORD said unto him, **Take thy father's young bullock, even the second bullock of seven years old, and throw down the altar of Baal that thy father hath, and cut down the grove that *is* by it:**

26 And build an altar unto the LORD thy God upon the top of this rock, in the ordered place, and take the second bullock, and offer a burnt sacrifice with the wood of the grove which thou shalt cut down.

27 Then Gideon took ten men of his servants, and did as the LORD had said unto him: and *so* it was, because he feared his father's household, and the men of the city, that he could not do *it* by day, that **he did *it* by night**.

28 And **when the men of the city arose early in the morning, behold, the altar of Baal was cast down, and the grove was cut down that *was* by it, and the second bullock was offered upon the altar *that was* built.**

29 And they said one to another, Who hath done this thing? And when they enquired and asked, they said, Gideon the son of Joash hath done this thing.

30 Then the men of the city said unto Joash, Bring out thy son, that he may die: because he hath cast down the altar of Baal, and because he hath cut down the grove that *was* by it.

31 And Joash said unto all that stood against him, Will ye plead for Baal? will ye save him? he that will plead for him, let him be put to death whilst *it is yet* morning: if he *be* a god, let him plead for himself, because *one* hath cast down his altar.

32 Therefore on that day he called him Jerubbaal, saying, Let Baal plead against him, because he hath thrown down his altar.

33 Then all the Midianites and the Amalekites and the children of the east were gathered together, and went over, and pitched in the valley of Jezreel.

34 But **the Spirit of the LORD came upon Gideon, and he blew a trumpet; and Abiezer was gathered after him.**

35 And he sent messengers throughout all Manasseh; who also was gathered after him: and he sent messengers unto Asher, and unto Zebulun, and unto Naphtali; and they came up to meet them.

GIDEON PRAYED FOR SIGNS TO WIN THE WAR
Judges 6:37 Behold, I will put a fleece of wool in the floor; *and* if the dew be on the fleece only, and *it be* dry upon all the earth *beside*, then shall I know that thou wilt save Israel by mine hand, as thou hast said.

38 And it was so: for he rose up early on the morrow, and thrust the fleece together, and wringed the dew out of the fleece, a bowl full of water.

39 And Gideon said unto God, **Let not thine anger be hot against me, and I will speak but this once: let me prove, I pray thee, but this once with the fleece; let it now be dry only upon the fleece, and upon all the ground let there be dew.**
40 And God did so that night: for it was dry upon the fleece only, and there was dew on all the ground.

GOD'S INSTRUCTION IN CHOOSING THE RIGHT MEN
Judges 7:4 And the LORD said unto Gideon, The people *are* yet *too* many; bring them down unto the water, and I will try them for thee there: and it shall be, ***that* of whom I say unto thee, This shall go with thee, the same shall go with thee; and of whomsoever I say unto thee, This shall not go with thee, the same shall not go.**
5 So he brought down the people unto the water: and **the LORD said unto Gideon, Every one that lappeth of the water with his tongue, as a dog lappeth, him shalt thou set by himself**; likewise every one that boweth down upon his knees to drink.
6 And the number of them that lapped, *putting* their hand to their mouth, were three hundred men: but all the rest of the people bowed down upon their knees to drink water.
7 And the LORD said unto Gideon, **By the three hundred men that lapped will I save you**, **and deliver the Midianites into thine hand**: and let all the *other* people go every man unto his place.

GIDEON DELIVERED ISRAEL AGAINST MIDIANITES
Judges 8:28 Thus was Midian subdued before the children of Israel, so that they lifted up their heads no more. And **the country was in quietness forty years in the days of Gideon.**

AFTER GIDEON'S DEATH
Judges 8:32 And Gideon the son of Joash died in a good old age, and was buried in the sepulchre of Joash his father, in Ophrah of the Abiezrites.
33 And it came to pass, as soon as Gideon was dead, that the children of Israel turned again, and went a whoring after Baalim, and made Baalberith their god.
34 And **the children of Israel remembered not the LORD their God, who had delivered them out of the hands of all their enemies on every side:**

35 **Neither shewed they kindness to the house of Jerubbaal,** *namely*, **Gideon, according to all the goodness which he had shewed unto Israel**.

6. TOLA

Judges 10:1 And after Abimelech there arose to defend Israel Tola the son of Puah, the son of Dodo, a man of Issachar; and he dwelt in Shamir in mount Ephraim.

2 And he judged Israel twenty and three years, and died, and was buried in Shamir.

7. JAIR

Judges 10:3 And after him arose Jair, a Gileadite, and judged Israel twenty and two years.

4 And he had thirty sons that rode on thirty ass colts, and they had thirty cities, which are called Havothjair unto this day, which *are* in the land of Gilead.

5 And Jair died, and was buried in Camon.

6 And the children of Israel did evil again in the sight of the LORD, and served Baalim, and Ashtaroth, and the gods of Syria, and the gods of Zidon, and the gods of Moab, and the gods of the children of Ammon, and the gods of the Philistines, and forsook the LORD, and served not him.

7 And the anger of the LORD was hot against Israel, and he sold them into the hands of the Philistines, and into the hands of the children of Ammon.

8 And that year they vexed and oppressed the children of Israel: eighteen years, all the children of Israel that *were* on the other side Jordan in the land of the Amorites, which *is* in Gilead.

9 Moreover the children of Ammon passed over Jordan to fight also against Judah, and against Benjamin, and against the house of Ephraim; so that Israel was sore distressed.

10 And the children of Israel cried unto the LORD, saying, We have sinned against thee, both because we have forsaken our God, and also served Baalim.

11 And the LORD said unto the children of Israel, *Did* not *I deliver you* from the Egyptians, and from the Amorites, from the children of Ammon, and from the Philistines?

12 The Zidonians also, and the Amalekites, and the Maonites, did oppress you; and ye cried to me, and I delivered you out of their hand.

13 **Yet ye have forsaken me, and served other gods: wherefore I will deliver you no more.**

14 **Go and cry unto the gods which ye have chosen; let them deliver you in the time of your tribulation.**

15 And **the children of Israel said unto the LORD, We have sinned: do thou unto us whatsoever seemeth good unto thee; deliver us only, we pray thee, this** day.

16 And **they put away the strange gods from among them, and served the LORD: and his soul was grieved for the misery of Israel**.

17 Then the children of Ammon were gathered together, and encamped in Gilead. And the children of Israel assembled themselves together, and encamped in Mizpeh.

18 And the people *and* princes of Gilead said one to another, What man *is he* that will begin to fight against the children of Ammon? he shall be head over all the inhabitants of Gilead.

8. SAMSON, THE NAZARITE AGAINST PHILISTINES

SAMSON MARRIED A PHILISTINE WOMAN

Judges 14:1 And Samson went down to Timnath, and saw a woman in Timnath of the daughters of the Philistines.

2 And **he came up, and told his father and his mother, and said, I have seen a woman in Timnath of the daughters of the Philistines: now therefore get her for me to wife**.

3 Then his father and his mother said unto him, *Is there* never a woman among the daughters of thy brethren, or among all my people, that thou goest to take a wife of the uncircumcised Philistines? And Samson said unto his father, Get her for me; for she pleaseth me well.

4 But his father and his mother knew not that it *was* of the LORD, that he sought an occasion against the Philistines: for at that time the Philistines had dominion over Israel.

5 Then went Samson down, and his father and his mother, to Timnath, and came to the vineyards of Timnath: and, behold, a young lion roared against him.

6 And the Spirit of the LORD came mightily upon him, and he rent him as he would have rent a kid, and *he had* nothing in his hand: but he told not his father or his mother what he had done.

7 And he went down, and talked with the woman; and she pleased Samson well.

8 And after a time he returned to take her, and he turned aside to see the carcase of the lion: and, behold, *there was* a swarm of bees and honey in the carcase of the lion.

9 And he took thereof in his hands, and went on eating, and came to his father and mother, and he gave them, and they did eat: but he told not them that he had taken the honey out of the carcase of the lion.

10 So his father went down unto the woman: and Samson made there a feast; for so used the young men to do.

11 And it came to pass, when they saw him, that they brought thirty companions to be with him.

SAMSON'S RIDDLES FOR THE THIRTY PHILISTINES

Judges 14:12 And Samson said unto them, I will now put forth a riddle unto you: if ye can certainly declare it me within the seven days of the feast, and find *it* out, then I will give you thirty sheets and thirty change of garments:

13 But if ye cannot declare *it* me, then shall ye give me thirty sheets and thirty change of garments. And they said unto him, Put forth thy riddle, that we may hear it.

14 **And he said unto them**, *Out of the eater came forth meat, and out of the strong came forth sweetness.* And they could not in three days expound the riddle.

15 And it came to pass on the seventh day, that they said unto Samson's wife, Entice thy husband, that he may declare unto us the riddle, lest we burn thee and thy father's house with fire: have ye called us to take that we have? *is it* not *so*?

16 And Samson's wife wept before him, and said, Thou dost but hate me, and lovest me not: thou hast put forth a riddle unto the children of my people, and hast not told *it* me. And he said unto her, Behold, I have not told *it* my father nor my mother, and shall I tell *it* thee?

17 And she wept before him the seven days, while their feast lasted: and it came to pass on the seventh day, that he told her, because she lay sore upon him: and she told the riddle to the children of her people.

SAMSON' KILLED THE THIRTY PHILISTINES FROM ASHKELON

Judges 14:18 And the men of the city said unto him on the seventh day before the sun went down, *What is sweeter than* *honey? and what is stronger than a lion?* And **he said unto them,** *If ye had not plowed with my heifer, ye had not found out my riddle.*

19 And **the Spirit of the LORD came upon him**, and he went down to Ashkelon, and **slew thirty men of them, and took their spoil, and gave change of garments unto them which expounded the riddle**. And his anger was kindled, and he went up to his father's house.

20 **But Samson's wife was** *given* **to his companion, whom he had used as his friend.**

SAMSON BURNED THE CORN FIELDS OF THE PHILISTINES

Judges 15:1 But it came to pass within a while after, in the time of wheat harvest, that Samson visited his wife with a kid; and he said, I will go in to my wife into the chamber. But her father would not suffer him to go in.

2 And her father said, I verily thought that thou hadst utterly hated her; therefore I gave her to thy companion: *is* not her younger sister fairer than she? take her, I pray thee, instead of her.

3 And Samson said concerning them, Now shall I be more blameless than the Philistines, though I do them a displeasure.

4 And Samson went and caught three hundred foxes, and took firebrands, and turned tail to tail, and put a firebrand in the midst between two tails.

5 And when he had set the brands on fire, he let *them* go into the standing corn of the Philistines, and burnt up both the shocks, and also the standing corn, with the vineyards *and* olives.

SAMSON KILLED A THOUSAND PHILISTINES

Judges 15:6 Then the Philistines said, Who hath done this? And they answered, Samson, the son in law of the Timnite, because he had taken his wife, and given her to his companion. And the Philistines came up, and burnt her and her father with fire.

7 And Samson said unto them, Though ye have done this, yet will I be avenged of you, and after that I will cease.

8 And he smote them hip and thigh with a great slaughter: and he went down and dwelt in the top of the rock Etam.

9 Then the Philistines went up, and pitched in Judah, and spread themselves in Lehi.

10 And the men of Judah said, Why are ye come up against us? And they answered, To bind Samson are we come up, to do to him as he hath done to us.

11 Then three thousand men of Judah went to the top of the rock Etam, and said to Samson, Knowest thou not that the Philistines *are* rulers over us? what *is* this *that* thou hast done unto us? And he said unto them, As they did unto me, so have I done unto them.

12 And they said unto him, We are come down to bind thee, that we may deliver thee into the hand of the Philistines. And Samson said unto them, Swear unto me, that ye will not fall upon me yourselves.

13 And they spake unto him, saying, No; but we will bind thee fast, and deliver thee into their hand: but surely we will not kill thee. And they bound him with two new cords, and brought him up from the rock.

14 *And* **when he came unto Lehi, the Philistines shouted against him**: and **the Spirit of the LORD came mightily upon him, and the cords that** *were* **upon his arms became as flax that was burnt with fire, and his bands loosed from off his hands.**

15 And he found a new jawbone of an ass, and put forth his hand, and took it, and slew a thousand men therewith.

16 And Samson said, **With the jawbone of an ass, heaps upon heaps, with the jaw of an ass have I slain a thousand men.**

17 And it came to pass, when he had made an end of speaking, that he cast away the jawbone out of his hand, and called that place Ramathlehi.

18 And he was sore athirst, and called on the LORD, and said, Thou hast given this great deliverance into the hand of thy servant: and now shall I die for thirst, and fall into the hand of the uncircumcised?

19 But **God clave an hollow place that** *was* **in the jaw, and there came water thereout; and when he had drunk, his spirit came again, and he revived: wherefore he called the name thereof Enhakkore, which** *is* **in Lehi unto this day.**

20 And **he judged Israel in the days of the Philistines twenty years.**

SAMSON LOVED DELILAH

Judges 16:4 And it came to pass afterward that he loved a woman in the valley of Sorek, whose name was Delilah.

5 And the lords of the Philistines came up unto her, and said unto her, Entice him, and see wherein his great strength *lieth*, and by what *means* we may prevail against him, that we may bind him to afflict him: and **we will give thee every one of us eleven hundred** *pieces* **of silver.**

DELILAH ASKED SAMSON ABOUT THE SOURCE OF HIS STRENGTH
Judges 16:6 And Delilah said to Samson, Tell me I pray thee, wherein thy great strength lieth, and wherewith thou mightest be bound to afflict thee.

SAMSON MADE HIS STORY THREE TIMES
1. Judges 16:7 And Samson said unto her, If they bind me with seven green withs that were never dried, then shall I be weak, and be as another man.
2. Judges 16:11 And he said unto her, If they bind me fast with new ropes that never were occupied, then shall I be weak, and be as another man.
3. **Judges 16**:13 And Delilah said unto Samson, Hitherto thou hast mocked me, and told me lies: tell me wherewith thou mightest be bound. And he said unto her, If thou weavest the seven locks of my head with the web.
14 And she fastened *it* with the pin, and said unto him, The Philistines *be* upon thee, Samson. And he awaked out of his sleep, and went away with the pin of the beam, and with the web.

FINALLY SAMSON TOLD DELILAH HIS SECRET
Judges 16:15And she said unto him, How canst thou say, I love thee, when thine heart *is* not with me? thou hast mocked me these three times, and hast not told me wherein thy great strength *lieth*.
16 And it came to pass, when she pressed him daily with her words, and urged him, *so* that his soul was vexed unto death;
17 That he told her all his heart, and said unto her, There hath not come a razor upon mine head; for **I** *have been* **a Nazarite unto God from my mother's womb: if I be shaven, then my strength will go from me, and I shall become weak, and be like any** *other* **man**

DELILAH SOLD SAMSON TO THE PHILISTINES

Judges 16:18 And when Delilah saw that he had told her all his heart, she sent and called for the lords of the Philistines, saying, Come up this once, for he hath shewed me all his heart. Then the **lords of the Philistines came up unto her, and brought money in their hand**.

19 And she made him sleep upon her knees; and she called for a man, and she caused him to shave off the seven locks of his head; and she began to afflict him, and his strength went from him.

20 And she said, The Philistines *be* upon thee, Samson. And he awoke out of his sleep, and said, I will go out as at other times before, and shake myself. And he wist not that the LORD was departed from him.

21 But **the Philistines took him, and put out his eyes, and brought him down to Gaza, and bound him with fetters of brass; and he did grind in the prison house.**

THE PHILISTINES THANKS DAGON THEIR god

Judges 16:22 Howbeit the hair of his head began to grow again after he was shaven.

23 **Then the lords of the Philistines gathered them together for to offer a great sacrifice unto Dagon their god, and to rejoice: for they said, Our god hath delivered Samson our enemy into our hand.**

24 And when the people saw him, they praised their god: for they said, Our god hath delivered into our hands our enemy, and the destroyer of our country, which slew many of us.

25 And it came to pass, when their hearts were merry, that they said, Call for Samson, that he may make us sport. And they called for Samson out of the prison house; and he made them sport: and they set him between the pillars.

26 And Samson said unto the lad that held him by the hand, Suffer me that I may feel the pillars whereupon the house standeth, that I may lean upon them.

27 **Now the house was full of men and women; and all the lords of the Philistines *were* there; and *there were* upon the roof about three thousand men and women**, that beheld while Samson made sport.

SAMSON PRAYED TO THE LORD HIS GOD

Judges 16 :28 And **Samson called unto the LORD**, and said, *O Lord GOD, remember me, I pray thee, and strengthen me, I pray thee, only this once, O God, that I may be at once avenged of the Philistines for my two eyes.*

29 And Samson took hold of the two middle pillars upon which the house stood, and on which it was borne up, of the one with his right hand, and of the other with his left.

30 And **Samson said, Let me die with the Philistines. And he bowed himself with *all his* might; and the house fell upon the lords, and upon all the people that *were* therein. So the dead which he slew at his death were more than *they* which he slew in his life**.

31 Then his brethren and all the house of his father came down, and took him, and brought *him* up, and buried him between
Zorah and Eshtaol in the buryingplace of Manoah his father. And **he judged Israel twenty years.**

9. SAMUEL: THE JUDGE AND THE PROPHET

GOD SAVED THE ISRAELITES FROM THE PHILISTINES

1Samuel 7:3 And **Samuel spake** unto all the house of Israel, saying, **If ye do return unto the LORD with all your hearts, *then* put away the strange gods and Ashtaroth from among you, and prepare your hearts unto the LORD, and serve him only: and he will deliver you out of the hand of the Philistines.**

4 Then **the children of Israel did put away Baalim and Ashtaroth, and served the LORD only**.

5 And Samuel said, Gather all Israel to Mizpeh, and I will pray for you unto the LORD.

6 And they gathered together to Mizpeh, and drew water, and poured *it* out before the LORD, and fasted on that day, and said there, We have sinned against the LORD. And Samuel judged the children of Israel in Mizpeh.

7 And when the Philistines heard that the children of Israel were gathered together to Mizpeh, the lords of the Philistines went up against Israel. And when the children of Israel heard *it*, they were afraid of the Philistines.

8 And the children of Israel said to Samuel, Cease not to cry unto the LORD our God for us, that he will save us out of the hand of the Philistines.

9 And Samuel took a sucking lamb, and offered *it for* a burnt offering wholly unto the LORD: and Samuel cried unto the LORD for Israel; and the LORD heard him.

10 And as Samuel was offering up the burnt offering, the Philistines drew near to battle against Israel: but **the LORD thundered with a great thunder on that day upon the Philistines, and discomfited them; and they were smitten before Israel.**

11 And the men of Israel went out of Mizpeh, and pursued the Philistines, and smote them, until *they came* under Bethcar.

12 Then Samuel took a stone, and set *it* between Mizpeh and Shen, and called the name of it Ebenezer, saying, Hitherto hath the LORD helped us.

13 **So the Philistines were subdued, and they came no more into the coast of Israel: and the hand of the LORD was against the Philistines all the days of Samuel.**

14 And the cities which the Philistines had taken from Israel were restored to Israel, from Ekron even unto Gath; and the coasts thereof did Israel deliver out of the hands of the Philistines. And there was peace between Israel and the Amorites.

15 And **Samuel judged Israel all the days of his life.**

PART 6
GOD ANOINTED DELIVERERS

'

CHAPTER III **KINGS OF ISRAEL**

1Samuel 8:7
*And **the LORD said unto Samuel**, Hearken unto the voice of the people in all that they say unto thee: for they have not rejected thee, **but they have rejected me, that I should not reign over them.** 8 According to all the works which they have done **since the day that I brought them up out of Egypt even unto this day, wherewith they have forsaken me, and served other gods, so do they also unto thee**.*

NATION OF ISRAEL ASKED FOR THEIR KING
1Samuel 8:1 And it came to pass, when Samuel was old, that he made his sons judges over Israel.

2 Now the name of his firstborn was Joel; and the name of his second, Abiah: *they were* judges in Beersheba.

3 And his sons walked not in his ways, but turned aside after lucre, and took bribes, and perverted judgment.

4 Then all the elders of Israel gathered themselves together, and came to Samuel unto Ramah,

5 And said unto him, Behold, thou art old, and thy sons walk not in thy ways: **now make us a king to judge us like all the nations.**

6 But the thing displeased Samuel, when **they said, Give us a king to judge us.** And Samuel prayed unto the LORD.

THE KING WILL RULE OVER GOD'S PEOPLE
1Samuel 8:9 Now therefore hearken unto their voice: howbeit yet protest solemnly unto them, and shew them the manner of the king that shall reign over them.

10 And Samuel told all the words of the LORD unto the people that asked of him a king.

11 And he said, This will be the manner of the king that shall reign over you: He will take your sons, and appoint *them* for

himself, for his chariots, and *to be* his horsemen; and *some* shall run before his chariots.

12 And he will appoint him captains over thousands, and captains over fifties; and *will set them* to ear his ground, and to reap his harvest, and to make his instruments of war, and instruments of his chariots.

13 And he will take your daughters *to be* confectionaries, and *to be* cooks, and *to be* bakers.

14 And he will take your fields, and your vineyards, and your oliveyards, *even* the best *of them*, and give *them* to his servants.

15 And he will take the tenth of your seed, and of your vineyards, and give to his officers, and to his servants.

16 And he will take your menservants, and your maidservants, and your goodliest young men, and your asses, and put *them* to his work.

17 He will take the tenth of your sheep: and ye shall be his servants.

18 And ye shall cry out in that day because of your king which ye shall have chosen you; and the LORD will not hear you in that day.

PEOPLE STILL INSISTED TO HAVE A KING

1Samuel 8:19 Nevertheless the people refused to obey the voice of Samuel; and they said, Nay; but we will have a king over us;

20 That we also may be like all the nations; and that our king may judge us, and go out before us, and fight our battles.

21 And Samuel heard all the words of the people, and he rehearsed them in the ears of the LORD.

22 And the LORD said to Samuel, Hearken unto their voice, and make them a king. And Samuel said unto the men of Israel, Go ye every man unto his city.

KINGS MUST RULE IN THE FEAR OF GOD

2Samuel 23:3The **God of Israel said, the Rock of Israel spake to me, He that ruleth over men *must be* just, ruling in the fear of God.**

4 And ***he shall be* as the light of the morning, *when* the sun riseth, *even* a morning without clouds; *as* the tender grass *springing* out of the earth by clear shining after rai**n.

5 Although my house *be* not so with God; yet he hath made with me an everlasting covenant, ordered in all *things*, and sure:

for *this* *is* all my salvation, and all *my* desire, although he make *it* not to grow.

THE FIRST FOUR KINGS OF ISRAEL

1. SAUL
1Samuel 9:1 **Now there was a man of Benjamin, whose name *was* Kish, the son of Abiel, the son of Zeror, the son of Bechorath, the son of Aphiah, a Benjamite, a mighty man of power**

2 And **he had a son, whose name *was* Saul**, a choice young man, and a goodly: and *there was* not among the children of Israel a goodlier person than he: from his shoulders and upward *he was* higher than any of the people.

1Samuel 9:15 Now the LORD had told Samuel in his ear a day before Saul came, saying,

16 To morrow about this time I will send thee a man out of the land of Benjamin, and thou shalt anoint him *to be* captain over my people Israel, that he may save my people out of the hand of the Philistines: for I have looked upon my people, because their cry is come unto me.

17 And **when Samuel saw Saul, the LORD said unto him, Behold the man whom I spake to thee of! this same shall reign over my people.**

2. DAVID
1Samuel 17:12 Now David *was* the son of that Ephrathite of Bethlehemjudah, whose name *was* Jesse; and he had eight sons: and the man went among men *for* an old man in the days of Saul.

13 And the three eldest sons of Jesse went *and* followed Saul to the battle: and the names of his three sons that went to the battle *were* Eliab the firstborn, and next unto him Abinadab, and the third Shammah.

14 And David *was* the youngest: and the three eldest followed Saul.

15 But David went and returned from Saul to feed his father's sheep at Bethlehem.

16 And the Philistine drew near morning and evening, and presented himself forty days.

17 And Jesse said unto David his son, Take now for thy brethren an ephah of this parched *corn*, and these ten loaves, and run to the camp to thy brethren;

18 And carry these ten cheeses unto the captain of *their* thousand, and look how thy brethren fare, and take their pledge.

19 Now Saul, and they, and all the men of Israel, *were* in the valley of Elah, fighting with the Philistines.

20 And David rose up early in the morning, and left the sheep with a keeper, and took, and went, as Jesse had commanded him; and he came to the trench, as the host was going forth to the fight, and shouted for the battle.

21 For Israel and the Philistines had put the battle in array, army against army.

22 And David left his carriage in the hand of the keeper of the carriage, and ran into the army, and came and saluted his brethren.

23 And as **he talked with them, behold, there came up the champion, the Philistine of Gath, Goliath by name, out of the armies of the Philistines, and spake according to the same words: and David heard** *them.*

24 And **all the men of Israel, when they saw the man, fled from him, and were sore afraid.**

25 And the men of Israel said, Have ye seen this man that is come up? surely to defy Israel is he come up: and it shall be, *that* the man who killeth him, the king will enrich him with great riches, and will give him his daughter, and make his father's house free in Israel.

26 And **David spake to the men that stood by him, saying, What shall be done to the man that killeth this Philistine, and taketh away the reproach from Israel? for who** *is* **this uncircumcised Philistine, that he should defy the armies of the living God?**

27 And the people answered him after this manner, saying, So shall it be done to the man that killeth him.

28 And Eliab his eldest brother heard when he spake unto the men; and Eliab's anger was kindled against David, and he said, Why camest thou down hither? and with whom hast thou left those few sheep in the wilderness? I know thy pride, and the naughtiness of thine heart; for thou art come down that thou mightest see the battle

GOLIATH THE PHILISTINE

1Samuel 17:2 And Saul and the men of Israel were gathered together, and pitched by the valley of Elah, and set the battle in array against the Philistines.

3 And the Philistines stood on a mountain on the one side, and Israel stood on a mountain on the other side: and *there was* a valley between them.

4 And there went out **a champion out of the camp of the Philistines, named Goliath, of Gath, whose height *was* six cubits and a span.**

5 And *he had* **an helmet of brass upon his head, and he *was* armed with a coat of mail; and the weight of the coat *was* five thousand shekels of brass.**

6 And *he had* **greaves of brass upon his legs, and a target of brass between his shoulders.**

7 And **the staff of his spear *was* like a weaver's beam; and his spear's head *weighed* six hundred shekels of iron: and one bearing a shield went before him.**

8 And he stood and cried unto the armies of Israel, and said unto them, Why are ye come out to set *your* battle in array? *am* not I a Philistine, and ye servants to Saul? choose you a man for you, and let him come down to me.

9 If **he be able to fight with me, and to kill me, then will we be your servants: but if I prevail against him, and kill him, then shall ye be our servants, and serve us.**

10 And **the Philistine said, I defy the armies of Israel this day; give me a man, that we may fight together.**

11 When Saul and all Israel heard those words of the Philistine, they were dismayed, and greatly afraid.

YOUNG DAVID KILLED GOLIATH

1Samuel 17:42 And when the Philistine looked about, and saw David, he disdained him: for he was *but* a youth, and ruddy, and of a fair countenance.

43 And the Philistine said unto David, *Am* I a dog, that thou comest to me with staves? And the Philistine cursed David by his gods.

44 And the Philistine said to David, Come to me, and I will give thy flesh unto the fowls of the air, and to the beasts of the field.

45 **Then said David to the Philistine, Thou comest to me with a sword, and with a spear, and with a shield: but I come to**

thee in the name of the LORD of hosts, the God of the armies of Israel, whom thou hast defied.

46 **This day will the LORD deliver thee into mine hand; and I will smite thee, and take thine head from thee; and I will give the carcases of the host of the Philistines this day unto the fowls of the air, and to the wild beasts of the earth; that all the earth may know that there is a God in Israel.**

47 **And all this assembly shall know that the LORD saveth not with sword and spear: for the battle** *is* **the LORD'S, and he will give you into our hands.**

48 And it came to pass, when the Philistine arose, and came and drew nigh to meet David, that David hasted, and ran toward the army to meet the Philistine.

49 And **David put his hand in his bag, and took thence a stone, and slang** *it*, **and smote the Philistine in his forehead, that the stone sunk into his forehead; and he fell upon his face to the earth.**

50 So David prevailed over the Philistine with a sling and with a stone, and smote the Philistine, and slew him; but *there was* no sword in the hand of David.

51 Therefore David ran, and stood upon the Philistine, and took his sword, and drew it out of the sheath thereof, and slew him, and cut off his head therewith. And when the Philistines saw their champion was dead, they fled.

KING DAVID

Psalm78:70 He *chose* David also his servant, and took him from the sheepfolds

2Samuel 6:21 And David said unto Michal, *It was* before **the LORD, which chose me before thy father,** and before all his house, to appoint me ruler over the people of the LORD, over Israel: therefore will I play before the LORD.

1Chronicles 28:4 Howbeit the LORD God of Israel **chose me before all the house of my father to be king over Israel for ever: for he hath chosen Judah** *to be* **the ruler;** and of the house of Judah, the house of my father; and among the sons of my father he liked me to make *me* king over all Israel:

3. SOLOMON

1Chronicles 28:5 And all of my sons, (for the LORD hath given me many sons) he hath chosen Solomon my son upon the throne of the kingdom of the LORD over Israel.

6 And he said unto me, **Solomon thy son, he shall build my house and my courts: for I have** *chosen* **him to be my son, and I will be his father.**

7 Moreover **I will establish his kingdom for ever,** *if* **he be constant to do my commandments and my judgments, as this day.**

9 And thou Solomon my son, know thou the God of thy father, and serve him with a perfect heart and with a willing mind: **for the LORD searcheth all hearts, and understandeth all the imaginations of the thoughts, if thou seek him, he will be found of thee; but if thou forsake him, he will cast thee off forever.**

4. REHOBOAM SON OF SOLOMON

1Kings 12:1 And Rehoboam went to Shechem: for all Israel were come to Shechem to make him king.

THE LORD CAUSED REHOBOAM TO HARDENED AGAINST THE CONGREGATION OF ISRAEL

1 Kings 11:26 And **Jeroboam the son of Nebat, an Ephrathite of Zereda**, Solomon's servant, whose mother's name *was* Zeruah, a widow woman, even he lifted up *his* hand against the king.

1Kings 12:2 And it came to pass, when Jeroboam the son of Nebat, who was yet in Egypt, heard *of it*, (for he was fled from the presence of king Solomon, and Jeroboam dwelt in Egypt;)

3 That they sent and called him. And Jeroboam and **all the congregation of Israel came, and spake unto Rehoboam, saying,**

4 **Thy father made our yoke grievous: now therefore make thou the grievous service of thy father, and his heavy yoke which he put upon us, lighter, and we will serve thee.**

5 And **he said unto them, Depart yet** *for* **three days, then come again to me. And the people departed.**

6 And king Rehoboam consulted with the old men, that stood before Solomon his father while he yet lived, and said, How do ye advise that I may answer this people?

7 And they spake unto him, saying, If thou wilt be a servant unto this people this day, and wilt serve them, and answer them, and speak good words to them, then they will be thy servants for ever.

8 But **he forsook the counsel of the old men, which they had given him, and consulted with the young men that were grown up with him,** *and* **which stood before him**:

9 And he said unto them, What counsel give ye that we may answer this people, who have spoken to me, saying, Make the yoke which thy father did put upon us lighter?

10 And **the young men that were grown up with him spake unto him, saying, Thus shalt thou speak unto this people that spake unto thee, saying, Thy father made our yoke heavy, but make thou** *it* **lighter unto us; thus shalt thou say unto them, My little** *finger* **shall be thicker than my father's loins.**

11 **And now whereas my father did lade you with a heavy yoke, I will add to your yoke: my father hath chastised you with whips, but I will chastise you with scorpions.**

12 So Jeroboam and all the people came to Rehoboam the third day, as the king had appointed, saying, Come to me again the third day.

13 And the king answered the people roughly, and forsook the old men's counsel that they gave him;

14 And spake to them after the counsel of the young men, saying, **My father made your yoke heavy, and I will add to your yoke: my father** *also* **chastised you with whips, but I will chastise you with scorpions.**

15 **Wherefore the king hearkened not unto the people; for the cause was from the LORD, that he might perform his saying, which the LORD spake by Ahijah the Shilonite unto Jeroboam the son of Nebat.**

16 So when all Israel saw that the king hearkened not unto them, the people answered the king, saying, What portion have we in David? neither *have we* inheritance in the son of Jesse: to your tents, O Israel: now see to thine own house, David. So Israel departed unto their tents.

ISRAEL REBELLED AGAINST THE HOUSE OF DAVID
1Kings 12:17 But *as for* the children of Israel which dwelt in the cities of Judah, Rehoboam reigned over them.

18 Then king Rehoboam sent Adoram, who *was* over the tribute; and all Israel stoned him with stones, that he died. Therefore king Rehoboam made speed to get him up to his chariot, to flee to Jerusalem.

19 So Israel rebelled against the house of David unto this day.

KINGDOM OF ISRAEL WAS DIVIDED
1Kings 12:20And it came to pass, **when all Israel heard that Jeroboam was come again, that they sent and called him unto the congregation, and made him king over all Israel:** there was none that followed the house of David, but the tribe of Judah only.

21 And when Rehoboam was come to Jerusalem, he assembled all the house of Judah, with the tribe of Benjamin, an hundred and fourscore thousand chosen men, which were warriors, to fight against the house of Israel, to bring the kingdom again to Rehoboam the son of Solomon.

THE LORD INTERFERED REHOBOAM'S PLAN TO FIGHT WITH ISRAEL
1Kings 12:22 But **the word of God came unto Shemaiah the man of God**, saying,

23 *Speak unto Rehoboam, the son of Solomon, king of Judah, and unto all the house of Judah and Benjamin, and to the remnant of the people, saying,*

24 **Thus saith the LORD**, *Ye shall not go up, nor fight against your brethren the children of Israel: return every man to his house; for this thing is from me*. They hearkened therefore to the word of the LORD, and returned to depart, according to the word of the LORD.

KINGDOM OF ISRAEL SINNED AGAINST GOD
1Kings 12:25 **Then Jeroboam built Schechem in mount Ephraim**, and dwelt therein; and went out from thence and built Penuel.

26 And **Jeroboam said in his heart**, Now shall the kingdom return to the house of David:

27 If this people go up to do sacrifice in the house of the LORD at Jerusalem, then shall the heart of this people turn again unto their lord, *even* unto Rehoboam king of Judah, and they shall kill me, and go again to Rehoboam king of Judah.

28 Whereupon **the king took counsel, and made two calves** *of* **gold, and said unto them, It is too much for you to go up to Jerusalem: behold thy gods, O Israel, which brought thee up out of the land of Egypt.**

29 **And he set the one in Bethel, and the other put he in Dan.**

30 And this thing became a sin: for the people went *to worship* before the one, *even* unto Dan.

31 And **he made an house of high places, and made priests of the lowest of the people, which were not of the sons of Levi.**

32 And Jeroboam ordained a feast in the eighth month, on the fifteenth day of the month, like unto the feast that *is* in Judah, and he offered upon the altar. So did he in Bethel, sacrificing unto the calves that he had made: and he placed in Bethel the priests of the high places which he had made.

33 So **he offered upon the altar which he had made in Bethel the fifteenth day of the eighth month,** *even* **in the month which he had devised of his own heart; and ordained a feast unto the children of Israel: and he offered upon the altar, and burnt incense.**

WARNING TO KING JEROBOAM OF ISRAEL

1Kings 14:7 Go, tell Jeroboam, Thus saith the LORD God of Israel, Forasmuch as I exalted thee from among the people, and made thee prince over my people Israel,

8 And rent the kingdom away from the house of David, and gave it thee: and *yet* thou hast not been as my servant David, who kept my commandments, and who followed me with all his heart, to do *that* only *which was* right in mine eyes;

9 **But hast done evil above all that were before thee: for thou hast gone and made thee other gods, and molten images, to provoke me to anger, and hast cast me behind thy back:**

10 Therefore, behold, I will bring evil upon the house of Jeroboam, and will cut off from Jeroboam him that pisseth against the wall, *and* him that is shut up and left in Israel, and will take away the remnant of the house of Jeroboam, as a man taketh away dung, till it be all gone.

BOOK OF RECORDS OF JUDAH AND ISRAEL

1. BOOK OF THE LAW/ BOOK OF THE COVENANT/ BOOK OF MOSES

Deuteronomy 29:29 **The secret** *things belong* **unto the LORD our** *God: but those things which are revealed belong unto us and to our children for ever, that we may do all the words of this law.*

Deuteronomy 31:24 **And it came to pass, when Moses had made an end of writing the words of this law in a book, until they were finished,**
Exodus 24:7 And he took the book of the covenant, and read in the audience of the people: and they said, All that the LORD hath said will we do, and be obedient.
Joshua 8: 33 And all Israel, and their elders, and officers, and their judges, stood on this side the ark and on that side before the priests the Levites, which bare the ark of the covenant of the LORD, as well the stranger, as he that was born among them; half of them over against mount Gerizim, and half of them over against mount Ebal; as Moses the servant of the LORD had commanded before, that they should bless the people of Israel.
34 And afterward he read all the words of the law, the blessings and cursings, according to all that is written in the book of the law.
35 There was not a word of all that Moses commanded, which Joshua read not before all the congregation of Israel, with the women, and the little ones, and the strangers that were conversant among them.
Josuah 24:26 And Joshua wrote these words in the book of the law of God, and took a great stone, and set it up there under an oak, that *was* by the sanctuary of the LORD.
Deuteronomy 29:27 And the anger of the LORD was kindled against this land, to bring upon it all the curses that are written in this book:
Joshua 23:6 Be ye therefore very courageous to keep and **to do all that is written in the book of the law of Moses,** that ye turn not aside therefrom *to* the right hand or *to* the left;

2Chronicles 34:15And Hilkiah answered and said to Shaphan the scribe, I have found the book of the law in the house of the LORD. And Hilkiah delivered the book to Shaphan.

Deuteronomy 31:26 Take this book of the law, and put it in the side of the ark of the covenant of the LORD your God, that it may be there for a witness against thee. /

Nehemiah 13:1 On that day they read in the book of Moses in the audience of the people; and **therein was found written, that the Ammonite and the Moabite should** not come into the congregation of God for ever;

2 **Because they met not the children of Israel with bread and with water, but hired Balaam against them, that he should curse them:** howbeit our God turned the curse into a blessing.

Joshua 1:8 **This book of the law shall not depart out of thy mouth; but thou shalt meditate therein day and night, that thou mayest observe to do according to all that is written therein:** for then thou shalt make thy way prosperous, and then thou shalt have good success.

2. BOOK OF THE RECORDS

Ezra 4:15 That search may be made in **the book of the records of thy fathers: so shalt thou find in the book of the records, and know that this city *is* a rebellious city**, and hurtful unto kings and provinces, and that they have moved sedition within the same of old time: for which cause was this city destroyed.

3. BOOK OF WARS OF THE LORD

Numbers 21:14 Wherefore it is said in **the book of the wars of the LORD**, What he did in the Red sea, and in the brooks of Arnon,

4. BOOK OF THE CHRONICLES OF THE KINGS OF JUDAH AND ISRAEL

2Chronicles 16:11 And, behold, the acts of Asa, first and last, lo, they *are* written in the book of the kings of Judah and Israel.

2Chronicles 35:27 And his deeds, first and last, behold, **they *are* written in the book of the kings of Israel and Judah.**

1Kings 14:29 Now **the rest of the acts of Rehoboam,** and all that he did, *are* they not written in **the book of the chronicles of the kings of Judah**?

5. BOOK OF JASPHER

Joshua 10:13 And **the sun stood still, and the moon stayed, until the people had avenged themselves upon their enemies.** *Is* **not this written in the book of Jasher? So the sun stood still in the midst of heaven, and hasted not to go down about a whole day.**

14 And **there was no day like that before it or after it, that the LORD hearkened unto the voice of a man: for the LORD fought for Israel**.

2Samuel 1:18 (Also he bade them teach the children of Judah *the use of* the bow: behold, *it is* written in **the book of Jasher.)**

6. BOOK OF JEREMIAH

Jeremiah 51:60 So Jeremiah wrote in a book all the evil that should come upon Babylon, *even* all **these words that are written against Babylon**.

61 And Jeremiah said to Seraiah, When thou comest to Babylon, and shalt see, and shalt read all these words;

62 Then shalt thou say, **O LORD, thou hast spoken against this place, to cut it off, that none shall remain in it, neither man nor beast, but that it shall be desolate for ever**.

63 And it shall be, when thou hast made an end of reading this book, *that* thou shalt bind a stone to it, and cast it into the midst of Euphrates:

64 And thou shalt say, Thus shall Babylon sink, and shall not rise from the evil that I will bring upon her: and they shall be weary. Thus far *are* the words of Jeremiah.

7. BOOK OF ACTS OF SOLOMON

1Kings 11:41 And the rest of the acts of Solomon, and all that he did, and his wisdom, *are* they not written **in the book of the acts of Solomon?**

PART 6
GOD ANOINTED DELIVERERS

CHAPTER IV **GOD REVEALED HIS PLAN TO THE PROPHETS**

2Chronicles 24:19
*Yet **he sent prophets to them, to bring them again unto the LORD**; and they testified against them: but they would not give ear.*

1Corinthians 14:3 But **he that prophesieth speaketh unto men** *to* **edification, and exhortation, and comfort.**

THE LORD GOD AND HIS SPIRIT SENT THE PROPHETS
Isaiah 48:16 *Come ye near unto me, hear ye this;* **I have not spoken in secret from the beginning; from the time that it was, there am I: and now the Lord GOD, and his Spirit, hath sent me.**

GOD GIVES INSTRUCTONS IN DREAM AND VISION

Numbers 12:6 *And he said, Hear now my words:* **If there be a prophet among you, I the LORD will make myself known unto him in a vision, and will speak unto him in a dream.**

Amos 3:7 Surely the LORD will do nothing, but **he revealeth his secret unto the servants the prophets.**
Job 33:14 For God speaketh once, yea twice, *yet man* perceiveth it not.
15 In a dream, in a vision of the night, when deep sleep falleth upon men, in slumberings upon the bed;
16 **Then he openeth the ears of men, and sealeth their instruction,**
17 That he may withdraw man *from his* purpose, and hide pride from man.

Hosea 12:10 I have also spoken by the prophets, and I have multiplied visions, and used similitudes, by the ministry of the prophets.

PROPHET WILL SPEAK IN THE NAME OF THE LORD
Deuteronomy18:15 **The LORD thy God will raise up unto thee a Prophet from the midst of thee, of thy brethren**, like unto me; unto him ye shall hearken;

18 **I will raise them up a Prophet from among their brethren, like unto thee, and will put my words in his mouth; and he shall speak unto them all that I shall command him.**

19 And it shall come to pass, *that* whosoever will not hearken unto my words which he shall speak in my name, I will require *it* of him.

1Samuel 9:9 (Beforetime in Israel, when a man went to enquire of God, thus he spake, Come, and let us go to the seer: for *he that is* now *called* a Prophet was beforetime called a Seer.)

A. ANCIENT PROPHECY OF THE WRATH OF GOD

THE COMING OF GREAT FLOOD

1. GIANTS WERE ON EARTH
Genesis 6:1 And it came to pass, when men began to multiply on the face of the earth, and daughters were born unto them,

2 That the sons of God saw the daughters of men that they *were* fair; and they took them wives of all which they chose.

4 There were giants in the earth in those days; **and also after that**, when the sons of God came in unto the daughters of men, and they bare *children* to them, the same *became* mighty men which *were* of old, men of renown.

2. HUMAN BEINGS WERE WICKED
Genesis 6:5 And GOD saw that the wickedness of man *was* great in the earth, and *that* every imagination of the thoughts of his heart *was* only evil continually.

6 And it repented the LORD that he had made man on the earth, and it grieved him at his heart.

7 And the LORD said, I will destroy man whom I have created from the face of the earth; both man, and beast, and the creeping

thing, and the fowls of the air; for it repenteth me that I have made them.

3. *GOD'S INSTRUCTION TO NOAH
Genesis 6:8 But Noah found grace in the eyes of the LORD.
Genesis 6:12 And God looked upon the earth, and, behold, it was corrupt; for all flesh had corrupted his way upon the earth.

13 And God said unto Noah, The end of all flesh is come before me; for the earth is filled with violence through them; and, behold, I will destroy them with the earth.

14 Make thee an ark of gopher wood; rooms shalt thou make in the ark, and shalt pitch it within and without with pitch.

15 And this *is the fashion* which thou shalt make it *of*: The length of the ark *shall be* three hundred cubits, the breadth of it fifty cubits, and the height of it thirty cubits.

16 A window shalt thou make to the ark, and in a cubit shalt thou finish it above; and the door of the ark shalt thou set in the side thereof; *with* lower, second, and third *stories* shalt thou make it.

17 And, behold, I, even I, do bring a flood of waters upon the earth, to destroy all flesh, wherein *is* the breath of life, from under heaven; *and* every thing that *is* in the earth shall die.

18 But with thee will I establish my covenant; and thou shalt come into the ark, thou, and thy sons, and thy wife, and thy sons' wives with thee.

19 And of every living thing of all flesh, two of every *sort* shalt thou bring into the ark, to keep *them* alive with thee; they shall be male and female.

20 Of fowls after their kind, and of cattle after their kind, of every creeping thing of the earth after his kind, two of every *sort* shall come unto thee, to keep *them* alive.

21 And take thou unto thee of all food that is eaten, and thou shalt gather *it*to thee; and it shall be for food for thee, and for them.

22 Thus did Noah; according to all that God commanded him, so did he.

Genesis 7:1 **And the LORD said unto Noah, Come thou and all thy house into the ark; for thee have I seen righteous before me in this generation.**

2 Of every clean beast thou shalt take to thee by sevens, the male and his female: and of beasts that *are* not clean by two, the male and his female.

3 Of fowls also of the air by sevens, the male and the female; to keep seed alive upon the face of all the earth.

4 For yet seven days, and I will cause it to rain upon the earth forty days and forty nights; and every living substance that I have made will I destroy from off the face of the earth.

5 **And Noah did according unto that the LORD commanded him.**

6 Noah was six hundred years old when the flood of waters was upon the earth

GOD'S COVENANT TO NOAH

Genesis 9:1 And **God blessed Noah and his sons, and said unto them, Be fruitful, and multiply, and replenish the earth.**

2 **And the fear of you and the dread of you shall be upon every beast of the earth, and upon every fowl of the air, upon all that moveth *upon* the earth, and upon all the fishes of the sea; into your hand are they delivered.**

3 **Every moving thing that liveth shall be meat for you; even as the green herb have I given you all things.**

4 But flesh with the life thereof, *which is* **the blood thereof, shall ye not eat.**

5 And surely your blood of your lives will I require; at the hand of every beast will I require it, and at the hand of man; at the hand of every man's brother will I require the life of man.

6 Whoso sheddeth man's blood, by man shall his blood be shed: for in the image of God made he man.

7 And you, be ye fruitful, and multiply; bring forth abundantly in the earth, and multiply therein.

8 And God spake unto Noah, and to his sons with him, saying,

9 And I, behold, I establish my covenant with you, and with your seed after you;

10 And with every living creature that *is* with you, of the fowl, of the cattle, and of every beast of the earth with you; from all that go out of the ark, to every beast of the earth.

11 **And I will establish my covenant with you; neither shall all flesh be cut off any more by the waters of a flood; neither shall there any more be a flood to destroy the earth.**

12 And God said, **This *is* the token of the covenant** which I make between me and you and every living creature that *is* with you, for perpetual generations:

13 **I do set my bow in the cloud, and it shall be for a token of a covenant between me and the earth.**

14 And it shall come to pass, when I bring a cloud over the earth, that the bow shall be seen in the cloud:

15 And I will remember my covenant, which *is* between me and you and every living creature of all flesh; and the waters shall no more become a flood to destroy all flesh.

16 **And the bow shall be in the cloud; and I will look upon it, that I may remember the everlasting covenant between God and every living creature of all flesh that *is* upon the earth.**

17 And God said unto Noah, **This *is* the token of the covenant, which I have established between me and all flesh that *is* upon the earth.**

NOAH'S FAMILY HISTORY

Genesis 5:1 This *is* the book of the generations of Adam. **In the day that God created man, in the likeness of God made he him;**

2 **Male and female created he them; and blessed them, and called their name Adam, in the day when they were created.**

3 And Adam lived an hundred and thirty years, and **begat *a son*** in his own likeness, after his image; and called his name **Seth:**

4 And the days of Adam after he had begotten Seth were eight hundred years: and he begat sons and daughters:

5 And **all the days that Adam lived were nine hundred and thirty years**: and he died.

6 And **Seth** lived an hundred and five years, and **begat Enos:**

7 And Seth lived after he begat Enos eight hundred and seven years, and begat sons and daughters:

8 And **all the days of Seth were nine hundred and twelve years**: and he died.

9 And **Enos** lived ninety years, and begat **Cainan:**

10 And Enos lived after he begat Cainan eight hundred and fifteen years, and begat sons and daughters:

11 And **all the days of Enos were nine hundred and five years**: and he died.

12 And **Cainan** lived seventy years, and begat **Mahalaleel**:

13 And Cainan lived after he begat Mahalaleel eight hundred and forty years, and begat sons and daughters:

14 And **all the days of Cainan were nine hundred and ten years**: and he died.

15 And **Mahalaleel** lived sixty and five years, and begat **Jared:**

16 And Mahalaleel lived after he begat Jared eight hundred and thirty years, and begat sons and daughters:

17 And **all the days of Mahalaleel were eight hundred ninety and five years**: and he died.

18 And **Jared** lived an hundred sixty and two years, and he begat **Enoch:**

19 And **Jared** lived after he **begat Enoch** eight hundred years, and begat sons and daughters:

20 And **all the days of Jared were nine hundred sixty and two years**: and he died.

21 And **Enoch** lived sixty and five years, and **begat Methuselah:**

22 And **Enoch walked with God a**fter he begat Methuselah three hundred years, and begat sons and daughters:

23 And **all the days of Enoch were three hundred sixty and five years**:

24 And **Enoch walked with God: and he *was* not; for God took him.**

25 **And Methuselah lived an** hundred eighty and seven years, and begat **Lamech:**

26 And Methuselah lived after he begat Lamech seven hundred eighty and two years, and begat sons and daughters:

27 And **all the days of Methuselah were nine hundred sixty and nine** years: and he died.

28 And **Lamech** lived an hundred eighty and two years, and **begat** a son:

29 And he called his name **Noah,** saying, This *same* shall comfort us concerning our work and toil of our hands, because of the ground which the LORD hath cursed.

30 And Lamech lived after he begat Noah five hundred ninety and five years, and begat sons and daughters:

31 And **all the days of Lamech** were **seven hundred seventy and seven years:** and he died.

32 And **Noah** was five hundred years old: and Noah **begat Shem, Ham, and Japheth.**

Genesis 9:28 And Noah lived after the flood three hundred and fifty years.

29And all the days of Noah were nine hundred and fifty years: and he died.

B. WISDOM TO INTERPRET DREAMS

THE TWO DREAMS OF THE KING OF EGYPT
Genesis 41:32 And **for that the dream was doubled unto Pharaoh twice**; *it is* **because the thing** *is* **established by God**, and God will shortly bring it to pass.

1 THE SEVEN LEAN AND ILL KINE DEVOURED THE SEVEN FAT KINE
Genesis 41:17 And Pharaoh said unto Joseph, In my dream, behold, I stood upon the bank of the river:
18 And, behold, there came up out of the river seven kine, fatfleshed and well favoured; and they fed in a meadow:
19 And, behold, seven other kine came up after them, poor and very ill favoured and leanfleshed, such as I never saw in all the land of Egypt for badness:
20 And the lean and the ill favoured kine did eat up the first seven fat kine:
21 And when they had eaten them up, it could not be known that they had eaten them; but they *were* still ill favoured, as at the beginning. So I awoke.

2. THE SEVEN THIN EARS OF CORN DEVOURED THE SEVEN GOOD EARS OF CORN
Genesis 41:22 And **I saw in my dream, and, behold, seven ears came up in one stalk, full and good:**
23 And, **behold, seven ears, withered, thin,** *and* **blasted with the east wind, sprung up after them:**
24 **And the thin ears devoured the seven good ears: and** I told *this* unto the magicians; but *there was* none that could declare *it* to me.

JOSEPH THE SON OF JACOB INTERPRETED THE DREAMS
Genesis 41:25 And Joseph said unto Pharaoh, The dream of Pharaoh *is* **one: God hath shewed Pharaoh what he** *is* **about to do.**
26 **The seven good kine** *are* **seven years; and the seven good ears** *are* **seven years: the dream** *is* **one.**

27 **And the seven thin and ill favoured kine that came up after them *are* seven years; and the seven empty ears blasted with the east wind shall be seven years of famine**.

28 This *is* the thing which I have spoken unto Pharaoh: **What God *is* about to do he sheweth unto Pharaoh.**

29 **Behold, there come seven years of great plenty throughout all the land of Egypt:**

30 **And there shall arise after them seven years of famine; and all the plenty shall be forgotten in the land of Egypt; and the famine shall consume the land;**

31 And the plenty shall not be known in the land by reason of that famine following; for it *shall be* very grievous.

C. VISION OF END TIMES

DANIEL
1. FOUR GREAT BEASTS

Daniel 7:1 In the first year of Belshazzar king of Babylon Daniel had a dream and visions of his head upon his bed: then he wrote the dream, *and* told the sum of the matters.

2 Daniel spake and said, I saw in my vision by night, and, behold, the four winds of the heaven strove upon the great sea.

3 And **four great beasts** came up from the sea, diverse one from another.

4 The first *was* like a lion, and had eagle's wings: I beheld till the wings thereof were plucked, and it was lifted up from the earth, and made stand upon the feet as a man, and a man's heart was given to it.

5 And behold another beast, a second, like to a bear, and it raised up itself on one side, and *it had* three ribs in the mouth of it between the teeth of it: and they said thus unto it, Arise, devour much flesh.

6 After this I beheld, and lo another, like a leopard, which had upon the back of it four wings of a fowl; the beast had also four heads; and dominion was given to it.

7 After this I saw in the night visions, and behold a fourth beast, dreadful and terrible, and strong exceedingly; and it had great iron teeth: it devoured and brake in pieces, and stamped the residue with the feet of it: and it *was* diverse from all the beasts that *were* before it; and it had ten horns.

8 I considered the horns, and, behold, there came up among them another little horn, before whom there were three of the first horns plucked up by the roots: and, behold, in this horn *were* eyes like the eyes of man, and a mouth speaking great things.

DANIEL'S INTERPRETATION (END TIMES PROPHESY)

FOUR KINGS OF THE FOUR KINGDOMS
Daniel 7:16 I came near unto one of them that stood by, and asked him the truth of all this. So he told me, and made me know the interpretation of the things.
17 **These great beasts, which are four,** *are* **four kings,** *which* shall arise out of the earth.
18 **But the saints of the most High shall take the kingdom, and possess the kingdom for ever, even for ever and ever.**
19 Then I would know the truth of the fourth beast, which was diverse from all the others, exceeding dreadful, whose teeth *were of* iron, and his nails *of* brass; *which* devoured, brake in pieces, and stamped the residue with his feet;
20 And of the ten horns that *were* in his head, and *of* the other which came up, and before whom three fell; even *of* that horn that had eyes, and a mouth that spake very great things, whose look *was* more stout than his fellows.

TRIBULATION PERIOD OF THE SAINTS
Daniel 8:24 And **his power shall be mighty, but not by his own power: and he shall destroy wonderfully, and shall prosper, and practise, and shall destroy the mighty and the holy people.**
25 And through his policy also he shall cause craft to prosper in his hand; and **he shall magnify** *himself* **in his heart, and by peace shall destroy many**: he shall also stand up against the Prince of princes; but he shall be broken without hand.
Daniel 7:21 I beheld, and **the same horn made war with the saints, and prevailed against them;**
Daniel 7:23 Thus he said, **the forth beast** shall be **the fourth kingdom upon earth**, which shall be diverse from all kingdoms, and shall devour the whole earth, and shall tread it down, and break it in pieces.

24 And **the ten horns out of this kingdom** *are* **ten kings** *that* **shall arise:** and another shall rise after them; and he shall be diverse from the first, and he shall subdue three kings.

25 **And he shall speak** *great* **words against the most High, and shall wear out the saints of the most High, and think to change times and laws:** and **they shall be given into his hand until a time and times and the dividing of time.**

2. DANIEL'S VISIONS OF HORNS DURING BABYLONIAN CAPTIVITY

Daniel 8:1 In **the third year of the reign of king Belshazzar** a vision appeared unto me, *even unto* me Daniel, after that which appeared unto me at the first.

2 And I saw in a vision; and it came to pass, when I saw, that I *was* at Shushan *in* the palace, which *is* in the province of Elam; and I saw in a vision, and I was by the river of Ulai.

3 Then I lifted up mine eyes, and saw, and, behold, there stood before the river a ram which had *two* horns: and the *two* horns *were* high; but one *was* higher than the other, and the higher came up last.

4 I saw the ram pushing westward, and northward, and southward; so that no beasts might stand before him, neither *was there any* that could deliver out of his hand; but he did according to his will, and became great.

5 And as I was considering, behold, **an he goat came from the west** on the face of the whole earth, and touched not the ground: and the goat *had* a notable horn between his eyes.

6 And he came to the ram that had *two* horns, which I had seen standing before the river, and ran unto him in the fury of his power.

7 And I saw him come close unto the ram, and he was moved with choler against him, and smote the ram, and brake his two horns: and there was no power in the ram to stand before him, but he cast him down to the ground, and stamped upon him: and there was none that could deliver the ram out of his hand.

8 Therefore the he goat waxed very great: and when he was strong, the great horn was broken; and for it came up four notable ones toward the four winds of heaven..

9 And out of one of them came forth a little horn, which waxed exceeding great, toward the south, and toward the east, and toward the pleasant *land*.

10 And it waxed great, *even* to the host of heaven; and it cast down *some* of the host and of the stars to the ground, and stamped upon them.

11 **Yea, he magnified** *himself* **even to the prince of the host, and by him the daily** *sacrifice* **was taken away, and the place of his sanctuary was cast down**.

12 And an host was given *him* against the daily *sacrifice* by reason of transgression, and it cast down the truth to the ground; and it practised, and prospered.

13 **Then I heard one saint speaking, and another saint said unto that certain** *saint* **which spake, How long** *shall be* **the vision** *concerning* **the daily** *sacrifice*, **and the transgression of desolation, to give both the sanctuary and the host to be trodden under foot?**

14 And **he said unto me, Unto two thousand and three hundred days; then shall the sanctuary be cleansed.**

INTERPRETATION OF HORNS (KINGDOMS UP TO END TIMES)

Daniel 8:15 And it came to pass, when I, *even* **I Daniel, had seen the vision, and sought for the meaning**, then, behold, there stood before me as the appearance of a man.

16 And I heard a man's voice between *the banks of* Ulai, which called, and said, Gabriel, make this *man* to understand the vision.

17 So he came near where I stood: and when he came, I was afraid, and fell upon my face: but he said unto me, Understand, O son of man: for at the time of the end *shall be* the vision.

18 Now as he was speaking with me, I was in a deep sleep on my face toward the ground: but he touched me, and set me upright.

19 And he said, Behold, I will make thee know what shall be in the last end of the indignation: for at the time appointed the end *shall be*.

20 The ram which thou sawest having *two* **horns** *are* **the kings of Media and Persia.**

21 And **the rough goat** *is* **the king of Grecia**: and **the great horn that** *is* **between his eyes** *is* **the first king.**

22 **Now that being broken, whereas four stood up for it, four kingdoms shall stand up out of the nation, but not in his power.**

23 And **in the latter time of their kingdom, when the transgressors are come to the full, a king of fierce**

countenance, and understanding dark sentences, shall stand up.

3. APOSTLE JOHN'S REVELATION: THE BEAST

Revelation 13:1 And I stood upon the sand of the sea, and **saw a beast rise up out of the sea, having seven heads and ten horns, and upon his horns ten crowns, and upon his heads the name of blasphemy.**

C. PROPHECIES

1. DAVID

PRAYER OF THE LORD IN HIS SUFFERINGS

Psalm 69:1 *(To the chief Musician upon Shoshannim, A Psalm of David.) Save me, O God; for the waters are come in unto my soul.*

2 I sink in deep mire, where there is no standing: I am come into deep waters, where the floods overflow me.

3 I am weary of my crying: my throat is dried: mine eyes fail while I wait for my God.

4 They that hate me without a cause are more than the hairs of mine head: they that would destroy me, being mine enemies wrongfully, are mighty: then I restored that which I took not away.

5 O God, thou knowest my foolishness; and my sins are not hid from thee.

6 Let not them that wait on thee, O Lord GOD of hosts, be ashamed for my sake: let not those that seek thee be confounded for my sake, O God of Israel.

7 Because for thy sake I have borne reproach; shame hath covered my face.

8 I am become a stranger unto my brethren, and an alien unto my mother's children.

9 For the zeal of thine house hath eaten me up; and the reproaches of them that reproached thee are fallen upon me.

13 But as for me, my prayer is unto thee, O LORD, in an acceptable time: O God, in the multitude of thy mercy hear me, in the truth of thy salvation.

16 Hear me, O LORD; for thy lovingkindness is good: turn unto me according to the multitude of thy tender mercies.

17 And hide not thy face from thy servant; for I am in trouble: hear me speedily.

19 Thou hast known my reproach, and my shame, and my dishonour: mine adversaries are all before thee.

20 Reproach hath broken my heart; and I am full of heaviness: and I looked for some to take pity, but there was none; and for comforters, but I found none.

21 They gave me also gall for my meat; and in my thirst they gave me vinegar to drink.

29 But I am poor and sorrowful: let thy salvation, O God set me up on high.

END TIMES PROPHECY: NATIONS AGAINST THE LORD

Acts 4:25 Who by the mouth of thy servant David hast said, Why did the heathen rage, and the people imagine vain things?

26 The kings of the earth stood up, and the rulers were gathered together against the Lord, and against his Christ**.**

Psalms 2:2 The kings of the earth set themselves, and **the rulers take counsel together, against the LORD, and against his anointed,** *saying,*

3 Let us break their bands asunder, and cast away their cords from us.

4 He that sitteth in the heavens shall laugh: the Lord shall have them in derision.

2. ELIJAH

PROPHESY: YEARS WITHOUT RAIN IN THE LAND

1Kings 16:29 And in the thirty and eighth year of Asa king of Judah began Ahab the son of Omri to reign over Israel: and Ahab the son of Omri reigned over Israel in Samaria twenty and two years.

30 **And Ahab the son of Omri did evil in the sight of the LORD above all that** *were* **before him.**

31 **And it came to pass, as if it had been a light thing for him to walk in the sins of Jeroboam the son of Nebat, that he took to wife Jezebel the daughter of Ethbaal king of the Zidonians, and went and served Baal, and worshipped him.**

32 And he reared up an altar for Baal in the house of Baal, which he had built in Samaria.

33 And Ahab made a grove; and Ahab did more to provoke the LORD God of Israel to anger than all the kings of Israel that were before him.

1Kings 17:1 And Elijah the Tishbite, *who was* of the inhabitants of Gilead, said unto Ahab, *As* the LORD God of Israel liveth, before whom I stand, there shall not be dew nor rain these years, but according to my word.

2 And the word of the LORD came unto him, saying,

3 Get thee hence, and turn thee eastward, and hide thyself by the brook Cherith, that *is* before Jordan.

4 And it shall be, *that* thou shalt drink of the brook; and I have commanded the ravens to feed thee there.

5 So he went and did according unto the word of the LORD: for he went and dwelt by the brook Cherith, that *is* before Jordan.

6 And the ravens brought him bread and flesh in the morning, and bread and flesh in the evening; and he drank of the brook.

7 And it came to pass after a while, that the brook dried up, because there had been no rain in the land.

3. AHAIJAH

PROPHESY: KINGDOM OF ISRAEL WILL BE DIVIDED

1Kings 11:29 And it came to pass at that time when Jeroboam went out of Jerusalem, that the prophet Ahijah the Shilonite found him in the way; and he had clad himself with a new garment; and they two *were* alone in the field:

30 And **Ahijah** caught the new garment that *was* on him, and rent it *in* twelve pieces:

31 And he said to Jeroboam, Take thee ten pieces: for thus saith the LORD, the God of Israel, Behold, **I will rend the kingdom out of the hand of Solomon, and will give ten tribes to thee:**

32 (But he shall have one tribe for my servant David's sake, and for Jerusalem's sake, the city which I have chosen out of all the tribes of Israel:)

33 **Because that they have forsaken me, and have worshipped Ashtoreth the goddess of the Zidonians, Chemosh the god of the Moabites, and Milcom the god of the children of Ammon, and have not walked in my ways, to do *that which is* right in mine eyes, and *to keep* my statutes and my judgments, as *did* David his father.**

34 Howbeit I will not take the whole kingdom out of his hand: but I will make him prince all the days of his life for David my servant's sake, whom I chose, because he kept my commandments and my statutes:

35 But I will take the kingdom out of his son's hand, and will give it unto thee, *even* ten tribes.

36 **And unto his son will I give one tribe, that David my servant may have a light alway before me in Jerusalem,** the city which I have chosen me to put my name there.

4. JEREMIAH

KINGDOM OF JUDAH WILL BE UNDER SIEGE BY BABYLON

Jeremiah 29:10 For thus saith the LORD, That after seventy years be accomplished at Babylon I will visit you, and perform my good word toward you, in causing you to return to this place.

5. EZEKIEL

BABYLONIANS WILL INVADE THE KINGDOM OF JUDAH

Ezekiel 5:7 Therefore thus saith the Lord GOD; Because ye multiplied more than the nations that *are* round about you, *and* **have not walked in my statutes, neither have kept my judgments, neither have done according to the judgments of the nations that** *are* **round about you;**

8 Therefore thus saith the Lord GOD; Behold, I, even I, *am* against thee, and will execute judgments in the midst of thee in the sight of the nations.

9 And I will do in thee that which I have not done, and whereunto I will not do any more the like, because of all thine abominations.

10 Therefore the fathers shall eat the sons in the midst of thee, and the sons shall eat their fathers; and I will execute judgments in thee, and the whole remnant of thee will I scatter into all the winds.

11 Wherefore, *as* I live, saith the Lord GOD; Surely, because thou hast defiled my sanctuary with all thy detestable things, and with all thine abominations, therefore will I also diminish *thee*; neither shall mine eye spare, neither will I have any pity.

12 **A third part of thee shall die with the pestilence, and with famine shall they be consumed in the midst of thee: and a**

third part shall fall by the sword round about thee; and I will scatter a third part into all the winds, and I will draw out a sword after them.

13 Thus shall mine anger be accomplished, and I will cause my fury to rest upon them, and I will be comforted: and they shall know that I the LORD have spoken *it* in my zeal, when I have accomplished my fury in them.

14 Moreover I will make thee waste, and a reproach among the nations that *are* round about thee, in the sight of all that pass by.

15 So it shall be a reproach and a taunt, an instruction and an astonishment unto the nations that *are* round about thee, when I shall execute judgments in thee in anger and in fury and in furious rebukes. I the LORD have spoken *it*

16 When I shall send upon them the evil arrows of famine, which shall be for *their* destruction, *and* which I will send to destroy you: and I will increase the famine upon you, and will break your staff of bread:

17 So will I send upon you famine and evil beasts, and they shall bereave thee; and pestilence and blood shall pass through thee; and I will bring the sword upon thee. I the LORD have spoken *it*.

Ezekiel 14:21 For thus saith the Lord GOD; How much more when I send my four sore judgments upon Jerusalem, the sword, and the famine, and the noisome beast, and the pestilence, to cut off from it man and beast?

22 Yet, behold, therein shall be left a remnant that shall be brought forth, *both* sons and daughters: behold, they shall come forth unto you, and ye shall see their way and their doings: and ye shall be comforted concerning the evil that I have brought upon Jerusalem, *even* concerning all that I have brought upon it.

23 And they shall comfort you, when ye see their ways and their doings: and ye shall know that I have not done without cause all that I have done in it, saith the Lord GOD.

END TIMES PROPHECIES

1. HAGGAI

THE COMING OF THE LORD OF HOSTS
Haggai 1:1 In the second year of Darius the king, in the sixth month, in the first day of the month, came the word of the LORD by Haggai the prophet unto Zerubbabel the son of Shealtiel,

governor of Judah, and to Joshua the son of Josedech, the high priest, saying,

2 Thus speaketh the LORD of hosts, saying, This people say, The time is not come, the time that the LORD'S house should be built.

3 Then came the word of the LORD by Haggai the prophet, saying,

4 *Is it* time for you, O ye, to dwell in your cieled houses, and this house *lie* waste?

5 Now therefore thus saith the LORD of hosts**; Consider your ways.**

6 **Ye have sown much, and bring in little; ye eat, but ye have not enough**; **ye drink, but ye are not filled with drink; ye clothe you, but there is none warm; and he that earneth wages earneth wages** *to put it* **into a bag with holes.**

7 Thus saith the LORD of hosts; Consider your ways.

8 Go up to the mountain, and bring wood, **and build the house; and I will take pleasure in it, and I will be glorified, saith the LORD.**

Haggai 2:6 For thus saith the LORD of hosts; Yet once, it *is* a little while, and I will shake the heavens, and the earth, and the sea, and the dry *land*;

7 And I will shake all nations, and the desire of all nations shall come: and I will fill this house with glory, saith the LORD of hosts.

8 The silver *is* mine, and the gold *is* mine, saith the LORD of hosts.

9 The glory of this latter house shall be greater than of the former, saith the LORD of hosts: and in this place will I give peace, saith the LORD of hosts.

Haggai 2:**22 And I will overthrow the throne of kingdoms, and I will destroy the strength of the kingdoms of the heathen; and I will overthrow the chariots, and those that ride in them; and the horses and their riders shall come down, every one by the sword of his brother.**

2. ISAIAH'S PROPHECIES

Isaiah 1:1 The vision of Isaiah the son of Amoz, which he saw concerning Judah and Jerusalem in the days of Uzziah, Jotham, Ahaz, *and* Hezekiah, kings of Judah.

2 Hear, O heavens, and give ear, O earth: for the LORD hath spoken, I have nourished and brought up children, and they have rebelled against me.

3 The ox knoweth his owner, and the ass his master's crib: *but* Israel doth not know, my people doth not consider.

4 Ah sinful nation, a people laden with iniquity, a seed of evildoers, children that are corrupters: they have forsaken the LORD, they have provoked the Holy One of Israel unto anger, they are gone away backward.

a. THE COMING OF THE REDEEMER OF ISRAEL (See Volume 2 Part 10 Chapter II)

Isaiah 11:1 And **there shall come forth a rod out of the stem of Jesse, and a Branch shall grow out of his roots:**

Isaiah 54:5 For thy Maker *is* thine husband; the LORD of hosts *is* his name; and thy Redeemer the Holy One of Israel; **The God of the whole earth shall he be called.**

Isaiah 53:11 **He shall see of the travail of his soul, *and* shall be satisfied: by his knowledge shall my righteous servant justify many; for he shall bear their iniquities.**

Isaiah 7:14 Therefore the Lord himself shall give you a sign; **Behold, a virgin shall conceive, and bear a son, and shall call his name Immanuel.**

b. THE HERITAGE OF THE NATION OF ISRAEL

Isaiah 54:17 **No weapon that is formed against thee shall prosper; and every tongue *that* shall rise against thee in judgment thou shalt condemn.** This *is* the heritage of the servants of the LORD, and their righteousness *is* of me, saith the LORD.

c. PUNISHMENT TO CHOSEN WHO DESPISED THE WORD OF GOD

Isaiah 5:1 Now will I sing to my wellbeloved a song of my beloved touching his vineyard. My wellbeloved hath a vineyard in a very fruitful hill:

2 And he fenced it, and gathered out the stones thereof, and planted it with the choicest vine, and built a tower in the midst of it, and also made a winepress therein: and he looked that it should bring forth grapes, and it brought forth wild grapes.

5 And now go to: I will tell you what I will do to my vineyard: **I will take away the hedge thereof, and it shall be eaten up;** and break down the wall thereof, and it shall be trodden down:

7 For **the vineyard of the LORD of hosts** *is* **the house of Israel, and the men of Judah his pleasant plant:** and he looked for judgment, but behold oppression; for righteousness, but behold a cry.

11 Woe unto them that rise up early in the morning, *that* they may follow strong drink; that continue until night, *till* wine inflame them!

12 And the harp, and the viol, the tabret, and pipe, and wine, are in their feasts: but they regard not the work of the LORD, neither consider the operation of his hands.

Isaiah 5:20 **Woe unto them that call evil good, and good evil;** that put darkness for light, and light for darkness; that put bitter for sweet, and sweet for bitter!

21 Woe unto *them that are* wise in their own eyes, and prudent in their own sight!

22 Woe unto *them that are* mighty to drink wine, and men of strength to mingle strong drink:

23 Which justify the wicked for reward, and take away the righteousness of the righteous from him!

24 Therefore **as the fire devoureth the stubble, and the flame consumeth the chaff, so their root shall the chaff, so their root shall be rottenness, and their blossom shall go up as dust: because they have cast away the law of the LORD of hosts, and despised the word of the Holy One of Israel.**

3. JEREMIAH

THE COMING BACK OF THE PEOPLE OF ISRAEL

Jeremiah 31:8 **Behold, I will bring them from the north country, and gather them from the coasts of the earth**, *and* with them the blind and the lame, the woman with child and her that travaileth with child together: a great company shall return thither.

9 **They shall come with weeping, and with supplications will I lead them**: I will cause them to walk by the rivers of waters in a straight way, wherein they shall not stumble: for I am a father to Israel, and Ephraim *is* my firstborn.

4. OBADIAH

JUDGMENT TO EDOM

Obadiah 1:1 The vision of Obadiah. Thus saith the Lord GOD concerning Edom; We have heard a rumour from the LORD, and an ambassador is sent among the heathen, Arise ye, and let us rise up against her in battle.

2 Behold, **I have made thee small among the heathen: thou art greatly despised**.

3 **The pride of thine heart hath deceived thee**, thou that dwellest in the clefts of the rock, whose habitation *is* high; that saith in his heart, Who shall bring me down to the ground?

4 Though thou exalt *thyself* as the eagle, and though thou set thy nest among the stars, thence will I bring thee down, saith the LORD.

5 If thieves came to thee, if robbers by night, (how art thou cut off!) would they not have stolen till they had enough? if the grapegatherers came to thee, would they not leave *some* grapes?

6 How are *the things* of Esau searched out! *how* are his hidden things sought up!

7 All the men of thy confederacy have brought thee *even* to the border: the men that were at peace with thee have deceived thee, *and* prevailed against thee; *they that eat* thy bread have laid a wound under thee: *there is* none understanding in him.

8 Shall **I not in that day, saith the LORD, even destroy the wise *men* out of Edom, and understanding out of the mount of Esau?**

9 **And thy mighty *men*, O Teman, shall be dismayed, to the end that every one of the mount of Esau may be cut off by slaughter**.

10 **For thy violence against thy brother Jacob shame shall cover thee, and thou shalt be cut off forever.**

17 **But upon mount Zion shall be deliverance, and there shall be holiness;** and the house of Jacob shall possess their possessions.

18 And the house of Jacob shall be a fire, and the house of Joseph a flame, and the house of Esau for stubble, and they shall kindle in them, and devour them; and **there shall not be *any* remaining of the house of Esau; for the LORD hath spoken *it*.**

21 And **saviours shall come up on mount Zion to judge the mount of Esau; and the Kingdom shall be the LORD'S.**

5. NAHUM

a. THE COMING OF GOD'S WRATH

Nahum 1:2 God *is* jealous, and the LORD revengeth; the LORD revengeth, and *is* furious; the LORD will take vengeance on his adversaries, and he reserveth *wrath* for his enemies.

3 The LORD *is* slow to anger, and great in power, and will not at all acquit *the wicked*: the LORD hath his way in the whirlwind and in the storm, and the clouds *are* the dust of his feet.

7 The LORD *is* good, a strong hold in the day of trouble; and he knoweth them that trust in him.

8 But with an overrunning flood he will make an utter end of the place thereof, and darkness shall pursue his enemies.

9 What do ye imagine against the LORD? he will make an utter end: affliction shall not rise up the second time.

10 For while *they be* folden together *as* thorns, and while they are drunken *as* drunkards, they shall be devoured as stubble fully dry.

b. THE LORD WILL AFFLICT HIS ENEMY

Nahum1:1 **The burden of Nineveh**. **The book of the vision of Nahum the** Elkoshite.

Nahum 1:11**There is *one* come out of thee**, **that imagineth evil against the LORD, a wicked counselor.**

12Thus saith the LORD; Though *they be* quiet, and likewise many, yet thus shall they be cut down, when he shall pass through. Though I have afflicted thee, I will afflict thee no more.

13 For now will I break his yoke from off thee, and will burst thy bonds in sunder.

14 And the LORD hath given a commandment concerning thee, ***that* no more of thy name be sown: out of the house of thy gods will I cut off the graven image and the molten image: I will make thy grave; for thou art vile.**

15 Behold upon the mountains the feet of him that bringeth good tidings, that publisheth peace! O Judah, keep thy solemn feasts, perform thy vows: for the wicked shall no more pass through thee; he is utterly cut off.

6. HABAKKUK

Habakkuk 3:1 A prayer of Habakkuk the prophet upon Shigionoth.

2 *O LORD, I have heard thy speech, and was afraid: O LORD, revive thy work in the midst of the years, in the midst of the years make known; in wrath remember mercy.*

6 He stood, and measured the earth: he beheld, and drove asunder the nations; and the everlasting mountains were scattered, the perpetual hills did bow: his ways *are* everlasting.

7 I saw the tents of Cushan in affliction: *and* the curtains of the land of Midian did tremble.

7. MICAH

Micha 1:1 The word of the LORD that came to Micah the Morasthite in the days of Jotham, Ahaz, *and* Hezekiah, kings of Judah, which he saw concerning Samaria and Jerusalem.

8. Ezekiel: GOD WILL DWELL IN THE MIDST OF JERUSALEM

Ezekiel 43 :7 And he said unto me, Son of man, the place of my throne, and the place of the soles of my feet, where I will dwell in the midst of the children of Israel for ever, and my holy name, shall the house of Israel no more defile, *neither* they, nor their kings, by their whoredom, nor by the carcases of their kings in their high places.

THE FORM AND PATTERN OF THE TEMPLE OF GOD IN MT ZION(Read Ezekiel Chapters 39-)

Ezekiel 43:**10** Thou son of man, shew the house to the house of Israel, that they may be ashamed of their iniquities: and let them measure the pattern.

11 And if they be ashamed of all that they have done, shew them the form of the house, and the fashion thereof, and the goings out thereof, and the comings in thereof, and all the forms thereof, and all the ordinances thereof, and all the forms thereof, and all the laws thereof: and write *it* in their sight, that they may keep the whole form thereof, and all the ordinances thereof, and do them.

12 This *is* the law of the house; Upon the top of the mountain the whole limit thereof round about *shall be* most holy. Behold, this *is* the law of the house.

CHAPTER V **GOD GAVE POWERS TO THE PROPHETS OF ISRAEL**

Micah 3:8
But truly I am full of power by the spirit of the LORD, and of judgment, and of might, to declare unto Jacob his transgression, and to Israel his sin.

Amos 2:11 **And I raised up of your sons for prophets**, **and of your young men for Nazarites.** *Is it* not even thus, O ye children of Israel? saith the LORD.

12 But ye gave the Nazarites wine to drink; and commanded the prophets, saying, Prophesy not.

A. FILLED WITH THE SPIRIT

1. MIGHT AND POWER TO DO MIRACLES

MOSES
Deuteronomy 34:10 And **there arose not a prophet since in Israel like unto Moses**, **whom the LORD knew face to face**,
Hosea 12:13 And **by a prophet the LORD brought Israel out of Egypt, and by a prophet was he preserved.**
Deuteronomy 34:11 In all the signs and the wonders, which the LORD sent him to do in the land of Egypt to Pharaoh, and to all his servants, and to all his land,
12 And in all that mighty hand, and in all the great terror which Moses shewed in the sight of all Israel.
Exodus 3:7 And the LORD said, I have surely seen the affliction of my people which *are* in Egypt, and have heard their cry by reason of their taskmasters; for I know their sorrows;
8 And I am come down to deliver them out of the hand of the Egyptians, and to bring them up out of that land unto a good land and a large, unto a land flowing with milk and honey; unto the

place of the Canaanites, and the Hittites, and the Amorites, and the Perizzites, and the Hivites, and the Jebusites.

10 Come now therefore, and I will send thee unto Pharaoh, that thou mayest bring forth my people the children of Israel out of Egypt.

ELIJAH

THE WIDOW FROM ZERAPHATH

1Kings 17:8 And the word of the LORD came to him saying,

9 Arise, get thee to Zarephath, which *belongeth* to Zidon, and dwell there: behold, I have commanded a widow woman there to sustain thee.

10 So he arose and went to Zarephath. And when he came to the gate of the city, behold, the widow woman *was* there gathering of sticks: and he called to her, and said, Fetch me, I pray thee, a little water in a vessel, that I may drink.

11 And as she was going to fetch *it*, he called to her, and said, Bring me, I pray thee, a morsel of bread in thine hand.

12 And she said, *As* the LORD thy God liveth, I have not a cake, but an handful of meal in a barrel, and a little oil in a cruse: and, behold, I *am* gathering two sticks, that I may go in and dress it for me and my son, that we may eat it, and die.

13 And **Elijah said unto her, Fear not; go *and* do as thou hast said: but make me thereof a little cake first, and bring *it* unto me, and after make for thee and for thy son.**

14 **For thus saith the LORD God of Israel, The barrel of meal shall not waste, neither shall the cruse of oil fail, until the day *that* the LORD sendeth rain upon the earth.**

15 **And she went and did according to the saying of Elijah: and she, and he, and her house, did eat *many* days.**

16 *And* **the barrel of meal wasted not, neither did the cruse of oil fail, according to the word of the LORD, which he spake by Elijah.**

ELIJAH SENT OBADIAH TO KING AHAB

1Kings 18:1 And it came to pass *after* many days, that the word of the LORD came to Elijah in the third year, saying, **Go, shew thyself unto Ahab; and I will send rain upon the earth.**

2 And Elijah went to shew himself unto Ahab. And *there was* a sore famine in Samaria.

3 And Ahab called Obadiah, which *was* the governor of *his* house. (Now Obadiah feared the LORD greatly

4 For it was *so*, when Jezebel cut off the prophets of the LORD, that Obadiah took an hundred prophets, and hid them by fifty in a cave, and fed them with bread and water.)

5 And Ahab said unto Obadiah, Go into the land, unto all fountains of water, and unto all brooks: peradventure we may find grass to save the horses and mules alive, that we lose not all the beasts.

6 So they divided the land between them to pass throughout it: Ahab went one way by himself, and Obadiah went another way by himself.

7 And as Obadiah was in the way, behold, Elijah met him: and he knew him, and fell on his face, and said, *Art* thou that my lord Elijah?

8 And he answered him, I *am*: go, tell thy lord, Behold, Elijah *is here*.

9 And he said, What have I sinned, that thou wouldest deliver thy servant into the hand of Ahab, to slay me?

10 *As* the LORD thy God liveth, there is no nation or kingdom, whither my lord hath not sent to seek thee: and when they said, *He is* not *there*; he took an oath of the kingdom and nation, that they found thee not.

11 And now thou sayest, Go, tell thy lord, Behold, Elijah *is here*.

12 And it shall come to pass, *as soon as* I am gone from thee, that the Spirit of the LORD shall carry thee whither I know not; and sowhen I come and tell Ahab, and he cannot find thee, he shall slay me: but I thy servant fear the LORD from my youth.

13 Was it not told my lord what I did when Jezebel slew the prophets of the LORD, how I hid an hundred men of the LORD'S prophets by fifty in a cave, and fed them with bread and water?

14 And now thou sayest, Go, tell thy lord, Behold, Elijah *is here*: and he shall slay me.

15 And Elijah said, *As* the LORD of hosts liveth, before whom I stand, I will surely shew myself unto him to day.

16 So Obadiah went to meet Ahab, and told him: and Ahab went to meet Elijah.

AHAB MET ELIJAH

1Kings 18:17 And it came to pass, when Ahab saw Elijah, that Ahab said unto him, *Art* thou he that troubleth Israel?

18 And he answered, I have not troubled Israel; **but thou, and thy father's house, in that ye have forsaken the commandments of the LORD, and thou hast followed Baalim.**
19 **Now therefore send,** *and* **gather to me all Israel unto mount Carmel, and the prophets of Baal four hundred and fifty, and the prophets of the groves four hundred, which eat at Jezebel's table.**
20 So Ahab sent unto all the children of Israel, and gathered the prophets together unto mount Carmel.

ELIJAH CHALLENGED THE FALSE PROPHETS AND THEIR FALSE gods
1Kings 18:21 And Elijah came unto all the people, and said, How long halt ye between two opinions? if the LORD *be* God, follow him: but if Baal, *then* follow him. And the people answered him not a word.
22 Then said Elijah unto the people, I, *even* I only, remain a prophet of the LORD; but Baal's prophets *are* four hundred and fifty men.
23 Let them therefore give us two bullocks; and let them choose one bullock for themselves, and cut it in pieces, and lay *it* on wood, and put no fire *under*: and I will dress the other bullock, and lay *it* on wood, and put no fire *under*:
24 And call ye on the name of your gods, and I will call on the name of the LORD: and the God that answereth by fire, let him be God. And all the people answered and said, It is well spoken.
25 And **Elijah said unto the prophets of Baal, Choose you one bullock for yourselves, and dress** *it* **first; for ye** *are* **many; and call on the name of your gods, but put no fire** *under.*
26 And they took the bullock which was given them, and they dressed *it*, and called on the name of Baal from morning even until noon, saying, **O Baal, hear us. But** *there was* **no voice, nor any that answered. And they leaped upon the altar which was made.**
27 **And it came to pass at noon, that Elijah mocked them, and said, Cry aloud: for he** *is* **a god; either he is talking, or he is pursuing, or he is in a journey,** *or* **peradventure he sleepeth, and must be awaked.**
28 And **they cried aloud, and cut themselves after their manner with knives and lancets, till the blood gushed out upon them.**

29 And it came to pass, when midday was past, and they prophesied until the *time* of the offering of the *evening* sacrifice, that *there was* **neither voice, nor any to answer, nor any that regarded**.

ELIJAH PRAYED TO THE LORD TO REVEAL HIS POWER
1Kings 18:30 And Elijah said unto all the people, **Come near unto me. And all the people came near unto him. And he repaired the altar of the LORD** *that was* **broken down.**

31 And **Elijah took twelve stones, according to the number of the tribes of the sons of Jacob, unto whom the word of the LORD came, saying, Israel shall be thy name:**

32 And with the stones he built an altar in the name of the LORD: and he made a trench about the altar, as great as would contain two measures of seed.

33 And he put the wood in order, and cut the bullock in pieces, and laid *him* on the wood, and said, Fill four barrels with water, and pour *it* on the burnt sacrifice, and on the wood.

34 And he said, Do *it* the second time. And they did *it* the second time. And he said, Do *it* the third time. And they did *it* the third time.

35 And the water ran round about the altar; and he filled the trench also with water.

36 **And it came to pass at** *the time of* **the offering of the** *evening* **sacrifice, that Elijah the prophet came near, and said, LORD God of Abraham, Isaac, and of Israel, let it be known this day that thou** *art* **God in Israel, and** *that* **I** *am* **thy servant, and** *that* **I have done all these things at thy word.**

37 *Hear me, O LORD, hear me, that this people may know that thou art the LORD God, and that thou hast turned their heart back again.*

38 **Then the fire of the LORD fell, and consumed the burnt sacrifice, and the wood, and the stones, and the dust, and licked up the water that** *was* **in the trench.**

39 **And when all the people saw** *it,* **they fell on their faces: and they said, The LORD, he** *is* **the God; the LORD, he** *is* **the God.**

40 And **Elijah said unto them, Take the prophets of Baal; let not one of them escape. And they took them: and Elijah brought them down to the brook Kishon, and slew them there.**

THE ABUNDANCE OF RAIN CAME

1Kings 18:41 And Elijah said unto Ahab, Get thee up, eat and drink; for *there is* a sound of abundance of rain.

42 So Ahab went up to eat and to drink. And Elijah went up to the top of Carmel; and he cast himself down upon the earth, and put his face between his knees,

43 And said to his servant, Go up now, look toward the sea. And he went up, and looked, and said, *There is* nothing. And he said, Go again seven times.

44 And it came to pass at the seventh time, that he said, Behold, there ariseth a little cloud out of the sea, like a man's hand. And he said, Go up, say unto Ahab, Prepare *thy chariot*, and get thee down, that the rain stop thee not.

45 And it came to pass in the mean while, that the heaven was black with clouds and wind, and there was a great rain. And Ahab rode, and went to Jezreel.

ELIJAH WAS TAKEN TO HEAVEN ALIVE

2 Kings 2:1 And it came to pass, when the LORD would take up Elijah into heaven by a whirlwind, that Elijah went with Elisha from Gilgal.

2 And Elijah said unto Elisha, Tarry here, I pray thee; for the LORD hath sent me to Bethel. And Elisha said *unto him, As* the LORD liveth, and *as* thy soul liveth, I will not leave thee. So they went down to Bethel.

3 And the sons of the prophets that *were* at Bethel came forth to Elisha, and said unto him, Knowest thou that the LORD will take away thy master from thy head to day? And he said, Yea, I know *it*; hold ye your peace.

4 And Elijah said unto him, Elisha, tarry here, I pray thee; for the LORD hath sent me to Jericho. And he said, *As* the LORD liveth, and *as* thy soul liveth, I will not leave thee. So they came to Jericho.

5 And the sons of the prophets that *were* at Jericho came to Elisha, and said unto him, Knowest thou that the LORD will take away thy master from thy head to day? And he answered, Yea, I know *it*; hold ye your peace.

6 And Elijah said unto him, Tarry, I pray thee, here; for the LORD hath sent me to Jordan. And he said, *As* the LORD liveth, and *as* thy soul liveth, I will not leave thee. And they two went on.

7 And fifty men of the sons of the prophets went, and stood to view afar off: and they two stood by Jordan.

8 And Elijah took his mantle, and wrapped *it* together, and smote the waters, and they were divided hither and thither, so that they two went over on dry ground.

9 And it came to pass, when they were gone over, that Elijah said unto Elisha, Ask what I shall do for thee, before I be taken away from thee. And Elisha said, I pray thee, let a double portion of thy spirit be upon me.

10 And he said, Thou hast asked a hard thing: *nevertheless*, if thou see me *when I am* taken from thee, it shall be so unto thee; but if not, it shall not be *so*.

11 And it came to pass, as they still went on, and talked, that, behold, *there appeared* a chariot of fire, and horses of fire, and parted them both asunder; and Elijah went up by a whirlwind into heaven.

12 And Elisha saw *it*, and he cried, My father, my father, the chariot of Israel, and the horsemen thereof. And he saw him no more: and he took hold of his own clothes, and rent them in two pieces.

ELIAS AND ELIJAH THE SAME PERSON

James 5:17 Elias was a man subject to like passions as we are, and **he prayed earnestly that   it might not rain:** and it rained not on the earth by the space of three years and six months.

18 And he prayed again, and the heaven gave rain, and the earth brought forth her fruit.

Luke 4:25 But I tell you of a truth, many widows were in **Israel in the days of Elias, when the heaven was shut up three years and six months, when great famine was throughout all the land;**

26 But unto none of them was **Elias sent, save unto Sarepta,** *a city* **of Sidon, unto a woman** *that was* **a widow.**

Romans 11:2 God hath not cast away his people which he foreknew. Wot ye not what the scripture saith of Elias? **How he maketh intercession to God against Israe**l, saying,

3 **LORD, they have killed thy prophets, and digged down thine altars; and I am left alone, and they seek my life.**

Matthew 11:14 **And if ye will receive it, this is Elias , which was for to come.**

15 He that hath ears to hear, let him hear.

Mark 9:12 And he answered and told them, Elias verily cometh first, and restoreth all things; and how it is written of the Son of man, that he must suffer many things, and be set at naught.

Matthew 17:10 And his disciples asked him, saying, Why then say the scribes **that Elias must first come?**

11 And **Jesus answered and said unto them, Elias truly shall first come, and restore all things,**

12 **But I say unto you, that Elias is come already, and they knew him not**, but have done unto him whatsoever they listed. Likewise shall also the Son of Man suffer of them.

Mark 9:13 But I say unto you, **that Elias is indeed come**, and they have done unto him, whatsoever they listed, as it written of him.

Luke 9:8 And of some, **that Elias had appeared; and of others, that one of the old prophets was risen again.**

Luke 1:17 **And he shall go before him in the spirit and power of Elias,** to turn the hearts of the fathers to the children, and the disobedient to the wisdom of the just; **to make ready a people prepared for the LORD.**

ELISHA
WATER OF JORDAN WAS PARTED
2Kings 2:13 He took up also the mantle of Elijah that fell from him, and went back, and stood by the bank of Jordan;

14 And he took the mantle of Elijah that fell from him, and smote the waters, and said, Where *is* the LORD God of Elijah? and when he also had smitten the waters, they parted hither and thither: and Elisha went over.

15 And when the sons of the prophets which *were* to view at Jericho saw him, they said, The spirit of Elijah doth rest on Elisha. And they came to meet him, and bowed themselves to the ground before him.

WATER WAS HEALED IN JERICHO
2Kings 2:19 And the men of the city said unto Elisha, Behold, I pray thee, the situation of this city *is* pleasant, as my lord seeth: but the water *is* naught, and the ground barren.

20 And he said, Bring me a new cruse, and put salt therein. And they brought *it* to him.

21 And **he went forth unto the spring of the waters, and cast the salt in there, and said, Thus saith the LORD, I have**

healed these waters; there shall not be from thence any more death or barren _land._

22 So the waters were healed unto this day, according to the saying of Elisha which he spake.

THE DEAD CHILD WAS RISEN FROM DEAD

2Kings 4:32 And when Elisha was come into the house, behold, the child was dead, _and_ laid upon his bed.

33 He went in therefore, and shut the door upon them twain, and prayed unto the LORD.

34 And he went up, and lay upon the child, and put his mouth upon his mouth, and his eyes upon his eyes, and his hands upon his hands: and he stretched himself upon the child; and the flesh of the child waxed warm.

35 Then he returned, and walked in the house to and fro; and went up, and stretched himself upon him: and the child sneezed seven times, and the child opened his eyes.

2. TO ANOINT KINGS

a. ANOINTING OF KING SAUL

Acts 13:21 And afterward they desired a king: and God gave unto them Saul, the son of Cis, a man of the tribe of Benjamin, by the space of forty years.

1Samuel 9:15 Now **the LORD had told Samuel in his ear a day before Saul came**, saying,

16 _To morrow about this time I will send thee a man out of the land of Benjamin, and thou shalt anoint him to be captain over my people Israel, that he may save my people out of the hand of the Philistines:_ for I have looked upon my people, because their cry is come unto me.

1Samuel 10:1 **Then Samuel took a vial of oil, and poured _it_ upon his head, and kissed him, and said**, _Is itnot because the LORD hath anointed thee to be captain over his inheritance?_

b. ANOINTING DAVID, THE SON OF JESSE

Acts 13:22 And when he had removed him, he raised up unto them David to be their king; to whom also he gave testimony, and said, I have found David the son of Jesse, a man after mine own heart, which shall fulfill all my will.

23 Of this man's seed hath God according to *his* promise raised unto Israel a Saviour, Jesus:
1Samuel 16:1 And the LORD said unto Samuel, How long wilt thou mourn for Saul, seeing I have rejected him from reigning over Israel? fill thine horn with oil, and go, I will send thee to Jesse the Bethlehemite: for I have provided me a king among his sons.
1Samuel 16:12 And he sent, and brought him in. Now he *was* ruddy, *and* withal of a beautiful countenance, and goodly to look to. And the LORD said, **Arise, anoint him: for this *is* he.**
13 **Then Samuel took the horn of oil, and anointed him in the midst of his brethren: and the Spirit of the LORD came upon David from that day forward**. So Samuel rose up, and went to Ramah.

c. ANOINTING HAZAEL TO BE THE KING OVER SYRIA
1Kings 19:15 And the LORD said unto him, Go, return on thy way to the wilderness of Damascus: and when thou comest, **anoint Hazael *to be* king over Syria:**

d. ANOINT KING AND PROPHET OVER ISRAEL
1Kings 19:16 **And Jehu the son of Nimshi shalt thou anoint *to be* king over Israel: and Elisha the son of Shaphat of Abelmeholah shalt thou anoint *to be* prophet in thy room**.

B. TO DELIVER MESSAGE FROM THE LORD

1. JONAH
Jonah 1:1 Now the word of the LORD came unto Jonah the son of Amittai, saying,
2 **Arise, go to Nineveh, that great city, and cry against it; for their wickedness is come up before me.**
Jonah 3:1 And the word of the LORD came unto Jonah the second time, saying,
2 Arise, go unto Nineveh, that great city, and preach unto it the preaching that I bid thee.
3 So Jonah arose, and went unto Nineveh, according to the word of the LORD. Now Nineveh was an exceeding great city of three days' journey.

4 **And Jonah began to enter into the city a day's journey, and he cried, and said,** *Yet forty days, and Nineveh shall be overthrown.*

5 **So the people of Nineveh believed God, and proclaimed a fast, and put on sackcloth**, from the greatest of them even to the least of them.

6 **For word came unto the king of Nineveh, and he arose from his throne, and he laid his robe from him, and covered** *him* **with sackcloth, and sat in ashes**.

7 **And he caused** *it* **to be proclaimed and published through Nineveh by the decree of the king and his nobles,** saying, Let neither man nor beast, herd nor flock, taste any thing: let them not feed, nor drink water:

8 But let man and beast be covered with sackcloth**, and cry mightily unto God: yea**, let them turn every one from his evil way, and from the violence that** *is* **in their hands.**

9 **Who can tell** *if* **God will turn and repent, and turn away from his fierce anger, that we perish not?**

10 And God saw their works, that they turned from their evil way; and **God repented of the evil, that he had said that he would do unto them; and he did** *it* not.

2. JEREMIAH

Jeremiah 26:2 Thus saith the LORD; Stand in the court of the LORD'S house, and speak unto all the cities of Judah, which come to worship in the LORD'S house, **all the words that I command thee to speak unto them; diminish not a word:**

3 **If so be they will hearken, and turn every man from his evil way,** that I may repent me of the evil, which I purpose to do unto them because of the evil of their doings.

4 And thou shalt say unto them, Thus saith the LORD; If ye will not hearken to me, to walk in my law, which I have set before you,

5 **To hearken to the words of my servants the prophets, whom I sent unto you, both rising up early, and sending** *them*, but ye have not hearkened;

6 Then will I make this house like Shiloh, and will make this city a curse to all the nations of the earth.

Jeremiah 51:60 **So Jeremiah wrote in a book all the evil that should come upon Babylon,** even all these words that are written against Babylon.

61 And Jeremiah said to Seraiah, When thou comest to Babylon, and shalt see, and shalt read all these words;

62 Then shalt thou say, O LORD, thou hast spoken against this place, to cut it off, **that none shall remain in it, neither man nor beast, but that it shall be desolate for ever.**

63 And it shall be, when thou hast made an end of reading this book, *that* thou shalt bind a stone to it, and cast it into the midst of Euphrates:

64 And thou shalt say, **Thus shall Babylon sink, and shall not rise from the evil that I will bring upon her:** and they shall be weary. Thus far *are* the words of Jeremiah.

3. MALACHI: RETURN TO GOD OF ISRAEL

Malachi 3:7 Even from the days of your fathers ye are gone away from mine ordinances, and have not kept *them*. **Return unto me, and I will return unto you, saith the LORD of hosts.** But ye said, Wherein shall we return?

10 **Bring ye all the tithes into the storehouse, that there may be meat in mine house, and prove me now herewith, saith the LORD of hosts, if I will not open you the windows of heaven, and pour you out a blessing, that *there shall* not *be room* enough *to receive it.***

11 **And I will rebuke the devourer for your sakes**, and he shall not destroy the fruits of your ground; neither shall your vine cast her fruit before the time in the field, saith the LORD of hosts.

C. GOD SHOWED HIS GLORY TO THE PROPHETS

1. EZEKIEL

VISION OF THE HOSTS OF HEAVEN: THE FOUR LIVING CREATURES

Ezekiel 1:3 The word of the LORD came expressly **unto Ezekiel the priest, the son of Buzi, in the land of the Chaldeans** by the river Chebar; and the hand of the LORD was there upon him.

4 And I looked, and, behold, a whirlwind came out of the north, a great cloud, and a fire infolding itself, and a brightness *was* about

it, and out of the midst thereof as the colour of amber, out of the midst of the fire.

5 Also out of the midst thereof *came* the likeness of four living creatures. **And this *was* their appearance; they had the likeness of a man.**

THE GLORY OF THE LORD (See Volume 3, Part 18 Chapter XV)
Ezekiel 1:27 And I saw as the colour of amber, as the appearance of fire round about within it, from the appearance of his loins even upward, and from the appearance of his loins even downward, **I saw as it were the appearance of fire, and it had brightness round about.**

28 As the appearance of the bow that is in the cloud in the day of rain, so *was* the appearance of the brightness round about. This *was* the appearance of the likeness of the glory of the LORD. And when I saw *it*, I fell upon my face, and I heard a voice of one that spake.

2. APOSTLE JOHN

Revelation 1:13 And in the midst of the seven candlesticks *one* like unto the Son of man, clothed with a garment down to the foot, and girt about the paps with a golden girdle.

14 **His head and *his* hairs *were* white like wool, as white as snow; and his eyes *were* as a flame of fire**;

15 **And his feet like unto fine brass, as if they burned in a furnace; and his voice as the sound of many waters**.

16 And he had in his right hand seven stars: and out of his mouth went a sharp twoedged sword: and his countenance *was* as the sun shineth in his strength.

17 And when I saw him, I fell at his feet as dead. And he laid his right hand upon me, saying unto me, Fear not; I am the first and the last:

18 I *am* he that liveth, and was dead; and, behold, I am alive for evermore, Amen; and have the keys of hell and of death.

19 Write the things which thou hast seen, and the things which are, and the things which shall be hereafter;

===

PART 7
THE CHILDREN OF DISOBEDIENCE

CHAPTER I **IDOLATERS**

Isaiah 40:25
To whom then will ye liken me, or shall I be equal? saith the Holy One. 26 Lift up your eyes on high, and behold who hath created these things, that bringeth out their host by number: he calleth them all by names by the greatness of his might, for that he is strong in power; not one faileth.

* THE TRUTH AND INSTRUCTION
Proverbs 23:23 Buy the truth, and sell *it* not; *also* wisdom, and instruction, and understanding.
John 8:32 And ye shall know the truth, and the truth shall make you free.

WORSHIP THE LIVING GOD
Isaiah 40:22 *It is* **he that sitteth upon the circle of the earth**, and the inhabitants thereof *are* as grasshoppers; that stretcheth out the heavens as a curtain, and spreadeth them out as a tent to dwell in:
23 That bringeth the princes to nothing; he maketh the judges of the earth as vanity.
24 Yea, they shall not be planted; yea, they shall not be sown: yea, their stock shall not take root in the earth: and he shall also blow upon them, and they shall wither, and the whirlwind shall take them away as stubble.
Deuteronomy 4:39 Know therefore this day, and consider *it* in thine heart, that **the LORD he** *is* **God in heaven above, and upon the earth beneath:** *there is* **none else.**
Nehemiah 9:6 **Thou,** *even* **thou,** *art* **LORD alone; thou hast made heaven, the heaven of heavens, with all their host, the earth, and all** *things* **that** *are* **therein, the seas, and all that** *is* **therein, and thou preservest them all; and the host of heaven worshippeth thee.**

7 **Thou *art* the LORD the God, who didst choose Abram**, and broughtest him forth out of Ur of the Chaldees, and gavest him the name of Abraham;

8 And foundest **his heart faithful before thee, and madest a covenant with him to give the land of the Canaanites, the Hittites, the Amorites, and the Perizzites, and the Jebusites, and the Girgashites, to give *it, I say*, to his seed,** and hast performed thy words; for thou *art* righteous:

9 And didst see the affliction of our fathers in Egypt, and heardest their cry by the Red sea;

10 And shewedst signs and wonders upon Pharaoh, and on all his servants, and on all the people of his land: for thou knewest that they dealt proudly against them. So didst thou get thee a name, as *it is* this day.

11 And thou didst divide the sea before them, so that they went through the midst of the sea on the dry land; and their persecutors thou threwest into the deeps, as a stone into the mighty waters.

12 Moreover thou leddest them in the day by a cloudy pillar; and in the night by a pillar of fire, to give them light in the way wherein they should go.

13 **Thou camest down also upon mount Sinai, and spakest with them from heaven, and gavest them right judgments, and true laws, good statutes and commandments**:

14 **And madest known unto them thy holy sabbath, and commandedst them precepts, statutes, and laws, by the hand of Moses thy servant**:

15 And gavest them bread from heaven for their hunger, and broughtest forth water for them out of the rock for their thirst, and promisedst them that they should go in to possess the land which thou hadst sworn to give them.

16 But **they and our fathers dealt proudly, and hardened their necks, and hearkened not to thy commandments,**

17 And **refused to obey, neither were mindful of thy wonders that thou didst among them; but hardened their necks, and in their rebellion appointed a captain to return to their bondage: but thou *art* a God ready to pardon, gracious and merciful, slow to anger, and of great kindness, and forsookest them not.**

18 Yea, when they had made them a molten calf, and said, This *is* thy God that brought thee up out of Egypt, and had wrought great provocations;

19 **Yet thou in thy manifold mercies forsookest them not in the wilderness: the pillar of the cloud departed not from them by day, to lead them in the way; neither the pillar of fire by night, to shew them light, and the way wherein they should go.**
20 **Thou gavest also thy good spirit to instruct them, and withheldest not thy manna from their mouth, and gavest them water for their thirst.**
21 Yea, **forty years didst thou sustain them in the wilderness, *so that* they lacked nothing; their clothes waxed not old, and their feet swelled not.**
22 Moreover **thou gavest them kingdoms and nations,** and didst divide them into corners: so they possessed the land of Sihon, and the land of the king of Heshbon, and the land of Og king of Bashan.
23 **Their children also multipliedst thou as the stars of heaven**, and broughtest them into the land, concerning which thou hadst promised to their fathers, that they should go in to possess *it*.
24 So the children went in and possessed the land, and thou subduedst before them the inhabitants of the land, the Canaanites, and **gavest them into their hands, with their kings, and the people of the land, that they might do with them as they would**.
25 And they took strong cities, and a fat land, and possessed houses full of all goods, wells digged, vineyards, and oliveyards, and fruit trees in abundance: so they did eat, and were filled, and became fat, and delighted themselves in thy great goodness.
26 Nevertheless they were disobedient, and rebelled against thee, and cast thy law behind their backs, and slew thy prophets which testified against them to turn them to thee, and they wrought great provocations.
27 Therefore **thou deliveredst them into the hand of their enemies, who vexed them: and in the time of their trouble,** when they cried unto thee, **thou heardest *them* from heaven; and according to thy manifold mercies thou gavest them saviours**, who saved them out of the hand of their enemies.
28 **But after they had rest, they did evil again before thee**: therefore leftest thou them in the hand of their enemies, so that they had the dominion over them: yet when they returned, and cried unto thee, thou heardest *them* from heaven; and **many times didst thou deliver them according to thy mercies;**

29 And testifiedst against them, that thou mightest bring them again unto thy law: yet they dealt proudly, and hearkened not unto thy commandments, **but sinned against thy judgments, (which if a man do, he shall live in them;) and withdrew the shoulder, and hardened their neck, and would not hear.**

30 Yet many years didst thou forbear them, and testifiedst against them by thy spirit in thy prophets: yet would they not give ear: therefore gavest thou them into the hand of the people of the lands.

31 **Nevertheless for thy great mercies' sake thou didst not utterly consume them, nor forsake them; for thou** *art* **a gracious and merciful God**.

32 Now therefore, our God, the great, the mighty, and the terrible God, who keepest covenant and mercy, let not all the trouble seem little before thee, that hath come upon us, on our kings, on our princes, and on our priests, and on our prophets, and on our fathers, and on all thy people, since the time of the kings of Assyria unto this day.

33 Howbeit thou *art* just in all that is brought upon us; for thou hast done right, **but we have done wickedly:**

34 **Neither have our kings, our princes, our priests, nor our fathers, kept thy law, nor hearkened unto thy commandments and thy testimonies, wherewith thou didst testify against them.**

35 For they have not served thee in their kingdom, and in thy great goodness that thou gavest them, and in the large and fat land which thou gavest before them, neither turned they from their wicked works.

36 Behold, we *are* servants this day, and *for* the land that thou gavest unto our fathers to eat the fruit thereof and the good thereof, behold, we *are* servants in it:

37 And it yieldeth much increase unto the kings whom thou hast set over us because of our sins: also they have dominion over our bodies, and over our cattle, at their pleasure, and we *are* in great distress.

38 And because of all this we make a sure *covenant*, and write *it*; and our princes, Levites, *and* priests, seal *unto it*.

Revelation 19:10 And I fell at his feet to worship him. And he said unto me, See *thou do it* not: I am thy fellowservant, and of thy brethren that have the testimony of Jesus: **worship God: for the testimony of Jesus is the spirit of prophecy**.

Revelation 22:8 And I John saw these things, and heard *them*. And when I had heard and seen, I fell down to worship before the feet of the angel which shewed me these things.

9 Then saith he unto me, See *thou do it* not: for I am thy fellowservant, and of thy brethren the prophets, and of them which keep the sayings of this book: **worship God.**

CHOSEN CHOSE TO DISOBEY

Colossians 3:6 *For which things' sake **the wrath of God cometh on the children of disobedience:***

Psalms 37:28 For the LORD loveth judgment, and forsaketh not his saints; they are preserved for ever: **but the seed of the wicked shall be cut off.**

Psalms 78:10 They kept not the covenant of God, and refused to walk in his law;

11 And forgat his works, and his wonders that he had shewed them.

1. THE MAKERS OF FALSE gods

Isaiah 44:9 They that make a graven image *are* all of them vanity; and their delectable things shall not profit; and they *are* their own witnesses; they see not, nor know; that they may be ashamed.

10 Who hath formed a god, or molten a graven image *that* is profitable for nothing?

Deuteronomy 4:16 Lest ye corrupt *yourselves*, and make you a graven image, the similitude of any figure, the likeness of male or female,

17 The likeness of any beast that *is* on the earth, the likeness of any winged fowl that flieth in the air,

18 The likeness of any thing that creepeth on the ground, the likeness of any fish that *is* in the waters beneath the earth:

19 And lest thou lift up thine eyes unto heaven, and when thou seest the sun, and the moon, and the stars, *even* all the host of heaven, shouldest be driven to worship them, and serve them, which the LORD thy God hath divided unto all nations under the whole heaven.

a. THE WORKMAN AND HIS METAL

Isaiah 44:11 Behold, all his fellows shall be ashamed: and the workmen, they *are* of men: let them all be gathered together, let them stand up; *yet* they shall fear, *and* they shall be ashamed together.

12 The smith with the tongs both worketh in the coals, and fashioneth it with hammers, and worketh it with the strength of his arms: yea, he is hungry, and his strength faileth: he drinketh no water, and is faint.

b. THE CARPENTER AND HIS WOOD

Isaiah 44:13 The carpenter stretcheth out *his* rule; he marketh it out with a line; he fitteth it with planes, and he marketh it out with the compass, and maketh it after the figure of a man, according to the beauty of a man; that it may remain in the house.

14 **He heweth him down cedars, and taketh the cypress and the oak,** which he strengtheneth for himself among the trees of the forest: he planteth an ash, and the rain doth nourish *it*.

15 **Then shall it be for a man to burn: for he will take thereof, and warm himself; yea, he kindleth *it*, and baketh bread; yea, he maketh a god, and worshippeth *it*; he maketh it a graven image, and falleth down thereto.**

16 **He burneth part thereof in the fire; with part thereof he eateth flesh; he roasteth roast, and is satisfied: yea, he warmeth *himself*, and saith, Aha, I am warm, I have seen the fire:**

2. IDOL WORSHIPERS

Isaiah 44:17 And **the residue thereof he maketh a god, *even* his graven image: he falleth down unto it, and worshippeth *it*, and prayeth unto it, and saith, Deliver me; for thou *art* my god.**

18 **They have not known nor understood: for he hath shut their eyes, that they cannot see; *and* their hearts, that they cannot understand.**

19 And none considereth in his heart, neither *is there* knowledge nor understanding to say, **I have burned part of it in the fire; yea, also I have baked bread upon the coals thereof; I have roasted flesh, and eaten *it*: and shall I make the residue thereof an abomination? shall I fall down to the stock of a tree?**

20 He feedeth on ashes: a deceived heart hath turned him aside, *that* **he cannot deliver his soul**, nor say, *Is there* not a lie in my right hand?

a. ABOMINATION TO THE LORD

2Kings 1:1 Then Moab rebelled against Israel after the death of Ahab.

2 And **Ahaziah fell down through a lattice in his upper chamber that** *was* **in Samaria**, and was sick: and **he sent messengers, and said unto them, Go, enquire of Baalzebub the god of Ekron whether I shall recover of this disease.**

3 But the angel of the LORD said to Elijah the Tishbite, Arise, go up to meet the messengers of the king of Samaria, and say unto them, *Is it* **not because** *there is* **not a God in Israel,** *that* **ye go to enquire of Baalzebub the god of Ekron?**

4 **Now therefore thus saith the LORD, Thou shalt not come down from that bed on which thou art gone up, but shalt surely die**. And Elijah departed.

5 And when the messengers turned back unto him, he said unto them, Why are ye now turned back?

6 And they said unto him, There came a man up to meet us, and said unto us, Go, turn again unto the king that sent you, and say unto him, Thus saith the LORD, *Is it* not because *there is* not a God in Israel, *that* thou sendest to enquire of Baalzebub the god of Ekron? therefore thou shalt not come down from that bed on which thou art gone up, but shalt surely die.

EVIL WILL COME TO THOSE WHO TRUSTED IN WICKEDNESS

Isaiah 47:9 But these two *things* **shall come to thee in a moment in one day, the loss of children, and widowhood: they shall come upon thee in their perfection for the multitude of thy sorceries,** *and* **for the great abundance of thine enchantments.**

10 **For thou hast trusted in thy wickedness: thou hast said, None seeth me. Thy wisdom and thy knowledge, it hath perverted thee**; and thou hast said in thine heart, I *am*, and none else beside me.

11 Therefore shall evil come upon thee; thou shalt not know from whence it riseth: and mischief shall fall upon thee; thou shalt not

be able to put it off: and desolation shall come upon thee suddenly, *which* thou shalt not know.

12 Stand now with thine enchantments, and with the multitude of thy sorceries, wherein thou hast laboured from thy youth; if so be thou shalt be able to profit, if so be thou mayest prevail.

13 Thou art wearied in the multitude of thy counsels. Let now the astrologers, the stargazers, the monthly prognosticators, stand up, and save thee from *these things* that shall come upon thee.

14 **Behold, they shall be as stubble; the fire shall burn them; they shall not deliver themselves from the power of the flame:** ***there shall*** **not** *be* **a coal to warm at,** *nor* **fire to sit before it.**

WORK OF THE FLESH

Galatians 5:17 For the flesh lusteth against the Spirit, and the Spirit against the flesh: and these are contrary the one to the other: so that ye cannot do the things that ye would.

18 But if ye be led of the Spirit, ye are not under the law.

19 **Now the works of the flesh are manifest**, which are *these*; Adultery, fornication, uncleanness, lasciviousness,

20 **Idolatry**, witchcraft, hatred, variance, emulations, wrath, strife, seditions, heresies,

21 Envyings, murders, drunkenness, revellings, and such like: of the which I tell you before, as I have also told *you* in time past, that **they which do such things shall not inherit the kingdom of God.**

b. TRANSGRESSORS FROM THE WOMB

Isaiah 48:8 Yea, thou heardest not; yea, thou knewest not; yea, from that time *that* thine ear was not opened: for I knew that thou wouldest deal very treacherously, and wast called a transgressor from the womb.

.

c. MADE SACRIFICES TO THE DEVILS

1Corinthians 10:19 What say I then? that the idol is any thing, or that which is offered in sacrifice to idols is any thing?

20 But I *say*, that **the things which the Gentiles sacrifice, they sacrifice to devils, and not to God: and I would not that ye should have fellowship with devils.**

d. SET THEIR HEARTS ON IDOLS

Ezekiel 14:2 And the word of the LORD came unto me, saying,

3 Son of man, these men have set up their idols in their heart, and put the stumblingblock of their iniquity before their face: should I be enquired of at all by them?

4 Therefore speak unto them, and say unto them, Thus saith the Lord GOD; **Every man of the house of Israel that setteth up his idols in his heart, and putteth the stumblingblock of his iniquity before his face, and cometh to the prophet; I the LORD will answer him that cometh according to the multitude of his idols;**

e. WORSHIPPING THE HOSTS OF HEAVEN

2Kings 17:16 And they left all the commandments of the LORD their God, and made them molten images, *even* two calves, and made a grove, **and worshipped all the host of heaven, and served Baal.**

2Chronicles 33:3 For he built again the high places which Hezekiah his father had broken down, and he reared up altars for Baalim, and made groves, and worshipped all the host of heaven, and served them.

Jeremiah 1:16 And I will utter my judgments against them touching all their wickedness, who have forsaken me, and have burned incense unto other gods, and worshipped the works of their own hands.

Jeremiah 16:11 Then shalt thou say unto them, **Because your fathers have forsaken me, saith the LORD, and have walked after other gods, and have served them, and have worshipped them, and have forsaken me, and have not kept my law;**

12 And ye have done worse than your fathers; for, behold, ye walk every one after the imagination of his evil heart, that they may not hearken unto me:

13 Therefore will I cast you out of this land into a land that ye know not, *neither* ye nor your fathers; and there shall ye serve other gods day and night; where I will not shew you favour.

Jeremiah 22:9 **Then they shall answer, Because they have forsaken the covenant of the LORD their God, and worshipped other gods, and served them.**

Deuteronomy 4:19 And lest thou lift up thine eyes unto heaven, and when thou seest the sun, and the moon, and the stars, *even* all the host of heaven, shouldest be driven to worship them, and serve them, which the LORD thy God hath divided unto all nations under the whole heaven.

Deuteronomy 8:19 And it shall be, if thou do at all forget the LORD thy God, and walk after other gods, and serve them, and worship them, I testify against you this day that ye shall surely perish.

Deuteronomy 11:16 Take heed to yourselves, that your heart be not deceived, and ye turn aside, and serve other gods, and worship them;

Deuteronomy 30:17 But if thine heart turn away, so that thou wilt not hear, but shalt be drawn away, and worship other gods, and serve them;

18 I denounce unto you this day, that ye shall surely perish, *and that* ye shall not prolong *your* days upon the land, whither thou passest over Jordan to go to possess it.

19 I call heaven and earth to record this day against you, *that* I have set before you life and death, blessing and cursing: therefore choose life, that both thou and thy seed may live:

20 That thou mayest love the LORD thy God, *and* that thou mayest obey his voice, and that thou mayest cleave unto him: for he *is* thy life, and the length of thy days: that thou mayest dwell in the land which the LORD sware unto thy fathers, to Abraham, to Isaac, and to Jacob, to give them.

1Kings 9:6 *But* if ye shall at all turn from following me, ye or your children, and will not keep my commandments *and* my statutes which I have set before you, **but go and serve other gods, and worship them:**

7 Then will I cut off Israel out of the land which I have given them; and this house, which I have hallowed for my name, will I cast out of my sight; and Israel shall be a proverb and a byword among all people:

Zephaniah 1:5 And **them that worship the host of heaven** upon the housetops; and them that worship *and* that swear by the LORD, and **that swear by Malcham**;

6 And them that are turned back from the LORD; and *those* that have not sought the LORD, nor enquired for him.

Acts 7:42 **Then God turned, and gave them up to worship the host of heaven**; **as it is written in the book of the prophets,** O ye house of Israel, have ye offered to me slain beasts and sacrifices *by the space of* forty years in the wilderness?

43 Yea, ye took up the tabernacle of Moloch, and the star of your god Remphan, figures which ye made to worship them: and I will carry you away beyond Babylon.

Deuteronomy 29:26 For they went and served other gods, and worshipped them, gods whom they knew not, and *whom* he had not given unto them:

f. WORSHIPPING THE SUN

Ezekiel 8:15 Then said he unto me, Hast thou seen *this*, O son of man? turn thee yet again, *and* thou shalt see greater abominations than these.

16 And he brought me into the inner court of the LORD'S house, and, behold, at the door of the temple of the LORD, between the porch and the altar, *were* about five and twenty men, with their backs toward the temple of the LORD, and their faces toward the east; and they worshipped the sun toward the east.

17 Then he said unto me, Hast thou seen *this*, O son of man? Is it a light thing to the house of Judah that they commit the abominations which they commit here? for they have filled the land with violence, and have returned to provoke me to anger: and, lo, they put the branch to their nose.

==

PART 8
GOD RENDERS PUNISHMENT

CHAPTER I LORD CHALLENGES IDOLS (gods)

Jeremiah 10:10
But the LORD is the true God, he is the living God, and an everlasting king: at his wrath the earth shall tremble, and the nations shall not be able to abide his indignation

Isaiah 45:15Verily thou art a God that hidest thyself, O God of Israel, the Saviour.

Jeremiah 10:1 Hear ye the word which the LORD speaketh unto you, O house of Israel:

2 Thus saith the LORD, **Learn not the way of the heathen, and be not dismayed at the signs of heaven; for the heathen are dismayed at them**.

A. IDOLS ARE NOTHING

Isaiah 41:22 Let them bring *them* forth, and shew us what shall happen: let them shew the former things, what they *be*, that we may consider them, and know the latter end of them; or declare us things for to come.

23 Shew the things that are to come hereafter, that we may know that ye *are* gods: yea, do good, or do evil, that we may be dismayed, and behold *it* together.

24 Behold, ye *are* of nothing, and your work of nought: an abomination *is he that* chooseth you.

Isaiah 41:29 Behold, **they are all vanity; their works are nothing: their molten images are wind and confusion.**

Isaiah 48:5 I have even from the beginning declared *it* to thee; before it came to pass I shewed *it* thee: lest thou shouldest say, Mine idol hath done them, and my graven image, and my molten image, hath commanded them.

Zechariah 10:2 **For the idols have spoken vanity, and the diviners have seen a lie, and have told false dreams; they** comfort in vain: therefore they went their way as a flock, they were troubled, because *there was* no shepherd.

Isaiah 42:8 **I *am* the LORD: that *is* my name: and my glory will I not give to another, neither my praise to graven images.**

Isaiah 42:16 And I will bring the blind by a way *that* they knew not; I will lead them in paths *that* they have not known: I will make darkness light before them, and crooked things straight. These things will I do unto them, and not forsake them.

17 They shall be turned back, they shall be greatly ashamed, that trust in graven images**, that say to the molten images, Ye *are* our gods.**

2Kings 17:14 Notwithstanding they would not hear, but hardened their necks, like to the neck of their fathers, that did not believe in the LORD their God.

15 And they rejected his statutes, and his covenant that he made with their fathers, and his testimonies which he testified against them; and **they followed vanity, and became vain**, and went after the heathen that *were* round about them, *concerning* whom the LORD had charged them, that they should not do like them.

B. FEAR NOT THE USELESS IDOLS (gods of nations)

Isaiah 46:1 Bel boweth down, Nebo stoopeth, their idols were upon the beasts, and upon the cattle: your carriages *were* heavy loaden; *they are* **a burden to the weary *beast.***

2 They stoop, they bow down together; they could not deliver the burden, but themselves are gone into captivity.

5 To whom will ye liken me, and make *me* equal, and compare me, that we may be like?

6 They lavish gold out of the bag, and weigh silver in the balance, *and* hire a goldsmith; and he maketh it a god: they fall down, yea, they worship.

7 They bear him upon the shoulder, they carry him, and set him in his place, and he standeth; from his place shall he not remove: yea, *one* shall cry unto him, yet can he not answer, nor save him out of his trouble.

Psalms 96:4 For the LORD *is* great, and greatly to be praised: he *is* to be feared above all gods.

5 For all the gods of the nations *are* idols: but the LORD made the heavens.

1Chronicles 16:25 For great is the LORD, and greatly to be praised**: he also is to be feared above all gods.**

Habakkuk 2:18 **What profiteth the graven image that the maker thereof hath graven it; the molten image, and a teacher of lies, that the maker of his work trusteth therein, to make dumb idols?**

19 Woe unto him that saith to the wood, **Awake; to the dumb stone, Arise, it shall teach! Behold, it** *is* **laid over with gold and silver, and** *there is* **no breath at all in the midst of it.**

Psalms 115:4 **Their idols** *are* silver and gold, the work of men's hands.

5 **They have mouths, but they speak not: eyes have they, but they see not:**

6 **They have ears, but they hear not: noses have they, but they smell not:**

7 **They have hands, but they handle** not: feet have they, but they walk not: neither speak they through their throat.

8 **They that make them are like unto them**; *so is* every one that trusteth in them.

Jeremiah 10:3 **For the customs of the people are vain: for one cutteth a tree out of the forest, the work of the hands of the workman, with the axe,**

4They deck it with silver and with gold; **they fasten it with nails and with hammers , that it move not.**

5 **They** *are* **upright as the palm tree, but speak not: they must needs be borne, because they cannot go. Be not afraid of them; for they cannot do evil, neither also** *is it* **in them to do good.**

Jeremiah 10:8 But they are altogether brutish and foolish: the stock *is* a doctrine of vanities.

9 Silver spread into plates is brought from Tarshish, and gold from Uphaz, the work of the workman, and of the hands of the founder: **blue and purple is their clothing: they are all the work of a cunning men.**

GOD'S ANGER AGAINST PEOPLE WHO PRAY AND BOW DOWN TO IDOLS

Matthew 7:21 **Not every one that saith unto me, Lord, Lord, shall enter into the kingdom of heaven; but he that doeth the will of my Father which is in heaven.**

22 Many will say to me in that day, Lord, Lord, have we not prophesied in thy name? and in thy name have cast out devils? and in thy name done many wonderful works?

23 And then will I profess unto them, I never knew you: depart from me, ye that work iniquity.

Jeremiah 10:11 Thus shall ye say unto them, The gods that have not made the heavens and the earth, *even* **they shall perish from the earth, and from under these heavens.**

14 Every man is brutish in *his* knowledge: **every founder is confounded by the graven image: for his molten image** *is* **falsehood, and** *there is* **no breath in them.**

15 **They** *are* **vanity,** *and* **the work of errors**: in the time of their visitation they shall perish.

Micah 1:7 **And all the graven images thereof shall be beaten to pieces, and all the hires thereof shall be burned with the fire, and all the idols thereof will I lay desolate:** for she gathered *it* of the hire of an harlot, and they shall return to the hire of an harlot.

C. GOD WARNS HIS PEOPLE WHO WORSHIP IDOLS

Nehemiah 9:17 And refused to obey, neither were mindful of thy wonders that thou didst among them; but hardened their necks, and in their rebellion appointed a captain to return to their bondage: but thou *art* a God ready to pardon, gracious and merciful, slow to anger, and of great kindness, and forsookest them not.

Isaiah 45:16 **They shall be ashamed, and also confounded, all of them: they shall go to confusion together that are makers of idols.**

Ezekiel 11:21 But *as for them* whose heart walketh after the heart of their detestable things and their abominations, I will recompense their way upon their own heads, saith the Lord GOD.

1. THEY WILL NEVER ENTER GOD'S REST

Psalms 95:3 **For the LORD is a great God, and a great King above all gods**.

Psalms 95:11 Unto whom **I sware in my wrath that they should not enter into my rest.**

Hebrews 4:1 Let us therefore fear, lest, a promise being left *us* of entering into his rest, any of you should seem to come short of it.

2 For unto us was the gospel preached, as well as unto them: but the word preached did not profit them, not being mixed with faith in them that heard *it*.

3 For we which have believed do enter into rest, as he said, As I have sworn in my wrath, if they shall enter into my rest: although the works were finished from the foundation of the world.

6 Seeing therefore it remaineth that some must enter therein, and they to whom it was first preached **entered not in because of unbelief**:

2. DISASTER WILL COME TO THE LAND

Ezekiel 14:12 The word of the LORD came again to me, saying,

13 Son of man, when the land sinneth against me by trespassing grievously, **then will I stretch out mine hand upon it, and will break the staff of the bread thereof, and will send famine upon it, and will cut off man and beast from it:**

3. GOD WILL PUNISH THE IDOL WORSHIPERS

Amos 5:25 Have ye offered unto me sacrifices and offerings in the wilderness forty years, O house of Israel?

26 **But ye have borne the tabernacle of your Moloch and Chiun your images, the star of your god, which ye made to yourselves.**

27 **Therefore will I cause you to go into captivity beyond Damascus, saith the LORD, whose name** *is* **The God of hosts.**

PEACE CAME TO THE LAND AFTER DESTROYING THE IDOLS

2Chronicles 15:16And also *concerning* Maachah the mother of **Asa the king**, he removed her from *being* queen, because she had made an idol in a grove: and Asa **cut down her idol, and stamped** *it***, and burnt** *it* **at the brook Kidron**.

17 But the high places were not taken away out of Israel: nevertheless the heart of Asa was perfect all his days.

18 And he brought into the house of God the things that his father had dedicated, and that he himself had dedicated, silver, and gold, and vessels.

19 And **there was no** *more* **war unto the five and thirtieth year of the reign of Asa.**

PART 8
GOD RENDERS PUNISHMENT

CHAPTER II **THE WRATH OF GOD IN ANCIENT TIMES**

Exodus 34:6
And the LORD passed by before him, and proclaimed, The LORD,
The LORD God, merciful and gracious, longsuffering, and
abundant in goodness and truth, 7Keeping mercy for thousands,
forgiving iniquity and transgression and sin, and that will by no
means clear the guilty; visiting the iniquity of the fathers upon the
children, and upon the children's children, unto the third and to
the fourth generation.

GOD'S PUNISHMENT

Psalms 94:12 Blessed *is* the man whom thou chastenest, O LORD, and teachest him out of thy law;
13That thou mayest give him rest from the days of adversity, until the pit be digged for the wicked.

1. GREAT FLOOD

Genesis 6:5 And GOD saw that the wickedness of man *was* great in the earth, and *that* every imagination of the thoughts of his heart *was* only evil continually.
6 And it repented the LORD that he had made man on the earth, and it grieved him at his heart.
7 And the LORD said, I will destroy man whom I have created from the face of the earth; both man, and beast, and the creeping thing, and the fowls of the air; for it repenteth me that I have made them.
8 But Noah found grace in the eyes of the LORD.
9 These *are* the generations of Noah: Noah was a just man *and* perfect in his generations, *and* Noah walked with God.
10 And Noah begat three sons, Shem, Ham, and Japheth.
11 The earth also was corrupt before God, and the earth was filled with violence.

12 And God looked upon the earth, and, behold, it was corrupt; for all flesh had corrupted his way upon the earth.

13 And God said unto Noah, The end of all flesh is come before me; for the earth is filled with violence through them; and, behold, I will destroy them with the earth.

Genesis 7:11 **In the six hundredth year of Noah's life** in the second month, the seventeenth day of the month, the same day **where all the fountains of the great deep broken up, and the windows of heaven were opened.**

12 And **the rain was upon the earth forty days and forty nights.**

21 And all flesh died that moved upon the earth, both of fowl, and of cattle, and of beast, and of every creeping thing that creepeth upon the earth, and every man:

22 All in whose nostrils was the breathed of life, of all that was in the dry land, died.

23 And every living substance was destroyed which was upon the face of the ground, both man, and cattle, and the creeping things, and the fowl of the heaven; and they were destroyed from the earth: and Noah only remained *alive*, and they that *were* with him in the ark.

24 And **the waters prevailed upon the earth an hundred and fifty days**.

2Peter 2:5 **And spared not the old world, but saved Noah, the eight person, a preacher of righteousness, bringing in the flood upon the world of the ungodly.**

2. DESTRUCTION OF SODOM AND GOMORRAH

2Peter 2:6 And **turning the cities of Sodom and Gomorrah into ashes** condemned them with an overthrow, **making them an ensample unto those that after should live ungodly;**

7**And delivered just Lot, vexed with the filthy conversation of the wicked:**

a. GOD DELIVERED WARNING BEFORE THE DESTRUCTION

Genesis 18:20 And the LORD said, Because the cry of Sodom and Gomorrah is great, and because their sin is very grievous;

21 I will go down now, and see whether they have done altogether according to the cry of it, which is come unto me; and if not, I will know.

Genesis 13:13 But the men of Sodom were wicked and sinners before the LORD exceedingly.

Genesis 19:1 And there came two angels to Sodom at even; and Lot sat in the gate of Sodom: and Lot seeing *them* rose up to meet them; and he bowed himself with his face toward the ground;

2 And he said, Behold now, my lords, turn in, I pray you, into your servant's house, and tarry all night, and wash your feet, and ye shall rise up early, and go on your ways. And they said, Nay; but we will abide in the street all night.

3 And he pressed upon them greatly; and they turned in unto him, and entered into his house; and he made them a feast, and did bake unleavened bread, and they did eat.

4 But before they lay down, the men of the city, *even* the men of Sodom, compassed the house round, both old and young, all the people from every quarter:

5 And **they called unto Lot, and said unto him, Where *are* the men which came in to thee this night? bring them out unto us, that we may know them**.

6 And Lot went out at the door unto them, and shut the door after him,

7 And said, I pray you, brethren, do not so wickedly.

8 Behold now, I have two daughters which have not known man; let me, I pray you, bring them out unto you, and do ye to them as *is* good in your eyes: only unto these men do nothing; for therefore came they under the shadow of my roof.

9 And they said, Stand back. And they said *again*, This one *fellow* came in to sojourn, and he will needs be a judge: now will we deal worse with thee, than with them. And they pressed sore upon the man, *even* Lot, and came near to break the door.

10 But the men put forth their hand, and pulled Lot into the house to them, and shut to the door.

11 And they smote the men that *were* at the door of the house with blindness, both small and great: so that they wearied themselves to find the door.

12 And the men said unto Lot, Hast thou here any besides? son in law, and thy sons, and thy daughters, and whatsoever thou hast in the city, bring *them* out of this place:

13 For we will destroy this place, because the cry of them is waxen great before the face of the LORD; and the LORD hath sent us to destroy it.

14 And Lot went out, and spake unto his sons in law, which married his daughters, and said, Up, get you out of this place; for the LORD will destroy this city. But he seemed as one that mocked unto his sons in law.

b. GOD SAVE LOT AND HIS FAMILY BEFORE HIS WRATH TO COME

Genesis 19:15 And when the morning arose, then **the angels hastened Lot**, saying, Arise, take thy wife, and thy two daughters, which are here; lest thou be consumed in the iniquity of the city.

16 And while he lingered, the men laid hold upon his hand, and upon the hand of his wife, and upon the hand of his two daughters; **the LORD being merciful unto him: and they brought him forth, and set him without the city.**

17 And it came to pass, when they had brought them forth abroad, that he said, **Escape for thy life; look not behind thee, neither stay thou in all the plain; escape to the mountain, lest thou be consumed.**

18 And Lot said unto them, Oh, not so, my Lord:

19 Behold now, thy servant hath found grace in thy sight, and thou hast magnified thy mercy, which thou hast shewed unto me in saving my life; and I cannot escape to the mountain, lest some evil take me, and I die:

20 Behold now, this city *is* near to flee unto, and it *is* a little one: Oh, let me escape thither, (*is* it not a little one?) and my soul shall live.

21 And he said unto him, See, I have accepted thee concerning this thing also, that I will not overthrow this city, for the which thou hast spoken.

22 Haste thee, escape thither; for I cannot do any thing till thou be come thither. Therefore the name of the city was called Zoar.

23 The sun was risen upon the earth when Lot entered into Zoar.

PUNISHMENT TO SODOM AND GOMORRAH

Genesis 19:24 Then the LORD rained upon Sodom and upon Gomorrah brimstone and fire from the LORD out of heaven;

25 And he overthrew those cities, and all the plain, and all the inhabitants of the cities, and that which grew upon the ground.

LOT'S WIFE DISOBEYED

Genesis 19:26 **But his wife looked back from behind him, and she became pillar of salt**.

PUNISHMENT TO THE SONS OF JUDAH

Genesis 38:1 And it came to pass at that time, that Judah went down from his brethren, and turned in to a certain Adullamite, whose name *was* Hirah.

2 And Judah saw there a daughter of a certain Canaanite, whose name *was* Shuah; and he took her, and went in unto her.

3 And she conceived, and bare a son; and he called his name Er.

4 And she conceived again, and bare a son; and she called his name Onan.

5 And she yet again conceived, and bare a son; and called his name Shelah: and he was at Chezib, when she bare him.

6 And Judah took a wife for Er his firstborn, whose name *was* Tamar.

7 **And Er, Judah's firstborn, was wicked in the sight of the LORD; and the LORD slew him.**

8 **And Judah said unto Onan**, *Go in unto thy brother's wife, and marry her, and raise up seed to thy brother.*

9 **And Onan knew that the seed should not be his; and it came to pass, when he went in unto his brother's wife, that he spilled *it* on the ground, lest that he should give seed to his brother.**

10 **And the thing which he did displeased the LORD: wherefore he slew him also.**

PART 8
GOD RENDERS PUNISHMENT

.

CHAPTER III **THE CURSE FROM GOD**

Genesis 12:3
And I will bless them that bless thee, and curse him that curseth thee: and in thee shall all families of the earth be blessed.

.

CURSE TO THOSE THAT WILL HARM ISRAEL

Jeremiah 2:3 Israel *was* holiness unto the LORD, *and* the firstfruits of his increase: all that devour him shall offend; evil shall come upon them, saith the LORD.

Deuteronomy 30:7 And the LORD thy God will put all these curses upon thine enemies, and on them that hate thee, which persecuted thee.

Numbers 22:12 And God said unto Balaam, Thou shalt not go with them; thou shalt not curse the people: for they *are* blessed.

(THURSDAY, Dec. 26, 2013 12:06 pm CA TIME posted in FB: Casting Out The Generation Of Curses)

A. ANCIENT MEN WERE CURSE FOR DISOBEDIENCE

1. ADAM

a. ADAM WILL DIE

Genesis 3:19 In the sweat of thy face shalt thou eat bread**, till thou return unto the ground; for out of it wast thou taken: for dust thou *art*, and unto dust shalt thou return.**

Romans 5:12 **Wherefore, as by one man sin entered into the world, and death by sin; and so death passed upon all men, for that all have sinned:**

Romans 6:23 **For the wages of sin *is* death; but the gift of God *is* eternal life through Jesus Christ our Lord.**

b. GOD CURSED THE EARTH (GROUND)

Genesis 3:17 And unto Adam he said, Because thou hast hearkened unto the voice of thy wife, and hast eaten of the tree, of which I commanded thee, saying, Thou shalt not eat of it: cursed *is* the ground for thy sake; in sorrow shalt thou eat *of* it all the days of thy life;

18 Thorns also and thistles shall it bring forth to thee; and thou shalt eat the herb of the field;

Genesis 5:29 And he called his name Noah, saying, This *same* shall comfort us concerning our work and toil of our hands, because of the ground **which the LORD hath cursed.**

2. EVE

Genesis 3:13 And the LORD God said unto the woman, What *is* this *that* thou hast done? And the woman said, The serpent beguiled me, and I did eat.

Genesis 3:16 Unto the woman he said, I will greatly multiply thy sorrow and thy conception; in sorrow thou shalt bring forth children; and thy desire *shall be* to thy husband, and he shall rule over thee.

GOD CURSED THE SERPENT AGAINST THE WOMAN AND HER SEED

Genesis 3:14 And **the LORD God said unto the serpent**, **Because thou hast done this, thou** *art* **cursed above all cattle, and above every beast of the field; upon thy belly shalt thou go, and dust shalt thou eat all the days of thy life:**

15 **And I will put enmity between thee and the woman, and between thy seed and her seed; it shall bruise thy head, and thou shalt bruise his heel.**

3. CAIN WAS CURSED

Genesis 4: 4 And Abel, he also brought of the firstlings of his flock and of the fat thereof. And the LORD had respect unto Abel and to his offering:

5 But unto Cain and to his offering he had not respect. And Cain was very wroth, and his countenance fell.

6 And the LORD said unto Cain, Why art thou wroth? and why is thy countenance fallen?

7 If thou doest well, shalt thou not be accepted? and if thou doest not well, sin lieth at the door. And unto thee *shall be* his desire, and thou shalt rule over him.

8 And Cain talked with Abel his brother: and it came to pass, when they were in the field, that Cain rose up against Abel his brother, and slew him.

9 And the LORD said unto Cain, Where *is* Abel thy brother? And he said, I know not: *Am* I my brother's keeper?

10 And he said, What hast thou done? the voice of thy brother's blood crieth unto me from the ground.

11 And now *art* thou cursed from the earth, which hath opened her mouth to receive thy brother's blood from thy hand;

12 **When thou tillest the ground, it shall not henceforth yield unto thee her strength; a fugitive and a vagabond shalt thou be in the earth**.

13 And Cain said unto the LORD, My punishment *is* greater than I can bear.

14 Behold, thou hast driven me out this day from the face of the earth; and from thy face shall I be hid; and I shall be a fugitive and a vagabond in the earth; and it shall come to pass, *that* every one that findeth me shall slay me.

15 And the LORD said unto him, **Therefore whosoever slayeth Cain, vengeance shall be taken on him sevenfold. And the LORD set a mark upon Cain, lest any finding him should kill him.**

B. CURSE DUE TO DISOBEDIENCE TO THE ORDINANCES OF GOD (ISRAEL)

Proverbs 3:33 The curse of the LORD *is* in the house of the wicked: but he blesseth the habitation of the just.

1. CURSES TO THE WORSHIPERS AND MAKERS OF IDOLS

Deuteronomy 27:15 Cursed *be* the man that maketh *any* graven or molten image, an abomination unto the LORD, the work of the hands of the craftsman, and putteth *it* in *a* secret *place*. And all the people shall answer and say, Amen.

Deuteronomy 29:16 (For ye know how we have dwelt in the land of Egypt; and how we came through the nations which ye passed by;

17 And ye have seen their abominations, and their idols, wood and stone, silver and gold, which *were* among them:)

18 Lest there should be among you man, or woman, or family, or tribe, whose heart turneth away this day from the LORD our God, **to go *and* serve the gods of these nations; lest there should be among you a root that beareth gall and wormwood;**

19 And it come to pass, when he heareth the words of this curse, that he bless himself in his heart, saying, I shall have peace, though I walk in the imagination of mine heart, to add drunkenness to thirst:

21 **And the LORD shall separate him unto evil out of all the tribes of Israel, according to all the curses of the covenant that are written in this book of the law:**

22 So that the generation to come of your children that shall rise up after you, and the stranger that shall come from a far land, shall say, when they see the plagues of that land, and the sicknesses which the LORD hath laid upon it;

23 *And that* the whole land thereof *is* brimstone, and salt, *and* burning, *that* it is not sown, nor beareth, nor any grass groweth therein, like the overthrow of Sodom, and Gomorrah, Admah, and Zeboim, which the LORD overthrew in his anger, and in his wrath:

24 Even all nations shall say, Wherefore hath the LORD done thus unto this land? what *meaneth* the heat of this great anger?

25 Then men shall say, Because they have forsaken the covenant of the LORD God of their fathers, which he made with them when he brought them forth out of the land of Egypt:

26 **For they went and served other gods, and worshipped them, gods whom they knew not**, and *whom* he had not given unto them:

27 And **the anger of the LORD was kindled against this land, to bring upon it all the curses that are written in this book:**

28 And **the LORD rooted them out of their land in anger, and in wrath, and in great indignation, and cast them into another land, as** *it is* **this day.**

29 The secret *things belong* unto the LORD our God: but those *things which are* revealed *belong* unto us and to our children for ever, that *we* may do all the words of this law.

2. CURSE TO THOSE WHO DO NOT CONFORM TO ALL THE WORDS OF THE LAW OF MOSES

Deuteronomy 27:26 Cursed *be* he that confirmeth not *all* the words of this law to do them. And all the people shall say, Amen.

3. CURSE TO THE PRIESTS WHO CORRUPTED THE LAW

Malachi 2:17 Ye have wearied the LORD with your words. Yet ye say, Wherein have we wearied *him*? When ye say, Every one that doeth evil *is* good in the sight of the LORD, and he delighteth in them; or, Where *is* the God of judgment?

Malachi 2:1 And now, O ye priests, this commandment *is* for you.

2 **If ye will not hear, and if ye will not lay** *it* **to heart, to give glory unto my name, saith the LORD of hosts, I will even send a curse upon you, and I will curse your blessings:** yea, I have cursed them already, because ye do not lay *it* to heart.

3 **Behold, I will corrupt your seed, and** spread dung upon your faces, *even* the dung of your solemn feasts; and *one* shall take you away with it.

4 And ye shall know that I have sent this commandment unto you, that my covenant might be with Levi, saith the LORD of hosts.

5 **My covenant was with him of life and peace; and I gave them to him** *for* **the fear wherewith he feared me, and was afraid before my name**.

6 The law of truth was in his mouth, and iniquity was not found in his lips: he walked with me in peace and equity, and did turn many away from iniquity.

7 **For the priest's lips should keep knowledge, and they should seek the law at his mouth: for he** *is* **the messenger of the LORD of hosts.**

8 **But ye are departed out of the way; ye have caused many to stumble at the law; ye have corrupted the covenant of Levi, saith the LORD of hosts**.

4. CURSES TO THOSE WHO DOESN'T LOVE THEIR NEIGHBORS

Deuteronomy 27:16 Cursed *be* he that setteth light by his father or his mother. And all the people shall say, Amen.

17 Cursed *be* **he that removeth his neighbour's landmark. And all the people shall say, Amen.**

18 Cursed *be* he that maketh the blind to wander out of the way. And all the people shall say, Amen.

19 Cursed *be* he that perverteth the judgment of the stranger, fatherless, and widow. And all the people shall say, Amen.

5. CURSES TO THOSE WITH SPIRIT OF LUSTS

Deuteronomy 27:20 Cursed *be* he that lieth with his father's wife; because he uncovereth his father's skirt. And all the people shall say, Amen.

21 Cursed *be* he that lieth with any manner of beast. And all the people shall say, Amen.

22 Cursed *be* he that lieth with his sister, the daughter of his father, or the daughter of his mother. And all the people shall say, Amen.

23 Cursed *be* he that lieth with his mother in law. And all the people shall say, Amen.

24 Cursed *be* he that smiteth his neighbour secretly. And all the people shall say, Amen.

6. CURSE TO THOSE WHO MURDER

Deuteronomy 27:25 Cursed *be* he that taketh reward to slay an innocent person. And all the people shall say, Amen.

C. CURSE TO THOSE WHO STEAL AND SWEAR FALSELY USING THE NAME OF THE LORD

Zechariah 5:1 Then I turned, and lifted up mine eyes, and looked, and behold a flying roll.

2 And he said unto me, What seest thou? And I answered, I see a flying roll; the length thereof *is* twenty cubits, and the breadth thereof ten cubits.

3 Then said he unto me, **This *is* the curse that goeth forth over the face of the whole earth: for every one that stealeth shall be cut off *as* on this side according to it; and every one that sweareth shall be cut off *as* on that side according to it.**

4 I will bring it forth, saith the LORD of hosts, and it shall enter into the house of the thief, and into the house of him that sweareth falsely by my name: and it shall remain in the midst of his house, and shall consume it with the timber thereof and the stones thereof.

D. CURSES TO THOSE WHO TRUSTED MAN'S WORD

Jeremiah 17:5 Thus saith the LORD; Cursed *be* the man that trusteth in man, and maketh flesh his arm, and whose heart departeth from the LORD.

FOUR GENERATIONS WILL SUFFER CURSES FROM THE LORD

Exodus 34:6 And the LORD passed by before him, and proclaimed, The LORD, The LORD God, merciful and gracious, longsuffering, and abundant in goodness and truth,

7 Keeping mercy for thousands, forgiving iniquity and transgression and sin, and that will by no means clear *the guilty*; visiting the iniquity of the fathers upon the children, and upon the children's children, unto the third and to the fourth *generation*.

Exodus 20:5 Thou shalt not bow down thyself to them, nor serve them: for I the LORD thy God *am* a jealous God, visiting the iniquity of the fathers upon the children unto the third and fourth *generation* of them that hate me;

Deuteronomy 28:45 Moreover all these curses shall come upon thee, and shall pursue thee, and overtake thee, till thou be destroyed; because thou hearkenedst not unto the voice of the LORD thy God, to keep his commandments and his statutes which he commanded thee:

Deuteronomy 29:20 The LORD will not spare him, but then the anger of the LORD and his jealousy shall smoke against that man, and **all the curses that are written in this book shall lie upon him, and the LORD shall blot out his name from under heaven**.

PART 8
GOD RENDERS PUNISHMENT

.

CHAPTER IV GOD'S PUNISHMENT TO MOSES' PEOPLE

Amos 3:2
You only have I known of all the families of the earth: therefore I will punish you for all your iniquities.

PEOPLE OF MOSES REFUSED GOD'S ORDER

Deuteronomy 1:18 And I commanded you at that time all the things which ye should do.

19 And when we departed from Horeb, we went through all that great and terrible wilderness, which ye saw by the way of the mountain of the Amorites, as the LORD our God commanded us; and **we came to Kadeshbarnea.**

20 And I said unto you, **Ye are come unto the mountain of the Amorites, which the LORD our God doth give unto us.**

21 **Behold, the LORD thy God hath set the land before thee: go up** *and* **possess** *it*, **as the LORD God of thy fathers hath said unto thee; fear not, neither be discouraged**.

22 And ye came near unto me every one of you, and said, **We will send men before us,** and they shall search us out the land, and bring us word again by what way we must go up, and into what cities we shall come.

23 And the saying pleased me well: and **I took twelve men of you, one of a tribe**:

24 And they turned and went up into the mountain, and **came unto the valley of Eshcol,** and searched it out.

25 And **they took of the fruit of the land in their hands, and brought** *it* **down unto us**, **and brought us word again, and said,** *It is* **a good land which the LORD our God doth give us**.

26 Notwithstanding ye would not go up, but rebelled against the commandment of the LORD your God:

27 **And ye murmured in your tents**, and said, Because the LORD hated us, he hath brought us forth out of the land of Egypt, to deliver us into the hand of the Amorites, to destroy us.

28 Whither shall we go up? our brethren have discouraged our heart, saying, The people *is* greater and taller than we; the cities *are* great and walled up to heaven; and moreover we have seen the sons of the Anakims there.

29 **Then I said unto you, Dread not, neither be afraid of them.**

30 **The LORD your God which goeth before you, he shall fight for you, according to all that he did for you in Egypt before your eyes;**

31 And in the wilderness, where thou hast seen how that the LORD thy God bare thee, as a man doth bear his son, in all the way that ye went, until ye came into this place.

32 Yet in this thing ye did not believe the LORD your God,

33 Who went in the way before you, to search you out a place to pitch your tents *in*, in fire by night, to shew you by what way ye should go, and in a cloud by day.

A. PUNISHMENT TO MIRIAM WHO SPOKE AGAINST MOSES

Numbers 12:1 And Miriam and Aaron spake against Moses because of the Ethiopian woman whom he had married: for he had married an Ethiopian woman.

2 And **they said**, *Hath the LORD indeed spoken only by Moses? hath he not spoken also by us? A*nd the **LORD heard** *it.*

4 **And the LORD spake suddenly unto Moses, and unto Aaron, and unto Miriam, Come out ye three unto the tabernacle of the congregation. And they three came out**.

5 And the LORD came down in the pillar of the cloud, and stood *in* the door of the tabernacle, and called Aaron and Miriam: and they both came forth.

6 And he said, Hear now my words: If there be a prophet among you, *I* the LORD will make myself known unto him in a vision, *and* will speak unto him in a dream.

7 My servant Moses *is* not so, who *is* faithful in all mine house.

8 **With him will I speak mouth to mouth, even apparently, and not in dark speeches; and the similitude of the LORD shall he behold: wherefore then were ye not afraid to speak against my servant Moses?**

9 And the anger of the LORD was kindled against them; and he departed.

10 And the cloud departed from off the tabernacle; and, **behold, Miriam** *became* **leprous,** *white* **as snow: and Aaron looked upon Miriam, and, behold,** *she was* **leprous.**

11 And **Aaron said unto Moses, Alas, my lord, I beseech thee, lay not the sin upon us, wherein we have done foolishly, and wherein we have** sinned.

12 Let her not be as one dead, of whom the flesh is half consumed when he cometh out of his mother's womb.

13 **And Moses cried unto the LORD, saying, Heal her now, O God, I beseech thee.**

14 And **the LORD said unto Moses, If her father had but spit in her face, should she not be ashamed seven days? let her be shut out from the camp seven days, and after that let her be received in** *again*.

15 **And Miriam was shut out from the camp seven days: and the people journeyed not till Miriam was brought in** *again*.

B. PUNISHMENT TO CHOSEN PEOPLE WITHOUT FAITH

1. THEY WILL ALL DIE IN THE WILDERNESS

Numbers 14:26 And the LORD spake unto Moses and unto Aaron, saying,

27 How long *shall I bear with* this evil congregation, which murmur against me? I have heard the murmurings of the children of Israel, which they murmur against me.

28 Say unto them, *As truly as* I live, saith the LORD, as ye have spoken in mine ears, so will I do to you:

29 **Your carcases shall fall in this wilderness; and all that were numbered of you, according to your whole number, from twenty years old and upward, which have murmured against me,**

Deuteronomy 1:35 Surely there shall not one of these men of this evil generation see that good land, which I sware to give unto your fathers,

Numbers 14:30 Doubtless ye shall not come into the land, *concerning* which I sware to make you dwell therein, save Caleb the son of Jephunneh, and Joshua the son of Nun.

31 But your little ones, which ye said should be a prey, them will I bring in, and they shall know the land which ye have despised.

32 But *as for* you, your carcases, they shall fall in this wilderness

33 And your children shall wander in the wilderness forty years, and bear your whoredoms, until your carcases be wasted in the wilderness.

34 After the number of the days in which ye searched the land, *even* forty days, each day for a year, shall ye bear your iniquities, *even* forty years, and ye shall know my breach of promise.

35 I the LORD have said, I will surely do it unto all this evil congregation, that are gathered together against me: in this wilderness they shall be consumed, and there they shall die.

36 And the men, which Moses sent to search the land, who returned, and made all the congregation to murmur against him, by bringing up a slander upon the land,

37 Even those men that did bring up the evil report upon the land, died by the plague before the LORD.

Deuteronomy 1: 40 But as for you, turn you, and take your journey into the wilderness by the way of the Red Sea.

Psalms 106:25 But murmured in their tents, and hearkend not unto the voice of the LORD,

26 Therefore he lifted up his hand against them, to overthrow them in the wilderness:

ONLY TWO CHOSEN PEOPLE COULD ENTER THE PROMISE LAND

Numbers 14:24 But **my servant Caleb**, because he had another spirit with him, and **hath followed me fully**, him will I bring into the land whereinto he went; and his seed shall possess it.

Numbers 14:38 But **Joshua the son of Nun, and Caleb the son of Jephunneh**, *which were* of the men **that went to search the land, lived** *still*

Deuteronomy 1:36 Save Caleb the son of Jephunneh; he shall see it, and to him will I give the land that he hath trodden upon, and to his children, because he hath wholly followed the LORD.

37 Also the LORD was angry with me for your sakes, saying, Thou also shalt not go in thither.

38 *But* **Joshua the son of Nun, which standeth before thee, he shall go in thither**: encourage him: **for he shall cause Israel to inherit it.**

39 Moreover your little ones, which ye said should be a prey, and **your children, which in that day had no knowledge between good and evil, they shall go in thither, and unto them will I give it, and they shall possess it.**

2. THE LORD LEFT HIS PEOPLE WHO DISOBEYED HIM

Numbers 14:39 And Moses told these sayings unto all the children of Israel: and the people mourned greatly.

40 And they rose up early in the morning, and gat them up into the top of the mountain, saying, Lo, we *be here*, and will go up unto the place which the LORD hath promised: for we have sinned.

41 And Moses said, Wherefore now do ye transgress the commandment of the LORD? but it shall not prosper.

42 Go not up, for the LORD *is* not among you; that ye be not smitten before your enemies.

43 For the Amalekites and the Canaanites *are* there before you, and ye shall fall by the sword: because ye are turned away from the LORD, therefore the LORD will not be with you.

44 But they presumed to go up unto the hill top: nevertheless the ark of the covenant of the LORD, and Moses, departed not out of the camp.

45 Then the Amalekites came down, and the Canaanites which dwelt in that hill, and smote them, and discomfited them, *even* unto Hormah.

THE ISRAELITES LOST THE BATTLE

Deuteronomy 1:41 Then ye answered and said unto me, We have sinned against the LORD, we will go up and fight, according to all that the LORD our God commanded us. And when ye had girded on every man his weapons of war, ye were ready to go up into the hill.

42 And **the LORD said unto me**, Say unto them, *Go not up, neither fight; for I am not among you; lest ye be smitten before your enemies.*

43 So I spake unto you; and **ye would not hear, but rebelled against the commandment of the LORD, and went presumptuously up into the hill.**

44 **And the Amorites, which dwelt in that mountain, came out against you, and chased you, as bees do, and destroyed you in Seir,** *even* **unto Hormah.**

45 **And ye returned and wept before the LORD; but the LORD would not hearken to your voice, nor give ear unto you**.

46 So ye abode in Kadesh many days, according unto the days that ye abode *there*.

C. ISRAEL GRUMBLED AGAINST GOD AND MOSES

WEPT FOR MEAT
Numbers 11:4 And the mixt multitude that *was* among them fell a lusting: and the children of Israel also wept again, and said, Who shall give us flesh to eat?

5 We remember the fish, which we did eat in Egypt freely; the cucumbers, and the melons, and the leeks, and the onions, and the garlick:

6 But now our soul *is* dried away: *there is* nothing at all, beside this manna, *before* our eyes.

GOD SENT QUAILS
Numbers 11:31 And there went forth a wind from the LORD, and brought quails from the sea, and let *them* fall by the camp, as it were a day's journey on this side, and as it were a day's journey on the other side, round about the camp, and as it were two cubits *high* upon the face of the earth.

32 And the people stood up all that day, and all *that* night, and all the next day, and they gathered the quails: he that gathered least gathered ten homers: and they spread *them* all abroad for themselves round about the camp.

PUNISHMENT TO THE MURMURERS AND COMPLAINERS

1. PLAGUES
Numbers 11:33 And while the flesh *was* yet between their teeth, ere it was chewed, the wrath of the LORD was kindled against the people, and **the LORD smote the people with a very great plague**.

34 And he called the name of that place Kibrothhattaavah: because there they buried the people that lusted.

35 *And* the people journeyed from Kibrothhattaavah unto Hazeroth; and abode at Hazeroth.

2.. GOD SENT FIERY SNAKES

Numbers 21:4 And they journeyed from mount Hor by the way of the Red sea, to compass the land of Edom: and the soul of the people was much discouraged because of the way.

5 And **the people spake against God, and against Moses, Wherefore have ye brought us up out of Egypt to die in the wilderness? for** *there is* **no bread, neither** *is there any* **water; and our soul loatheth this light bread.**

6 And **the LORD sent fiery serpents among the people, and they bit the people; and much people of Israel died.**

7 Therefore the people came to Moses, and said, We have sinned, for we have spoken against the LORD, and against thee; pray unto the LORD, that he take away the serpents from us. And Moses prayed for the people.

GOD COMMANDED MOSES TO MAKE A FIERY SERPENT OF BRASS

Numbers 21:8 And **the LORD said unto Moses**, *Make thee a fiery serpent, and set it upon a pole: and it shall come to pass, that every one that is bitten, when he looketh upon it, shall live.*

9 And Moses made a serpent of brass, and put it upon a pole, and it came to pass, that if a serpent had bitten any man, when he beheld the serpent of brass, he lived.

D. PEOPLE ENVIED MOSES AND AARON

Numbers 16:1 Now Korah, the son of Izhar, the son of Kohath, the son of Levi, and Dathan and Abiram, the sons of Eliab, and On, the son of Peleth, sons of Reuben, took *men*:

2 And they rose up before Moses, with certain of the children of Israel, two hundred and fifty princes of the assembly, famous in the congregation, men of renown:

3 And **they gathered themselves together against Moses and against Aaron,** and said unto them, *Ye take* too much upon you, seeing all the congregation *are* holy, every one of them, and the

LORD *is* among them: wherefore then lift ye up yourselves above the congregation of the LORD?

4 And **when Moses heard *it*, he fell upon his face:**

5 **And he spake unto Korah and unto all his company,** saying, Even to morrow the LORD will shew who *are* his, and *who is* holy; and will cause *him* to come near unto him: even *him* whom he hath chosen will he cause to come near unto him.

6 This do; Take you censers, Korah, and all his company;

7 And put **fire therein, and put incense in them before the LORD to morrow: and it shall be** *that* **the man whom the LORD doth choose, he** *shall be* **holy:** *ye take* **too much upon you, ye sons of Levi.**

8 And Moses said unto Korah, Hear, I pray you, ye sons of Levi:

9 *Seemeth it but* a small thing unto you, that the God of Israel hath separated you from the congregation of Israel, to bring you near to himself to do the service of the tabernacle of the LORD, and to stand before the congregation to minister unto them?

10 And he hath brought thee near *to him*, and all thy brethren the sons of Levi with thee: and seek ye the priesthood also?

11 For which cause *both* thou and all thy company *are* gathered together against the LORD: and what *is* Aaron, that ye murmur against him?

12 And **Moses sent to call Dathan and Abiram, the sons of Eliab: which said,** *We will not come up:*

13 *Is it a small thing that thou hast brought us up out of a land that floweth with milk and honey, to kill us in the wilderness, except thou make thyself altogether a prince over us?*

14 *Moreover thou hast not brought us into a land that floweth with milk and honey, or given us inheritance of fields and vineyards: wilt thou put out the eyes of these men? we will not come up.*

15 And Moses was very wroth, and said unto the LORD, Respect not thou their offering: I have not taken one ass from them, neither have I hurt one of them.

16 And Moses said unto Korah, Be thou and all thy company before the LORD, thou, and they, and Aaron, to morrow:

17 And take every man his censer, and put incense in them, and bring ye before the LORD every man his censer, two hundred and fifty censers; thou also, and Aaron, each *of you* his censer.

18 And they took every man his censer, and put fire in them, and laid incense thereon, and stood in the door of the tabernacle of the congregation with Moses and Aaron.

19 And Korah gathered all the congregation against them unto the door of the tabernacle of the congregation: and the glory of the LORD appeared unto all the congregation.

GOD'S PUNISHMENT TO KORAH , ABIRAM AND HIS MEN

Number 16:20 And **the LORD spake unto Moses** and unto Aaron, saying,

21 Separate yourselves from among this congregation, that **I may consume them in a moment**.

22 And they fell upon their faces, and said, O God, the God of the spirits of all flesh, shall one man sin, and wilt thou be wroth with all the congregation?

23 And the LORD spake unto Moses, saying,

24 Speak unto the congregation, saying, **Get you up from about the tabernacle of Korah, Dathan, and Abiram.**

25 And **Moses rose up and went unto Dathan and Abiram; and the elders of Israel followed him**.

26 And he spake unto the congregation, **saying, Depart, I pray you, from the tents of these wicked men, and touch nothing of theirs, lest ye be consumed in all their sins.**

27 So they gat up from the tabernacle of Korah, Dathan, and Abiram, on every side: and Dathan and Abiram came out, and stood in the door of their tents, and their wives, and their sons, and their little children.

28 And Moses said, Hereby ye shall know that the LORD hath sent me to do all these works; for *I have* not *done them* of mine own mind.

29 If these men die the common death of all men, or if they be visited after the visitation of all men; *then* the LORD hath not sent me.

30 But if the LORD make a new thing, and the earth open her mouth, and swallow them up, with all that *appertain* unto them, and they go down quick into the pit; then ye shall understand that these men have provoked the LORD.

31 And it came to pass, as he had made an end of speaking all these words, that the ground clave asunder that *was* under them:

32 And **the earth opened her mouth, and swallowed them up, and their houses, and all the men that** *appertained* **unto Korah, and all** *their* **goods.**

33 **They, and all that** *appertained* **to them, went down alive into the pit, and the earth closed upon them: and they perished from among the congregation.**

34 And all Israel that *were* round about them fled at the cry of them: for they said, Lest the earth swallow us up *also*.

35 And **there came out a fire from the LORD, and consumed the two hundred and fifty men that offered incense.**

Psalms 106:16 They envied Moses also in the camp, *and* Aaron the saint of the LORD.

17 The earth opened and swallowed up Dathan, and covered the company of Abiram.

18 And a fire was kindled in their company; the flame burned up the wicked.

PLAGUE KILLED MORE PEOPLE

Numbers 16:36 And the LORD spake unto Moses, saying,

37 Speak unto Eleazar the son of Aaron the priest, that he take up the censers out of the burning, and scatter thou the fire yonder; for they are hallowed.

38 **The censers of these sinners against their own souls,** let them make them broad plates *for* a covering of the altar: for they offered them before the LORD, therefore they are hallowed: and they shall be a sign unto the children of Israel.

39 And Eleazar the priest took the brasen censers, wherewith they that were burnt had offered; and they were made broad *plates for* a covering of the altar:

40 *To be* a memorial unto the children of Israel, that no stranger, which *is* not of the seed of Aaron, come near to offer incense before the LORD; that he be not as Korah, and as his company: as the LORD said to him by the hand of Moses.

41 But on the morrow all the congregation of the children of Israel murmured against Moses and against Aaron, saying, Ye have killed the people of the LORD.

42 And it came to pass, when the congregation was gathered against Moses and against Aaron, that they looked toward the tabernacle of the congregation: and, behold, the cloud covered it, and the glory of the LORD appeared.

43 And Moses and Aaron came before the tabernacle of the congregation.

44 And the LORD spake unto Moses, saying,

45 Get you up from among this congregation, that I may consume them as in a moment. And they fell upon their faces.

46 And Moses said unto Aaron, Take a censer, and put fire therein from off the altar, and put on incense, and go quickly unto the congregation, and make an atonement for them: for there is wrath gone out from the LORD; **the plague is begun.**

47 And **Aaron took as Moses commanded, and ran into the midst of the congregation; and, behold, the plague was begun among the people:** and he put on incense, and made an atonement for the people.

48 And **he stood between the dead and the living; and the plague was stayed**.

49 Now **they that died in the plague were fourteen thousand and seven hundred, beside them that died about the matter of Korah.**

50 And Aaron returned unto Moses unto the door of the tabernacle of the congregation: and the plague was stayed.

E. PEOPLE WORSHIPING THE GOLDEN CALF WERE KILLED

Psalm 106:19 **They made a calf in Horeb, and worshipped the molten image.**

20 Thus **they changed their glory into the similitude of an ox that eateth grass.**

21 **They forgat God their saviour**, which had done great things in Egypt;

22 Wondrous works in the land of Ham, *and* terrible things by the Red sea.

23 Therefore he said that he would destroy them, had not Moses his chosen stood before him in the breach, to turn away his wrath, lest he should destroy *them*.

Exodus 32:26 Then Moses stood in the gate of the camp, and said, Who *is* on the LORD'S side? *let him come* unto me. And all the sons of Levi gathered themselves together unto him.

27 And he said unto them, Thus saith the LORD God of Israel, Put every man his sword by his side, *and* go in and out from gate to gate throughout the camp, and slay every man his brother, and every man his companion, and every man his neighbour.

28 And the children of Levi did according to the word of Moses: and **there fell of the people that day about three thousand men.**

FOLLOWERS OF IDOL BAAL PERISHED BY PLAGUE

Exodus 32:34 Therefore now go, lead the people unto *the place* of which I have spoken unto thee: **behold, mine Angel shall go before thee: nevertheless in the day when I visit I will visit their sin upon them.**

35 And **the LORD plagued the people, because they made the calf, which Aaron made.**

Numbers 25:1 And Israel abode in Shittim, and **the people began to commit whoredom with the daughters of Moab.**

2 **And they called the people unto the sacrifices of their gods: and the people did eat, and bowed down to their gods.**

3 **And Israel joined himself unto Baalpeor: and the anger of the LORD was kindled against Israel.**

4 And the LORD said unto Moses, Take all the heads of the people, and hang them up before the LORD against the sun, that the fierce anger of the LORD may be turned away from Israel.

5 And Moses said unto the judges of Israel, Slay ye every one his men that were joined unto Baalpeor.

6 And, behold, **one of the children of Israel came and brought unto his brethren a Midianitish woman in the sight of Moses, and in the sight of all the congregation of the children of Israel, who** *were* weeping *before* **the door of the tabernacle of the congregation**.

7 And **when Phinehas,** the son of Eleazar, the son of Aaron the priest, saw *it*, he rose up from among the congregation, and **took a javelin in his hand;**

8 **And he went after the man of Israel into the tent, and thrust both of them through, the man of Israel, and the woman through her belly**. So the plague was stayed from the children of Israel.

9 And **those that died in the plague were twenty and four thousand.**

Psalms 106:28 **They joined themselves also unto Baalpeor, and ate the sacrifices of the dead.**

29 Thus they provoked *him* to anger with their inventions: and the plague brake in upon them.

30 Then stood up Phinehas, and executed judgment: and *so* the plague was stayed.

31 And that was counted unto him for righteousness unto all generations for evermore.

MOSES INSTRUCTIONS BEFORE ENTERING THE PROMISE LAND

Deuteronomy 4:1 Now therefore hearken, O Israel, unto the statutes and unto the judgments, which I teach you, for to do *them*, that ye may live, and go in and possess the land which the LORD God of your fathers giveth you.

2 **Ye shall not add unto the word which I command you, neither shall ye diminish** *ought* **from it, that ye may keep the commandments of the LORD your God which I command you.**

3 Your eyes have seen what the LORD did because of Baalpeor: for all the men that followed Baalpeor, the LORD thy God hath destroyed them from among you.

4 But ye that did cleave unto the LORD your God *are* alive every one of you this day.

F. MOSES WAS NOT ALLOWED TO ENTER THE PROMISE LAND

Psalm 106:32 **They angered** *him* **also at the waters of strife, so that it went ill with Moses for their sakes:**

33 Because **they provoked his spirit, so that he spake unadvisedly with his lips.**

Numbers 20:1 Then came the children of Israel, *even* the whole congregation, into the desert of Zin in the first month: and the people abode in Kadesh; and Miriam died there, and was buried there.

2 And there was no water for the congregation: and they gathered themselves together against Moses and against Aaron.

3 And the people chode with Moses, and spake, saying, Would God that we had died when our brethren died before the LORD!

4 And why have ye brought up the congregation of the LORD into this wilderness, that we and our cattle should die there?

5 And wherefore have ye made us to come up out of Egypt, to bring us in unto this evil place? it *is* no place of seed, or of figs, or of vines, or of pomegranates; neither *is* there any water to drink.

6 And Moses and Aaron went from the presence of the assembly unto the door of the tabernacle of the congregation, and they fell upon their faces: and the glory of the LORD appeared unto them.

7 And **the LORD spake unto Moses, saying**,

8 *Take the rod, and gather thou the assembly together, thou, and Aaron thy brother, and speak ye unto the rock before their eyes; and it shall give forth his water, and thou shalt bring forth to them water out of the rock: so thou shalt give the congregation and their beasts drink.*

9 And Moses took the rod from before the LORD, as he commanded him.

10 And **Moses and Aaron gathered the congregation together before the rock, and he said unto them**, *Hear now, ye rebels; must we fetch you water out of this rock?*

11 And Moses lifted up his hand, and with his rod he smote the rock twice: and the water came out abundantly, and the congregation drank, and their beasts *also*.

12 And **the LORD spake unto Moses and Aaron**, *Because ye believed me not, to sanctify me in the eyes of the children of Israel, therefore ye shall not bring this congregation into the land which I have given them.*

13 This *is* the water of Meribah; because the children of Israel strove with the LORD, and he was sanctified in them.

G. PUNISHMENT TO PEOPLE DOING ABOMINATION TO THE LORD

Deuteronomy 17:2 If there be found among you, within any of thy gates which the LORD thy God giveth thee, man or woman, that hath wrought wickedness in the sight of the LORD thy God, in transgressing his covenant,

3 And hath gone and served other gods, and worshipped them, either the sun, or moon, or any of the host of heaven, which I have not commanded;

4 And it be told thee, and thou hast heard *of it*, and enquired diligently, and, behold, *it be* true, *and* the thing certain, *that* such abomination is wrought in Israel:

5 Then shalt thou bring forth that man or that woman, which have committed that wicked thing, unto thy gates, *even* that man or that woman, and shalt stone them with stones, till they die.

WITNESSES NECESSARY TO IMPLEMENT PUNISHMENT

Deuteronomy 17:6 At the mouth of two witnesses, or three witnesses, shall he that is worthy of death be put to death; *but* **at the mouth of one witness he shall not be put to death.**

7 The hands of the witnesses shall be first upon him to put him to death, and afterward the hands of all the people. So thou shalt put the evil away from among you.

8 If there arise a matter too hard for thee in judgment, between blood and blood, between plea and plea, and between stroke and stroke, *being* matters of controversy within thy gates: then shalt thou arise, and get thee up into the place which the LORD thy God shall choose;

9 And thou shalt come unto the priests the Levites, and unto the judge that shall be in those days, and enquire; and they shall shew thee the sentence of judgment:

10 And thou shalt do according to the sentence, which they of that place which the LORD shall choose shall shew thee; and thou shalt observe to do according to all that they inform thee:

11 According to the sentence of the law which they shall teach thee, and according to the judgment which they shall tell thee, thou shalt do: thou shalt not decline from the sentence which they shall shew thee, *to* the right hand, nor *to* the left.

12 And the man that will do presumptuously, and will not hearken unto the priest that standeth to minister there before the LORD thy God, or unto the judge, even that man shall die: and thou shalt put away the evil from Israel.

PART 8
GOD RENDERS PUNISHMENT

CHAPTER V **ISRAEL'S DISOBEDIENCE**

. IN JOSHUA'S TIME

GOD ALLOWED ISRAEL TO LOSE THE BATTLE AGAINST A-I

Joshua 7:1 But the children of Israel committed a trespass in the accursed thing: for Achan, the son of Carmi, the son of Zabdi, the son of Zerah, of the tribe of Judah, took of the accursed thing: **and the anger of the LORD was kindled against the children of Israel**.

2 And Joshua sent men from Jericho to Ai, which *is* beside Bethaven, on the east side of Bethel, and spake unto them, saying, Go up and view the country. And the men went up and viewed Ai.

3 And they returned to Joshua, and said unto him, Let not all the people go up; but let about two or three thousand men go up and smite Ai; *and* make not all the people to labour thither; for they *are but* few.

4 So there went up thither of the people about three thousand men: and they fled before the men of Ai.

5 **And the men of Ai smote of them about thirty and six men: for they chased them** *from* **before the gate** *even* **unto Shebarim, and smote them in the going down:** wherefore the hearts of the people melted, and became as water.

6 And Joshua rent his clothes, and fell to the earth upon his face before the ark of the LORD until the eventide, he and the elders of Israel, and put dust upon their heads.

7 And Joshua said, Alas, O Lord GOD, wherefore hast thou at all brought this people over Jordan, to deliver us into the hand of the Amorites, to destroy us? would to God we had been content, and dwelt on the other side Jordan!

8 O Lord, what shall I say, when Israel turneth their backs before their enemies!

9 For the Canaanites and all the inhabitants of the land shall hear *of it*, and shall environ us round, and cut off our name from the earth: and what wilt thou do unto thy great name?

10 **And the LORD said unto Joshua, Get thee up; wherefore liest thou thus upon thy face?**

11 **Israel hath sinned, and they have also transgressed my covenant which I commanded them: for they have even taken of the accursed thing, and have also stolen, and dissembled also, and they have put *it* even among their own stuff.**

12 **Therefore the children of Israel could not stand before their enemies, *but* turned *their* backs before their enemies, because they were accursed: neither will I be with you any more, except ye destroy the accursed from among you.**

ACHAN'S LOOT FROM JERICHO

Joshua 7:21 When I saw among the spoils a goodly Babylonian garment, and two hundred shekles of silver, and a wedge of gold of fifty shekels weight then I coveted them, and took them;, and behold, they are hid in the earth in the midst of my tent, and the silver under it.

22 So Joshua sent messengers, and they ran unto the tent; and, behold, *it was* hid in his tent, and the silver under it.

23 And they took them out of the midst of the tent, and brought them unto Joshua, and unto all the children of Israel, and laid them out before the LORD.

ACHAN, HIS FAMILY AND ANIMALS WERE PUT TO DEATH

Joshua 7:24 And Joshua, and all Israel with him, took Achan the son of Zerah, and the silver, and the garment, and the wedge of gold, and his sons, and his daughters, and his oxen, and his asses, and his sheep, and his tent, and all that he had: and **they brought them unto the valley of Achor.**

25 And Joshua said, Why hast thou troubled us? the LORD shall trouble thee this day. **And all Israel stoned him with stones, and burned them with fire, after they had stoned them with stones.**

26 **And they raised over him a great heap of stones unto this day. So the LORD turned from the fierceness of his anger.** Wherefore the name of that place was called, The valley of Achor, unto this day.

B. THE TIME OF JUDGES

Judges 2:18 And **when the LORD raised them up with judges, then the LORD was with the judge, and delivered them out of the hand of their enemies all the days of the judge**, for it repented the LORD because of their groanings by reason of them that oppressed them and vexed them.

THE SIN OF ISRAEL: WORSHIPPING IDOLS

1Corinthians 10:22 Do we provoke the LORD to jealousy? Are we stronger than he?

1. AFTER JOSHUA"S DEATH

Judges 2:8 And **Joshua the son of Nun, the servant of the LORD died**, being an hundred and ten years old.

10 And also all that generation were gathered unto their fathers: and there arose another generation after them, which knew not the LORD, nor yet the works which he had done for Israel. **Deuteronomy 32**:16 **They provoked him (God) to jealousy with strange gods, with abominations provoked they him to anger.**

17 They sacrificed unto devils, not to God; to gods whom they knew not, to new *gods that* came newly up, whom your fathers feared not.

18 Of the Rock *that* begat thee thou art unmindful, and hast forgotten God that formed thee.

19 And when the LORD saw *it*, he abhorred *them*, because of the provoking of his sons, and of his daughters.

20 And he said, I will hide my face from them, I will see what their end *shall be*: for they *are* a very froward generation, children in whom *is* no faith.

21 They have moved me to jealousy with *that which is* not God; they have provoked me to anger with their vanities: and I will move them to jealousy with *those which are* not a people; I will provoke them to anger with a foolish nation.

DISOBEDIENCE OF THE PEOPLE OF ISRAEL TO GOD'S COMMANDMENTS

Judges 3:6 And **they took their daughters to be their wives, and gave their daughters to their sons, and served their gods.**

7 And the children of Israel did evil in the sight of the LORD, and forgat the LORD their God, and **served Baalim and the groves.**

THE ANGER OF THE LORD AGAINST ISRAEL

Judges 2:14 And the anger of the LORD was hot against Israel, and **he delivered them into the hands of spoilers that spoiled them, and he sold them into the hands of their enemies round about,** so that they could not any longer stand before their enemies.

15 Whithersoever they went out, the hand of the LORD was against them for evil, as the LORD had said, and as the LORD had sworn unto them: and they were greatly distressed.

THE PEOPLE OF ISRAEL CONTINUED SINNING AGAINST THE LORD

Judges 2:17 And yet they would not hearken unto their judges, but they went a whoring after other gods, and bowed themselves unto them: they turned quickly out of the way which their fathers walked in, obeying the commandments of the LORD; *but* they did not so

19 And it came to pass, **when the judge was dead,** *that* **they returned, and corrupted** *themselves* **more than their fathers, in following other gods to serve them**, and to bow down unto them; they ceased not from their own doings, nor from their stubborn way.

THE LORD WAS HOT WITH ANGER AGAINST ISRAEL

Judges 2:20 And the anger of the LORD was hot against Israel; and he said, Because that this people hath transgressed my covenant which I commanded their fathers, and have not hearkened unto my voice;

21 **I also will not henceforth drive out any from before them of the nations which Joshua left when he died:**

22 That through them I may prove Israel, whether they will keep the way of the LORD to walk therein, as their fathers did keep *it*, or not.

23 Therefore the LORD left those nations, without driving them out hastily; neither delivered he them into the hand of Joshua.

Judges 3: 8 Therefore the anger of the LORD was hot against Israel, and **he sold them into the hand of Chushanrishathaim king of Mesopotamia: and the children of Israel served Chushanrishathaim eight years.**

2. AFTER THE DEATH OF EHU, THE JUDGE

Judges 4:1 **And the children of Israel again did evil in the sight of the LORD, when Ehud was dead.**

2 **And the LORD sold them into the hand of Jabin king of Canaan**, that reigned in Hazor; the captain of whose host *was* Sisera, which dwelt in Harosheth of the Gentiles.

3. AFTER THE DEATH OF GIDEON

Judges 8:33 And it came to pass, **as soon as Gideon was dead, that the children of Israel turned again, and went a whoring after Baalim, and made Baalberith their god.**

34 And the children of Israel remembered not the LORD their God, who had delivered them out of the hands of all their enemies on every side:

35 Neither shewed they kindness to the house of Jerubbaal, *namely*, Gideon, according to all the goodness which he had shewed unto Israel.

4. AFTER JARID'S DEATH

Judges 10:3 And after him arose Jair, a Gileadite, and judged Israel twenty and two years.

5 And **Jair died,** and was buried in Camon.

6 And the children of Israel did evil again in the sight of the LORD, and **served Baalim, and Ashtaroth, and the gods of Syria, and the gods of Zidon, and the gods of Moab, and the gods of the children of Ammon, and the gods of the Philistines, and forsook the LORD, and served not him.**

GOD'S SOLD THEM TO THE HANDS OF PHILISTINES AND AMMON

Judges 10:7 And the anger of the LORD was hot against Israel, and **he sold them into the hands of the Philistines, and into the hands of the children of Ammon.**

8 And that year they vexed and oppressed the children of Israel: eighteen years, all the children of Israel that *were* on the other side Jordan in the land of the Amorites, which *is* in Gilead.

9 Moreover **the children of Ammon passed over Jordan to fight also against Judah, and against Benjamin, and against the house of Ephraim; so that Israel was sore distressed**.

ISRAEL CRIED TO GOD

Judges 10:10 And the children of Israel cried unto the LORD, saying, **We have sinned against thee, both because we have forsaken our God, and also served Baalim**.

THE LORD ANSWERED ISRAEL

Judges 10:11 And **the LORD said unto the children of Israel**, *Did* **not** *I deliver you* **from the Egyptians, and from the Amorites, from the children of Ammon, and from the Philistines?**

12 **The Zidonians also, and the Amalekites, and the Maonites, did oppress you; and ye cried to me, and I delivered you out of their hand.**

13 **Yet ye have forsaken me, and served other gods: wherefore I will deliver you no more.**

14 **Go and cry unto the gods which ye have chosen; let them deliver you in the time of your tribulation.**

ISRAEL ASKED DELIVERANCE FROM THE LORD

Judges 10:15 And the children of Israel said unto the LORD, *We have sinned: do thou unto us whatsoever seemeth good unto thee; deliver us only, we pray thee, this day.*

16 **And they put away the strange gods from among them, and served the LORD: and his soul was grieved for the misery of Israel.**

C. GOD PUNISHED ELI'S SONS

1Samuel 2:12 Now the sons of Eli *were* sons of Belial; **they knew not the LORD**.

13 And the priests' custom with the people *was, that*, when any man offered sacrifice, the priest's servant came, while the flesh was in seething, with a fleshhook of three teeth in his hand;

14 And he struck *it* into the pan, or kettle, or caldron, or pot; all that the fleshhook brought up the priest took for himself. So they did in Shiloh unto all the Israelites that came thither.

15 Also before they burnt the fat, the priest's servant came, and said to the man that sacrificed, Give flesh to roast for the priest; for he will not have sodden flesh of thee, but raw.

16 And *if* any man said unto him, Let them not fail to burn the fat presently, and *then* take *as much* as thy soul desireth; then he would answer him, *Nay*; but thou shalt give *it me* now: and if not, I will take *it* by force.

17 Wherefore the sin of the young men was very great before the LORD: for men abhorred the offering of the LORD.

1Samuel 2:22 Now Eli was very old, and heard all that his sons did unto all Israel; and how they lay with the women that assembled *at* the door of the tabernacle of the congregation.

23 And he said unto them, Why do ye such things? for I hear of your evil dealings by all this people.

24 Nay, my sons; for *it is* no good report that I hear: ye make the LORD'S people to transgress.

25 If one man sin against another, the judge shall judge him: but if a man sin against the LORD, who shall intreat for him? Notwithstanding they hearkened not unto the voice of their father, because the LORD would slay them.

GOD'S WARNING TO ELI

1Samuel 3:13 For I have told him that I will judge his house for ever for the iniquity which he knoweth; because his sons made themselves vile, and he restrained them not.

14 And therefore I have sworn unto the house of Eli, that the iniquity of Eli's house shall not be purged with sacrifice nor offering for ever.

1Samuel 2:33 And the man of thine, *whom* I shall not cut off from mine altar, *shall be* to consume thine eyes, and to grieve thine heart: and all the increase of thine house shall die in the flower of their age.

34 And this *shall be* a sign unto thee, that shall come upon thy two sons, on Hophni and Phinehas; in one day they shall die both of them.

1Samuel 3:11 And **the LORD said to Samuel,** *Behold, I will do* ***a thing in Israel, at which both the ears of every one that heareth it shall tingle.***

12 *In that day I will perform against Eli all things which I have spoken concerning his house: when I begin, I will also make an end.*

THE TWO SONS OF ELI WERE SLAIN AND THE ARK OF GOD WAS TAKEN BY PHILISTINES

1Samuel 4:1 And the word of Samuel came to all Israel. Now Israel went out against Philistines to battle, and pitched beside Ebenezer: and the Philistines pitched in Aphek.

2And the Philistines put themselves in array against Israel: and when they joined battle, Israel was smitten before the Philistines: and they slew of the army in the field four thousand men

3 And when the people were come into the camp, the elders of Israel said, Wherefore hath the LORD smitten us to day before the Philistines? Let us fetch the ark of the covenant of the LORD out of Shiloh unto us, that, when it cometh among us, it may save us out of the hand of our enemies.

4 so the people sent to Shiloh, that they might bring from thence the ark of covenant of the LORD of Hosts, which dwelleth between the cherubims: and the two sons of Eli, Hopni and Phinehas were there with the ark other covenant of God.

10 And the Philistines fought, and Israel was smitten, and they fled every man into his tent: and there was a very great slaughter; for there fell of Israel thirty thousand footmen.

11 And **the ark of God was taken; and the two sons of Eli, Hophni and Phinehas, were slain**.

12 And there ran a man of Benjamin out of the army, and came to Shiloh the same day with his clothes rent, and with earth upon his head.

13 And when he came, lo, Eli sat upon a seat by the wayside watching: for his heart trembled for the ark of God. And when the man came into the city, and told *it*, all the city cried out.

14 And when Eli heard the noise of the crying, he said, What *meaneth* the noise of this tumult?

And the man came in hastily, and told Eli.

15 Now Eli was ninety and eight years old; and his eyes were dim, that he could not see.

16 And the man said unto Eli, I *am* he that came out of the army, and I fled to day out of the army. And he said, What is there done, my son?

17 And **the messenger answered and said, Israel is fled before the Philistines, and there hath been also a great slaughter among the people, and thy two sons also, Hophni and Phinehas, are dead, and the ark of God is taken.**

18 And it came to pass, **when he made mention of the ark of God, that he fell from off the seat backward by the side of the gate, and his neck brake, and he died: for he was an old man, and heavy. And he had judged Israel forty years.**

19 **And his daughter in law, Phinehas' wife, was with child,** *near* **to be delivered: and when she heard the tidings that the ark of God was taken, and that her father in law and her husband were dead, she bowed herself and travailed; for her pains came upon her.**

20 **And about the time of her death the women that stood by her said unto her,** Fear not; for thou hast born a son. But she answered not, neither did she regard *it*.

21 And she named the child Ichabod, saying, The glory is departed from Israel: because the ark of God was taken, and because of her father in law and her husband.

22 And she said, The glory is departed from Israel: for the ark of God is taken.

D. UZZAH'S PUNISHMENT FOR TOUCHING THE ARK OF COVENANT

2Samuel 6:1 Again, David gathered together all *the* chosen *men* of Israel, thirty thousand.

2 And David arose, and went with all the people that *were* with him from Baale of Judah, to bring up from thence the ark of God, whose name is called by the name of the LORD of hosts that dwelleth *between* the cherubims.

3 And they set the ark of God upon a new cart, and brought it out of the house of Abinadab that *was* in Gibeah: and Uzzah and Ahio, the sons of Abinadab, drave the new cart.

4 And they brought it out of the house of Abinadab which *was* at Gibeah, accompanying the ark of God: and Ahio went before the ark.

5 And David and all the house of Israel played before the LORD on all manner of *instruments made of* fir wood, even on harps, and on psalteries, and on timbrels, and on cornets, and on cymbals

6 And **when they came to Nachon's threshingfloor, Uzzah put forth** *his hand* **to the ark of God, and took hold of it; for the oxen shook** *it.*

7 **And the anger of the LORD was kindled against Uzzah; and God smote him there for** *his* **error; and there he died by the ark of God.**

8 And **David was displeased, because the LORD had made a breach upon Uzzah: and he called the name of the place Perezuzzah to this day.**

DAVID BROUGHT BACK THE ARK TO THE CITY OF DAVID

Luke 2:4 *And Joseph also went up from Galilee, out of the city of Nazareth, into Judaea,* **unto the city of David, which is called Bethlehem**; *(because he was of the house and lineage of David:)*

2Samuel 6:9 **And David was afraid of the LORD that day**, and said, **How shall the ark of the LORD come to me?**

10 So David would not remove the ark of the LORD unto him into the city of David: but David carried it aside into the house of Obededom the Gittite.

11 **And the ark of the LORD continued in the house of Obededom the Gittite three months: and the LORD blessed Obededom, and all his household.**

12 And it was told king David, saying, The LORD hath blessed the house of Obededom, and all that *pertaineth* unto him, because of the ark of God. **So David went and brought up the ark of God from the house of Obededom into the city of David with gladness**.

13 And it was *so*, that when they that bare the ark of the LORD had gone six paces, he sacrificed oxen and fatlings.

14 And **David danced before the LORD with all** *his* **might**; and **David** *was* **girded with a linen ephod.**

15 **So David and all the house of Israel brought up the ark of the LORD with shouting, and with the sound of the trumpet.**

MICHAL DESPISED DAVID DANCING IN THE STREET

1Chronicles 15:27 And David *was* clothed with a robe of fine linen, and all the Levites that bare the ark, and the singers, and Chenaniah the master of the song with the singers: David also *had* upon him an ephod of linen.

28 Thus all Israel brought up the ark of the covenant of the LORD with shouting, and with sound of the cornet, and with trumpets, and with cymbals, making a noise with psalteries and harps.

29 And it came to pass, *as* **the ark of the covenant of the LORD came to the city of David**, that **Michal the daughter of Saul looking out at a window saw king David dancing and playing: and she despised him in her heart**.

2Samuel 6:16 And as the ark of the LORD came into the city of David, Michal Saul's daughter looked through a window, and saw king David leaping and dancing before the LORD; and she despised him in her heart.

17 And they brought in the ark of the LORD, and set it in his place, in the midst of the tabernacle that David had pitched for it: and David offered burnt offerings and peace offerings before the LORD.

18 And as soon as David had made an end of offering burnt offerings and peace offerings, he blessed the people in the name of the LORD of hosts.

19 And he dealt among all the people, *even* among the whole multitude of Israel, as well to the women as men, to every one a cake of bread, and a good piece *of flesh*, and a flagon *of wine*. So all the people departed every one to his house.

E. PUNISHMENT TO MICHAL WHO INSULTED DAVID, THE ELECT

2Samuel 6:20 Then David returned to bless his household. And **Michal the daughter of Saul came out to meet David, and said, How glorious was the king of Israel to day, who uncovered himself to day in the eyes of the handmaids of his servants, as one of** the vain fellows shamelessly uncovereth himself!

21 And **David said unto Michal,** *It was* **before the LORD, which chose me before thy father, and before all his house, to appoint me ruler over the people of the LORD, over Israel: therefore will I play before the LORD.**

22 **And I will yet be more vile than thus, and will be base in mine own sight: and of the maidservants which thou hast spoken of, of them shall I be had in honour**.

23 **Therefore Michal the daughter of Saul had no child unto the day of her death.**

PART 8
GOD RENDERS PUNISHMENT

CHAPTER VI **KINGS' DISOBEDIENCE TO GOD**

KINGS DISOBEYED GOD'S INSTRUCTIONS

Nehemiah 9:33 Howbeit thou *art* just in all that is brought upon us; for **thou hast done right, but we have done wickedly:**

34 **Neither have our kings, our princes, our priests, nor our fathers, kept thy law, nor hearkened unto thy commandments and thy testimonies, wherewith thou didst testify against them.**

35 **For they have not served thee in their kingdom, and in thy great goodness that thou gavest them,** and in the large and fat land which thou gavest before them, **neither turned they from their wicked works.**

1. SAUL
*GOD'S INSTRUCTION TO SAUL

1Samuel 15:1 Samuel also said unto Saul, The LORD sent me to anoint thee *to be* king over his people, over Israel: now therefore hearken thou unto the voice of the words of the LORD.

2 **Thus saith the LORD of hosts**, I remember *that* which Amalek did to Israel, how he laid *wait* for him in the way, when he came up from Egypt.

3 **Now go and smite Amalek, and utterly destroy all that they have, and spare them not; but slay both man and woman, infant and suckling, ox and sheep, camel and ass.**

REJECTED THE WORD OF THE LORD

1Samuel 15:4 And Saul gathered the people together, and numbered them in Telaim, two hundred thousand footmen, and ten thousand men of Judah.

5 And Saul came to a city of Amalek, and laid wait in the valley.

6 And Saul said unto the Kenites, Go, depart, get you down from among the Amalekites, lest I destroy you with them: for ye

shewed kindness to all the children of Israel, when they came up out of Egypt. So the Kenites departed from among the Amalekites.

7 And Saul smote the Amalekites from Havilah *until* thou comest to Shur, that *is* over against Egypt.

8 And he took Agag the king of the Amalekites alive, and utterly destroyed all the people with the edge of the sword.

9 **But Saul and the people spared Agag, and the best of the sheep, and of the oxen, and of the fatlings, and the lambs, and all** *that was* **good, and would not utterly destroy them**: but every thing *that was* **vile and refuse, that they destroyed**

TOO LATE FOR REPENTANCE SAUL WAS REJECTED BY GOD

1Samuel 15:23 For rebellion *is as* the sin of witchcraft, and stubbornness *is as* iniquity and idolatry. Because thou hast rejected the word of the LORD, **he hath also rejected thee from** *being* **king.**

24 **And Saul said unto Samuel, I have sinned: for I have transgressed the commandment of the LORD, and thy words: because I feared the people, and obeyed their voice**.

25 **Now therefore, I pray thee, pardon my sin, and turn again with me, that I may worship the LORD.**

26 And Samuel said unto Saul, **I will not return with thee: for thou hast rejected the word of the LORD, and the LORD hath rejected thee from being king over Israel.**

1Samuel 15:35 And Samuel came no more to see Saul until the day of his death: nevertheless Samuel mourned for Saul: and the LORD repented that he had made Saul king over Israel.

2. KING DAVID DID NOT CONSULT GOD

1Chronicles 21:1 And **Satan stood up against Israel, and provoked David to number Israel**.

2 And David said to Joab and to the rulers of the people, Go, number Israel from Beersheba even to Dan; and bring the number of them to me, that I may know *it*.

3 **And Joab answered, The LORD make his people an hundred times so many more as they** *be*: **but, my lord the king,** *are* **they not all my lord's servants? why then doth my lord require this thing? why will he be a cause of trespass to Israel**?

4 Nevertheless the king's word prevailed against Joab. Wherefore Joab departed, and went throughout all Israel, and came to Jerusalem.

5 And Joab gave the sum of the number of the people unto David. And all *they of* Israel were a thousand thousand and an hundred thousand men that drew sword: and Judah *was* four hundred threescore and ten thousand men that drew sword.

6 But Levi and Benjamin counted he not among them: for the king's word was abominable to Joab.

7 And God was displeased with this thing; therefore he smote Israel.

8 And David said unto God, I have sinned greatly, because I have done this thing: but now, I beseech thee, do away the iniquity of thy servant; for I have done very foolishly.

10 Go and tell David, saying Thus saith the LORD, I offer thee three things: choose thee one of them, that I may do it unto thee

11 So Gad came to David, and said unto him, Thus saith the LORD, Choose thee

12 Either three years' famine; or three months to be destroyed before thy foes, while that the sword of thine enemies overtaketh *thee*; or else three days the sword of the LORD, even the pestilence, in the land, and the angel of the LORD destroying throughout all the coasts of Israel. Now therefore advise thyself what word I shall bring again to him that sent me.

13 And David said unto Gad, I am in a great strait: let me fall now into the hand of the LORD; for very great *are* his mercies: but let me not fall into the hand of man.

14 So the LORD sent pestilence upon Israel: and there fell of Israel seventy thousand men.

15 And God sent an angel unto Jerusalem to destroy it: and as he was destroying, the LORD beheld, and he repented him of the evil, and said to the angel that destroyed, It is enough, stay now thine hand. And the angel of the LORD stood by the threshingfloor of Ornan the Jebusite.

DAVID REPENTED HIS SIN

1Chronicles 21:16 And David lifted up his eyes, and saw the angel of the LORD stand between the earth and the heaven, having a drawn sword in his hand stretched out over Jerusalem. Then David and the elders *of Israel, who were* clothed in sackcloth, fell upon their faces.

17 And David said unto God, *Is it* not I *that* commanded the people to be numbered? even I it is that have sinned and done evil indeed; but *as for* these sheep, what have they done? let thine hand, I pray thee, O LORD my God, be on me, and on my father's house; but not on thy people, that they should be plagued.

18 Then the angel of the LORD commanded Gad to say to David, that David should go up, and set up an altar unto the LORD in the threshingfloor of Ornan the Jebusite.

19 And David went up at the saying of Gad, which he spake in the name of the LORD.

20 And Ornan turned back, and saw the angel; and his four sons with him hid themselves. Now Ornan was threshing wheat.

21 And as David came to Ornan, Ornan looked and saw David, and went out of the threshingfloor, and bowed himself to David with *his* face to the ground.

22 Then David said to Ornan, Grant me the place of *this* threshingfloor, that I may build an altar therein unto the LORD: thou shalt grant it me for the full price: that the plague may be stayed from the people.

23 And Ornan said unto David, Take *it* to thee, and let my lord the king do *that which is* good in his eyes: lo, I give *thee* the oxen *also* for burnt offerings, and the threshing instruments for wood, and the wheat for the meat offering; I give it all.

24 And king David said to Ornan, Nay; but I will verily buy it for the full price: for I will not take *that* which *is* thine for the LORD, nor offer burnt offerings without cost.

25 So David gave to Ornan for the place six hundred shekels of gold by weight.

26 And David built there an altar unto the LORD, and offered burnt offerings and peace offerings, and called upon the LORD; and he answered him from heaven by fire upon the altar of burnt offering.

27 And the LORD commanded the angel; and he put up his sword again into the sheath thereof.

28 At that time when David saw that the LORD had answered him in the threshingfloor of Ornan the Jebusite, then he sacrificed there.

3. KING SOLOMON DISOBEYED GOD'S COMMAND

2Chronicles 7:15 Now mine eyes shall be open, and mine ears attent unto the prayer *that is made* in this place.

16 For now have I chosen and sanctified this house, that my name may be there for ever: and mine eyes and mine heart shall be there perpetually.

17 And as for thee, if thou wilt walk before me, as David thy father walked, and do according to all that I have commanded thee, and shalt observe my statutes and my judgments;

18 Then will I stablish the throne of thy kingdom, according as I have covenanted with David thy father, saying, There shall not fail thee a man *to be* ruler in Israel.

19 **But if ye turn away, and forsake my statutes and my commandments, which I have set before you, and shall go and serve other gods, and worship them;**

20 **Then will I pluck them up by the roots out of my land which I have given them; and this house, which I have sanctified for my name, will I cast out of my sight, and will make it *to be* a proverb and a byword among all nations.**

21 And this house, which is high, shall be an astonishment to every one that passeth by it; so that he shall say, Why hath the LORD done thus unto this land, and unto this house?

22 And it shall be answered, Because they forsook the LORD God of their fathers, which brought them forth out of the land of Egypt, and laid hold on other gods, and worshipped them, and served them: therefore hath he brought all this evil upon them.

a. KING SOLOMON MARRIED WOMEN FROM OTHER NATIONS

1Kings 11:1 But king Solomon loved many strange women, together with the daughter of Pharaoh, women of the Moabites, Ammonites, Edomites, Zidonians, *and* Hittites;

2 Of the nations *concerning* which the LORD said unto the children of Israel, Ye shall not go in to them, neither shall they come in unto you: *for* surely they will turn away your heart after their gods: Solomon clave unto these in love.

3 And he had seven hundred wives, princesses, and three hundred concubines: and his wives turned away his heart.

Nehemiah 13:26 Did not Solomon king of Israel sin by these things? yet among many nations was there no king like him, who was beloved of his God, and God made him king over all Israel: nevertheless even him did outlandish women cause to sin.

27 Shall we then hearken unto you to do all this great evil, to transgress against our God in marrying strange wives?

b. KING SOLOMON WORSHIPED IDOLS

1Kings 11:4 For it came to pass, when Solomon was old, *that* his wives turned away his heart after other gods: and his heart was not perfect with the LORD his God, as *was* the heart of David his father.

5 **For Solomon went after Ashtoreth the goddess of the Zidonians, and after Milcom the abomination of the Ammonites.**

6 And **Solomon did evil in the sight of the LORD,** and went not fully after the LORD, as *did* David his father.

7 **Then did Solomon build an high place for Chemosh, the abomination of Moab, in the hill that *is* before Jerusalem, and for Molech, the abomination of the children of Ammon.**

8 **And likewise did he for all his strange wives, which burnt incense and sacrificed unto their gods.**

PUNISHMENT: THE LORD DIVIDED THE KINGDOM OF SOLOMON

1Kings 11:9 And the LORD was angry with Solomon, because his heart was turned from the LORD God of Israel, which had appeared unto him twice,

10 And had commanded him concerning this thing, that he should not go after other gods: but he kept not that which the LORD commanded.

11 **Wherefore the LORD said unto Solomon**, Forasmuch as this is done of thee, and thou hast not kept my covenant and my statutes, which I have commanded thee, **I will surely rend the kingdom from thee, and will give it to thy servant**.

12 Notwithstanding in thy days I will not do it for David thy father's sake: *but* I will rend it out of the hand of thy son.

13 Howbeit I will not rend away all the kingdom; *but* will give one tribe to thy son for David my servant's sake, and for Jerusalem's sake which I have chosen.

4. GOD WILL BRING EVIL TO KING AHAB'S WIFE AND CHILDREN

I Kings 21:17 And the word of the LORD came to Elijah the Tishbite, saying,

18 Arise, go down to meet Ahab king of Israel, which *is* in Samaria: behold, *he is* in the vineyard of Naboth, whither he is gone down to possess it.

19 And thou shalt speak unto him, saying, Thus saith the LORD, Hast thou killed, and also taken possession? And thou shalt speak unto him, saying, Thus saith the LORD, In the place where dogs licked the blood of Naboth shall dogs lick thy blood, even thine.

20 And Ahab said to Elijah, Hast thou found me, O mine enemy? And he answered, I have found *thee*: because thou hast sold thyself to work evil in the sight of the LORD.

21 Behold, I will bring evil upon thee, and will take away thy posterity, and will cut off from Ahab him that pisseth against the wall, and him that is shut up and left in Israel,

22 And will make thine house like the house of Jeroboam the son of Nebat, and like the house of Baasha the son of Ahijah, for the provocation wherewith thou hast provoked *me* to anger, and made Israel to sin.

23 And of Jezebel also spake the LORD, saying, The dogs shall eat Jezebel by the wall of Jezreel.

24 Him that dieth of Ahab in the city the dogs shall eat; and him that dieth in the field shall the fowls of the air eat.

25 But there was none like unto Ahab, which did sell himself to work wickedness in the sight of the LORD, whom Jezebel his wife stirred up.

26 **And he did very abominably in following idols,** according to all *things* as did the Amorites, whom the LORD cast out before the children of Israel.

27 And it came to pass, when Ahab heard those words, that he rent his clothes, and put sackcloth upon his flesh, and fasted, and lay in sackcloth, and went softly.

28 And the word of the LORD came to Elijah the Tishbite, saying,

29 Seest thou how Ahab humbleth himself before me? because he humbleth himself before me, I will not bring the evil in his days: *but* in his son's days will I bring the evil upon his house.

5. KING UZZIAH DISOBEYED GOD'S LAW BY BURNING THE INCENSE

2Chronicles 26:15 And he made in Jerusalem engines, invented by cunning men, to be on the towers and upon the bulwarks, to shoot arrows and great stones withal. And his name spread far abroad; for he was marvellously helped, till he was strong.

16 **But when he was strong, his heart was lifted up to** *his* **destruction**: for he transgressed against the LORD his God, **and went into the temple of the LORD to burn incense upon the altar of incense**.

17 And **Azariah the priest went in after him, and with him fourscore priests of the LORD**, *that were* valiant men:

18 And they withstood Uzziah the king, and said unto him, *It appertaineth* **not unto thee, Uzziah, to burn incense unto the LORD, but to the priests the sons of Aaron, that are consecrated to burn incense: go out of the sanctuary; for thou hast trespassed; neither** *shall it be* **for thine honour from the LORD God.**

19 **Then Uzziah was wroth,** and *had* a censer in his hand to burn incense: and while he was wroth with the priests, the leprosy even rose up in his forehead before the priests in the house of the LORD, from beside the incense altar.

20 And Azariah the chief priest, and all the priests, looked upon him, and, **behold, he** *was* **leprous in his forehead,** and they thrust him out from thence; yea, himself hasted also to go out, because the LORD had smitten him.

21 And **Uzziah the king was a leper unto the day of his death**, and dwelt in a several house, *being* a leper; for he was cut off from the house of the LORD: and Jotham his son *was* over the king's house, judging the people of the land.

6. KING MANASSEH OF JUDAH DID ABOMINATIONS TO THE LORD

2Chronicles 33:1 Manasseh *was* twelve years old when he began to reign, and he reigned fifty and five years in Jerusalem:

2 But did *that which was* evil in the sight of the LORD, **like unto the abominations of the heathen, whom the LORD had cast out before the children of Israel.**

3 **For he built again the high places which Hezekiah his father had broken down, and he reared up altars for Baalim, and**

made groves, and worshipped all the host of heaven, and served them.

4 Also he built altars in the house of the LORD, whereof the LORD had said, In Jerusalem shall my name be for ever.

5 And he built altars for all the host of heaven in the two courts of the house of the LORD.

6 And **he caused his children to pass through the fire in the valley of the son of Hinnom: also he observed times, and used enchantments, and used witchcraft, and dealt with a familiar spirit, and with wizards**: he wrought much evil in the sight of the LORD, to provoke him to anger.

7 **And he set a carved image, the idol which he had made, in the house of God**, of which God had said to David and to Solomon his son, In this house, and in Jerusalem, which I have chosen before all the tribes of Israel, will I put my name for ever:

PUNISHMENT TO THE KINGDOM OF JUDAH

2Kings 21:1 Manasseh *was* twelve years old when he began to reign, and reigned fifty and five years in Jerusalem. And his mother's name *was* Hephzibah.

2 And he did *that which was* evil in the sight of the LORD, after the abominations of the heathen, whom the LORD cast out before the children of Israel.

3 For **he built up again the high places which Hezekiah his father had destroyed**; and he reared up altars for Baal, and made a grove, as did Ahab king of Israel; and **worshipped all the host of heaven, and served them.**

4 And he built altars in the house of the LORD, of which the LORD said, In Jerusalem will I put my name.

5 And **he built altars for all the host of heaven in the two courts of the house of the LORD.**

6 And **he made his son pass through the fire, and observed times, and used enchantments, and dealt with familiar spirits and wizards: he wrought much wickedness in the sight of the LORD, to provoke** *him* **to anger.**

7 And **he set a graven image of the grove** that he had made in the house, of which the LORD said to David, and to Solomon his son, In this house, and in Jerusalem, which I have chosen out of all tribes of Israel, will I put my name for ever:

8 **Neither will I make the feet of Israel move any more out of the land which I gave their fathers;** *only if they will observe to*

do according to all that I have commanded them, and according to all the law that my servant Moses commanded them.

9 But **they hearkened not: and Manasseh seduced them to do more evil than did the nations whom the LORD destroyed before the children of Israel.**

10 And the LORD spake by his servants the prophets, saying,

11 Because Manasseh king of Judah hath done these abominations, *and* hath done wickedly above all that the Amorites did, which *were* before him, and **hath made Judah also to sin with his idols:**

12 Therefore thus saith the LORD God of Israel, Behold, I *am* bringing *such* evil upon Jerusalem and Judah, that whosoever heareth of it, both his ears shall tingle.

13 And I will stretch over Jerusalem the line of Samaria, and the plummet of the house of Ahab: and I will wipe Jerusalem as *a man* wipeth a dish, wiping *it*, and turning *it* upside down.

14 And **I will forsake the remnant of mine inheritance, and deliver them into the hand of their enemies;** and they shall become a prey and a spoil to all their enemies;

15 Because they have done *that which was* evil in my sight, and have provoked me to anger, since the day their fathers came forth out of Egypt, even unto this day.

16 **Moreover Manasseh shed innocent blood very much, till he had filled Jerusalem from one end to another; beside his sin wherewith he made Judah to sin, in doing *that which was* evil in the sight of the LORD.**

GOD PUNISHED MANNASEH

2Chronicles 33:11 Wherefore the LORD brought upon them the captains of the host of the king of Assyria, which took Manasseh among the thorns, and bound him with fetters, and carried him to Babylon.

MANNASEH HUMBLED HIMSELF TO GOD

2Chronicles 33:12 And when he was in affliction, he besought the LORD his God, and humbled himself greatly before the God of his fathers,

13 And prayed unto him: and he was intreated of him, and heard his supplication, and brought him again to Jerusalem into his kingdom. Then Manasseh knew that the LORD he *was* God.

14 Now after this he built a wall without the city of David, on the west side of Gihon, in the valley, even to the entering in at the fish gate, and compassed about Ophel, and raised it up a very great height, and put captains of war in all the fenced cities of Judah.

15 And he took away the strange gods, and the idol out of the house of the LORD, and all the altars that he had built in the mount of the house of the LORD, and in Jerusalem, and cast *them* out of the city.

16 And he repaired the altar of the LORD, and sacrificed thereon peace offerings and thank offerings, and commanded Judah to serve the LORD God of Israel.

17 Nevertheless the people did sacrifice still in the high places, *yet* unto the LORD their God only.

7. JEHOIAKIM KING OF JUDAH BURNED THE WORDS OF THE LORD

Jeremiah 36:21 So the king sent Jehudi to fetch the roll: and he took it out of Elishama the scribe's chamber. And Jehudi read it in the ears of the king, and in the ears of all the princes which stood beside the king.

22Now the king sat in the winterhouse in the ninth month: and *there was a fire* on the hearth burning before him.

23And it came to pass, *that* when Jehudi had read three or four leaves, **he cut it with the penknife, and cast** *it* **into the fire that** *was* **on the hearth, until all the roll was consumed in the fire that** *was* **on the hearth**.

27 Then the word of the LORD came to Jeremiah, after that the king had burned the roll, and the words which Baruch wrote at the mouth of Jeremiah, saying,

28 Take thee again another roll, and write in it all the former words that were in the first roll, which Jehoiakim the king of Judah hath burned.

29 And thou shalt say to Jehoiakim king of Judah, Thus saith the LORD; Thou hast burned this roll, saying, Why hast thou written therein, saying, **The king of Babylon shall certainly come and destroy this land, and shall cause to cease from thence man and beast?**

30 Therefore thus **saith the LORD of Jehoiakim king of Judah**; He shall have none to sit upon the throne of David: and his dead body shall be cast out in the day to the heat, and in the night to the frost.

31 And **I will punish him and his seed and his servants for their iniquity; and I will bring upon them, and upon the inhabitants of Jerusalem, and upon the men of Judah, all the evil that I have pronounced against them; but they hearkened not**.

32 Then took Jeremiah another roll, and gave it to Baruch the scribe, the son of Neriah; who wrote therein from the mouth of Jeremiah all the words of the book which Jehoiakim king of Judah had burned in the fire: and there were added besides unto them many like words.

8. NEBUCHADNEZZAR THE KING OF BABYLON
GOD WARNED THE KING THROUGH HIS DREAM

Daniel 4:4 I Nebuchadnezzar was at rest in mine house, and flourishing in my palace:

5 I saw a dream which made me afraid, and the thoughts upon my bed and the visions of my head troubled me.

6 Therefore made I a decree to bring in all the wise *men* of Babylon before me, that they might make known unto me the interpretation of the dream.

8 But at the last Daniel came in before me, whose name *was* Belteshazzar, according to the name of my god, and in whom *is* the spirit of the holy gods: and before him I told the dream, *saying*,

9 O Belteshazzar, master of the magicians, because I know that the spirit of the holy gods *is* in thee, and no secret troubleth thee, tell me the visions of my dream that I have seen, and the interpretation thereof.

10 **Thus *were* the visions of mine head in my bed**; I saw, and behold **a tree in the midst of the earth, and the height thereof *was* great.**

11 The tree grew, and was strong, and the height thereof reached unto heaven, and the sight thereof to the end of all the earth:

12 The leaves thereof *were* fair, and the fruit thereof much, and in it *was* meat for all: the beasts of the field had shadow under it, and the fowls of the heaven dwelt in the boughs thereof, and all flesh was fed of it.

13 **I saw in the visions of my head upon my bed, and, behold, a watcher and an holy one came down from heaven;**

14 He cried aloud, and said thus, **Hew down the tree, and cut off his branches, shake off his leaves, and scatter his fruit:** let the beasts get away from under it, and the fowls from his branches:

15 **Nevertheless leave the stump of his roots in the earth, even with a band of iron and brass, in the tender grass of the field; and let it be wet with the dew of heaven, and** *let* **his portion** *be* **with the beasts in the grass of the earth:**

16 **Let his heart be changed from man's, and let a beast's heart be given unto him; and let seven times pass over him.**

17 **This matter** *is* **by the decree of the watchers, and the demand by the word of the holy ones: to the intent that the living may know that the most High ruleth in the kingdom of men, and giveth it to whomsoever he will, and setteth up over it the basest of men.**

18 This dream I king Nebuchadnezzar have seen. Now thou, O Belteshazzar, declare the interpretation thereof, forasmuch as all the wise *men* of my kingdom are not able to make known unto me the interpretation: but thou *art* able; for the spirit of the holy gods *is* in thee.

19 Then Daniel, whose name *was* Belteshazzar, was astonied for one hour, and his thoughts troubled him. The king spake, and said, Belteshazzar, let not the dream, or the interpretation thereof, trouble thee. Belteshazzar answered and said, **My lord, the dream** *be* **to them that hate thee, and the interpretation thereof to thine enemies.**

20 **The tree that thou sawest, which grew, and was strong, whose height reached unto the heaven, and the sight thereof to all the earth;**

21 **Whose leaves** *were* **fair, and the fruit thereof much, and in it** *was* **meat for all; under which the beasts of the field dwelt, and upon whose branches the fowls of the heaven had their habitation:**

22 It *is* thou, O king, that art grown and become strong: for thy greatness is grown, and reacheth unto heaven, and thy dominion to the end of the earth.

23And **whereas the king saw a watcher and an holy one coming down from heaven, and saying, Hew the tree down, and destroy it; yet leave the stump of the roots thereof in the earth, even with a band of iron and brass, in the tender grass of the field; and let it be wet with the dew of heaven,** and *let* his portion *be* with the beasts of the field, till seven times pass over him;

24 **This *is* the interpretation**, O king, and this *is* the decree of the most High, which is come upon my lord the king:

25 That they shall drive thee from men, and thy dwelling shall be with the beasts of the field, and they shall make thee to eat grass as oxen, and they shall wet thee with the dew of heaven, and seven times shall pass over thee, till thou know that the most High ruleth in the kingdom of men, and giveth it to whomsoever he will.

26 And whereas they commanded to leave the stump of the tree roots; thy kingdom shall be sure unto thee, after that thou shalt have known that the heavens do rule.

27 Wherefore, O king, let my counsel be acceptable unto thee, and **break off thy sins by righteousness, and thine iniquities by shewing mercy to the poor; if it may be a lengthening of thy tranquillity**.

KING NEBUCHADNEZZAR WAS PUNISHED FOR BEING PROUD

Proverbs 16:5 *Every one that is proud in heart is an abomination to the LORD: though hand join in hand, he shall not be unpunished.*

Daniel 4:28 All this came upon the king Nebuchadnezzar.

29 At the end of twelve months he walked in the palace of the kingdom of Babylon.

30 The king spake, and said, Is not this great Babylon, that I have built for the house of the kingdom by the might of my power, and for the honour of my majesty?

31 While the word *was* in the king's mouth, there fell a voice from heaven, *saying*, O king Nebuchadnezzar, to thee it is spoken; The kingdom is departed from thee.

32 And they shall drive thee from men, and thy dwelling *shall be* with the beasts of the field: they shall make thee to eat grass as oxen, and seven times shall pass over thee, until thou know that the most High ruleth in the kingdom of men, and giveth it to whomsoever he will.

33 The same hour was the thing fulfilled upon Nebuchadnezzar: and he was driven from men, and did eat grass as oxen, and his body was wet with the dew of heaven, till his hairs were grown like eagles' *feathers*, and his nails like birds' *claws*.

34 And at the end of the days I Nebuchadnezzar lifted up mine eyes unto heaven, and mine understanding returned unto me, and I blessed the most High, and I praised and honoured him that liveth for ever, whose dominion *is* an everlasting dominion, and his kingdom *is* from generation to generation:

KING NEBUCHADNEZZAR GAVE HONOR AND PRAISES TO GOD

Daniel 4:36 At the same time my reason returned unto me; and for the glory of my kingdom, mine honour and brightness returned unto me; and my counsellors and my lords sought unto me; and I was established in my kingdom, and excellent majesty was added unto me.

37 Now I Nebuchadnezzar praise and extol and honour the King of heaven, all whose works *are* truth, and his ways judgment: and those that walk in pride he is able to abase.

9. BELSHAZZAR OF BABYLON DISHONOR GOD

Daniel 5:1 Belshazzar the king made a great feast to a thousand of his lords, and drank wine before the thousand.

2 Belshazzar, whiles he tasted the wine, commanded to bring the golden and silver vessels which his father Nebuchadnezzar had taken out of the temple which *was* in Jerusalem; that the king, and his princes, his wives, and his concubines, might drink therein.

3 Then they brought the golden vessels that were taken out of the temple of the house of God which *was* at Jerusalem; and the king, and his princes, his wives, and his concubines, drank in them.

4 They drank wine, and praised the gods of gold, and of silver, of brass, of iron, of wood, and of stone.

GOD GAVE HIS WARNING

Daniel 5:5 In the same hour came forth fingers of a man's hand, and wrote over against the candlestick upon the plaister of the wall of the king's palace: and the king saw the part of the hand that wrote.

6 Then the king's countenance was changed, and his thoughts troubled him, so that the joints of his loins were loosed, and his knees smote one against another.

7 The king cried aloud to bring in the astrologers, the Chaldeans, and the soothsayers. *And* the king spake, and said to the wise *men* of Babylon, Whosoever shall read this writing, and

shew me the interpretation thereof, shall be clothed with scarlet, and *have* a chain of gold about his neck, and shall be the third ruler in the kingdom.

8 Then came in all the king's wise *men*: but they could not read the writing, nor make known to the king the interpretation thereof.

9 Then was king Belshazzar greatly troubled, and his countenance was changed in him, and his lords were astonied.

DANIEL WAS NEEDED TO INTERPRET THE WRITINGS ON THE WALL

Daniel 5:10 *Now* the queen, by reason of the words of the king and his lords, came into the banquet house: *and* the queen spake and said, O king, live for ever: let not thy thoughts trouble thee, nor let thy countenance be changed:

11 There is a man in thy kingdom, in whom *is* the spirit of the holy gods; and in the days of thy father light and understanding and wisdom, like the wisdom of the gods, was found in him; whom the king Nebuchadnezzar thy father, the king, *I say*, thy father, made master of the magicians, astrologers, Chaldeans, *and* soothsayers;

12 For as much as an excellent spirit, and knowledge, and understanding, interpreting of dreams, and shewing of hard sentences, and dissolving of doubts, were found in the same Daniel, whom the king named Belteshazzar: now let Daniel be called, and he will shew the interpretation.

DANIEL WAS BROUGHT TO THE KING

Daniel 5:13 Then was Daniel brought in before the king. *And* the king spake and said unto Daniel, *Art* thou that Daniel, which *art* of the children of the captivity of Judah, whom the king my father brought out of Jewry?

15 And now the wise *men*, the astrologers, have been brought in before me, that they should read this writing, and make known unto me the interpretation thereof: but they could not shew the interpretation of the thing:

16 And I have heard of thee that thou canst make interpretations, and dissolve doubts: **now if thou canst read the writing, and make known to me the interpretation thereof, thou shalt be clothed with scarlet, and *have* a chain of gold about thy neck, and shalt be the third ruler in the kingdom.**

17 Then Daniel answered and said before the king, **Let thy gifts be to thyself, and give thy rewards to another; yet I will read the writing unto the king, and make known to him the interpretation.**

BELSHAZZAR SINNED AGAINST THE LORD GOD
Daniel 5:22 And thou his son, O Belshazzar, hast not humbled thine heart, though thou knewest all this;
23 But hast lifted up thyself against the Lord of heaven; and they have brought the vessels of his house before thee, and thou, and thy lords, thy wives, and thy concubines, have drunk wine in them; and thou hast praised the gods of silver, and gold, of brass, iron, wood, and stone, which see not, nor hear, nor know: and the God in whose hand thy breath *is*, and whose *are* all thy ways, hast thou not glorified:

DANIEL REMINDED THE KING ABOUT THE FATE OF HIS FATHER
Daniel 5:18 O thou king, the most high **God gave Nebuchadnezzar thy father a kingdom, and majesty, and glory, and honour:**
19 And for the majesty that he gave him, all people, nations, and languages, trembled and feared before him: whom he would he slew; and whom he would he kept alive; and whom he would he set up; and whom he would he put down.
20 But when his heart was lifted up, and his mind hardened in pride, **he was deposed from his kingly throne, and they took his glory from him:**
21 And he was driven from the sons of men; and his heart was made like the beasts, and his dwelling *was* with the wild asses: they fed him with grass like oxen, and his body was wet with the dew of heaven; till he knew that the most high God ruled in the kingdom of men, and *that* he appointeth over it whomsoever he will.

JUDGMENT TO BELSHAZZAR WERE WRITTEN ON THE WALL
Daniel 5:24 Then was the part of the hand sent from him; and this writing was written.
25 And this *is* the writing that was written, **ME-NE, MENE, TE-KEL, U-PHAR-SIN.**

26 This *is* the interpretation of the thing: **MENE**; *God hath numbered thy kingdom, and finished it.*

27 **TEKEL**; *Thou art weighed in the balances, and art found wanting.*

28 PERES; Thy kingdom is divided, and given to **the Medes and Persians**.

29 Then commanded Belshazzar, and **they clothed Daniel with scarlet, and** *put* **a chain of gold about his neck, and made a proclamation concerning him, that he should be the third ruler in the kingdom.**

30 In that night was **Belshazzar the king of the Chaldeans slain.**

31 **And Darius the Median took the kingdom,** *being* **about threescore and two years old.**

10. GOD PUNISHED KING HEROD

Acts 12:1 Now about that time **Herod the king** stretched forth *his* hands to vex certain of the church.

2 And **he killed James the brother of John with the sword.**

3 And **because he saw it pleased the Jews, he proceeded further to take Peter also**. (Then were the days of unleavened bread.)

4 And when he had apprehended him, he put *him* in prison, and delivered *him* to four quaternions of soldiers to keep him; intending after Easter to bring him forth to the people.

Acts 12:19 And when Herod had sought for him, and found him not, he examined the keepers, and commanded that *they* should be put to death. And he went down from Judaea to Caesarea, and *there* abode.

20 And Herod was highly displeased with them of Tyre and Sidon: but they came with one accord to him, and, having made Blastus the king's chamberlain their friend, desired peace; because their country was nourished by the king's *country*.

21 And **upon a set day Herod, arrayed in royal apparel, sat upon his throne, and made an oration unto them.**

22 And **the people gave a shout,** *saying, It is* **the voice of a god, and not of a man**.

23 **And immediately the angel of the Lord smote him, because he gave not God the glory: and he was eaten of worms, and gave up the ghost.**

==

PART 8
GOD RENDERS PUNISHMENT

CHAPTER VII **THE DIVIDED KINGDOMS LED TO CAPTIVITY**

A. GOD'S WARNING TO THE TEN TRIBES OF ISRAEL

1. WILL BE SCATTERED AMONG NATIONS

Deuteronomy 28:64 And **the LORD shall scatter thee among all people, from the one end of the earth even unto the other; and there thou shalt serve other gods, which neither thou nor thy fathers have known,** *even* **wood and stone.**

Ezekiel 6:8 Yet will I leave a remnant, that ye may have *some* **that shall escape the sword among the nations,** when ye shall be scattered through the countries.

9 And **they that escape of you shall remember me among the nations whither they shall be carried captives, because I am broken with their whorish heart, which hath departed from me, and with their eyes, which go a whoring after their idols: and they shall lothe themselves for the evils which they have committed in all their abominations.**

10 And they shall know that I *am* the LORD, *and that* I have not said in vain that I would do this evil unto them.

11 Thus saith the Lord GOD; Smite with thine hand, and stamp with thy foot, and say, Alas for all the evil abominations of the house of Israel! for they shall fall by the sword, by the famine, and by the pestilence.

12 **He that is far off shall die of the pestilence; and he that is near shall fall by the sword; and he that remaineth** and is besieged shall die by the famine: thus will I accomplish my fury upon them.

2. ISRAEL WILL NOT FIND REST AND PEACE

Deuteronomy 28:65 And among these nations shalt thou find no ease, neither shall the sole of thy foot have rest: but the LORD shall give thee there a trembling heart, and failing of eyes, and sorrow of mind:

66 And thy life shall hang in doubt before thee; and thou shalt fear day and night, and shalt have none assurance of thy life:

67 In the morning thou shalt say, Would God it were even! and at even thou shalt say, Would God it were morning! for the fear of thine heart wherewith thou shalt fear, and for the sight of thine eyes which thou shalt see.

ISRAEL CONTINUED SINNING AGAINST GOD

Jeremiah 2:13 For my people have committed two evils; they have forsaken me the fountain of living waters, *and* hewed them out cisterns, broken cisterns, that can hold no water.

2Kings 17:7 For *so* it was, that the children of Israel had sinned against the LORD their God, which had brought them up out of the land of Egypt, from under the hand of Pharaoh king of Egypt, and had feared other gods,

8 And walked in the statutes of the heathen, whom the LORD cast out from before the children of Israel, and of the kings of Israel, which they had made.

9 And the children of Israel did secretly *those* things that *were* not right against the LORD their God, and they built them high places in all their cities, from the tower of the watchmen to the fenced city.

10 And **they set them up images and groves in every high hill**, and under every green tree:

11 And there they burnt incense in all the high places, as *did* the heathen whom the LORD carried away before them; and wrought wicked things to provoke the LORD to anger:

12 For they served idols, whereof the LORD had said unto them, Ye shall not do this thing.

Hosea 9:10 I found Israel like grapes in the wilderness; I saw your fathers as the firstripe in the fig tree at her first time: *but* they went to Baalpeor, and separated themselves unto *that* shame; and *their* abominations were according as they loved.

11 *As for* Ephraim, their glory shall fly away like a bird, from the birth, and from the womb, and from the conception.

12 Though they bring up their children, yet will I bereave them, *that there shall* not *be* a man *left*: yea, woe also to them when I depart from them!

13 Ephraim, as I saw Tyrus, *is* planted in a pleasant place: but Ephraim shall bring forth his children to the murderer.

14 Give them, O LORD: what wilt thou give? give them a miscarrying womb and dry breasts.

15 All their wickedness *is* in Gilgal: for there I hated them: for the wickedness of their doings I will drive them out of mine house, I will love them no more: all their princes *are* revolters.

16 Ephraim is smitten, their root is dried up, they shall bear no fruit: yea, though they bring forth, yet will I slay *even* the beloved *fruit* of their womb.

17 My God will cast them away, because they did not hearken unto him: and they shall be wanderers among the nations.

ALL THE PROPHETS AND SEERS WARNED THE PEOPLE
2Kings 17:13 Yet the LORD testified against Israel, and against Judah, by all the prophets, *and by* all the seers, saying, Turn ye from your evil ways, and keep my commandments *and* my statutes, according to all the law which I commanded your fathers, and which I sent to you by my servants the prophets.

14 Notwithstanding they would not hear, but hardened their necks, like to the neck of their fathers, that did not believe in the LORD their God.

15 And they rejected his statutes, and his covenant that he made with their fathers, and his testimonies which he testified against them; and they followed vanity, and became vain, and went after the heathen that *were* round about them, *concerning* whom the LORD had charged them, that they should not do like them.

PEOPLE DISOBEYED AND REBELLED AGAINST GOD
Nehemiah 9:26 Nevertheless they were disobedient, and rebelled against thee, and cast thy law behind their backs, and slew thy prophets which testified against them to turn them to thee, and they wrought great provocations.

27 Therefore thou deliveredst them into the hand of their enemies, who vexed them: and in the time of their trouble, when they cried unto thee, thou heardest *them* from heaven; and according to thy manifold mercies thou gavest them saviours, who saved them out of the hand of their enemies.

28 But after they had rest, they did evil again before thee: therefore leftest thou them in the hand of their enemies, so that they had the dominion over them: yet when they returned, and cried unto thee, thou heardest *them* from heaven; and many times didst thou deliver them according to thy mercies;

29 And testifiedst against them, that thou mightest bring them again unto thy law: yet they dealt proudly, and hearkened not unto thy commandments, but sinned against thy judgments, (which if a man do, he shall live in them;) and withdrew the shoulder, and hardened their neck, and would not hear.

30 Yet many years didst thou forbear them, and testifiedst against them by thy spirit in thy prophets: yet would they not give ear: therefore gavest thou them into the hand of the people of the lands.

31 Nevertheless for thy great mercies' sake thou didst not utterly consume them, nor forsake them; for thou *art* a gracious and merciful God.

THE TEN TRIBES OF ISRAEL LEFT ALL THE COMMANDMENTS OF THE LORD

2Kings 17:16 And they left all the commandments of the LORD their God, and made them molten images, *even* two calves, and made a grove, and worshipped all the host of heaven, and served Baal.

17 And they caused their sons and their daughters to pass through the fire, and used divination and enchantments, and sold themselves to do evil in the sight of the LORD, to provoke him to anger.

18 Therefore the LORD was very angry with Israel, and removed them out of his sight: there was none left but the tribe of Judah only.

19 Also Judah kept not the commandments of the LORD their God, but walked in the statutes of Israel which they made.

20 And the LORD rejected all the seed of Israel, and afflicted them, and delivered them into the hand of spoilers, until he had cast them out of his sight.

21 For he rent Israel from the house of David; and they made Jeroboam the son of Nebat king: and Jeroboam drave Israel from following the LORD, and made them sin a great sin.

22 For the children of Israel walked in all the sins of Jeroboam which he did; they departed not from them;

23 Until the LORD removed Israel out of his sight, as he had said by all his servants the prophets. So was Israel carried away out of their own land to Assyria unto this day.

THE KINGDOM OF ISRAEL WAS CARRIED AWAY INTO ASSYRIA

2Kings 17:1 In the twelfth year of **Ahaz king of Judah** began **Hoseah the son of Elah to reign in Samaria over Israel nine years.**

2 And he did *that which was* evil in the sight of the LORD, but not as the kings of Israel that were before him.

3 Against him came up Shalmaneser king of Assyria; and Hoshea became his servant, and gave him presents.

4 And the king of Assyria found conspiracy in Hoshea: for he had sent messengers to So king of Egypt, and brought no present to the king of Assyria, as *he had done* year by year: therefore the king of Assyria shut him up, and bound him in prison.

5 Then the king of Assyria came up throughout all the land, and went up to Samaria, and besieged it three years.

6 In the ninth year of Hoshea the king of Assyria took Samaria, and carried Israel away into Assyria, and placed them in Halah and in Habor *by* the river of Gozan, and in the cities of the Medes.

Hosea 10:1 Israel *is* an empty vine, he bringeth forth fruit unto himself: according to the multitude of his fruit he hath increased the altars; according to the goodness of his land they have made goodly images.

2 Their heart is divided; now shall they be found faulty: he shall break down their altars, he shall spoil their images.

3 For now they shall say, We have no king, because we feared not the LORD; what then should a king do to us?

4 They have spoken words, swearing falsely in making a covenant: thus judgment springeth up as hemlock in the furrows of the field.

5 The inhabitants of Samaria shall fear because of the calves of Bethaven: for the people thereof shall mourn over it, and the priests thereof *that* rejoiced on it, for the glory thereof, because it is departed from it.

6 **It shall be also carried unto Assyria** *for* **a present to king Jareb: Ephraim shall receive shame, and Israel shall be ashamed of his own counsel.**

7 *As for* Samaria, her king is cut off as the foam upon the water.

8 The high places also of Aven, the sin of Israel, shall be destroyed: the thorn and the thistle shall come up on their altars; and they shall say to the mountains, Cover us; and to the hills, Fall on us.

9 O Israel, thou hast sinned from the days of Gibeah: there they stood: the battle in Gibeah against the children of iniquity did not overtake them.

10 *It is* in my desire that I should chastise them; and the people shall be gathered against them, when they shall bind themselves in their two furrows.

11 And Ephraim *is as* an heifer *that is* taught, *and* loveth to tread out *the corn*; but I passed over upon her fair neck: I will make Ephraim to ride; Judah shall plow, *and* Jacob shall break his clods.

12 Sow to yourselves in righteousness, reap in mercy; break up your fallow ground: for *it is* time to seek the LORD, till he come and rain righteousness upon you.

13 Ye have plowed wickedness, ye have reaped iniquity; ye have eaten the fruit of lies: because thou didst trust in thy way, in the multitude of thy mighty men.

14 Therefore shall a tumult arise among thy people, and all thy fortresses shall be spoiled, as Shalman spoiled Betharbel in the day of battle: the mother was dashed in pieces upon *her* children.

15 So shall Bethel do unto you because of your great wickedness: in a morning shall the king of Israel utterly be cut off.

OTHER NATIONS WERE TAUGHT TO FEAR THE LORD OF ISRAEL

2Kings 17:24 And the king of Assyria brought *men* from Babylon, and from Cuthah, and from Ava, and from Hamath, and from Sepharvaim, and placed *them* in the cities of Samaria instead of the children of Israel: and they possessed Samaria, and dwelt in the cities thereof.

25 And *so* it was at the beginning of their dwelling there, *that* they feared not the LORD: therefore the LORD sent lions among them, which slew *some* of them.

26 Wherefore they spake to the king of Assyria, saying, The nations which thou hast removed, and placed in the cities of Samaria, know not the manner of the God of the land: therefore he hath sent lions among them, and, behold, they slay them, because they know not the manner of the God of the land.

27 Then the king of Assyria commanded, saying, Carry thither one of the priests whom ye brought from thence; and let them go and dwell there, and let him teach them the manner of the God of the land.

28 Then one of the priests whom they had carried away from Samaria came and dwelt in Bethel, and taught them how they should fear the LORD.

OTHER NATIONS FEARED GOD BUT SERVE OTHER gods
2Kings 17:29 Howbeit every nation made gods of their own, and put *them* in the houses of the high places which the Samaritans had made, every nation in their cities wherein they dwelt.

30 And the men of Babylon made Succothbenoth, and the men of Cuth made Nergal, and the men of Hamath made Ashima,

31 And the Avites made Nibhaz and Tartak, and the Sepharvites burnt their children in fire to Adrammelech and Anammelech, the gods of Sepharvaim.

32 So they feared the LORD, and made unto themselves of the lowest of them priests of the high places, which sacrificed for them in the houses of the high places.

33 They feared the LORD, and served their own gods, after the manner of the nations whom they carried away from thence.

34 Unto this day they do after the former manners: they fear not the LORD, neither do they after their statutes, or after their ordinances, or after the law and commandment which the LORD commanded the children of Jacob, whom he named Israel;

35 With whom the LORD had made a covenant, and charged them, saying, Ye shall not fear other gods, nor bow yourselves to them, nor serve them, nor sacrifice to them:

36 But the LORD, who brought you up out of the land of Egypt with great power and a stretched out arm, him shall ye fear, and him shall ye worship, and to him shall ye do sacrifice.

37 And the statutes, and the ordinances, and the law, and the commandment, which he wrote for you, ye shall observe to do for evermore; and ye shall not fear other gods.

38 And the covenant that I have made with you ye shall not forget; neither shall ye fear other gods.

39 But the LORD your God ye shall fear; and he shall deliver you out of the hand of all your enemies.

40 Howbeit they did not hearken, but they did after their former manner.

41 **So these nations feared the LORD, and served their graven images,** both their children, and their children's children: as did their fathers, so do they unto this day.

B. PUNISHMENT TO THE DIVIDED KINGDOM OF ISRAEL

Nehemiah 1:8 Remember, I beseech thee, the word that thou commandedst thy servant Moses, saying, **If ye transgress, I will scatter you abroad among the nations:**

9 **But if ye turn unto me, and keep my commandments, and do them; though there were of you cast out unto the uttermost part of the heaven,** yet will I gather them from thence, and will bring them unto the place that I have chosen to set my name there.

1. THE CHILDREN OF ISRAEL WERE SCATTERED AMONG NATIONS

Jeremiah 50:33 *Thus saith the LORD of hosts; The children of Israel and the children of Judah were oppressed together: and all that took them captives held them fast; they refused to let them go.*

Isaiah 5:13Therefore my people are gone into captivity, because *they have* no knowledge: and their honourable men *are* famished, and their multitude dried up with thirst.

Ezekiel 20:23 **I lifted up mine hand unto them also in the wilderness, that I would scatter them among the heathen, and disperse them through the countries;**

24 **Because they had not executed my judgments**, but had despised my statutes, and had polluted my sabbaths, and their eyes were after their fathers' idols.

25 Wherefore I gave them also statutes *that were* not good, and judgments whereby they should not live;

26 And I polluted them in their own gifts, in that they caused to pass through *the fire* all that openeth the womb, that I might make them desolate, to the end that they might know that I *am* the LORD.

27 Therefore, son of man, speak unto the house of Israel, and say unto them, Thus saith the Lord GOD; Yet in this your fathers have blasphemed me, in that they have committed a trespass against me.

28 *For* when I had brought them into the land, *for* the which I lifted up mine hand to give it to them, then they saw every high hill, and all the thick trees, and they offered there their sacrifices,

and there they presented the provocation of their offering: there also they made their sweet savour, and poured out there their drink offerings.

31 For when ye offer your gifts, when ye make your sons to pass through the fire, ye pollute yourselves with all your idols, even unto this day: and shall I be enquired of by you, O house of Israel? *As* I live, saith the Lord GOD, I will not be enquired of by you.

2. THE KINGDOM OF JUDAH WAS GONE INTO CAPTIVITY

Lamentations 1:3 Judah is gone into captivity because of affliction, and because of great servitude: she dwelleth among the heathen, she findeth no rest: all her persecutors overtook her between the straits.

4 The ways of Zion do mourn, because none come to the solemn feasts: all her gates are desolate: her priests sigh, her virgins are afflicted, and she *is* in bitterness.

5 Her adversaries are the chief, her enemies prosper; for the LORD hath afflicted her for the multitude of her transgressions: her children are gone into captivity before the enemy.

6 And from the daughter of Zion all her beauty is departed: her princes are become like harts *that* find no pasture, and they are gone without strength before the pursuer.

7 Jerusalem remembered in the days of her affliction and of her miseries all her pleasant things that she had in the days of old, when her people fell into the hand of the enemy, and none did help her: the adversaries saw her, *and* did mock at her sabbaths.

Lamentations 2:1 How hath the Lord covered the daughter of Zion with a cloud in his anger, *and* cast down from heaven unto the earth the beauty of Israel, and remembered not his footstool in the day of his anger!

2 The Lord hath swallowed up all the habitations of Jacob, and hath not pitied: he hath thrown down in his wrath the strong holds of the daughter of Judah; he hath brought *them* down to the ground: he hath polluted the kingdom and the princes thereof.

3 He hath cut off in *his* fierce anger all the horn of Israel: he hath drawn back his right hand from before the enemy, and he burned against Jacob like a flaming fire, *which* devoureth round about.

4 He hath bent his bow like an enemy: he stood with his right hand as an adversary, and slew all *that were* pleasant to the eye in

the tabernacle of the daughter of Zion: he poured out his fury like fire.

5 The Lord was as an enemy: he hath swallowed up Israel, he hath swallowed up all her palaces: he hath destroyed his strong holds, and hath increased in the daughter of Judah mourning and lamentation.

6 And he hath violently taken away his tabernacle, as *if it were of* a garden: he hath destroyed his places of the assembly: the LORD hath caused the solemn feasts and sabbaths to be forgotten in Zion, and hath despised in the indignation of his anger the king and the priest.

7 The Lord hath cast off his altar, he hath abhorred his sanctuary, he hath given up into the hand of the enemy the walls of her palaces; they have made a noise in the house of the LORD, as in the day of a solemn feast.

8 The LORD hath purposed to destroy the wall of the daughter of Zion: he hath stretched out a line, he hath not withdrawn his hand from destroying: therefore he made the rampart and the wall to lament; they languished together.

9 Her gates are sunk into the ground; he hath destroyed and broken her bars: her king and her princes *are* among the Gentiles: the law *is* no *more*; her prophets also find no vision from the LORD.

THE CHOSEN WERE IN GREAT SHOCK

Lamentations 2:10 The elders of the daughter of Zion sit upon the ground, *and* keep silence: they have cast up dust upon their heads; they have girded themselves with sackcloth: the virgins of Jerusalem hang down their heads to the ground.

11 Mine eyes do fail with tears, my bowels are troubled, my liver is poured upon the earth, for the destruction of the daughter of my people; because the children and the sucklings swoon in the streets of the city.

12 They say to their mothers, Where *is* corn and wine? when they swooned as the wounded in the streets of the city, when their soul was poured out into their mothers' bosom.

13 What thing shall I take to witness for thee? what thing shall I liken to thee, O daughter of Jerusalem? what shall I equal to thee, that I may comfort thee, O virgin daughter of Zion? for thy breach *is* great like the sea: who can heal thee?

14 **Thy prophets have seen vain and foolish things for thee: and they have not discovered thine iniquity, to turn away thy captivity; but have seen for thee false burdens and causes of banishment.**

15 All that pass by clap *their* hands at thee; they hiss and wag their head at the daughter of Jerusalem, *saying, Is* this the city that *men* call The perfection of beauty, The joy of the whole earth?

16 All thine enemies have opened their mouth against thee: they hiss and gnash the teeth: they say, We have swallowed *her* up: certainly this *is* the day that we looked for; we have found, we have seen *it*.

17 The LORD hath done *that* which he had devised; he hath fulfilled his word that he had commanded in the days of old: he hath thrown down, and hath not pitied: and he hath caused *thine* enemy to rejoice over thee, he hath set up the horn of thine adversaries.

18 **Their heart cried unto the Lord**, *O wall of the daughter of Zion, let tears run down like a river day and night: give thyself no rest; let not the apple of thine eye cease.*

19 *Arise, cry out in the night: in the beginning of the watches pour out thine heart like water before the face of the Lord: lift up thy hands toward him for the life of thy young children, that faint for hunger in the top of every street.*

20 *Behold, O LORD, and consider to whom thou hast done this. Shall the women eat their fruit, and children of a span long? shall the priest and the prophet be slain in the sanctuary of the Lord?*

21 *The young and the old lie on the ground in the streets: my virgins and my young men are fallen by the sword; thou hast slain them in the day of thine anger; thou hast killed, and not pitied.*

22 **Thou hast called as in a solemn day my terrors round about, so that in the day of the LORD'S anger none escaped nor remained: those that I have swaddled and brought up hath mine enemy consumed.**

LAMENTATIONS OF OF THE CHOSEN PEOPLE
Lamentations 1:10 The adversary hath spread out his hand upon all her pleasant things: for she hath seen *that* the heathen entered into her sanctuary, whom thou didst command *that* they should not enter into thy congregation.

11 All her people sigh, they seek bread; they have given their pleasant things for meat to relieve the soul: see, *O LORD, and consider; for I am become vile.*

12 Is it nothing to you, all ye that pass by? behold, and see if there be any sorrow like unto my sorrow, which is done unto me, wherewith the LORD hath afflicted me in the day of his fierce anger.

13 From above hath he sent fire into my bones, and it prevaileth against them: he hath spread a net for my feet, he hath turned me back: he hath made me desolate and faint all the day.

14 The yoke of my transgressions is bound by his hand: they are wreathed, and come up upon my neck: he hath made my strength to fall, the Lord hath delivered me into their hands, from whom I am not able to rise up.

15 The Lord hath trodden under foot all my mighty *men* in the midst of me: he hath called an assembly against me to crush my young men: the Lord hath trodden the virgin, the daughter of Judah, *as* in a winepress.

16 For these *things* I weep; mine eye, mine eye runneth down with water, because the comforter that should relieve my soul is far from me: my children are desolate, because the enemy prevailed.

17 Zion spreadeth forth her hands, *and there is* none to comfort her: the LORD hath commanded concerning Jacob, *that* his adversaries *should be* round about him: Jerusalem is as a menstruous woman among them.

18 The LORD is righteous; for I have rebelled against his commandment: hear, I pray you, all people, and behold my sorrow: my virgins and my young men are gone into captivity.

BURNING OF THE TEMPLE IN JERUSALEM

Amos 2:4 Thus saith the LORD; For three transgressions of Judah and for four, I will not turn away *the punishment* thereof; because they have despised the law of the LORD, and have not kept his commandments, and their lies caused them to err, after the which their fathers have walked:

5 But **I will send a fire upon Judah, and it shall devour the palaces of Jerus**alem.

THE ELECTS WERE BROUGHT TO BABYLON

Jeremiah 32:2 For then the king of Babylon's army besieged Jerusalem: and Jeremiah the prophet was shut up in the court of the prison, which *was* in the king of Judah's house.

Daniel 1:6 Now among these were of the children of Judah, **Daniel, Hananiah, Mishael, and Azariah:**

Zechariah 1:12 Then the angel of the LORD answered and said, O LORD of hosts, how long wilt thou not have mercy on Jerusalem and on the cities of Judah, against which thou hast had indignation these **threescore and ten years?**

SUFFERINGS OF THE CAPTIVES

Lamentaions 3:1 I *am* the man *that* hath seen affliction by the rod of his wrath.

2 He hath led me, and brought *me into* darkness, but not *into* light.

3 Surely against me is he turned; he turneth his hand *against me* all the day.

4 My flesh and my skin hath he made old; he hath broken my bones.

5 He hath builded against me, and compassed *me* with gall and travail.

6 He hath set me in dark places, as *they that be* dead of old.

7 He hath hedged me about, that I cannot get out: he hath made my chain heavy.

8 Also when I cry and shout, he shutteth out my prayer.

9 He hath inclosed my ways with hewn stone, he hath made my paths crooked.

10 He *was* unto me *as* a bear lying in wait, *and as* a lion in secret places..

11 He hath turned aside my ways, and pulled me in pieces: he hath made me desolate.

12 He hath bent his bow, and set me as a mark for the arrow.

13 He hath caused the arrows of his quiver to enter into my reins.

14 I was a derision to all my people; *and* their song all the day.

15 He hath filled me with bitterness, he hath made me drunken with wormwood.

16 He hath also broken my teeth with gravel stones, he hath covered me with ashes.

17 And thou hast removed my soul far off from peace: I forgat prosperity.

18 And I said, My strength and my hope is perished from the LORD:

19 Remembering mine affliction and my misery, the wormwood and the gall.

20 My soul hath *them* still in remembrance, and is humbled in me.

21 This I recall to my mind, therefore have I hope.

22 *It is of* the LORD'S mercies that we are not consumed, because his compassions fail not

PRAYER OF THE CAPTIVES

Lamentations 1:20 *Behold, O LORD; for I am in distress: my bowels are troubled; mine heart is turned within me; for I have grievously rebelled: abroad the sword bereaveth, at home there is as death.*

21 They have heard that I sigh: there is none to comfort me: all mine enemies have heard of my trouble; they are glad that thou hast done it: thou wilt bring the day that thou hast called, and they shall be like unto me.

22 Let all their wickedness come before thee; and do unto them, as thou hast done unto me for all my transgressions: for my sighs are many, and my heart is faint.

PRAYER TO LEARN THE COMMANDMENTS OF THE LORD

Ezra 9:10 *And now, O our God, what shall we say after this? for we have forsaken thy commandments,*

Psalms 119:60 *I made haste, and delayed not to keep thy commandments.*

Psalms 119:66 *Teach me good judgment and knowledge: for I have believed thy commandments.*

Psalms 119:73 *JOD. Thy hands have made me and fashioned me: give me understanding, that I may learn thy commandments.*

Psalms 119:86 *All thy commandments are faithful: they persecute me wrongfully; help thou me.*

Ezra 9:14 *Should we again break thy commandments, and join in affinity with the people of these abominations? wouldest not thou be angry with us till thou hadst consumed us, so that there should be no remnant nor escaping?*

15 O LORD God of Israel, thou art righteous: for we remain yet escaped, as it is this day: behold, we are before thee in our

trespasses: for we cannot stand before thee because of this.

NEHEMIAH'S PRAYER FOR THE NATION OF ISRAEL
Nehemiah 1:1 The words of Nehemiah the son of Hachaliah. And it came to pass in the month Chisleu, in the twentieth year, as I was in Shushan the palace,

2 **That Hanani, one of my brethren, came, he and *certain* men of Judah; and I asked them concerning the Jews that had escaped, which** were left of the captivity, and concerning Jerusalem.

3 And **they said** unto me, *The remnant that are left of the captivity there in the province are in great affliction and reproach: the wall of Jerusalem also is broken down, and the gates thereof are burned with fire.*

4 And it came to pass, when I heard these words, that **I sat down and wept, and mourned *certain* days, and fasted, and prayed before the God of heaven,**

5 **And said**, *I beseech thee, O LORD God of heaven, the great and terrible God, that keepeth covenant and mercy for them that love him and observe his commandments:*

6 *Let thine ear now be attentive, and thine eyes open, that thou mayest hear the prayer of thy servant, which I pray before thee now, day and night, for the children of Israel thy servants, and confess the sins of the children of Israel, which we have sinned against thee: both I and my father's house have sinned.*

7 *We have dealt very corruptly against thee, and have not kept the commandments, nor the statutes, nor the judgments, which thou commandedst thy servant Moses.*

10 *Now these are thy servants and thy people, whom thou hast redeemed by thy great power, and by thy strong hand.*

11 *O Lord, I beseech thee, let now thine ear be attentive to the prayer of thy servant, and to the prayer of thy servants, who desire to fear thy name: and prosper, I pray thee, thy servant this day, and grant him mercy in the sight of this man. For I was the king's cupbearer.*

PART 8
GOD RENDERS PUNISHMENT

CHAPTER VIII **FALSE PROPHET**

Proverbs 25:14
Whoso boasteth himself of a false gift is like clouds and wind without rain.

A. PROPHET SPEAKING LIES

1. HANANIAH (Before the captivity of Babylon)

Jeremiah 28:1 And it came to pass the same year, in the beginning of the reign of Zedekiah king of Judah, in the fourth year, *and* in the fifth month, *that* **Hananiah the son of Azur the prophet, which *was* of Gibeon**, spake unto me in the house of the LORD, in the presence of the priests and of all the people, saying,

2 Thus speaketh the LORD of hosts, the God of Israel, saying, I have broken the yoke of the king of Babylon.

3 Within two full years will I bring again into this place all the vessels of the LORD'S house, that Nebuchadnezzar king of Babylon took away from this place, and carried them to Babylon:

4 And I will bring again to this place Jeconiah the son of Jehoiakim king of Judah, with all the captives of Judah, that went into Babylon, saith the LORD: for I will break the yoke of the king of Babylon.

5 Then the prophet Jeremiah said unto the prophet Hananiah in the presence of the priests, and in the presence of all the people that stood in the house of the LORD,

6 Even the prophet Jeremiah said, Amen: the LORD do so: the LORD perform thy words which thou hast prophesied, to bring again the vessels of the LORD'S house, and all that is carried away captive, from Babylon into this place.

7 Nevertheless hear thou now this word that I speak in thine ears, and in the ears of all the people;

8 The prophets that have been before me and before thee of old prophesied both against many countries, and against great kingdoms, of war, and of evil, and of pestilence.

437

9 The prophet which prophesieth of peace, **when the word of the prophet shall come to pass, *then* shall the prophet be known, that the LORD hath truly sent him.**

10 Then Hananiah the prophet took the yoke from off the prophet Jeremiah's neck, and brake it.

11 And **Hananiah spake in the presence of all the people, saying, Thus saith the LORD; Even so will I break the yoke of Nebuchadnezzar king of Babylon from the neck of all nations within the space of two full years. And the prophet Jeremiah went his way.**

12 **Then the word of the LORD came unto Jeremiah *the prophet*, after that Hananiah the prophet had broken the yoke from off the neck of the prophet Jeremiah, saying,**

13 *Go and tell Hananiah, saying, Thus saith the LORD; Thou hast broken the yokes of wood; but thou shalt make for them yokes of iron.*

14 *For thus saith the LORD of hosts, the God of Israel; I have put a yoke of iron upon the neck of all these nations, that they may serve Nebuchadnezzar king of Babylon; and they shall serve him: and I have given him the beasts of the field also.*

15 *Then said the prophet Jeremiah unto Hananiah the prophet, Hear now, Hananiah; The LORD hath not sent thee; but thou makest this people to trust in a lie.*

16 *Therefore thus saith the LORD; Behold, I will cast thee from off the face of the earth: this year thou shalt die, because thou hast taught rebellion against the LORD.*

17 **So Hananiah the prophet died the same year in the seventh month.**

*GOD'S INSTRUCTION TO THE PEOPLE OF JUDAH
Jeremiah 29:8 For thus **saith the LORD of hosts, the God of Israel; Let not your prophets and your diviners, that be in the midst of you, deceive you, neither hearken to your dreams which ye cause to be dreamed.**

9 **For they prophesy falsely unto you in my name: I have not sent them, saith the LORD.**

2. SHEMAIAH THE NEHELAMITE, AND HIS SEED (under Babylon Captivity) **Jeremiah** 29:20 Hear ye therefore the word of the LORD, all ye of the captivity, whom I have sent from Jerusalem to Babylon:

21 **Thus saith the LORD of hosts,** the God of Israel, of Ahab the son of Kolaiah, and of Zedekiah the son of Maaseiah, which prophesy a lie unto you in my name; *Behold, I will deliver them into the hand of Nebuchadrezzar king of Babylon; and he shall slay them before your eyes;*

22 *And of them shall be taken up a curse by all the captivity of Judah which are in Babylon, saying, The LORD make thee like Zedekiah and like Ahab, whom the king of Babylon roasted in the fire;*

23 *Because they have committed villany in Israel, and have committed adultery with their neighbours' wives, and have spoken lying words in my name, which I have not commanded them; even I know, and am a witness*, **saith the LORD.**

Jeremiah 29:31 Send to all them of the captivity, saying, Thus **saith the LORD concerning Shemaiah the Nehelamite**; *Because that Shemaiah hath prophesied unto you, and I sent him not, and he caused you to trust in a lie:*

32 **Therefore thus saith the LORD**; *Behold,* ***I will punish Shemaiah the Nehelamite, and his seed***: *he shall not have a man to dwell among this people; neither shall he behold the good that I will do for my people, saith the LORD; because he hath taught rebellion against the LORD.*

3.THE HOLY GHOST BLINDED BARJESUS (Apostles' time)

Acts 13:5 And when they were at Salamis, they preached the word of God in the synagogues of the Jews: and they had also John to *their* minister.

6 And when they had gone through the isle unto Paphos, they found a certain sorcerer, **a false prophet, a Jew, whose name** ***was* Barjesus:**

7 Which was with the deputy of the country, Sergius Paulus, a prudent man; who called for Barnabas and Saul, and desired to hear the word of God.

8 But **Elymas the sorcerer (for so is his name by interpretation) withstood them, seeking to turn away the deputy from the faith**.

9 **Then Saul, (who also *is called* Paul,) filled with the Holy Ghost, set his eyes on him,**

10 **And said, O full of all subtilty and all mischief, *thou* child of the devil, *thou* enemy of all righteousness, wilt thou not cease to pervert the right ways of the Lord?**

11 And now, behold, the hand of the Lord *is* upon thee, and thou shalt be blind, not seeing the sun for a season. And immediately there fell on him a mist and a darkness; and he went about seeking some to lead him by the hand.

B. ISSUE OF CORRUPTION
GEHAZI, SERVANT OF PROPHET ELISHA

2Kings 5:1 Now Naaman, captain of the host of the king of Syria, was a great man with his master, and honourable, because by him the LORD had given deliverance unto Syria: he was also a mighty man in valour, *but he was* a leper

2 And the Syrians had gone out by companies, and had brought away captive out of the land of Israel a little maid; and she waited on Naaman's wife.

3 And she said unto her mistress, Would God my lord *were* with the prophet that *is* in Samaria! for he would recover him of his leprosy.

4 And *one* went in, and told his lord, saying, Thus and thus said the maid that *is* of the land of Israel.

5 And the king of Syria said, Go to, go, and I will send a letter unto the king of Israel. And he departed, and took with him ten talents of silver, and six thousand *pieces* of gold, and ten changes of raiment.

6 And he brought the letter to the king of Israel, saying, Now when this letter is come unto thee, behold, I have *therewith* sent Naaman my servant to thee, that thou mayest recover him of his leprosy

ELISHAS' INSTRUCTIONS TO NAMAAN

2Kings 5:7 And it came to pass, when the king of Israel had read the letter, that he rent his clothes, and said, *Am* I God, to kill and to make alive, that this man doth send unto me to recover a man of his leprosy? wherefore consider, I pray you, and see how he seeketh a quarrel against me.

8 And it was *so*, when Elisha the man of God had heard that the king of Israel had rent his clothes, that he sent to the king, saying, Wherefore hast thou rent thy clothes? let him come now to me, and he shall know that there is a prophet in Israel.

9 So Naaman came with his horses and with his chariot, and stood at the door of the house of Elisha.

10 And Elisha sent a messenger unto him, saying, **Go and wash in Jordan seven times, and thy flesh shall come again to thee, and thou shalt be clean**.

11 But Naaman was wroth, and went away, and said, Behold, I thought, He will surely come out to me, and stand, and call on the name of the LORD his God, and strike his hand over the place, and recover the leper.

12 *Are* not Abana and Pharpar, rivers of Damascus, better than all the waters of Israel? may I not wash in them, and be clean? So he turned and went away in a rage.

13 And his servants came near, and spake unto him, and said, My father, *if* the prophet had bid thee *do some* great thing, wouldest thou not have done *it*? how much rather then, when he saith to thee, Wash, and be clean?

14 **Then went he down, and dipped himself seven times in Jordan, according to the saying of the man of God: and his flesh came again like unto the flesh of a little child, and he was clean.**

ELISHA REFUSED THE PAYMENT

2Kings 5:15 And he returned to the man of God, he and all his company, and came, and stood before him: and he said, Behold, now I know that *there is* no God in all the earth, but in Israel: now therefore, I pray thee, take a blessing of thy servant.

16 But he said, *As* **the LORD liveth, before whom I stand, I will receive none. And he urged him to take *it*;** but he refused.

17 And Naaman said, Shall there not then, I pray thee, be given to thy servant two mules' burden of earth? for thy servant will henceforth offer neither burnt offering nor sacrifice unto other gods, but unto the LORD.

18 In this thing the LORD pardon thy servant, *that* when my master goeth into the house of Rimmon to worship there, and he leaneth on my hand, and I bow myself in the house of Rimmon: when I bow down myself in the house of Rimmon, the LORD pardon thy servant in this thing.

19 And **he said unto him, Go in peace**. So he departed from him a little way.

20 But **Gehazi, the servant of Elisha the man of God, said,** *Behold, my master hath spared Naaman this Syrian, in not receiving at his hands that which he brought: but, as the LORD liveth, I will run after him, and take somewhat of him.*

21 So Gehazi followed after Naaman. And when Naaman saw *him* running after him, he lighted down from the chariot to meet him, and said, *Is* all well?

22 And he said, *All is well. My master hath sent me, saying, Behold, even now there be come to me from mount Ephraim two young men of the sons of the prophets: give them, I pray thee, a talent of silver, and two changes of garments.*

23 And Naaman said, Be content, take two talents. And he urged him, and bound two talents of silver in two bags, with two changes of garments, and laid *them* upon two of his servants; and they bare *them* before him.

24 And when he came to the tower, he took *them* from their hand, and bestowed *them* in the house: and he let the men go, and they departed.

CURSE AND PUNISHMENT TO GEHAZI AND HIS SEEDS

2Kings 5:25 But he went in, and stood before his master. And Elisha said unto him, Whence *comest thou*, Gehazi? And he said, Thy servant went no whither.

26 And he said unto him, Went not mine heart *with thee*, when the man turned again from his chariot to meet thee? *Is it* a time to receive money, and to receive garments, and oliveyards, and vineyards, and sheep, and oxen, and menservants, and maidservants?

27 **The leprosy therefore of Naaman shall cleave unto thee, and unto thy seed for ever**. And **he went out from his presence a leper** *as white* **as snow.**

GOD SENT THE LYING SPIRIT TO THE PROPHETS

2Chronicles 18:19 And **the LORD said, Who shall entice Ahab king of Israel, that he may go up and fall at Ramothgilead?** And one spake saying after this manner, and another saying after that manner.

20 Then **there came out a spirit, and stood before the LORD, and said, I will entice him. And the LORD said unto him, Wherewith?**

21 And he said, *I will go out, and be a lying spirit in the mouth of all his prophets*.

And the LORD said, *Thou shalt entice him, and thou shalt also prevail: go out, and do even so.*

1Kings 22:22 And the LORD said unto him, Wherewith? And he said, I will go forth, and I will be a lying spirit in the mouth of all his prophets. And he said, Thou shalt persuade him, and prevail also: go forth, and do so**.**

*GOD'S INSTRUCTION: LISTEN NOT TO THE FALSE PROPHET

Jeremiah 23:16 Thus saith the LORD of hosts, Hearken not unto the words of the prophets that prophesy unto you: they make you vain: they speak a vision of their own heart, *and* not out of the mouth of the LORD.

17 They say still unto them that despise me, The LORD hath said, Ye shall have peace; and they say unto every one that walketh after the imagination of his own heart, No evil shall come upon you.

18 For who hath stood in the counsel of the LORD, and hath perceived and heard his word? who hath marked his word, and heard *it*?

HAVE NO VISION AND GOD WILL NOT ANSWER

Micah 3:5 Thus saith the LORD concerning the prophets that make my people err, that bite with their teeth, and cry, Peace; and he that putteth not into their mouths, they even prepare war against him.

6 Therefore night *shall be* unto you, that **ye shall not have a vision**; and it shall be dark unto you, that ye shall not divine; and the sun shall go down over the prophets, and the day shall be dark over them.

7 Then shall the seers be ashamed, and the diviners confounded: yea, they shall all cover their lips; **for *there is* no answer of God**.

GOD'S ANGER IS UPON THE FALSE PROPHET

Ezekiel 13:3 **Thus saith the Lord GOD; Woe unto the foolish prophets, that follow their own spirit, and have seen nothing!**

Jeremiah 23:30 Therefore, **behold, I *am* against the prophets, saith the LORD, that steal my words every one from his neighbour.**

31 **Behold, I *am* against the prophets, saith the LORD, that use their tongues, and say, He saith.**

32 **Behold, I *am* against them that prophesy false dreams, saith the LORD, and do tell them, and cause my people to err**

by their lies, and by their lightness; yet I sent them not, nor commanded them: therefore they shall not profit this people at all, saith the LORD.

Ezekiel 13:4 O Israel, thy prophets are like the foxes in the deserts.

5 Ye have not gone up into the gaps, neither made up the hedge for the house of Israel to stand in the battle in the day of the LORD.

6 They have seen vanity and lying divination, saying, The LORD saith: and the LORD hath not sent them: and they have made *others* to hope that they would confirm the word.

7 Have ye not seen a vain vision, and have ye not spoken a lying divination, whereas ye say, The LORD saith *it*; albeit I have not spoken?

8 Therefore thus saith the Lord GOD; Because ye have spoken vanity, and seen lies, therefore, behold, I *am* against you, saith the Lord GOD.

9 And mine hand shall be upon the prophets that see vanity, and that divine lies: they shall not be in the assembly of my people, neither shall they be written in the writing of the house of Israel, neither shall they enter into the land of Israel; and ye shall know that I *am* the Lord GOD.

10 Because, even because they have seduced my people, saying, Peace; and *there was* no peace; and one built up a wall, and, lo, others daubed it with untempered *morter*:

11 Say unto them which daub *it* with untempered *morter*, that it shall fall: there shall be an overflowing shower; and ye, O great hailstones, shall fall; and a stormy wind shall rend *it*.

12 Lo, when the wall is fallen, shall it not be said unto you, Where *is* the daubing wherewith ye have daubed *it*?

13 Therefore thus saith the Lord GOD; I will even rend *it* with a stormy wind in my fury; and there shall be an overflowing shower in mine anger, and great hailstones in *my* fury to consume *it*.

14 So will I break down the wall that ye have daubed with untempered *morter*, and bring it down to the ground, so that the foundation thereof shall be discovered, and it shall fall, and ye shall be consumed in the midst thereof: and ye shall know that I *am* the LORD.

15 Thus will I accomplish my wrath upon the wall, and upon them that have daubed it with untempered *morter*, and will say unto you, The wall *is* no *more*, neither they that daubed it;

16 *To wit*, the prophets of Israel which prophesy concerning Jerusalem, and which see visions of peace for her, and *there is* no peace, saith the Lord GOD.

GOD WILL PUNISH THE FALSE PROPHET
Jeremiah 23:14 I **have seen also in the prophets of Jerusalem an horrible thing: they commit adultery, and walk in lies: they strengthen also the hands of evildoers**, that none doth return from his wickedness: they are all of them unto me as Sodom, and the inhabitants thereof as Gomorrah.

15 Therefore thus **saith the LORD of hosts** concerning the prophets; *Behold, I will feed them with wormwood, and make them drink the water of gall: for from the prophets of Jerusalem is profaneness gone forth into all the land.*

19 Behold, a whirlwind of the LORD is gone forth in fury, even a grievous whirlwind: it shall fall grievously upon the head of the wicked.

20 **The anger of the LORD shall not return, until he have executed, and till he have performed the thoughts of his heart: in the latter days ye shall consider it perfectly**.

21 I have not sent these prophets, yet they ran: I have not spoken to them, yet they prophesied.

22 But if they had stood in my counsel, and had caused my people to hear my words, then they should have turned them from their evil way, and from the evil of their doings.

EVERLASTING PUNISHMENT UPON THE FALSE PROPHET
Jeremiah 23:33 And when this people, or the prophet, or a priest, shall ask thee, saying, What *is* the burden of the LORD? thou shalt then say unto them, What burden? **I will even forsake you, saith the LORD.**

34 And *as for* the prophet, and the priest, and the people, that shall say, The burden of the LORD**, I will even punish that man and his house**.

35 Thus shall ye say every one to his neighbour, and every one to his brother, What hath the LORD answered? and, What hath the LORD spoken?

36 And the burden of the LORD shall ye mention no more: **for every man's word shall be his burden; for ye have perverted the words of the living God, of the LORD of hosts our God.**

37 Thus shalt thou say to the prophet, What hath the LORD answered thee? and, What hath the LORD spoken?

38 But since ye say, The burden of the LORD; therefore thus saith the LORD; Because ye say this word, The burden of the LORD, and I have sent unto you, saying, Ye shall not say, The burden of the LORD;

39 **Therefore, behold, I, even I, will utterly forget you, and I will forsake you, and the city that I gave you and your fathers,** *and cast you* **out of my presence:**

40 **And I will bring an everlasting reproach upon you, and a perpetual shame, which shall not be forgotten.**

===

MY DEAR BROTHERS AND SISTERS IN CHRIST JESUS, 4/29/13

Many people are wondering **why God allowed evil to manifest in some people's lives.** The Word of God from the Holy Scriptures will explains everything. Some of us **blame or point our finger to Him or to other people,** and make God and others responsible to be the source of our stress, and emotional disasters in life, Why don't we begin **to look first at our spiritual life. Is our belief and religious practices in accordance with the teachings of the LORD? Are we still following the traditions of man not the word of God?** May the LORD bless you with wisdom and understanding to learn and keep His WORD and start depending on His grace .

===

==

PART 8
GOD RENDERS PUNISHMENT

.

CHAPTER IX **GOD LEFT HIS CHOSEN**

Isaiah 59:*2*

But your iniquities have separated between you and your God, and your sins have hid his face from you, that he will not hear.

TRANSGRESSING AND LYING AGAINST THE LORD

Isaiah 59:3 For your hands are defiled with blood, and your fingers with iniquity; your lips have spoken lies, your tongue hath muttered perverseness.

4 None calleth for justice, nor *any* pleadeth for truth: they trust in vanity, and speak lies; they conceive mischief, and bring forth iniquity.

5 They hatch cockatrice' eggs, and weave the spider's web: he that eateth of their eggs dieth, and that which is crushed breaketh out into a viper.

6 Their webs shall not become garments, neither shall they cover themselves with their works: their works *are* works of iniquity, and the act of violence *is* in their hands.

7 Their feet run to evil, and **they make haste to shed innocent blood: their thoughts *are* thoughts of iniquity; wasting and destruction *are* in their paths.**

8 The way of peace they know not; and *there is* **no judgment in their goings: they have made them crooked paths: whosoever goeth therein shall not know peace.**

Isaiah 59:12 **For our transgressions are multiplied before thee**, and our sins testify against us: for our transgressions *are* with us; and *as for* our iniquities, we know them;

13 **In transgressing and lying against the LORD, and departing away from our God**, **speaking oppression and revolt, conceiving and uttering from the heart words of falsehood.**

*GOD'S INSTRUCTION TO KEEP AWAY FROM IDOLS

Exodus 20:5 Thou shalt not bow down thyself to them, nor serve them: for I the LORD thy God *am* a jealous God, visiting the iniquity of the fathers upon the children unto the third and fourth *generation* of them that hate me;

Nahum 1:2 **God *is* jealous**, and the LORD revengeth; the LORD revengeth, and *is* furious; the LORD will take vengeance on his adversaries, and **he reserveth *wrath* for his enemies.**

Acts 17:24 God made the world and all things therein, seeing that he is LORD of heaven and earth, dwelleth not in temples made with hands;

25 **Neither is worshipped with men's hands, as though he needed anything, seeing he giveth to all life, and breath and all things;**

Ezekiel 14:2 And the word of the LORD came unto me, saying,

3 **Son of man, these men have set up their idols in their heart, and put the stumblingblock of their iniquity before their face:** should I be enquired of at all by them?

4 Therefore speak unto them, and say unto them, **Thus saith the Lord GOD**; *Every man of the house of Israel that setteth up his idols in his heart, and putteth the stumblingblock of his iniquity before his face, and cometh to the prophet; I the LORD will answer him that cometh according to the multitude of his idols;*

5 That I may take the house of Israel in their own heart, because **they are all estranged from me through their idols.**

GOD WILL LEFT ISRAEL UPON WORSHIPING IDOLS

Deuteronomy 31:16 And the LORD said unto Moses, Behold, thou shalt sleep with thy fathers; and **this people will rise up, and go a whoring after the gods of the strangers of the land**, whither they go *to be* among them, and **will forsake me, and break my covenant which I have made with them.**

17 **Then my anger shall be kindled against them in that day, and I will forsake them, and I will hide my face from them**, and they shall be devoured, and many evils and troubles shall befall them; so that they will say in that day, Are not these evils come upon us, because our God *is* not among us?

18 And **I will surely hide my face in that day for all the evils which they shall have wrought, in that they are turned unto other gods.**

19 Now therefore write ye this song for you, and teach it the children of Israel: put it in their mouths, that this song may be a witness for me against the children of Israel.

20 For when I shall have brought them into the land which I sware unto their fathers, that floweth with milk and honey; and they shall have eaten and filled themselves, and waxen fat; then will they turn unto other gods, and serve them, and provoke me, and break my covenant.

21 And it shall come to pass, **when many evils and troubles are befallen them, that this song shall testify against them as a witness; for it shall not be forgotten out of the mouths of their seed: for I know their imagination which they go about, even now,** before I have brought them into the land which I sware.

22 Moses therefore wrote this song the same day, and taught it the children of Israel.

CHOSEN CHOSE TO DISOBEY GOD
A. CHOSEN WORSHIP IDOLS

Romans 1:21 Because that, when they knew God, they glorified *him* not as God, neither were thankful; **but became vain in their imaginations, and their foolish heart was darkened.**

22 Professing themselves to be wise, they became fools,

23 And **changed the glory of the uncorruptible God into an image made like to corruptible man, and to birds, and fourfooted beasts, and creeping things**.

Psalm 106:20 Thus **they changed their glory into the similitude of an ox that eateth grass.**

RESULTING TO SEXUAL SIN

Romans 1:24 Wherefore God also gave them up to uncleanness through the lusts of their own hearts, to dishonour their own bodies between themselves:

25 **Who changed the truth of God into a lie, and worshipped and served the creature more than the Creator, who is blessed for ever. Amen.**

26 **For this cause God gave them up unto vile affections: for even their women did change the natural use into that which is against nature:**

27 **And likewise also the men, leaving the natural use of the woman, burned in their lust one toward another; men with**

men working that which is unseemly, and receiving in themselves that recompence of their error which was meet.

B. NO KNOWLEDGE OF GOD
Hosea 4:6 **My people are destroyed for lack of knowledge , because thou hast rejected knowledge, I will also reject thee,** that thou shalt be no priest to me: seeing thou hast forgotten the law of thy God, **I will also forget thy children.**
Hosea 4:1 Hear the word of the LORD, ye children of Israel: for the LORD hath a controversy with the inhabitants of the land, because *there is* **no truth, nor mercy, nor knowledge of God in the land.**
2 By swearing, and lying, and killing, and stealing, and committing adultery, they break out, and blood toucheth blood.
3 **Therefore shall the land mourn, and every one that dwelleth therein shall languish, with the beasts of the field, and with the fowls of heaven; yea, the fishes of the sea also shall be taken away**.
1John 5:19 And we know that we are of God, and the whole world lieth in wickedness.
20 **And we know that the Son of God is come, and hath given us an understanding, that we may know him that is true, even in his Son Jesus Christ. This is the true God, and eternal life.**

1. GOD LEFT THEM TO POVERTY
Hosea 4:7 As they were increased, so they sinned against me: *therefore* **will I change their glory into shame.**
8 They eat up the sin of my people, and they set their heart on their iniquity.
9 And there shall be, like people, like priest: and I will punish them for their ways, and reward them their doings.
10 **For they shall eat, and not have enough:** they shall commit whoredom, and shall not increase: because they have left off to take heed to the LORD.
11 **Whoredom and wine and new wine take away the heart.**

2. GOD HEARS NOT THE SINNERS (FB 09/05/2014 7:30 pm)
a. BECAUSE OF SINS
John 9:31 Now we know that **God heareth not sinners**: but **if any man be a worshipper of God, and doeth his will. Him he heareth.**

Isaiah 59:2 But **your iniquities have separated between you and your God**, and **your sins have hid his face from you, that he will not hear.**

b. PRAYERS BASED ON THE LUSTS OF FLESH

Isaiah 1:15 And when ye spread forth your hands, I will hide mine eyes from you: yea, when ye make many prayers, I will not hear: your hands are full of blood.

James 4:2 Ye lust, and have not: ye kill, and desire to have, and cannot obtain: ye fight and war, yet ye have not, because ye ask not.

3 Ye ask, and receive not, because ye ask amiss, that ye may consume *it* upon your lusts.

4 Ye adulterers and adulteresses, know ye not that the friendship of the world is enmity with God? **whosoever therefore will be a friend of the world is the enemy of God.**

5 Do ye think that the scripture saith in vain, The spirit that dwelleth in us lusteth to envy?

Micah 3:4 Then shall they cry unto the LORD, but **he will not hear them: he will even hide his face from them at that time,** as they have behaved themselves ill in their doings.

c. PRAYING TO THE IDOLS

Jeremiah 11:10 They are turned back to the iniquities of their forefathers, which refused to hear my words; and they went after other gods to serve them: the house of Israel and the house of Judah have broken my covenant which I made with their fathers.

11 Therefore thus saith the LORD, Behold, I will bring evil upon them, which they shall not be able to escape; and though they shall cry unto me, I will not hearken unto them.

12 Then shall the cities of Judah and inhabitants of Jerusalem go, and cry unto the gods unto whom they offer incense: but they shall not save them at all in the time of their trouble.

13 **For *according to* the number of thy cities were thy gods**, O Judah; **and *according to* the number of the streets of Jerusalem have ye set up altars to *that* shameful thing,** *even* altars to burn incense unto Baal.

14 Therefore pray not thou for this people, neither lift up a cry or prayer for them: for I will not hear *them* in the time that they cry unto me for their trouble.

1John 5:21 *Little children, **keep yourselves from idols**. Amen.*

d. THE PRETENSE OF LONG PRAYING TO COVER UP EXPLOITATIONS

Mark 12:40 Which devour widows' houses, and **for a pretence make long prayers: these shall receive greater damnation.**

Luke 20:47 Which devour widows' houses, and for a shew make long prayers: the same shall receive greater damnation.

Matthew 23:14 Woe unto you, scribes and Pharisees, hypocrites! for ye devour widows' houses, and for a pretence make long prayer: therefore ye shall receive the greater damnation.

e. MAKE A VOW TO THE LORD AND NOT PAY

Ecclesiastes 5:1 Keep thy foot when thou goest to the house of God, and be more ready to hear, than to give the sacrifice of fools: for they consider not that they do evil.

2 Be not rash with thy mouth, and let not thine heart be hasty to utter *any*thing before God: for God *is* in heaven, and thou upon earth: therefore let thy words be few.

3 For a dream cometh through the multitude of business; and a fool's voice *is known* by multitude of words.

4 When thou vowest a vow unto God, defer not to pay it; for *he hath* no pleasure in fools: pay that which thou hast vowed.

5 Better *is it* that thou shouldest not vow, than that thou shouldest vow and not pay.

Numbers 30:2 If a man vow a vow unto the LORD, or **swear an oath to bind his soul with a bond; he shall not break his word, he shall do according to all that proceedeth out of his mouth**.

f. PRAYING WITH A PROUD HEART

Luke 18:11 The Pharisee stood and prayed thus with himself, God, I thank thee, that I am not as other men are, extortioners, unjust, adulterers, or even as this publican.

g. PRAYING AND FASTING FOR STRIPE, DEBATE AND SMITE

Isaiah 58:3 Wherefore have we fasted, *say they*, and thou seest not? *wherefore* have we afflicted our soul, and thou takest no knowledge? Behold, in the day of your fast ye find pleasure, and exact all your labours.

4 Behold, ye fast for strife and debate, and to smite with the fist of wickedness: ye shall not fast as *ye do this* day, to make your voice to be heard on high.

5 Is it such a fast that I have chosen? a day for a man to afflict his soul? *is it* to bow down his head as a bulrush, and to spread sackcloth and ashe s*under him*? wilt thou call this a fast, and an acceptable day to the LORD?

6 *Is* not this the fast that I have chosen? to loose the bands of wickedness, to undo the heavy burdens, and to let the oppressed go free, and that ye break every yoke?

C. EVIL PRACTICES THAT SEPARATE YOU FROM GOD

Isaiah 42:5 *Thus saith God the LORD, he that created the heavens, and stretched them out; he that spread forth the earth, and that which cometh out of it;* **he that giveth breath unto the people upon it, and spirit to them that walk therein:**

Deuteronomy 32:20 And **he said**, *I will hide my face from them*, I will see what their end *shall be:* for they *are* a very froward generation, children in whom *is* no faith.

Isaiah 30:1 Woe to the rebellious children, saith the LORD, **that take counsel, but not of me; and that cover with a covering, but not of my spirit, that they may add sin to sin:**

Ezekiel 14:6 Therefore say unto the house of Israel, Thus **saith the Lord GOD; Repent**, and **turn** *yourselves* **from your idols; and turn away your faces from all your abominations.**

7 **For every one of the house of Israel, or of the stranger that sojourneth in Israel, which separateth himself from me, and setteth up his idols in his heart, and putteth the stumblingblock of his iniquity before his face, and cometh to a prophet to enquire of him concerning me; I the LORD will answer him by myself:**

8 And I will set my face against that man, and will make him a sign and a proverb, and **I will cut him off from the midst of my people; and ye shall know that I** *am* **the LORD.**

9 **And if the prophet be deceived when he hath spoken a thing**, I the LORD have deceived that prophet, and I will stretch out my hand upon him, and **will destroy him from the midst of my people Israel.**

10 And **they shall bear the punishment of their iniquity: the punishment of the prophet shall be even as the punishment of him that seeketh** *unto him*;

GOD LEFT THEM TO BE SUBDUED BY THEIR ENEMIES

Psalms 81:8 Hear, O my people, and I will testify unto thee: **O Israel, if thou wilt hearken unto me;**

9 **There shall no strange god be in thee; neither shalt thou worship any strange god**.

10 I *am* the LORD thy God, which brought thee out of the land of Egypt: open thy mouth wide, and I will fill it.

11 But my people would not hearken to my voice; and Israel would none of me.

12 **So I gave them up unto their own hearts' lust: *and* they walked in their own counsels.**

13 Oh that my people had hearkened unto me, *and* Israel had walked in my ways!

14 I should soon have subdued their enemies, and turned my hand against their adversaries.

15 The haters of the LORD should have submitted themselves unto him: but their time should have endured for ever.

16 He should have fed them also with the finest of the wheat: and with honey out of the rock should I have satisfied thee.

D. PRACTICES ABOMINATIONS TO THE LORD

2Corinthians 11:3 **But I fear, lest by any means, as the serpent beguiled Eve through his subtilty, so your minds should be corrupted** from the simplicity that is in Christ.

Deuteronomy 18:10 There shall not be found among you *any one* that maketh his son or his daughter to pass through the fire, *or* that useth divination, *or* an observer of times, or an enchanter, or a witch,

11 Or a charmer, or a consulter with familiar spirits, or a wizard, or a necromancer.

12 For all that do these things *are* an abomination unto the LORD: and because of these abominations the LORD thy God doth drive them out from before thee.

Isaiah 19:3 And **the spirit of Egypt shall fail in the midst thereof; and I will destroy the counsel thereof**: and they shall seek to the idols, and to the charmers, and to them that have familiar spirits, and to the wizards.

1. PRAYING TO DEAD

Isaiah 8:19 And when they shall say unto you, Seek unto them that have familiar spirits, and unto wizards that peep, and that mutter: **should not a people seek unto their God**? for the living to the dead?

Isaiah 29:4 And thou shalt be brought down, *and* shalt speak out of the ground, and thy speech shall be low out of the dust, and thy voice shall be, as of one that hath a familiar spirit, out of the ground, and **thy speech shall whisper out of the dust**.

SEEK AFTER FAMILIAR SPIRITS

Leviticus 19:31 Regard not them that have familiar spirits, neither seek after wizards, to be defiled by them: I *am* the LORD your God.

Leviticus 20:6 And the soul that turneth after such as have familiar spirits, and after wizards, to go a whoring after them, **I will even set my face against that soul,** and will cut him off from among his people.

PUNISHMENT DURING THE TIME OF MOSES

Leviticus 20:27A man also or woman that hath a familiar spirit, or that is a wizard, **shall surely be put to death: they shall stone them with stones: their blood** *shall be* **upon them.**

SAUL DIED FOR HIS TRANSGRESSION

1Chronicles 10:13 So Saul died for his transgression which he committed against the LORD, *even* against the word of the LORD, which he kept not, and also for asking *counsel* of *one that had* a familiar spirit, to enquire *of it;*

14 And enquired not of the LORD: therefore he slew him, and turned the kingdom unto David the son of Jesse.

2. WITCHCRAFT PRACTICES SIN AGAINST THE LORD

1Samuel 15:23 For **rebellion** *is as* **the sin of witchcraft**, **and stubbornness** *is as* **iniquity and idolatry. Because thou hast rejected the word of the LORD,** he hath also rejected thee from *being* king.

a. CONSULTER TO DIVINERS (FORTUNE TELLER)

Jeremiah 27:9 Therefore hearken not ye to your prophets, nor to your diviners, nor to your dreamers, nor to your enchanters, nor to your sorcerers, which speak unto you, saying, Ye shall not serve the king of Babylon:

10 For **they prophesy a lie unto you,** to remove you far from your land; and that I should drive you out, and ye should perish.

Jeremiah 29:8 For thus saith the LORD of hosts, the God of Israel; **let not your prophets and your diviners**, that *be* in the midst of you, **deceive you, neither hearken to your dreams** which ye cause to be dreamed.

Zechariah 10:2 For the idols have spoken vanity, and **the diviners have seen a lie, and have told false dreams; they comfort in vain:** therefore they went their way as a flock, they were troubled, because *there was* no shepherd.

b. STARGAZERS (HOROSCOPE OF THE STARS)

Daniel 5:15 And now **the wise *men*, the astrologers,** have been brought in before me, that they should read this writing, and make known unto me the interpretation thereof: but **they could not shew the interpretation of the thing:**

Jeremiah 10:2 **Thus saith the LORD, Learn not the way of the heathen, and be not dismayed at the signs of heaven; for the heathen are dismayed at them.**

Isaiah 47:13 Thou art wearied in the multitude of thy counsels. Let now the astrologers, the stargazers, the monthly prognosticators, stand up, and save thee from *these things* that shall come upon thee.

14 Behold, **they shall be as stubble; the fire shall burn them; they shall not deliver themselves from the power of the flame:** *there shall* not *be* a coal to warm at, *nor* fire to sit before it

SOURCE OF WITCHCRAFT PRACTICES: OLD BABYLON

Ezekiel 21:21 For the king of Babylon stood at the parting of the way, at the head of the two ways, **to use divination**: he made *his* arrows bright, **he consulted with images, he looked in the liver**.

22 At his right hand was the divination for Jerusalem, to appoint captains, to open the mouth in the slaughter, to lift up the voice with shouting, to appoint *battering*rams against the gates, to cast a mount, *and* to build a fort.

23 And it shall be unto them as a false divination in their sight, to them that have sworn oaths: but he will call to remembrance the iniquity, that they may be taken.

3. SIN TO SACRIFICE THEIR CHILDREN TO DEATH (FALSE DOCTRINE)

2Chronicles 33:6 And **he caused his children to pass through the fire** in the valley of the son of Hinnom: also he observed times, and used enchantments, and used witchcraft, and dealt with a familiar spirit, and with wizards: **he wrought much evil in the sight of the LORD, to provoke him to anger**.

2Kings 17:17 And they caused their sons and their daughters to pass through the fire, and used divination and enchantments, and sold themselves to do evil in the sight of the LORD, to provoke him to anger.

2Kings 21:6 And **he made his son pass through the fire, and observed times, and used** enchantments, and dealt with familiar spirits and wizards: he wrought much wickedness in the sight of the LORD, **to provoke *him* to anger.**

4. FOLLOWING THE WISDOM OF THIS WORLD

a. GOD LEFT EVEN KING TO HIS MISFORTUNES

2Chronicles 16:6   Then Asa the king took all Judah; and they carried away the stones of Ramah, and the timber thereof, wherewith Baasha was building; and he built therewith Geba and Mizpah.

7 And at that time Hanani the seer came to Asa king of Judah, and said unto him, Because thou hast relied on the king of Syria, and not relied on the LORD thy God, therefore is the host of the king of Syria escaped out of thine hand.

8 Were not the Ethiopians and the Lubims a huge host, with very many chariots and horsemen? yet, because thou didst rely on the LORD, he delivered them into thine hand.

9 For the eyes of the LORD run to and fro throughout the whole earth, to shew himself strong in the behalf of *them* whose heart *is* perfect toward him. Herein thou hast done foolishly: therefore from henceforth thou shalt have wars.

10 Then Asa was wroth with the seer, and put him in a prison house; for *he was* in a rage with him because of this *thing*. And Asa oppressed *some* of the people the same time.

12 And Asa in the thirty and ninth year of his reign was diseased in his feet, until his disease *was* exceeding *great*: yet in his disease he sought not to the LORD, but to the physicians.

13 And Asa slept with his fathers, and died in the one and fortieth year of his reign.

14 And they buried him in his own sepulchres, which he had made for himself in the city of David, and laid him in the bed which was filled with sweet odours and divers kinds *of spices* prepared by the apothecaries' art: and they made a very great burning for him.

b. GOD GAVE THEM OVER TO REPROBATE MIND

Romans 1:28 And even as they did not like to retain God in *their* knowledge, God gave them over to a reprobate mind, to do those things which are not convenient;

29 Being filled with all unrighteousness, fornication, wickedness, covetousness, maliciousness; full of envy, murder, debate, deceit, malignity; whisperers,

30 Backbiters, haters of God, despiteful, proud, boasters, inventors of evil things, disobedient to parents,

31 Without understanding, covenantbreakers, without natural affection, implacable, unmerciful:

Ephesians 4:18 **Having the understanding darkened, being alienated from the life of God through the ignorance that is in them, because of the blindness of their heart**:

19 Who being past feeling have given themselves over unto lasciviousness, to work all uncleanness with greediness.

c. GOD HARDENED THE SPIRIT

Deuteronomy 2:30 But Sihon king of Heshbon would not let us pass by him: for the LORD thy God hardened his spirit, and made his heart obstinate, that he might deliver him into thy hand, as *appeareth* this day.

31 And the LORD said unto me, Behold, I have begun to give Sihon and his land before thee: begin to possess, that thou mayest inherit his land.

32 Then Sihon came out against us, he and all his people, to fight at Jahaz.

33 And the LORD our God delivered him before us; and we smote him, and his sons, and all his people.

5. ESTABLISHED THEIR OWN RIGHTEOUSNESS

Romans 10:2 *For I bear them record that they have a zeal of God, but not according to knowledge.*
3 For they being ignorant of God's righteousness, and going about to establish their own righteousness, have not submitted themselves unto the righteousness of God.

Romans 11:8 *(*According as it is written, **God hath given them the spirit of slumber, eyes that they should not see, and ears that they should not hear;) unto this day**.
Deuteronomy 29:2 And Moses called unto all Israel, and said unto them, Ye have seen all that the LORD did before your eyes in the land of Egypt unto Pharaoh, and unto all his servants, and unto all his land;
3 The great temptations which thine eyes have seen, the signs, and those great miracles:
4 Yet the LORD hath not given you an heart to perceive, and eyes to see, and ears to hear, unto this day.
Romans 11:9 And David saith, Let their table be made a snare, and a trap, and a stumbling block, and a recompense unto them:
10 Let their eyes be darkened that they may not see, and bow down their back alway.

6. THE JEWS' SIN OF MARRYING WOMEN FROM OTHER NATIONS
Nehemiah 13:23 In those days also saw I Jews *that* had married wives of Ashdod, of Ammon, *and* of Moab:
24 **And their children spake half in the speech of Ashdod, and could not speak in the Jews' language,** but according to the language of each people.
25 **And I contended with them, and cursed them, and smote certain of them, and plucked off their hair, and made them swear by God,** *saying***, Ye shall not give your daughters unto their sons, nor take their daughters unto your sons, or for yourselves.**
26 **Did not Solomon king of Israel sin by these things?** yet among many nations was there no king like him, who was beloved of his God, and God made him king over all Israel: nevertheless even him did outlandish women cause to sin.

GOD'S COMPASSION TO FORGIVE THE CHOSEN PEOPLE

Leviticus 26:41 And *that* I also have walked contrary unto them, and have brought them into the land of their enemies; **if then their uncircumcised hearts be humbled, and they then accept of the punishment of their iniquity:**

42 **Then will I remember my covenant with Jacob, and also my covenant with Isaac, and also my covenant with Abraham will I remember; and I will remember the land.**

43 The land also shall be left of them, and shall enjoy her sabbaths, while she lieth desolate without them: and they shall accept of the punishment of their iniquity: because, even because they despised my judgments, and because their soul abhorred my statutes.

44 **And yet for all that, when they be in the land of their enemies, I will not cast them away, neither will I abhor them, to destroy them utterly, and to break my covenant with them: for I *am* the LORD their God.**

45 **But I will for their sakes remember the covenant of their ancestors**, whom I brought forth out of the land of Egypt in the sight of the heathen, that I might be their God: **I *am* the LORD**.

46 These *are* the statutes and judgments and laws, which the LORD made between him and the children of Israel in mount Sinai by the hand of Moses.

*GOD'S INSTRUCTIONS TO ISRAEL

Ezekiel 18:30 Therefore I will judge you, O house of Israel, every one according to his ways, saith the Lord GOD. **Repent, and turn *yourselves* from all your transgressions; so iniquity shall not be your ruin.**

31 Cast away from you all your transgressions, whereby ye have transgressed; and make you a new heart and a new spirit: for why will ye die, O house of Israel?

32 For I have no pleasure in the death of him that dieth, saith the Lord GOD: wherefore turn *yourselves*, and live ye.

GOD'S PROMISE TO HIS CHOSEN UNDER CAPTIVITY IN BABYLON

Jeremiah 29:10 For thus **saith the LORD, *That after seventy years* be accomplished at Babylon I will visit you, and perform**

my good word toward you, in causing you to return to this place**.

11 For I know the thoughts that I think toward you, saith the LORD, thoughts of peace, and not of evil, to give you an expected end.

12 Then **shall ye call upon me**, and ye shall go and pray unto me, and I will hearken unto you.

13 And **ye shall seek me, and find *me,*** when ye shall search for me with all your heart.

14 And **I will be found of you, saith the LORD: and I will turn away your captivity, and I will gather you from all the nations, and from all the places whither I have driven you, saith the LORD;** and I will bring you again into the place whence I caused you to be carried away captive.

PRAYER TO OBEY THE LORD

Psalms 119:127 *Therefore I love thy commandments above gold; yea, above fine gold.* 131 *I opened my mouth, and panted: for I longed for thy commandments.* 143 *Trouble and anguish have taken hold on me: yet thy commandments are my delights.*

151 *Thou art near, O LORD; and all thy commandments are truth.* 166 **LORD, I have hoped for thy salvat***ion, and done thy commandments.* 172 ***My tongue shall speak of thy word: for all thy commandments are righteousness****. 176 / I have gone astray like a lost sheep; seek thy servant; **for I do not forget thy commandments.***

Psalms 119:19 I am a stranger in the earth*: hide not thy commandments from me. 21 Thou hast rebuked the proud that are cursed, which do err from thy commandments. 32 I will run the way of thy commandments, when thou shalt enlarge my heart.33 HE. Teach me, O LORD, the way of thy statutes; and I shall keep it unto the end.34 Give me understanding, and I shall keep thy law; yea, I shall observe it with my whole heart.35 **Make me to go in the path of thy commandments***; for therein do I delight.47 And I will delight myself in thy commandments, which I have loved. 48 My hands also will I lift up unto thy commandments, which I have loved; and I will meditate in thy statutes.Amen LORD.*

CHAPTER X **JUDGMENT OF SOUL UPON DEATH**

Hebrews 9:27
And as it is appointed unto men once to die, but after this the judgment:

THE SOULS OF THE RICH MAN AND LAZARUS

Luke 16:19 There was a certain rich man, which was clothed in purple and fine linen, and fared sumptuously every day:

20 And there was a certain beggar named Lazarus, which was laid at his gate, full of sores,

21 And desiring to be fed with the crumbs which fell from the rich man's table: moreover the dogs came and licked his sores.

22 **And it came to pass, that the beggar died, and was carried by the angels into Abraham's bosom: the rich man also died, and was buried**;

23 **And in hell he lift up his eyes, being in torments**, and seeth Abraham afar off, and Lazarus in his bosom.

24 And he cried and said, Father Abraham, have mercy on me, and send Lazarus, that he may dip the tip of his finger in water, and cool my tongue; for I am tormented in this flame.

25 But Abraham said, Son, remember that thou in thy lifetime receivedst thy good things, and likewise Lazarus evil things: but now he is comforted, and thou art tormented.

26 And beside all this, between us and you there is a great gulf fixed: so that they which would pass from hence to you cannot; neither can they pass to us, that *would come* from thence.

27 **Then he said**, *I pray thee therefore, father, that thou wouldest send him to my father's house:*

28 *For I have five brethren; that he may testify unto them, lest they also come into this place of torment.*

29 **Abraham saith unto him**, *They have Moses and the prophets; let them hear them.*

30 **And he said,** *Nay, father Abraham: but if one went unto them from the dead, they will repent.*

31 **And he said unto him,** *If they hear not Moses and the prophets, neither will they be persuaded, though one rose from the dead.*

LORD JESUS SPOKE WHERE THE SOUL GOES AFTER DEATH

Matthew 7:21 *Not every one that saith unto me, LORD, LORD, shall enter into the kingdom of heaven; but he that doeth the will of my Father which is in heaven.*

Matthew18:3And said, Verily I say unto you, Except ye be converted, and become as little children, ye shall not enter into the kingdom of heaven.

1. KINGDOM OF HEAVEN(See Volume 2 Part 11 ChapterII)
Matthew 5:20 **For I say unto you, That except your righteousness shall exceed** *the righteousness* **of the scribes and Pharisees, ye shall in no case enter into the kingdom of heaven.**
Psalms 49:15 But **God will redeem my soul from the power of the grave: for he shall receive me. Selah.**

THE SOULS WORSHIPING GOD IN HEAVEN
Revelation 6:9 And when he had opened the fifth seal, **I saw under the altar the souls of them that were slain for the word of God**, and for the testimony which they held:
10 And they cried with a loud voice, saying, *How long, O Lord, holy and true, dost thou not judge and avenge our blood on them that dwell on the earth?*
11 And white robes were given unto every one of them; and it was said unto them, that they should rest yet for a little season, **until their fellowservants also and their brethren, that should be killed a**s they *were*, should be fulfilled.
Revelation 20:4 And I saw thrones, and they sat upon them, and judgment was given unto them: **and** *I saw* **the souls of them that were beheaded for the witness of Jesus, and for the word of God, and which had not worshipped the beast, neither his**

image, neither had received *his* mark upon their foreheads, or in their hands; and they lived and reigned with Christ a thousand years.

THE SOUL OF MOSES WAS WITH ELIAS CAME FROM HEAVEN

Mark 9:2 And after six days Jesus taketh *with him* Peter, and James, and John, and leadeth them up into an high mountain apart by themselves: and he was transfigured before them

3 And his raiment became shining, exceeding white as snow; so as no fuller on earth can white them.

4 **And there appeared unto them Elias with Moses: and they were talking with Jesus.**

5 And Peter answered and said to Jesus, Master, it is good for us to be here: and let us make three tabernacles; one for thee, and one for Moses, and one for Elias.

SOULS ARE GOING TO HEAVEN TO SIT DOWN WITH THE PROPHETS

Matthew 8:11 And I say unto you, **That many shall come from the east and west, and shall sit down with Abraham, and Isaac, and Jacob, in the kingdom of heaven.**

Matthew 5:19 **Whosoever therefore shall break one of these least commandments, and shall teach men so,** *he shall be called the least in the kingdom of heaven*: **but whosoever shall do and teach** *them,* **the same shall be called great in the kingdom of heaven.**

Acts 14:22 Confirming **the souls of the disciples,** *and* exhorting them to continue in the faith, and that we must through much tribulation **enter into the kingdom of God.**

THE ELECT CAN'T DELIVER THE SOUL OF THEIR CHILDREN

Ezekiel 14:20 Though Noah, Daniel, and Job, *were* in it, *as* I live, saith the Lord GOD, **they shall deliver neither son nor daughter**; **they shall** *but* **deliver their own souls by their righteousness.**

Ezekiel 18:4 **Behold all souls are mine; as the soul of the father; so also the souls of the son is mine: the soul that sinneth, it shall die.**

2. HELL

Proverbs 9:18 But he knoweth not that the dead are there and that her guests are in the depths of hell.

Job 26:6 Hell is naked before him, and destruction hath no covering.

Deuteronomy 32:22 For a fire is kindled in mine anger, and **shall burn unto the lowest hell, and shall consume the earth with her increase, and set on fire the foundations of the mountains**.

2Samuel 22:6 The **sorrows of hell** compassed me about; **the snares of death prevented** me;

Psalms 18:5 The sorrows **of hell** compassed me about; **the snares of death prevented me.**

Psalms 116:3 The sorrow of death compassed me, **and the pains of hell got hold upon me; I found trouble and sorrow.**

Isaiah 5:14 Therefore hell hath enlarged herself, and opened her mouth without measure: and their glory, and their multitude, and their pomp, and he that rejoiceth, **shall descend into it.**

Isaiah 14:9 **Hell from beneath is moved for thee to meet** *thee* **at thy coming: it stirreth up the dead for thee,** *even* **all the chief ones of the earth; it hath raised up from their thrones all the kings of the nations.**

Mark 9:44, 46,48   Where **the worm dieth not, and the fire is not quenched.**

49 **For everyone shall be salted with fire**, and every sacrifice shall be salted with salt.

Psalm 63:9 **But those** *that* **seek my soul, to destroy** *it***, shall go into the lower parts of the earth.**

GOD DELIVERED JESUS FROM HELL

Psalms 16:10 **For thou wilt not leave my soul in hell**; neither wilt thou suffer thine Holy One to see corruption.

Psalm 86:12 I will praise thee, O Lord my God, with all my heart: and I will glorify thy name for evermore.

13 For great is thy mercy toward me: and **thou hast delivered my soul from the lowest hell.**

Acts 2:27 Because **thou wilt not leave my soul in** hell, neither wilt thou suffer thine Holy One to see corruption.

Acts 2:31 He seeing this before spake of the resurrection of Christ, that **his soul was not left in hell, neither his flesh did see corruption.**

Proverbs 23:14 Thou shalt beat him with the rod, and **shalt deliver his soul from hell.**

LOSING ONE'S SOUL

Matthew 16:26 **For what is a man profited, if he shall gain the whole world, and lose his own soul? or what shall a man give in exchange for his soul?**

Mark 8:34And when he had called the people *unto him* with his disciples also, he said unto them, Whosoever will come after me, let him deny himself, and take up his cross, and follow me.

35 For whosoever will save his life shall lose it; but whosoever shall lose his life for my sake and the gospel's, the same shall save it.

36 For what shall it profit a man, if he shall gain the whole world, and lose his own soul?

37 Or what shall a man give in exchange for his soul?

THE SOUL WILL GO TO HELL

Psalms 55:15 *Let death seize upon them, and let them go down quick into hell: for wickedness is in their dwellings, and among them.*

Isaiah 28:15 Because ye have said, We have made a covenant with death, and **with hell** are we at agreement; when the overflowing scourge shall pass through, it shall not come unto us: **for we have made lies our refuge, and under falsehood have we hid ourselves:**

Psalms 2:8 Ask of me, and **I shall give** *thee* **the heathen** *for* **thine inheritance, and the uttermost parts of the earth** *for* **thy possession**.

GOD THE DESTROYER OF LOST SOULS

Matthew 10:28 And fear not them which kill the body, but are not able to kill the soul: but rather fear him which is able to destroy both soul and body in hell.

GOD WILL SET HIS FACE AGAINST THIS SOUL

Psalm 9:17 *The wicked shall be turned into hell, and all the nations that forget God.*

Leviticus 20:6 And the soul that turneth after such as have familiar spirits, and after wizards, to go a whoring after them, I will even set my face against that soul, and will cut him off from among his people.

Proverbs 6:32 **But whoso committeth adultery with a woman lacketh understanding: he that doeth it destroyeth his own soul**.

Job 27:8 For what *is* the hope of the hypocrite, though he hath gained, when God taketh away his soul?

Proverbs 21:10 **The soul of the wicked desireth evil:** his neighbor findeth no favour in his eyes.

Galatians 5:17 For the flesh lusteth against the Spirit, and the Spirit against the flesh: and these are contrary the one to the other: so that ye cannot do the things that ye would.

18 But if ye be led of the Spirit, ye are not under the law.

19 Now the works of the flesh are manifest, which are *these*; Adultery, fornication, uncleanness, lasciviousness,

20 Idolatry, witchcraft, hatred, variance, emulations, wrath, strife, seditions, heresies,

21 Envyings, murders, drunkenness, revellings, and such like: of the which I tell you before, as I have also told *you* in time past, that they which do such things shall not inherit the kingdom of God.

Proverbs 5:5 Her feet go down to death; **her steps take hold on hell.**

Matthew 7:21 Not every one that saith unto me, Lord, Lord, shall enter into the kingdom of heaven; but he that doeth the will of my Father which is in heaven.

22 Many will say to me in that day, Lord, Lord, have we not prophesied in thy name? and in thy name have cast out devils? and in thy name done many wonderful works?

23 And then will I profess unto them, I never knew you: depart from me, ye that work iniquity.

WICKED SOULS

Ezekiel 18:20 The soul that sinneth, it shall die. **The son shall not bear the iniquity of the father, neither shall the father bear the iniquity of the son: the righteousness of the righteous shall be upon him, and** the wickedness of the wicked shall be upon him.

Romans 2:9 **Tribulation and anguish, upon every soul of man that doeth evil, of the Jew first, and also of the Gentile;**

Proverbs 28:5 **Evil men understand not judgment**: but they that seek the LORD understand all *things*.

THE SINNERS

1Corinthians 3:3 For ye are yet carnal: for whereas *there is* among you envying, and strife, and divisions, are ye not carnal, and walk as men?

Ezekiel 15:7 And I will set my face against them; **they shall go out from *one* fire, and *another* fire shall devour them;** and ye shall know that **I *am* the LORD, when I set my face against them.**

IDOL WORSHIPERS

1Chronicles 16:26 For all the gods of the people are idols: but the LORD made the heavens.

NONBELIEVERS

John 8:24   I said therefore unto you, that **ye shall die in your sins: for if ye believe not that I am he, ye shall die in your sins.**

 John 3:18 He that believeth on him is not condemned: but **he that believeth not is condemned already, because he hath not believed in the name of the only begotten Son of God.**

19 And this is the condemnation, that light is come into the world, and men loved darkness rather than light, because their deeds were evil.

20 For every one that doeth evil hateth the light, neither cometh to the light, lest his deeds should be reproved.

John 3:36 He that believeth on the Son hath everlasting life: and **he that believeth not the Son shall not see life; but the wrath of God abideth on him.**

John 5:44 **How can ye believe, which receive honour one of another, and seek not the honour that *cometh* from God only?**

PHARISEES AND SCRIBES OF ISRAEL WHO PERSECUTED THE PROPHETS

Matthew 23:29 Woe unto you, scribes and Pharisees, hypocrites! because ye build the tombs of the prophets, and garnish the sepulchres of the righteous,

30 And say, If we had been in the days of our fathers, we would not have been partakers with them in the blood of the prophets.

31 Wherefore ye be witnesses unto yourselves, that ye are the children of them which killed the prophets.

32 Fill ye up then the measure of your fathers.

33 *Ye* serpents, *ye* generation of vipers, how can ye escape the damnation of hell?

34 Wherefore, behold, I send unto you prophets, and wise men, and scribes: and *some* of them ye shall kill and crucify; and *some* of them shall ye scourge in your synagogues, and persecute *them* from city to city:

35 That upon you may come all the righteous blood shed upon the earth, from the blood of righteous Abel unto the blood of
Zacharias son of Barachias, whom ye slew between the temple and the altar.

BACKBITERS

Matthew 12:34 O generation of vipers, how can ye, being evil, speak good things? **for out of the abundance of the heart the mouth speaketh.**

35 A good man out of the good treasure of the heart bringeth forth good things: and **an evil man out of the evil treasure bringeth forth evil things.**

36 But I say unto you, **That every idle word that men shall speak, they shall give account thereof in the day of judgment**.

37 For by thy words thou shalt be justified, and by thy words thou shalt be condemned.

1Timothy 6:4 **He is proud**, knowing nothing, but doting about questions and strifes of words, whereof cometh envy, strife, railings, evil surmisings,

5 Perverse disputings of men of corrupt minds, and destitute of the truth, supposing that gain is godliness: from such withdraw thyself.

Romans 1:30 Backbiters, haters of God, despiteful, proud, boasters, inventors of evil things, disobedient to parents,

31Without understanding, covenantbreakers, without natural affection, implacable, unmerciful:

32Who knowing the judgment of God, that they which commit such things are worthy of death, not only do the same, but have pleasure in them that do them.

Proverbs 6:16 These six *things* doth the LORD hate: yea, seven *are* an abomination unto him:

17 A proud look, a lying tongue, and hands that shed innocent blood,

18 An heart that deviseth wicked imaginations, feet that be swift in running to mischief,

19 A false witness *that* speaketh lies, and he that soweth discord among brethren.

Psalms 101:5Whoso privily slandereth his neighbour, him will I cut off: him that hath an high look and a proud heart will not I suffer.

Luke 12:3 **Therefore whatsoever ye have spoken in darkness shall be heard in the light;** and that which ye have spoken in the ear in closets shall be proclaimed upon the housetops.

James 3:6 And the tongue *is* a fire, a world of iniquity: so is the tongue among our members, that it defileth the whole body, and setteth on fire the course of nature; and **it is set on fire of hell**.

MURDERER

Matthew 5:21 Ye have heard that it was said by them of old time, Thou shalt not kill; and **whosoever shall kill shall be in danger of the judgment:**

22 But I say unto you, That whosoever is angry with his brother without a cause shall be in danger of the judgment: and whosoever shall say to his brother, Raca, shall be in danger of the council: but whosoever shall say, **Thou fool, shall be in danger of hell fire.**

ADULTERER

Proverbs 6:32 *But* whoso committeth adultery with a woman lacketh understanding: **he *that* doeth it destroyeth his own soul.**
Matthew 5:28 But I say unto you, That whosoever looketh on a woman to lust after her hath committed adultery with her already in his heart.

29 And if thy right eye offend thee, pluck it out, and cast *it* from thee: for it is profitable for thee that one of thy members should perish, and not *that* thy whole body should be cast into hell.

30 **And if thy right hand offend thee**, cut it off, and cast it from thee: for it is profitable for thee that one of thy members should perish, and not *that* **thy whole body shall be cast into hell**

Matthew 18:9 And if thine eye offend thee, pluck it out, and cast *it* from thee: it is better for thee to enter into life with one eye, rather than having two eyes to be cast into hell fire.

Mark 9:47 And if thine eye offend thee, pluck it out: it is better for thee to enter into the kingdom of God with one eye, than having two eyes to be cast into hell fire:

Matthew 5:32 But I say unto you, That whosoever shall put away his wife, saving for the cause of fornication, causeth her to commit adultery: and whosoever shall marry her that is divorced committeth adultery.

Luke 16:18 Whosoever putteth away his wife, and marrieth another, committeth adultery: and whosoever marrieth her that is put away from *her* husband committeth adultery.

Proverbs 9:13 **A foolish woman** *is* **clamorous:** *she is* **simple, and knoweth nothing**.

14 For she sitteth at the door of her house, on a seat in the high places of the city,

15 **To call passengers who go right on their ways:**

16 Whoso *is* simple, let him turn in hither: and *as for* him that wanteth understanding, **she saith to him,**

17 **Stolen waters are sweet, and bread** *eaten* **in secret is pleasant**.

18 But he knoweth not that the dead *are* there; *and* *that* **her guests** *are* **in the depths of hell.**

CHILD ABUSER

Mark 9:36 And he took a child, and set him in the midst of them: and when he had taken him in his arms, he said unto them,

42 And whosoever shall offend one of *these* little ones that believe in me, it is better for him that a millstone were hanged about his neck, and he were cast into the sea.

Matthew 18:3 And said, Verily I say unto you, Except ye be converted, and become as little children, ye shall not enter into the kingdom of heaven.

4 Whosoever therefore shall humble himself as this little child, the same is greatest in the kingdom of heaven.

5 And whoso shall receive one such little child in my name receiveth me.

6 But whoso shall offend one of these little ones which believe in me, it were better for him that a millstone were hanged about his neck, and *that* he were drowned in the depth of the sea.

7 Woe unto the world because of offences! for it must needs be that offences come; but woe to that man by whom the offence cometh!

8 Wherefore if thy hand or thy foot offend thee, cut them off, and cast *them* from thee: it is better for thee to enter into life halt or maimed, rather than having two hands or two feet to be cast into everlasting fire.

9 And if thine eye offend thee, pluck it out, and cast *it* from thee: it is better for thee to enter into life with one eye, rather than having two eyes to be cast into hell fire.

10 **Take heed that ye despise not one of these little ones; for I say unto you, That in heaven their angels do always behold the face of my Father which is in heaven.**

DOCTRINE OF RELIGION

Matthew 23:15 Woe unto you, scribes and Pharisees, hypocrites! for ye compass sea and land to make one proselyte, and when he is made, ye make him twofold more the child of hell than yourselves.

Matthew 23:33 *Ye* serpents, *ye* generation of vipers, **how can ye escape the damnation of hell?**

EVIL DOERS

Mark 9:43 And if thy hand offend thee, cut it off: it is better for thee to enter into life maimed, than having two hands to go into hell, into the fire that never shall be quenched:

45 And if thy foot offend thee, cut it off: it is better for thee to enter halt into life, than having two feet to be cast into hell, into the fire that never shall be quenched:

SUFFERINGS OF THE LIVING SOULS OF THE HEATHEN

Romans 2:9 **Tribulation and anguish, upon *every soul of man that doeth evil**, of the Jew first, and also of the Gentile;

2Peter 2:14 Having eyes full of adultery, and that cannot cease from sin; **beguiling unstable souls:** an heart they have exercised with covetous practices; **cursed children**:

Isaiah 57:20 But **the wicked** *are* **like the troubled sea, when it cannot rest, whose waters cast up mire and dirt.**

21 *There is* **no peace, saith my God, to the wicked**

APPOINTED TIME TO ENTER INTO JUDGMENT WITH GOD

Proverbs 2:8 He keepeth the paths of judgment, and preserveth the way of his saints.

Ecclesiastes 8:6 Because to every purpose there is time and judgment, therefore the misery of man *is* great upon him.

7 For he knoweth not that which shall be: for who can tell him when it shall be?

Jeremiah 8:7 **Yea, the stork in the heaven knoweth her appointed times**; and the turtle and the crane and the swallow observe the time of their coming; **but my people know not the judgment of the LORD.**

Job 34:20 In a moment shall they die, and the people shall be troubled at midnight, and pass away: and the mighty shall be taken away without hand.

21 For his eyes *are* upon the ways of man, and he seeth all his goings.

22 *There is* no darkness, nor shadow of death, where the workers of iniquity may hide themselves

23 For he will not lay upon man more *than right*; that he should enter into judgment with God.

Job 7:1 *Is there* **not an appointed time to man upon earth?** *are not* his days also like the days of an hireling?

DEATH OF THE WICKED

Job 21:17 How oft is the candle of the wicked put out! and *how oft* cometh their destruction upon them! *God* distributeth sorrows in his anger.

18 They are as stubble before the wind, and as chaff that the storm carrieth away.

20 His eyes shall see his destruction, and **he shall drink of the wrath of the Almighty**.

21 For what pleasure *hath* he in his house after him, when the number of his months is cut off in the midst?

22 Shall *any* teach God knowledge? seeing he judgeth those that are high.

23 One dieth in his full strength, being wholly at ease and quiet.

24 His breasts are full of milk, and his bones are moistened with marrow.

25 And another dieth in the bitterness of his soul, and never eateth with pleasure.

26 They shall lie down alike in the dust, and the worms shall cover them.

27 **Behold, I know your thoughts, and the devices *which* ye wrongfully imagine against me.**

28 For ye say, **Where *is* the house of the prince? and where *are* the dwelling places of the wicked?**

29 Have ye not asked them that go by the way? and do ye not know their tokens,

30 **That the wicked is reserved to the day of destruction? they shall be brought forth to the day of wrath.**

31 Who shall declare his way to his face? and who shall repay him *what* he hath done?

32 Yet shall he be brought to the grave, and shall remain in the tomb.

Job 27: 9 **Will God hear his cry when trouble cometh upon him?**

Job 7:9 As the cloud is consumed and vanisheth away: so **he that goeth down to the grave shall come up no more.**

10 **He shall return no more to his house, neither shall his place know him anymore**.

Job 10:21 Before **I go whence I shall not return, even to the land of darkness, and the shadow of death;**

22 **In the land of darkness itself; and of the shadow of death, without any order, and where the light is in darkness.**

Job 28:3 He setteth **an end to darkness,** and searcheth out all perfection: **the stones of darkness, and the shadow of death.**

DEATH WILL CLAIM THE WICKED 'S FAMILY

Job 27:13 This *is* the portion of a wicked man with God, and the heritage of oppressors, *which* they shall receive of the Almighty.

14 If his children be multiplied, *it is* for the sword: and his offspring shall not be satisfied with bread.

15 Those that remain of him shall be buried in death: and his widows shall not weep.

16 Though he heap up silver as the dust, and prepare raiment as the clay;

17 He may prepare *it*, but the just shall put *it* on, and the innocent shall divide the silver.

18 He buildeth his house as a moth, and as a booth *that* the keeper maketh.

19 The rich man shall lie down, but he shall not be gathered: he openeth his eyes, and he *is* not.

20 Terrors take hold on him as waters, a tempest stealeth him away in the night.

21 The east wind carrieth him away, and he departeth: and as a storm hurleth him out of his place.

22 For *God* shall cast upon him, and not spare: he would fain flee out of his hand.

23 *Men* shall clap their hands at him, and shall hiss him out of his place.

PHYSICAL DEATH OF THE SINNER

2Samuel 22:5 When the waves of death compassed me, the floods of ungodly men made me afraid;

Proverbs 11:7 **When a wicked man dieth, *his* expectation shall perish: and the hope of unjust *men* perisheth.**

2Peter 2:9 The Lord knoweth how to deliver the godly out of temptations, and to reserve the unjust unto the day of judgment to be punished:

GOD RESERVES THE UNJUST TO BE PUNISHED

2 Peter 2:4 For if God spared not the angels that sinned, but cast *them*down to hell, and delivered *them* into chains of darkness, to be reserved unto judgment;

8(For that righteous man dwelling among them, in seeing and hearing, vexed *his* righteous soul from day to day with *thei r*unlawful deeds;)

9The Lord knoweth how to deliver the godly out of temptations, and to reserve the unjust unto the day of judgment to be punished:

10But chiefly them that walk after the flesh in the lust of uncleanness, and despise government. Presumptuous *are they*, selfwilled, they are not afraid to speak evil of dignities.

PRAYERS TO THE SALVATION OF THE SOUL

Psalms 30:3 *O LORD, thou hast brought up my soul from the grave: thou hast kept me alive, that I should not go down to the pit. Amen*

Psalms 41:4 *I said, LORD, be merciful unto me: heal my soul; for I have sinned against thee.*

Psalms 103:1 *A Psalm* of David.) *Bless the LORD, O my soul: and all that is within me, bless his holy name.*

2 *Bless the LORD, O my soul, and forget not all his benefits:*

Psalms 35:9*And my soul shall be joyful in the LORD: it shall rejoice in his salvation.*

Psalms 142:7*Bring my soul out of prison, that I may praise thy name: the righteous shall compass me about; for thou shalt deal bountifully with me.*

Psalms 25:20 *O keep my soul, and deliver me: let me not be ashamed; for I put my trust in thee.*

Psalms 26:9 *Gather not my soul with sinners, nor my life with bloody men:*

10 In whose hands is mischief, and their right hand is full of bribes.

11 But as for me, I will walk in mine integrity: redeem me, and be merciful unto me.

12 My foot standeth in an even place: in the congregations will I bless the LORD.

Psalms 143:6 *I stretch forth my hands unto thee: my soul thirsteth after thee, as a thirsty land. Selah.*

11 *Quicken me, O LORD, for thy name's sake: for thy righteousness' sake bring my soul out of trouble.*

Psalms 86:2 *Preserve my soul; for I am holy: O thou my God, save thy servant that trusteth in thee. Amen.*

==

PART 9
MYSTERY OF BODY, SOUL AND SPIRIT

CHAPTER I **THE LIVING SOUL**

Isaiah 26:8 Yea, in the way of thy judgments, O LORD, have we waited for thee; **the desire of *our* soul *is* to thy name, and to the remembrance of thee.**

9 **With my soul have** I desired thee in the night; yea, **with my spirit within me** will I seek thee early: for when thy judgments *are* in the earth, the inhabitants of the world will learn righteousness.

A. BODY

Psalms 115:17 **The dead praise not the LORD, neither any that go down into silence.**

Romans 12:1 I beseech you therefore, brethren, by the mercies of God, that ye present your bodies a living sacrifice, holy, acceptable unto God, *which is* your reasonable service.

2 And be not conformed to this world: but be ye transformed by the renewing of your mind, that ye may prove what *is* that good, and acceptable, and perfect, will of God.

Psalm 104:29 Thou hidest thy face, they are troubled**: thou takest away their breath, they die, and return to their dust.**

DEATH LOST ALL MEMORIES UNDER THE SUN

Ecclesiastes 9:5 For **the living know that they shall die**; **but the dead know not anything**, neither have they anymore a reward; **for the memory of them is forgotten**.

6 **Also their love, and their hatred, and their envy, is now perished, neither have they anymore a portion for ever in anything that is under the sun.**

Psalms 88:10 Wilt thou shew wonders to the dead? Shall the dead arise *and* praise thee? Selah.

Job 14:20 Thou prevailest for ever against him, and **he passeth: thou changest his countenance, and sendest him away.**

21 His sons come to honour, and **he knoweth** *it* **not**; and they are brought low, **but he perceiveth** *it* **not of them.**
22 But **his flesh upon him** shall have pain, **and his soul within him** shall mourn.

SHADOW OF PHYSICAL DEATH

Job 38:17 (The Lord said), *Have the gates of death been opened unto thee? Or hast thou seen the doors of the shadow of death?*

Jeremiah 13:16 **Give glory to the LORD your God, before he cause darkness,** and before your feet stumble upon the dark mountains, and, while ye look for light, **he turn it into the shadow of death, and make it gross darkness.**
Job 14:10 **But man dieth, and wasteth away: yea, man giveth up the ghost and where is he?**

B. THE LIVING SOUL
Genesis 2:7 And **the LORD God formed** *man of the dust* **of the ground, and breathed into his nostrils** *the breathed of life*; **and man became a** *living soul.*
1Corinthians 15:45 And so it is written, **The** *first man* **Adam was made a living soul**; the *last Adam was made a quickening spirit.*
Romans 13:1 Let every soul be subject unto the higher powers. For there is no power but of God: the powers that be are ordained of God.
2 **Whosoever therefore resisteth the power, resisteth the ordinance of God**: and **they that resist shall receive to themselves damnation.**
Matthew 16:26 **For what is a man profited if he shall gain the whole world, and** *lose his own soul? Or what shall a man give in exchange of his soul*?

1. SAVING OF SOUL
Job 12:10 **In** whose hand is the soul of every living thing, and the breath of all mankind.
Psalms 62:1 (To the chief Musician, to Jeduthun, A Psalm of David.) Truly **my soul waiteth upon God: from him** *cometh* **my salvation.**

James 1:21 Wherefore lay apart all filthiness and superfluity of naughtiness, and receive with meekness the engrafted word, which is able **to save your souls**.

James 5:19 Brethren, if any of you do err from the truth, and **one convert him**;

20   Let him know, that he which converteth the sinner from the error of his way **shall save a soul from death**, and **shall hide a multitude of sins.**

Hebrews 10:39 But we are not of them who draw back unto perdition; but **of them that believe to the saving of the soul.**

ATONEMENT OF SOUL

Romans 7:22 *For I delight in the law of God after the inward man :*

a. ANCIENT PEOPLE: THROUGH THEIR FAITH
(See Volume 3, Part 16 Chapter I)

b. TIME OF MOSES AND BEFORE CHRIST: THROUGH THE BLOOD OFFERINGS

Leviticus 17:11 *For the life of the flesh is in the blood: and I have given it to you upon the altar to make an atonement for your souls: for it is the blood that maketh an atonement for the soul.*

Exodus 30:15 The rich shall not give more, and the poor shall not give less than half a shekel, when *they* give an offering unto the LORD, to make an atonement for your souls.

16 And thou shalt take the atonement money of the children of Israel, and shalt appoint it for the service of the tabernacle of the congregation; that it may be a memorial unto the children of Israel before the LORD, to make an atonement for your souls.

Numbers 15:28 And **the priest shall make an atonement for the soul that sinneth ignorantly,** when he sinneth by ignorance before the LORD, to make an atonement **for him; and it shall be forgiven him.**

Leviticus 4:26 And he shall burn all his fat upon the altar, as the fat of the sacrifice of peace offerings: and the priest shall make an atonement for him as concerning his sin, and it shall be forgiven him.

35 And he shall take away all the fat thereof, as the fat of the lamb is taken away from the sacrifice of the peace offerings; and the priest shall burn them upon the altar, according to the offerings made by fire unto the LORD: and the priest shall make anatonement for his sin that he hath committed, and it shall be forgiven him.

Leviticus 5:6 And he shall bring his trespass offering unto the LORD for his sin which he hath sinned, a female from the flock, a lamb or a kid of the goats, for a sin offering; and the priest shall make an atonement for him concerning his sin.

10 And he shall offer the second *for* a burnt offering, according to the manner: and the priest shall make an atonement for him for his sin which he hath sinned, and it shall be forgiven him.

13 And the priest shall make an atonement for him as touching his sin that he hath sinned in one of these, and it shall be forgiven him: and *the remnant* shall be the priest's, as a meat offering.

16 And he shall make amends for the harm that he hath done in the holy thing, and shall add the fifth part thereto, and give it unto the priest: and the priest shall make an atonement for him with the ram of the trespass offering, and it shall be forgiven him.

18 And he shall bring a ram without blemish out of the flock, with thy estimation, for a trespass offering, unto the priest: and the priest shall make an atonement for him concerning his ignorance wherein he erred and wist *it* not, and it shall be forgiven him.

Leviticus 6:7 And the priest shall make an atonement for him before the LORD: and it shall be forgiven him for any thing of all that he hath done in trespassing therein.

Leviticus 7:7 As the sin offering *is,* so *is* the trespass offering: *there is* one law for them: the priest that maketh atonement therewith shall have *it*

c. THROUGH THE BLOOD OF CHRIST

1Peter 4:6 **For for this cause was the gospel preached also to them that are dead**, that they might be judged according to men in the flesh, but live according to God in the spirit..

Galatians 3:22 But the scripture hath concluded all under sin, **that the promise by faith of Jesus Christ might be given to them that believe.**

2. PURIFICATION OF SOUL
1Peter 1:19 But **with the precious blood of Christ, as of a lamb without blemish and without spot:**
20 Who verily was foreordained before the foundation of the world, but was manifest in these last times for you,
21 Who by him do believe in God, that raised him up from the dead, and gave him glory; that your faith and hope might be in God.
22 **Seeing ye have purified your souls in obeying the truth through the Spirit unto unfeigned love of the brethren,** *see that ye* love one another with a pure heart fervently:

LIVING SOUL THAT LIVE BY FAITH
Hebrews 10:38 Now the just shall live by faith: but if *any man* draw back, my soul shall have no pleasure in him.
39 But we are not of them who draw back unto perdition; **but of them that believe to the saving of the soul.**

PEACEFUL LIVING
Jeremiah 6:16 Thus saith the LORD, Stand ye in the ways, and see, and ask for the old paths, where *is* the good way, and walk therein, and ye shall find rest for your souls. But they said, We will not walk *therein.*
Jeremiah 31:25 For I have satiated the weary soul, and I have replenished every sorrowful soul.
Isaiah 26:9 **With my soul have I desired thee in the night; yea, with my spirit within me will I seek thee early: for when thy judgments** *are* **in the earth, the inhabitants of the world will learn righteousness.**

GOD PRESERVES THEIR SOULS
Psalms 97:10 Ye that love the LORD, hate evil**: he preserveth the souls of his saints;** he delivereth them out of the hand of the wicked.

3. GOD CLAIMS THE SOUL OF HIS ELECT

Psalms 124:7 *Our soul is escaped as a bird out of the snare of the fowlers: the snare is broken, and we are escaped.*

Genesis 35:18 And it came to pass, as her soul was in departing, (for she died) that she called his name Benoni: but his father called him Benjamin.

19 And Rachel died, and was buried in the way to Ephrath, which *is* Bethlehem.

Ezekiel 18:4 **Behold all souls are mine** ; as the soul of the father, so also the soul of the son is mine: **the soul of the sinneth, it shall die.**

Matthew 22:37 Jesus said unto him, **Thou shalt love the Lord thy God with all thy heart, and with all thy soul, and with all thy mind**.

Psalms 119:167 My soul hath keep thy testimonies; and I love them exceedingly.

Psalms 119:129   PE. Thy testimonies *are* wonderful: therefore doth my soul keep them..

Psalms 119:175 **Let my soul live, and it shall praise thee**; and let thy judgments help me.

Psalms 130:6 My soul *waiteth* for the Lord more than they that watch for the morning: *I say, more than* they that watch for the morning.

Psalms 138:3 In the day when I cried thou answeredst me, *and* strengthenedst me *with* strength in my soul.

Psalms 30:3 O LORD, thou hast brought up my soul from the grave: thou hast kept me alive, that I should not go down to the pit.

Psalms 86:13 For great *is* thy mercy toward me: and thou hast delivered my soul from the lowest hell.

Psalms 56:13 For thou hast delivered my soul from death: *wilt* not *thou deliver* my feet from falling, that I may walk before God in the light of the living?

Ezekiel 33:5 He heard the sound of the trumpet, and took not warning; his blood shall be upon him. But he that taketh warning shall deliver his soul.

GOD WILL REDEEM THE SOUL FROM THE POWER OF GRAVE

James 1:21 Wherefore lay apart all filthiness and superfluity of naughtiness, and **receive with meekness the engrafted word, which is able to save your souls.**

Psalms 34:22   The LORD redeemeth the soul of his servants: and none of them that trust in him shall be desolate.

Psalms 49:15But God will redeem my soul from the power of the grave: for he shall receive me. Selah.

GOD SENT BACK THE SOUL OF THE DEAD CHILD

1Kings 17:17   And it came to pass after these things, *that* the son of the woman, the mistress of the house, fell sick; and his sickness was so sore, that there was no breath left in him.

18 And she said unto Elijah, What have I to do with thee, O thou man of God? art thou come unto me to call my sin to remembrance, and to slay my son?

19 And he said unto her, Give me thy son. And he took him out of her bosom, and carried him up into a loft, where he abode, and laid him upon his own bed.

20 And he cried unto the LORD, and said, O LORD my God, hast thou also brought evil upon the widow with whom I sojourn, by slaying her son?

21 And he stretched himself upon the child three times, and cried unto the LORD, and said, **O LORD my God, I pray thee, let this child's soul come into him again.**

22 **And the LORD heard the voice of Elijah; and the soul of the child came into him again, and he revived.**

23 And Elijah took the child, and brought him down out of the chamber into the house, and delivered him unto his mother: and Elijah said, See, thy son liveth.

24 And the woman said to Elijah, Now by this I know that thou *art* a man of God, *and* that the word of the LORD in thy mouth *is* truth.

4. RESURRECTION OF THE DEAD AFTER THE WRATH OF GOD

Job 14:12 So man lieth down, and riseth not: till the heavens *be* no more, they shall not awake, nor be raised out of their sleep.

13 O that thou wouldest hide me in the grave, that thou wouldest keep me secret, **until thy wrath be past, that thou wouldest appoint me a set time, and remember me!**

14 If a man die, shall he live *again*? **all the days of my appointed time will I wait, till my change come.**

15 Thou shalt call, and I will answer thee: thou wilt have a desire to the work of thine hands.

TROUBLED SOULS

JOB'S TRIBULATION AND SICKNESS
Job 14:22 **But his flesh upon him shall have pain**, and **his soul within him shall mourn.**

Job 10:1 My **soul is weary of my life**; I will leave my complaint upon myself I will speak in **the bitterness of my soul.**

MOSES WAS STRESSED OUT
Numbers 11:10 Then Moses heard the people weep throughout their families, every man in the door of his tent: and the anger of the LORD was kindled greatly; Moses also was displeased.

11 And Moses said unto the LORD, **Wherefore hast thou afflicted thy servant? and wherefore have I not found favour in thy sight, that thou layest the burden of all this people upon me?**

12 **Have I conceived all this people? have I begotten them, that thou shouldest say unto me, Carry them in thy bosom, as a nursing father beareth the sucking child, unto the land which thou swarest unto their fathers?**

13 Whence should I have flesh to give unto all this people? for they weep unto me, saying, Give us flesh, that we may eat.

14 **I am not able to bear all this people alone, because** *it is* **too heavy for me.**

15 And if thou deal thus with me, kill me, **I pray thee, out of hand, if I have found favour in thy sight; and let me not see my wretchedness.**

HANNAH'S PROBLEM
1Samuel 1:1 Now there was a certain man of Ramathaimzophim, of mount Ephraim, and his name *was* Elkanah, the son of

Jeroham, the son of Elihu, the son of Tohu, the son of Zuph, an Ephrathite:

2 And he had two wives; the name of the one *was* Hannah, and the name of the other Peninnah: and Peninnah had children, but Hannah had no children.

3 And this man went up out of his city yearly to worship and to sacrifice unto the LORD of hosts in Shiloh. And the two sons of Eli, Hophni and Phinehas, the priests of the LORD, *were* there.

4 And when the time was that Elkanah offered, he gave to Peninnah his wife, and to all her sons and her daughters, portions:

5 But unto Hannah he gave a worthy portion; for he loved Hannah: but **the LORD had shut up her womb.**

6 **And her adversary also provoked her sore, for to make her fret,** because the LORD had shut up her womb.

7 And *as* he did so year by year, when she went up to the house of the LORD, so she provoked her; therefore she wept, and did not eat.

1Samuel 1:10 And she *was* in bitterness of soul, and prayed unto the LORD, and wept sore.

11 And **she vowed a vow, and said**, *O LORD of hosts, if thou wilt indeed look on the affliction of thine handmaid, and remember me, and not forget thine handmaid*, **but wilt give unto thine handmaid a man child, then I will give him unto the LORD all the days of his life, and there shall no razor come upon his head.**

COME TO THE LORD ALL TROUBLED SOULS

Matthew 11:28 Come unto me, all ye that labour and are heavy laden, and **I will give you rest**.

29 Take my yoke upon you, and learn of me; for I am meek and lowly in heart: and ye shall find rest unto your souls.

30 For my yoke is easy, and my burden is light.

1Peter 4:19 **Wherefore let them that suffer according to the will of God commit the keeping of their souls** to him in well-doing, as unto a faithful Creator.

2Corinthians 1:3 Blessed *be* God, even the Father of our Lord Jesus Christ, the Father of mercies, and the God of all comfort;

4 **Who comforteth us in all our tribulation, that we may be able to comfort them which are in any trouble, by the comfort wherewith we ourselves are comforted of God.**

5 For as the sufferings of Christ abound in us, so our consolation also aboundeth by Christ.

6 And whether we be afflicted, *it is* for your consolation and salvation, which is effectual in the enduring of the same sufferings which we also suffer: or whether we be comforted, *it is* for your consolation and salvation.

7 And our hope of you *is* stedfast, knowing, that as ye are partakers of the sufferings, so *shall ye be* also of the consolation.

8 For we would not, brethren, have you ignorant of our trouble which came to us in Asia, that we were pressed out of measure, above strength, insomuch that we despaired even of life:

9 **But we had the sentence of death in ourselves, that we should not trust in ourselves, but in God which raiseth the dead:**

10 **Who delivered us from so great a death, and doth deliver: in whom we trust that he will yet deliver *us*;**

PRAYER OF THE TROUBLED SOUL

Psalm 88:1 (A Song *or* Psalm for the sons of Korah, to the chief Musician upon Mahalath Leannoth, Maschil of Heman the Ezrahite.)

O LORD God of my salvation, I have cried day and night before thee:

2 Let my prayer come before thee; incline thine ear unto my cry;

*3 For **my soul is full of troubles: and my life draweth nigh unto the grave.***

9 Mine eyes mourneth by reason of affliction: LORD, I have called daily upon thee, I have stretched out my hands unto thee.

14 LORD, Why castest thou off my soul? Why hidest thy face from me?

*Psalm 41:4 I said , **LORD, be merciful unto me: heal my soul; for I have sinned against thee.***

*Psalm 120:2 **Deliver my soul, O LORD from lying lips, and from deceitful tongue. Amen***

===

CHAPTER II **SPIRIT OF GOD IN MAN**

Ecclesiastes 12:7
Then shall the dust return to the earth as it was: and
the spirit shall return unto God who gave it.

GOD'S BREATH OF LIFE

Job 27:3 All the while my breath *is* in me, and **the spirit of God**
***is* in my nostrils**;

Job 33:4The Spirit of God hath made me, and **the breath of the**
Almighty hath given me life.

Isaiah 42:5 Thus saith God the LORD, he that created the
heavens, and stretched them out; he that spread forth the earth,
and that which cometh out of it; **he that giveth breath unto the**
people upon it, and spirit to them that walk therein:

Zechariah 12:1 The burden of the word of the LORD for Israel,
saith the LORD, which stretcheth forth the heavens, and layeth
the foundation of the earth, and **formeth the spirit of man within**
him

Job32:8 But there is a spirit in man: and the inspiration of the
Almighty giveth them understanding.

1Corinthians 2:11 For what man knoweth the things of a man,
save **the spirit of man which is in him?** even so the things of
God knoweth no man, but the Spirit of God.

12 **Now we have received**, not the spirit of the world, but **the**
spirit which is of God; that we might know the things that are
freely given to us of God.

THE SPIRIT OF LIFE LEFT

Ecclesiastes 8:8 *There is* **no man that hath power over the**
spirit to retain the spirit; neither *hath he* **power in the day of**
death: and *there is* no discharge in *that* war; neither shall
wickedness deliver those that are given to it.

Genesis 6:3 And the LORD said, My spirit shall not always strive with man, for that he also *is* **flesh: yet his days shall be an hundred and twenty years.**

Isaiah 29:10 For the LORD hath poured out upon you the spirit of deep sleep, and hath closed your eyes: the prophets and your rulers, the seers hath he covered.

Isaiah 40:6 The voice said, Cry. And he said, What shall I cry? All flesh *is* grass, and all the goodliness thereof *is* as the flower of the field:

7 The grass withereth, the flower fadeth: because the spirit of the LORD bloweth upon it: surely the people *is* grass.

Ecclesiastes 3:19 For that which befalleth the sons of men befalleth beasts; even one thing befalleth them: as the one dieth, so dieth the other; yea, **they have all one breath**; so that a man hath no preeminence above a beast: for all *is* vanity.

20 All go unto one place; all are of the dust, and all turn to dust again.

21 **Who knoweth the spirit of man that goeth upward, and the spirit of the beast that goeth downward to the earth?**

Psalms 146:4 **His breath goeth forth, he returneth to his earth; in that very day his thoughts perish.**

James 2:26 **For as the body without the spirit is dead, so faith without works is dead also.**

MAN SUCCUMB TO PHYSICAL DEATH

Ecclesiastes 9:12 **For man also knoweth not his time:** as the fishes that are taken in an evil net, and as the birds that are caught in the snare; **so** *are* **the sons of men snared in an evil time, when it falleth suddenly upon them.**

1. GIVING UP THE SPIRIT

Job 34:14 *If he set his heart upon man,* **if he gather unto himself his spirit and his breath;**
15 *All flesh shall perish together, and man shall turn again unto dust.*

Job 10:18 Wherefore then hast thou brought me forth out of the womb? **Oh that I had given up the ghost, and no eye had seen me!**

Genesis 25:8**Then Abraham gave up the ghost, and died** in a good old age, an old man, and full *of years*; and was gathered to his people.

Genesis 35:29 And **Isaac gave up the ghost**, and died, and was gathered unto his people, *being* old and full of days: and his sons Esau and Jacob buried him.

Psalms 104:29 Thou hidest thy face, they are troubled: **thou takest away their breath, they die**, and return to their dust.

a. LORD JESUS GAVE UP HIS SPIRIT

Matthew 27:45 Now from the sixth hour there was darkness over all the land unto the ninth hour.

46 And about the ninth hour Jesus cried with a loud voice, saying, **Eli, Eli, lama sabachthani?** that is to say, **My God, my God, why hast thou forsaken me**?

50 **Jesus** when he had cried again with a loud voice, **yielded up the ghost.**

John 19:30 When Jesus therefore had received the vinegar**, he said, It is finished: and he bowed his head, and gave up the ghost.**

b. STEPHEN THE MAN FULL OF FAITH

Acts 6:5 And the saying pleased the whole multitude: and **they chose Stephen, a man full of faith and of the Holy Ghost,** and Philip, and Prochorus, and Nicanor, and Timon, and Parmenas, and Nicolas a proselyte of Antioch:

8And Stephen, full of faith and power, did great wonders and miracles among the people.

9Then there arose certain of the synagogue, which is called *the synagogue* of the Libertines, and Cyrenians, and Alexandrians, and of them of Cilicia and of Asia, disputing with Stephen.

Acts 7:55 But **he, being full of the Holy Ghost**, looked up stedfastly into heaven, and saw the glory of God, and Jesus standing on the right hand of God,

56 And said, Behold, I see the heavens opened, and the Son of man standing on the right hand of God.

57 Then they cried out with a loud voice, and stopped their ears, and ran upon him with one accord,

58 And cast *him* out of the city, and stoned *him*: and the witnesses laid down their clothes at a young man's feet, whose name was Saul.

59 And they stoned Stephen, calling upon *God*, and saying, **LORD Jesus, receive my spirit**.

60 And he kneeled down, and cried with a loud voice, LORD, lay not this sin to their charge. And when he had said this, he fell asleep.

c. ALIVE AGAIN WHEN THE SPIRIT COMES BACK

Luke 8:41 And, behold, there came a man named Jairus, and he was a ruler of the synagogue: and he fell down at Jesus' feet, and besought him that he would come into his house:

42 For he had one only daughter, about twelve years of age, and she lay a dying. But as he went the people thronged him.

49 While he yet spake, there cometh one from the ruler of the synagogue's *house*, saying to him, Thy daughter is dead; trouble not the Master.

50 But when Jesus heard *it*, he answered him, saying, Fear not: believe only, and she shall be made whole.

51 And when he came into the house, he suffered no man to go in, save Peter, and James, and John, and the father and the mother of the maiden.

52 And all wept, and bewailed her: but he said, Weep not; she is not dead, but sleepeth.

53 And they laughed him to scorn, knowing that she was dead.

54 **And he put them all out, and took her by the hand, and called, saying, Maid, arise.**

55 **And her spirit came again, and she arose straightway:** and he commanded to give her meat.

Mark 5:22 And, behold, there cometh one of the rulers of the synagogue, Jairus by name; and when he saw him, he fell at his feet,

23 And besought him greatly, saying, My little daughter lieth at the point of death: *I pray thee*, come and lay thy hands on her, that she may be healed; and **she shall live**.

24 And *Jesus* went with him; and much people followed him, and thronged him.

35 While he yet spake, there came from the ruler of the synagogue's *house certain* which said, Thy daughter is dead: why troublest thou the Master any further?

36 As soon as Jesus heard the word that was spoken, he saith unto the ruler of the synagogue, Be not afraid, only believe.

37 And he suffered no man to follow him, save Peter, and James, and John the brother of James.

38 And he cometh to the house of the ruler of the synagogue, and seeth the tumult, and them that wept and wailed greatly.

39 And when he was come in, he saith unto them, Why make ye this ado, and weep? the damsel is not dead, but sleepeth.

40 And they laughed him to scorn. But when he had put them all out, he taketh the father and the mother of the damsel, and them that were with him, and entereth in where the damsel was lying.

41 And **he took the damsel by the hand, and said unto her, Talitha cumi; which is, being interpreted, Damsel, I say unto thee, arise.**

42 And straightway the damsel arose, and walked; for she was *of the age* of twelve years. And they were astonished with a great astonishment.

43 And he charged them straitly that no man should know it; and commanded that something should be given her to eat.

GOD WILL GIVE OR TAKE AWAY HIS SPIRIT UPON MAN

Numbers 11:16 And the LORD said unto Moses, Gather unto me seventy men of the elders of Israel, whom thou knowest to be the elders of the people, and officers over them; and bring them unto the tabernacle of the congregation, that they may stand there with thee.

17 And I will come down and talk with thee there: **and I will take of the spirit which *is* upon thee, and will put *it* upon them;** and they shall bear the burden of the people with thee, that thou bear *it* not thyself alone.

Numbers 11**:25** And **the LORD came down in a cloud**, and spake unto him, **and took of the spirit that *was* upon him, and gave *it* unto the seventy elders: and it came to pass, *that*, when the spirit rested upon them, they prophesied, and did not cease.**

THE SPIRIT OF GOD DWELLS IN THE ELECT

Numbers 14:24 But my servant **Caleb, because he had another spirit with him**, and hath followed me fully, him will I bring into the land whereinto he went; and his seed shall possess it.

Numbers 11:26 But there remained two *of the* men in the camp, the name of the one *was* Eldad, and the name of the other Medad:

and the spirit rested upon them; and they *were* of them that were written, but went not out unto the tabernacle: and they prophesied in the camp.

1Peter 4:14 **If ye be reproached for the name of Christ, happy** *are ye*; **for the spirit of glory and of God resteth upon you:** on their part he is evil spoken of, but on your part he is glorified.

1John 3:24 And **he that keepeth his commandments dwelleth in him, and he in him**. And hereby **we know that he abideth in us, by the Spirit which he hath given us.**

BROKEN SPIRIT

Proverbs 12:25 **Heaviness in the heart of man, maketh it stoop**: but a good word maketh it glad.

Proverbs 15:13 A merry heart maketh a cheerful countenance: but **by sorrow of the heart the spirit is broken.**

Proverbs 17:22 A merry heart doeth good like a medicine but **a broken spirit drieth the bones**.

VISION TROUBLED THE SPIRIT

Daniel 2:1 And in the second year of the reign of Nebuchadnezzar Nebuchadnezzar dreamed dreams, wherewith his spirit was troubled, and his sleep brake from him.

2 Then the king commanded to call the magicians, and the astrologers, and the sorcerers, and the Chaldeans, for to shew the king his dreams. So they came and stood before the king.

3 And the king said unto them, I have dreamed a dream, and my spirit was troubled to know the dream.

THE CANDLE OF GOD

Ephesians 3:16 **That he would grant you**, according to the riches of his glory, **to be strengthened with might by his Spirit in the inner man;**

Proverbs 20:27 **The spirit of man** *is* **the candle of the LORD, searching all the inward parts of the belly.**

1Peter 3:4 But *let it be* **the hidden man of the heart**, in that **which is not corruptible**, *even the ornament* of a meek and **quiet spirit, which is in the sight of God of great price**.

2Corinthians 4:16 For which cause we faint not; **but though our outward man perish, yet the inward** *man* **is renewed day by day.**

THE LORD WEIGHED THE SPIRITS.

Numbers 23:19 **God** *is* **not a man, that he should lie; neither the son of man, that he should repent:** hath he said, and shall he not do *it*? or hath he spoken, and shall he not make it good?

20 Behold, I have received *commandment* to bless: and he hath blessed; and **I cannot reverse it**.

Proverbs 16:2 All **the ways of man are clean in his own eyes; but the LORD weigheth the spirits.**

RECEIVING THE TRUTH

1Thessalonians 2:13 *For this cause also thank we God without ceasing, because,* **when ye received the word of God which ye heard of us, ye received it not as the word of men, but as it is in truth, the word of God, which effectually worketh also in you that believe. Amen**

===

===

BRINGING MANY SONS INTO GLORY

HOLY BIBLE STUDY RESOURCES
KJV BIBLE

VOLUME I **GOD PRESERVES HIS CHOSEN PEOPLE**
Subject Index

===

PART 1
GOD'S WORD TO ALL GENERATIONS

CHAPTER 1 **THE HOLY BIBLE WAS WRITTEN**
p 93-96

1Corinthians 10:11

THE HOLY SCRIPTURES: GOD IS THE AUTHOR
Isaiah 41:4; 1Corinthians 14:33; Deuteronomy 32:4

A.THE HOLY GHOST MOVED THE PROPHETS
Hebrews 1:1; 2Samuel 23:2; Ezekiel 2:1, 2; Ezekiel 3:10; Ezekiel 3:24 -27; 2Peter 1:21; Luke 1:70-75

*B. GOD INSTRUCTIONS TO THE PROPHETS

1. WRITE DOWN THE WORDS
Psalms 102:18; Jeremiah 36:2, 4; Habakkuk 2:2, 3; Isaiah 8:1; Isaiah 30:8

2. HEAR GOD'S INSTRUCTIONS
Deuteronomy 32:1, 2, 3; Proverbs 8:32-36

C. LORD JESUS WARNS NOT TO ALTER THE WORD OF GOD
Proverbs 30:6

1. BLASHPEMY AGAINST THE HOLY GHOST
Matthew 12:31, 32; Mark 3:29, 30

2. THE LORD SHALL BLOT OUT NAME FROM UNDER THE HEAVEN.
2Peter 1:20, 21; Exodus 32:33; Revelation 22:18-19; Deuteronomy 29:20

PART 1
GOD'S WORD TO ALL GENERATIONS

CHAPTER II **IMPORTANCE OF THE HOLY SCRIPTURES**
p97-104

Isaiah 55:11

A. GOD'S WORD IS WISDOM
Proverbs 2:10, 11; Proverbs 8:6-11

THE LORD GIVES WISDOM TO UNDERSTAND GOD'S WORD
Proverbs 2:6; Colossians 2:2, 3

WISDOM FROM ABOVE IS PURE AND PEACEFUL
Daniel 2:20; James 3:17

GOD GIVES WISDOM THAT REVEALS THE DEEP AND SECRET THINGS
Daniel 2:21-22

IF ANY ONE LACK WISDOM, LET HIM ASK GOD IN FAITH
Mark 9:23; Jeremiah 33:3; James 1:5, 6

PRAY FOR WISDOM AND UNDERSTANDING
Ephesians 1:17-20

DANIEL PRAISING GOD
Daniel 2:23

B.THE WORD OF GOD WILL LAST FOREVER

1. BREAD FROM HEAVEN
Matthew 4:4; John 6:32, 33

2. THE WORD OF GOD IS PURE
Proverbs 30:5; 2Samuel 22:31; Psalms 18:30; Psalms 12:6

3. THE WORD OF GOD IS TRUE FROM THE BEGINNING
John 17:17; Psalms 119:160; 1Thessalonians 2:13

4. THE WORD OF GOD SHALL NOT PASS AWAY
Luke 21:33, Isaiah 40:8 ; Isaiah 55:11

C.THE SCRIPTURES IS ALL ABOUT GOD
Revelation 1:8; Revelation 22:13

1. GOD GIVES HOPE AND MERCY
Romans 5:5; Romans 11:32; Romans 15:4

2. GOD GIVES EVERLASTING LIFE
John 4:14; Psalms 36:9

*D. FOR INSTRUCTION IN RIGHTEOUSNESS
2Timothy 3:16-17

E. GOD SHOWS ALL HIS WONDERFUL WORKS
Psalms 111:6; Psalms 111:4, 3; 1Samuel 2:2; Deuteronomy 32:4

F. THE PLAN OF GOD
Romans 16:26; Proverbs 2:8, 9; Psalms 102:26; Psalms 33:11;
Proverbs 19:21

REVELATION OF LORD JESUS CHRIST
Hebrews 10:7; Luke 24:27; Galatians 3:22; Romans 10:11; John 5:39; Acts 18:28

LEADS TO GOSPEL OF CHRIST
1Peter 1:25; 2Timothy 3:15; 1Thessalonians 1:5, 6

G. THE LORD'S REMINDER TO ALL GENERATIONS
Deuteronomy 32:5-7

1. GOD WILL ALWAYS HELP AND STRENGTHEN HIS CHILDREN
Psalms 127:1 -5; Isaiah 41:10, 11

2. COMING OF THE WRATH OF GOD
2Chronicles 34:21; 2Kings 22:13

ALL GENERATIONS MUST PRAISE GOD
Psalms145:4-13

PRAYER TO PRAISE GOD
 Psalms 145:1-3
==

PART 2
THE SCRIPTURES SPEAK ABOUT GOD'S PLAN

CHAPTER I GOD'S PLAN FOR HIS CHOSEN
p105-107

Ephesians 1:9, 10

SINGLE PLAN OF GOD FOR ALL HIS CHOSEN
Isaiah 64:4, 5; Romans 16:25, 26; 2Peter 3:7; Acts 17:31; Hebrews 9:26, 28

THE LORD GOD WILL LIVE AMONG HIS PEOPLE
1Kings 8:27; 2Chronicles 6:18

1. TABERNACLE OF THE CONGREGATION IN WILDERNESS
Leviticus 26:11, 12

2. THE LORD'STABERNACLE WILL BE IN MOUNT ZION
Psalms 15:1-5; Isaiah 16:5

ZION WILL BE THE HABITATION OF GOD
Psalms 132:11-18; Psalms 122:5

INHERITANCE OF THE SAINTS
James 2:5; 1Peter 1:4, 5

PRAYER PRAISING THE LORD'S FAITHFULNESS
Psalms 89:5, 6; Revelation 1:6

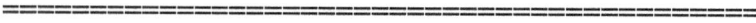

===

PART 2
THE SCRIPTURES SPEAK ABOUT GOD'S PLAN

CHAPTER II **IMPLEMENTATION OF GOD'S PLAN**
p108-113

A. GOD REVEALED HIMSELF
1John 5:7, 8, 6

THE MYSTERY OF GODLINESS
1Timothy 3:16; John 4:24; 2Corinthians 3:17; Ephesians 3:5

1. GOD IN HEAVENLY KINGDOM
Psalms 8:1; Isaiah 45:5, 6, 7; Exodus 3:14, 15; Exodus 6:3; Psalms 83:18; Isaiah 26:4; Isaiah 12:2; Genesis 22:14 ; Exodus 17:15, 16; Judges 6:24; Psalms 68:4; Psalms 113:4

CREATOR OF HEAVENS
Genesis 1:1, 8; Isaiah 50:3; Isaiah 48:13; Psalms 103:19; Job 26:9; Deuteronomy 10:14; Matthew 5:34

2. GOD'S WORD
John 1:1; 1 Peter 1: 20, 21; Proverbs 8:22-31

LORD JESUS THE WORD OF GOD
Hebrews 11:3; Colossians 1:15-17; John 1:3, 10-14

3 THE HOLY SPIRIT IS GOD'S BREATH
Psalms 33:6

CREATOR OF THE HOSTS OF HEAVEN
Job 26: 13; Psalm104: 4; Nehemiah 9:6; Isaiah 40:26; Jeremiah 33:22; 1Kings 22:19; Psalms 103:20-22

THE HOST OF HEAVEN WAS SEEN BY JACOB
Genesis 32:1-2

PRAYER PRAISING GOD FOR HIS WORKS IN ALL PLACES OF HIS DOMINION
Psalm 148:1, 2; Psalm 103:20-22

B. GOD THE CREATOR OF EARTH AND MAN
Psalm 115:15; Proverbs 3:19 ,20; Psalms 90:2; Isaiah 46:9-10; Zechariah 12:1

C.THE MIGHTY GOD
Deuteronomy 10:17

===

PART 2
THE SCRIPTURES SPEAK ABOUT GOD'S PLAN

CHAPTER III **MYSTERY OF GOD'S CREATION**
p114-126

Job 37:12; Psalms 19:1 -6

IN THE BEGINNING

1. CREATION OF EARTH
2Peter 3:5; Genesis 1:2; Jeremiah 51:15; Jeremiah 10:12 ; Psalms 115:15, Psalms 104:5, 6; Job 38:4 -7; Job 26:7-12

a. THROUGH GOD'S WORD EVERYTHING WAS CREATED
Psalms 33:9; Job 37:2 -5

FIRST DAY: THERE WAS LIGHT
Genesis 1:3-5; Job 38: 1, 12, 13, 24

SECOND DAY: A FIRMAMENT IN THE MIDST OF THE
WATERS
Genesis 1:6- 8; Jeremiah 51:16; Jeremiah 10:13; Psalms 147:8;
Job 37:6, 16, 17; Job 38:9 -10; Job 37:10,11; Psalms 147:16-18

THIRD DAY THE WATERS UNDER THE HEAVEN BE
GATHERED TOGETHER
Genesis 1:9; Job 38:11, 8; 2Samuel 22:16; Psalms 18:15;
Genesis1:10 ; Job 38:25-27; Genesis 1:11-13

FOURTH DAY: LIGHTS IN HEAVEN TO DIVIDE THE DAY
FROM THE NIGHT
 Genesis 1:14-19

THE STARS IN HEAVEN
Job 38:31-33

FIFTH DAY: WATERS BRING FORTH ABUNDANTLY THE
MOVING CREATURE AND FOWLS THAT FLY ABOVE
THE EARTH
Genesis 1:20-23

SIXTH DAY:GOD CREATED MAN IN HIS OWN IMAGE
AND FORMED EVERY BEAST OF THE FIELD
Genesis 1:27; Genesis 2:18 , 19; Genesis 1:24, 25; Genesis 1:31

SEVENTH DAY: GOD BLESSED THE SEVENTH DAY AND
RESTED
Genesis 2:1-3

b. GOD CREATED EARTH FOR THE CHILDREN OF MEN
Isaiah 45:18; Isaiah 48:13; Psalms 115:16

c. NO EARTHLY BEING COMES FROM HEAVEN EXCEPT THE SON OF MAN
Isaiah 45:12; John 3:13; John 3:31; Proverbs 30:4; Psalms 33:13-14

2. CREATION OF MAN
Genesis1:26

a. GOD GAVE US LIFE WHICH IS HIS SPIRIT OF LIFE
Genesis 2:7; Psalms 119:25; Job 33:4; Isaiah 42:5

b. MAN WAS FORMED FROM DUST
 Genesis 1:27; Psalm 33:15; Job 42:2; Psalm 103:14

3. THE WORKS OF GOD FOR HIS PEOPLE
(According to His Plan and Purpose)
 James 1:18; Job 35:11

a. MAN WAS CREATED IN GOD'S OWN IMAGE AND LIKENESS

1.GOD IS BEAUTIFUL
Psalms 27:4; Psalms 29:2; Psalm50:2; Psalms 90:17; Psalms 96:9; Isaiah 33:17; Psalms 104:1

GOD'S BEAUTY MANIFESTS IN HIS CREATION
Romans 1:19, 20

2.THE FIRST MAN WITH EVERLASTING LIFE
Genesis 2:16-17; Genesis 3:22

3.ADAM'S DOMINION OVER GOD'S CREATIONS
Genesis 1:26; Genesis 2:20

THE FIRST MAN UNDERSTAND AND COULD TALK WITH ANIMALS
Genesis 3:1-5

 b. GOD CREATED A WOMAN AS THE HELPER OF MAN
Genesis 2:21-24

GOD BLESSED THE FIRST MAN TO BE FRUITFUL
Genesis 1:28

c. GOD WAS VISIBLE AND COMMUNED WITH ADAM
AND EVE
Genesis 3:8, 9

d. LORD GOD THE PROVIDER
Psalms 103:13; Genesis 2:8; Genesis 2:9; Genesis 1:29 -30

GOD THAT MADE THE WORLD AND ALL THE THINGS
THEREIN
Acts 17:24-27

GOD'S LANGUAGE WAS THE ONLY LANGUAGE OF MEN
Genesis 11:1

PRAISING GOD FOR ALL HIS WONDERFUL CREATIONS
Psalms 148:1-6, Psalms 69:34; Psalms 104:24-31; Psalms 148:7-
    14

==

PART 2
THE SCRIPTURES SPEAK ABOUT GOD'S PLAN

CHAPTER IV **SEPARATION OF ANCIENT MEN FROM HIS CREATOR**
p127-134

Isaiah 40:22

*FIRST INSTRUCTION OF GOD
Genesis 2:16-17

A. DISOBEDIENCE OF THE FIRST MAN
Genesis 3:6-13

ADAM AND EVE WERE SENT OUT FROM THE GARDEN
OF EDEN
Genesis 3:22-24

*GOD'S INSTRUCTION TO NOAH
Genesis 9:4-6

B. AFTER NOAH'S FLOOD
Genesis 11:2 -4

C. THE LORD GOD IMPLEMENTED HIS POWER TO ALL
MEN

1. GOD CONFOUNDED THE LANGUAGE OF MAN
 Genesis 11:1, 5-7

2. GOD SCATTERED PEOPLE ABROAD UPON THE FACE
OF THE EARTH
 Genesis 11:8, 9; Genesis 10:5

GOD DIVIDED THE NATIONS IN THE DAYS OF PELEG
Genesis 10:1, 21-25; 1Chronicles 1:19

THE GENERATIONS OF SHEM
Genesis 11:10-19

3. GOD DIVIDED TO THE NATIONS THEIR INHERITANCE
Deuteronomy 32:8, 9; Acts 17:26-27; Genesis 10:32

ANCIENT KINGDOM OF MEN FROM NOAH'S SONS

a. THE SONS OF SHEM

KINGDOM OF ASSYRIA
Genesis 10:21, 22; Genesis 10:11, 12

KINGS IN THE LAND OF EDOM FROM THE SONS OF
ESAU
1Chronicles 1:34-50

DUKES OF EDOM
1Chronicles 1:51-54

b. THE SONS OF HAM

KINGDOM OF BABEL (Babylon)
Genesis 10:6-10

SODOM, AND GOMORRAH AND NATIONS OF CANAAN
Genesis 10:6, 13-19

PHILISTINES
1Chronicles 1:9-12

c. THE SONS OF JOPETH
Genesis 10:2-4

4. THE MOST HIGH GOD RULES OVER THE KINGDOMS
OF MEN
Daniel 4:17

KING SOLOMON
 1Chronicles 28:5, 6

KING NEBUCHADNEZAR OF BABYLON
 Daniel 4:25; Daniel 5:21
==

PART 3
GOD CALLED HIS PEOPLE

CHAPTER I GOD CHOSE HIS PEOPLE FROM THE BEGINNING
p 135-147

Ephesians 1:4-6

THE MYSTERY OF ADOPTION

A. NAMES WRITTEN IN HEAVEN
Hebrews 12:23-25; Isaiah 8:18

B. PREDESTINATED ACCORDING TO THE PURPOSE OF HIM
 Romans 9: 11; Matthew 20:16; Ephesians 1:11 ; Romans 8:28-30; 2Timothy 1:9,10; 2Thessalonians 2:13, 14; Ephesians 2:10

*GOD'S INSTRUCTION TO THE CHOSEN(NATION OF ISRAEL)
Exodus 19:5-6

GOD CHOSE THE PRINCES OF THE TRIBES OF ISRAEL
Numbers 1:16; Genesis 32:28; Ezekiel 34:24; 1Kings 11:34;

GOD CHOSE THE POOR AND FOOLISH THINGS OF THIS WORLD
 1Corinthians 1:26-30; James 2:5; 1Thessalonians 4:7

THE MYSTERY OF GOD'S MIND
 Isaiah 55:8 -9; Job 42:2

1. GOD IS THE POTTER, PEOPLE ARE CLAY
Isaiah 64:8; Jeremiah 18:4: 2Timothy 2:20, 21; Isaiah 45:9-11; Romans 9:18-24

GOD FASHIONED MAN FROM DUST
Job 10:8,9,11,12; Job 33:6; Job 12:10; Jeremiah 18:6; Isaiah 29:16

2. GOD KNOWS THE HEART OF PEOPLE
Proverbs 15:3; 1Samuel 16:7; Jeremiah 17:10; 1John 3:19-21; 1Kings 8:38-39

3 GOD KNOWS HIS CHOSEN
Psalms 100:3; Ezekiel 11:5 ;John 6: 64; Psalms 1:6; Psalms 37:18; Psalms 44:21; Psalms 94:11; Hebrews 4:13

a. INSIDE THE MOTHER'S WOMB
Psalms 139:13-16

1.GOD CHOSE ISAAC BEFORE HE WAS BORN
Genesis 17:19; Genesis 17:21

JACOB AND ESAU
Genesis 25:21-23

2.GOD CHOSE JACOB
Romans 9:13-17; Isaiah 44:2; Psalms 135:4; Isaiah 41:8,9

3.SAMSON
Judges 13:1-5

4. GOD CHOSE SOLOMON BEFORE HE WAS BORN
1Kings 8:16-20

b. NO ONE COULD ESCAPE FROM THE POWER OF GOD
 Jeremiah 23:23,24; ob 23:13 -14; Psalms 139:9-12; Job 34:16-29

c. GOD KNOWS THE THOUGHTS AND IMAGINATIONS OF
MAN
1Chronicles 28:9, Psalms 69:5

d. GOD KNOWS WHERE THE SOUL GOES AFTER DEATH
Psalms 139:7, 8

THE WHOLE DUTY OF MAN
 Ecclesiastes 12:13, 14

THE CHOSEN MUST ALWAYS READY TO MEET THE
LORD

PARABLES OF THE WISE AND FOOLISH VIRGINS
Matthew 25:1 -7

FOOLISH VIRGINS NOT ALLOWED TO BE WITH THE
BRIDEGROOM
Matthew 25:8-13

PEOPLE WILL PASSED AWAY LIKE GRASS
2Peter 3:8; Psalms 90:4-10; Psalms 103:15-16

REMEMBER THE CREATOR WHILE WE ARE YOUNG
Ecclesiastes 12:1-6

PRAYER TO THE ALL KNOWING GOD
Psalm 139:1-7

==

PART 3
GOD CALLED HIS PEOPLE

CHAPTER II **SEED**
p148-157

Acts 3:25

GOD CALLED HIS CHOSEN PEOPLE, SEED
Matthew 13:38, 39; Psalms 105:6; Numbers 23:21 ,23

GOD'S COVENANT TO ABRAHAM AND HIS SEED
Genesis 17:1-7,9

A. GOD GAVE THE PROMISE LAND TO ABRAHAM AND
HIS SEED
Genesis 15:18-21

GOD GAVE THE LAND OF CANAAN (ISRAEL) TO ISAAC
SEED
Genesis 17:8; Deuteronomy 34:4; Deuteronomy 1:8; Genesis
28:13; Genesis 13:15; Exodus 33:1; Genesis 35:12

THE CHOSEN PEOPLE

ISAAC THE PROMISE OF GOD WAS MADE
Genesis 26:24; Genesis 28:4; Genesis 21:12

1. THE SEED OF PROMISE FROM ISAAC
Isaiah 61:9; Joshua 24:3; Romans 9:7-10,12

NATION OF ISRAEL FROM JACOB'S SEED
Isaiah 46:3,4; Isaiah 44:1; Isaiah 41:8; Hosea 1:10;
Deuteronomy 7:6-8,10; 2Samuel 7:23,24; Deuteronomy 4:37,38;
Deuteronomy 10:15; 1Peter 2:9

THE LORD CAME FROM THE TRIBE OF JUDAH
Psalm 78:68; Hebrews 7:14; Isaiah 65:9

 GOD CHOSE DAVID TO BE THE KING OF ISRAEL
FOREVER (End times)
1Chronicles 28:4

THE FAMILY OF ISRAEL (GOD'S CHOSEN PEOPLE)
Romans 3:1-2; Genesis 28:1-4; Isaiah 45:4

a.JACOB'S TWO WIVES AND TWO HANDMAIDS
Genesis 29:16-31

b. TWELVE SONS OF JACOB (TWELVE TRIBES OF
ISRAEL)

.LEAH 'S FOUR SONS: REUBEN, SIMEON, LEVI AND
JUDAH
Genesis 29:32-35

BILHAH'S (RACHEL'S HANDMAID) TWO SONS: DAN,
AND NAPHTALI
Genesis 30:1-8

ZILPAH (LEAH'S HANDMAID) TWO SONS :GAD AND
ASHER
 Genesis 30:9 -13

LEAH'S OTHER TWO SONS AND A DAUGHTER:
ISSACHAR AND ZEBULON
Genesis 30:14-21

TWO SONS OF RACHEL(JOSEPH AND BENJAMIN)
Genesis 30:22 -24 ; Genesis 35:16-18

2. GENTILES THE OTHER CHOSEN
Acts 10:34-35

GENTILES THE WORSHIPERS OF IDOLS
1Corinthians 10:20; 1Corinthians 12:2; Ephesians 2:11-12

THE GENTILES WERE CALLED TO BECOME THE
CHILDREN OF GOD
 Romans 9:24-26; Genesis 22:18; Galatians 3:8
==

PART 3
GOD CALLED HIS PEOPLE

CHAPTER III **GOD REVEALED HIMSELF TO GENTILES**
p158-179
Psalms 33:12

GOD FREED HIS CHOSEN FROM BONDAGE

A. GOD SENT JOSEPH TO EGYPT(THE LAND OF HAM)
Psalm 105:16-22

B. GOD OF ISRAEL SENT MOSES TO PHARAOH
Psalms 105:23 -26; Exodus 7:1-7; Exodus 6:1, 10, 11;
Exodus 5:1-3

C. GOD SHOWED HIS POWER TO GENTILES
Acts 7:36; Jeremiah 32:20, 21; Deuteronomy 4:34; Deuteronomy
7:19; Deuteronomy 26:8; Deuteronomy 34:11, 12; Deuteronomy
6:22

THE LORD DID SIGNS AND WONDERS TO EGYPT
Psalms 105:27

1. TURNED THEIR WATERS INTO BLOOD
Psalms 105:29; Exodus 7:17-25

2. BROUGHT FORTH FROGS IN ABUNDANCE
Psalms 105:30; Exodus 8:1-14

3. THERE CAME DIVERS SORTS OF FLIES AND LICE
FROM DUST
Psalms 105:31; Exodus 8:16-20;Exodus 8:21-25

4. PLAGUE TO THE ANIMALS OF THE EGYPTIANS
Exodus 9:1-8

5. BOIL BREAKING FORTH WITH BLAINS UPON
EGYPTIANS.
Exodus 9:9-17

6. HAIL FOR RAIN, AND FLAMING FIRE IN THEIR LAND
Psalms 105:32; Exodus 9:22-34

7. THE LOCUSTS AND CATERPILLARS DEVOURED THE
KINGDOM'S FARM
Psalms 105:34, 35; Exodus 10:12-19

8. THREE DAYS OF THICK DARKNESS IN ALL THE LAND
OF EGYPT
Exodus 10:20 -29

9. THE LORD PASSOVER TO ALL THE FIRSTBORN OF
EGYPT
Psalms 105:36; Exodus 11:1-8; Exodus 12:1-13, 21-30

THE FEAST OF GOD'S PASSOVER THROUGH OUT ALL
GENERATIONS
Exodus 12:14-16

OBSERVANCE OF THE FIRST FEAST OF UNLEAVENED
BREAD
Exodus 12:17-20

10. THE RED SEA PARTED
Exodus 14:18; Exodus 14:4-17, 19-31

D. DANIEL UNDER BABYLONIAN CAPTIVITY

KING NEBUDCHANEZZAR'S DREAMS TROUBLED HIM
Daniel 2:1-6, 10-13

DANIEL PRAYED AND GAVE THANKS TO THE LORD
Daniel 2:17-23

GOD REVEALED SECRETS IN THE LATTER DAYS
Daniel 2:27-30

KING NEBUCHADNEZZAR'S DREAMS

1. THE GREAT IMAGE
Daniel 2:31-33

2. THE STONE CUT OUT WITHOUT HANDS
Daniel 2:34-35

DANIEL INTERPRETED THE DREAMS
Daniel 2:36 -43

THE COMING OF THE KINGDOM OF GOD IN THE NEW
EARTH
 Daniel 2:44, 45

E. SAUL/PAUL WAS CALLED TO MINISTER THE
GENTILES (After the Resurrection of the LORD Jesus)
Acts 22:21, 14-16

THE TESTIMONY OF PAUL

1. PAUL WAS NAMED SAUL OF TARSUS
Acts 22: 1-5

2. LORD JESUS BLINDED SAUL
 Acts 22:6 -13

SAUL BECAME THE APOSTLE OF CHRIST
1Timothy 1:12,13,15,16; 1Timothy 2:7, 8

PAUL'S TEACHING AGAINST IDOLATRY
Acts 17:22-31

PRAYER OF APOSTLE PAUL FOR THE GENTILES
BELIEVERS
Ephesians 3:14-21

PART 4
FIRST AGREEMENT TO THE NATION OF ISRAEL

CHAPTER I **THE ORDINANCES OF GOD**
p180-190

Nehemiah 9:13

GOD SHOWED HIS GLORY TO MOSES AND OTHERS
Exodus 24:9-18

GOD COMMANDED MOSES TO CUT TWO TABLES OF STONE
Psalms 94:12; Exodus 34:1 -10

THE FIRST BLOWING OF TRUMP

GOD WILL SHOW HIMSELF TO THE PEOPLE OF ISRAEL
Exodus 19:9

PEOPLE MUST SANCTIFY AND WEAR CLEAN CLOTHES BEFORE SEEING THE LORD
Exodus 19:10-17

THE LORD CAME DOWN TO GIVE HIS LAWS
Deuteronomy 33:2-4; Exodus 19:18-25; Exodus 20:18-21

THE ORDINANCES OF GOD
Deuteronomy 4:2; Deuteronomy 4:7-8: Deuteronomy 9:10; Deuteronomy 6:1

TEN COMMANDMENTS
First Commandment: THOU SHALT HAVE NONE OTHER gods BEFORE ME
Exodus 20:1-3; Deuteronomy 5:6-7

Second Commandment: THOU SHALT NOT BOW DOWN
AND SERVE THE IDOLS
Exodus 20:4-6; Deuteronomy 5:8-10

Third Commandment: THOU SHALT NOT TAKE THE NAME
OF THE LORD THY GOD IN VAIN
 Exodus 20:7; Deuteronomy 5:11

Fourth Commandment: KEEP THE SABBATH DAY
Deuteronomy 5:12-14; Exodus 20:8-11

Fifth Commandment: HONOUR THY FATHER AND THY
MOTHER
Deuteronomy 5:16; Exodus 20:12

Sixth Commandment: THOU SHALT NOT KILL
Deuteronomy 5:17; Exodus 20:13

Seventh Commandment: THOU SHALT NOT COMMIT
ADULTERY
Deuteronomy 5:18; Exodus 20:14

Eighth Commandment: THOU SHALT NOT STEAL
Deuteronomy 5:19; Exodus 20:15

Ninth Commandment: THOU SHALT NOT BEAR FALSE
WITNESS AGAINST THY NEIGHBOUR.
Deuteronomy 5:20; Exodus 20:16

Tenth Commandment: NEITHER SHALT THOU DESIRE THY
NEIGHBOR'S WIFE
Deuteronomy 5:21; Exodus 20:17

*GOD'S INSTRUCTIONS TO THE NATION OF ISRAEL
Deuteronomy 10:12, 13

1. KEEP THE COMMANDMENTS AND LAWS
Psalms 19:7; Proverbs 7:1-3; Deuteronomy 7:10, 11;
Deuteronomy 4:5,6

2. OBEY THE COMMANDMENTS
Psalms 19:8 ;Deuteronomy 5:32-33, Deuteronomy 6:2-6

3. THE PEOPLE MUST NOT MAKES IDOLS OF god
Exodus 20:22-23; Isaiah 42:5-8; Leviticus 26:1

4 DO NOT WORSHIP THE HOSTS OF HEAVEN AND ANY GRAVEN IMAGES
Deuteronomy 4:15-19; Deuteronomy 17:3, 4; Colossians 2:18

5. TEACH THE CHILDREN THE COMMANDMENTS AND FEAR OF THE LORD
Deuteronomy 31:12, 13; Deuteronomy 4:9-11;
Psalms 78:1-8; Deuteronomy 6:7-9

===

PART 4
FIRST AGREEMENT TO THE NATION OF ISRAEL

CHAPTER II FEASTS AND TRADITIONS
p 191-196

THE ARK OF THE COVENANT
Exodus 25:16-22

MOVING OUT OF THE ARK OF THE COVENANT
Numbers10:33-36

FEASTS OF THE LORD
Deuteronomy16:12; Leviticus 23:1-4

1. LORD'S PASSOVER
Leviticus 23:5; Exodus 13:3,4 ; Deuteronomy 16:1-11

2. FEAST OF TRUMPET
Leviticus 23:23 -25

3. DAY OF ATONEMENT (FORGIVENESS OF SIN)
Leviticus 23:27-32

4. FEAST OF DEDICATION
John 10:22

 5. FEASTS OF SHELTERS,"FEAST OF BOOTHS' OR FEAST OF TENTS
 Leviticus 23:42-44

6. FEAST OF PURIM
Esther 9:17-21

THE LORD COMMANDED HIS PEOPLE TO APPEAR BEFORE HIM
Deuteronomy16:16, 17

 7. FEAST OF UNLEAVENED BREAD
Leviticus 23:6-8

8. THE FEAST OF WEEKS OF THE FIRSTFRUITS OF WHEAT HARVEST
 Numbers 28:26; Exodus 23:16; Exodus 23:19; Exodus 34:22; Exodus 34:26

9. THE FEAST OF TABERNACLES
Leviticus 23:34-38; Deuteronomy 16:13-15; Leviticus 23:39-41
==

PART 4
FIRST AGREEMENT TO THE NATION OF ISRAEL

CHAPTER III **GOD CHOSE LEVITES TO BE THE PRIEST**
p197-211

AARON WAS THE HEAD OF THE HOUSE OF LEVI
Numbers 17:1 -11

AARON AND HIS SONS ANOINTED PRIESTS OF ISRAEL
Numbers 18:1-8; Deuteronomy 21:5

A. THE HIGH PRIEST AND PRIEST
Exodus 40:12-15; Exodus 40:27-32

GOD TOOK LEVITES TO DO THE SERVICE IN THE TABERNACLE
Numbers 8:13-19

THE MINISTER OF CONGREGATION
Numbers 8:23-26

THE HOLY GARMENT OF THE PRIEST
Leviticus 8:6-9, 12, 13

THE SHARE OF THE PRIEST
Leviticus 7:33

B.. RULES ABOUT TITHES
Leviticus 27:30-32; Deuteronomy 12:5-7; Deuteronomy14:22-29

TITHES BE GIVEN TO THE SONS OF LEVI
Hebrews 7:5; Deuteronomy 26:12, 13

FIRST TITHE
ABRAHAM TO THE HIGH PRIEST OF GOD
Hebrews 7:1-4

MELCHIZEDEK BLESSED ABRAM
Genesis 14:18-20

C. THE FIRSTFRUITS OFFERINGS OF ISRAEL TO THE LORD
Leviticus 23:10; Deuteronomy 26:1 -9; Leviticus 2:12-16; Numbers 18:12-14; Deuteronomy 26:10

GOD CLAIMED THE FIRSTBORN BOTH OF MAN AND OF BEAST
Exodus 13:2, 15; Numbers 18:15-19

PRAYER OFFERING THE FIRST FRUITS OF THE LAND
Deuteronomy 26:10

D. THE LORD COMMANDED ISRAEL TO MAKE THEIR OWN TRUMPETS
Numbers 10:1-3

*GOD'S INSTRUCTIONS IN BLOWING THE TRUMPET
Numbers 10:8

THE PURPOSE OF BLOWING THE TRUMPET
Nehemiah 4:20

1. JOURNEY FROM MOUNT SINAI
Numbers 10:4-7

2. IN THE DAY OF FEAST AND CELEBRATION
Numbers 10:10; Psalms 81:3

3. TO GO WAR WITHIN THE LAND OF ISRAEL
Numbers 10:9

*GOD'S .INSTRUCTIONS ABOUT THE FALL OF JERICHO
Joshua 6:2-10

THE BLOWING OF TRUMPETS

1. THE FALL OF JERICO
Joshua 6:11-21

2. THE TRUMPET SOUNDED FOR VICTORY AGAINST MOAB
Judges 3:27 -30

3. THE SPIRIT OF THE LORD CAME UPON GIDEON AGAINST MIDIANITES
Judges 6:33-35; Judges 7:16-25

4. VICTORY OF KING SAUL AND JONATHAN AGAINST PHILISTINES
1Samuel 13:3, 4

5. BLOWING THE TRUMPET STOP THE FIGHTS BETWEEN
PEOPLE OF ISRAEL AND JUDAH(After The Death Of King
Saul)
2samuel 2:10,12-28

6. THE PRIESTS AS WATCHMAN SHALL BLOW THE
TRUMPHET IN THE SECOND COMING OF CHRIST (Vol 3
Part 18 chapter VI)
==

PART 4
FIRST AGREEMENT TO THE NATION OF ISRAEL

CHAPTER IV **THE BLOOD COVENANT**
p212-224

Leviticus 4:20,

ATONEMENT OF SIN
Leviticus 4:5;1Chronicles6:49; 2Chronicles29:24: Leviticus 4:31

THE PLACE TO OFFER THE BURNT OFFERINGS
Deuteronomy 12:13, 14, 26

THE ALTAR
Exodus 20:24-26; Exodus 40:6, 7-11; Leviticus 8:10, 11

SPRINKLE THE BLOOD AROUND THE ALTAR
Leviticus 1:5; Leviticus 8:15; Leviticus 8:19;
Exodus 24:8;*Exodus 23:18; Exodus 34:25;
Leviticus 4:16, 18; Leviticus 4:6, 17; Leviticus 4:30; Leviticus 4:7
Exodus 24:6; Leviticus 1:11; Leviticus 1:15; Leviticus 3:2;
Leviticus 3:8; Leviticus 3:13; Leviticus 7:14

PREPARATION OF THE BURNT OFFERING
Leviticus 8:14-36

THE BURNT OFFERINGS
Leviticus 7:2; Deuteronomy15: 21 -23; Deuteronomy 12:27;
Leviticus 6:27; Deuteronomy 12:15, 16, 18, 19

MEAT OFFERINGS
Leviticus 2:1-4

1. BREAD OFFERINGS
Numbers 28:1-2; Leviticus 23:17; Leviticus 23:20

2. TWO LAMBS FOR CONTINUAL OFFERING
Numbers 28:3-8

3. SABBATH OFFERINGS
Numbers 28:9-10

4 BEGINNING OF MONTH'S OFFERING
Numbers 28:11-14

5. SIN OFFERING (ATONEMENT)
Leviticus 5:9; Numbers 28:15, 22, 23; Leviticus 6:30; Leviticus 4:25; Leviticus 4:34

6. PASSOVER OFFERING
Numbers 28:16-21

7. SEVENTH MONTH ON THE FIRST DAY OFFERING
Numbers 29:1-6

8. TENTH DAY OF THIS SEVENTH MONTH HOLY CONVOCATION
Numbers 29:7-11

9. FIFTEENTH DAY OF THE SEVENTH MONTH
 First Day, Numbers 29:12-16
Second Day, Numbers 29:17-19

 Third Day, Numbers 29:20-22

 Fourth Day, Numbers 29:23-25

Fifth Day , Numbers 29:26-28

 Sixth Day, Numbers 29:29-31

Seventh Day, Numbers 29:32-34
Eight Day, Number 29:35 -39

OFFERINGS FOR DEFILING THE LAW
1. SINNED BY THE DEAD
Numbers 6:9-11

2. LAW OF SEPERATION DEFILED
Numbers 6:12, 13

3. PEACE OFFERINGS
Numbers 6:14-21

===

PART 4
FIRST AGREEMENT TO THE NATION OF ISRAEL

CHAPTER V **THE LAW OF SABBATH**
p225-229

Psalms 19:7;Psalm 119:1,2

*GOD'S INSTRUCTIONS
Deuteronomy 11:16 Leviticus 26;2

THE LAW OF SABBATH GIVEN TO NATION OF ISRAEL
Exodus 31:13; Exodus 31:16; Deuteronomy 5:15; Leviticus 24:8

DAYS OF SABBATH HOLY CONVOCATION
Leviticus 23:24; Leviticus 23:32; Leviticus 23:39; Leviticus 25:4;
Leviticus 25:8-9

IMPLEMENTING THE LAW OF SABBATH
Exodus 20:11

1. KEEP IT HOLY
Exodus 20:8; Leviticus 19:30; Leviticus 26:2

2. NO WORK FOR EVERYBODY
Exodus 20:10; Leviticus 23:3; Deuteronomy 5:14

3. BAKE FOOD BEFORE THE DAY OF SABBATH
Exodus 16:23

4. NO MAN GO OUT OF HIS PLACE ON SABBATH
Exodus 16:29

5. NO KINDLING OF FIRE IN THE DAY OF SABBATH
Exodus 35:3

6. OBSERVE SABBATH IN THE PROMISE LAND
Leviticus 25:2; Leviticus 25:6

7. THE EAST GATE OF THE INNER COURT WILL BE
OPENED ON SABBATH
Ezekiel 46:1, 3

8. THE PRINCE PART TO GIVE THE BURNT OFFERINGS
DURING SABBATH
Ezekiel 45:17; Ezekiel 46:4; Ezekiel 46:12

GOD WILL BLESS THOSE WHO KEEP THE SABBATH
Isaiah 56:1-7

 PUNISHMENT TO ISRAELITES WHO VIOLATES THE
SABBATH

1. PUT TO DEATH
Exodus 31:14, 15; Exodus 35:2

2. AFFLICT THE SOUL
Leviticus 16:31

==

PART 4
THE FIRST AGREEMENT TO THE NATION OF ISRAEL

CHAPTER VI **OTHER LAWS FOR SANCTIFICATION**
p230-234

A. DO NOT EAT BLOOD
Deuteronomy 12:23-25; Leviticus 7:26; Leviticus 3:17; Leviticus 7:27

B. MEAT THAT CAN BE EATEN
Deuteronomy 14:4-6

ANIMALS WHICH THE ISRAELITES NOT ALLOW TO EAT
Deuteronomy 14:3, 7-10- 21

C. LAW OF NAZARITE
Numbers 6:1-8

D. LAWS ABOUT THE GENTILES
Deuteronomy 23:3, 4, 7,8

E.MAKE THE CAMP OF THE CHOSEN HOLY
Deuteronomy 23:14-18; Deuteronomy 23:1,2

F. THE LAW OF MARRYING THE WIDOW
Deuteronomy 25:4-12

G. NOT ALLOWED TO CUT HAIR FOR THE DEAD
Deuteronomy 14:1

H. LAW OF PUNISHMENT FOR THE WICKED
Deuteronomy 25:1 -3

I. DIVORCE
Leviticus 22:13; Deuteronomy 24:1-5

==

PART 4
THE FIRST AGREEMENT TO THE NATION OF ISRAEL

CHAPTER VII **GOD'S ECONOMY**
p235-241

*GOD'S INSTRUCTIONS

A. TAKING CARE OF ANIMALS
Leviticus 19:19

B. THE LEND UPON USURY
Deuteronomy 23:19-23; Leviticus 25:36, 37

C. RULES ABOUT GATHERING THE NEIGHBORS CROPS
Deuteronomy 23:24, 25

D. THE SEVENTH YEAR THE YEAR OF RELEASE
Deuteronomy 15:10, 15; Deuteronomy 15:4, 1-3, 9-14

E. THE SEVENTH YEAR: THE SABBATH OF REST
Leviticus 25:1-7

BLESSING COMES IN THE SIXTH YEAR
Leviticus 25:20-22

F. YEAR OF JUBILE
Leviticus 25:17, 23, 8-16

REDEMPTION OF POSSESSION
Leviticus 25:24-38

NEVER FORCE THE POOR BROTHER TO BECOME YOUR
SLAVE
Leviticus 25:55; Leviticus 25:39-44

REDEEMING CHILDREN OF THE STRANGERS
Leviticus 25:45-54

MOSES WROTE THE WORDS AND LAW OF THE
COVENANT
Exodus 34:27-35; Deuteronomy 31:9-11

===

PART 5
TEST OF FAITH

CHAPTER I **JOB'S SUFFERINGS**
p242-248

JOB'S LIFE BEFORE GOD CALLED HIM
Job 29:5-12

GOD GAVE JOB WISDOM AND UNDERSTANDING
Proverbs 3:13; Job 29:4; Job 27:3, 4, 6; Job 29:13-16;
Job 28:12, 13, 28

JOB WAS BLESSED WITH PROVISIONS AND CHILDREN
Job 1:1-3

SATAN BROUGHT TRAGEDIES TO JOB (See Workings of
Satan to Job Volume 2 Part 14 Chapter I)
Job 1:13-22

 JOB GOT SICKNESS
Job 2:9, 10; Job 30:17-19 , 30

THREE FRIENDS OF JOB CONDEMNED HIM
Job 2:11-13; Job 3:1, 25, 26

1. ELIPHAZ THE TEMANITE
Job 4:1, 8, 9

2. BILDAD THE SHUHITE
Job 8:1, 3, 4,13, 20, 22

3. ZOPHAR THE NAAMATHITE
Job 11:1-5; Job11:11, 13, 14, 20

JOB'S OWN RIGHTEOUSNESS
Job34:4-6

GOD'S WRATH AGAINST PERSON WITH A PROUD
HEART
Job 40:10-14

ELIHU WITNESSED THE EXCHANGED BETWEEN JOB
AND HIS FRIENDS
Job 32:2, 3

JOB REPENTED
Job 42:1-6

THE LORD BLESSED JOB TWICE AS MUCH AS HE HAD
BEFORE.
Job 42:7 -17

ELIHU WROTE DOWN THE BOOK OF JOB
Job 32:15-17; Job 19:23; Job 31:35-37
==

PART 5
TEST OF FAITH

CHAPTER II **A BLESSING OR A CURSE**
p249-268
Deuteronomy 30:19

OBEDIENCE TO ESTABLISH HIS COVENANT TO ISRAEL
Leviticus 25:18; Leviticus 26:9-13; Deuteronomy 30:20; Isaiah
1:19; Deuteronomy 7:11-12 ; Deuteronomy 12:28;
1Kings 2:3

.*GOD'S INSTRUCTIONS UPON REACHING CANAAN
Deuteronomy 12:32; Deuteronomy 14:2; Deuteronomy 12:29-31

1. DESTROY THOSE SEVEN NATIONS
Deuteronomy 9:5; Deuteronomy 7:1-2; Psalms 78:54-55

2. NEVER MARRY SONS AND DAUGHTERS OF OTHER
NATIONS
Deuteronomy 7:3-4

3. DON'T MAKE MOLTEN gods
Exodus 34:15-17

4. DON'T OFFER THE SON OR DAUGHTER AS SACRIFICE
TO FALSE god
Deuteronomy 12:31; Deuteronomy 18:10

5. DON'T TALK TO THE SPIRIT OF THE DEAD AND TO CONSULT WIZARD
Deuteronomy 18:11

6. DESTROY THE IDOLS IN THE LAND
Exodus 34:11 -13; Deuteronomy 12:1-3; Deuteronomy 7:5; 2 Kings 23:4

7. ISRAEL NOT ALLOWED TO ATTEND BURIAL OF THE OTHER NATIONS
Isaiah 14:20

TWO CHOICES FOR THE CHOSEN
Deuteronomy 11:26-28

A. BLESSINGS TO ISRAEL UPON OBEDIENCE TO THE LAWS
Deuteronomy 28:2

1. PROSPERITY TO THE FAMILY OF ISRAEL
Deuteronomy 29:9; Deuteronomy 7:13; Deuteronomy 28:8, 12; Deuteronomy 28:5; ; Leviticus 26:3 -5

2. GOD WILL BLESS ISRAEL WITH GOOD HEALTH
Deuteronomy 7:14; Deuteronomy 28:3, 4, 6

3. NO ENEMY COULD HARM THEM
Deuteronomy7:15; Deuteronomy 28:7; Exodus 23:22, 23; Leviticus 26:6 -8

FEAR NOT THE REPROACH OF MEN
Isaiah 51:7

SALVATION WILL CONTINUE FOREVER
Isaiah 51:8

GOD IS IN CONTROL
Isaiah 51:13

GOD WILL GIVE COMFORT
Isaiah 51:12

GOD WILL COVER THE CHOSEN
Psalms 105:7 -15; 1Chronicles 16:16 -22

4. THE BLESSING OF LONG LIFE AND PEACE
Proverbs 3:1-7

LENGTHEN THE DAYS OF LIFE OF THE ELECT AND
OFFSPRING
1Kings 3:14; Deuteronomy 4:40; Deuteronomy 6:2, 3

5. THE LORD WILL ESTABLISH ISRAEL AS A HOLY
NATION
Deuteronomy 28:13, 14; Deuteronomy 26:16-19; Deuteronomy
28:1; Deuteronomy 28:9-10

GOD BLESSED ISRAEL
Number 6:22-27

MOSES BLESSED ISRAEL BEFORE HIS DEATH
Deuteronomy33:1-29

B. CURSES DUE TO DISOBEDIENCE
Exodus 34:7

1. POVERTY AND PESTILENCE TO THE HERDS AND
PLANTS
Deuteronomy 28:15-21

2. ISRAEL WILL SUFFER FROM SICKNESS
Deuteronomy 28:22-30

3. THE ENEMIES WILL COME TO DESTROY ISRAEL
Deuteronomy 28:31-37

4. POVERTY WILL NEVER LEFT THEM
Deuteronomy 28:38-48

5. OTHER NATIONS WILL BRING THEM INTO CAPTIVITY
Deuteronomy 28:49 -57

6. ISRAEL WILL SUFFER PLAGUES FROM THE LORD
Deuteronomy 28:58-63

7. ISRAEL WILL LIVE WITH WORRIES AND A
TREMBLING HEART
Deuteronomy 28:64-68

8. WRATH OF GOD WILL COME TO PEOPLE OF
DISOBEDIENCE
2Chronicles 34:21; 2Kings 22:13

JUDGMENT TO ISRAEL UPON BREAKING THE
COVENANT
Leviticus 26:15

1. WILL BREAK THE PRIDE OF THEIR POWER
Leviticus 26:16 -24

2. PESTILENCE WILL COME AND BE DELIVERED IN THE
HAND OF THEIR ENEMIES
Leviticus 26:25-40

3. ISRAEL WILL BE BROUGHT TO THE LAND OF THEIR
ENEMIES
Leviticus 26:41 -46

THE ELECT BLESSED THE LORD
1Chronicles 29:10-13
==

PART 6
GOD ANOINTED DELIVERERS

CHAPTER I **TO PRESERVE GOD'S CHOSEN**
p269-283

A. GOD WOULD NOT LIKE HIS PEOPLE TO PERISH

JONAH WAS SENT TO NINEVEH (GENTILES)
Jonah 3:1-9

GOD SHOWED HIS REASON TO JONAH
Jonah 3:10; Jonah 4:1-11

B. GOD'S ELECT WILL INHERIT THE LAND OF ISRAEL
Isaiah 65:9

C. GOD ANOINTED DELIVERERS OF ISRAEL

1. MOSES AGAINST AMALEK
Exodus 17:8-16

MOSES' VICTORIES AGAINST THE KINGS OF HESHBON
AND BASHAN
Deuteronomy 29:2-8

MOSES LAID HAND ON JOSHUA TO TAKE CHARGE
Numbers 27:18-23; Deuteronomy 3:28; Deuteronomy 34:9

2. JOSHUA, THE SON OF NUN
Joshua 1:5

LED THE ISRAELITES INTO THE PROMISE LAND
(CANAAN)
Joshua 1:1-9

GOD WAS WITH JOSHUA THE ELECT

a. JORDAN RIVER DRIED UP
Joshua 3:7-17

TWELVE STONES FOR THE MEMORIAL IN JORDAN
Joshua 4:1-9;20

b. GOD WAS WITH JOSHUA IN JERICHO

RAHAB HID THE MESSENGERS OF ISRAEL
Joshua 2:1-24

RAHAB AND HER FAMILY WERE SPARED IN THE FALL
OF JERICHO
Joshua 6:6-10; Joshua 6:22-27

c. GOD FOUGHT FOR ISRAEL AGAINST FIVE KINGS
Joshua 10:5-14 ,16-20 ,22-29;39-42

D. ESTHER WAS DESTINED TO SAVE THE LIVES OF JEWS
Esther 2:5-7,15-17

THE KING ORDERED TO KILL ALL THE JEWS IN ONE
DAY
Esther 3:13 -14, Esther 4:1-12

MORDECAI ASKED ESTHER FOR THE DELIVERANCE OF
ALL THE JEWS
 Ester 4:13-17

ESTHER EXPOSED THE EVIL PLAN OF HAMAN
Esther 7:2-10

==

PART 6
GOD ANOINTED DELIVERERS

CHAPTER II **THE JUDGES**
p284-301

Judges 2:18

NATIONS WITHIN THE PROMISE LAND
Judges 2:22; Judges 2:21, 23; Judges 3:1-5; Acts 13:19

ISRAEL CRIED FOR GOD'S HELP
Judges 3:9; Acts 13:20; Judges 2:16, 17, 19

THE JUDGES OF ISRAEL
2 Samuel 7:10, 11

1. OTHNIEL AGAINST THE KING OF MESPOTAMIA
Judges 3:10, 11
2. EHUD AGAINST THE KING OF MOAB
Judges 3:12-30

3. SHAMGAR AGAINST PHILISTINES
Judges 3: 31

4. DEBORAH AGAINST CAPTAIN SISERA OF THE
CANAANITES
Judges 4:1-24

5. GIDEON AGAINST MIDIAN
Judges 6:1-7

THE ANGEL OF THE LORD APPEARED TO GIDEON
Judges 6:11-22

THE LORD'S MESSAGE TO GIDEON
Judges 6:23-35

GIDEON PRAYED FOR SIGNS TO WIN THE WAR
Judges 6:37-40

GOD'S INSTRUCTION IN CHOOSING THE RIGHT MEN
Judges 7:4-7

GIDEON DELIVERED ISRAEL AGAINST MIDIANITES
Judges 8:28

AFTER GIDEON'S DEATH
Judges 8:32-35

6. TOLA
Judges 10:1, 2

7. JAIR
Judges 10:3-18

8. SAMSON, THE NAZARITE AGAINST PHILISTINES

SAMSON MARRIED A PHILISTINE WOMAN
Judges 14:1-11
SAMSON'S RIDDLES FOR THE THIRTY PHILISTINES
Judges 14:12-17

SAMSON' KILLED THE THIRTY PHILISTINES FROM
ASHKELON
Judges 14:18-20

SAMSON BURNED THE CORN FIELDS OF THE
PHILISTINES
Judges 15:1-5

SAMSON KILLED A THOUSAND PHILISTINES
Judges 15:6-20

SAMSON LOVED DELILAH
Judges 16:4, 5

DELILAH ASKED SAMSON ABOUT THE SOURCE OF HIS
STRENGTH
Judges 16:6

SAMSON MADE HIS STORY THREE TIMES
1. Judges 16:7
2. Judges 16:11
3. Judges 16:13, 14

FINALLY SAMSON TOLD DELILAH HIS SECRET
Judges 16:15 -17

DELILAH SOLD SAMSON TO THE PHILISTINES
Judges 16:18-21

THE PHILISTINES THANKS DAGON THEIR god
Judges 16:22-27

SAMSON PRAYED TO THE LORD HIS GOD
Judges 16:28-31

9. SAMUEL: THE JUDGE AND THE PROPHET

GOD SAVED THE ISRAELITES FROM THE PHILISTINES
1Samuel 7:3 -15

===

PART 6
GOD ANNOINTED DELIVERERS

CHAPTER III **KINGS OF ISRAEL**
p302-314

1Samuel 8:7, 8

NATION OF ISRAEL ASKED FOR THEIR KING
1Samuel 8:1-6

THE KING WILL RULE OVER GOD'S PEOPLE
1Samuel 8:9-18

PEOPLE STILL INSISTED TO HAVE A KING
1Samuel 8:19-22

KINGS MUST RULE IN THE FEAR OF GOD
 2Samuel 23:3 -5

THE FIRST FOUR KINGS OF ISRAEL

1. SAUL
1Samuel 9:1, 2, 15-17

 2. DAVID
1Samuel 17:12 -28

GOLIATH THE PHILISTINE
1Samuel 17:2-11

YOUNG DAVID KILLED GOLIATH
 1Samuel 17:42-51

KING DAVID
Psalms 78:70; 2Samuel 6:21; 1Chronicles 28:4

 3. SOLOMON
 1Chronicles 28:5-7,9

4. REHOBOAM SON OF SOLOMON
1Kings 12:1

THE LORD CAUSED REHOBOAM TO HARDENED AGAINST THE CONGREGATION OF ISRAEL
1 Kings 11:26; 1Kings 12:2-16

ISRAEL REBELLED AGAINST THE HOUSE OF DAVID
1Kings 12:17-19

KINGDOM OF ISRAEL WAS DIVIDED
1Kings 12:20, 21

THE LORD INTERFERED REHOBOAM'S PLAN TO FIGHT WITH ISRAEL
1Kings12:22-24

KINGDOM OF ISRAEL SINNED AGAINST GOD
1Kings 12:25-33

WARNING TO KING JEROBOAM OF ISRAEL
1Kings 14:7 -10

BOOK OF RECORDS OF JUDAH AND ISRAEL

1. BOOK OF THE LAW/ BOOK OF THE COVENANT/ BOOK OF MOSES
Deuteronomy 29:29; Deuteronomy 31:24; Exodus 24:7; Joshua 8:33-35; Jusuah24:26; Deuteronomy 29:27; Joshua 23:6; 2Chronicles 34:15; Deuteronomy 31:26; Nehemiah 13:1, 2; Joshua 1:8

2. BOOK OF THE RECORDS
Ezra 4:15

3. BOOK OF WARS OF THE LORD
Numbers 21:14

4. BOOK OF THE CHRONICLES OF THE KINGS OF JUDAH AND ISRAEL
2Chronicles 16:11; 2Chronicles 35:27; 1Kings 14:29

5. BOOK OF JASPHER
Joshua 10:13, 14; 2Samuel 1:18

6. BOOK OF JEREMIAH
Jeremiah 51:60-64

7. BOOK OF ACTS OF SOLOMON
1Kings 11:41
===

PART 6
GOD ANOINTED DELIVERERS

CHAPTER IV **GOD REVEALED HIS PLAN TO HIS PROPHETS**
p315-336

2Chronicles 24:19; 1Corinthians 14:3

THE LORD GOD AND HIS SPIRIT SENT THE PROPHETS
Isaiah 48:16

GOD GIVES INSTRUCTONS IN A DREAM AND VISION
Numbers12:6; Amos 3:7; Job 33:14-17; Hosea 12:10

PROPHET WILL SPEAK IN THE NAME OF THE LORD
Deuteronomy18:15, 18, 19; 1Samuel 9:9

A. ANCIENT PROPHECY OF THE WRATH OF GOD

THE COMING OF GREAT FLOOD

1. GIANTS WERE ON EARTH
Genesis 6:1, 2, 4

2. HUMAN BEINGS WERE WICKED
Genesis 6:5-7

3. *GOD'S INSTRUCTION TO NOAH
Genesis 6:8, 12-22; Genesis 7:1-6

GOD'S COVENANT TO NOAH
Genesis 9:1-17

NOAH'S FAMILY HISTORY
Genesis 5:1-32; Genesis 9:28,29

B. WISDOM TO INTERPRET DREAMS
THE TWO DREAMS OF THE KING OF EGYPT
Genesis 41:32

1. THE SEVEN LEAN AND ILL KINE DEVOURED THE
SEVEN FAT KINE
Genesis 41:17 -21

2. THE SEVEN THIN EARS OF CORN DEVOURED THE
SEVEN GOOD EARS OF CORN
Genesis 41:22-24

JOSEPH THE SON OF JACOB INTERPRETED THE DREAMS
 Genesis 41:25-31

C. VISION OF END TIMES

DANIEL

1. FOUR GREAT BEASTS
Daniel 7:1-8

DANIEL'S INTERPRETATION (END TIMES PROPHESY)

FOUR KINGS OF THE FOUR KINGDOMS
Daniel 7:16- 20

TRIBULATION PERIOD OF THE SAINTS
Daniel 8:24, 25; Daniel 7:21, 23-25

2. DANIEL'S VISIONS OF HORNS DURING BABYLONIAN
CAPTIVITY
Daniel 8:1-14

INTERPRETATION OF HORNS (KINGDOMS UP TO END TIMES)
Daniel 8:15-23

3. APOSTLE JOHN'S REVELATION

THE BEAST
Revelation 13:1

D. PROPHECIES
 1. David

PRAYER OF THE LORD IN HIS SUFFERINGS
Psalm 69:1-9, 13, 16, 17, 19-21, 29

END TIMES PROPHECY : NATIONS AGAINST THE LORD
Acts 4:25-26; Psalms 2: 2-4

2. ELIJAH
PROPHESY: YEARS WITHOUT RAIN IN THE LAND
1Kings 16:29-33; 1King 17:1-7

3. AHAIJAH

PROPHESY: KINGDOM OF ISRAEL WILL BE DIVIDED
1Kings 11:29-36

4. JEREMIAH

KINGDOM OF JUDAH WILL BE UNDER SIEGE BY BABYLON
Jeremiah 29:10

5. EZEKIEL

BABYLONIANS WILL INVADE THE KINGDOM OF JUDAH
 Ezekiel 5:7-17; Ezekiel 14:21-23

END TIME PROPHECIES

1. HAGGAI

THE COMING OF THE LORD OF HOSTS
Haggai 1:1-8: Haggai 2:6 -9, 22

2. ISAIAH PROPHECIES
Isaiah 1:1-4

a. THE COMING OF THE REDEEMER OF ISRAEL (See Volume 2, Part 10 Chapter II)
Isaiah 11:1; Isaiah 54:5; Isaiah 53:11; Isaiah 7:14

b. THE HERITAGE OF THE NATION OF ISRAEL
Isaiah 54:17

c. PUNISHMENT TO CHOSEN WHO DESPISED THE WORD OF GOD
Isaiah 5:1, 2, 5, 7, 11, 12; Isaiah 5:20-24

3. .JEREMIAH

THE COMING BACK OF THE PEOPLE OF ISRAEL
Jeremiah 31:8, 9

4. OBADIAH

JUDGMENT TO EDOM
Obadiah 1:1-10, 17, 18, 21

5. NAHUM

a. THE COMING OF GOD'S WRATH
Nahum 1:2, 3, 7-10

b. THE LORD WILL AFFLICT HIS ENEMY
Nahum1:1,11-15

6. HABAKKUK
Habakkuk 3:1, 2, 6, 7

7. MICAH
Micah 1:1

8. Ezekiel: GOD WILL DWELL IN THE MIDST OF
JERUSALEM
Ezekiel 43 :7

THE FORM AND PATTERN OFTHE TEMPLE OF GOD IN
MT ZION(Read Ezekiel Chapters 39-)
Ezekiel 43:10-12
===

PART 6
GOD ANOINTED DELIVERERS

CHAPTER V **GOD GAVE POWERS TO THE PROPHETS OF ISRAEL**
p337-349

Micah 3:8; Amos 2:11,12

A. FILLED WITH THE SPIRIT

1.OF MIGHT AND POWER TO DO MIRACLES

MOSES
Deuteronomy 34:10; Hosea 12:13; Deuteronomy 34:11-12;
Exodus 3:7, 8, 10

ELIJAH

THE WIDOW FROM ZERAPHATH
1Kings17:8-16

ELIJAH SENT OBADIAH TO KING AHAB
1Kings 18:1-16

AHAB MET ELIJAH
1Kings 18:17-20

ELIJAH CHALLENGED THE FALSE PROPHETS AND
THEIR FALSE gods
1Kings 18:21-29

ELIJAH PRAYED TO THE LORD TO REVEAL HIS POWER
1Kings 18:30-40

THE ABUNDANCE OF RAIN CAME
1Kings 18:41-45

ELIJAH WAS TAKEN TO HEAVEN ALIVE
2Kings 2:1-12

ELIAS AND ELIJAH THE SAME PERSON
James 5:17, 18; Luke 4:25-26; Romans 11:2, 3; Matthew 11:14,
15; Mark 9:12; Matthew 17:10 -12; Mark 9:13; Luke 9:8;
Luke 1:17

ELISHA

WATER OF JORDAN WAS PARTED
2Kings 2:13, 14, 15

WATER WAS HEALED IN JERICHO
2Kings 2:19-22

THE DEAD CHILD WAS RISEN FROM DEAD
2Kings 4:32-35

2. TO ANOINT KINGS

a. ANOINTING OF KING SAUL
Acts 13:21; 1Samuel 9:15, 16; 1Samuel 10:1

b. ANOINTING DAVID, THE SON OF JESSE
Acts 13:22, 23; 1Samuel 16:1, 12, 13

c. ANOINTING HAZAEL TO BE THE KING OVER SYRIA
1King 19:15

d. ANOINT KING AND PROPHET OVER ISRAEL
1King 19:16

B. TO DELIVER MESSAGE FROM THE LORD

1. JONAH
Jonah 1:1, 2; Jonah 3:1-10

2. JEREMIAH
Jeremiah 26:2-6

JEREMIAH'S PROPHECY AGAINST BABYLON
Jeremiah 51:60-64

3. MALACHI : RETURN TO GOD OF ISRAEL
Malachi 3:7, 10, 11

C. GOD SHOWED HIS GLORY TO THE PROPHETS

1. EZEKIEL

VISION OF THE HOSTS OF HEAVEN: THE FOUR LIVING
CREATURES
Ezekiel 1:3-5

THE GLORY OF THE LORD (See Volume 3 Part 18 Chapter
XV)
Ezekiel 1:27, 28

2. APOSTLE JOHN
Revelation 1:13 ⁻19
===

PART 7
THE CHILDREN OF DISOBEDIENCE

CHAPTER I IDOLATERS
p350-360

Isaiah 40:25, 26

THE TRUTH AND INSTRUCTION
Proverbs 23:23; John 8:32

WORSHIP THE LIVING GOD
Isaiah 40:22-24; Deuteronomy 4:39; Nehemiah 9:6-38 ;
Revelation 19:10; Revelation 22:8, 9

CHOSEN CHOSE TO DISOBEY GOD
Colossians 3:6; Psalms 37:28; Psalms 78:10, 11

1. THE MAKERS OF FALSE gods
Isaiah 44:9 -10; Deuteronomy 4:16-19

 a. THE WORKMAN AND HIS METAL
Isaiah 44:11-12

b. THE CARPENTER AND HIS WOOD
Isaiah 44:13-16

2. IDOL WORSHIPERS
 Isaiah 44:17-20

a. ABOMINATION TO THE LORD
 2Kings 1:1-6

 EVIL WILL COME TO THOSE WHO TRUSTED IN
WICKEDNESS
Isaiah 47:9-14

WORK OF THE FLESH
Galatians 5:17 -21

b. TRANSGRESSORS FROM THE WOMB
 Isaiah 48:8

c. MADE SACRIFICES TO THE DEVILS
 1Corinthians 10:19, 20

d. SET THEIR HEARTS ON IDOLS
 Ezekiel 14:2-4

e. WORSHIPPING THE HOSTS OF HEAVEN
2Kings 17:16; 1Chronicles 33:3; Jeremiah 1:16; Jeremiah 16:11-13; Jeremiah 22:9; Deuteronomy 4:19;Deuteronomy 8:19; Deuteronomy 11:16; Deuteronomy 30:17-20; 1Kings 9:6,7; Zephaniah 1:5, 6; Acts 7:42, 43; Deuteronomy 29:26

f. WORSHIPPING THE SUN
Ezekiel 8:15-17

==

PART 8
GOD RENDERS PUNISHMENT

CHAPTER I LORD CHALLENGES IDOLS (gods)
p361-365

Jeremiah 10:1 ,2; Isaiah 45:15;

A. IDOLS ARE NOTHING
Isaiah 41:22 -24; Isaiah 41:29; Isaiah 48:5;Zechariah 10:2; Isaiah 42:8, Isaiah 42:16-17, 2Kings17:14-15

B. FEAR NOT THE USELESS IDOLS (gods of nations)
 Isaiah 46:1,2. 5-7, Psalms 96:4-5, 1Chronicles 16:25;
Habakkuk 2:18 -19; Psalms 115:4-8, Jeremiah 10:3-5; Jeremiah 10:8, 9

GOD'S ANGER AGAINST PEOPLE WHO PRAY AND BOW DOWN TO IDOLS
Matthew 7:21-23; Jeremiah 10:11, 14, 15;
Micah 1:7

C. GOD WARNS HIS PEOPLE WHO WORSHIP IDOLS
Nehemiah 9:17; Isaiah 45:16, Ezekiel 11:21

1. THEY .WILL NEVER ENTER GOD'S REST
 Psalm 95:3; Psalms 95:11; Hebrews 4:1-3,6

2 DISASTER WILL COME TO THE LAND
Ezekiel 14:12-13

3 GOD WILL PUNISH THE IDOLWORSHIPERS
Amos 5:25 -27

D. PEACE CAME TO THE LAND AFTER DESTROYING THE
IDOLS
2Chronicles 15:16-19

==

PART 8
GOD RENDERS PUNISHMENT

CHAPTER II **THE WRATH OF GOD IN ANCIENT TIMES**
p366-370

Exodus 34:6,7

GOD'S PUNISHMENT
Psalms 94:12,13

1. GREAT FLOOD
Genesis 6:5-13; Genesis 7:11, 12, 21-24, 2Peter 2:5

2. DESTRUCTION OF SODOM AND GOMORRAH
2Peter 2:6,7

a. GOD'S DELIVERED WARNING BEFORE THE
DESTRUCTION
Genesis 18:20-21; Genesis 13: 13; Genesis 19:1-14

b. GOD SAVED LOT AND HIS FAMILY BEFORE HIS
WRATH TO COME
Genesis 19:15 -23

PUNISHMENT TO SODOM AND GOMORRAH
Genesis 19:24, 25

LOT'S WIFE DISOBEYED
Genesis 19:26

==

PART 8
GOD RENDERS PUNISHMENT

. CHAPTER III **THE CURSE FROM GOD**
p371-377

Genesis 12:3

CURSE THOSE THAT WILL HARM ISRAEL
Jeremiah 2:3 Deuteronomy 30:7 Numbers 22:12

A. ANCIENT MEN WERE CURSE FOR DISOBEDIENCE

1. ADAM

a. ADAM WILL DIE
Genesis 3:19; ; Romans 5:12; Romans 6:23

b. GOD CURSED THE EARTH (GROUND)
Genesis 3:17,18;Genesis 5:29

2. EVE
Genesis 3:13,16

GOD CURSED THE SERPENT AGAINST THE WOMAN
AND HER SEED
Genesis 3: 14,15

3. CAIN WAS CURSED
Genesis 4:4-15

B. CURSE DUE TO DISOBEDIENCE TO THE ORDINANCES
OF GOD (ISRAEL)
Proverbs 3:33

1. CURSES TO THE WORSHIPERS AND MAKERS OF IDOLS
Deuteronomy 27:15; Deuteronomy 29:16 -29

2. CURSE TO THOSE WHO DO NOT CONFORM TO ALL THE WORDS OF THE LAW OF MOSES
Deuteronomy 27:26

3. CURSE TO THE PRIESTS WHO CORRUPTED THE LAW
Malachi 2:17; Malachi 2:1-8

4. CURSES TO THOSE WHO DOESN'T LOVE THEIR NEIGHBORS
Deuteronomy 27:16-19

5. CURSES TO THOSE WITH SPIRIT OF LUSTS
Deuteronomy 27:20-24

6. CURSE TO THOSE WHO MURDER
Deuteronomy 27:25

C CURSE TO THOSE WHO STEAL AND SWEAR FALSELY USING THE NAME OF THE LORD
 LORD
Zechariah 5:1-4

D. CURSES TO THOSE WHO TRUSTED MAN'S WORD
Jeremiah 17:5

FOUR GENERATIONS WILL SUFFER CURSES FROM THE LORD
Exodus 34:6.7; ; Exodus 20:5; Deuteronomy 28:45; Deuteronomy 29:20

===

PART 8
GOD RENDERS PUNISHMENT

. CHAPTER IV GOD'S PUNISHMENT TO MOSES' PEOPLE

Amos 3:2

PEOPLE OF MOSES REFUSED GOD'S ORDER
Deuteronomy 1:18-33

A. PUNISHMENT TO MIRIAM WHO SPOKE AGAINST MOSES
Numbers 12:1-2,4-15

B. PUNISHMENT TO CHOSEN PEOPLE WITHOUT FAITH

1. THEY WILL ALL DIE IN THE WILDERNESS
Numbers 14:26-29, Deuteronomy 1:35, Numbers 14:30-37; Deuteronomy 1:40, Psalms 106:25, 26

ONLY TWO CHOSEN PEOPLE COULD ENTER THE PROMISE LAND
Numbers 14:24; Numbers 14:38; Deuteronomy 1:36-39

2. THE LORD LEFT HIS PEOPLE WHO DISOBEYED HIM
Numbers 14:39-45

THE ISRAELITES LOST THE BATTLE
Deuteronomy 1:41-46

C. ISRAEL GRUMBLED AGAINST GOD AND MOSES

WEPT FOR MEAT
Numbers 11: 4-6

GOD SENT QUAILS
Numbers 11: 31,32

PUNISHMENT TO THE MURMURERS AND COMPLAINERS

1. PLAGUES
Numbers 11: 33-35

2. GOD SENT FIERY SNAKES
Numbers 21:4-7

GOD COMMANDED MOSES TO MAKE A FIERY
SERPENT OF BRASS
Numbers 21:8, 9

D. PEOPLE ENVIED MOSES AND AARON,
Numbers 16:1-19

GOD'S PUNISHMENT TO KORAH, ABIRAM AND HIS MEN
Number 16:20-35; Psalms 106:16-18

PLAGUE KILLED MORE PEOPLE
Numbers 16:36 -50

E. PEOPLE WORSHIPING THE GOLDEN CALF WERE
KILLED
Psalm 106:19-23, Exodus 32:26 -28

FOLLOWERS OF IDOL BAAL PERISHED BY PLAGUE
Exodus 32:34, 35; Numbers 25:1-9; Psalm 106:28-31;

MOSES INSTRUCTIONS BEFORE ENTERING THE
PROMISE LAND
Deuteronomy 4:1-4

F. MOSES WAS NOT ALLOWED TO ENTER THE PROMISE
LAND
Psalm 106:32,33; Numbers 20:1-13

G. PUNISHMENT TO PEOPLE DOING ABOMINATION TO
THE LORD
Deuteronomy 17:2-5

WITNESSES NECESSARY TO IMPLEMENT PUNISHMENT
Deuteronomy 17:6-12

==

PART 8
GOD RENDERS PUNISHMENT

CHAPTER V ISRAEL'S DISOBEDIENCE
p393-403

A. IN JOSHUA'S TIME

GOD ALLOWED ISRAEL TO LOSE THE BATTLE AGAINST A-I
Joshua 7:1-12

ACHAN'S LOOT FROM JERICHO
Joshua 7:21-23

ACHAN, HIS FAMILY AND ANIMALS WERE PUT TO DEATH
Joshua 7:24-26

B. THE TIME OF JUDGES
Judges 2:18

THE SIN OF ISRAEL: WORSHIPPING IDOLS
1Corinthians 10:22

1. AFTER JOSHUA'S DEATH
Judges 2:8, 10; Deuteronomy 32:16-21

DISOBEDIENCE OF THE PEOPLE OF ISRAEL TO GOD'S COMMANDMENTS
Judges 3:6-7

THE ANGER OF THE LORD AGAINST ISRAEL
Judges 2:14-15

THE PEOPLE OF ISRAEL CONTINUED SINNING AGAINST THE LORD
Judges 2:17, 19

THE LORD WAS HOT WITH ANGER AGAINST ISRAEL
Judges 2:20-23, Judges 3:8

2. AFTER THE DEATH OF EHU, THE JUDGE
Judges 4:1-2

3. AFTER THE DEATH OF GIDEON
Judges 8:33-35

4. AFTER JARID'S DEATH
Judges 10:3-6

GOD'S SOLD THEM TO THE HANDS OF PHILISTINES AND
AMMON
Judges 10:7-9

ISRAEL CRIED TO GOD
Judges 10:10

THE LORD ANSWERED ISRAEL
Judges 10:11-14

ISRAEL ASKED DELIVERANCE FROM THE LORD
Judges 10:15-16

C.GOD PUNISHED THE SONS OF THE OF THE ELECT

ELI'S SON DIDN'T SHOW RESPECT TO THE OFFERINGS
 1Samuel 2:12-17; 1Samuel 2:22-25

GOD'S WARNING TO ELI
 1Samuel 3:13-14;1Samuel 2:33,34; 1 Samuel 3:11,12

THE TWO SONS OF ELI WERE SLAIN AND THE ARK OF
COVENANT WAS TAKEN BY PHILISTINES
1 Samuel 4:1-4, 10-22

D. UZZAH'S PUNISHMENT FOR TOUCHING THE ARK OF
COVENANT
2Samuel 6:1-8

DAVID BROUGHT BACK THE ARK OF COVENANT TO
THE CITY OF DAVID
Luke 2:4; 2Samuel 6:9-15

MICHAL DESPISED DAVID DANCING IN THE STREET
1Chronicles 15:27-29; 2Samuel 6:16-19

E. PUNISHMENT TO MICHAL WHO INSULTED DAVID, THE ELECT
2Samuel 6:20-23

===

PART 8
GOD RENDERS PUNISHMENT

.

CHAPTER VI **KINGS DISOBEDIENCE TO GOD**
p404-421

KINGS DISOBEYED GOD'S INSTRUCTIONS
 Nehemiah 9:33-35

1. SAUL

*GOD'S INSTRUCTION TO SAUL
1Samuel 15:1-3

REJECTED THE WORD OF THE LORD
1Samuel 15:4-9

TOO LATE FOR REPENTANCE, SAUL WAS REJECTED BY GOD
1Samuel 15:23-26, 35

2. KING DAVID DID NOT CONSULT GOD
1Chronicles 21:1-10-15

DAVID REPENTED HIS SIN
1Chronicles 21:16-28

3. KING SOLOMON DISOBEYED GOD'S COMMAND
2 Chronicles 7:15-22

a. KING SOLOMON MARRIED WOMEN FROM OTHER NATIONS
 1Kings 11:1-3; Nehemiah 13:26, 27

b. KING SOLOMON WORSHIPED IDOLS
1Kings 11:4-8

PUNISHMENT: THE LORD DIVIDED THE KINGDOM OF
SOLOMON
1Kings 11:9-13

4. GOD WILL BRING EVIL TO KING AHAB'S WIFE AND
CHILDREN
I Kings 21:17-29

5.KING UZZIAH DISOBEYED GOD'S LAW BY BURNING
THE INCENSE
2Chronicles 26:15 -21

6. KING MANASSEH OF JUDAH DID ABOMINATIONS TO
THE LORD
2Chronicles 33:1-7

PUNISHMENT TO THE KINGDOM OF JUDAH
2Kings 21:1-1 6

GOD PUNISHED MANNASEH
2Chronicles 33:11

MANNASEH HUMBLED HIMSELF TO GOD
2Chronicles 33:12-17

7. JEHOIAKIM KING OF JUDAH BURNED THE WORDS OF
THE LORD
Jeremiah 36:21-23,27-32

8. NEBUCHADNEZZAR THE KING OF BABYLON

GOD WARNED THE KING OF BABYLON THROUGH HIS
DREAM
Daniel 4: 4 -6,8-27

KING NEBUCHADNEZZAR WAS PUNISHED FOR BEING
PROUD
Proverbs 16:5; Daniel 4:28-34

KING NEBUCHADNEZZAR GAVE HONOR AND PRAISES
TO GOD
Daniel 4:36-37

9. BELSHAZZAR OF BABYLON DISHONOR GOD
Daniel 5:1-4

GOD GAVE HIS WARNING
Daniel 5:5-9

DANIEL WAS NEEDED TO INTERPRET THE WRITINGS
ON THE WALL
Daniel 5:10-12

DANIEL WAS BROUGHT TO THE KING
Daniel 5:13-15, 17

BELSHAZZAR SINNED AGAINST THE LORD GOD
Daniel 5:22, 23

DANIEL REMINDED THE KING ABOUT THE FATE OF HIS
FATHER
Daniel 5:18-21

JUDGMENT TO BELSHAZZAR WERE WRITTEN ON THE
WALL
Daniel 5:24-29-31

10. GOD PUNISHED KING HEROD
Acts 12:1-4; Acts 12:19-23

==

PART 8
GOD RENDERS PUNISHMENT

CHAPTER VII **THE DIVIDED KINGDOMS LED TO CAPTIVITY**
p422-436

A. GOD 'S WARNING TO THE TEN TRIBES OF ISRAEL

1.WILL BE SCATTERED AMONG NATIONS
Deuteronomy 28:64; Ezekiel 6:8-12

2. ISRAEL WILL NOT FIND REST AND PEACE
Deuteronomy 28:65, 66, 67

ISRAEL CONTINUED SINNING AGAINST GOD
Jeremiah 2:13, 2 Kings 17:7-12; Hosea 9:10 -17

ALL THE PROPHETS AND SEERS WARNED THE PEOPLE
2Kings 17:13-15

PEOPLE DISOBEYED AND REBELLED AGAINST GOD
Nehemiah 9:26-31

THE TEN TRIBES OF ISRAEL LEFT ALL THE
COMMANDMENTS OF THE LORD
2Kings 17:16 -23

THE KINGDOM OF ISRAEL WAS CARRIED AWAY INTO
ASSYRIA
2Kings 17:1-6; Hosea 10:1-15

OTHER NATIONS WERE TAUGHT TO FEAR THE LORD OF
ISRAEL
2Kings 17:24-28

OTHER NATIONS FEARED GOD BUT SERVE OTHER gods
2 Kings 17:29 -41

B. PUNISHMENT TO THE DIVIDED KINGDOM OF
ISRAEL
Nehemiah 1:8-9

1. THE CHILDREN OF ISRAEL WERE SCATTERED
AMONG NATIONS
Jeremiah 50:33 ; Isaiah 5:13; Ezekiel 20:23 -31

2. THE KINGDOM OF JUDAH WAS GONE INTO
CAPTIVITY
Lamentations 1:3-7; Lamentation 2:1-9

THE CHOSEN WERE IN GREAT SHOCK
Lamentation 2:10-22

LAMENTATIONS OF OF THE CHOSEN PEOPLE
Lamentation 1:10-18

BURNING OF THE TEMPLE IN JERUSALEM
Amos 2:4,5

THE ELECTS WERE BROUGHT TO BABYLON
Jeremiah 32:2; Daniel 1:6; Zechariah 1:12

SUFFERINGS OF THE CAPTIVES
Lamentations 3:1-22

PRAYER OF THE CAPTIVES
Lamentations 1:20-22

 PRAYER TO LEARN THE COMMANDMENTS OF THE
LORD
Ezra 9:10; Psalms 119:60, 66, 73, 86; Ezra 9:14,15

NEHEMIAH'S PRAYER FOR THE NATION OF ISRAEL
Nehemia 1:1-7, 10, 11
==

PART 8
GOD RENDERS PUNISHMENT

CHAPTER VIII **FALSE PROPHET**
p437-446

Proverbs 25:14

A. PROPHET SPEAKING IN LIES

1.HANANIAH (Before the captivity of Babylon)
Jeremiah 28:1-17

*GOD'S INSTRUCTION TO THE PEOPLE OF JUDAH
Jeremiah 29:8, 9

2..SHEMAIAH THE NEHELAMITE, AND HIS SEED(under Babylon's Captivity)
Jeremiah 29:20-23, 31, 32

3.THE HOLY GHOST BLINDED BARJESUS (Apostles' time)
Acts 13:5-11

B. ISSUE OF CORRUPTION

GEHAZI, SERVANT OF PROPHET ELISHA
2Kings 5:1-6

ELISHAS' INSTRUCTIONS TO NAMAAN
2Kings 5:7-14

ELISHA REFUSED THE PAYMENT
2Kings 5:15-24

CURSE AND PUNISHMENT TO GEHAZI AND HIS SEEDS
2Kings 5: 25-27

GOD SENT THE LYING SPIRIT TO THE PROPHETS
2Chronicles 18:19-21; 1Kings 22:22

*GOD'S INSTRUCTION:LISTEN NOT TO THE FALSE PROPHET
Jeremiah 23:16-18

HAVE NO VISION AND GOD WILL NOT ANSWER
Micah 3:5-7

GOD'S ANGER IS UPON THE FALSE PROPHET
Ezekiel 13:3; Jeremiah 23:30-32; Ezekiel 13:4-16

GOD WILL PUNISH THE FALSE PROPHET
Jeremiah 23:14, 15, 19-22

EVERLASTING PUNISHMENT UPON THE FALSE
PROPHET
Jeremiah 23:33-40

===

PART 8
GOD RENDERS PUNISHMENT

CHAPTER IX **GOD LEFT HIS CHOSEN**
p447-461

Isaiah 59:2

TRANSGRESSING AND LYING AGAINST THE LORD
Isaiah 59:3-8, 12,13

*GOD'S INSTRUCTION TO KEEP AWAY FROM IDOLS
Exodus 20:5, Nahum1:2; Acts 17:24, 25; Ezekiel 14:2 -5

GOD WILL LEFT ISRAEL UPON WORSHIPING IDOLS
Deuteronomy 31:16-22

CHOSEN CHOSE TO DISOBEY GOD

A. CHOSEN WORSHIP IDOLS
Romans 1:21-23; Psalm 106:20

RESULTING TO SEXUAL SIN
Romans 1:24-27

B. NO KNOWLEDGE OF GOD
Hosea 4:6,1-3; 1John 5:19-20

1.GOD LEFT THEM TO POVERTY
Hosea 4:7-11

2. GOD HEARS NOT THE SINNERS
(Posted in FB 09/05/2014 7:30 pm)

a. BECAUSE OF SINS
John 9:31; Isaiah 59:2

b. PRAYERS BASED ON THE LUSTS OF FLESH
Isaiah 1:15; James 4:2-5; Micah 3:4

c. PRAYING TO THE IDOLS
Jeremiah 11: 10 -14; 1John 5:21

d. THE PRETENSE OF LONG PRAYING TO COVER UP
EXPLOITATIONS
Mark 12:40; Luke 20:47; Matthew 23:14

e. MAKE A VOW TO THE LORD AND NOT PAY
Ecclesiastes 5:1-5; Numbers 30:2

f. PRAYING WITH A PROUD HEART
Luke 18:11

g. PRAYING AND FASTING FOR STRIPE, DEBATE AND
SMITE
Isaiah 58: 3-6

C. YOUR EVIL THAT SEPARATE FROM GOD
Isaiah 42:5; Deuteronomy 32:20; Isaiah 30:1; Ezekiel 14:6-10

GOD LEFT THEM TO BE SUBDUED BY THEIR ENEMIES
Psalms 81:8-16

D. PRACTICES ABOMINATIONS TO THE LORD
 2Corinthians 11:3, Deuteronomy 18:10-12; Isaiah 19:3

1. PRAYING TO DEAD
Isaiah 8:19; Isaiah 29:4

SEEK AFTER FAMILIAR SPIRITS
Leviticus 19:31; Leviticus 20:6

PUNISHMENT DURING THE TIME OF MOSES
Leviticus 20:27

SAUL DIED FOR HIS TRANSGRESSION
1 Chronicles 10:13,14

2. WITCHCRAFT PRACTICES SIN AGAINST THE LORD
Samuel 15:23

a. CONSULTER TO DIVINERS (FORTUNE TELLER)
Jeremiah 27:9, 10; Jeremiah 29:8; Zechariah 10:2

b. STARGAZERS (HOROSCOPE OF THE STARS)
Daniel 5:15; Jeremiah 10:2; Isaiah 47:13, 14

SOURCE OF WITCHCRAFT PRACTICES: OLD BABYLON
Ezekiel 21:21-23

3. SIN TO SACRIFICE THEIR CHILDREN TO DEATH
(FALSE DOCTRINE)
2Chronicles 33:6; 2Kings 17:17; 2Kings 21:6

4. FOLLOWING THE WISDOM OF THIS WORLD

a. GOD LEFT EVEN KING TO HIS MISFORTUNES
2 Chronicles 16:6-14

b. GOD GAVE THEM OVER TO REPROBATE MIND
Romans 1:28-31; Ephesians 4:18, 19

c. GOD HARDENED THE SPIRIT
Deuteronomy 2:30-33

5. ESTABLISHED THEIR OWN RIGHTEOUSNESS,
Romans 10:2,3; Romans 11:8; Deuteronomy 29:2-4; Romans
11:9,10

6. THE JEWS' SIN OF MARRYING WOMEN FROM OTHER
NATIONS
Nehemia 13:23 -26

GOD'S COMPASSION TO FORGIVE THE CHOSEN PEOPLE
Leviticus 26:41-46

GOD'S INSTRUCTIONS TO ISRAEL
Ezekiel 18:30-32

GOD'S PROMISE TO HIS CHOSEN UNDER CAPTIVITY IN BABYLON
Jeremiah 29:10-14

PRAYER TO OBEY THE LORD
Psalms 119:127, 131, 143, 151, 166, 172, 176; Psalms 119:19, 21, 32-35, 47, 48

===

PART 8
GOD RENDERS PUNISHMENT

CHAPTER X JUDGMENT OF SOUL UPON DEATH
p462-476

Hebrews 9:27

THE SOULS OF THE RICH MAN AND LAZARUS
Luke16:19-31

LORD JESUS SPOKE WHERE THE SOUL GOES AFTER DEATH
Matthew 7:21; Matthew18:3

1. KINGDOM OF HEAVEN (See Volume 2 Part 11 ChapterII)
Matthew 5:20 ; Psalms 49:15

THE SOULS WORSHIPING GOD IN HEAVEN
 Revelation 6:9-11 ;Revelation 20:4

THE SOUL OF MOSES WAS WITH ELIAS CAME FROM HEAVEN
Mark 9:2 -5

SOULS ARE GOING TO HEAVEN TO SIT DOWN WITH THE PROPHETS
Matthew 8:11; Matthew 5:19; Acts 14:22

THE ELECT CAN'T DELIVER THE SOUL OF THEIR
CHILDREN
Ezekiel 14:20; Ezekiel 18:4

2. HELL
Proverbs 9:18 ; Job 26:6 ;Deuteronomy 32:22; 2Samuel 22:6;
Psalms 18:5 ; Psalms 116:3; Isaiah 5:14; Isaiah 14:9;
Mark 9:44, 46, 48, 49 ; Psalm 63:9

 GOD DELIVERED JESUS FROM HELL
Psalms 16:10; Psalm 86:12,13; Acts 2:27; Acts 2:31; Proverbs
23:14

LOSING ONE'S SOUL
Matthew 16:26 ; Mark 8:34-37

THE SOUL WILL GO TO HELL
Psalms 55:15; Isaiah 28:15; Job 27:8; Psalms 2:8

GOD THE DESTROYER OF LOST SOULS
Matthew 10:28

GOD WILL SET HIS FACE AGAINST THIS SOUL
Psalms 9:17;   Leviticus 20:6 ;   Proverbs 6:32; Proverbs
21:10;Galatians 5:17 -21; Proverbs 5:5; Matthew 7:21-23

WICKED SOULS
Ezekiel 18: 20; Romans 2:9; Proverbs 28:5

THE SINNERS
1Corinhians 3:3; Ezekiel 15:7

IDOL WORSHIPERS
1Chronicles 16:26

NON BELIEVERS
John 8:24; John 3:18-20; John 3:36; John 5:44

PHARISEES AND SCRIBES OF ISRAEL WHO PERSECUTED
THE PROPHETS
Matthew 23:29-35

BACKBITERS
Matthew 12:34-37; 1Timothy 6:4, 5; Romans 1:30-32;
Proverbs 6:16-19; Psalms 101:5; Luke 12:3; James 3:6

MURDERER
Matthew 5:21 -22

ADULTERER
Proverbs 6:32 ;Matthew 5: 28-30; Matthew 18:9; Mark 9:47;
Matthew 5:32 ;Luke 16:18; Proverbs 9:13-18

CHILD ABUSER
Mark 9:36,42;Matthew 18:3-10

DOCTRINE OF RELIGION
Matthew 23:15; Matthew 23:33

EVIL DOERS
Mark 9:43,45

SUFFERINGS OF THE LIVING SOULS OF THE HEATHEN
Romans 2:9; 2Peter 2:14; Isaiah 57: 20, 21

APPOINTED TIMES TO ENTER INTO JUDGMENT WITH
GOD
Proverbs 2:8; Ecclesiastes 8:6,7; Jeremiah 8:7; Job 34: 20-23; Job
7:1

DEATH OF THE WICKED
Job 21:17, 18, 20-32; Job 27:9; Job 7:9 ,10; Job 10:21, 22; Job
28:3

DEATH WILL CLAIM THE WICKED 'S FAMILY
Job 27:13-23

PHYSICAL DEATH OF THE SINNER
2Samuel 22:5; Proverbs 11:7; 2Peter 2:9

GOD RESERVES THE UNJUST TO BE PUNISHED
2 Peter 2:4,8,9,10

PRAYER FOR THE SALVATION OF THE SOUL
Psalms 30:3; Psalms 41:4; Psalms 103:1,2; Psalm 35:9;
Psalms 142:7; Psalms 25:20, Psalms 26:9-12; Psalms 143:6, 11;
Psalms 86:2

==

PART 9
MYSTERY OF THE BODY, SOUL AND SPIRIT

CHAPTER 1 **THE LIVING SOUL**
p477-486

Isaiah 26:8-9

A. BODY
Psalm 115:17; Romans 12:1-2; Psalm 104:29

DEATH LOST ALL MEMORIES UNDER THE SUN
Ecclesiastes 9:5,6; Psalms 88:10; Job 14:20-22

SHADOW 0F PHYSICAL DEATH
Job 38:17; Jeremiah 13: 16; Job 14: 10

 B. LIVING SOUL
Genesis 2:7; 1Corinthians 15:45; Romans 13:1, 2; Matthew 16:26

1. SAVING OF SOUL
Job 12:10 ;Psalms 62:1; James 1:21; James 5:19, 20 ; Hebrews
10:39

ATONEMENT OF SOUL
Romans 7:22

a. ANCIENT PEOPLE: THROUGH THEIR FAITH
(See Vol.3 Part16 Chapter 1)

b. TIME OF MOSES AND BEFORE CHRIST: THROUGH THE
BLOOD OFFERINGS
Leviticus 17:11; Exodus 30:15, 16; Numbers 15:28 ; Leviticus
4:26,35; Leviticus 5:6,10,13,16,18; Leviticus 6:7; Leviticus 7:7

c. THROUGH THE BLOOD OF CHRIST
1Peter 4:6; Galatians 3:22

2. PURIFICATION OF SOUL
1Peter 1:19-22

LIVING SOUL THAT LIVE BY FAITH
 Hebrews 10:38-39

PEACEFUL LIVING,
 Jeremiah 6:16: Jeremiah 31:25; Isaiah 26:9

GOD PRESERVES THEIR SOULS,
 Psalm 97:10

3.GOD CLAIMS THE SOUL OF HIS ELECT
Psalm 124:7; Genesis 35:18,19 ; Ezekiel 18:4;   Matthew 22:37;
Psalm 119:167, 129, 175; Psalm 130:6; Psalms 138:3;
Psalms 30:3; Psalms 86:13; Psalms 56:13 Ezekiel 33:5

GOD WILL REDEEM THE SOUL FROM THE POWER OF
GRAVE
James 1:21; Psalm 34:22; Psalm 49:15

GOD SENT BACK THE SOUL OF THE DEAD CHILD
1Kings 17:17-24

4. RESURRECTION OF THE DEAD AFTER THE WRATH OF
GOD
Job 14:12-15

TROUBLED SOULS

JOB'S TRIBULATION AND SICKNESS
Job 14:22; Job 10:1

MOSES WAS STRESSED OUT
Numbers 11:10-15

HANNAH'S PROBLEM
1Samuel 1:1-7; 1Samuel 1:10,11

COME TO THE LORD ALL TROUBLED SOULS
 Matthew 11:28-30; 1 Peter 4: 19; 2Corinthians1:3-10

PRAYER OF THE TROUBLED SOUL
Psalm 88:1- 3, 9, 14; Psalm 41:4; Psalm 120:2
===

PART 9
MYSTERY OF BODY, SOUL AND SPIRIT

CHAPTER II **SPIRIT OF GOD IN MAN**
p487-493

Ecclesiastes 12:7

GOD'S BREATH OF LIFE
Job 27:3; Job 33:4; Isaiah 42:5; Zechariah 12:1 ; Job32:8
1Corinthians 2:11,12

THE SPIRIT OF LIFE LEFT
Ecclesiastes 8:8; Genesis 6:3 ; Isaiah 29:10; Isaiah 40:6.7;
Ecclesiastes 3:19-21; Psalms 146:4; James 2:26

MAN SUCCUMB TO PHYSICAL DEATH
Ecclesiastes 9:12

GIVING UP THE SPIRIT
Job 34:14,15; Job 10:18; Genesis 25:8; Genesis 35:29;
Psalms 104:29

a. LORD JESUS GAVE UP HIS SPIRIT
Matthew27:45, 46, 50; John 19: 30

b. STEPHEN THE MAN FULL OF FAITH
Acts 6:5, 8, 9; Acts 7:55 -60

c. ALIVE AGAIN WHEN THE SPIRIT COMES BACK
Luke 8:41, 42, 49-55; Mark 5:22- 24, 35-43

GOD WILL GIVE OR TAKE AWAY HIS SPIRIT UPON MAN
Numbers 11:16, 17, 25

THE SPIRIT OF GOD DWELLS IN THE ELECT
Numbers 14:24; Numbers 11:26; 1Peter 4:14, 1John 3:24

BROKEN SPIRIT
Proverbs 12:25; Proverbs 15:13 ; Proverbs 17:22

VISION TROUBLED THE SPIRIT
Daniel 2:1-3

2. THE CANDLE OF GOD
Ephesians 3:16; Proverbs 20:27; 1Peter 3:4; 2Corinthians 4:16

THE LORD WEIGHED THE SPIRITS.
Numbers 23:19,20; Proverbs 16:2

RECEIVING THE TRUTH
1Thessalonians 2:13

===

ACKNOWLEDGMENT

Psalms 113:2
Blessed be the name of the LORD from this time forth and for evermore.

My short **life's greatest testimony:** Now I believe that nothing is impossible to God. If we ask Him through prayers, He will answer according to His own will and to serve His purpose which is saving the soul of His chosen and give us spiritual blessings.

Even though I was lost, a none-believer for nineteen years, since 1971 to 1990, He had never forsaken me. He answered the prayers of my mom and dad as well as the prayers of my fourteen siblings. They were petitioning for God's mercy with regards to the salvation of my soul which was indeed in the brink of destruction. A miracle, happened in one moment of time when God lifted me out from darkness, away from the workings of the principalities and powers that deceived and blinded me spiritually for many years. The LORD saved my soul by revealing Himself through His Word, giving me wisdom and understanding about His message of salvation as written in the Scriptures. **And now at His time**, he called me as part of His plan to spread His gospel to the chosen.

It is amazing and truly unbelievable by human perspective, how God works in the lives of His people. I had experienced His power even though I had little knowledge of Him. At first, I didn't know what to write and how to start this book, a rich bible study resources. Of course it is by no way of replacing the authority of the Bible, but rather to glorify the LORD even more and to answer his calling to preach His gospel. So I first started with prayers, begging God through our LORD Jesus to show me the way on how to serve Him. It was like solving a puzzle, or going to the unknown of God's Word and supernaturally unlocking the mysteries of the Bible.

I could not accomplish the writings of the whole text without the guidance and enlightenment from my God and His Holy Spirit who helped me put the ideas in my soul. God said, I will put the words in your mouth, as what He said to all His prophets in the Holy Bible. Truly, the great resources of knowledge about knowing God, his wonderful works and His plan for His people are fully recorded in the Scriptures. Praise God.

I glorify and give my thanks and praises to our Almighty God through our LORD Jesus Christ and the Holy Spirit. Through Their mighty power and guidance, these books, volume 1, 2 &3 will serve their purpose: to be a rich bible study resources, to reveal GOD's plan of salvation, to preach the Gospel of Christ and the truth of His instructions to all the chosen and elect.

I also give my heartfelt thanks to all these people that God brought into my life, leading to my spiritual journey and became a follower, a servant of the LORD and to have a wonderful relationship with Christ and the Holy Spirit that sealed the salvation of my soul.

First: my appreciation to my own brother, Samuel V. Sendon who shared me Ephesians 1:17-19. He instructed me to memorize and pray it. It was the prayer of Apostle Paul, asking God for wisdom and understanding to know HIM. I did pray every night up to verse 20 for two years and God amazingly answered my prayers. Since then, God changed my life spiritually.

I extend my appreciation and thanks to Kathy White. She was the first one to hear the concept of the book. Furthermore, I am equally indebted to Jack White and Mike White for allowing me to use their internet. They are blessings to me from the LORD as well as Miss Lois Becker who was always with me when I typed portions of my manuscript.

I am very grateful to Thelma Simmons who gave me a copy of The Holy Bible KJV (Thru the Bible Radio Network Special Edition 1976). The glorious Bible became my primary reference and the crossed reference was The Official King James Bible online, which was very helpful during the editing and proof reading. Thelma was the one who introduced me to this wonderful family (White) wherein book, Volume 1,2 & 3 were written in Lois' house, few days a week for a three years and five months excluding the tedious proof reading.

God is good to show me the Bible maps online which are of public domain. Credit is for those people with God's wisdom and bright ideas who created websites: http://www.sacred-texts.com/; http://www.Biblenews1.com/ Larry Wood; American Bible Society, Bible Times, BIBLES NET.COM. These ancient maps are absolutely vital in understanding the historical backgrounds of the places, showing the various geographical locations found in the Scriptures from the Old Testament to New Testament. This is absolutely necessary for the Bible study.

I'm truly indebted and thankful to Brother Prof. Erwin Pajares who is the author of the book *Positive Mind: In a Negative World.* He tirelessly answered all my questions and provided knowledgeable information on how to publish and print this book. I really appreciated the help of my niece, Kresta de Guzman-Klassen to edit the Synopsis. and to my only son, Diwa who helped me in re-formatting the manuscript. He was truly a gift from God who helped me to finalize the details before the book printing.

I also give my great appreciation to Create.Space.Com for the printing, publication and marketing of this book

I was also inspired and very pleased sharing the verses according to God's plan of salvation to my husband, Francisco Ramos Jr., my daughters: Liwanag, Sinag, Laya, Bayan and all my siblings through phone calls or online social media. I was spiritually joyful for their interest and thirst in hearing the Word of God. Finally, I extend my regards to my son Diwa and my youngest daughter Pilipinas, who shared valuable insights and criticism in writing the manuscript.

Thank you and God bless.

Herminia Sendon Ramos 03/02/2014

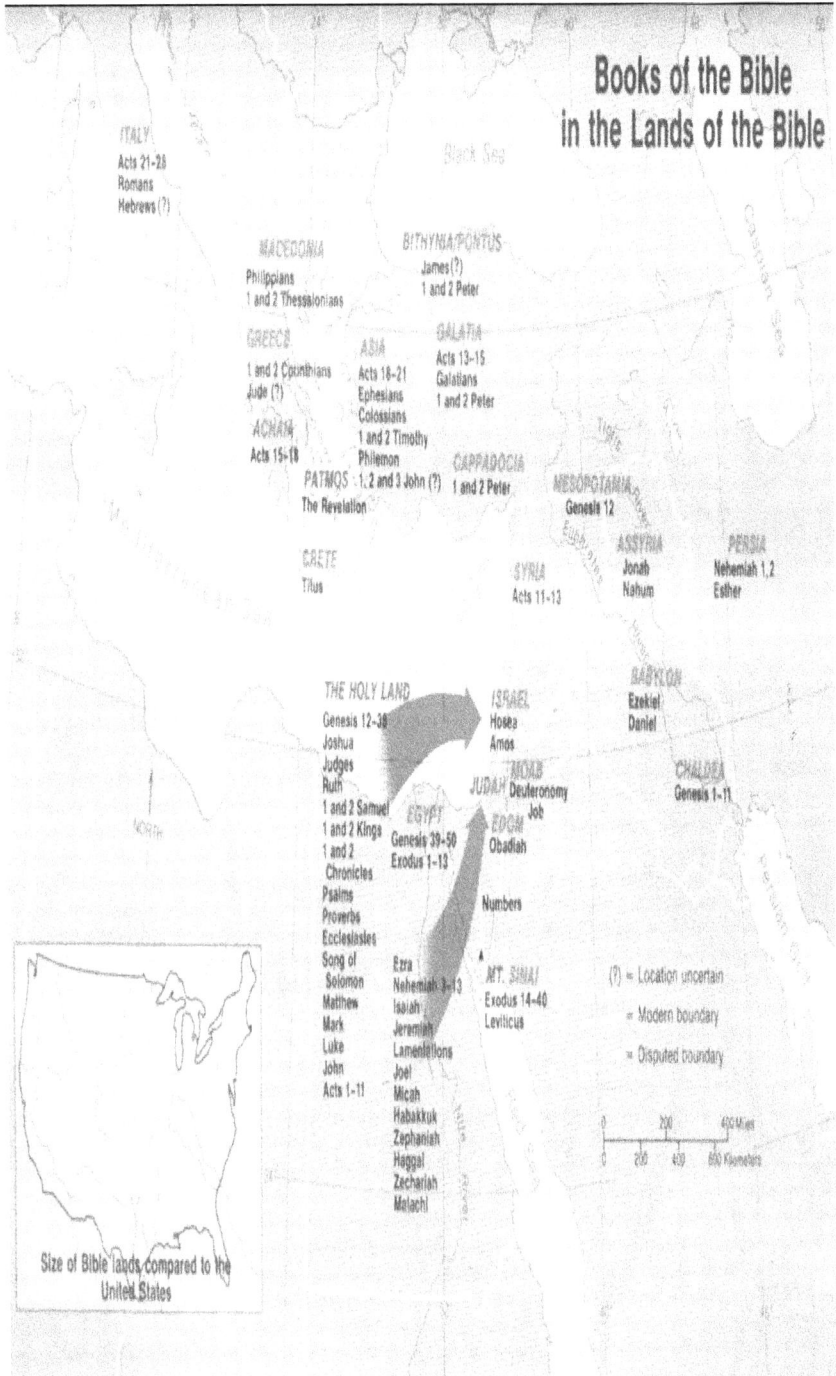

Books of the Bible
in the Lands of the Bible

ITALY
Acts 21-28
Romans
Hebrews (?)

Black Sea

MACEDONIA
Philippians
1 and 2 Thessalonians

BITHYNIA/PONTUS
James (?)
1 and 2 Peter

GREECE
1 and 2 Corinthians
Jude (?)

ASIA
Acts 18-21
Ephesians
Colossians
1 and 2 Timothy
Philemon

GALATIA
Acts 13-15
Galatians
1 and 2 Peter

ACHAIA
Acts 15-18

PATMOS : 1, 2 and 3 John (?)
The Revelation

CAPPADOCIA
1 and 2 Peter

MESOPOTAMIA
Genesis 12

CRETE
Titus

SYRIA
Acts 11-13

ASSYRIA
Jonah
Nahum

PERSIA
Nehemiah 1, 2
Esther

THE HOLY LAND
Genesis 12-38
Joshua
Judges
Ruth
1 and 2 Samuel
1 and 2 Kings
1 and 2
Chronicles
Psalms
Proverbs
Ecclesiastes
Song of
Solomon
Matthew
Mark
Luke
John
Acts 1-11

ISRAEL
Hosea
Amos

MOAB
JUDAH Deuteronomy
Job

EGYPT
Genesis 39-50
Exodus 1-13

EDOM
Obadiah

Numbers

Ezra
Nehemiah 3-13
Isaiah
Jeremiah
Lamentations
Joel
Micah
Habakkuk
Zephaniah
Haggai
Zechariah
Malachi

MT. SINAI
Exodus 14-40
Leviticus

BABYLON
Ezekiel
Daniel

CHALDEA
Genesis 1-11

(?) = Location uncertain

= Modern boundary

= Disputed boundary

0   200   400 Miles
0   200   400   600 Kilometers

Size of Bible lands compared to the
United States

APPENDIX 2 Satellite pictures are credited to NASA(Larry Wood)

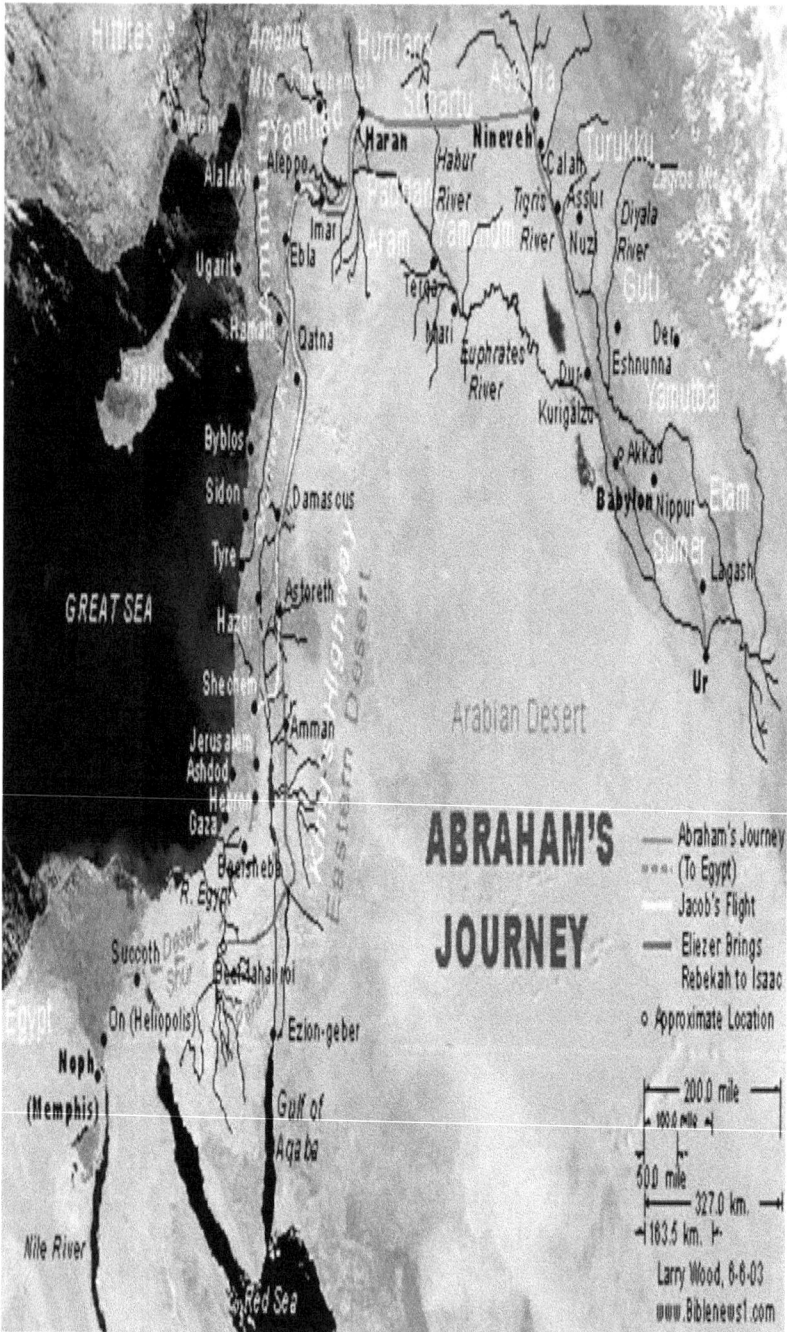

ABRAHAM'S JOURNEY

Legend:
- —— Abraham's Journey
- ∙∙∙ (To Egypt)
- —— Jacob's Flight
- —— Eliezer Brings Rebekah to Isaac
- ○ Approximate Location

Scale:
- 200.0 mile
- 100.0 mile
- 50.0 mile
- 327.0 km.
- 163.5 km.

Larry Wood, 6-6-03
www.Biblenews1.com

APPENDIX 3 Satellite pictures are credited to NASA(Larry Wood)

ROUTE OF THE EXODUS

573

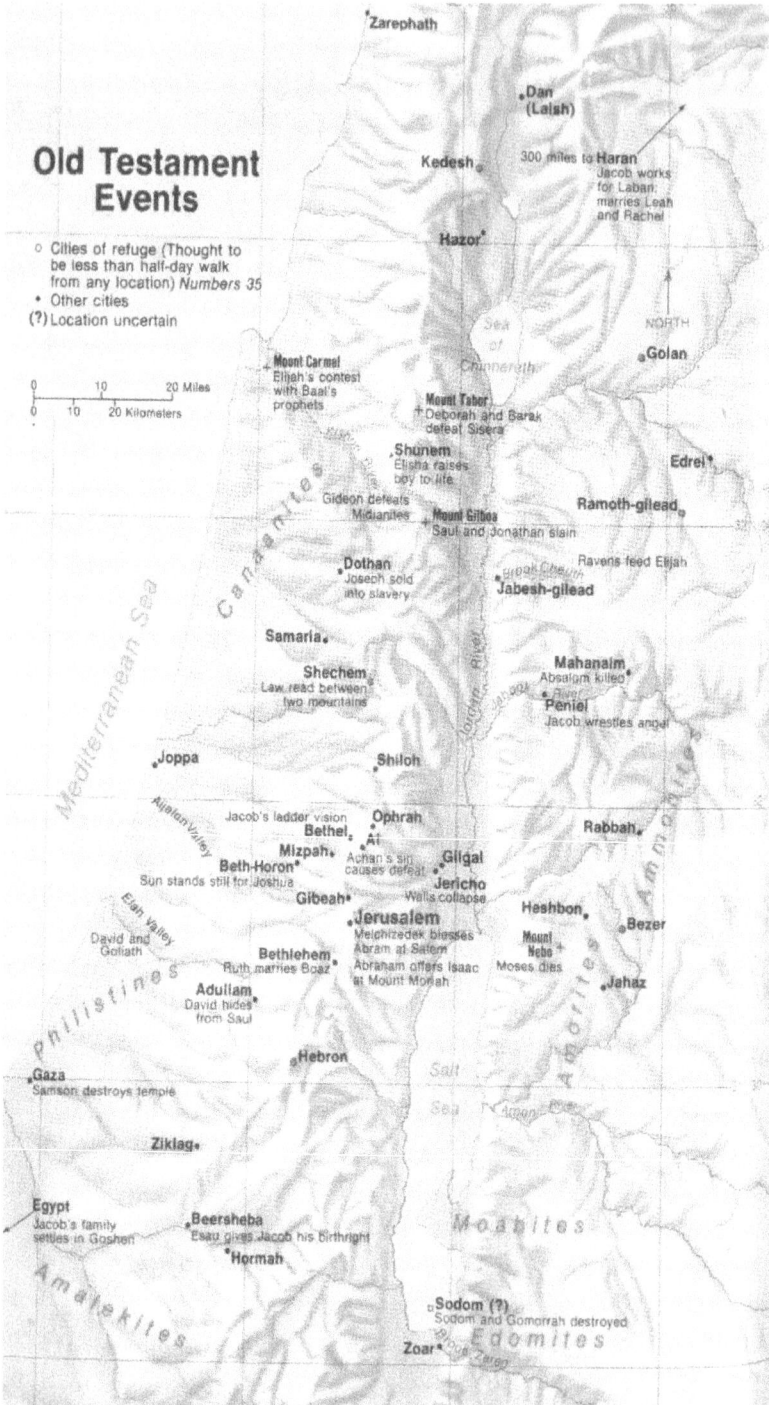

CANAAN
AFTER THE CONQUEST,
as divided amongst the tribes

Scale of English Miles.

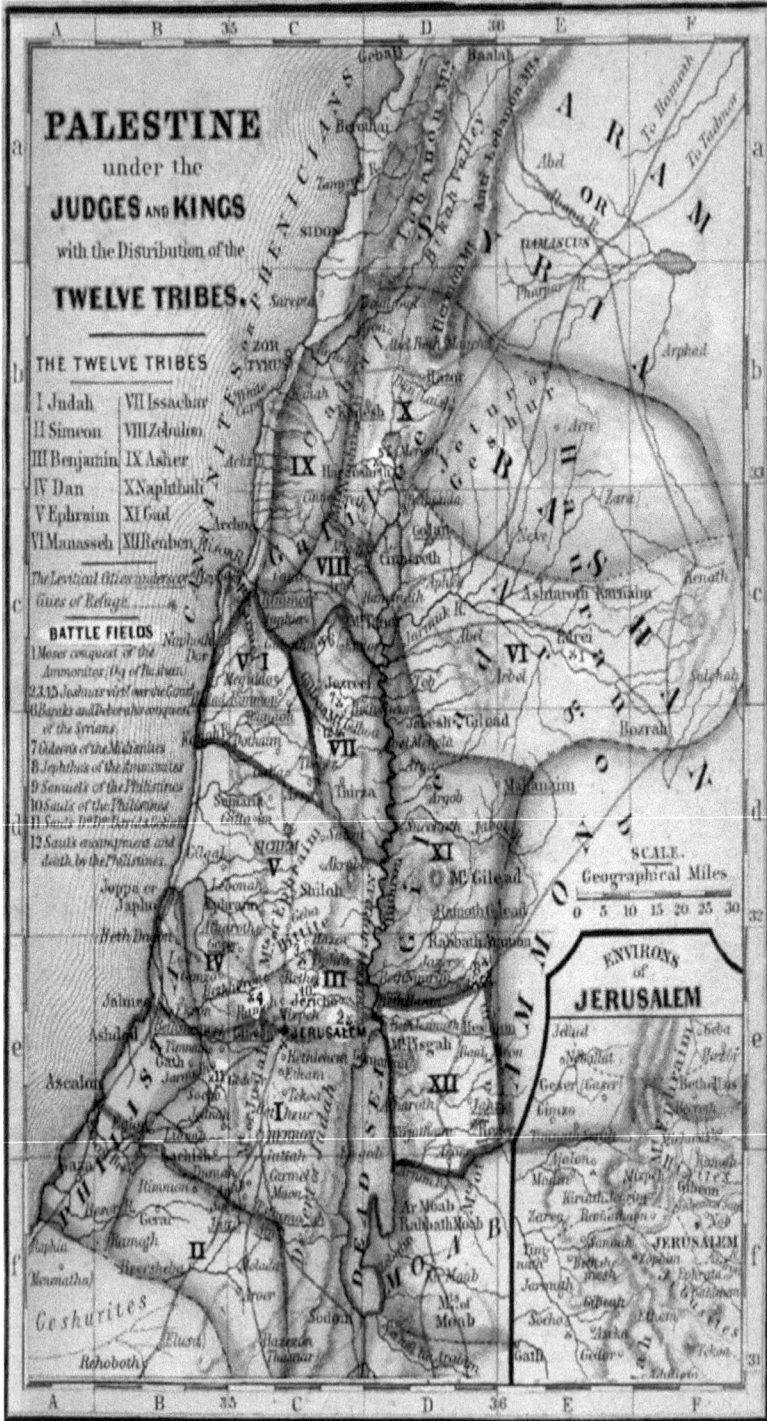

APPENDIX 7 Satellite pictures are credited to NASA(Larry Wood)

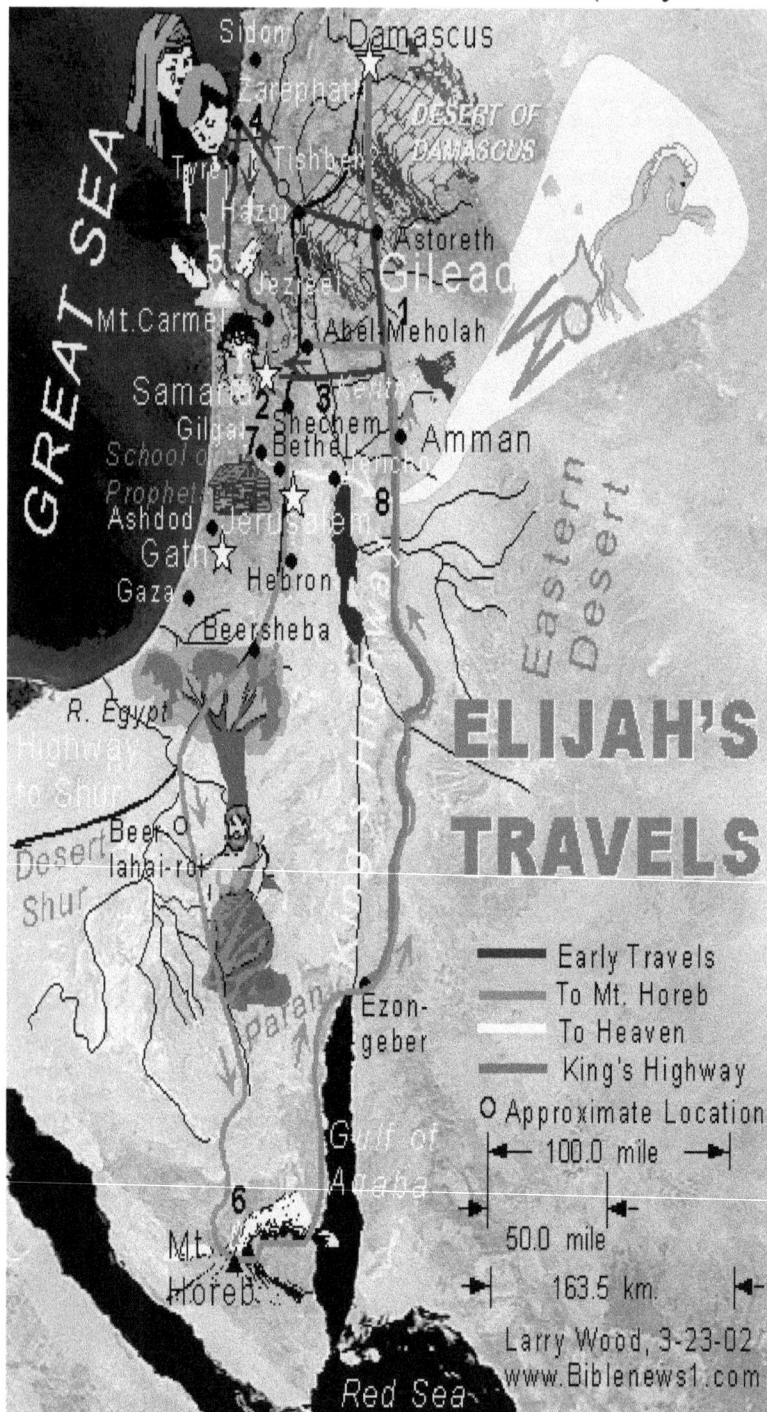

APPENDIX 9 Published in 1888 by the American Bible
Society

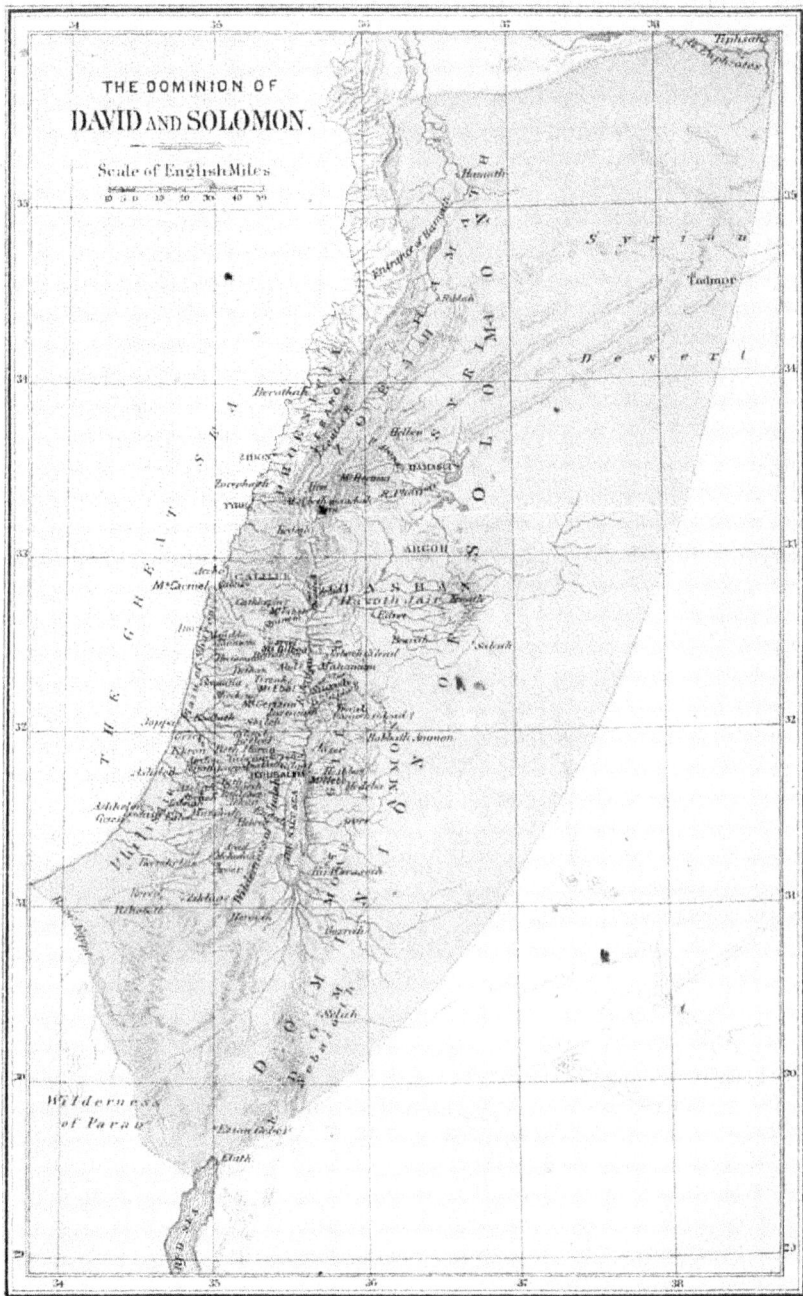

THE DOMINION OF
DAVID AND SOLOMON.

Scale of English Miles

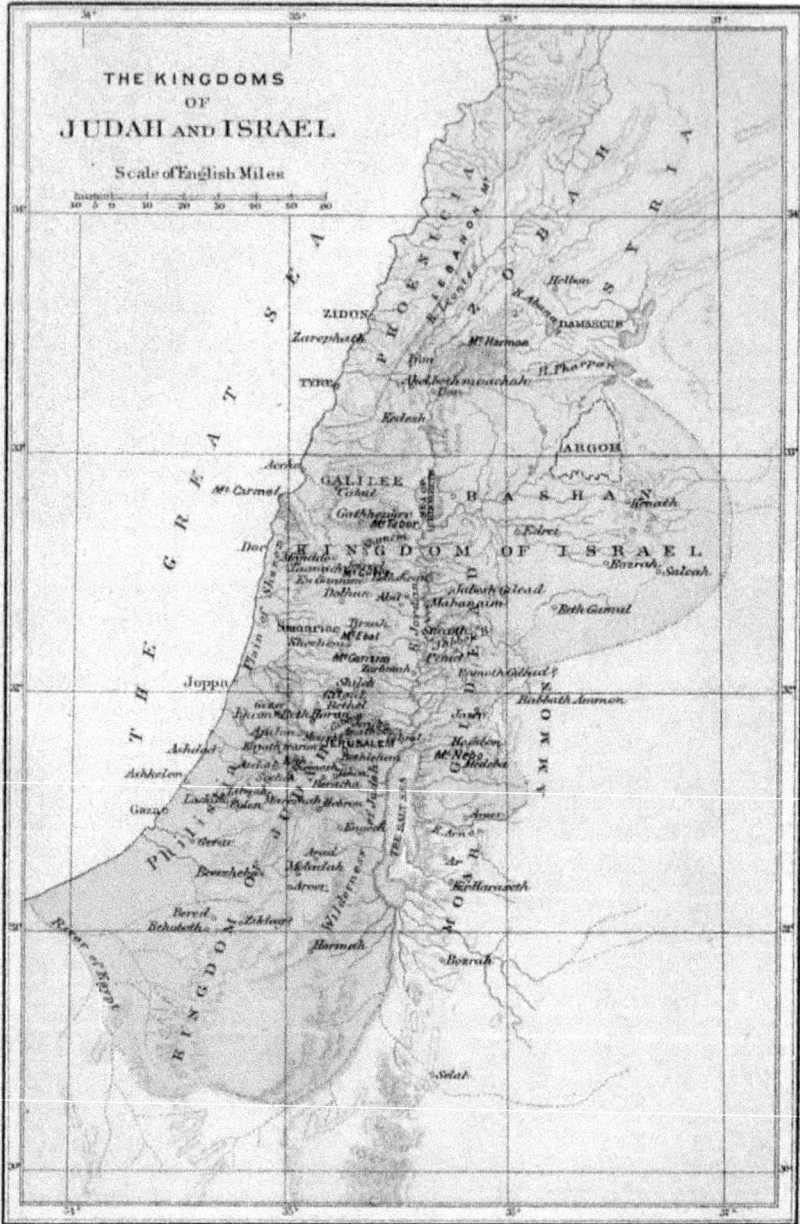

THE KINGDOMS
OF
JUDAH AND ISRAEL.

Scale of English Miles